# Decisions for Sustainability

Decisions by individuals, organizations and nations shape the well-being of humans and other species, the environment and sustainability. *Decisions for Sustainability* examines how we can make better decisions concerning our future sustainability. It incorporates sociological, psychological and economic perspectives to highlight our strengths and weaknesses in decision-making and suggest strategies to influence both individual and societal decisions. Sustainability challenges – from local land use and toxic contamination to climate change and biodiversity loss – illustrate how we might make better decisions and what factors lead to conflict. How we use science in the face of uncertainty is also examined, and a range of ethical criteria for good decisions are proposed. Emphasizing the need for diversity in decision-making and clarifying the relationship between reform and societal transformation, this book provides a comprehensive view of what we know about decision-making and how we can do better in the face of sustainability challenges.

**Thomas Dietz** is a University Distinguished Professor at Michigan State University. His work has shaped understanding of sustainability decision-making, the drivers of environmental change and the relationship between science and values. He has chaired or served on more than twenty national or international science assessments and US National Research Council committees. In 2005, he was corecipient of the Sustainability Science Award from the Ecological Society of American. Dietz is a fellow of the American Association for the Advancement of Science and has participated in dozens of consensus-building efforts on climate, biodiversity and sustainability.

# Decisions for Sustainability

## Facts and Values

**Thomas Dietz**
Michigan State University

 CAMBRIDGE
UNIVERSITY PRESS

**CAMBRIDGE**
UNIVERSITY PRESS

Shaftesbury Road, Cambridge CB2 8EA, United Kingdom

One Liberty Plaza, 20th Floor, New York, NY 10006, USA

477 Williamstown Road, Port Melbourne, VIC 3207, Australia

314–321, 3rd Floor, Plot 3, Splendor Forum, Jasola District Centre,
New Delhi – 110025, India

103 Penang Road, #05–06/07, Visioncrest Commercial, Singapore 238467

Cambridge University Press is part of Cambridge University Press & Assessment,
a department of the University of Cambridge.

We share the University's mission to contribute to society through the pursuit of
education, learning and research at the highest international levels of excellence.

www.cambridge.org
Information on this title: www.cambridge.org/9781009169417

DOI: 10.1017/9781009169400

First published 2023

*A catalogue record for this publication is available from the British Library.*

*Library of Congress Cataloging-in-Publication Data*
Names: Dietz, Thomas, author.
Title: Decisions for sustainability: facts and values / Thomas Dietz, Michigan State University.
Description: 1 Edition. | New York, NY: Cambridge University Press, [2023] | Includes bibliographical references
and index.
Identifiers: LCCN 2022057924 | ISBN 9781009169417 (hardback) | ISBN 9781009169424 (paperback) |
ISBN 9781009169400 (ebook)
Subjects: LCSH: Sustainability. | Sustainable development – Social aspects. | Sustainable development – Economicl
aspects. | Decision making.
Classification: LCC HC79.E5 D5474 2023 | DDC 304.2–dc23/eng/20230112
LC record available at https://lccn.loc.gov/2022057924

ISBN 978-1-009-16941-7 Hardback
ISBN 978-1-009-16942-4 Paperback

Cambridge University Press & Assessment has no responsibility for the persistence
or accuracy of URLs for external or third-party internet websites referred to in this
publication and does not guarantee that any content on such websites is, or will
remain, accurate or appropriate.

To Linda, who has shared so much of this journey with me and has made possible the best of my life; to Alexandra, Adam, Marta, Elizabeth, Maximilian, Cecilia, Geronimo and Hope, who will live in the world we have shaped and in their turn reshape it; and to Darwin, Bailey, Maggie and Ben, who have reminded me that we share the planet with others.

# Contents

# Figures

# Tables

# Boxes

# Acknowledgments

The arguments in this book have evolved for many years, and over that time my thinking has been shaped by many friends and collaborators. So, the list of those who deserve acknowledgment is vast. I will undoubtedly forget some; to them, I apologize.

First and foremost, I acknowledge my human family: Alex, Adam, Marta, Elizabeth, Max, Cecilia, Gimo, Hope and most of all Linda. They give my life meaning and comfort. So too have our canine companions, Darwin, Bailey, Maggie and Ben. My parents, Glen and Nora, always nurtured and supported my aspirations.

Several colleagues have given me extensive, detailed and very thoughtful comments on drafts: Shahzeen Attari, Paul McLaughlin, Kristian Nielsen, Matt Sanderson, Mike Vandenbergh and Cam Whitley; as did the anonymous reviewers for Cambridge University Press. I hope I have adequately reflected their insights.

Much of my initial thinking in these issues emerged while I was an undergraduate, and a number of friends and faculty, several of them musicians or historians rather than scientists, shaped my perspective. For long friendship and inspiration, I thank Alex Bevan, Kerry Blech, Rolly Brown, Andy Cohen, G. Dennis Cooke, Tom Grace, Howard Hobbs, Tom Lough, Owen Lovejoy, Olaf Prufer, Nancy Rogers, Bud Shane, Barbara Taylor, Bruce Way, Gene Wenninger and George Whitney.

I was fortunate to learn immensely from peers and faculty while in graduate school. For serving as mentors and colleagues, I thank Linda Benner, Ruth Dixon, Bruce Hackett, Kathy Holden, Tom Love, Ben Orlove, Karen Paige, Dan Ray, Pete Richerson, Gordon Rausser, Sy Schwartz, Tim Tardiff, Phil Terry. Ed Vine. and especially my advisors, Jim McEvoy and Jim Cramer.

A special acknowledgment is owed to my friend of longest duration, John Barone. We went to school together K–PhD, he led the Cuyahoga River project, is first author on my first published paper, taught me a great deal about the physical aspects of environmental issues, was a comrade in much that we did at Kent State and remains a dear friend and source of insights and laughs.

Over the years, I have benefited immensely from many collaborators. Much of what is here reflects their insights. These include especially those who Linda Kalof calls "the rhizomes" – the network of our students who continue to be an inspiring community. In chronological order of their PhDs: Steve Whitfield, Cynthia Warrick, Annette Hanada, Mike Slimak, Desiree DiMauro, Robin Sweeney, Vivian Nolan, Mitch Baer, Nancy Kanbar, Chris Oliver, Amy Fitzgerald, Joe Greenblott, Rachael Shwom, David Bidwell, Lori Baralt, Jennifer Kelly, Ryan Gunderson, Cam Whitley, Seven Mattes, Stephen Vrla, Mark Suchyta and Nathan Poirier. A joy of my career has been to meet scholars who became friends: Joe Arvai, Rich Borden, Mel Bowers, Chien-fe Chen, Bill Clark, Nives Dolšak, Ken Frank, Scott Frey, Jonathan Gilligan, Larry Hamilton, Ryan Haupt, Andrew Jorgenson, Bonnie McCay, Aaron

McCright, Ted Parson, Sandy Marquart-Pyatt, Pam Matson, Seven Mattes, Emilio Moran, Richard Moss, Kristian Nielsen, Lin Ostrom, Aseem Prakash, Jiaguo Qi, Ortwin Renn, Louie Rivers, John Robinson, Gene Rosa, Tom Rudel, Steve Schneider, Margaret Shannon, Linda Steg, Paul Stern, Lee Talbot, Paul Thompson, Seth Tuler, Mike Vandenbergh, Tom Webler, Kyle Whyte, Don Worster, Richard York and Jinhua Zhao. Jack Liu has led many important collaborations in which he has graciously included me, among them fruitful work with wonderful emerging scholars, including Xiadong Chen, Min Gong Chung, Zhenci Xu, Wu Yang and Hongbo Yang. I have the special good fortune of having Linda Kalof and Adam Douglas Henry as both family and collaborators. For two decades, Carl Taylor has shared wisdom, insight and guidance; I am honored to call him a friend and cherish our special connection as we walked parallel paths.

Organizations matter. I have had the good luck to be part of Michigan State's Environmental Science and Policy Program, the Department of Sociology and the Center for Systems Integration and Sustainability as well as the University of Vermont's Gund Institute. Each has provided intellectual and material support. For the last two decades, much of my work has been supported by Michigan AgBio Research (the "Experiment Station").

The team at Cambridge University Press assembled to produce the book have been exemplary; I thank Sapphire Duveau, Sarah Lambert, Matt Lloyd and Preethika Ramalingam, and especially Linsey Hague for their work. Rachel Kelly did amazing work tracking down sources for examples used throughout the book. Jihan Mohammed provided very nuanced insights into the implications of terms such as "third world." I thank Susan Kendall and Scout Calvert who gave me expert and wise advice on how to make this book as accessible to students as possible via working constructively with libraries.

# Introduction

We arrive at decisions as a result of necessity ... or luck.

Jerry Garcia[1]

All models are wrong. Some models are useful.

George E. P. Box[2]

Noble friends,
That which combined us was most great, and let not
A leaner action rend us. What's amiss,
May it be gently heard: When we debate
Our trivial difference loud, we do commit
Murder in healing wounds: then, noble partners,
The rather, for I earnestly beseech,
Touch you the sourest points with sweetest terms,
No curstness grow to the matter.

*Antony and Cleopatra*, Act 2, Scene 2

The Cuyahoga River caught fire in 1969. The "burning river" became a major symbol of the environmental movement as the first Earth Day in 1970 approached.[3] It was not the first time pollutants on the Cuyahoga had ignited, and steps were underway to address the problem.

The fire was in the industrial "flats" in downtown Cleveland where the river flowed into Lake Erie. Akron, 45 miles south and upriver, was another major source of pollution. Still further upriver, the Cuyahoga flowed through my hometown, Kent, Ohio. Kent started as a mill town powered by the river. By the late 1960s, people in Kent were aware of pollution but thought the river was beautiful. A dam and waterfall were the center of town, and the major park was on the river.[4] In 1971, I was part of a team of fourteen undergraduates at Kent State University who studied the river within the boundaries of Kent, a five-mile stretch.[5] That experience began the thinking that led to this book.

Members of our research team had been involved in organizing Kent State's version of the first Earth Day, which we called "Project Earth." Earth Day was on April 22, 1970, but events stretched before and after that.[6] Project Earth was scheduled for May 6. It never happened. The campus was closed on May 4 after four students were killed and nine wounded by the Ohio National Guard.[7] Studying a local ecosystem was a way to link science to our politics and ethics. The relationship between science and politics, facts (how the world is) and values (how we would like it to be), understanding and action, is the central theme of this book. The term "sustainability" would not come into common use until the 1980s (see Chapters 1 and 2). But the themes of sustainability – reducing stress on the environment while improving the well-being of humans and other species – were central to our thinking and engagement at Kent State.

Our study anticipated the arguments I will make in the book. It was highly interdisciplinary, looking at the hydrology, water chemistry and biology of the river, the opinion of the Kent community and the economics of the river in Kent. We knew the history of the area, including the displacement of Indigenous people by settler colonists. Standing Rock in the middle of Cuyahoga near the northern border of Kent was known as a site for deliberation by Native American communities.[8] The abolitionist John Brown had run a tannery in Kent and the remnants of his building were in the middle of our study area, linking to the fight against slavery. Kent had been a site of fierce union struggles in the 1930s.[9] In addition to that context, we also learned from the community. A survey we conducted revealed that the public in Kent loved the river, knew it had great potential for recreation and were eager for a clean-up and better public access.[10] Those views became evidence in the struggle that led to the creation of the Cuyahoga River National Park.

Work on sustainability emphasizes being "place-based," but "place" makes sense only by linking the local to the global.[11] Our study showed the interplay between Kent and the larger political-economic system. We identified four major issues in our stretch of the river. The first had a local cause and a local solution – some practices at the drinking water treatment plant were unnecessarily degrading the river. The second – a lack of investment in public access to the river – could be partially solved by local governments but also required state and federal action. The third was that the flow of water in the Cuyahoga River through Kent was controlled by the City of Akron. Akron takes its water from Lake Rockwell upstream of Kent. In times when the Lake was low, Akron would cut the flow over the Lake Rockwell dam to a trickle, generating serious problems for the river ecosystem. The flow problems required a regional solution and federal assistance, including the eventual removal of the dam in downtown Kent. The most serious problems were the discharge of toxic heavy metals and hydrochloric and sulfuric acids used in industrial "pickling" of metals and electroplating. The companies generating this pollution were national, with publicly traded stock, so they were resistant to any local pressure to reform. This local place-based problem could be solved only by state and national policy change and enforcement. While we did not articulate it at the time, in each of these issues there is a tension between narrow self-interest and the larger public good. That tension is central to most environmental decisions.

Studying the Cuyahoga started my thinking about how to make decisions in the face of serious problems and important opportunities. Global environmental change has been transforming the planet. Long-standing problems of inequality, poverty, prejudice, and violence persist. Emerging robotic, nano, information, bio and cognitive technologies have immense potential for good and ill. To avoid catastrophes, to craft a better world, we will have to make good decisions, decisions that foster sustainability and justice. We need decisions that enhance human well-being and the well-being of other species and that reduce the stress humans place on the biosphere. In pursuit of that goal, I explore the concept of sustainability, and what we know about how we make decisions, and offer some thoughts on how we might do better. At the start of this journey, I acknowledge that my focus on justice, human well-being, other species and the biosphere reflects my values and that people differ in what they consider important.

Following the logic of George E. P. Box in the epigraph, I suspect much of what I have to say will be wrong.[12] But I hope that even my errors will advance your thinking. That is the nature of the scientific enterprise. We offer ideas and evidence. We discuss them. Better understanding emerges from the discussion. Our understanding always evolves. Little that I say is original. I am building on large intellectual traditions and most of my contribution, such as it may be, comes from rearranging those traditions. As Jean-Luc Godard seems to have said: "It's not where you take things from, it's where you take them to."[13]

## I.1    The Plan of the Book

My goal in this book is to explore how understanding both decision-making and sustainability might help us make better decisions. Chapter 1 engages the idea of decisions that shape our impacts on the environment and on well-being. Chapter 2 reviews how the concept of sustainability emerged and how it relates to the idea of growth. Chapter 3 reviews three major approaches to understanding individual decision-making. Chapter 4 asks how we can distinguish between facts and values. Chapter 5 proposes criteria for good decisions. Chapter 6 identifies sources of conflict that make it hard to make good decisions. Chapter 7 examines the relations between gradual progress and radical transformation. Chapter 8 focuses on how we might make better decisions as individuals. Chapter 9 examines how we might structure public discourse to yield better group decisions. I have tried to structure each chapter so that it can be read on its own. As a result, a number of key issues are revisited in multiple chapters.

There are six ideas that shape what follows in this book: cultural evolution and the need for diversity, altruism versus self-interest, the need to be explicit about facts and values, the importance of moving across disciplinary boundaries, the idea of deliberation and the importance of a critical assessment of society. The arguments in the chapters that follow are based on them. I hope that will be obvious as you read through the chapters, but I thought it would be useful to make them explicit here.

## I.2    Six Perspectives

### I.2.1    Cultural Evolution

Most of human behavior, and certainly most of our decisions, are substantially influenced by culture – what we learn from others. Culture is our dominant mode of adaptation. As Henrich puts it, culture is "the secret of our success" – where success is meant in the simple and problematic sense that we have become a dominant species in Earth's biosphere.[14] Understanding cultural evolution is essential for understanding social change, and thus for seeing how we can move towards a just and sustainable future.

The cultural evolution perspective I use has five key elements.[15] First, culture is viewed as the information we acquire from others, whether by direct teaching, by observing or by discussion. The culture of a group can be thought of as the rules that shape decisions and influence actions.

Some of those rules are written in laws or in the formal procedures that tell us what to do and how to do it. Other rules are more informal: values, norms and beliefs held by members of the group.[16] Different people hold different views and individual views change over time. We can define subpopulations based on their values, norms and beliefs (e.g., conservatives, liberals), or we can define subpopulations based on demographic characteristics (e.g., gender identity, race/ethnicity, age, place of residence, social class) and examine their subcultures.

Second, cultural change is driven by social learning and selection that favors some values, norms, beliefs and practices over others.[17] Box I.1 provides two examples of the process of cultural evolution. Culture influences our decisions and shapes our actions. In turn, other individuals, human and nonhuman, as well as the nonliving parts of the environment, respond to those actions. That response creates a form of selection. If I get a strong positive reaction from my peers by saying climate change is a serious issue, that strengthens my belief in climate change and encourages others to take climate change seriously. If I get a strong negative reaction, I am likely to let go of that belief, and so will others who observe the negative reaction.[18] Over time, the content of culture evolves from these selective pressures. Some elements of culture become more legitimate, others less so. And individuals (influencers), social movements and organizations work very hard to shape cultural change in directions they favor – a key element of ever-changing preferences in music and art but also of political change as the powerful try to shape culture to serve their interests. So, I define power as "the ability to influence the situation so as to ensure that others behave as desired, that is, the ability to influence the rules upon which others act."[19] (While I focus on individuals, organizations and movements also shape cultural evolution; see Box I.2.)

Change also happens as we learn from new groups, as we generate new ideas and sometimes from errors in copying others. These processes constantly generate variation within a group. Then, selection acts on this variation, favoring some values, beliefs, norms and practices while suppressing others. This overall process – variation and selective retention – is evolution. The same general mechanism applies to the evolution of culture, to genetic evolution, to the selection of algorithms in genetic programming.[20] Evolution is a very general process, but the details are very different for culture, genes and algorithms.

---

## Box I.1 Two Examples of cultural evolution

In the United States in the early 1960s, the honorific for adult women, Miss or Mrs., signaled their marital status. But all adult men, married and unmarried, were given the honorific Mr. Starting with the new wave of the women's/feminist movement in the late 1960s, Ms., an honorific for women that does not signal marital status, became common. Ms. had been in the dictionary for centuries. What changed was the norm that it, not Mrs. or Miss, should be used for adult women. Gender-neutral pronouns were also promoted in the early 1970s. I was captivated by a novel, *The Cook and The Carpenter*, that used gender neutrality in writing, in particular the pronoun thon ("that one"), to show deep gender biases in our thinking.[21] But while Ms. became standard, "thon," which has been in dictionaries since the 1930s, did not catch on, nor, at first, did other gender-neutral pronouns. In the last two decades, the singular, gender-neutral "they" has become common to respect the preferences of nonbinary, transgender and gender-nonconforming people. These continuing changes are an example of cultural evolution actively promoted by a social movement. New norms about pronouns do not transform gender relations or end discrimination and bias, but they do reduce some microaggressions and can help many people feel a bit more accepted and acknowledged. And they raise our awareness of issues around gender identity and that awareness can facilitate further change.

Technological change is also an evolutionary process. Starting about 9,500 years ago, the Indigenous people of the North American Great Lakes region may have been the first to make copper tools (arrowheads, knives, axes) and art.[22] But after about 4,500 years, copper was not used much. Why was copper abandoned? The copper in the area is exceptionally pure and thus rather soft. The arrowheads and other tools made from it are not much better than well-crafted stone tools and are much harder to make.[23] Climate change – a dry period – probably made efficient tools very important. Using stone rather than copper saves time and effort. Copper was gradually abandoned except for art and awls, where even the soft copper is better than stone. Technological and environmental change were intertwined and shaped in part by context – the kinds of copper available. Giving up copper was not a step backwards but just selection favoring the best tools when resources were scarce.

Third, evolutionary thinking is grounded in population thinking, a core idea of Charles Darwin's *On the Origin of Species*.[24] Population thinking sees large patterns, including social structure, generated by the actions of individuals. But those large patterns in turn shape individual action. It is a holistic way of thinking about humans and their interactions with each other, with other species and with the biosphere. But unlike some systems-based approaches, population thinking doesn't assume "the system" has a reality distinct from the parts.[25] Box I.2 examines how population thinking links individual decision-making with decision by organizations like corporations and governments.

### Box I.2  Networks, organizations and institutions

"US formally withdraws from Paris agreement" (BBC News, November 4, 2020)

"U.S. officially rejoins Paris Agreement on climate change" (NPR News, February 19, 2021)

"GM announces electric Chevy Silverado pickup that can go 400 miles on a single charge" (CNN Business, April 6, 2021)

These news stories seem to be saying that the US government and GM are making decisions. Why do I focus on decisions by individuals? Aren't the decisions that matter those by organizations: governments, corporations, social movement groups, churches and so on?[26] As consumers, some of us decide to buy a car with low greenhouse gas emissions. A state government can impose standards on all new cars, a car rental company can insist on low emissions from the hundreds of thousands of cars they buy each year and car manufacturers can decide to produce vehicles that emit less.

It can be convenient to talk about the United States or GM making a decision. The term "organization" implies something that we think of in ways very similar to the way we think about people.[27] And in many legal systems, including in the United States, organizations that have been created by "incorporating" have legal rights; they are "juristic persons." So, talking about decision made by organizations seems natural.

But until major decisions are turned over to artificial intelligence, people make the decisions even when, for convenience, we say a government or a corporation does. Before an important decision is reached there is usually discussion. Even in a dictatorship, the dictator will have a circle of advisors.[28] Politics is the actions, including discussion, trying to influence decisions. There may be very clear rules about who makes the decision, about the criteria they should use, about who they should consult with and how. There are always informal flows of information making connections outside of the formal organization. For governments, we call these policy networks, and they include members of the legislature and the executive branch of government but also lobbyists, political commentators, social movements, experts and ordinary citizens who try to make their views heard.[29] Similar networks exist within and between private corporations, and there are many links between governments and corporations as they try to influence each other. And even within a corporation with a formal chain of command determined by legally binding written rules, we cannot understand decision-making without taking account of the individuals involved and informal networks both within and stretching outside the formal organizational structure.[30] So, while it is sometimes useful to think of the California state government or National Rent a Car acting as if they were a person, we have to be careful that approach doesn't mislead us.[31]

Thinking about organizations reminds us of a key point of the evolutionary perspective: individuals are always embedded in larger structures. We live in networks of others who we observe and learn from, who observe and learn from us, with whom we share resources and have conversations. Just as decisions by organizations involve individuals, individual decisions are embedded in larger structures that nearly always include organizations.

Social movements are special social networks that include organizations, strongly committed and active individuals and those less active but supportive of the movement, who may or may not be members of movement organizations. Movements are one of the most important ways that cultural change occurs. Movements influence how we think about issues and are key to struggles to bring about changes in policies in government, corporations and other organizations. Throughout the book, I will refer repeatedly to the environmental movement and movements to promote social justice and overcome bias – they are central to what has happened and to change in the future.[32]

The term "institution" is used to describe not only the networks interacting to produce decisions, including the organizations, but also the formal, written rules and the informal rules – the norms – that shape those interactions.[33] Cultural change in those rules can have important consequences for both human well-being and the environment. So, moving towards sustainability is often talked about as changing institutions that shape both individual and organizational decisions.

Political economies are sets of institutions that shape how members of societies act, and thus what happens in response to those actions. In evolutionary terms, they are selective regimes, albeit ones that can be reshaped by the actions of those with power.[34] Terms like "capitalism," "communism," "fascism," and "socialism" are very broad descriptions of types of political economies; real political economies will always be complex hybrids of these abstractions. Ostrom emphasized distinctions across governance by markets, by central governments and by communities in order to make the point that in reality there are no pure forms – all governance mechanisms are a hybrid that involve aspects of all three.[35] We can ask what kinds of decisions are degrading human well-being or the environment, and how those decisions are being and might be shaped by institutional arrangements. We can then try to change institutions to do better. I will return to this in Chapter 9, but note here that invoking the abstract terms for "isms" in political conflict often generates more heat than light and makes it harder to find solutions.[36]

Fourth, cultural evolution takes place in ecosystems filled with humans and other species as well as the physical environment – coupled human and natural systems.[37] The ecological theorist G. Evelyn Hutchinson titled one of his books *The Ecological Theater and the Evolutionary Play*.[38] I think of the cultural evolutionary play in the human ecological theater. Change and structure are inextricably intertwined, and one cannot understand one without considering the other. Everything we do as humans has effects on other species and the environment, and other species and the environment are constantly influencing us, even when we are not aware of it.

Finally, a cultural evolution perspective draws attention to the vital importance of diversity. Selection requires diversity. This is true in genetic evolution, where genetic diversity is essential for coping with change.[39] In cultural evolution, having multiple values, beliefs and norms – multiple perspectives – engaged in a discussion is essential for evolution in the face of social, technological and environmental change. Without such diversity, there is no basis for adaptive response to changes and no chance for hybrid ideas. Even in small groups, diverse ideas seem more important for problem-solving than the overall level of expertise, although both matter.[40] When we move from individuals to organizations, markets or democracies, diversity remains important, although power and social structure can influence the degree to which diversity facilitates problem-solving. My emphasis on diversity is driven not just by a concern with fairness but also by an understanding of the importance of diversity for finding effective solutions to complex, rapidly changing and very pressing problems.[41]

The evolutionary perspective is a powerful tool for understanding change and the relationship between individuals and larger structures. Evolution can hone marvelous adaptations, and paying attention to evolutionary processes will help us develop better approaches to a just and sustainable future. But the scientific power of evolutionary explanations does not imply that the outcome of the evolutionary process is always ethically desirable.[42] Understanding evolution can help us make decisions that guide us towards the future we want. But desirable outcomes are not "natural" or inevitable. The next two sections elaborate on these points.

## I.2.2    Altruism versus Self-Interest

Do we act from narrow assessment of what matters for ourselves and close family members? Or are we often altruistic, taking account of the effects of our decisions on other humans, on other species, on the biosphere itself? The contrast between altruism and self-interest, and the scope of altruism, is a central theme in evolutionary theory and in nearly all the social sciences.[43]

It can be hard to maintain altruism in a social group. If you bear a personal cost from being altruistic (and that is really what we mean by altruism), there will be selection against acting altruistically. If altruistic actions benefit the larger group, then that benefit might outweigh the costs to you. So, when do the benefits to the group from altruism outweigh the costs to the individual? When can altruism towards those who are not close kin persist and even spread rather than being selected out and disappearing? For genetic evolution, the general answer is: only under very special conditions, such as among bees and ants.[44] Cultural evolution proceeds differently than genetic evolution, and altruism can persist and spread via cultural dynamics.[45] But cultural evolution can also favor homophily (sometimes called "tribalism") – situations where we are more attentive to, and trust more, those we resemble.[46] I will argue this tendency is a major obstacle to making good decisions. Unfortunately, the assignment of similarity and difference is often based on arbitrary cues such as physical appearance, religion or social class, or accents and other language patterns. So, cultural evolution can support caring for the well-being of others but also racism and other prejudices.

## I.2.3    Explicit about Facts, Values and Ethics

I use the term "facts" to mean beliefs about the state of the world, "values" to refer to what each of us sees as important and "ethics" as the rules we favor when values are in conflict, either in a decision by a single individual or across individuals. A long-standing debate in the social sciences and philosophy asks whether facts can be distinguished from values.[47] Chapter 4 examines the issue in detail. But to preview, I follow the position of pragmatist philosophers from John Dewey forward: For practical purposes, it is possible to distinguish facts from values and is often useful to do so. I view science as a powerful tool for assessing statements of fact.

Like any aspect of culture, science evolves. Science is always uncertain and always influenced by values and by power and biases. If we are careful about restraining those influences, we can come to understandings that are useful for decisions. For the last 500 years or so, much of the work we label "science" has emerged from Europe and its settler colonies. That science was driven by the needs of colonialism, capitalism and militarism, as well as by the hope of advancing human well-being and by curiosity. Earlier, what we call science was much more global. In the twenty-first century, the Western dominance in science is transforming into a planet-wide network, which has strong implications for what is studied and how it is studied.[48] As I will emphasize throughout the book, science is often necessary but often not sufficient for learning the facts we need to make decisions. All human cultures have evolved sophisticated understandings of their environments. Joining those understandings with those that emerge from science is crucial for dealing with most sustainability decisions. In engaging these multiple perspectives, we also should appreciate that making a distinction between facts and values is not the only way of assessing what matters in decisions, although it is usually a good strategy.

We are in a period of rapid evolution in our understandings of how to incorporate multiple perspectives into decision-making, sometimes called "decolonizing science." For example, Rebekah Sinclair uses Indigenous logics to remind us that when we speak of individual decision-making, the "individual" is embedded in and has been shaped by their culture and interactions with others.[49] We also might make decision-making less anthropocentric by taking into account the interests of other species.[50] In my discussion, I will emphasize the importance of contextual understandings, an approach intended to engage and learn from the ongoing thinking about decolonizing understandings and moving away from anthropocentrism.

I considered dropping the terms "facts" and "values" entirely to emphasize the tentative nature of "facts" and that the fact/value distinction, if used naïvely, is counterproductive. But I have found that, for many people, the terms "facts" and "values" link with their thinking and their experience in decision-making. So, the terms are useful for carrying forward a discussion that unpacks what constitutes a "fact" and the relationship of facts and values.

I will argue in Chapter 4 that science has developed some useful norms about how to decide what should be viewed as a fact; norms that, when working well, lead to understandings that are resonant with reality.[51] But the process of science, and the tentative facts that emerge, are never perfect; the process is ongoing and often challenged by those with power who want to shape public beliefs. Keeping scientific assessment of facts as free from the influences of bias and power is a constant struggle. In Chapter 3, I will discuss the social psychological research that shows that, as individuals, we use both values and beliefs about facts in making decisions and that our values influence our beliefs, even, as in science, we have to struggle to moderate the influence of values and power on our assessment of the facts.

Economics and decision sciences have long been explicit about the distinction between a descriptive statement of how the world works and an ethical statement of what is best. Most economists and decision scientists support a utilitarian ethical theory, arguing that decisions should provide the greatest good for the greatest number. There are many other ethical theories, and some of them are deployed in policy analysis, as we will see in Chapter 5. But too often those calling for action on sustainability problems are not clear about the ethical theories that underpin their analyses.

Scientists who want to influence decision-making should be thoughtful and articulate about the ethical positions they advocate. People will differ in what is important to them, their values, and in the ethical theories they advocate to resolve value conflicts. For the discussion to progress, clarity about the ethical theories in play is essential.[52] (That is not to say you must pick only one theory; in Chapter 5, I argue in favor of seven.) If we combine a descriptive theory of how the world works, values about what is important and ethical theories of how to weigh value differences across people and across outcomes, we may be able to produce sound prescriptive ideas about what we should do to make things better, to move towards sustainability.

### I.2.4    Integrating across Disciplines

The Greek poet Archilocus said "a fox knows many things but a hedgehog knows one big thing." Isaiah Berlin drew on the metaphor to characterize scholarship – some scholars are interdisciplinary foxes,[53] but others are specialist hedgehogs. Science probably advances most effectively when we have diversity in styles – both hedgehogs and foxes. The Rosetta Stone, looted from Egypt by Napoleon's troops, was the basis for understanding Egyptian hieroglyphics and thus gaining insight into an important ancient African civilization. Deciphering it required work by both the hedgehog Jean François Champollion and the fox, Thomas Young – neither alone could have figured it out.[54]

From the start, I have embraced interdisciplinary approaches. My Ph.D. is in ecology with a specialization in human ecology. I have always had joint faculty appointments in sociology departments and at least one other academic unit that focused on the environment. Given the urgency of the sustainability problems we face, we need to speed the cumulation of knowledge by integrating across disciplinary boundaries. One goal of this book is to provide links between perspectives so we can build a better-connected network that allows us to learn from each other.[55]

Academic disciplines are aggregations of theories, methods and research topics. Their boundaries come from the history of professional societies and university departments. Most social science disciplines were organized to address the problems of the late nineteenth and early twentieth centuries.[56] Disciplines have built knowledge and honed methods for studying those problems. But disciplinary boundaries are often impediments to the flow of information and can retard the advance of our understanding. We need different configurations of research to address new problems, including sustainability.

We can learn a lot by treating disciplinary traditions with respect even as we develop a more inclusive perspective. Often critiques of a discipline address a stereotype rather than making a legitimate engagement with the core active thinking in the discipline. Even when I am critical, I hope that I am doing so with respect and with reasonable accuracy. One cost of my approach is that I cannot review in detail some of the rich and extensive literatures I engage. If a topic interests or seems important to you, take my summary as a starting point for delving into the references so that you can engage the subtleties of what is known and learn from emerging scholarship.

### I.2.5    Deliberation

Jazz music is our art form that was created to codify democratic experience and give us a model for it. Jazz music was invented to let us know how to listen to each other, how to negotiate.

The real power of jazz and the inner vision of jazz is that a group of people can come together and create art, improvise art and negotiate their agendas with each other and that negotiation is the art. (Wynton Marsalis)[57]

Communication is a crucial part of cultural evolution. We learn by observing the actions of others and by trial and error, but we also learn by engaging in deliberation with others.

Humans are exceptionally adept both at imitating others and in our linguistic ability. While language can be used to deceive and misdirect, it is also a powerful tool for understanding each other and for making decisions together. In Chapter 4, I argue that science is best understood as a process of cultural evolution where the rules that structure scientific deliberation move us to better understandings of reality. Chapters 5 and 9 offer a number of suggestions about how deliberation can be used to make decisions in the face of differing values. Overall, I suggest that deliberative approaches are the best way for moving forward towards sustainability.

The deliberative approach argues that good decisions are ones that arise from fair and competent discussions that engage all parties that are interested in or impacted by a decision. I will discuss the idea of fair and competent deliberation in Chapter 5.[58] Briefly, fair means engaging all interested and affected parties so that they have an effective voice in the decision – fairness in process. It also means that the outcomes of the decision process are evaluated for how they differentially impact various groups, giving special attention to disproportionate harm to the most vulnerable – that is fairness in outcomes. Competent means taking careful account of both facts and values, including diversity and uncertainty about both.

Deliberative approaches to decision-making seem to have been used in many societies across much of human history, and Indigenous perspectives may have had great influence on Western thinking about democracy.[59] In the quotes above, Wynton Marsalis invokes jazz performance as an example of this kind of deliberation, noting that the interaction is itself the essence of the outcome. My own engagement with deliberative theory started with the work of Jürgen Habermas, perhaps the most influential theorist of deliberation.[60] But I soon turned back to the pragmatist philosopher John Dewey, who is a major source for my thinking not just about deliberation but about how to approach problems of facts and values in decision-making.[61] The argument for deliberative processes in environmental and sustainability decisions arose in the 1980s.[62] A comprehensive review of that literature by the US National Research Council in *Public Participation in Environmental Assessment and Decision Making* concluded that:

When done well, public participation improves the quality and legitimacy of a decision and builds the capacity of all involved to engage in the policy process. It can lead to better results in terms of environmental quality and other social objectives. It also can enhance trust and understanding among parties. Achieving these results depends on using practices that address difficulties that specific aspects of the context can present.[63]

I will discuss the tradition of using deliberative approaches for sustainability decision-making in more detail in Chapter 9. In some cases, deliberation is used in policy analysis; in some cases, it is used in specific decisions; and in some, it supports ongoing management of ecosystems.[64]

Habermas and other theorists of deliberation argue about the governance of society as a whole rather than the specific decisions that aggregate into that governance. The argument is that a society is rational if and only if there is a public sphere where deliberative decision-making occurs. Feminist critiques of Habermas emphasize that most historical forms of the public sphere have favored the privilege of affluent white males over the interests of women, people of color, other disadvantaged humans and other species. In particular, Fraser has argued that in many contemporary societies it is easy for a political deliberation to be dominated by white male elites to the exclusion of others.[65] She notes that those excluded, who are also often subject to discrimination and violence, create counter-publics, spaces for discussion where their experience and concerns are articulated. Such counter-publics can initiate strategies for social change. In my view, it is crucial that deliberative processes engage such counterpublics not only to ensure that the processes are truly fair and competent but also because these views and perspectives will speed the evolution of social learning.

### I.2.6    Human Ecology: Structural and Critical

These five perspectives intersect in "structural human ecology."[66] Structural human ecology is not a specific theory but a "theory group" – a network of scholars sharing similar substantive interests, methods and approaches. The term "structural human ecology" was coined by Rosa to cover an evolving set of perspectives.[67]

York and Mancus propose a critical human ecology, allied with structural human ecology, to bring together Marxian and human ecological traditions.[68] Marxism and human ecology share a grounding in materialist approaches – taking the world as more than a social construction – and both examine historical perspectives on cultural evolution. The idea of differential power across people, organizations and nations is part of structural human ecology but the critical approach emphasizes those forces. This book is a bridge between structural and critical human ecology. The term "critical" implies moving beyond a scientific description to make ethical judgments and, in the case of critical human ecology, judgements about sustainability.[69]

Ideas of justice and sustainability raised by critical human ecology help us imagine utopias. Utopias are societies that do not exist but that would be free of the injustices of contemporary societies, societies in which humans, other species and the environment would thrive.[70] Do we get to utopia by a series of reforms or by a total transformation of society? Do reforms facilitate or block transformation? Voltaire popularized an Italian proverb on this issue: "In his writings, a wise Italian says that the best is the enemy of good."[71] I will discuss the issue of reform versus transformation in Chapter 7.

If a critical human ecology is to influence decision-making, it must proceed from an understanding of how we make decisions. Here, Robinson's advocacy of "backcasting" suggests a way of integrating utopian thinking with the kinds of analysis done in structural human ecology.[72] A community can envision a future it wants and then work backwards to find a path towards that desired future. The approach requires identification of the obstacles in the way of the desired future. Those who understand structure, cultural evolution and decision-making can help find a path around the obstacles. Reality will never follow the path projected, but continued engagement can lead to adaptive governance towards sustainability.

## I.3    The Contexts That Shaped My Thinking

The ideas that underpin human ecology and cultural evolution permeate my thinking and this book. The research I have done instantiated that perspective in problems of decision-making. The Cuyahoga River Project demonstrated the need for interdisciplinary work and showed that science can influence decision-making and that communities often have clear priorities about what they would like. Earth Day and the killings at Kent and Jackson State showed both the importance of diverse voices and the role power can have in blocking moves towards sustainability.

In the 1970s at the University of California, Davis, I worked with my first graduate advisor, Jim McEvoy, to develop methods to assess the social impacts of government decisions.[73] In the United States, the National Environmental Policy Act of 1969 called for analysis of environmental impacts before government decisions were made; similar requirements emerged in many countries and for international projects.[74] If a dam was proposed to provide hydroelectric power and prevent flooding, the logic of assessment says that before a decision is made all the environmental and social impacts of the proposed dam should be identified and analyzed to the extent possible and compared to reasonable alternatives, perhaps several smaller dams, as well as with the alternative of no dam construction. The hope was that requiring such assessments would clarify what was at stake and encourage consideration of what we would now call sustainability. There has been an understandable tendency to try to routinize these often complex, expensive and time-consuming analyses by using computer simulation models to project impacts. As we analyzed the potential impacts of a hypothetical dam in the Sierra Nevada foothills of California, it became clear that the impacts that mattered most to those who would be affected were not captured by the models. The communities cared about lifestyle; the models projected employment and tax revenues. While such models might be useful, they can dominate the discussion, leading to "bad numbers driving out good paragraphs" in the analysis. This led to my interest in processes that engage interested and affected parties in deliberation with each other and with researchers. It was also at Davis that I began working on energy conservation with Jim Cramer, Ed Vine and others (see Box 8.1), leading to my interest in individual and household environmental decision-making.

The 1970s were a time of strong conflict about the increased use of nuclear power. Nuclear proponents wanted decisions made on what they held to be an objective basis – one that would largely disenfranchise voices of the public and social movements in favor of technical analysis and, in particular, risk analysis. The complexities of dealing with toxic pollutants also encouraged the use of risk analysis. I will discuss risk analysis in Chapters 2, 3, 4 and 6. Briefly, risk analysis usually produces quantitative estimates of how many lives will be lost under alternative decisions and often of the economic costs of the decisions. When analyses become highly technical, value assumptions can get buried and the voices of those interested in and/or impacted by discussion are ignored, just as they are when simulation models are the primary basis for impact assessment. Like the deliberative turn in impact analysis, many of us argued for embedding the formal analysis in deliberative processes engaging interested and impacted parties.[75]

In the 1980s, I was working at George Washington and George Mason University and was in daily contact with people working on risk issues for the federal government but also for law and consulting firms, corporate lobbies, environmental groups, labor unions and other organizations. Bob Rycroft and I studied the network of these "risk professionals."[76] Our work made clear that decisions emerge from an interplay of individuals and organizations, with individuals shaping but also being influenced by the organizations where they worked and by their contact with others in the system. It was population thinking applied to the policy system centered "inside the beltway" in Washington, DC.

These research programs shaped the thinking reflected in this book. As I will emphasize repeatedly, the bulk of evolution in my thinking has been dominated by scholars and experiences in the Western, Educated, Industrial, Rich, Democratic (WEIRD) and capitalist parts of the world, and that is typical of much research on decision-making. But voices of people of color, of the working class and poor, of people from the third world and of Indigenous people have long been a part of discourse on environmental issues – for example, they were central to the first Earth Day in 1970 – but have seldom been adequately engaged and empowered.[77] We must also be attentive to gender identity and disability. My hope is that we can develop ways of making decisions that make use of science and of some of the ethical traditions I describe in the book but also better incorporate other perspectives, including other epistemologies and other ethical systems. Our thinking about environmental decision-making has become richer and more sophisticated in the half-century since Earth Day. I hope the next decades will see further evolution in ways that will help us move towards sustainability with fairness and competence.

## I.4    The Triplets

In working on the ideas in this book, I was struck by how often triplets emerge. We expect dichotomies: thesis and antithesis, yin and yang, structure and power, nature and society, markets and governments. But it can be dangerous to describe the world in binary categories with everything and everyone forced into one of two categories. Triplets are common in thinking about human ecological systems. I suggest there are three major approaches to understanding decision-making: the rational actor model, a social psychological framework and a framework that emphasizes heuristics and biases. These are reviewed in Chapter 3. In Chapter 4, I suggest that there are three major ethical traditions that dominate policy analysis and much collective decision-making: anarchism/libertarianism, utilitarianism and a deliberative approach.[78] The triple bottom line – care about profits, the planet and people – is a common way of engaging sustainability (see Chapter 7). Ostrom discusses the triplet of government, market and community in environmental decision-making.

I am not attributing any deep meaning to these triplets, although the number 3 has some interesting features. It is the last prime number before we hit the first non-prime, 4. Three objects produce three pairs of objects. Trinities appear in several world religions. But I see this as just an interesting coincidence and a sign that dichotomies are a bit too simple to capture important aspects of human ecology. As Ostrom's work makes clear, moving from a binary to a triplet frees us to imagine more complicated hybrids and intersections.

## I.5    Limitations

We need to engage a diversity of scholarly disciplines in decision-making. We also need many other perspectives. I bring perspectives from my personal experiences and from my research, both of which are strongly centered in my social position and are very US-centric.[79] I have noted my analysis is grounded in Western, Educated, Industrial, Rich, Democratic (WEIRD) parts of the world that are mostly in a capitalist political economy.[80] The amount of variation, the variety of contexts I have experienced and studied, is limited. The perspectives of those with different experiences and positions within the United States as well as those who bring understandings from experiences from the rest of the world need to be part of the conversation. Happily, efforts are underway to increase diversity in both the research literature and the deliberative processes that can help us make good decisions. Standpoint theorists such as Sandra Harding remind us of how essential such diversity of perspectives is for sound science. The approach echoes the Vulcan celebration of "Kul-Ut-Shan," "Infinite Diversity in Infinite Combinations" (IDIC).[81]

Even when I disagree with an argument, I try to present its logic. The most obvious example is that I try to take seriously the rational actor model and the kind of utilitarian ethics closely associated with it in policy analysis and decision-making. I also try to take seriously libertarian offshoots of anarchist views. I am critical of these approaches, but by thinking carefully about them we learn how to develop better theory and more powerful and nuanced ethical stances. I do not want to minimize the damage that can be done by narrow ethical views and by the decisions they legitimate. I emphasize Ostrom's admonition that there are no pure forms, and when rhetoric demonizes or canonizes it is often referring to something abstracted from reality – a stereotype or oversimplification that distracts us from serious analysis of serious issues. I have tried to follow the admonition of Lepidus in the epigram, disagreeing, but disagreeing gently, as I believe that approach more quickly advances the understanding we urgently need.

Finally, while I make frequent reference to the rapidly developing animal studies literature, most work on sustainability and decision-making has not gone nearly far enough to incorporate perspectives from animal studies.[82] This is ironic since human life and our cultural evolution and biological evolution have always been in interplay with other species. Indeed, the first artworks by humans include representations of other animals, indicating their significance to us. There are at least two ways the animal studies literature can contribute substantially to sustainability decisions. First, it calls for us to broaden our ethical scope to move beyond anthropocentrism and include consideration of the well-being of other species, even trying to incorporate their voices in our deliberation, the idea of "Who Will Speak for Wolf?" Second, our scientific frameworks need to take account of other species as sentient beings with agency who actively reshape their worlds even as humans do. The cultural evolutionary perspective I advocate needs to better incorporate not just our interactions with other humans and with an "environment" but also our interactions with species, many of whom also have culture, with their own lives and interests. These themes appear throughout the book but I think far more has to be done to fully incorporate them into our thinking about sustainability.

## I.6    Coda

We are faced with the necessity of making many decisions that will influence the future of the planet, including our species and the others with whom we share the biosphere. While we will need luck to avoid catastrophe, luck alone will not suffice. My goal is to encourage discussions that link thinking about sustainability with thinking about decision-making. Such conversations are underway, as are the decisions that are influencing the future. My hope is that, by expanding those conversations, we may learn to do better. To paraphrase Jerry Garcia: Things are happening, and we have to try to figure out what they are.[83]

In trying to figure out what is happening, several ideas guide me. Our decisions as individuals and in communities, organizations and governments and globally are shaped by institutions and culture that in turn are the result of both cultural evolution and by the exercise of power. In order to make better decisions, we need to shape the contexts in which we make decisions. The evolutionary perspective underpins what follows in the book, always tempered by an awareness of inequities in the power to shape decisions. I acknowledge the limits of our ability to make decisions. And I spend some time discussing the process of science. Science, for all its flaws at any point in time, seems to have developed a set of norms and institutions that tend towards self-correction in deciding how to describe the world, in what constitutes a fact. Making decisions about sustainability is more complex because we have to take account of both facts and of diverse values. But by identifying what might make for a good decision, and what gets in the way of good decisions, we may be able to shape processes that facilitate good decisions. We will make mistakes, but if we learn from those mistakes, we may be able to shape the evolution of decision-making in ways that support sustainability and are attentive to the voices of those interested in and impacted by our decisions. This view started with my experiences in Kent and has evolved to what you will read here.

# 1    Sustainability and Decisions

I went back to Ohio
But my pretty countryside
Had been paved down the middle
By a government that had no pride
The farms of Ohio had been replaced by shopping malls.
"My City Was Gone," The Pretenders

The song "My City Was Gone" laments sprawl development. Chrissie Hynde grew up in Cuyahoga Falls, Ohio, in the 1950s and 1960s.[1] My family often visited my Uncle Les, Aunt Mabel and cousins Jerry, Carl and Eileen there. In the 1950s, the drive from Kent took us past farm fields and scattered houses. Then things changed. Aunt Mabel got a job less than a mile from their suburban house at Montgomery Ward, a department store at the first large shopping center in the area. Long-standing family-owned businesses in downtown Kent and Cuyahoga Falls had trouble competing with the big-box and chain stores; many were gone by the late 1960s. By then, the drive from Kent to Cuyahoga Falls was mostly past housing and commercial developments rather than open land.

Paul McLaughlin captures Hynde's lament in the term "Genericville." You can drive around such a place (walking is difficult and dangerous) with only weather, vegetation and soil indicating if you are in New England, the Midwest, the South, California or elsewhere. This provides predictability – the same menu at every franchise restaurant in a chain no matter where it is located and whatever the season. When my family vacationed by car in the 1950s, finding a place to eat where the food was safe and tasty was a challenge. "Look for where the truckers eat" was the rule. The American Automobile Association gained the trust of American travelers from their rating system for restaurants and motels, as Michelin had in France. In Genericville, distant corporate headquarters enforce restaurant-quality standards and food safety. Often the soups, chopped salad greens and hamburger patties are shipped in from kitchens hundreds or thousands of miles away. Little or nothing is based on the local context. Any real sense of place, season and local identity is lost. Genericville minimizes diversity and local character in favor of efficiency, predictability and profitability.[2]

A conference in Fairfax County in the Northern Virginia suburbs of Washington, DC, asking "Are current patterns of land development sustainable?," prompted my thinking about the meaning of sustainability. These suburbs have been growing very rapidly for decades. From the year 2000 to 2010, Loudon County, about 35 miles from Washington, nearly doubled in population, adding about 170,000 people over that decade.[3] Developments were extending ever further into the farmland that surrounded them. A few small towns, with histories stretching back to before the Revolutionary War, were starting to thwart the plans of developers. When a community resisted sprawl, development would leapfrog, with the result that some old towns and small areas of farmland were surrounded by Genericville.

These suburbs have some of the worst traffic congestion in the United States. The DC Metro rapid transit system was designed in the 1960s to handle commuting between downtown Washington and the inner suburbs. By the 1990s, most commuting was from one suburban location to another – something hard to do on the Metro. Rapid growth was putting a strain on the water system even though this is a relatively wet part of the United States. I've been told by experts that some communities downstream from newer developments were drinking water that was "recycled." So much water was being taken by upstream users that, by the time a glass of water is drawn from a tap downstream, on average that water had already been processed through a municipal water treatment system – a sewage treatment plant.[4] Northern Virginia could be a poster child for the problems of sprawl. If sustainability involves thinking about economic development, the environment and quality of life, it made sense to discuss issues of sustainability in Northern Virginia. However, for most participants at the conference the key issue was that sprawl growth might not be able to continue. It might not be sustainable in the sense of continuing without change.[5] The discussions were almost the antithesis of what is normally meant by "sustainable development."

Ironically, Northern Virginia has a model of what a community might be. Reston, Virginia, was founded in 1964 by Robert E. Simon (hence RESton) and was perhaps the first planned community in the contemporary United States. The original development surrounded the artificial Lake Anne and was modeled after Portofino, Italy. Community design gave preference to walking over driving. Lake Anne Plaza was the hub of the development, with a plaza, restaurants and other businesses on the first floor and apartments on the second and third floors. My wife Linda and I and our golden retriever Darwin lived in a townhouse complex about a mile away. The kitchens were small by design to encourage dining in the community. Air-conditioning used cool water from the bottom of Lake Anne so there would be no noisy outside compressors that could discourage conversations and disrupt tranquility. The National Wildlife Federation had designated the community a "backyard wildlife habitat." Simon's ideal was that people could live, work and relax in the community and that one could live there comfortably from childhood to old age. The proximity of work, home, stores and schools could ease gendered divisions of labor. Reston was also intended to be a racially integrated community at a time when that was innovative. There is a fifteen-story high-rise apartment building on the plaza and apartments, townhouses and single-family dwellings are tastefully intermixed. All the businesses in the plaza were locally owned. Reston was a refuge from the sprawl of the rest of Fairfax County. It could have been a model for the development that dominated the rest of the region – clusters of high density with amazing amenities. But "old" Reston was a quaint anomaly. The typical pattern for Northern Virginia, and even Reston outside the original development, was a sprawl of single-family houses, apartment/condo complexes, big-box stores and strip malls. Unlike the historic district of Reston, cars, roads and parking lots dominate most of the Northern Virginia suburbs of Washington, DC, a pattern that now impacts communities fifty or more miles away. But it is not uniform. Thirty miles away, Hillsboro,

Virginia, has found ways to preserve its small-town character in the face of pressure from sprawl and the commuting that dominate the area around it.[6] Unlike Reston, where Simon had the resources to plan the community from the start, in Hillsboro the changes have come from hard work by a broad coalition, engaging state and federal as well as local resources.

At the conference, the contrast between my expectations for a discussion of sustainability in Northern Virginia, perhaps invoking Reston, and the expectations of those promoting development was startling. It made me wonder if the term "sustainability" is useful in guiding our decisions. A few years later, I was at a meeting between agricultural researchers and the heads of organizations representing agribusinesses. One researcher emphasized that his group was moving to focus more on sustainable agriculture. The president of a powerful group responded, quite sharply, "Whose agriculture isn't sustainable?" It became clear that these organizations had a different view of organic farming, free range animal husbandry, local sourcing of food and similar moves that many of us would interpret as "more sustainable." In their minds, these forms of agriculture were economic anomalies and impractical. They strongly supported a "right to farm" law to keep agriculture "sustainable." "Right to farm" was usually promoted as a way of keeping new migrants to the countryside from objecting to traditional agricultural practices – a matter of sustainability for contemporary agriculture. We have lived in an area of Vermont with working farms as neighbors. It is certainly true that new residents from the suburbs are sometimes startled by the smell that comes from spreading cow manure on pasture. One can understand the desire to keep folks "from away," as native Vermonters put it, from blocking such farming practices.[7] But "right to farm" laws often have been used by large corporate agricultural operations, including huge concentrated animal feeding operations (CAFOs), to defend against lawsuits from neighbors and to supersede local zoning and other restrictions.[8] So, once again, I had encountered a group with strong views about sustainability as they defined it but with a perspective very different from mine.

## 1.1 Small Examples and Grand Challenges

We face huge and transformational challenges. Some of these are continuations of problems of coercion, discrimination and inequality that have been with us since humans first transformed ecosystems and were caught in hierarchical political and economic structures. They are still so prevalent around the globe and within the United States that they require urgent action, and in too many places they are getting worse.[9]

Global environmental change (GEC) – climate change, biodiversity loss, alteration of biogeochemical cycles, widespread dispersion of persistent toxics and plastics – began millennia ago. The pace of GEC greatly accelerated with European colonialism, capitalism and the industrial revolution and accelerated again after World War II with global markets, more powerful technologies and much larger human populations in most parts of the world. Some fear that we are exceeding planetary boundaries – putting so much stress on the environment that ecosystems are being overwhelmed, with catastrophic results for humans and other life on earth.[10]

Problems are emerging that will be equally challenging. Novel technologies will transform the world and generate new issues by changing how we impact the environment and engage with other humans and other species. Among them:

(1) Nanotechnology: the ability to build tiny machines, the size of small insects or even as small as specks of dust;
(2) Biotechnology: directly intervening in the genetics of humans and other organisms;
(3) Information technology: artificial intelligences with far greater capacity than humans;
(4) Cognitive and neurotechnology: understanding of how our brains work but also unprecedented abilities to intervene in our brains and minds;
(5) Robotics: machines that can mimic and exceed human abilities.

They are not distinct technologies. As each develops, they draw on the others.

These technologies raise profound ethical and policy issues. They will make us confront what we mean by "human," creating new moral dilemmas. Debates about genetically modified organisms in the food supply, about privacy and access to personal information on the Internet and about robots (automation) displacing jobs have been going on for decades. Further debates are developing about whether we should:

• allow combat robots to make "kill" decisions without human intervention;
• permanently alter the genes of wild populations of plants and animals;
• alter the genes of a human to enhance their capabilities.

As with sustainability, good decisions about these emerging challenges will have to be made based on the best possible understanding of the available facts and by thoughtful engagement with our values. Lessons we learn about decision-making for problems of sustainability can teach us a great deal about how to proceed.

Given these huge challenges, why do I so often invoke small decisions, for example how we should manage land development at the local and regional level? As I emphasized in the Introduction, small decisions shape, and are shaped by, larger structures and give us a way to think about and ultimately influence them. As those local changes aggregate across the planet, the biosphere is changed.[11] My hope is that thinking about the small and sometimes the local can help make the issues involved in decisions more transparent and closer to most of our experiences.

Understanding land use also requires us to confront the historical interplay of land use with discrimination and inequality.[12] Northeastern Ohio, Northern Virginia and indeed all the land in the United States were once occupied and tended by Indigenous peoples. They were largely displaced by settler colonists from Europe. It is estimated that more than 50 million Indigenous people, 90 percent of the population of the Americas, died as a result of direct violence initiated by the colonists, by newly introduced diseases and by social and ecological disruption. The impacts on ecosystems were so large that they probably influenced the global climate. When areas formerly tended by Indigenous people went fallow it seems to have reduced greenhouse gases in the atmosphere enough to contribute to the "Little Ice Age" of about 1500–1850.[13] The Indigenous people who survived often were displaced from the ecosystems that had coevolved with their cultures. Whyte offers the striking argument that many Indigenous people have already lived through the dystopias usually described in science fiction.[14]

Kent, where I grew up, is located at the Great Divide that separates the Gulf of Mexico and North Atlantic watersheds. It had long been home to a sophisticated set of people who portaged between the Cuyahoga and the Tuscarawas rivers, and thus the two continental watersheds, in large networks of trade and cultural exchange – Kent is in Portage County. It seems likely that much of the Indigenous population there had been killed by the spread of European diseases before settler colonists arrived, but Ottawa, Ojibwa, Haudenosaunee (Iroquois) and Wyandot peoples were in the area. The word "Cuyahoga" probably comes from the Wyandot term for "crooked river." The political systems of the peoples of Northeastern North America were a major inspiration for Europeans who observed that many Indigenous societies were democratic and egalitarian, with broad decisions based on deliberation. It was a sharp contrast to the more hierarchical and authoritarian societies of Europe.[15]

While slavery was not prevalent in Kent, the site of John Brown's tannery on the Cuyahoga invoked the struggle for abolition. Soon after the first Europeans began to colonize the Americas, an economy based on slavery started to grow. About 2 percent of what would be the US population was in bondage by the time the Declaration of Independence and the Constitution were written. In what would become the Confederacy, the fraction was more than one-third and remained at that level until the Civil War. Many of the compromises enshrined in the Constitution came from demands to maintain the slave economy in the new nation.[16] When the Civil War ended slavery, racism and discrimination against African Americans evolved into new forms. Such discrimination has also damaged the lives of Latinx people, people of Asian ancestry, Native Americans and other Indigenous peoples. Indeed, at various points and places in US history nearly every ethnic group except those of English ancestry has been subject to discrimination. But discrimination based on the social construct of race has been and continues to be the most pervasive and pernicious form of prejudice. Land use reminds us of this history: The patterns we see today have been shaped by discrimination through laws, private policies and practices, and hostility and result in environmental injustice.

Reflection on the small examples like local land use can make clear how larger forces shape our lives and reveal how change initiated by individuals acting together can lead to larger structural changes that reshape society towards justice and sustainability. This interplay between individual action and larger structures is a key element of the evolutionary perspective discussed in the Introduction. Consider the abolition of slavery in the British Empire. In the late eighteenth and early nineteenth centuries, slavery and the sugar production it supported were big business, perhaps as powerful as the oil industry is now.[17] In 1787, a dozen British citizens formed what seems to be the first European organization to fight slavery. The movement that evolved used public education, lobbying, boycotts and other tactics common today. In 1807, the British involvement in the slave trade was abolished, followed by the outlawing of slavery in British colonies in 1833. Why did this happen? Part of the explanation is persistent and skillful action by those formerly in bondage and their allies in the abolition movement. Structural factors mattered too. This was a time when the rise of factories was changing the shape of the British capitalist economy and thus the profitability of slavery. In 1804, a slave revolt in Haiti established an independent country, and there were many other acts of resistance throughout the Americas by those in bondage. Colombia, Peru, Chile, Argentina, Bolivia, Paraguay, Mexico and several European nations had abolished slavery before Britain did. Both individual action and larger structures mattered and were constantly shaping each other even as they do around sustainability and justice issues today.

The history of social change also demonstrates the importance of diversity. In the case of abolition, those still in bondage, those who had escaped from bondage and the European-ancestry abolitionists were constantly collaborating with and learning from each other. To understand a situation and to interpret our values in light of that understanding requires deliberation with others whose experiences and perspectives differ from our own. Such engagement is essential in finding ways forward. As we wrestle with the triplet of old problems, global environmental change and emerging technologies, we need the wisdom and understandings that come from having diverse voices in the discussions that shape our decisions; and we have much to learn from past struggles to transform society.

## 1.2    Does the Idea of Sustainability Help Us Make Decisions?

We all seem to favor sustainability, but do we have so many different understandings of sustainability that the idea has become meaningless? Is calling for sustainability just another way of saying we should "do good?" I am not alone in raising these questions – many have commented that sustainability may have come to mean so many different things that it now means little. If the concept of sustainability is deployed by nearly everyone, is seen by everyone as largely compatible with their present objectives and is viewed by thoughtful scholars as contested, is the term still useful? Are there ways of thinking about sustainability that are helpful? In the terms of the pragmatist John Dewey, I want to examine what work sustainability does for us as we try to make complex and difficult decisions. What approaches to sustainability can help us deal with the serious challenges we face as we move through the twenty-first century? And in turn, can thinking about how we make decisions and how we might do better at decision-making help us move towards sustainability?

Tom Burns offers an important insight when he notes that terms like "sustainability," and especially definitions of it, emerge from complicated deliberations.[18] Those deliberating will usually differ in their assessment of the facts, in values they hold and in the contexts in which they will experience the outcomes of decisions. So, it should not be surprising that, in trying to resolve conflicts and reach a consensus, contradictions and imprecision characterize the terms used. Chapter 2 will explore the evolution of the concept of sustainability. For now, we can say that sustainability means caring about both human well-being and the stress we place on the environment and on other species.[19] Improving human well-being while reducing environmental stress seems uncontroversial – nearly everyone agrees with these two goals. But moving from those very general goals to a specific decision raises many complications and conflicts.

The decision of how to commute to work or school provides an example. Car travel has huge impacts globally. In the United States, cars are responsible for about 17 percent of total greenhouse gas emissions.[20] So, our transportation decisions matter. When I lived in Davis, California, many people commuted by bicycle. Recent estimates for bicycle commuting are 3 percent in Washington, DC, 1.4 percent in Lansing, Michigan, 2.5 percent in Sacramento, California, but 19 percent in Davis, California (data are only for the work commute and are for the period 2008–2012). Why the differences? The biophysical environment matters. Davis and Sacramento are pretty flat with mild winters – freezing weather is rare. The physical layout of the city impacts the time spent commuting. As was the case for Reston, land use policy decisions have made Davis compact. The longest commute within the city is only a few miles. Davis has also been an innovator in energy efficiency, including bicycle-friendly policies as well as a strong university/town bus system. There are bicycle lanes on all streets, physical barriers between bicycle and car lanes on many, an extensive network of bicycle-only paths, lots of bicycle parking and police that enforce bicycle traffic rules (including no bicycle riding on sidewalks, stop signs and even speed limits). Political decisions have shaped infrastructure to make bicycling safe and convenient.

What might I consider when making a decision about how to commute to work and, in particular, whether to bike, and how does that lead to more biking in Davis than other places? Most people would care about the monetary costs, safety, convenience, discomfort, exercise and time, and many of us care about the environmental impact. The monetary cost differences between bicycling and driving are probably the same across cities, although cars are probably more expensive to operate in larger cities. Safety will be higher in Davis because of policies and infrastructure that favor bikes. The unpleasantness of biking in winter will be less in Davis than in places with colder climates. The time cost of bicycling will usually be less in Davis because of its compact design and priority given to bikes. The environmental benefits and personal health benefits of bikes versus cars will be the same across cities for the same distance commuted. And, in Davis, because so many people travel by bike, the idea of bicycles as the typical way to get around – the norm – is much stronger than elsewhere. Different people will have different values and face different personal constraints and thus apply different weights to different criteria. Moreover, the decision may differ from day to day, depending on the weather and daily schedules. It's clear many things enter into a simple decision, with some of them shaped by the biophysical environment and many by long-standing policies.

In many ways, deciding whether or not to commute by bike is simple. I can roughly assess all the factors I've listed, including the chance of bad weather. When making choices about what food to buy, or where to live, or what candidates or policies to support, even more things have to be considered, and it can be hard to get the facts about the consequences of our choices in part because we have to predict the future and that always involves uncertainty. Individuals, households, communities, governments at all levels from the local to the global, private corporations, nongovernmental organizations, all make decisions that are consequential for the environment and for human well-being. These decisions will have impacts for years to come. Decisions that influence climate change will have impacts that persist for centuries. How does the idea of sustainability help? In the case of the bicycle commute, taking account of the environmental and human well-being might highlight the reduction in pollution and health benefits of biking and encourage me to think about how bicycling versus driving influences others in the community. So, sustainability encourages me to think about impacts beyond myself.

The *Oxford English Dictionary* tells us that the word "decision" comes to us from Latin via French. The origins are in the Latin term "decider," which means "to cut off" as well as to decide.[21] The idea of making a decision has been grounded in the idea of "cutting off" some options in favor of others. If actions result from habit, if there is no choice, if there are no options that are "cut off," then there is no decision.[22]

## 1.3    Kinds of Decisions

Most of us are aware that our choices as consumers have an impact on the environment. We can decide to buy organic, to save energy, to recycle, to bicycle. We may also be aware of the impacts of our consumer decisions on the well-being of other humans and other animals and look for products that are "fair trade," from companies that treat their workers well, opt for vegan food, or look for the animal welfare rating of animal-based foods. But how do my actions influence sprawl suburban development and large-scale agriculture? Consumer choices matter. I can favor local stores over the big chains and shop downtown. I might be able to choose to live in the city rather than the suburbs, depending on what I can afford and other constraints. But for these larger-scale impacts, it's clear that my political choices as a citizen matter too.

The six roles illustrated in Figure 1.1 can help us think about our sustainability decisions.[23] Each role involves decisions that can influencing the well-being of humans and other species and the stress we place on the biosphere. In thinking about how we can move towards sustainability, we should consider all five roles, not focus narrowly on only one.

**Figure 1.1**  Decision-making roles
Adapted from Figure 1 in Nielsen et al. (2021).

(1) Consumer. Decisions about how we use energy and water, what kinds of products we buy, whether we commute by bicycle, etc.

Most research on environmental decision-making has focused on the consumer role. Some criticize this focus on the grounds that we "cannot consume our way to sustainability." In Chapter 7, I will examine the links between reforms, like changes in consumption, and large-scale transformations. For now, I note that I know of no one who argues that changes in consumption alone will get us to a just and sustainable future. But our actions as consumers, as managers of the environmental inputs and outputs of our household, should be taken seriously for two reasons. First, they have substantial consequences. My colleagues and I have estimated that household-level decisions about direct energy consumption are responsible for 38 percent of US greenhouse gas emissions – emissions larger than those of any country except China and (of course) the United States itself.[24] We further estimate that effective programs to deploy on-the-shelf technology could reduce those emissions enough to reduce overall US emissions by 7.4 percent, more than the total emissions of France. This includes only direct energy consumption: electricity used in the house and the fuels used for heating and transportation. So, the total impact of household consumption, including impacts via decisions about food, clothing and other goods, is even larger and the potential for reductions greater.[25] Second, and perhaps more important, our decisions as consumers send signals to those who produce what we consume, and that has undoubtedly encouraged some corporations to offer more sustainable products. Such shifts can have effects throughout the supply chain for consumer products. For example, we have argued that a move towards labeling the greenhouse gas emission from products (carbon labeling) will strongly encourage companies to reduce those emissions so that their products appear more desirable.[26]

(2) Citizen. Decisions about voting, signing petitions, posting on social media, donating money to causes we support and otherwise engaging in politics.

Actions in this role range from the routine, such as voting or expressing opinions on social media, to the more committed, such as being active in social movements or political campaigns. Some who engage in activism are professionals employed by organizations to influence policy, so citizen action can overlap with organizational membership. But others are activists who are deeply committed even if they are not paid for their engagement.[27] In Chapter 9, I will discuss political engagement in democracies. I emphasize that some activists are not citizens in the legal sense; I'm using the term to cover political action no matter who engages.

(3) Role model. Making decisions visible to others.

Norms – what we think we should do, what we think others think we should do, what we think others are doing – are among the most powerful influences on our decisions (see Chapter 3). Whenever our decisions are visible to others, we are signaling what actions are appropriate. Being aware of how our actions may influence others may encourage us to make those decisions visible.

(4) Organizational participant. Engaging with an organization as a member, employee or other participant.

Most of us are regularly engaged with a number of organizations. If you work for an organization or participate in voluntary organizations, you can have some influence on the decisions of those organizations, and organizational decisions can have huge impacts on the environment and human well-being.[28] For example, many students and faculty are pressing universities to be more sustainable. As noted in the Introduction, even if an organization has very formal decision-making rules, informal networks always have an influence.

(5)  Investor. Owner of stocks or other investments in organizations.

In capitalist economies, private investors can have a tremendous influence on the behavior of private corporations, and many investors are pressing for more sustainable corporate actions.[29] Just a little more than half of US families own some stock, much of it in the form of retirement or other long-term savings. This ownership is not evenly distributed: The wealthiest 1 percent in the United States own about half of all those stocks. Large organizations, including investment firms, pension funds and universities, also own a substantial amount of stock, so organizations as well as individuals can pressure for more sustainable policies by corporations. Corporate action will be discussed further in Chapter 7.

(6)  Resource manager. Managing large or small landscapes.

Many of us manage landscapes or directly extract resources from ecosystems on a small scale, such as when we make decisions about how to care for a yard or plant a garden. Each plot is small, but overall about 2 percent of the land area of the United States is in lawns, substantially more than the area of the next largest crop, corn. Some lawns are managed with more environmental impact per acre than many farmed crops, but others are managed to protect wildlife.[30] Some people, such as farmers and foresters, manage substantial resources either as individuals or as part of a community or workers in an organization.[31] Many people are installing solar photovoltaic arrays to generate electricity on their property, making them producers as well as consumers, "prosumers."[32]

Everyone can engage in some ways in most of these roles, but the most affluent have a special responsibility.[33] The richest 1 percent of people in the world (roughly those with incomes above US$109,000 per year; to be in the richest 1 percent within the United States you need an income of $546,000 a year) have huge impacts on the environment through each of the six roles. They have generated much of the current stress on the environment and thus have leverage for taking action to reduce that stress. "With great power must also come – great responsibility."[34]

Inequality, problematic in itself, degrades our ability to achieve sustainability.[35] Inequality also means that the less affluent and powerful have unique experiences and insights about the adverse consequences of the structures and constraints resulting from past and current decisions. The most effective strategies for change require diversity in understanding, ideas and actions – we have to mobilize the experience and creativity of the 99 percent as well as the resources of the 1 percent.

Organizations as well as individuals can have multiple roles. A corporation is a consumer of what it needs to produce its products and otherwise support its activities and can have tremendous effects through its supply chain.[36] It can also act as a role model for other similar corporations and as a resource manager. Many corporations engage in political actions, since in the United States corporations have rights similar to those of citizens. Government agencies, churches, nonprofit organizations and other organizations can also have substantial impact in multiple ways.

## 1.4    Context Matters

Gene Rosa used to say that the central finding of sociology is that "Context Matters."[37] When we think about how history and context shape our decisions, we are engaging the sociological imagination: "the awareness of the relationship between personal experience and the wider society."[38] Our personal lives, with their troubles and joys and individual decisions, are embedded in larger social processes and structures. We need a way of thinking about both our power and how structure creates opportunities for and constraints on our ability to act.

Deciding where to live is an example. Where you live influences how you will commute, how much time you will spend outdoors, what consumer choices you have, your health, who you will interact with in your neighborhood, your access to shopping, recreation and other opportunities, how much influence you can have on government, and much more. So, it's an important choice, but it's a choice that is shaped by the history of land use decisions.

In many US cities, minority neighborhoods have been "redlined" – marked too risky for mortgages and other funding.[39] As a result, less was invested in buildings, parks and green space and the neighborhoods were often the site for highways and industry. Redlined areas became less desirable, with lower housing prices. Those with enough income to avoid them will do so, while those who have to seek moderately priced housing will settle there. Over the long term, these cumulating decisions increased the amount of land covered by buildings and pavement and reduced the amount of green space, factors that contribute to heat islands. So, some of the urban health problems from climate change can be traced back to racist decisions made about investments nearly a century ago. So too can some of the impact of the COVID-19 pandemic on minority communities. Such neighborhoods are often "multiply deserted areas" with limited access to food, health care, green space and public services, and the industrial facilities located there have often been a source of toxic contamination.[40]

Why don't people living in these neighborhoods move? First, the financial cost of moving can be substantial and residents often can't afford to buy or rent in more expensive neighborhoods. Second, one strategy for dealing with poverty and economic uncertainty is to rely on a network of friends and family, and that can require being near those who can help. Third, we all become attached to where we live for any length of time, and neighborhoods with challenges are also familiar homes and communities to many who live there.[41]

In the face of these multiple challenges, redlined communities have responded in diverse ways. Informal mechanisms compensate for the lack of access to formal institutions. In many cases, despite the obstacles imposed by past and present discrimination, these communities have been able to develop important community infrastructure and local businesses that provide important lessons for innovation and resilience.[42]

The consequences of redlining show how constraints on today's choices have been shaped by decisions made in the past. The interplay between context and choice, between structure and power, is central to the rest of the book. So, it will be useful to see how this dynamic plays out in the way we assess facts through research, in how we understand social change and in how inequality can have pernicious effects.

### 1.4.1  Our Understandings Are Context-Dependent

For some kinds of facts, and some kinds of science, results are very context-dependent, while for others it is not. I will discuss this in some detail in Chapter 4. Some sciences, like physics and chemistry, have strong "invariance" principles. If the speed of light is measured accurately in Cleveland in 1887, given Einstein's insight that the speed of light is a constant, we can assume that the measurement applies throughout most of history across the universe.[43] Context doesn't matter all that much, so it is much easier to be cumulative and to reduce uncertainty. But for much of the science we need for sustainability, results are very context-dependent. Facts will vary across contexts – across ecosystems, across countries, across time periods, across subgroups within the human population. Science can still establish facts, but we have to be careful in applying findings made in one context to another.

Economic decisions are a good example. As we will see in Chapter 3, nearly everyone has trouble making decisions about the future. It's sometimes suggested that people are poor and disadvantaged because of bad decision-making. But something more subtle is at work: People are often making decisions that are well adapted to difficult circumstances.[44] How have African Americans and other people of color responded to limited access to and discrimination by mainstream financial organizations such as banks and credit unions?[45] The redlining discussed at the beginning of this section is part of this discrimination, but it also influences the ability to start a business, to get an education, to deal with emergencies, and much more. One response is to depend on social networks and community. When a family living in such a context has a windfall, or when it needs a loan, it makes far better sense to turn to trusted members of one's extended family and social network than to a distant and often discriminatory organization.[46] Sharing good fortune builds social resources that can be called upon in difficult times. Later reciprocity of kin and friends may be more accessible than a small savings account. If one ignores the context in which these financial decisions are made, they might seem irrational and inefficient. But in the context of limited access to financial organizations and discrimination, relying on social ties for reciprocity makes a great deal of sense.[47]

Low-income people and people facing discrimination have often evolved approaches that differ from those used by the more affluent and favored but that are well suited to adapting to the situations they face. There are many other examples of cultures evolving strategies that work well in that context but that seem "irrational" or "inefficient" if the context is ignored. For example, African peoples who depend on cattle seem to harvest those cattle at a slower rate than might seem economically optimal. But if we take account of the need to deal with periodic droughts, then what seem like inefficiencies can also be buffers against disaster.[48] In contrast, some seemingly "rational" strategies may be very vulnerable in the face of change. We have also seen how the seemingly efficient strategy of "just in time production," where factories depend on regular deliveries of supplies to continue manufacturing, quickly fell apart in the COVID-19 pandemic.[49]

The challenge for research is trying to understand these effects of context and not overgeneralize from one circumstance to another. The challenge for policy is to design policies and programs that will work well in the contexts where they will play out. What works well in one place with a particular set of opportunities and constraints might be an abysmal failure somewhere else. As I will emphasize repeatedly, engaging with people who know the context in which decisions are made can be immensely helpful in getting it right.

While context dependency makes the science we do to inform sustainability decisions especially difficult, it is also an exciting part of our science. Acknowledging that context matters is only the first step. We want to go beyond documenting differences across contexts to understand how context affects what we observe at the individual level. Comparing economic strategies of disadvantaged communities to the mainstream reveals discrimination and lack of access but also resourcefulness in using social networks. By comparing across contexts, we gain insights into how social structure – the distribution of power, information, access to resources and so on – matters.

## 1.4.2  Context and Choice Are Two Views of the Same Process

As I argued in the Introduction, population thinking breaks down the dichotomy between structure and power.[50] As the housing example demonstrates, current choices are constrained by the history of previous decisions by others. Still other constraints are the result of the biophysical environment. But what is physically and biologically possible is shaped substantially by past decisions about technologies and resources. We develop new technologies to solve problems but also to make profits or gain power. New technologies may or may not have the consequences intended but usually have unintended and unanticipated consequences.[51] Fossil fuels became the major energy source of energy for industrial societies starting in the eighteenth century, but research on their potential to alter the climate didn't emerge until the second half of the nineteenth century and only became robust in the late twentieth century. Chlorofluorocarbons (CFCs) were introduced to make refrigeration and air-conditioning cheaper and safer. The discovery that they destroy stratospheric ozone and thus increase exposure to dangerous ultraviolet radiation on the earth's surface came later. Power plays a role in what we know about technology. There is a long history of industrial interests repressing and obfuscating science that demonstrates harm to public health and the environment.[52] And we have a tendency to invest far more in developing technologies and science useful for production than in science that helps us understand the impacts of our technologies and economic activities, a point I will revisit throughout the book.

Within a given context, we make decisions and engage in activities that have consequences for the future and thus reshape the context in which we live. Some responses to our actions are favorable to us, some are not. But the responses to our actions are not fixed. Many species, and especially humans, actively shape the responses to their actions – a socially constructed adaptive landscape.[53] This is the purpose of policy and law – to change what responses occur when an action is taken. Some responses are hard to change: lead is toxic whatever claims are made by the lead industry; the climate is changing even when government agencies are forbidden from using the term "climate change."[54] By choosing what technologies to develop and which lines of research to ignore, by investing in infrastructure for cars but not for bicycles or public transportation, by redlining some neighborhoods and investing in others, we shape the response from the biophysical environment to a substantial degree.[55] Our decisions are constrained by existing structures. But we can work to change those structures. From an evolutionary perspective, history is open-ended. What has happened and what will happen are the result of the interplay of the structures in place and the actions we take, and so our actions can shape the future but only if we address constraints and opportunities imposed by structure.[56] As Marx put it : "Men [*sic*] make their own history, but they do not make it as they please; they do not make it under self-selected circumstances, but under circumstances existing already, given and transmitted from the past."[57]

### 1.4.3   The Effects of Context Can Be Pernicious Because of Inequality

At least since 1970, we have been aware that the adverse effects of human stress on the environment are not evenly distributed.[58] Structural human ecology has examined how nations differ in the stress they place on the environment and their vulnerability to environmental change, especially climate change and the loss of ecosystem services.[59] These differences are driven in large part by the structure of the global political economy – by the public and private agreements that shape trade, other political and economic policies and much else – as well as constraints imposed by the biophysical environment.[60] There also are huge gaps within nations, with the poor and those facing discrimination disproportionately exposed to environmental threats.[61]

The forms these inequities take seem almost without end: exposure to toxics in the air, a lack of access to safe drinking water, living in dwellings with lead paint, cooking on stoves that pollute the microenvironment in which a family lives, holding jobs that are health risks, not having access to air-conditioning in times of dangerous heat waves, living in communities at risk from toxic dump sites, lacking access to resources to recover from natural disasters, and others. The term "risk" indicates that while the outcome for any individual cannot be predicted with certainty, we can assess the probability of bad outcomes for an individual and the proportion of the population who will have bad outcomes. The idea of risk has become central to sustainability decisions.[62] Stratification by risk seems to apply to every social category that reduces the power of individuals and communities to act. Differences in income, social class, race and ethnicity, gender identity, age, disability, geographic location within a nation and in which nation someone lives, and their intersections, often lead to power differences.[63] Power differences produce increased exposure to environmental health and safety risks and decreased ability to make choices as individuals or communities to respond to those risks.

The constraints people face have to be at the center of our thinking about sustainability. Many residents of Flint, Michigan, didn't have a choice that allowed them regular access to clean water.[64] Residents in some Native American communities cannot avoid exposure to radioactive tailings from uranium mines. Many workers throughout the world don't have a choice of earning a living without exposing themselves to health risks. Apartment dwellers usually don't have a choice about how efficient their furnace or hot water heater is. Income and discrimination limit the ability to choose where to live. Our theories and research strategies have to examine these constraints so we can understand them better. The constraints are also ethical issues that influence what actions we should take. Research on sustainability decision-making needs to provide a better understanding of what steps we can take to redress these wrongs.[65]

Focusing on decision-making can clarify the constraints and obstacles people face. It can also reveal how decisions by elites shape social structure and thus constraints. At present, there is often a division in how we approach these two aspects of the relationship between power and decision-making. The disadvantaged are most often studied using ethnography, survey and experimental methods, while the powerful are most often studied using historical accounts. This is understandable. Political and economic elites are not likely to respond to surveys, participate in experiments or allow an ethnographer routine access to their decision-making processes. But more could be done to better understand elite decision-making. Consider a comparison of the preferences of Yale Law School students (historically an elite group, many of whom come to occupy powerful positions in government and the private sector), University of California, Berkeley law students (a rather privileged group compared to the general population but not nearly as elite as Yale Law students) and a representative sample of the US population.[66] The Yale Law students overwhelmingly identified themselves as Democrats, but they differed from the public in having much stronger preferences for economic efficiency over equality and were much more likely to be self-interested rather than altruistic.[67]

As these elite students pursue their careers, they will differ from the average American by giving more weight to efficiency over equality and will be more inclined to favor their personal interests than the common good. We don't know the extent to which gaining admittance to Yale Law School selects for these values and the extent to which their training at Yale reenforces them. This is only one study, any single study can be flawed,and I am singling out Yale among all elite universities simply because that was the focus of the study. Still, it shows how individual characteristics can lead to elite decisions that differ substantially from the preferences of most Americans. And those decisions will in turn cumulate into policies, programs and social structures that affect nearly everyone.[68]

In thinking about sustainability, we have to remember that the decisions of some matter more than the decisions of others. The cumulative impact of thousands or millions of decisions by individual consumers can have immense consequences for sustainability.[69] But so too do the decisions of a small number of the most powerful in society; as noted, the global affluent have disproportional impact and disproportional opportunities to make changes.[70] While those opportunities can bring about positive change, there will also be those who fight to preserve an unequal status quo that they perceive benefits them.

## 1.5    Local Decisions and Global Change

The dynamics of land use in most places are the result of decisions by local landowners, businesspeople, families and governments. But the context of those decisions is shaped by the global political economy, national and state policies and many nonlocal interests – places across the globe are coupled.[71] Some of the consequences are local – the changes in the character of communities. Some of the most substantial impacts are on other species, who see their habitat altered, with species that have trouble with human-dominated landscapes displaced by commensal species – those who can deal with us as neighbors.[72] As local land use changes occur across the globe, those changes become a major driver of biodiversity loss and climate change.[73]

The idea of sustainability is intended to help us make better decisions about land use and other actions. The goal is to improve the well-being of humans and other species while reducing damage to the environment. Thinking about sustainability is the result of an evolution in our thinking about the problems we face and what constitutes an ethical way to make decisions. While much of the book examines our current understandings, Chapter 2 provides the background on how we came to those understandings.

# 2 Sustainability Evolving

## 2.1 Things Change

My mother, Nora Elizabeth O'Brien, was born in 1910.[1] She graduated from high school in 1928. Soon after, the stock market crashed and the global Great Depression started. By then, she was working as a secretary at the Davey Tree Expert Company in Kent and weathered the Depression there. She continued to work after marrying but took six years off when I was born. She returned to work in a small unit of five women who ran the duplicating technology of the 1950s and 1960s. This was before dry process photocopying ("Xerox") machines, let alone desktop computers and printers. The Addressograph/Multigraph machinery used to mass-produce letters to customers occupied about 80 square feet and when running produced a noise level that I am sure would violate today's government workplace safety standards.

It was the only place in the company where women had some autonomy. They occupied the entire top floor (the "third floor" in everyone's conversation) of the small downtown office building that was company headquarters and saw their male supervisor only a few times a day. I later realized that my mother's circle of friends included women who worked outside the home and did not have children and women who had children but did not work outside the home. She was the only woman in her network of friends who was a mother and worked outside the home. And given a traditional gender division of labor, she was responsible for all housework and all cooking except when my father occasionally made traditional German food (mostly homemade sauerkraut and sausages).

My father, Glen Dietz, was born in 1912.[2] His family feared for his life in the flu pandemic of 1918.[3] While he was in high school, his father was injured at work. The company's worker compensation plan was to fire injured workers. (This was before unions led to more reasonable public and private policies.) To help support his family, my father dropped out of high school. His first job was as a farm worker in Ohio celery fields, using the "short-handled hoe" (El Cortito) that the United Farm Workers of America, led by Cesar Chavez, later fought to ban.[4] During the late 1930s, he was involved in several strikes and union actions, part of the rise of the labor movement in the United States. Some of these, such as the 1936 strike by the machinists' union against Black & Decker, became violent when strikebreakers attacked union pickets.[5] As the Depression ended and World War II began, he found a unionized job at Goodyear Aircraft (later renamed Aerospace), a branch of the tire company that built blimps to patrol for submarines off the US coast. But shortly after that he was drafted at age thirty. He and my mother had been dating for several years; they married while he was on leave before being shipped to Italy. Their relationship was controversial with her family because he was a German American Protestant and my mother was an Irish American Catholic. Theirs was described as a "mixed marriage." Because of his age, the Army made him a telephone lineman, the assumption being that this was a bit less risky and strenuous than simply being an infantryman. Telephone lines often had to be run to forward observers near German front lines. He won a Bronze Star for doing his job under artillery and sniper fire near Velletri, Italy. After the war in Europe ended, he assumed he would be sent on the invasion of Japan and thus be in combat for several more years. Before that happened, the war ended with the first (and thankfully so far only) use of nuclear weapons in war. He returned to my mother in Ohio and resumed work at Goodyear as a journeyman machinist and eventually an inspector, working for years on the "SUBROC," a nuclear-armed missile that could be fired from a submarine torpedo tube while underwater, and on other Navy contracts. When Goodyear transferred most of its Aerospace operations to Arizona, he decided to move towards retirement rather than go there (see Chapter 7).

Both my mother and my father were viewed as "white" in a community with some African Americans but very few people of other races. In their generation, strong distinctions were made across European ethnicities and religions. Irish, Italian and Polish Americans, the most common ethnic groups in Kent, were seen as very distinct groups and there were terms for derogatory stereotyping for those and many other groups. There were also strong class lines – I never met someone with a college degree socially until I was in high school, where some of my new friends had college-graduate parents, including physicians and college professors.

My parents' personal stories, with their troubles and joys, are embedded in some of the major changes and public issues of the twentieth century: the globalization that led to a worldwide flu pandemic, the Great Depression, the rise of unions, World War II, the relative prosperity for the American working class during the 1950s and 1960s, changes in fertility and marriage, changes in gender roles and, in reaction to union strength, corporate jobs moving to places where unions and the laws supporting them were weak.[6] This was also the period when contemporary ideas about the environment, economic and population growth and ultimately sustainability evolved. Tracing that evolution provides some insights into why sustainability has come to mean so many different things. Just as my parents' lives were shaped in part by large historical processes, so too sustainability thinking was influenced by these same events and processes.[7] My parents' history demonstrates the sociological imagination, the intertwining of the public and the personal.[8] And it also shows how individuals shape and are shaped by larger forces. Neither were politically active but my father was a staunch supporter of his union, the United Auto Workers. My mother provided a model of a mother who worked outside the home.

## 2.2    Economic Growth, the Environment and Democracy

The idea of sustainability emerged amid three major issues that dominated policy discussions in the second half of the twentieth century. The first was how to enhance human well-being. For most of this period, human well-being was equated with income, or at the national level, with gross domestic product (GDP), a measure of the total amount of economic activity taking place in a country.[9] World War II had cost 50–80 million deaths, or 2–3.5 percent of the world's population, about the same amount as World War I and the 1918 flu pandemic combined. In some countries, including the Soviet Union, several nations in Eastern Europe and areas in the Pacific and East Asia where combat took place, the death toll may have been more than 10 percent.[10] In contrast, the US death toll of 419,400 soldiers, while terrible, was only 0.3 percent of the population then and less than current US losses from the COVID-19 pandemic in total number of deaths (roughly 1 million, about 0.3 percent of the population, on April 19, 2022). In many countries, the war also devastated the physical manufactured resources – machinery, factories, refineries, railroads and bridges – used for production of goods and services.[11] Investments in infrastructure were essential for economic growth, and the World Bank and the United States invested in rebuilding its allies' infrastructure as well as that of former enemies Germany, Italy and Japan.[12]

At the end of World War II, the Soviet Union supported Communist governments in the nations it had retaken from the Nazis, including the eastern part of Germany. The period immediately after World War II saw a number of Communist-led strikes in Western Europe and growing electoral success by Communist and other parties of the left.[13] The seeming success of the left fanned militant anti-Communism. It also encouraged "expanding the pie" so everyone would have some share in the increasing income. Unions won bargaining power within industry, while union-backed social programs provided a "safety net" against risks such as illness and unemployment. In the United States, government support for college educations expanded. So did support for home purchases and for highway construction, both of which encouraged sprawl development and often increased racial segregation. The hope was that these reforms would reduce the pressure for more radical changes within nations – what Schnaiberg called the great compromise.[14] Economic growth was also seen as essential for "winning" the Cold War between capitalist and Communist nations – both sides argued its system was best at producing growth, and both sides needed to invest in the military. The emergence of what President Dwight Eisenhower termed the military-industrial complex provided a mechanism through which public funds could be used to finance investment both in industrial production for defense and in the public infrastructure, such as roads and ports, that supported it.[15]

Simon Kuznets observed that in the United States and the United Kingdom economic growth first made income inequality worse but further growth reduced inequality.[16] (The pattern where growth first makes things worse and then makes them better is often called the Kuznets curve.) If you accept the argument that growth ultimately leads to lower levels of inequality, even the vexing problem of inequality might be resolved through growth. This is a core idea in the great compromise but also motivated the "trickle down" economic theory of the Reagan era – the benefits of growth would trickle down from the elites to everyone else without the need for social policy to reduce the burden of inequality.

Figure 2.1 shows the trajectory of inequality in the United States – it is a graph of how much of all income goes to the richest 1 percent of the US population (now roughly those making more than $546,000 a year), tracing the conflict between the richest and the rest of us over the last century. In the "Gilded Age," after the US Civil War, there was a vast expansion of

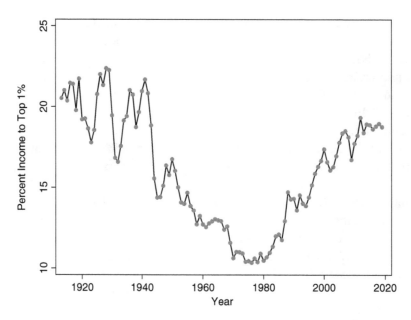

**Figure 2.1** Share of income of the top 1 percent in the United States
Key dates: 1929 – start of the Great Depression; 1945 – end of World War II;
1981 – Ronald Reagan becomes president.
Data from World Inequality Database, https://wid.world/data/#countrytime
series/sptinc_p99p100_992_j/US/1913/2019/eu/k/p/yearly/s (accessed October
12, 2021).

capitalist economic activity, growing inequality and an increased concentration of economic and political power in the hands of the most wealthy. The same period saw the rise of "trusts" and "combines," in which one or a few corporations so strongly dominated a market that they could control prices. This is the antithesis of the logic of the competition that is supposed to make capitalist markets efficient in allocating resources.[17]

Around the start of the twentieth century, unions and other social movements pushed for actions to regulate the market, while women and Black, Indigenous and People of Color (BIPOC) mobilized against discrimination.[18] Struggles around local pollution and against contamination of food and water also emerged then. The period around the Great Depression and World War II saw substantial advances in these reforms of the capitalist market economy, including the great compromise. These accomplishments between 1940 and 1980 often left women and especially BIPOC communities behind.[19]

Those on the right opposed to these reforms began to gain power in the Republican Party during the 1964 presidential candidacy of Barry Goldwater.[20] In the late 1960s and early 1970s, Richard Nixon was successful in aligning some elements of the working class with the right, and at the same time poised the Republican Party against the civil rights movement in his "Southern Strategy."[21] Starting in 1981, Ronald Reagan and Republican Speaker of the House Newt Gingrich made politics more ideological and rolled back many of the reforms that had been part of the great compromise. At the same time, some corporate executives, notably Jack Welsh, CEO of General Electric, broke long-standing great compromise policies that had reduced inequality.[22] Libertarian/free market theories, discussed in this chapter and in Chapters 3 and 5, provided an intellectual rationale for these policy changes. The result was a rise in inequality and challenges to environmental protection. Putnam and Garrett label this trajectory "I–We–I" and argue that it was driven by value change over time, with shifts from narrow self-interest to more altruistic values and empathy and then back to self-interest.[23] But shifts in political power also matter. Some of the shifts towards self-interest may be driven by cutting back social safety nets, thus putting individuals and families more at risk from unemployment and health problems and forcing them to focus on self-interest. Unions were a powerful force calling for solidarity and a social safety net.[24] But corporations moving jobs to states with anti-union laws and the decline of unionized jobs overall have weakened this voice and opened up an opportunity for anti-immigrant and other emotionally charged arguments about economic decline in economically stressed communities. All this has prevented society from addressing public issues and reduced them to personal troubles and creates a selective regime favoring self-interest, while the shift of income to the most wealthy makes it harder for non-elites to organize politically.[25] All this happened while the United States was moving from its global economic dominance after World War II to one where US companies faced international competition and were themselves globalizing, often moving production to other countries. At the same time, large investors, especially hedge funds, placed strong emphasis on short-term profits and forced corporations to do the same.

As the industrialized nations sustained substantial levels of economic growth, in the 1950s and 1960s attention turned to "development" in the "third world" or the "less developed countries."[26] Development was the process by which the "less developed" nations, mostly former colonies of the eighteenth- and nineteenth-century imperial powers, would transform their economies into something resembling that of the developed nations.[27] They would increase GDP per capita and thus, it was argued, alleviate poverty and enhance human well-being.[28] Initially, much of the attention was focused on continuing the extraction of raw materials from these countries that supported economic activity in the richer countries.[29] Around 1980, the idea of sustainable development entered the discourse and will be the subject of the next section.

The environment was the second major focus of the late twentieth century. While the origins of the environmental movement in the United States can be traced to the seventeenth century, there was an important change in the nature of environmental discourse in the late 1960s, marked by the publication of Rachel Carson's *Silent Spring* in 1962 and by the first Earth Day on April 22, 1970.[30] A link was forged between traditional advocacy for what we would now call biodiversity and growing awareness of air and water pollution and other toxins in the environment.[31] The dialogue among those holding these two sets of concerns broadened and deepened thinking about the environment. It juxtaposed, as Burch put it, "The Peregrine Falcon and the Urban Poor," linking endangered species with social justice and impacts on humans.[32] The emerging new movement also connected environmental concerns with criticisms of the Vietnam War and militarization and with counterculture discussions of lifestyle and choice of technology.[33]

Environmental justice was very much a part of the discourse fifty years ago. Some Earth Day organizers had strong ties to the civil rights movement. Inequality and injustice were themes in many Earth Day talks and people of color were active as both speakers at and organizers of Earth Day events.[34] In contrast, the traditional conservation movement had advocated for national parks and other conservation areas that displaced Indigenous people, and some movement leaders, including John Muir, held views that are troubling.[35] Historically, Indigenous people have lived for generations in nearly every terrestrial environment on earth. Many ecosystems we label "wild" or "natural" are the result of a long coevolution between Indigenous people and the ecosystems in which they lived. Yosemite National Park, a gem of the US National Park system, illustrates the history.[36] In 1864, President Abraham Lincoln granted the land in the Yosemite Valley to California as a state park; it became a National Park in 1890. From the first European incursion, Indigenous practices for harvesting resources and managing the land were discouraged, and the many Indigenous groups who had been engaged with the park ecosystems for centuries were forced out. Ironically, the cessation of their management practices led to a loss of biodiversity and to plant growth that obscured the magnificent vistas in the valley.[37]

The systematic displacement of these peoples from their home ecosystems is one of the great tragedies of human history and includes the slave trade, the great dying of Indigenous peoples after European invasion and many cases of migration caused either by direct use of force or by discriminatory economic actions and explicit policy. The struggle to find appropriate ways to move from this legacy of settler colonialism and racism towards more just and inclusive ways of protecting the environment, and particularly better ways of dealing with "wild" areas, continues. However we define sustainability, dealing with these injustices must be at the core of our decisions.[38]

The third major policy focus was democracy. The nineteenth century saw the decline of monarchies as major seats of power in industrial nations. The struggle against fascism dominated politics from the 1930s until the end of World War II. Then came the "Cold War" conflict between the capitalist nations of the West and the Communist nations. After the collapse of the Soviet Union, democracy was widely accepted as the legitimate form of governance.[39] Indeed, Fukuyama suggested that the triumph of liberal democracy represented the "end of history."[40] He argued that we were at "the end point of mankind's ideological evolution and the universalization of Western liberal democracy as the final form of human government."[41]

Democracy was not an invention of Western nations in the 1700s, let alone in the twentieth century. We usually trace democracy to Greek city-states, like Mytilene, that were more connected to what we now think of as the "Middle East" than to Western Europe. And across the thousands of years of history of food foraging, horticultural and agricultural societies, there were many forms of governance, often relatively egalitarian, with decision-making processes that we would now describe as deliberation towards consensus.[42] Indeed, it appears that key European writers on freedom, equality and democracy were strongly influenced by the political and economic systems and eloquent arguments of Indigenous peoples, particularly the French encounters with the peoples of northeastern North America. These cultures contrasted sharply with the hierarchical and unequal societies of the Europeans. Cultural evolution towards greater democracy and freedom in what we now call Western nations may have been a spread of ideas and examples from Indigenous peoples even as those cultures were being devastated by conquest and settler colonialism.

After World War II, liberation movements around the world invoked the growing emphasis on democracy and pointed to the contradiction between what was being said and reality. In the United States, the civil rights movement built on a long history of struggle by African Americans, Native Americans, Latinx Americans, Asian Americans and their allies to push for equality and an end to racism.[43] These struggles laid the groundwork not only for each other but also for the environmental, women's/feminist, gay liberation, disability rights and other movements. Around the world, people organized to gain independence from colonial rule and throw off authoritarian rulers.[44]

Figure 2.2 traces a measure of democracy that emphasizes deliberative processes that, as I noted in the Introduction, are a major theme in the book.[45] The solid line is for the world, indicating how the global human population is governed by weighting each country's democracy score by its size. The dashed plot is for the United States. The general pattern has been a rise in democracy across the twentieth and early twenty-first century, but with a downturn starting about 2010.

In addition to these political contexts, science and technological change have substantially transformed the world during the period from World War II to the present. Scientific and technological advances in World War II were of crucial importance, including antibiotics, highly accurate bomb sights, computers, jet aircraft, radar, rockets and nuclear weapons.[46] After the war, government investment in research for the military, medicine, other practical applications and for science in general became routine, linking federal agencies to universities and to the private sector. I will elaborate on some of these dynamics in Chapter 4.

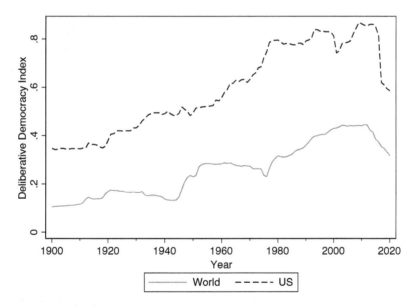

**Figure 2.2** Trends in democracy in the world and the United States
Data are from the Varieties of Democracy Project (V-Dem), www.v-dem.net/data_analysis/VariableGraph/ (accessed February 22, 2022).

## 2.3    Sustainable Development and Sustainability

### 2.3.1    The Origins of Sustainability Thinking

In the midst of these post–World War II trends, sustainability emerged as the intersection between promoting human well-being and protecting the environment. Lester Brown was the first to use the concept of sustainability in its contemporary form. The goal of a sustainable society was first discussed at a meeting of the Club of Rome in 1968 and first appeared in print in *The Limits to Growth* report in 1972.[47]

The core ideas of sustainability in the United States go back further, at least to the writings of John Wesley Powell, George Perkins Marsh and Aldo Leopold. Many historians trace the ancestry of the concept and the term to Hans Carl von Carlowitz and his *Sylvicultura oeconomica, oder haußwirthliche Nachricht und Naturmäßige Anweisung zur wilden Baum-Zucht* in 1713.[48] The first legal statement of the ideas of sustainability in the United States may be in the National Park Service Enabling Act of 1916: "which purpose is to conserve the scenery and the natural and historic objects and the wild life therein and to provide for the enjoyment of the same in such manner and by such means as will leave them unimpaired for the enjoyment of future generations" (National Park Service Enabling Act of 1916 §1, 16 U.S.C. 1). The idea of using "ecology" to help plan the use of natural resources, taking into account future generations, appears in a UN Economic and Social Council resolution in 1959.[49] The popularity of the term "sustainable development" can be traced to the famed Brundtland report, *Our Common Future*.[50] John Robinson emphasizes the contrast between discussions of sustainable development and sustainability.[51] I will follow his lead in framing this discussion.

*Our Common Future* offers what has become the standard definition of sustainable development: a process that "meets the needs of current generations without compromising the ability of future generations to meet their own needs."[52] This framing is wholly anthropocentric. The protection of ecosystems and biodiversity is a priority to the extent that they are needed by humans. However, the first articulation of sustainable development was by a group with a traditional conservation focus: the International Union for Conservation of Nature (IUCN).[53] Lee Talbot, the secretary-general of the IUCN, and others argued that the goals of conservation could not be realized without paying attention to problems of human well-being. But the shift to human well-being as the primary objective of sustainability, while taking account of the environment as either a goal in itself or a constraint on human well-being, seems to take off with the Brundtland report or perhaps its precursor, the *North–South: A Program for Survival*, the Brandt report.[54]

### 2.3.2    Promoting Growth

The "sustainable development" school of thought emphasized the need for economic growth even while paying attention to the harm done to the environment.[55] For example, *Our Common Future* calls for a five-to-tenfold increase in industrial activity to meet the needs of the poor. But the sustainable development approach recognized that economic growth depended not just on the physical resources (machinery, buildings, roads, canals, etc.) that had been emphasized in development theory up to that point but also on natural resources, which were often referred to as "natural capital."[56] *Our Common Future* is attentive to the problems of the poorest people in the world.[57] But economic growth was still considered the key approach to improving human well-being. Evidence that policies and institutions intended to promote economic growth often ignore, and even exacerbate, inequality was not central to the discussion.

In both the capitalist West and the Communist nations, development projects usually took the form of building new physical infrastructure, such as road systems, ports, dams, and irrigation systems. During its first twenty years, two-thirds of the World Bank's loans were to build transportation and electrical systems.[58] Agriculture was transformed by the "Green Revolution": new seed types and the irrigation systems, pesticides and fertilizers to support them. Sustainable development began to raise concerns with the environmental and social impacts of these traditional development projects.

Development funds were usually loans, not gifts. Sometimes large parts of these loans were siphoned out of productive use via corruption. Some projects were ill-conceived from the start or were based on assumptions that were not attentive to the local context where projects were implemented. So, many projects never produced their anticipated benefits. Meanwhile, paying off the loans became a crippling expense for many nations. In exchange for renegotiations of their debts, the World Bank, the International Monetary Fund and the lender nations required indebted governments to make "structural adjustments"[59] The advocates of these requirements believed that well-functioning capitalist market institutions, low taxes and free trade would lead to economic growth and growth would alleviate poverty, what are usually called neoliberal policies.[60] Problems of inequality were seen as secondary to problems of productivity, that is, output per worker or per person, and would be solved by the Kuznets curve.[61] Some argued that the adverse effects of economic growth on the environment also would be resolved by affluence as nations moved along an environmental version of the Kuznets curve. A parallel theory of ecological modernization also argued that increasing affluence would reduce stress on the environment.[62] In some ways, the imposition of these neoliberal policies was an extension of long-standing US foreign policy, which throughout the twentieth century has acted both overtly and covertly (through supporting coups and insurrections) to block socialist parties from holding power.[63] The kinds of policies imposed by structural adjustments were also adopted by many rich countries as conservatives like Reagan and Thatcher took power in the 1980s.[64] Most research indicates that structural adjustments have been problematic for both human well-being and the environment.[65]

### 2.3.3   Questioning Growth

Conventional economic development theory and sustainable development theory differ fundamentally in the importance assigned to the environment but not about the desirability of economic growth.[66] In the 1970s, a number of arguments for limits to growth such as Paul Ehrlich's influential *The Population Bomb* and the highly visible *Limits to Growth* attracted broad attention.[67] The Carter administration's *Global 2000* report, which was suppressed by the Reagan administration, was largely about the effects of population and economic growth.[68] These analyses were sometimes very simplistic, have often been dismissed as neo-Malthusian and have been subject to scholarly and political critiques.[69] But the models did initiate serious questions about whether continuous increases in economic activity and human population were possible given the resulting stress on the environment. While not garnering as much public attention, Kenneth Boulding and Herman Daly were laying the groundwork for arguments that economic growth as conventionally defined – an increase in GDP – was not an adequate goal.[70] Daly, in particular, was an early advocate for alternative ways of measuring human well-being.[71] The debate about the desirability and feasibility of growth, including recent calls for "degrowth," remains a central part of sustainability discussions.[72] A rethinking of the benefits of growth raises the questions of how we produce well-being and thus what is necessary for improved well-being of humans and other species.

The idea of limits to growth is that, at some point, increased human population and expanded economic activity will not be sustainable. Eventually, we would disrupt ecosystems in ways that are irreparable or we would exhaust critical natural resources with dire consequences for human well-being and devastating results for other species. Discussions of climate change often invoke visions of catastrophe and the resulting dystopia, a trope that also was common when the risk of nuclear war seemed very high. Dystopian images may be powerful motivators, but they might also lead both to despair and to rejecting all but perfect solutions to problems (see Chapter 3). In my view, dystopias and utopias are useful in the same way – neither is likely but they can help us think through what we want and don't want and develop strategies towards a desirable future.

The influence of ecological thinking is evident in the sometimes explicit and sometimes implicit use of the concept of "carrying capacity" in these discussions.[73] In ecology, the carrying capacity of an environment for a species is the maximum number of individuals the environment can support in perpetuity – the sustainable population size.[74] The idea of "planetary boundaries" is similar but more subtle.[75] The boundaries are levels of change in biospheric processes that can be exceeded only at great risk. Most ecological analyses take the characteristics of a species as fixed and that makes the idea of carrying capacity useful.[76] With a species that is undergoing very rapid cultural evolution, it is not clear that carrying capacity is helpful.

A debate among prominent environmental scientists, with Paul Ehrlich and John Holdren on one side and Barry Commoner on the other, prompted work to try to understand the drivers of human stress on the environment. Box 2.1 describes this literature.

The multiplicative nature of the equation emphasizes that population does not have an impact independent of affluence and technology, affluence does not have an impact independent of population and technology and technology does not have an impact independent of population and affluence. Consider the effects on greenhouse gas emissions as population and affluence increase. In many countries, electricity generation is an important source of greenhouse gas emissions. In the United States, it is about 25 percent of emissions.[84] Increased population and affluence will lead to more use of electricity. If electricity is generated by burning coal, one form of T, then substantial emissions result. If electricity is generated from solar technologies, we have far fewer greenhouse gas emissions.[85] So, P and A could increase and with them the use of electricity, but the impact (I) of that increase depends on what technologies are used to generate the electricity, and the mix of technologies used will depend on past and present decisions. For example, it is conceivable that if US programs to support the development of low-cost photovoltaic technologies started in the Carter administration in the

## Box 2.1  Understanding the drivers

The debate between Ehrlich and Holdren and Commoner produced the IPAT equation.[77] IPAT is "Impact equals population times affluence times technology" or

$$I = P * A * T$$

I is some measure of stress on the environment, such as the emission of a toxic chemical or deforestation. (We use I for "Impact," but in most applications of IPAT, I is a measure of stress on the environment, such as greenhouse gas emissions, not a measure of how the environment responds, such as change in global average temperature.) P is the size of the human population.[78] A is affluence, which we can interpret as consumption or as the amount of economic activity per capita. T is everything else. It is labeled "technology" but it is intended to capture all the other factors that moderate the effects of population and affluence in generating stress on the environment: infrastructure, culture, institutions, climate and whatever else might matter. That is, IPAT says:

$$\text{Stress on the environment} = (\text{Population}) * (\text{Affluence}/\text{population})$$
$$* (\text{environmental stress}/\text{affluence})$$

For example, in 2019 greenhouse gas emissions for the United States were about 6,558 million metric tonnes, the human population was about 328 million and GDP per capita was about $65,000. So, we can use those numbers to solve for T, which is about 0.31 kilograms per dollar of GDP.[79] This allows us to analyze what happens if population or affluence increases, or if we reduce emissions per unit affluence – that is, change the value of the terms in the equation.

The Kaya identity, a modified version of IPAT, is extremely influential in discussions of climate policy.[80] Kaya breaks the T term of IPAT into two terms, modeling I as the product of population, per capita affluence, energy use per unit affluence and greenhouse gas emissions per unit energy use. But, unfortunately, Kaya has all the weaknesses of IPAT, so for simplicity I will focus on IPAT as an example; my concerns for the most part also apply to Kaya.

Gene Rosa, Richard York and I proposed an alternative to IPAT, called STIRPAT (for "stirp," which means descendent, of IPAT).[81] STIRPAT uses data to estimate how much a change in P or A or other things influence I. It has been used in many studies; our original papers have been cited several thousand times and it is now common to see "STIRPAT" in the title of research papers. The STIRPAT approach has shown that inequality can increase harm to the environment, that the environmental movement can decrease it, that a 1 percent increase in population usually leads to a 1–1.5 percent increase in environmental stress, and much else.[82] To explain the difference between STIRPAT and IPAT, we have to think about nonlinear regression models. Since that gets a bit complicated rather quickly, I will use the IPAT model as a trope for discussing the drivers of environmental stress in the rest of the chapter. I emphasize that while IPAT can be useful for such a conceptual discussion, it is not terribly useful to quantify IPAT; that is the reason we developed STIRPAT.[83]

1980s had been continued, then the cost of solar photovoltaics would be substantially lower today and they would be a larger part of our electricity supply than the 2 percent at present.[86] But when Ronald Reagan became president in 1981, he and other Republicans cut those programs, a decision that probably had an impact on the current cost of solar.

The IPAT equation provides a way of thinking about the impacts of growth. To keep environmental impacts at the same level, we must decrease T as quickly as PA increases. There are three ways in which impacts can change. *Scale* is just PA, the total amount of economic activity. T can then be broken into two components. One is *composition* – what we consume. The other is *technique* – the processes and equipment we use. For example, in many areas of the world, drinkable fresh water is in short supply and climate change is making the problem worse. Increasing population size and affluence tend to increase demand for water – the scale effect. However, what people living in those areas consume also matters. Some may opt for conventional lawns that require extensive watering, others may decide to use native plants that do just fine with natural rainfall. And the choice of technology matters too. We can install equipment that uses less water, such as low flow showerheads. At a larger scale, public and private policies can encourage efficiency in water use and discourage water-intensive activities such as irrigated agriculture. Altogether, changes in composition of consumption and in the technology used can have substantial impacts.[87]

Technological improvement and cultural change – changes in content or technique – have substantially reduced some forms of environmental stress in some places. For example, air and water pollution in most developed nations is less than it was in the 1960s despite substantial growth in affluence and some growth in population. The Cuyahoga River no longer catches on fire, and in many countries using gasoline does not produce lead pollution, nor is lead used in paint. Globally, the use of ozone-depleting substances has been drastically reduced.[88] This is because policies mandated better air and water pollution control technologies for factories, farms, automobiles and other sources of pollution. Some products, like leaded gasoline, lead-based paint and ozone-depleting compounds, were phased out of use.[89]

For other environmental stressors, such as greenhouse gas emissions, land use change and plastic waste, there has been no reduction but rather substantial increases. Emissions of greenhouse gases have led to levels of carbon dioxide in the atmosphere larger than at any point in the last 800,000 years.[90] As a result, the climate seems to be moving into similarly uncharted territory. Emissions of $CO_2$ from burning fossil fuels has also shifted the pH (the acidity) of the oceans in ways unprecedented in recent geological history.[91] It is very hard to estimate the number of species that have gone extinct, but it is reasonable to believe that habitat loss and now climate change and ocean acidification will lead to a rapid increase in the rate of extinction as the twenty-first century unfolds.[92] The populations of many commercially important species of fish have collapsed as well.[93] These changes in fish populations may reflect not only the fate of a single species but potentially large transitions in entire marine ecosystems. Human action is having major transformative effects on the biosphere at a pace that is without precedent in human history and has rarely been seen in the history of life on earth.

## 2.3.4  From Limits to Risks

When the three witches forecast Macbeth's future as king, Banquo is skeptical, saying: "If you can look into the seeds of time, and say which grain will grow and which will not, speak then unto me" (*Macbeth* Act 1, Scene 3). Caution about forecasts seems prudent; in a sense, Banquo is asking the witches to offer evidence of the accuracy of their forecast. Decisions based on inaccurate predictions can lead to trouble. But decisions inevitably require assumptions about the future, and so not using a forecast is assuming things won't change, and that too is a forecast.

The scientific community looks to the future with projections rather than predictions. A projection is an "if–then" statement and is usually accompanied by a statement of uncertainty.[94] For example, population projections tell us what the future population of a nation or the world will be *if* birth rates, death rates and migration rates follow a particular trajectory in the future. The projections will be highly accurate *if* the trajectory of birth, death and migration rates follow those trajectories, and they will be inaccurate to the extent that they deviate from the assumed trajectories. Since we cannot know with certainty what will happen to fertility, mortality and migration, we cannot know the future population with certainty. Indeed, the projections are often the rationale for taking steps to change the things that drive them. If rapid population growth is believed a problem, a nation can encourage reduced fertility.[95] If massive climate change will be a problem, we can try to reduce greenhouse gas emissions below what might have happened. Indeed, as I noted in the Introduction, Robinson has offered the useful insight that, rather than forecasting, we should "backcast" – decide on the future we want and then find ways to get from where we are now to the future we want.[96]

Unfortunately, in political debate the uncertainty in current projections, estimates and understanding is often mobilized as an argument against action. There is uncertainty in all science, just as there is uncertainty in all of our efforts to anticipate the future. As Rosa pointed out in an important essay I will discuss in Chapter 4, the challenge is to understand the kinds of uncertainty we face and make decisions taking that understanding into account.[97]

Concern about the future involves another deep complexity. While some human and natural systems behave in ways that can be described simply by a straight line or a linear equation, many cannot – they are, in the jargon, nonlinear. This nonlinearity can lead to surprises – the system can behave in ways that are very hard to predict from its recent history.[98] For example, it has been very common for the amount of fish caught in a large area to remain steady or even increase year by year until suddenly, and seemingly without warning, there is a sharp decrease, not a gradual decline. Mullon and colleagues estimate that only about one-third of fishery collapses over the last fifty years have been gradual declines rather than a series of wild fluctuations or an abrupt drop.[99] In the case of climate change, there is reason to believe that, as the planet warms, changes in ecosystems, including the oceans, may lead to fundamental changes in the carbon cycle, leading to increased concentrations of greenhouse gases in the atmosphere from natural sources that will accelerate climate change.[100] Often it is hard to see impending change, so it can be very hard to know when we are on the verge of such a transition.[101]

As noted in the Introduction, starting about 1980, debates about environmental policy tried to capture uncertainty by focusing on risk.[102] For a technology such as a nuclear power plant, risk analysis requires identifying the different ways in which the plant might fail, the consequences of each kind of failure and the probabilities of each. For the release of a toxic substance, a risk analysis would take account of what exposure will do to humans and other species and how much exposure is likely. Often the outcomes are described in terms of loss of life or in monetary terms. The literature on risk analysis is huge, with debates about how best to define the term and how to carry out risk analyses.[103]

In 1983, one of William Ruckelshaus' first actions as administrator of the US Environmental Protection Agency (EPA) was to give a speech to the National Academy of Sciences discussing the tension between technical analysis and the broader aims of democratic decision-making.[104] Ruckelshaus had been appointed after Reagan's first EPA administrator, Ann Gorsuch (mother of Associate Supreme Court Justice Neil Gorsuch), was forced to resign amidst controversy about her bias in favor of industry. Risk assessments were meant to provide a "scientific" basis for making decisions, including incorporating risk and uncertainty into benefit-cost analysis, an influential method of policy analysis discussed in Box 5.4.

Risk analysis had long been used in engineering, notably the analysis of nuclear power safety and of specific missions of the US space program. In the 1970s, research made clear that individual perceptions of risk were often influenced by mental shortcuts, a topic discussed in more detail in Chapter 3. The hope was that a formal risk analysis would avoid the errors these shortcuts introduced and lead to consensus on the best decision to make. This assumes that controversy is caused by an "information deficit," a view described in more detail in Chapters 6 and 8.

Most risk analyses pay little attention to differences in values and to the unequal distribution of costs, benefits and risks. Nonetheless, the focus on risk analysis has led to increased understanding of how human actions can lead to harm to humans, other species and the biosphere and encouraged a careful examination of the degree of uncertainty in our current understanding and projections about the future.[105] Indeed, recent ideas about how to think about global environmental change, such as the planetary boundaries approach mentioned in Section 2.3.3, can be thought of as a form of risk analysis. Risk analysis is a useful tool for handling uncertainty as long as we don't believe that it can resolve most conflicts. Conflicts are based on more than disagreement about facts, a point I will return to in Chapter 6. There are still some who feel that better science alone will lead to better decisions, ignoring values and inequities. But now risk analysis is often framed as "adaptive risk management" with a vision that the scientific analysis is done in active deliberation with interested and affected parties, a theme I will discuss further in Chapter 8.

## 2.4   Sustainability and Growth

Ideas around human well-being, the environment and sustainability have evolved from a focus on the desirability of economic growth to a concern with limits and the use of risk as a way of framing our thinking. The older ideas are still present; many still argue that economic growth is the best way to deal with our problems, and the idea of limits and the disasters that may occur if we exceed them are very much part of the climate discourse. But other ideas are now part of our conversation: the triple bottom line, weak versus strong sustainability and a move from sustainable development to just sustainability. I will note each of them.

**Triple bottom line.** The triple bottom line approach argues that, in making decisions, corporations and governments should pay attention not just to the economic bottom line of profits but also to the environment (the planet) and human well-being (people).[106] I will discuss this approach and its merits and limits in Chapter 7.

**Weak versus strong sustainability.** The idea of weak and strong sustainability emerges from realizing that multiple resources are needed to provide human well-being: physical resources (stuff – machinery, buildings, etc.) but also by the use of the environment (natural resources), human skills and abilities (human resources) and social relationships such as trust and network ties (social resources).[107] How much of each kind of resource will we need to achieve a good level of well-being, and how much will future generations need? Under weak sustainability, it is assumed that we can substitute one kind of resource for another. It may be appropriate to decide to cut a forest if the resulting profits are invested in education (human resources) and dams and roads (physical resources). The logic is that while one kind of resource is being depleted, future generations will overall be better off because of the investment in other kinds of resources. Strong sustainability assumes that little or no substitution is possible, so we need to make decisions that preserve adequate stocks of all four types of resources. Both of these approaches to sustainability have become part of scholarly as well as practical discourse.[108]

**Just sustainability.** Here, I mean the term "just" in two ways. First is a move away from "sustainable development" to simply "sustainability." I also mean just in the sense that work on sustainability is increasingly focusing on issues of social justice, that we always have to think about the implications of decisions for those who are most at risk. A justice focus is reflected in some of the goals for sustainability described in the next section.

Sustainable development was a step away from views that argued economic growth was all that mattered and that other problems will be handled as societies become more affluent.[109] But within the logic of sustainable development, there are branches of thinking, notably environmental Kuznets curve and ecological modernization theories, that suggest that increased affluence and the societal changes that come with it will solve environmental problems.[110] The stream of thinking labeled "sustainability" does not privilege economic growth or profits as fundamentally more important than other concerns. Sustainability questions not only the feasibility but also the desirability of unlimited expansions of human population and economic activity.

The centuries-long debate about the effects of population growth has led to a broad consensus that population growth at levels currently projected may have substantially adverse, albeit not catastrophic, consequences on human well-being and the environment.[111] The burden of proof is on those who argue that the benefits of further population growth outweigh the risks.[112] At least since the 1970s, we have also come to question the benefits of economic growth.[113] We know that increases in affluence, in the scale of the economy, can have both positive and adverse effects and that the relationship between affluence and both the environment and human well-being may be very context-specific.

More recent work unpacks these ideas to redefine growth and to examine what a "no-growth" or "degrowth" society would look like.[114] Thinking about the links between growth, no growth and degrowth requires analysis of the effects on the well-being of humans, which has been the historical justification for growth, as well as consideration of other species, and of shifts in power, since the pressure for growth is strongly connected with the distribution of power in contemporary societies.[115] It quickly engages the debate about reform versus societal transformation that I will discuss in Chapter 7.

## 2.5    Goals, Metrics and Decisions

In 2015, the United Nations General Assembly endorsed seventeen Sustainable Development Goals (SDGs) (see Figure 2.3). The Goals were meant as a call to action, ways in which the world community can improve human well-being and reduce stress on the environment. By being specific about what needs to change in order to achieve sustainability, the hope was that they would guide decisions as a global consensus on fact and values.

**Figure 2.3** The United Nations Sustainable Development Goals (SDGs)
*Source*: www.un.org/sustainabledevelopment/news/communications-material/ (accessed July 15, 2020).

The history of the SDGs to some degree recapitulates the history of the sustainability discourse outlined in Sections 2.2 and 2.3. In 2001, the United Nations, the Organisation for Economic Co-operation and Development, the World Bank and the International Monetary Fund agreed to eight Millennium Development Goals (MDGS): eradicate extreme poverty and hunger, achieve universal primary education, promote gender equality and empower women, reduce child mortality, improve maternal health, combat HIV/AIDS and other diseases, ensure environmental sustainability and establish a global partnership for development.[116] The MDGs emphasized various aspects of human well-being and in particular the alleviation of poverty. This was a counterpoint to assuming economic growth would alleviate poverty and enhance well-being.[117] However, only one MDG focused on the environment. In 2012, Colombia proposed that the United Nations develop sustainable development goals. That led to the current set of goals, seven of which focus on environmental themes.

One reasonable criticism of the SDGs is that they are vague despite the 169 targets that are intended to guide action towards the Goals.[118] There are important areas of well-being and justice, such as the situation of Indigenous peoples and of people with disabilities, that could be given more emphasis in the SDGs. But, imperfect as they are, the SDGs do have some value in influencing our thinking and research and ultimately decision-making. First, they serve as a set of internationally agreed upon norms that broaden the scope of what should be taken into account in decision-making, shifting away from a narrow focus on growth or even on poverty reduction, important as that is. Second, they allow some degree of tracking, examination of differential progress across regions or groups and assessment of positive and negative synergies across goals.[119] For example, we were able to use reasonable, albeit imperfect, indicators to examine regional differences in progress towards the goals in China.[120] We found that while progress was being made in rural areas, problems related to conventional economic growth and the associated industrialization and urbanization were becoming more prevalent. In another analysis, we found that international trade helps rich nations achieve the SDGs but slows the progress of less affluent nations.[121] Critiques of the SDGS as well as using them to examine differential progress across groups and regions and the examination of positive and negative synergies can be a productive way of improving our understanding of and ultimately decision-making about sustainability.[122]

Another stream of literature attempts to develop single overall metrics for sustainability. When policy focused on economic growth alone, GDP served as a master indicator of progress.[123] Typically, GDP is reported for countries and is a key metric in discussions of economic policy, where increases in GDP are seen as good, decreases as bad. For example, a recession is defined as a decrease in GDP over two successive quarters of the year, that is, over six months. While the idea of GDP goes back to the seventeenth century, the first calculation of it appears to be by Simon Kuznets in 1934.[124] It is understandable that, during the Great Depression, when 20–25 percent of the labor force in Europe and North America were unemployed, there was keen interest in determining how much economic activity was taking place and in monitoring how that changed over time. When GDP is divided by population to produce GDP per capita, there is a tendency to interpret that number as an indicator of human well-being. Even in reporting his initial calculations, Kuznets cautioned against this: "The welfare of a nation can, therefore, scarcely be inferred from a measurement of national income as defined above."[125] Despite this warning, GDP per capita was the focus of the efforts to encourage economic growth and development just described. This emphasis on economic activity per se was understandable during the Depression and perhaps after World War II. However, we have come to realize that GDP per capita, while measuring what it intends to measure, is, as Kuznets warned us, not a good measure of human well-being and certainly not of sustainability.

There are many measures proposed as alternatives to GDP.[126] Some correct GDP to capture what it misses: damage to the environment, depletion of natural resources (both forms of natural capital), labor not captured in the economy such as much of the work of women and others whose efforts are in the household, socially dysfunctional activities that do appear in economic transactions (car crashes, for example, create economic activity through medical care and car repair) and many others.

Many scholars have been urging the use of direct measures of human well-being. The motivation goes back to Kuznets' argument – that GDP per capita is not a measure of well-being – and more recent research that shows that while affluence as measured by GDP per capita has some relationship to well-being, they are not the same thing.[127] The general pattern seems to be that increasing affluence improves well-being as one moves from very low to moderate levels of affluence but after that the link between well-being and affluence breaks down, an argument articulated by Richard Easterlin fifty years ago.[128] There is an emerging consensus that survey data can provide meaningful measures of subjective well-being – how individuals feel about their lives – and that such measures, aggregated to nations or states, are a useful complement to the standard economic indicators such as GDP per capita or unemployment rates.[129] The animal studies literature admonishes us to consider not only our own welfare but that of other species as well but those concerns have not been incorporated into indicators as yet. In the sociological literature, life expectancy at birth (roughly, the average length of life or the average age at death in the year for which it was reported) is used as a well-being measure since it captures the effects of many of the factors included in the SDGs.[130]

We might think about sustainability simply as trying to enhance human well-being while minimizing the stress humans place on the environment. We can ask how efficient we are at producing human well-being, where the criteria for efficiency is the damage we do to the environment, what has been called the ecological efficiency of well-being.[131] Figure 2.4 shows an example of this kind of analysis, graphing greenhouse gas emissions per capita, a major stress on the environment, versus life expectancy.[132] (Note that the shading indicates the affluence of the nation and the circle size its population. The greenhouse gas emissions reflect emissions from consumption not from production; so, if a good is produced in one country and imported to another the emissions are assigned to the importing country.) It appears that moving from very low to moderate levels of emissions is associated with improved well-being. But after a fairly low threshold, there is little relationship between environmental stress and well-being, suggesting that stress could be reduced without reducing well-being. The desirable upper-left area of the graph is labeled Goldemberg's corner after José Goldemberg, who argued that basic human needs could be met with only modest energy consumption; a similar point was made by Mazur and Rosa even earlier.[133] Why do countries fall where they do on the curve? If we answer that question, we can develop strategies to improve well-being and lessen environmental stress.

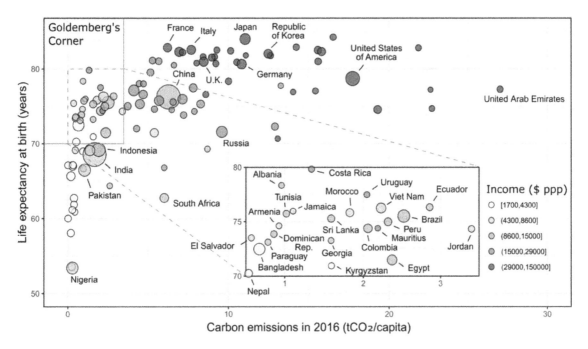

**Figure 2.4** Relationship between life expectancy and greenhouse gas emissions
*Source:* Roberts et al. (2020).

We know, for example, that inequality substantially reduces the ecological efficiency of well-being.[134]

My sense is that we are in a time of transition where we are moving from critiques of economic growth towards alternative formulations of sustainability. If we frame sustainability as enhanced well-being for humans and other species and reduced stress on the environment, we can have meaningful and inclusive discussions about what we mean by each of these concepts.[135] Those discussions will sometimes have to be global. But local discussions are also essential to reflect specific contexts and the historical experience of diverse communities, such as the examples of land use development in Chapter 1. This approach allows us to move from abstract arguments about sustainability towards methods for measuring change. It also encourages research programs that inform us about what policies and what forms of political economic institutions facilitate and retard progress. The history with which I began the chapter shows how individual lives are shaped by larger contexts; the research and discussions I advocate are intended to unpack those constraints, what shaped them and how they can be changed, and what changes we would like.

The idea of sustainability evolved in the late twentieth century, in the context of increased attention to the environment, questions about the outcomes of economic growth and a growing acceptance of democracy. Environmental concern remains strong among the public in most nations, and while some environmental problems have been addressed, the loss of biodiversity and the widespread dispersion of toxic substances remain problematic, and climate change looms as a dominant problem.[136] The move to think beyond simple expansion of economic growth continues. Recent years have seen an increase in inequality (see Figure 2.1) and a return to a situation where some corporations are so large as to dominant the market. And since about 2010, more and more nations seem to be slipping away from the ideal of democratic deliberation as a form of governance (see Figure 2.2). So, the context in which we make decisions continues to change.

Decision-making is, and always has been, difficult. I am much influenced by John Dewey and the pragmatists. I wonder what "work" the idea of sustainability, in its various forms, can do for us in making decisions even as the context evolves. And I also wonder how careful thinking about decision-making can help us make better decisions given a goal of sustainability. The overall question that motivates the book is: "How can we make better decisions?" The rest of the book is a journey, following a road, no simple highway, to explore that question. While much of that journey will have to do with how we make decisions together, it will be useful first to briefly review what we know about individual decision-making. That is the subject of Chapter 3.

# 3     How We Make Decisions

Should I buy an electric car or a hybrid or a conventional gas-fueled car? A carbon tax policy will increase the cost of gasoline with the goal of reducing greenhouse gas emissions. Should I support it? Should I pay extra for products that are animal welfare–friendly, organic, locally produced and/or fair trade? Should I support a measure to ban wolf hunting?

Some of our decisions are made as consumers, some as citizens, some in other roles described in Chapter 1. Some of our decisions have direct impacts on sustainability. For example, by using less gasoline I reduce greenhouse gas emissions and air pollution. Nearly all of our decisions have indirect effects by sending signals about what we favor and what we don't. Those signals happen through political activities, through what we buy and because people observe what we do and say. The direct effects of individual decisions can matter when they cumulate across a large number of people. The indirect effects can have even greater impact by changing the policies and ultimately the actions of public and private organizations.[1] Since the actions of organizations are influenced by individual decisions, what we know about individual decisions is a good starting point on the road we will follow in the book.

A substantial part of all social science research is about understanding how we make decisions. There are three grand traditions: the rational actor model, social psychological models and the heuristics and biases approach. Each of these traditions has a huge literature. Unfortunately, they are not very well integrated. Work in one tradition often ignores work on similar problems in the other literatures. There are exceptions that combine traditions but the easiest way forward is to start by looking at them one at a time.

## 3.1   The Rational Actor Model

The rational actor model (RAM) has been the dominant view of human decision-making for at least a century.[2] The RAM postulates that we make decisions by choosing what will maximize our personal benefits, called our utility, relative to costs and subject to constraints. The key constraints are the amount of money and time we have.[3] The RAM is used in all the social sciences, has been monolithic in economics and strongly influences most discussions of public and private policy. As we will see, the RAM is a descriptive theory (a positive theory in the language often used in economics) of how people make decisions. But it is also an ethical theory of how people ought to make decisions. The ethical theory and the descriptive theory can be distinguished but they are closely linked and most who use the descriptive theory also accept the ethical theory.[4] Since money and time are unequally distributed in most societies, applications of the RAM that ignore those inequalities may be unrealistic and reenforce those inequalities.

The RAM assumes that we pick the option that does best for our utility and "cut off" other options that do less well for our utility. We can think of utility roughly as the happiness, enjoyment or satisfaction you receive from an action or state of the world. A core assumption in the RAM is that we know our preferences – know how much utility will come with each choice we might make.[5] Another is that we are rational in the sense that the relationship among preferences makes logical sense.[6] One way of thinking about the relationship between the RAM and the social psychological approaches discussed in Section 3.3 is that social psychology is a theory of what our preferences are, while the RAM describes how we make choices to realize those preferences. Similarly, the heuristics and biases literature discussed in Section 3.4 examines how people deviate from the strong assumptions about decision-making used in the traditional versions of the RAM.

How does the RAM say we decide what option to select and which to cut off? As an ethical theory, how does the RAM propose we ought to make decisions? While the formal theory is best expressed mathematically, it can also be thought of as a series of steps.[7] Let's take a simple choice, like choosing whether to buy an organic versus a conventional apple. When faced with this decision, if I am following the RAM, I would take the following steps:

(1) List all the alternative choices I can make. For this "toy" example, it's just a choice between organic and conventional.

(2) For each alternative, list all the possible outcomes, including estimates of the point in the future at which those outcomes would occur. The outcomes are the enjoyment of the apple and, if I think organic is better for me and for the planet, the perceived impacts on my health and on the environment. The enjoyment comes now, health and environmental impacts later. The price I have to pay for the apple is an immediate cost and usually will be higher for the organic than for the conventional apple. For this example, I will ignore time constraints, assuming both kinds of apples are readily available on the shelf in front of me. But many people live in areas with limited food availability (food "deserts") where an organic apple might take some time to find.[8]

(3) For each outcome at each point in time, estimate the utility I would get from its occurrence. Both the gains in utility from the good things and the losses from the bad things count. The big source of utility is enjoying the apple. If I think organic applies are better for my health, I would also derive some utility from those benefits. And if I think organic is less harmful to the environment and I care about the environment, there is also some utility there. The negative is the cost of the apples, which is higher for the organic. All these utilities have to be expressed in the same units or I won't be able to compare them.[9]

(4) Estimate the probability of each outcome occurring. The price is certain. Assuming I like apples, the enjoyment is pretty certain but it's not 100 percent because I might get a bad apple. The health and environmental outcomes are less certain.

(5) Discount each utility of each outcome for the time at which it occurs and its uncertainty. For the apple, since health and perhaps environmental benefits are in the future and are not as certain as the immediate satisfaction of eating, those utilities would be down-weighted,

or in the language of the RAM, discounted over time. Discounting is controversial, and it has a huge impact when we evaluate decisions with impacts in the future, as they are for most environmental and sustainability decisions.[10]

(6) Add all these resulting expected discounted utilities up for each choice. I then get an expected utility for the organic apple and conventional apple.

(7) Pick the choice that yields the greatest expected discounted utility.

I have simplified the full theory, but the example captures the basic logic of the RAM.

Is this how I decide what kind of apple to buy? Of course not. It is a very laborious set of steps, and one demanding too much information that is hard to obtain, such as the impacts on my health and the environment. Even a RAM proponent could argue that this process would be foolish rather than rational for such a small decision. After all, our time is worth something.

I do not intend this example to mock the RAM. Almost inevitably, if one picks a routine decision to use as an example, the demands of the RAM are far beyond what is reasonable to expect of us. If we are making a big decision, such as purchasing a car or a house or deciding what college to attend, it does make sense to work through some of these kinds of calculations.[11] In the case of major public decisions, the RAM logic is used in benefit-cost policy analysis (see Box 5.4).

If the RAM seems unrealistic, why is it so influential in the study of decision-making? First, we might behave "as if" we did these calculations. We may have shortcuts that produce roughly the same results as the elaborate calculations I have just described. Second, we may make rational choices "on average." While any individual choice may deviate substantially from what would be expected given the RAM, when we look across many people the model still predicts well because the flaws in each individual's decision process average out. Third, in some ways the RAM is the best developed and most analytically powerful theory of individual decision-making we have and thus should be the starting point from which we move in building alternative theories.[12]

Finally, the popularity of the RAM resonates with a common set of beliefs, especially among the richest and most powerful, that markets are the best way to make decisions and allocate resources, the neoliberal ideas discussed in Chapter 2.[13] In capitalist societies, the rich have benefited from the market and are in a position to influence education and policy in ways that ensure those benefits continue. The RAM makes sense to them as a way of justifying what happens in markets. Some of the most affluent have made substantial investments in organizations to promote the use of the RAM and praise the benefits of a free market, for example the American Enterprise Institute (www.aei.org), Cato Institute (www.cato.org) and the Heritage Foundation (www.heritage.com). We don't see as large a set of well-funded organizations critical of the market – critics of the market seldom have the funds to endow such organizations.[14] Real markets that have been shaped by the actions of the powerful may deviate substantially from the hypothetical markets assumed in many applications of the RAM, and many powerful advocates of free markets actually favor policies that distort the market, with substantial adverse impacts on the environment and human well-being.[15]

While the core of RAM modeling is about decision-making in markets under monetary constraints, it has been expanded far beyond that. Starting in the 1960s, economists led by Gary

Becker turned their attention to topics that had not been within the domain of economic analysis, including fertility, marriage, crime and discrimination.[16] A key contribution of their work was to emphasize that time as well as money is a constraint in making decisions.

In parallel with arguments about the family, crime and other phenomenon, public choice theorists applied the logic of the RAM to politics. My former colleagues James Buchanan and Gordon Tullock, among others, argued that individual self-interest on the part of voters, politicians and bureaucrats was the most effective way to understand the dynamics of government.[17] The approach has found advocates in political science and also in legal scholarship. It appears to have had substantial influence on efforts to reshape the nature of American democracy by the Koch family and their allies so as to minimize the influence of government.[18]

The RAM assumes we are all wholly self-interested. In making a decision, we take account only of the effects on our own utility, perhaps including close kin.[19] As Adam Smith put it: "We are not ready to suspect any person of being defective in selfishness."[20] Becker builds this assumption into his view of economics: "The combined assumptions of maximizing behavior, market equilibrium, and stable preferences, used relentlessly and unflinchingly, form the heart of the economic approach as I see it."[21]

The argument that our decisions are wholly self-interested is not universally accepted. If human behavior is shaped by cultural evolution, some degree of altruism is likely, as I argued in the Introduction. Some elaborations of the RAM incorporate concern with others into an individual's preferences.[22] The contrast between self-interest and altruism leads us to social psychological theories of decision-making.

While much of this discussion has been critical of the RAM, I see the RAM as complementary to the other two streams of decision-making theory. The massive and very sophisticated literature on the RAM is centrally about money and time constraints on decision-making and the way our interactions, in attempting to realize our preferences, lead to general patterns of behavior. A survey of any microeconomics text shows that this is the focus of much of economics – it is about action under constraint and the overall outcomes of market interactions. Social psychological theories focus on what shapes the preferences that are deployed as a starting point in the RAM.

## 3.2     From Isolated Individuals to Groups

A key feature of the most common version of the RAM is that is that your decisions only influence my decisions through prices. The price captures the actions of other people in producing apples – the supply – and the actions of other people buying apples – the demand. In the theory, supply and demand produce the price, and I consider the price in making decisions. In Chapter 8, I will discuss markets and prices as a way of combining individual decisions into group decisions. But sometimes the actions of others matter in ways that may not be adequately captured by market prices; and sometimes we are making decisions in a different context than the market-based social interactions assumed by the RAM.

In a recent campaign for the Vermont state legislature, one candidate argued that Vermont should lead the way in reducing greenhouse gas emissions. Her opponent criticized such actions, arguing that even if Vermont did a lot it wouldn't matter unless other states and other countries did too. If all states and countries followed the logic of not acting because others may not, no one will take action.[23] This is the problem of the commons, often described in terms of a community grazing sheep. Suppose I live in a village that has land used for grazing sheep. The land is a commons – no one owns it; its use is open to everyone in the village. If everyone puts out no more than three sheep each and the human population of the village doesn't change, the ecosystem on the common land is stable. From year to year, it regenerates itself. If most people put out four or more sheep, then there is too much grazing, the grass ecosystem degrades and soon there is no more grass for grazing. If I follow the strict RAM, my decision-making might look something like the following.

If I graze only three sheep, but most of my neighbors put out four or even more, the commons will be overgrazed despite my actions, and I will suffer the consequences with everyone else despite my careful actions to try to sustain the commons. Indeed, for the year or two before the grazing is ruined, my family will get the benefits of only three sheep while my neighbors will get the benefits of the extra sheep they graze. Unless I can trust my neighbors not to put out extra sheep, or have some way of making sure they don't, the rational thing for me to do, at least in the narrow sense of the RAM, is to put out the extra sheep. If everyone is a rational actor, everyone will do this and the grazing commons will collapse, making us all worse off than if we could have found a way to cooperate. That is the logic of the candidate opposing climate change action – it doesn't make sense to act unless we know everyone else will too. This is often called the "tragedy of the commons" because a bad outcome is predicted.[24] I prefer the term "drama of the commons" because, in real commons, sometimes the outcome is a tragic collapse but there are happy endings too.[25]

In formal terms, commons are a resource where access is nonexcludable (open access, anyone can use it) and uses are subtractable (my use of it can degrade your use).[26] Ostrom argued that neither excludability or subtractability are absolutes but depend to some extent on technology. Barbed wire converted the open access commons of much of western North American grazing land to closed access.[27] Before barbed wire, enclosing the land was not practical; after barbed wire, it was. There are some resource uses that are effectively not subtractable, such as clean air to breathe or beautiful viewscapes. Seemingly nonsubtractable goods are subject to congestion effects. If too many of us are crowded on a hiking trail, then our experience is degraded even if the viewscape itself is not.[28] Timescale matters if the system is renewable. A road system or the electromagnetic spectrum can become congested but is instantly renewable – once use declines, the problem disappears, although for roads wear over time degrades the infrastructure. One of my original mentors in environmental sociology, Tom Lough, estimated that fossil fuels could be treated as a renewable resource at then (1970) current levels of per capita consumption if the human population of the earth was around 10 million. (At the time, the world population was 3.7 billion; now, it is 8 billion.)

Climate change is a commons problem.[29] It does not matter much where a long-lasting greenhouse gas is emitted since it ends up mixed into the atmosphere, so emissions of greenhouse gases anywhere in the world contribute to climate change everywhere in the world. If one state or country sharply curtails its emissions but others do not, the climate still changes, albeit not as much or as quickly. One can think of sustainability as defined by the Brundtland report (see Chapter 2) as a commons problem with a focus on future generations. Current resource use may cause harm to ecosystems and deplete resources so they are not available to future generations, who would be worse off as a result.[30]

Decisions made in coordination with others is one of the central issues in any science that studies behavior, including not just the social but the ecological and evolutionary sciences. It is becoming an issue in computer science and robotics as artificial entities interact with each other and with biological entities. The problem goes by many names: the commons but also the collective action problem, the problem of social traps and the undersupply of public goods, among other things.

Watch a few episodes of most police dramas and a familiar trope will appear that involves a two-person version of the problem. Suppose a suspect named Selina is being questioned by the police. She is confronted with a dilemma by Harvey, the prosecutor. If she confesses and her accomplice, Ivy, does not, then Harvey will not press charges against Selina but will go for a maximum sentence for Ivy. If both Selina and Ivy confess, Harvey can use the confessions to get convictions with moderate sentences for both of them. If Selina does not confess but Ivy does, Harvey prosecutes Selina and lets Ivy off. If both Selina and Ivy keep the code of silence, omertà, then Harvey can convict them only on minor charges. The result that follows from Selina's decision depends on what Ivy does, and vice versa. The ideal solution would be for both to keep silent. Can they trust each other to do that? What does the RAM predict will happen? This problem, for obvious reasons, is called Prisoner's Dilemma. It is one of the foundations of a branch of the RAM called game theory.[31]

In the Prisoner's Dilemma, our preferences seem clear. Both Selina and Ivy would like to minimize their prison sentences. But the best strategy to do that depends on what the other person does, so a utility-maximizing decision depends on an assessment of trust. Selina and Ivy might care about each other and that could influence their decisions. But the simple application of the RAM assumes we care only about ourselves, so Selina and Ivy will both confess and both will be worse off than if both kept silent.

The RAM approach assumes that decisions are made purely based on self-interest; there is no altruism. It sees trusting others as problematic. But cultural evolutionary theory suggests altruism may not be rare, and a lot of research suggests that the strict assumptions of the RAM may not be realistic in many situations.[32] That is our next topic.

## 3.3    Values, Beliefs, Norms, Empathy, Trust, Identity, Polarization and Emotions

**Values.** Most scholars who have thought about decision-making acknowledge that more than narrow self-interest is at play in many of our decisions. Drawing on theories of cultural evolution and on feminist ethics, Paul Stern, Linda Kalof and I began exploring the role of altruism in environmental decision-making. Starting with our initial analysis, we made the distinction between altruism directed towards other humans (humanistic altruism) and altruism directed towards other species and the biosphere itself (biospheric altruism).[33]

We quickly decided that it would be advantageous to integrate our work with the existing social psychological literature on values developed by Milton Rokeach and expanded by Shalom Schwartz.[34] The term "values" is used in everyday language to indicate something fundamentally important: "The principles or moral standards of a person or social groups, the generally accepted or personally held judgment of what is valuable and important in life."[35] Values are views about what is desirable that can be applied across specific decisions and that are used to guide decisions. That is, values shape our preferences but are more general than the specific preferences we use in making a decision.[36] In deciding which apple to buy, if I have altruistic concerns with the biosphere, that will lean my preference towards an organic apple. My self-interest values will be focused on price, enjoyment and possible health effects for me.

In studies on environmental and sustainability decision-making, there are four major value clusters that emerge in nearly every group studied, although the details differ in interesting ways.[37] The four key values emerge as two polar opposites: self-interest versus altruism; traditional values versus openness to change (see Figure 3.1).[38]

Self-interest is just what the term implies – a focus on your own welfare and perhaps that of your immediate family. It is what lies at the heart of the RAM. Altruism is the opposite – a concern with the well-being of others. In the Rokeach/Schwartz tradition, no distinction is made between altruism towards other humans and concern with the environment. We have expanded the measurements used by Schwartz and his colleagues to capture that distinction. People who care about other species and the planet also care about other humans and the two values are tightly linked.[39] This contradicts a charge sometimes made against environmentalists – that they do not care about people. Altruism both towards the biosphere and towards other humans leads to greater concern with the environment, while embracing self-interest values and traditional values typically leads to less concern with the environment.

Because many decisions about the environment and sustainability involve a commons, it makes theoretical sense that the distinction between self-interest and the two forms of altruism

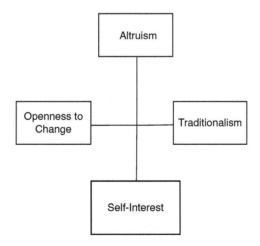

**Figure 3.1** General relationship among values

would be useful in understanding them.[40] If I am narrowly self-interested, then I may ignore the effects of my actions on the common good. In contrast, if I give value to the well-being of other humans, other species or the biosphere, I may make decisions to protect the common good. The arguments in feminist ethics that influence our work maintain that members of groups that have suffered from oppression may be especially attentive to the well-being of others.[41]

The theoretical argument for the influence of the other major value axis – tradition versus openness to change – is less clear. However, in many nations, certainly in the United States, the environmental movement in its post–Rachel Carson/Earth Day form is associated with changes from business as usual, with new technologies and lifestyles and with progressive politics.[42] In turn, over time, conservatives and those associated with what they perceive as "traditional" American values became opposed to environmentalism. Some studies do show that tradition-alism can be an important influence on environmentalism and a few studies find an effect of openness to change.[43] In an important addition to the approach, Steg and colleagues have argued for the importance of hedonism.[44] Some pro-environmental decisions are perceived to result in a reduction of pleasure or comfort. Hedonism plays an important role in some if not all environmentally consequential decisions.

I see values as the precursors to preferences and decisions. If someone uses the RAM, values indicate what outcomes are of greatest importance to them, although the simplest form of the RAM would suggest that only outcomes that feed self-interest matter. But if humanistic or biospheric altruism are important to me, the effects of my decisions on others will influence my preferences. If I hold hedonistic values, then the perceived hassle of pro-environmental choices will matter. If I am making a quick decision without much careful analysis (I will describe this kind of decision-making in Section 3.4), then the values are a guide for what kind of clues to look for. I might ask: How is this choice related to preserving traditions, to enhancing my personal well-being, to providing new experiences for me, to taking care of others and the environment? Most people hold all these values to some extent, so what matters are which values are most important to a person, and other things matter as well. Values are the first step in a chain of decision-making that can lead to altruistic behavior.

**VBN Theory.** To explain pro-environmental decisions, especially support for the environ-mental movement, Paul Stern, Linda Kalof and I elaborated our work to embed values in a causal chain. We built on the work of Heberlein and others who applied Schwartz's ideas to the environment.[45] What has come to be called values–beliefs–norms (VBN) theory has been successfully applied to a wide variety of political and consumer environmental actions in many places around the world, has itself evolved and has been linked to other theories to provide a more robust understanding of how we make decisions about the environment and sustainability.[46] I won't detail the theory here but will briefly discuss two key elements of it, beliefs and norms, and then mention other social psychological factors that influence our decisions.

**Beliefs.** In VBN theory, we assume that causal influence moves from values to general beliefs to specific beliefs. Values make us more or less attentive to new information – if we care about the well-being of others and the environment, we are more likely to pick up on new information about social and environmental problems. General beliefs are broad assessments of how the world works. For example, I may accept or reject the belief that the environment is quite susceptible to human action, or that government generally does a good job. VBN doesn't assume people are coolly rational and objective in assessing new information. Our values shape what we believe to be true in general, and what we believe to be true in general influences our assessment of specific new information. This tendency, biased assimilation of new information, is well documented, with different disciplines having different terms to describe it.[47] Even if this bias is slight, it can lead to a cascading effect.[48] We may initially take a position on a public issue without much careful thought. Over time, that position can be reenforced until it becomes quite elaborate and impervious to new information.

**Norms.** Norms are very influential in shaping behavior.[49] Norms come in several "flavors." A *descriptive norm* is my understanding of how most people act or what they believe.[50] A *prescriptive norm* is what I think other people think I should do. A *personal norm* is what I think I should do. All three influence our decisions. Intriguing evidence suggests that we are very attentive to changing norms – we care about trends.[51] For example, providing information that a growing number of people are limiting meat consumption increases interest in meatless meals even though it is clear that most people in the United States eat meat.

Ostrom emphasized the importance of norms in governing commons. Communities that have strong norms and the ability to perpetuate them, and when necessary enforce them, can be highly successful at sustaining commons resources like forests or fisheries. Norms are often used to encourage pro-environmental behavior. Schultz and colleagues gave households a comparison of their household's energy use over the last month to that of the average consumption of neighbors, a descriptive norm. Those who were using more energy than their neighbors reduced their use substantially, while those who were using less tended to increase consumption, a rebound effect.[52] To counter the rebound, frugal users received a "smiley face" on their usage report. The smiley face is invoking a prescriptive norm – letting someone know how others feel about their behavior. There are many other examples of the effective use of norms to influence sustainability decisions.[53] The combination of descriptive and prescriptive norms seemed to effectively reduce consumption, especially when it is clear that the descriptive and prescriptive norms refer to peers.

**Empathy.** The logic of extending scope of concern to others suggested by feminist theory implies that empathy – the ability to understand and care about the situation of others, including nonhumans – should be closely related to altruism. While empathy has been studied extensively, that research has not been linked to the work on altruism. A better integration would allow deeper consideration of how far the scope of altruism extends, how "tribalism" that narrows the scope of concern might be overcome and how concern with other humans and concern with other species are linked.[54] Empathy is probably important to cultural change. Media, daily experience and both informal conversations and the structured deliberative processes I emphasize can help develop empathy beyond just those we already know and lead to decisions that take account of well-being broadly, not just among those we know best. But these mechanisms can also be deployed to define "others" who are outside the scope of ethical consideration, part of the polarization dynamics I will discuss later in this section. I suspect that one of the most powerful impacts of unions in the United States from the 1930s until the 1980s was their ability to encourage empathy not only for their members but for workers in general and even for anyone dealing with economic hardship.

**Trust.** Trust is the belief that others will do what is expected of them – that they will follow the norms you think apply to them. Trust is a sort of glue that holds societies together.[55] If the outcomes of my actions depend on what you do, then being able to predict your actions, to rely on you to do what you say you will do, is crucial to my decisions. As we saw, trust is central in the Prisoner's Dilemma, where my decision hinges on whether I trust my confederate.[56] Perhaps as a result, we seem to have a strong aversion to having our trust betrayed.[57]

In a large population, trust cannot be based solely on the experience of personal interactions. Even if you have an extensive social network, it can be hard to access someone who has direct experience with the person you may need to trust. (Internet reviews help us get around this problem in our role as consumers.) Both the general reputations of individuals and groups and even generalized trust ("Most people can be expected to do the right thing") become increasingly important as the range of people with whom we interact becomes larger. The structure of social networks will also matter a great deal in shaping how information flows, including our descriptive norms about what we think others believe and are doing.[58]

It is not surprising that trust influences our decisions about what actions should be taken around environmental and technological risks.[59] Steve Whitfield led a study looking at how trust influences support for nuclear power. One of the major findings is that public support for or opposition to nuclear power hinges very much on trust. Those who trust the nuclear industry and the federal agencies involved support nuclear power. Those who do not trust the industry and that part of government do not support nuclear power. When we take account of trust, the more concerned one is with climate change, the more one supports nuclear power. This seems to me a very reasonable assumption on the part of members of the public. The average citizen (the average respondent to the survey) does not have the time or the technical background to read the risk assessments on nuclear power and weigh the evidence underpinning them. This is something that is reasonably delegated to industry, and government, and the environmental groups who act as watchers of the watchmen.[60] If you trust those organizations, then you feel nuclear power is a viable option. If you do not trust them, you are wary of nuclear power since it will not be adequately monitored and policed.

**Identity.** VBN theory suggests that, instead of doing a RAM-style analysis, we may make a decision based on the view "This is the right thing for someone like me to do," a personal norm. The concept of identity clarifies the idea of "someone like me." Who you see as similar to you depends on your perception of your identity and your perception of their identity. Theorists stretching from Meade and Dewey to Rokeach have emphasized the strong tie between values and personal identity.[61] Our values help us define who we are, who is like us and who is not like us and help coordinate our actions with others.[62] Biospheric values seem closely linked to identity as an environmentalist. In turn, environmentalist identity is a strong predictor of environmental decisions, one way values influence our decisions.[63] And values are linked to feelings of connection with nature, another form of identity.

Identity is to some degree context-dependent – we can shift across roles like those introduced in Chapter 1. If I am interacting with friends or family, in that role I may give more weight to altruistic values than if I am in the role of a consumer interacting with a salesperson or bargaining at a yard sale. People differ in the degree to which the values they deploy vary across roles. For some people, there may be very little variation, while for others shifts across contexts and thus across roles may be very substantial.[64]

**Emotions.** Seeing someone make a decision that is consistent with our values and norms is gratifying. We have an even stronger negative reaction to seeing someone make decisions that violate our values and norms. Strong emotions can make us deviate from the RAM and may encourage us to use the heuristics and biases shortcuts described in Section 3.4. We know that both positive and negative emotions are strongly related to concern with and willingness to take action on climate change. It is unclear how much our emotions cause or are caused by our decisions and actions and whether positive or negative emotions motivate complacency or action.[65] And while strong emotions can evoke immediate action, the effect may not last longer than the emotional state itself. I will return to the issue of complacency in Chapter 7. To summarize, while we know emotions matter in sustainability decisions, we need to better understand just how they work.

**Polarization.** The combination of biased assimilation (BA) of new information and homophily (H), paying attention to only those like us, can lead to polarization (P) – ever increasing gaps in values, beliefs and norms – in both policy networks and the general public.[66] I will call this dynamic BAHP. Because values and identity are closely linked to emotions, polarization can produce negative feelings towards those with different views.[67] In Chapter 4, I will argue that science is in large part a set of norms for overcoming BAHP when we try to establish facts.

The dynamics of BAHP are reenforced by limits on altruism. I have contrasted narrow self-interest with altruism towards all other humans and the biosphere. The dynamics of cultural evolution can produce altruism, but it is easier to maintain altruism towards a group than it is towards everyone (see Introduction). Unfortunately, we often define the group of those "like us" based on minor, superficial cues about them, cues that may lead to deep prejudice including racism and stereotyping of both the in-group and the out-group. The outgroup can be seen as so dissimilar that their motives are suspect and their statements viewed with suspicion – they are not trusted. This tendency has been well documented in policy systems. It seems to be the basis of political polarization among the general public and facilitates decisions based on emotion and that ignore a careful weighing of evidence and of other views.[68] At its most extreme, it has led to some of the great tragedies of human history, including slavery, the displacement of Indigenous peoples and the Holocaust. It is one of the most serious sources of poor decisions about sustainability. But it may be possible to encourage broader empathy and thus overcome this dynamic. I will revisit the effects on decision-making in Chapter 6 and how we might do better in Chapter 9.

We all engage in biased assimilation and homophily. Doing so is not unreasonable. Being skeptical of new information that is inconsistent with what you already believe simply assumes your beliefs are reasonably accurate. We are more comfortable with those similar to us as interactions are smoother. But biased assimilation and homophily reduce the diversity of beliefs and values we consider. When we need social learning to cope with changing circumstances, as we certainly do to move towards sustainability, the lack of diversity slows evolution. And when biased assimilation and homophily lead to polarization, learning can be blocked and social conflict amplified. I will discuss these dynamics in Chapter 9. In the United States, while political polarization seems to have increased in the twenty-first century, it may be only 20 percent of the population who are involved, although they are those most engaged in political processes.[69] But both polarization itself and research on it are evolving rapidly, so what we know as I write may have changed by the time you read this.

What causes what? VBN theory proposes that causation flows primarily from values to general beliefs to more specific beliefs and then to norms and then to decisions. In some situations, causation may flow backwards up this chain. If I make a decision consistent with my norms, beliefs and values, it probably strengthens them. But if I make a decision that is contradictory to them, it may lead to shifts in norms, beliefs and values. For example, if I have a personal norm that I should minimize my purchase of new clothing but on impulse buy something new, I may be more likely to notice others buying new clothes, weakening the descriptive norm that supports avoiding clothing purchases. Theories of decision-making are partial explanations that capture general patterns but there will always be exceptions and instances that contradict the general pattern.

**Integrating theories.** Many other theories have been offered to explain environmental decision-making; there are too many to review all of them here. Unfortunately, in the current research literature the theories are really a cacophony, with most studies invoking one theory or another but rarely attempting to integrate across them.[70] And when more than one theory is engaged, too often the framing is a "battle of the bands," in which theories are viewed as in competition rather than as complementary. But each theory captures a different aspect of decision-making. By integrating them, we can develop a richer, more nuanced and more context-sensitive approach.[71] I hold out hope that future work will provide a more catholic approach to theory.

After VBN, perhaps the most common approach to understanding pro-environmental action is the theory of planned behavior (TPB). TPB is a general-purpose approach to understanding what leads us to make decisions and take actions. It has been applied hundreds of times to dozens of kinds of behavior.[72] Its basic formulation proposes that a behavior can be predicted by someone's attitudes towards the behavior, their perception of social pressure to carry out the behavior (a prescriptive norm), their view of their ability to carry out the behavior and their intention to carry out the behavior. The key feature of TPB research is that each of these components is measured with specific reference to the behavior studied. For example, a TPB approach to the adoption of residential photovolta-ics (RPV) would measure attitudes towards RPV, perceived social pressure to install (or to not install) and perceived feasibility of RPV for that residence. As Ajzen, a parent of the theory, has put it, TPB has high fidelity and predictive ability. In contrast, VBN, especially values, will have less predictive ability but higher "bandwidth," in the sense that the same variables can predict a wide variety of decisions. To quote Ajzen: "General attitudes and values can help explain a broad range of behaviors, but they account for relatively little variance in any one behavior; whereas behavior specific measures of attitudes, subjective norms, perceptions of control, and intentions can explain a great deal of variance, but only for the particular behavior of interest."[73] Indeed, the two theories are probably best seen as a causal chain, with values as general predictors of a wide variety of behaviors that influence not only the other components of VBN theory but also the components of TPB. In an analysis of fifty-six studies of VBN and TPB, Klöckner finds support for just such a causal chain connecting the two theories.[74]

A theory of self-regulation complements VBN and TPB by focusing on the steps that have to be taken to carry out an action.[75] If VBN theory stops with a person deciding "I ought to minimize my purchase of new clothes to reduce my impact on the environment," self-regulation theory sees that personal norm as a goal. The context matters – it might be easy or difficult to carry out pro-sustainability actions. The theories are intended to cover a middle range where action is feasible.[76] Since context is shaped by history and can be changed, changing the constraints of context to make pro-sustainability decisions by consumers easier to implement can be an important way to encourage such decisions.

The VBN model, and most models that come from social psychology, are not unlike the RAM in that they suggest we make choices after careful review of what matters to us. I have suggested that VBN is a complement to the RAM that explains the bases for our preferences. Both the RAM and social psychological theories are modeling what is called deliberate, System II or "Slow" decisions in which we think through what matters to us.[77] However, we often make decisions quickly without taking the time for detailed analysis of alternatives, processes labeled affective, System I or "Fast" decisions. The social psychological tradition in which VBN is embedded also acknowledges and provides some insights for fast as well as slow decision-making. In fast decision-making, we look for clues that help us quickly assess our choices without thinking through implications in detail. Some of those clues are about what values are at play and what role we should adopt in making the decision.[78] Research on System I decision-making provides a substantial complement to both VBN theory and the RAM.

## 3.4    Heuristics, Biases and Fast Decisions

Even as the RAM was expanding to cover more than "economic" decisions and was gaining influence in policy, other lines of research in the social sciences were questioning its adequacy as a description of how we make decisions. Seventy-five years ago, Herbert Simon suggested that the amount of time and information needed to carry out the calculations required to maximize expected utility is too great – we cannot use that approach on a routine basis.[79] In his view, our rationality was not comprehensive but worked only within bounds.[80] He argued that often we "satisfice." We look for a choice that is "good enough" rather than spending time looking for the absolute best.

Buying a new car or finding an apartment shows how satisficing works. In any urban area, I will be faced with hundreds, even thousands, of choices. Applying a rational actor calculus to assess all these options would be overwhelming. A simpler approach is "elimination by aspects."[81] Pick some key criteria: "Car must cost less than $15,000" or "Car must have a combined EPA mileage rating of at least 40 miles per gallon." That will drop the number of candidate cars substantially, perhaps to a manageable number where more detailed comparisons that look like the RAM can be applied. Elimination by aspects approximates the RAM for the options you analyze, but it differs from the full RAM.[82] If I use these criteria, I would eliminate a car that costs $15,100 even though it might be highly desirable on all the other criteria that matter to me and thus might be the "best" choice under the RAM. In the case of apples, I might use a rule that I will only buy organic applies – at most stores that would eliminate most of the possible choices and allow me to focus on just a few. Elimination by aspects is just one approach to understanding how we make decisions in the face of great complexity and uncertainty.[83]

The literature describing these alternatives to the RAM is often labeled "heuristics and biases" for the shortcuts we use in System I or "fast" decisions.[84] The shortcuts are called heuristics in that they are fast and practical tools for simplifying a decision. However, they often lead to decisions that are quite different from what we would do if we followed the RAM, thus the use of the term "biases" to describe the literature: the heuristics bias us away from a RAM decision. Unlike the RAM, with its single strong core theory, or the social psychological approach with a moderate number of variables that seem to influence our preferences, the heuristics and biases literature identifies many specific shortcuts in decision-making. Satisficing through elimination by aspects is just one example.

Critiques of the RAM have gone from "outsider" work that was often ignored in economics and policy to a popular topic in both research and policy discussions. The innovative work by Kahneman, Tversky and others identifying these heuristics and biases and developing a model that incorporates some of them led to Kahneman winning the Nobel Prize in Economics in 2002.[85] Work inspired by the heuristics and biases approach has flourished. Indeed, it has become sufficiently influential that economists have taken up experimental methods that were developed by psychologists for studying how people actually make decisions, creating the neologisms "experimental economics" and "behavioral economics."[86] A parallel literature has examined political heuristics – the shortcuts we use in making political decisions – and the approach is beginning to have some influence in sociology as well.[87] The tradition has inspired important work on perceptions of risk and uncertainty that are central to decision-making about the environment and sustainability that I will review in Section 3.5.

Anchoring is one of the most important heuristics and can serve as an example of how we may go astray in making decisions. Anchoring is a starting point bias. We begin thinking about a decision problem from some starting point that is easy to bring to mind. The problem with anchoring is that we often minimize how different things are from the anchor.

Attari and colleagues asked people to compare how much energy is used by various activities and appliances (e.g. running the dishwasher, running a laptop computer for an hour) compared to a 100 watt light bulb.[88] They found that, overall, most people somewhat overestimated the amount of energy used by things that used little and substantially underestimated the amount of energy used by the things that use a lot. Figure 3.2 illustrates this. The dotted line shows where people would be if they knew accurately the amount of energy used. The squares and circles show the average estimates of energy used, and the solid curve shows the pattern of those responses. This is a logarithmic scale, so each tick mark indicates ten times more energy used. For example, on average people think a dishwasher uses about 200 watt-hours when in fact the average dishwasher uses

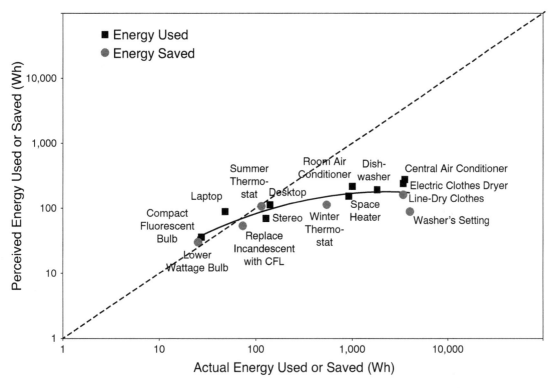

**Figure 3.2** Actual versus perceived energy consumption in the household
The actual energy used by household appliances (horizontal axis) versus the amount of energy people think the appliances use. The dotted line is how people would respond if they were perfectly accurate. Image provided by Shahzeen Attari based on Attari et al. (2009) and reprinted with permission.

about 1,800 watt-hours. People are underestimating dishwasher energy use by about a factor of 9.

What are they thinking? Most of us don't have a very intuitive sense of the flow of electricity through the devices we use. So, the people in this study seem to be using an anchoring heuristic that keeps their estimates near the 100 watt light bulb. This biases their estimates of how much energy is used at the high end downward and at the low end upward. As a result, people will misunderstand the best strategies for reducing their energy consumption. Attari also looked at perceptions of household water consumption and found the errors were much smaller than for energy.[89] This makes sense. We have a much better sense of a gallon of water than of a watt-hour of electrical use.

Even experts have trouble making estimates of electrical consumption, although they are more accurate than the average consumer. Happily providing some simple information that gives consumers multiple anchors can move a long way towards correcting misperceptions. Similar patterns of misunderstanding have been found with food – our estimates of the environmental impacts tend to be inaccurate but are easily corrected with labeling. But the basic point remains – we use shortcuts in making decisions, and while they are useful, they can also lead us astray.[90]

Anchoring effects can be deployed to influence decisions. Cialdini, in *Influence: The Psychology of Persuasion*, showed the many ways in which our decisions are manipulated, usually to the economic or political advantage of those doing the manipulation and at a cost to us. Cialdini not only conducted important experiments in the laboratory and in field settings; he also signed up to be trained as and work as a "persuader" – a salesperson or marketer – to see how our choices are manipulated in the market. Twenty-five years later, Thaler and Sunstein revisited this subject with *Nudge: Improving Decisions about Health, Wealth and Happiness*.[91] Their point is the same as Cialdini's – the way we normally make decisions can lead to some bad outcomes. Perhaps the most well worked and striking examples go back to the anchoring effect, which is also labeled "set point bias" or "starting point bias" in these literatures. Starting points matter immensely, as the work of Attari and colleagues demonstrates. Thaler and Sunstein summarize the many studies that show that when people are offered options about what packages to pick as part of their employee benefits, the options that are defaults – what you get if you do not choose – are dispropor-tionately chosen. Television networks know that if you watch their show at 8:00, you are quite likely to not switch channels when the 8:30 show comes on and build schedules so popular shows provide a lead to new shows. If a voter favors a candidate for a prominent office, for example, president of the United States, then they are more likely to vote for other candidates of the same party in that election than if there is not a favored candidate for a prominent office.[92]

One implication of all this research is that we ought to design policies and programs so that they will be easy for people to make decisions that match their preferences and easy for them to implement those decisions once made. Design principles can be used to shape policies and programs. Design principles are generalizations from scientific understanding that can inform planning of programs and policies to make them effective. The ethical justification for the principles is that if a government agency, a private utility or a nonprofit has decided to promote energy efficiency, then they should look to these design principles as ways of making it easy for the energy consumer to take action. How these principles are best implemented will depend on the context, and it is best to apply design principles in deliberation with those who will be affected by the program or policy. Chapters 8 and 9 provide a more extensive discussion of design principles.

While not usually considered a heuristic, we are biased towards stories as a way to understand the world. This is understandable. We have spent most of our cultural evolutionary history in groups where we share information through stories, so telling and listening to stories is something that comes naturally, and stories can have a strong effect on our perception of facts and can highlight some values over others. They can be a powerful tool for communicating about science and sustainability. But, like all of the processes studied in the heuristics and biases literature, stories can distort decision-making. In Box 3.1, I offer some thoughts about stories and science as ways of conveying facts.

## Box 3.1  Stories versus science

There are many passionate calls for the presentation of scientific evidence in the form of stories. The hope is that this will make science more persuasive to the public. We seem to find stories more compelling than a scientific narrative based on coherent theory and the assessment of evidence. But I am cautious about stories. For me, the scientific method is a process intended to reduce the influence of well-told stories in developing a factual understanding of the world. Religious narratives, whether of the sun god Huitzilopochtli chasing his siblings the moon and stars or of the Lord making the sun and the moon stand still (Joshua 10:13), often seem more compelling stories than gravitational forces, a heliocentric solar system and complex orbital dynamics. Most of us prefer the scientific narrative to the religious one as a factual description not because it is a more entertaining story but because it is better according to the rules we accept as the scientific method. (Of course, as Darwin said, "There is grandeur in this view.")

There may be reasons to tell stories in service of science. I have used stories to introduce many of the themes in the book as a way of trying to clarify what motivates the discussion. But we have to be careful that the influence of a well-told story does not substitute for an understanding of why we prefer the solar system model of Copernicus and Newton to the wonderful narratives of various religions. Such stories used in place of evidence can have problematic influences on public discourse. For example, in Box 5.5 I argue our beliefs about government inefficiency come from us making judgments based on anecdotes and stories rather than on systematic evidence about government performance. The power of stories is a potential source of distortion in deliberative processes that I view as crucial for integrating facts and values in decision-making (see Chapters 4 and 8). We need fair and competent discourse so every position has equal footing based on its logic and sincerity. But a compelling story and a compelling storyteller may have an inappropriate advantage in such circumstances.

I am not arguing we should not use stories – they are compelling in their ability to make facts concrete and context-specific and to articulate values and norms. But they also can be used to distort, can entrain emotions, can play into BAHP and can be manipulated by the powerful. Perhaps the counter to these problems is hearing a multiplicity of stories and discussing them in deliberative processes of the sort I advocate in Chapter 9.

## 3.5  Risk Perception

One of the major issues in the heuristics and biases literature is how people handle risk and uncertainty in making decisions. We do not do it very well, or at least we do it differently than the RAM suggests we should.[93] For example, suppose I ask, "Which kills more people per year, sharks or bees?" I suspect many people will say sharks. But deaths from bee stings seem to be far more common than deaths from shark attacks.[94] Shark attacks get far more coverage than fatalities from bee stings, which are usually the result of an unfortunate allergic reaction to the sting. We give greater weight to the things we can think about easily and tend to overestimate their probability while underestimating the probability of things where examples do not come readily to mind. In addition, we tend to think that things that are out of our control are riskier than things we feel we can control and that things that have dread outcomes are riskier than those that have outcomes that, while bad, are not dread.[95] Shark attacks may seem less under our control and more dreadful than a bee sting reaction.

We also tend to confuse uncertainty in scientific understanding with a lack of any understanding at all. A group of scientists may reach a consensus that the probability that the climate is changing is 95 percent. To scientists, that is pretty strong evidence. But an assertion of 95 percent probability, rather than an assertion of absolute certainty, seems to be interpreted by many not trained in probabilistic reasoning as a statement that scientists do not know whether the climate is changing.[96] This tendency to expect science to be close to absolute certainty has led to relatively effective campaigns to delay action on key environmental problems by emphasizing scientific uncertainty, a point discussed further in Chapter 4.[97] Uncertainty in environmental conflict and the political efforts to exploit it will be discussed in more detail later in this section and in Chapter 6.

One reaction to these findings, and to the many other studies that have replicated and expanded on them, is to conclude that we are pretty incompetent at handling probabilities and other quantitative concepts. In some sense that is true – if you want to make a decision that follows the prescriptions of the RAM, it is probably a good idea to be methodical, to check your judgments, perhaps to use a formal procedure, some software or a consultant. Clearly, the RAM describes a decision-making process that is hard for people to do. Most of what it requires involves tasks most people find very difficult. The things we do well – social interaction, pattern recognition, language processing – do not have much value in the RAM model. This suggests a criterion for a good decision process: that it complements our weaknesses and builds on our strengths.[98]

The heuristics and biases we use in most decisions may be the result of cultural evolution that selected for ways of making decisions that worked well over most of human history.[99] Loss aversion – viewing a loss of a given amount as having greater weight than a gain of the same amount – is a very common bias away from the strict RAM. But it seems a very appropriate strategy when the loss we are avoiding could put us over the edge into catastrophe. Or consider the availability heuristic applied to the problem of avoiding a lion for people who live near lions.

---

### Box 3.2  The risk depends on who you are

The heuristics may reflect an approach to decision-making that works well when the key features of the environment are best thought of as processes with memory – what will happen next depends a lot on what just happened. In contemporary society, our statistical tools and many approaches to decision-making assume that events are not dependent on recent history in the sense that the flips of a fair coin are purely independent: knowing what just happened should not change your guess as to what happens next. With a fair coin, the probability of a heads after three heads in a row is still 50 percent. The coin, the dice and the roulette wheel have no memory of what just happened. But in the ecosystems and social systems in which humans have spent most of their existence, most processes do have memory. The lion may still be hanging around, the fish may still be abundant in a particular patch of river, the grove of trees may still have fruit, the group that lives near that mountain may still be friendly. For these kinds of processes, recent events are often a very good guide to the future. The heuristics and biases may reflect that. In particular, the availability heuristic is a tendency to give greater weight to what is easy to recall, either because something happened recently or because it was dramatic.

If what happened yesterday is a good guide to today, then the availability heuristic could lead to better decisions than assuming all data should get equal weight. It may also be that the availability heuristics, with its tendency to emphasize the dramatic, gives special cognitive weight to disasters from which it would be impossible to recover, short-circuiting the kind of risk calculation that follows from the RAM but providing a decision-making process that is simple and quick to implement. This logic may also underpin loss aversion. In some abstract sense, the loss and gain of $1,000 may be equivalent (and utility theory assumes that it is). But for someone at the economic margin, while gaining $1,000 might be very nice, losing $1,000 could be catastrophic. This again emphasizes the importance of context-sensitive analysis. What may be "rational" for a high-income family might be very irrational for a family at the edge of poverty where one economic mishap (lost work from illness, a car breakdown, etc.) can mean, for example, loss of housing and homelessness that can set off a cycle of self-reinforcing negative events.[100] This in turn can lead groups who have a long history of having to make decisions in the face of disadvantage and a lack of power to develop strategies that work in those contexts but look far different from what might be expected under a "one-size-fits-all" view of decision-making.[101]

Police shootings of African Americans and other minorities are a particularly tragic example of these heuristics. African American men and women, American Indian/Alaska Native men and women and Latino men face higher lifetime risk of being killed by police than do their white peers.[102] Many factors contribute to these discrepancies, but there has been a tendency to treat them as routine and even inevitable. The Black Lives Matter movement is an effort to highlight egregious cases of the use of force against people of color, pointing to the most recent incidents in what has been a long and troubling history.[103] It is an example of the sort of critical analysis I referred to in the Introduction – to resolve a problem we first must become aware of it as a problem. There are undoubtedly heuristics at work in the decisions that produce such tragic outcomes. First, it seems likely that police are often using cognitive shortcuts in assessing risks in encounters with the public. Sometimes the shortcuts are based on explicit racism. At other times, while the outcome is racist, the bias is not an explicit racial prejudice but assignment of probabilities of risk that are keying on race rather than more objective criteria – a more implicit bias. The encounters are fraught with emotion and require quick decisions, thus encouraging the use of cognitive shortcuts and System I.[104] Of course, the behavior of the persons interacting with the police matters. But at least in the United States it seems clear that race/ethnicity entrains biases that lead cognitive shortcuts to produce bad decisions in too many cases. We can hope that the attention being drawn to the issue can lead to more deliberation among police, researchers and especially the communities impacted, and that in turn could lead to institutions, policies and procedures that reduce violence overall, especially the disproportionate share of violence visited on people of color.

On average, the probability of a lion attack may be low. But if last week a lion chased someone else in your group, using the availability heuristic to increase your assessment of lion risk is probably reasonable – the "availability" of the risk from a lion to your thinking accurately reflects the risk. It is a means of incorporating useful information. As Box 3.2 elaborates, how to process risk information depends a great deal on who you are.

Since we have trouble handling probabilities, how do we assess the risks of contemporary life? In an innovative series of studies, Fischhoff, Slovic, Lichtenstein and others asked people to rate a large number of technological risks such as nuclear reactor accidents, hang-gliding, smoking tobacco, coal mining accidents and more on scales that described how the risks were perceived.[105] They found that people tend to categorize risks along two basic dimensions:

(1)  How much dread do people have of the outcome?
     People have a greater dread of death by homicide than death by suicide, and death by shark attack is more dread than death by bee sting, for example.

(2)  How much control do you have over the risk?
     You have (or at least most people think they have) more control over suicide than over airplane accidents, and over bee stings than shark attacks, for example.

They also asked people to rank how common (how probable) harm from each risk is. If people are using the RAM, then the assessment of probability should not be influenced by perception of personal control or dread.[106] Rather, it should be a strict accounting of the sort that an actuary would do for an insurance company. The probability estimate would be how many people died of cancer divided by how many people in the population might have died of cancer (the number at risk). But in fact the perceived dread and perceived control have a strong influence on assessed probability. We think things we dread are more probable than those we do not – most people think heart attack deaths (less dread) are less common than cancer deaths (more dread) and shark attacks seem to produce more worry than bee stings. Perceived ability to control the risk has the same kind of effect. If you think you have a lot of control (suicide, bee stings, car accidents), you underrate the risk relative to things over which you think you have less control (homicide, shark attacks, airplane accidents). These basic ideas have led to a great deal of research trying to better understand how people perceive risks.[107]

This understanding of how we think about risks has been deployed in debates about policy decisions since the 1960s and was part of the evolution of the risk focus in policy described in Chapter 2. To review, because we have trouble understanding uncertainty, some draw the conclusion that the public should not have much say in decisions that involve environmental and technological risk.[108] Others argue that our difficulties in handling risk suggest that we should make use of formal procedures to assess risk. Many of us argue that such formal analyses need to be embedded in processes that link the scientific analysis with deliberation with the public – those interested in or who will be impacted by decisions about risk.[109] I will return to the theme of how to incorporate uncertainty into our decision-making throughout the rest of the book.

## 3.6    Towards Synthesis

The RAM, social psychological theories that invoke values, norms, beliefs and other factors and the heuristics and biases literature are the major traditions that inform our understanding of environmental decision-making and that should inform and be informed by our thinking about sustainability. The heuristics and biases literature emerged at least in part as a reaction to the RAM.[110]

Contrasting them is to contrast slow, deliberate decision-making with fast, affective decision-making. VBN and related theories occupy an intermediate ground between the two. With its emphasis on altruism, VBN contrasts with the emphasis on narrow self-interest that is typical of most RAM applications. But the idea of moving through a process of consulting values, beliefs and norms in making a decision seems a slow, thoughtful process in contrast to the fast, affective process of using heuristics and biases to make decisions. However, values are closely linked to identity, and things that are linked to values or identity will produce an emotional response. VBN theory and related approaches can be seen as a theory of how we search for clues in fast, affective decision-making.[111] So, VBN ideas can be deployed in models of either fast or slow decision-making.

In trying to synthesize across the traditions, the differences in methodologies may matter as much or more than the theoretical differences. In most applications of the RAM, the formal model of maximization of utility under constraints suggests parameters to be estimated – for example, the degree to which demand for energy increases with increasing income or decreases with increasing prices for energy or for competing goods, or time discount rates for future costs and benefits and so on. The parameters in the model are then estimated with data from any of a variety of sources, most often survey data or data on aggregate units such as countries, states or cities but sometimes from experiments. VBN is usually represented as a causal path from values to beliefs to risk, and the model is usually estimated using survey data or sometimes experimental data. Values may influence our decisions directly but they also influence our beliefs and norms and so have both direct and indirect effects on decisions. Indirect effects are not much emphasized in most RAM applications. The heuristics and biases literature is dominated by experiments in the laboratory or the field. While there are exceptions, the tendency for researchers in one tradition to use the dominant methodology is strong and can be a major barrier to communication. Experimentalists worry about the ability to draw conclusions about causation from nonexperimental data; researchers who use representative samples worry about the degree to which findings from experiments can be generalized. Perhaps the best approach is to acknowledge that all methods have their strengths and weaknesses and that our understanding advances most quickly when problems are approached deploying multiple theories and multiple methods.[112]

Each of these three theoretical traditions offers some important insights into how people make decisions. We don't expect individual decisions to be highly predictable. Each of us face a set of constraints and concerns that are only partially captured by any of the theories. But the theories are powerful enough that they can help us develop ways to influence decisions, as we will see in Chapters 8 and 9. We need more synthetic work that better understands how the three traditions can best complement one another, especially work on how decisions differ across contexts. That is, part of integrating the theories is developing a theory of contexts.[113] A theory of contexts will clarify when we decide based on rational self-interest, when a variety of values and norms are in play, when the shortcuts of heuristics and biases dominate, when heuristics and biases interact with the process of the RAM and VBN and when we don't make much use of heuristics and biases and how power and inequality influence decisions. I have emphasized how these traditions have been applied to sustainability. But they also apply to nearly all decision-making, and we can learn a great deal by making comparisons of what we know about the dynamics of sustainability decisions with other kinds of decisions. Box 3.3 examines the early stages of our understanding of responses to the COVID-19 pandemic as an example.

---

### Box 3.3  Individual decision-making in the COVID-19 pandemic

Research on the pandemic is still evolving, but we have some tentative insights that illustrate the ideas in this chapter. Our actions in the pandemic impacted us as individuals but also impacted others. That is typical of sustainability decisions. Many of the individual actions advocated by public health officials, in particular "social distancing," wearing masks and getting vaccinated, reduce the risk of infection to each of us when we do them. But they also reduce the risk of the virus spreading to others. Both self-interest and altruism are in play. During the initial stages of the pandemic, in many countries and regions compliance with social distancing measures was very high, even when the measures were voluntary. What was shaping these actions? Initial analyses of risk perception indicated that most people saw the risks to others as much higher than their own risk.[114] So, altruism and personal norms mattered. People believed that they had an obligation to act.

In the United States, by late April 2020, a contrarian narrative began to circulate, instantiated in demonstrations protesting business closures, mask-wearing and other measures intended to slow the spread of the virus. When vaccines became available, arguments against them circulated. While research on the dynamics and funding of these campaigns is ongoing, they seem to resemble the disinformation campaigns mounted against many environmental policy initiatives. Now, polarization in beliefs about the nature of the pandemic, in risk perceptions and in willingness to take action is unfortunately much like the polarization around climate change.[115] Clearly, as the pandemic continues to evolve and research on it emerges, there will be lessons applicable to sustainability.

---

We want theories of decision-making not only to describe how we make decisions but to offer some insights into how to make better decisions for sustainability.[116] To move very far towards better decisions, we have to invoke an ethical theory. The RAM is closely linked to utilitarian ethics. Yet neither the VBN nor heuristics and biases literatures have an affiliated ethical theory. Before we examine how the theories might better engage with sustainability, it will be essential to ask what constitutes good decisions and the obstacles that impede making good decisions. That is the subject explored in the rest of the book. The first step will be to consider the relationship between facts and values, between "is" and "ought."

# 4    Facts and Values

I once was at lunch with a distinguished economist and a distinguished ecologist. They disagreed over the importance of tropical deforestation. At first, their debate was about the facts. How fast is tropical rain forest disappearing?[1] What will follow on those landscapes when the forest is cut? What will happen to the species lost from the lumbered tracts? Before we had moved from the salads to the main course, it was clear that there was little disagreement between them on the best available answers to these questions – on the facts. Then the conversation took an interesting turn:[2]

ECOLOGIST: "So you agree we are losing tropical rain forest very quickly, that it will be replaced with scrub and that many species will disappear as a result."
ECONOMIST: "Yes, but I don't think it matters much."

The conversation paused for a moment. These thoughtful researchers had come to agreement about the facts. The differences in their positions on deforestation rested not on different beliefs about the facts but on the importance they assigned to biodiversity – on values. But much of the discussion of values that followed was in the language of facts. How much wealth would logging create? How long could an economy based on harvesting the forest last and what would follow? What ecosystem services would be lost and how would that impact human well-being? How much income could be generated from sustainable uses of the forest that involved little logging?[3] Such statements about facts were more common than statements about the relative value of biodiversity and of human welfare and economic growth.

I offer this stylized conversation to make two points. First, both facts and values matter when we make decisions about sustainability. Deciding if deforesting an area is a good thing or a bad thing depends on knowing what is happening and projecting what will happen – assessing facts and our uncertainty about them. But it also requires trade-offs, and trade-offs are based on values. Second, we seem to be more comfortable debating facts than values. Since values are close to our identities, challenges to them may seem threatening and emotionally charged. So disagreements will often focus on facts even when value differences are a cause for disagreement.

In Chapter 3, I argued that we have a strong tendency to let our values influence our assessment of the facts via biased assimilation. Science has gained authority as a way of assessing the facts that we hope is relatively free from those influences.[4] How well does science do that? I will begin by describing the process of science and how it is structured to try to reduce the influence of values and power in deciding what the facts are. Box 4.1 notes that some scholars (strong constructionists) believe facts are just assertions of values, while others (positivists) feel it is relatively easy to find facts using science. The rest of the chapter will discuss how values come into science and the role of power in shaping science.

## Box 4.1 Can we distinguish facts from values?

In our daily lives, we have little problem differentiating between statements like "This coffee was grown organically" and "I ought to buy organic coffee." The first is a statement of facts, the second an ethical assertion about what we ought to do (a personal norm) that reflects our values. The distinction between "is" and "ought" seems clear. But at least since Plato's account of Socrates' discussion with Meno more than twenty-two centuries ago, there has been some debate about our ability to separate facts from values.[5]

Values–beliefs–norms (VBN) theory argues that our values and what we already believe will influence how we assess new information – that is, we are subject to biased assimilation. This is not irrational. We cope with a huge amount of information coming from the biophysical environment, nonhumans we are interacting with and other humans. The explosion of electronic media may or may not mean we are exposed to more information than in the past. We are certainly exposed to different sorts of information, and especially information that is not grounded in a context of our local physical environment nor in interactions with others we know well.[6] We have to filter and organize what would otherwise be a cacophony of information. This is not new for our species. We have always filtered and organized the input from our senses.[7] Some of these filters and organizing tools are the cognitive shortcuts of Chapter 3. They include using our values as filters and thus being more likely to accept as true assertions of facts that are harmonious with our values and less likely to accept those that aren't.

Does the signal of reality get through the filtering influence of our cognitive shortcuts and value biases? Strong social constructionists hold that it is not meaningful to speak of an objective reality – all we have are socially constructed impressions.[8] But others, "realists," argue that science can provide relatively clear and unambiguous information about the facts of the world.[9] Debates about whether or not there is an objective reality (ontology) and whether we can understand it (epistemology) seem esoteric, but they matter for our decisions.

Current debates about drawing a distinction between facts and values, and the effort to understand why science seems to produce consensus statements that describe the world accurately, flow from the Vienna school of logical positivists.[10] Positivists hold that there is an objective reality and that we can extract statements of fact from it. One of their major tenets is that one can clearly separate statements of fact from other kinds of statements, such as statements about what is important (values) or about what we ought to do (prescriptive norms). Their very assertive ideas about the nature of scientific knowledge prompted ongoing debate, inspiring the work of many of the most influential philosophers of science of the late twentieth century.[11] The strongest reactions have evolved into the "strong program" of argument about the social construction of science.

The strong constructionists hold that scientific assertions are mostly the result of values and biases and should be viewed very skeptically and not given much greater weight than other assertions of fact. If reality is just a construction, then scientific arguments about anthropogenic climate change are nothing more than a form of political argument. So are concerns about exposure to toxic pollutants.[12] At the other end of the spectrum, there are those who feel that science will give clear guidance about what decisions to make. Those holding this view believe that to the extent that there is scientific uncertainty, it can be handled through technical procedures such as risk analysis (see Chapters 2 and 3).

The feminist theorist Donna Haraway, the sociologist Gene Rosa and many philosophers urge us to move beyond a rather pointless dichotomy contrasting scientific assertions as taken-for-granted truths and giving no special privilege to scientific assertion of facts.[13] Instead, we need to learn from both these views. That is the approach I take in this chapter.

## 4.1   How Do We Come to Facts?

Science is a conversation that is guided by strong norms. The hope is that over time the consensus in the conversation evolves towards a good approximation of reality.[14] Peer-reviewed publications are the core of the conversation.[15] Typically, a publication is reviewed by two or more experts in the field and an editor makes a decision to publish (or not publish or to revise) based on those reviews.[16] In some fields, such as the social sciences, the review process is "double-blind" so that the authors do not know who wrote the reviews and the reviewers are not given the identity of the author. This double-blind approach is intended to minimize the effects of prestige – the paper from the famous professor at the world's top university will have no better chance of getting accepted than the paper from the unknown scholar at a less prestigious place.[17] The system is not perfect, but it helps. However, in the physical and biological sciences, peer review is often "single-blind" – the author does not know who reviewed the paper, but the reviewers know who wrote the paper. This is a bit less scientific since single-blind review is subject to the effects of prestige in assessing the work.[18]

A strong norm of the scientific conversation is that what is to be accepted as true must be resonant with empirical observation and be coherent with what is already known. Scientists are human, so factors of friendship and animosity, prestige, personal ambition and myriad other processes influence what is taken as consensus and how long it takes for an assertion of fact to be accepted as consensus.[19] Indeed, there is a plausible argument that "scientific progress advances one funeral at a time" – that consensus is reached as proponents of older ideas die out.[20] But if science is a deliberative process in which our views evolve, the value of scientific norms is not that they operate perfectly in every case. Rather, over time the norms incorporate diverse views and move the consensus towards a better understanding of reality.

The consensus should not come by invoking authority, either human or divine, or by arguing that the nature of the world can be determined by what we desire it to be.[21] For example, the motto of the Royal Society (the full name is The Royal Society of London for Improving Natural Knowledge; it is one of the oldest scientific organizations) is "Nullius in verba" ("Take nobody's word for it"). The process is imperfect. Some researchers manage to publish papers that are fraudulent. Some proportion of all papers contain errors that, while not intentional, were not detected by the authors or in the peer-review process. So, we generally want to see more than one study reach the same conclusion before we feel we have a reasonable handle on the facts.

The norms of the scientific conversation continue to evolve. It is now common for a journal to require a statement as to what each author on the paper contributed to the research. This allows clarity about who is responsible for any errors that may later be detected and militates against the prestigious or the powerful having their names added to papers as a courtesy. Most journals require a statement of financial disclosure and conflict of interests to help militate against research that might be tainted by monetary influences.[22] They also require that the data used in the analysis be made available for other researchers who want to replicate the study, and all US federal funding agencies I know about also have a strong requirement for open access to the data from research they fund.[23] When I started my career, few if any journals had any of these requirements. Now, most of them do – the norms are changing towards more openness about potential biases and better ability to check results. These changes are in response to a growing awareness of problems that have been uncovered by the scientific community and science journalists. Fraudulent analyses often have turned out to be the work of one member of a larger team, so indicating who was responsible for what helps clarify responsibility. Studies whose results favor some financial interests over others now reveal, to at least some degree, the interests of the researchers. Errors in methods can be detected via careful scrutiny and reanalysis. As problems are noticed, the community takes steps to correct them. The attention given to errors and even fraud in recent years is not a crisis in science but evidence of the scientific process at work. A published paper is not an irrefutable demonstration of fact; it is a turn in the conversation and others may disagree with it and show why it should not be believed. Eventually consensus emerges but only after extended discussion and sometimes rather fierce arguments.

That is the ideal. Historically, science has been dominated by white, cis male, ableist, WEIRD perspectives, and access to the scientific conversation has been difficult for others because of both direct bias and structural barriers. For example, the insightful theories, methodologies and insights of W. E. B. DuBois and several innovative women were largely absent from mainstream sociology for decades because of racist, class and gender biases.[24] Had that work been part of the ongoing discussion, our understanding of society would have advanced much more quickly. Since the mid-twentieth century, thinkers from the global south like Fanon and Freire have articulated how our intellectual traditions are shaped by power relationships, including colonialism and capitalism.[25] We not only are becoming more aware of the limits and biases of the tradition I discuss but are trying to effectively and respectfully incorporate other voices and perspectives. Increased diversity in views allows us to make more rapid progress in the science we need for sustainability.[26]

Values still, and indeed must, play a role in scientific decisions. To keep them from dominating our views about facts, we have to understand how values influence the process of science. The next section will describe six ways in which the values of scientists influence their decisions. I will then turn to the ways in which larger social forces, and particularly the interests of the powerful, can shape both science and the influence of science in informing the beliefs we use in making decisions.

## 4.2    Values and Scientists

The strongest value held by most scientists is a commitment to the scientific process. If I say I am a scientist, I am saying I hold what philosophers call epistemic values – shared views about how we go about establishing facts.[27] From those values follow the norms of how research is conducted and reported. However, within this general set of norms, there are still a lot of decisions that must be made by scientists in pursuing their work. These decisions involve other values, not just the epistemic ones. Elliott's taxonomy of six ways that non-epistemic values influence decision-making in science is useful for thinking about these decisions.[28]

First, values influence what scientists decide to study. Scientists' choices are certainly influenced by their sense of what they enjoy doing, what they feel competent doing and what they feel will be rewarded by the larger community. But many scientists also care a great deal that their work is useful to society, although they may differ in their views about what is useful. Power comes into such decisions through funding and the prestige accorded to different fields. For example, a researcher who decides to pursue work on genetic technologies or nanotechnologies or artificial intelligence can look for funding from industry as well as foundations and the federal government. They also might end up with lucrative patents or be able to start a profitable private firm. A researcher who wants to study what causes poverty and the consequences of poverty on both individuals and society may be able to obtain funding from foundations and government but is unlikely to be supported by industry, obtain patents or start a for-profit firm based on their research.

Second, scientists influence decisions about where funds should be allocated for research and here again judgments based on values, norms and beliefs come into play. On committees that decide on funding, arguments are usually about both how much a given field of research will contribute, including how "ready" the field is to make big advances in fundamental knowledge, and how useful the research will be. Work that deeply advances fundamental knowledge but has little immediate use and work that is useful but doesn't contribute much to knowledge both sometimes get supported, although the weight given to each of these criteria depends on the priorities of the organization doing the funding. The US National Science Foundation emphasizes fundamental knowledge while also taking account of usefulness. Agencies like the US Department of Agriculture or the Environmental Protection Agency want to advance fundamental knowledge but have a primary responsibility to fund research that allows them to do a better job in meeting the goals assigned to them by Congress. But in every discussion I've been in, both criteria matter.

Third, scientists must decide how to approach a problem. If you decide that research on cancer is very important, there are value judgments involved in deciding on how much emphasis to place on research on cancer prevention, including carcinogens in the environment, versus on cures for cancer.[29] Or if you decide reducing hunger and malnutrition is important, you might work on technology such as genetically modified organisms and the use of agricultural chemicals to increase the quantity and nutritional quality of the crops produced. You might focus on organic and sustainable agriculture. Or you might examine the institutions and incentives that drive good and bad practices in production, distribution (including waste) and ultimately consumption of food.[30] These may not be mutually exclusive logically, but usually a single researcher can't do all of them and so must make choices based on both personal preferences for what kinds of research they find satisfying and what lines of research they think will have the greatest social benefits.

Fourth, scientists must make decisions about what kind of model they will develop. A model is a description of how the world works. Sometimes this is simply prose but often it is expressed in one or more equations and/or in computer simulations. Richard Levins suggested that we would like our models to be general (applicable to many circumstances rather than just one or a few), precise (yielding detailed descriptions rather than generalities) and realistic (capturing what is going on in the messiness of the real world).[31] But he argued that no model can do well on more than two out of the three criteria. Elliott notes that when scientists are trying to inform decisions, they must construct and deploy models quickly and at moderate costs. This leads to value judgments about which of Levins' three criteria to emphasize in modeling.[32]

Elliott's fifth argument about values in science focuses on how scientists handle uncertainty. How humans process uncertainty was a major theme of Chapter 3 and will occupy much of the rest of this chapter. His sixth point of entry for values is in how scientists chose to present their results and engage with the public, especially around policy decisions. Some of the finest scientists I have had the privilege to work with have taken very different approaches to this problem even though they all struck me as deeply passionate about doing work that would improve human well-being and protect the environment.[33] The climatologist Steve Schneider and ecologist Paul Ehrlich match the model of public scientists: They often appeared on television, were frequently interviewed in all media and were authors of many popular books and articles. In contrast, the political scientist Elinor Ostrom focused her energies on her scientific work and in conversations with those who manage commons and who are affected by that management, and seldom engaged with the mass media.[34] Choosing what to convey beyond writing for and speaking to professional audiences depends both on what one views as useful and appropriate and on personal style and preferences.[35] In Box 4.2, I discuss ways in which effective communication between scientists and the general public can be facilitated.

The norms of science are intended to reduce the risk that these six types of decisions by scientists, shaped by individual values, interfere with developing statements of fact that are good approximations of reality. The norms work over time, as multiple studies accumulate and as more voices are brought into the conversation. In my view, they are reasonably effective.[36]

Larger societal forces also shape what we know, in particular the active campaigns to shape risk perceptions noted throughout the book.[37] Some of the most important biases are those that cause far more investment in some kinds of sciences than others. Schnaiberg makes a useful distinction between production sciences, such as typical applications of engineering, economics and chemistry, that are intended to produce things and impact sciences such as ecology and sociology that try to help us understand how changing things affects us, other species and the biosphere.[38] We badly underinvest in impact science relative to the investment we make in production sciences. For example, the effort spent on inventing new chemicals overwhelms our ability to understand how those chemicals might impact ecosystems. After a new product has become common, even ubiquitous, we slowly learn of its adverse effects. While there have been substantial advances in the impact sciences since the mid-twentieth century, the investment in them still lags far behind investment in the production sciences.[39]

Trying to adhere to the idealized norms of scientific discourse would be difficult enough on a level playing field; the direct intrusion of power and the cultural assumptions that have emerged from the past exercise of power make it much harder to adhere to the norms. Good decisions require accurate assessment of the facts. But scientific facts are always uncertain to some degree. As we saw in Chapter 3, it can be difficult to handle uncertainty in making decisions. How should we think about uncertainty in our assessment of facts?

---

## Box 4.2  Should scientists be science communicators?

Do scientists have an obligation to communicate their science with the public? In the eighteenth century, most scientists funded themselves with earned or, more often, inherited fortunes. But now a large portion of all scientists are educated at public universities, work at public universities and/or have their research supported by public funds. That creates some obligation to communicate outside the scientific community. What does that imply for science?

All scientists should have some training in how to communicate effectively with the press, with the public and with those involved in the policy system. Scientists whose work engages them with or has special impacts on particular communities should be engaged in communication with those communities and learn how to do that in an effective and ethical way. Communication is two-way – scientists have as much or more to learn from communities as the communities learn from scientists. I will expand on this in Section 4.4 and Chapter 9. Many interdisciplinary programs are working on ways to incorporate training in communication without placing undue burden on already busy students and faculty, even as they also include training on how to communicate across disciplines.[40] But I don't believe better science communication will come from trying to make every scientist an expert at being a mass media influencer or a Jane Goodall, Steve Schneider or Paul Ehrlich. Rather, effective science communication requires an institutional solution.[41]

The US Land Grant universities have some experience with this. Faculty often have part of their time allocated to the "Extension" service focused on outreach and engagement. Someone with a 25 percent Extension appointment might be expected to do more outreach and engagement and a bit less research and teaching. Extension is centered around agriculture and natural resources but has always been broader than that. The Home Economics tradition has led to outreach around families and children, for example. Carl Taylor at Michigan State used his Extension appointment to support his work with urban youth in Detroit and other Michigan cities and continues to have major impacts there. Land grant extension is not the only model for science communication, but it does establish the point that extensive engagement with the public needs to be part of the workload of those scientists who do it, that effective communications will often involve collaboration with those who are experts on communications and that such collaboration is often facilitated by organizations designed for such linkages.

Throughout the book, I argue for linking scientific analysis to public deliberation. This redefines communication away from a one-way flow of information from scientists to the public to an ongoing discourse that assumes that there are multiple forms of expertise, including expertise on how to conduct such deliberations. At its best, the history of land grant extension uses this model. In deploying science for sustainability, scientists need to be informed about and have some training in how to be effective participants. But the engagement of scientists and of interested and affected parties can be greatly facilitated by what are sometimes called bridging organizations that have ongoing relationships with multiple forms of expertise, including expertise grounded in the community and expertise in and experience with deliberation.[42]

## 4.3    HERO

It is not particularly useful to see science as purely the results of power struggles with no special authority in getting at facts or to see science as the smoothly functioning, always unbiased path to truth. Donna Haraway makes this clear in her insightful analysis "Situated knowledges." I want to pursue the nuanced approach she advocates, drawing also on the work of Gene Rosa.[43]

Rosa proposed we think about science for decision-making in terms of an approach he labeled HERO (Hierarchical Epistemology, Realist Ontology).[44] His starting point is a realist ontology: There exists a world independent of our comprehension of it. Factual statements should be evaluated by the degree to which they seem to capture that reality. Science is a process of producing statements that have high accuracy in representing the world, and ideally the process should lead to increases in that accuracy over time as the scientific conversation unfolds.

Rosa asks why we sometimes have scientific assertions that most of us accept as essentially value-free while other scientific assertions seem more influenced by biases, politics and values and thus very susceptible to power. He suggests that two variables can help explain these differences: ostensibility and repeatability.[45] Ostensibility is the degree to which the evidence is accessible, visible and agreed-upon. Repeatability is the degree to which there are multiple examples. Ostensibility and repeatability come into play in different ways in different fields of science, so Box 4.3 examines ways of classifying science. I add a third element to his two, political power, the efforts of those with power to influence the scientific consensus.

## Box 4.3  Types of science

Differences in ostensibility and repeatability are often turned into invidious comparisons between the "hard" and "soft" sciences. When someone insists on differentiating "hard" and "soft" sciences, I sometimes invoke a comparison of the "hard" and "easy" sciences. The "easy" sciences are those where strong invariance principles make it easy to accumulate data across space and time, where there are few practical or ethical restrictions on experimentation and where sample sizes are often in the millions, billions or even higher. By this logic, much of physics and chemistry are "easy" sciences. In contrast, we have fields where we must be cautious about assuming invariance and instead wrestle with context dependence, where experiments may not be feasible or ethical and where sample sizes are always modest. These fields, including much of ecology and the social sciences, are the "hard" sciences.

My point is not to push these distinctions but to argue that if we need to lump different areas of science into clusters, we should ask about the purpose for defining these clusters and be thoughtful about the features that are important for the distinctions being made. The historical distinctions that have been crystallized in academic structures of departments and professional societies are roughly between the physical, biological and social sciences. That may be useful for a first approximation, but fields such as biochemistry, biological anthropology and cognitive science make clear that disciplinary distinctions are historical artifacts of the organization of European and North American universities. We need to understand the basis of such distinctions, use them when appropriate and avoid them when they are misleading and based on historical differences that are no longer useful. The rise of interdisciplinary fields of research demonstrates the importance of being flexible in thinking about science, and that has been true since new fields like biochemistry, biophysics, biological engineering and computer science emerged in the mid-twentieth century.

I find it useful to distinguish experimental sciences with strong invariance principles from the historical/evolutionary sciences where things tend to vary across contexts. (This is roughly the same as my "easy/hard" distinction but without the playful language.) Contemporary experimental physics, such as the search for the Higgs boson and the work that is done at Michigan State's Facility for Rare Isotope Beams, may be the prototypical example of the former type of science. Experiments can manipulate the phenomena of interest, sample sizes are immense and the emergent laws are assumed applicable across most of time and space. Most of the social sciences and ecology are examples of historical and evolutionary sciences. It is often not possible or ethical to experimentally manipulate key variables, samples sizes are modest – in the case of historical process, the sample size may be 1 – and things seem very context-specific. Some parts of the social sciences (e.g., cognitive science and much of psychology, "experimental economics") are experimental. Some parts of the physical (e.g., much of astronomy, climatology and geology) and biological (e.g., much of evolutionary biology and ecology) are historical sciences. The distinction is useful because the logic and methods for establishing facts are resonant within the experimental and within the historical sciences and somewhat discordant across these lines.

The idea of ostensibility and repeatability allows us to assess lines of scientific evidence and evaluate conclusions about facts in ways that are useful for understanding decisions about sustainability. As Rosa succinctly put it, ostensibility means "Do you see what I see in the examples?" while repeatability means "The examples will repeat themselves." The importance of ostensibility and repeatability is clear if we think about science as a conversation about what goes on in the world.[46] Those engaged in the conversation can reach consensus more readily when participants in the conversation can point to examples and others agree that they are seeing the same thing. Consensus-building is further enhanced when there are multiple examples.[47] However, whatever the degree of ostensibility and repeatability, those with power can influence consensus, as can power embedded in cultural assumptions. I will return to that issue in Section 4.4. But first, it's useful to examine cases where the effects of power and cultural biases are relatively minor and then turn to cases where they are influential and may even dominate the scientific conversation.

Many examples from the physical sciences illustrate the process of reaching scientific consensus when there is high ostensibility and repeatability. One of the most common experiments in introductory physics labs is rolling balls made of materials with very different densities and thus masses down an inclined plane.[48] This replicates Galileo's fabled experiment of dropping two balls, one made of a very dense material, one of a less dense material, off the leaning tower of Pisa. Galileo was testing the idea that the speed of falling objects on earth is independent of their mass. His hypothesis contradicts Aristotle's view that the heavy objects fall faster than lighter ones.[49] Every year, students in many thousands of schools around the world test the same idea using the same basic logic. The inclined plane allows for slower speeds and easier measurement of how long it takes each ball to reach the bottom than does just dropping the balls. The experiment is highly ostensible. You simply observe whether one ball reaches the bottom before the other ball does. Because it is easy to do, it is highly repeatable. Surely this experiment has been done millions of times.[50] Many other experiments in physics and chemistry undoubtedly also have been subject to millions of replications, and as techniques in molecular biology become cheaper and easier, I suspect we will see tens to hundreds of thousands of replications there too. In contrast, those in the ecological and social sciences cannot draw on this vast amount of replication. Indeed, sadly, relatively few serious social science courses are offered in high school. In college, most social science courses don't engage students in data analysis let alone collection of new data.[51]

High repeatability and ostensibility give us "normal" science, the sort of science most of us learn about in high school. There are objective facts – a realist ontology. We have clear and defensible ways of determining what those facts are – a positivist epistemology. But, unfortunately, as Rosa pointed out to us, when we make sustainability decisions, both repeatability and ostensibility can become problematic.

The exposure to toxic substances is tragically common: lead in gasoline and paint, aboveground testing of nuclear weapons, Minamata mercury contamination, Love Canal, Three Mile Island, Bhopal, Chernobyl, Fernald, *Exxon Valdez*, *Deepwater Horizon*, Fukushima, Flint. The list spans the planet and involves both old and new technologies. Some examples are localized. Others cover large regions or the globe.[52] There are always complex ethical issues. But, for the moment, let's review the difficulty involved in establishing the facts.

A chemical spill in West Virginia provides an example. About 300,000 people in the Charleston region of western West Virginia had to deal with contamination of their drinking water by a spill of 4-methylcyclohexanemethanol (MCHM) into the Elk River.[53] The compound is used to "clean" coal – it is used to remove impurities that contribute to air pollution. The difficulty in assessing the risk from the spill seems all too typical. The toxicity of MCHM is not well understood. Prior to the spill, there were only a few studies using in vitro screening ("in glass" – lab testing that doesn't use animals) or exposures of laboratory rats to assess toxicity. The compound was grandparented into a list of chemicals for which further testing was not mandated in the 1976 Toxic Substances Control Act, which greatly reduced the incentive to test. The evidence that does exist suggests that these compounds may pose relatively low risk to human health at exposures below 1 part per million, but that evidence is so limited that it must be viewed as not particularly authoritative. The facility that produced the spill had not been inspected in perhaps two decades. A week after the spill, Freedom Industries, the company owning the facility, declared bankruptcy so financial responsibility for the spill is muddied. Eleven days after the spill, Freedom Industries announced that a mixture of glycol ethers, termed "PPH," was also spilled. Again, the toxicity of these compounds was not well studied but there was some disputed evidence that they pose risks to animal reproduction. At least one researcher, detected formaldehyde, a serious carcinogen, in local water supplies. Formaldehyde might be produced as the materials spilled broke down into other compounds. The company initially announced a spill of 7,500 gallons, while some government agencies suggested only 5,000 gallons. But, by seventeen days after the spill, the estimate was increased to 10,000 gallons. The company that supplies water to local communities initially felt that their filtration systems could handle the contamination but then saw that their filters were overwhelmed.

The low ostensibility and repeatability of information available for decision-making around this spill seems clear. The toxicities of the compounds spilled have not been much studied even in the laboratory and there are no studies in humans or wildlife. As is often the case, it is not just the initial compounds spilled that matter; risks also come from the compounds into which they degrade. Formaldehyde is a serious and well-studied health risk, but it was hard to know how much of it was in the drinking water supply. The exposure to humans in the communities affected came through a complicated route: chemicals spilled in the river, water taken from the river into the drinking water system then through the pipes of the water system into individual homes and businesses and thus into tap water. Even seemingly simple facts – how much of what was spilled – seem to shift over time. Studies done since the spill seem to indicate that the effects on humans and other species will be relatively small, although these estimated effects are very uncertain.[54] But whatever the final outcomes, it is clear that government officials and residents, in making decisions about what to do, were faced with very substantial uncertainties.

I picked the Elk River example because it is a relatively simple case. The effects of the spill may be short-lived in that it is plausible that most of the problematic compounds have dropped in concentration to minor levels and it appears that they are only moderately toxic. In contrast, in Flint, Michigan, a decision driven by a neoliberal policy to cut city expenses caused substantial lead contamination of the drinking water, with outcomes that are still uncertain but more dire. We know a lot about the toxicity of lead, the most notable contaminant in the drinking water, including, tragically, that the effects of lead exposure in children can last a lifetime.[55] But here the problem is embedded in a context of industrial decline, segregation and racism, unemployment and a myriad of other problems.[56] Even looking only at the water problem, assessing the risks is immensely complex, with exposures varying substantially from neighborhood to neighborhood and household to household.

What does it take to assess the risks we face from, for example, a chemical exposure of the sort that occurred in West Virginia or in Flint? One of the first steps in assessing the risks faced in response to potential exposure to a chemical is to determine its toxicity.[57] Thinking about the molecular structure of a potentially toxic compound and modeling its behavior when it interacts with biologically important molecules is a starting point, but real biology in living cells is much more complicated than the best current models, so this step, while informative, and highly ostensible and repeatable, is not sufficient for making risk decisions. A next step from theory is "in vitro" toxicity. Bacteria or cultured cells from animals grown in lab containers are exposed to the chemical. Again, this is highly ostensible and repeatable science and gives some sense of how living cells react to the compound. But while this is a closer approximation to the risks that may be faced by humans and other animals, it is still not sufficient to understand what will happen as the organ systems of an animal deal with a novel compound. A further step is animal testing, usually on rats and mice. While this allows some understanding of what happens physiologically, there are still many uncertainties – for example, how to extrapolate "from mice to men" (*sic*) or how to compare the high doses used in laboratory studies (high doses are needed to keep the number of animals tested low) to the doses of human exposures.[58] And the ethics of exposing nonhumans to toxic substances, observing the effects while they are alive and then "sacrificing" them are problematic.[59]

Rosa emphasized the importance of context in assessing scientific conclusions.[60] We can have science with high ostensibility and repeatability when we are studying phenomena that don't change much across contexts. For running balls of different mass down an inclined plain, we expect essentially the same results no matter where on earth or, by and large, where in the universe we do the experiment. And we expect roughly the same results at whatever point in cosmological history we conduct the experiment. If we take account of the reaction dynamics of a compound whose toxicity we are assessing, then given the same chemical environment (other molecules present, pressure, temperature, etc.), we also expect strong invariance – we should get the same results if the work is done in Medellín, Mombasa or Montreal. But each species and each organ system within a single species may respond somewhat differently. The degree of ostensibility and repeatability almost inevitably declines as we move from basic chemistry to physiological processing and ultimately to toxicology.

Nor do the complexities end there. Science is built around developing generalizations that are robust across contexts, often by understanding why context has the effects it does. But many, perhaps most, environmental and sustainability decisions are about very particular contexts. The issue to members of the public who may have drunk water that was contaminated is not about the scientific abstractions based on reasonably ostensible and repeatable science. Rather, the issue is what risk they, and their children and their companion animals, face. To answer that, we must estimate how much exposure they have. That is immensely complex, involving the dynamics of the chemicals in surface and ground water through the drinking water systems and into hundreds or thousands of home plumbing systems. It requires estimating individual habits in water use, exposure to other chemicals that might exacerbate or perhaps ameliorate the effects of the compound and variation across individuals by age, gender, ethnicity, disease status and many other characteristics that might influence how the exposure will affect them.

We have moved from a domain of highly ostensible and repeatable science – how a molecule behaves in a particular set of conditions – to one where we must extrapolate from that science to a hugely complicated problem. And we are no longer in a discussion about "statistical deaths" projected in a model but rather about possible illness to real people, including children, and companion animals (see Chapter 6). We must think carefully about how to use our scientific understanding of facts. The conditions – ostensibility and repeatability – that give us high confidence in the fact established by science in some domains – the speed of falling objects – do not carry the same weight in many situations where we must assess facts to make a decision.

I am not arguing that scientific assertions about facts should be given no more weight than assertions coming from "common sense" or obscure websites. I am arguing that, because of the modest levels of ostensibility and repeatability involved, most decisions about the environment and sustainability do not flow directly from scientific assessment of facts. Rather, in circumstances of low ostensibility and repeatability, the deep and legitimate concerns of those impacted must be integrated with our best scientific understanding, including an accurate assessment of how uncertain that science may be. Rosa referred to this problem as one of postnormal science.[61]

In Chapter 9, I will turn to the problems of how to make collective decisions in situations in the face of substantial uncertainty. But first I want to add one more criterion that underpins our trust in scientific assertions of fact in addition to ostensibility and repeatability. I want to examine the influence of power on our ability to assess facts.

## 4.4   The Problem of Power

Ostensibility and repeatability are important because they help us reach agreement about facts. When ostensibility and/or repeatability are low, it is harder to reach consensus. Then homophily and biased assimilation can more easily influence science. Bias in favor of prior beliefs can guard against too rapid adoption of ideas that are not well supported but also retard the acceptance of ideas that ultimately become the consensus. Prior beliefs can be formal statements of science, but they can also be deeply held and even unconscious biases. For example, Gould documented the sad history of efforts to look at variation in human intelligence and showed how subtle and pernicious gender, racial and ethnic prejudices can be in influencing the outcome of seemingly objective and methodologically rigorous measurements.[62]

There is great variation in the degree to which consensus about scientific facts is influenced by power. While physicists and the public that pays attention to science may care a great deal about experiments to detect gravity waves, the outcomes are not of much concern in larger-scale societal politics.[63] When we turn to the scientific conclusions that we need to make decisions about sustainability, very powerful individuals and organizations see their interests at stake. Billions of dollars in potential profits may depend in substantial degree on the outcome of laboratory toxicity testing – if a chemical that has great commercial value is found to be dangerous, substantial potential profits might be lost. Millions of dollars in remediation costs and damages may ride on the outcome of assessing risks from chemical spills, radioactive leaks and other industrial accidents. When we move to climate change, some of the largest industries in the world – oil and coal companies – see threats. They have a direct interest in what conclusions are drawn from the scientific conversation and will act forcefully to influence that conclusion.[64]

We have seen these efforts to shape scientific consensus throughout the twentieth century, and it continues today. Assessments of risks from lead in gasoline and other consumer products, cigarette smoking, ozone depletion, acid precipitation and now climate change have all been the subject of concerted campaigns by those who saw their financial interests at risk.[65] These campaigns are the direct exercise of power – funding of research, advertising campaigns, lobbying and other activities to push the scientific consensus towards a conclusion favorable to their interests. A common strategy is to "manufacture uncertainty" – create doubt about scientific findings that show risk and might lead to regulation. Often these efforts include attacks on those sounding warmings about risk. When Rachel Carson raised concerns about pesticides, she was castigated as a Communist and called "hysterical" (a very gendered term).[66]

Sometimes the campaigns of the powerful manifest themselves in donations to political campaigns and in communication via television ads, op-ed pieces, reports and books. Sometimes the approach is built into the regulatory process. The process of setting standards, rules for testing and other details of decision-making has great influence on what outcomes flow from a law or regulation.[67] Setting up the mechanisms by which a law will be enforced is usually the work of government agencies in consultation with those who are interested in or affected by the law. It is slow and tedious work and usually very technical. But it has a huge impact on how a law influences what happens. Engaging effectively in these discussions and negotiations requires persistence and substantial sophistication about the scientific, engineering and legal details of what is being proposed.[68] In my experience, these discussions can sound as if they are being conducted in a foreign language unless one is familiar with a very substantial vocabulary of technical terms.[69] This puts the economically powerful at an advantage. In a study in the early 1980s, we found that for every PhD scientist working on policy issues in Washington for an environmental group, there were eight PhD scientists working on policy issues for corporations and their trade associations.[70] So, for example, if the US Environmental Protection Agency proposed rules for the regulation of a toxic substance, there were likely to be eight careful analyses by experts concerned that the regulation was too costly and stringent for every one analysis from an expert concerned that public health was not being adequately protected and that the proposed rules were too loose. The ability of corporations and the organizations they fund to hire expertise swamps that of environmental groups and thus over time builds in a pressure towards regulation that will be less strict than might be ideal in balancing risk, benefits and costs to the public.[71]

The power to shape actions is not limited to direct engagement in policy debates. It also comes in the form of "taken-for-granted" assumptions and how issues are framed. Around many environmental issues, but especially around climate change, the scientific community has been surprised, even shocked, by the pushback against a steadily growing scientific consensus. There are clearly several elements to this.

The rather complex patterns of evidence involved in understanding exposure to toxics via drinking water, ecosystem dynamics under human intervention or transformational changes in the climate system may be uncomfortable for those whose model of science comes from problems with high ostensibility and reliability.[72] There is some evidence that increased understanding of science increases acceptance of uncertain science, but those results seem to vary across issues and political ideology and other beliefs.[73] It appears that, for conservatives, more education and greater self-assessed understanding of climate change lead to more skepticism about the reality and seriousness of the problem.[74] We need more research on how views of science influence stances on policy issues like climate change, biotechnology, nanotechnology and other complex science-based issues, and the HERO framework might be a source of hypotheses.[75] But it seems plausible that when we are dealing with science with modest ostensibility and repeatability and where results can be very context-specific, biased assimilation and homophily and ultimately polarization (BAHP) play a major role in decision-making.

The two figures inspired by Rosa's work map areas of science by ostensibility and repeatability and then by the degree powerful interests are at play.[76] In Figure 4.1, the vertical axis is the degree to which the evidence offered in the scientific conversation on an issue is ostensible, with ostensibility decreasing as you look up the scale. The other dimension is the degree to which it is repeatable, with repeatability decreasing as you move from left to right. Rosa argued that when an issue can be examined with methods that have high repeatability and ostensibility, then we are in the domain of "normal" science of the sort that is taught in introductory physics and chemistry courses and that matches what are probably the most common public images of science. Determining the speed with which balls of different density fall is extremely repeatable and quite ostensible. Even though the evidence for gravity waves requires a long chain of reasoning through complex instrumentation and analysis, the trust in physics developed over the last century or so lets us see the results as reasonably ostensible and quite repeatable in principle even if not something that can be done in many laboratories. However, for many issues related to environment and sustainability, neither ostensibility nor repeatability is very high. As we have seen, the risks from toxic contamination, from climate change, from many environmental and sustainability problems, must be judged based on science that is far more context-specific and far less ostensible and repeatable than the simple model of studying falling objects. To reflect this, the upper right of the graph is the domain called postnormal science.

Rosa's point is that we must be cautious about factual claims grounded in science when we move to domains of low ostensibility and repeatability. Confidence can spill over from the

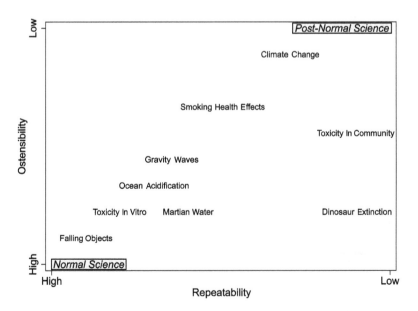

**Figure 4.1** Ostensibility and repeatability in scientific knowledge claims

domains of normal science to assertions on topics where ostensibility and repeatability are low.[77] Science is still our best tool for assessing facts but must be used in decision-making with a sense of uncertainties and context dependence. Not doing this can raise the suspicion of interested and affected parties. As Rosa put it: "The typical objections of laypersons, then, is not to science per se . . . but to institutions that attempt to maintain a monopoly on knowledge claims and which sometimes misapply abstract science to the peculiarities of local settings."[78]

Figure 4.2 adds a third dimension – the degree to which powerful interests care about the consensus that emerges from the scientific process. The vertical axis combines ostensibility and repeatability from Figure 4.1 into a score where low scores represent normal science and high scores postnormal features. The horizontal axis indicates the degree to which the powerful care about the outcomes of the scientific discourse. When the interests of the powerful are engaged, further caution about scientific consensus is warranted. The upper right area is where science is likely to be publicly contentious, values will influence assessment of facts and BAHP processes can slow the emergence of broad consensus. Over time, the normal process of science can lead to trustworthy assessment of facts even in the face of such powerful interests. That is relatively easy in the lower left area. It can take longer in the upper right area. We have a good understanding of the risks of lead exposure and cigarette smoking despite substantial resistance by the industries involved. But reaching scientific consensus took decades longer than would have been the case if those industries had not launched strong campaigns to shape the science to their benefit, and the cost of that delay was many lives damaged and lost.[79]

In situations where the science has relatively low ostensibility and repeatability, it can be much harder to overcome the influence of powerful actors with strong interest in what are accepted as facts. In cases of local toxics contamination, the complexity of the system

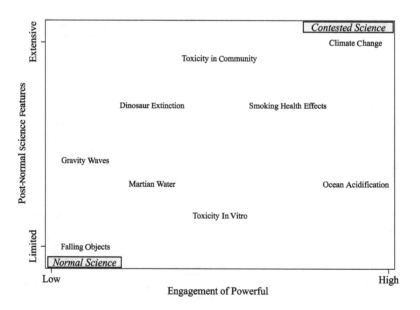

**Figure 4.2** Power and contention in science

generating risks and the limited ability to model that system in detail may mean that a strong consensus never emerges. But even when the science remains quite uncertain, there are policy processes that can lead to decisions that are well grounded in science and accepted as legitimate by all interested and affected parties. I will discuss these in Chapter 9. The key point is that because science must be deployed in a way sensitive to the local context, many types of expertise have to be effectively engaged in the conversations that are attempting to establish the facts, including Indigenous and local knowledge.[80]

Finally, I want to emphasize that I use the terms "expertise" and "facts" here to be consistent with the overall language of the book and most of the discussions in the field. I have also emphasized the importance of bringing diverse voices into the conversation, and especially those voices that have traditionally been excluded. In adding that needed diversity, it's important to realize that terms like "facts," "values" or "expertise" have to be assessed critically and defined contextually. This requires discussion with voices that have not been part of the conversation that shaped the use of those terms and who may find them inappropriate.[81] I believe the terms have been and will be useful in the context of the book, but they may need to be redefined or replaced as our thinking evolves.

## 4.5    Back to Values and Facts

The VBN theory described in Chapter 3 argues that our values are filters shaping our beliefs, and that general beliefs, such as believing the biosphere can be impacted by human action, shape more specific beliefs, such as accepting climate change as a serious threat.[82] General beliefs and values have the most influence when the science has limited ostensibility and repeatability and when powerful interests try to shape our perceptions, often by suggesting the science is very uncertain. Over time, as evidence has become more ostensible and reliable and as opposition by powerful interests has moderated, the influence of values and general beliefs may diminish.[83]

Uncertain facts are a major challenge to decision-making. But we are often uncertain about values as well. By value uncertainty, I mean that many decisions about sustainability and the environment require us to think about situations and potential outcomes that are far from our day-to-day experience. In the case of climate change, we are anticipating changes in the biosphere that will unfold over many decades, and even centuries, and that are unprecedented in human history. In general, we have entered an era – the Anthropocene – where human actions have a very strong effect on the biosphere and where there is no ecosystem not influenced by human actions.[84] In response, people have expanded the values they consult in taking actions from narrow self-interest or even altruism towards other humans to include concern with other species and the biosphere itself.[85]

When confronted with a decision that requires us to analyze changes that are familiar to us, most people are probably reasonably competent at comparing the choices to what they value. The trade-offs may be difficult, but we have lots of practice making them. We may approximate the rational actor model (RAM) or use a reasonable set of shortcuts via heuristics and biases. But in the case of environment and sustainability problems, we are often dealing with relatively novel issues and the link to our values are uncertain and each of us may feel value conflicts.[86] When the issues are politicized, as they often are, campaigns attempt to short circuit careful thought that would allow us to assess how our choices lead to outcomes that match or don't match our value priorities. Rather than a balanced review of the costs, risks and benefits of moving away from fossil fuels, we are confronted with images of polar bears and rhetoric about coal mining jobs. We are faced with value uncertainty because the problems are not familiar to us (low repeatability), the links to our values are not obvious (low ostensibility) and powerful actors are trying to tell us what to think. The three factors that require us to be humble about our assertions of facts also should suggest humility and caution in assessing the implications for various choice outcomes for our values.

At any point in time, science is imperfect, with scientists subject to all the challenges in making decisions that are faced by all humans, subject to biases and the influence of power and often reflecting prejudice and discriminatory views. But the norms and institutions of science have evolved, and continue to evolve, in a way that tries to reduce the influence of these biases. As we think about what constitutes a good decision and what gets in the way of making good decisions, science offers hope that we can shape norms and institutions in ways that lead to better decisions, however imperfect our efforts may be at any point in time. I am not arguing that the norms of science alone are sufficient for good decisions since decisions require engaging values as well as facts. I am suggesting that science gives an example of an evolutionary history that, slowly and with missteps, leads to better decisions. The hope is that we can shape the evolution of decision-making processes in ways that lead to better decisions about sustainability.

Chapters 8 and 9 will discuss how we can make good decisions in the face of these obstacles. But first I need to discuss what constitutes a good decision, why we have conflict in making decisions and why some standard approaches for introducing sustainability into decision-making may not be sufficient. Those will be the topics of Chapters 5 and 6.

# 5     What Is a Good Decision?

In 2005, the Detroit Zoo moved its two elephants, Winky and Wanda, to the Performing Animal Welfare Society's (PAWS) ARK 2000 Sanctuary in California. This was not an easy decision.[1] Elephants are very popular at zoos, and many other zoos were upset, fearing the precedent might cost them attendance. Why did the zoo do this? How could we know if this is a good decision? Both facts and values were involved. The facts, briefly, were (1) elephants are very popular at zoos and help attendance and revenues and (2) elephants have evolved to live in large multigenerational social groups and wander across miles of landscape. The values involve the revenues of the zoo, the ability to educate the public about elephants and the well-being of Winky and Wanda.

The story of Winky and Wanda is about a very specific decision. We also have to think about criteria for decision-making when we think about large-scale problems. When I started working on climate change in the 1980s, most researchers dismissed solar radiation management as a way to reduce climate risks. Solar radiation management would inject particles into the atmosphere to reduce the amount of solar energy that can be trapped by greenhouse gasses. There were (and are) great uncertainties that made the implications of solar radiation management unclear. Intentionally modifying the climate to compensate for our unintentional modifications raises complex value problems. As decades have passed with little progress in reducing greenhouse gas emissions, many of us feel that some research on solar radiation management is needed – it might prove the only way to avoid some catastrophic accelerations in climate change. But even the most ardent advocates of solar radiation management acknowledge that there are many scientific and value questions that have to be addressed before making decisions about whether or not or how to deploy it.[2]

We want to make "good" decisions about elephants in zoos, about solar radiation management, about any sustainability issue. But what is a good decision? I have been surprised, bemused and often dismayed by how little of the literature on sustainability and environmental policy discusses the criteria that make a decision good.[3] Many environmental conflicts are driven, in part, by differing views about what constitutes a good decision and by a lack of discussion about those differences. In this chapter, I offer seven criteria or pillars for calling a decision "good."[4] The first three are about the outcomes that follow from a decision. The other four are about the decision-making process itself.[5]

You may find some of the criteria make sense to you and reject others or find some essential and others trivial. These are starting points for discussion, not strong conclusions. I favor a deliberative approach: Criteria for good decisions should emerge from a broad discussion. As the quote from George E. P. Box in the Introduction emphasizes, much of what I say may be wrong, but I hope it is useful.

In this discussion, it's important to again distinguish facts ("what is") from values ("what ought to be"). In Chapter 4, I focused on the logic of distinguishing facts and values and the influence both of the scientific method and of power in shaping our understanding of facts. Here, I will use the distinction in identifying decision criteria. Box 5.1 offers some history of the distinction.

---

### Box 5.1  Positive and normative

John Neville Keynes, the father of the famous economist John Maynard Keynes, proposed dividing economics into "positive" and "normative" approaches.[6] In his schema, statements about what we think is true are labeled positive statements and are the domain of science. Positive statements are beliefs about the world. For him, positive does not mean "affirmative." Rather, the term has its origins in positivist approaches to the philosophy of science – an approach that takes the observed world as real and knowable without much difficulty (see Box 4.1). Statements about what ought to happen are labeled normative and are the domain of ethics.[7] Keynes' argument is that we should not confuse normative and positive statements in making decisions.

Hume noted what is now called the naturalistic fallacy, that we can confuse "is" and "ought."[8] Some, often labeled conservatives, hold traditional values and argue that the past and/or the way things are now are the best ways to organize the world, explicitly equating "is" and "ought." For example, many in the United States feel the Constitution is the best guidance we have for policy decisions.[9] Some environmentalists argue that we should restore ecosystems to something resembling their historical state.[10] Those who value tradition usually do so because they feel that traditional social arrangements reflect great wisdom (e.g., confidence that the framers of the US Constitution got it right), a long period of social evolution or other reasons subtler than "that's the way it's always been." The implication is that policies can't do much to make the world better.[11]

---

We have to pay attention to the way things are as a starting point in making decisions. We want to design courses of action, including policies, programs and social arrangements, that will work – that will produce the results we hope for. This requires accurate assessment of the facts. The rational actor model (RAM) assumes that people make decisions by being self-interested and maximizing utility. But if people are sometimes altruistic or don't make choices carefully and rationally, as discussed in Chapter 3, then the policies that will work are different from those that might be justified if people were fully rational and only self-interested.[12]

Before moving on to the seven pillars I propose, I will review the three major normative theories that most often are deployed in conflicts about sustainability decision-making. They appear across my seven criteria. In Box 5.2, I briefly describe other important ethical theories that are worthy of careful consideration but are less frequently invoked in the policy debates I have seen.

## Box 5.2  Rights, virtues and capabilities

If you have explored the ethics literature, you might ask why I have not included rights or Kantian theory, virtue ethics and capabilities theory. My focus is on the theories that are deployed regularly in the sustainability conflicts I know about. Other theories may have a lot to contribute, and to some extent I will engage them in my seven suggested criteria. Briefly, the logic of each is as follows.[13]

Rights theory, usually associated with Kant, argues that an ethical decision is one that respects the rights of others.[14] Some versions emphasize a social contract in which we come to agreement about our obligations to respect each other; other versions make more abstract appeals, such as asking if a rule would be acceptable if applied to everyone. Sometimes only humans are seen as having rights but the ideas of rights theory can be extended to other species.

Virtue theory traces back to Aristotle, as do most other Western ethical traditions. Ethical decisions are those that are based on and implement virtues.[15] The virtues usually advocated include honesty, compassion and justice; they have remarkable resonance with the values of social psychological theory. Since these values are often anthropocentric, some theorists have argued to extend the set to include harmony with nature or the preservation of ecosystems, a move much like including biospheric altruism in social psychological value theory. That extends virtues to include our treatment of species and ecosystems. Thompson argues that virtue theory is often about creating a social context, a cultural selective regime in my terms (e.g., values and norms), that facilitates the practice of virtues, so, again, I see strong links to social psychological theory.[16]

Nussbaum has argued that ethical decisions are those that ensure that people have the means to fulfill their potential to realize their capabilities.[17] The approach emerged around criticisms that development policy had a too narrow focus on economic growth (see Chapter 2). It emphasizes looking at individuals in their context and has been easily extended to considerations of gender inequality, ableism and nonhumans and to dialogue with Indigenous perspectives. The UN Sustainable Development Goals reflect an articulation of conditions needed for humans to achieve their capabilities.

## 5.1  The Big Three Ethical Theories

Three ethical theories dominate contemporary discussions of policy analysis: utilitarianism, the deliberative approach and anarchism/libertarianism.[18] By policy analysis, I mean work that tries to clarify what the effects of a collective decision will be and often goes on to recommend a decision. Policy analysis can inform collective decisions by governments but also by any organization or by a community, as is the case for the community management of common resources discussed in Chapter 3. Each approach provides a strong goal that can be used to evaluate decisions but there are variations within each.[19] I think the "big three" ethical positions are valuable but not sufficient to inform us; we need other perspectives as well.[20]

Utilitarian policy analysis is built on the assumption that people make carefully calculated decisions based on clear personal preferences – the rational actor model of Chapter 3.[21] It is the most extensively developed way of assessing policies and underpins both benefit-cost analysis and risk analysis (see Box 5.4). It can be traced to Bentham and Mill in eighteenth- and nineteenth-century England, as modern capitalism was taking shape. For utilitarians, a good individual decision is one that increases the "utility" for the individual, and a good collective decision increases the overall utility for society when one sums across changes in individual utilities. The catchphrase is "the greatest good for the greatest number" (in the original, "it is the greatest happiness of the greatest number that is the measure of right and wrong").[22]

What constitutes utility and how should we measure it? For Bentham and Mill, utility was, roughly, happiness. This idea in Western philosophy – good decisions are those that increase happiness – stretches back at least to Epicurus, who was teaching in Athens, Mytilene and Lampsacus around 300 BCE. And it was undoubtedly present in many Indigenous philosophies as well. In applications of utilitarianism to policy analysis, happiness usually is equated with utility, and utility is usually conceptualized in monetary terms. But increasingly, we are looking at direct measures of happiness and life satisfaction as guides to how well a society is doing, with the hope that these measurements can inform policy (see Chapter 2).

Whose welfare is included in utilitarian analysis? Utilitarian policy analysis is anthropocentric and often focuses on the utility of the inhabitants of a nation. But the perspective can be broadened. Starting with Bentham, utilitarians have been leaders in advocating for animals, arguing that the welfare of nonhuman animals deserves consideration.[23]

Deliberative decision-making has its origins in the idea that democracy is a good way to make decisions (see the Introduction and Chapter 9). Unlike the utilitarian approach that examines the outcomes of our choices, deliberative theory focuses on the processes we use to make choices, calling for processes that are fair and competent (I will discuss what is meant by those terms under Criterion 5 in Section 5.6). Like utilitarianism, deliberative theory has generated a huge theoretical literature as well as a substantial literature on good practices. But, with a few exceptions, the literatures on utilitarianism and deliberative ethics do not inform each other.[24]

Libertarianism or anarchism is a third major approach in contemporary policy debates. In this tradition, the fundamental criterion for good decision-making is enhancing individual liberty. While libertarian thinking has influence in environmental policy debates, its theoretical underpinnings may be less familiar than the utilitarian or deliberative approach and deserve some attention.[25] Contemporary libertarianism seems to have its origins in anarchist thought, although this is not often acknowledged in popular libertarian discussions.[26] The term "libertarian" was closely associated, indeed interchangeable, with the term "anarchism" in many discussions outside and, until World War II, within the United States.[27] But "anarchist" has become a pejorative term in many contemporary discussions, invoking the idea of someone who wants chaos. Certainly, terrorist acts by anarchists in the late nineteenth and early twentieth centuries did little to enhance the image of anarchist theory.[28] Even today, a major strain of anarchist thinking calls for provocations to force authority into revealing its true nature, which anarchists see as repressive. But most anarchist theorists are not advocates of terror.[29]

A major difference between libertarians in the United States and the mainstream of anarchist thinking seems to be that those who self-label as libertarians are deeply concerned about the adverse effects of government power. So are anarchists. But anarchists are also concerned about power vested in any organization, public or private, while libertarians seem to be comfortable with the concentration of power in corporations.[30] Libertarianism and some forms of utilitarianism are linked by arguments that unfettered markets allow for human freedom, that such "free" markets will lead to maximization of human well-being and that governments are inevitably inept and inefficient even when well intentioned.[31]

This position is very nicely and briefly articulated by Edwards. His argument against federal programs and policies is grounded in assumptions about markets versus organizations: "The driving force behind market economies is that voluntary exchanges are mutually beneficial" and that "government does not have enough knowledge to make good decisions, and it lacks the flexibility to change directions when it makes mistakes."[32] Absent from the analysis are the unequal distributions of power in the market, the ability of market actors to shape state policy to their own interests and the fact that even if a hypothetical market of small actors behaved in the ways assumed, the market composed of huge corporations involves large bureaucracies subject to many of the same problems as large government agencies. For all of the political discussion of government inefficiency in the libertarian literature, there is relatively little systematic overview of the many studies examining just how well government does in providing services when compared to the private sector.[33]

While utilitarianism focuses on outcomes – a good decision enhances utility – and deliberative approaches focus on processes – good decisions come from good processes – libertarianism is largely about what decisions *shouldn't* do – they shouldn't interfere with individual freedoms. Libertarianism is worth highlighting as a separate approach from utilitarianism because not all libertarians are utilitarians and not all utilitarians are libertarians. One might hold to a libertarian view even if one doesn't believe in the assumptions about human decision-making that imply free choice leads to utility maximization for society. Freedom of choice might be valued in itself without regard to the societal consequences.

Each of these theories focuses on one criterion. Utilitarians label as good those outcomes that provide greatest satisfaction to the greatest number of people. Deliberative theorists argue that good decisions (or at least the best we can do) are those that emerge from processes of decision-making that are participatory, competent in handling facts and values and fair in processes and outcomes. Libertarians argue that freedom of choice is paramount and best served by strong and clear property rights.[34]

These three ideas about how to make decisions may be useful as guidance but they do not strike me as sufficient. As noted, I have seen remarkably little discussion of the full range of criteria that might be considered in evaluating the quality of decisions we make about sustainability.[35] Thus my suggestion of seven criteria include but go beyond these three ethical theories.

## 5.2    Criterion 1: Enhance Well-Being

Decisions about sustainability are intended to improve human well-being and the well-being of the biophysical environment and other species.[36] To use sustainability as a criteria, we first have to decide how to define well-being. A common approach in policy analysis is to use a utilitarian logic and assume that changes in income are measures of changes in well-being (see Box 5.4).

But emphasizing well-being does not require a utilitarian analysis and certainly need not assume that market prices are a good indicator of societal values, an assumption built into many utilitarian policy analyses (see Chapter 9). In particular, as noted in Chapter 2, there is growing interest in measuring human well-being directly rather than using prices, income or other economic measures as an indicator of well-being. (Recall that the founders of utilitarianism talked about "happiness.")

Even if there is agreement about how to define well-being, there can be sharp conflicts about the importance to assign to humans versus other species and across different species of nonhumans and to the importance of individuals versus species versus ecosystems.[37] The controversy about Winky and Wanda was about human versus elephant well-being. In parts of the US west, wild horses and burros reach populations that strain local ecosystems.[38] Some people view them as invasive species destroying ecosystems and thus harming the well-being of other species. Others see them as noble animals whose own well-being is crucial, and still others as competitors with human cattle productions in a region where grazing land and water are scarce, focusing on human well-being, or at least the well-being of ranchers.

To simplify a bit, for some, only human well-being matters. The well-being of the environment must be considered only to the extent that it influences human well-being. This position is commonly labeled anthropocentrism.[39] Ecocentrists feel that importance should be assigned to certain states or conditions of the biophysical environment independent of the contribution of those states or conditions to human well-being.[40] For the anthropocentrist, the concept of environmental well-being does not have intrinsic ethical weight, while for the ecocentrist it does.[41] For those who partake of both value systems, both matter. Many Indigenous people hold that there is a seamless connection between humans and other species and ecosystems so that even the idea of these distinctions seems problematic.[42]

Understanding the implications of alternative courses of action for human well-being is daunting. Assessing the well-being of other species or of ecosystems as a whole is at least as daunting. Making trade-offs between these two forms of well-being is even more complex. These challenges apply when we try to make individual decisions. The problems multiply for group decisions by a household, community, nation or collection of nations. We seldom know with any great degree of certainty what will happen as a result of our actions. And even if we had complete and certain knowledge, the difficult weighing of alternatives and trade-offs would apply.[43]

A substantial amount of the literature in ethics and policy analysis wrestles with these complicated problems of what we should value and, given some set of values, how we can assess impacts on the things we care about, manage the trade-offs and take proper account of uncertainty. This literature and the tools and concepts within it can go a long way towards clarifying the issues and showing the difficulties. Trade-offs across different impacts remain an issue for almost every decision we make. For a utilitarian, the trade-offs can be handled by estimating how the utility of humans and perhaps other species will change as a result of different decisions.

In a hypothetical technocratic world, we might imagine an app that moves through all the above considerations and points towards a decision.[44] In practice, few of us would be comfortable with relegating an important decision to such a rigid and hidden process.[45] As Box 5.3 points out, we are already facing this problem with the emergence of self-driving cars and other applications of artificial intelligence (AI).

---

## Box 5.3  Artificial intelligence and technocratic decision-making

In the Introduction, I suggested that thinking about environmental and sustainability decisions may be a useful testbed for thinking about other challenges, especially those posed by emerging technologies. It is clear that "deep thinking" by multilayered neural networks and genetic algorithms has already reached impressive decision-making power. Playing a game of chess or an even more complex game of go or poker is really just a sequence of decisions in response to the decisions made by one's opponent, with clear objective and rules. The ability of software to defeat even the most sophisticated human decision makers in chess, go and poker demonstrates the impressive decision-making power of AI.

These games have a single objective. When multiple criteria must be included in a decision, ethical issues emerge. Self-driving vehicles will sometimes have to decide whether to put passengers at risk to avoid harming pedestrians or to favor the passengers over the pedestrians. In surveys, most people agree that, in general, AIs for self-driving cars should use a utilitarian calculus, taking the action that saves the most lives overall. But they would prefer to purchase a self-driving car that would give preference to saving the passengers, presumably including themselves. (As one might expect, there is a great deal of complexity and variation in people's preferences.)[46] So, even the relatively simple case of a self-driving car is ethically complex, involving the distinction between self-interest and altruism discussed in Chapter 3.

There have also been efforts to use AI to make decisions "objective." For example, it has been suggested that AI could be used to predict the probability of criminal recidivism and thus offer advice about sentencing, parole and other decisions in the justice system. But critical analysis of this approach has revealed some very troubling issues. AI applications do not try to develop a causal model of what factors are influencing a variable; they focus on correlation. Distinguishing between causation and correlation is a fundamental issue in statistics applied to the social sciences, and much work in statistical analysis tries to find better ways of assessing the plausibility of causal assertions. AI applied to marketing can be very successful with simply predicting based on correlation. If an AI knows you liked some movies, that can be useful in predicting what other movies you might like even if there is no understanding about what factors cause your preferences. However, when applied to the criminal justice system in a society with a long history of racism and other biases, the AI algorithms easily pick up on the results of racism and thus propose harsher treatment of minorities. Essentially, society's prejudices become embedded in the AI because it has ignored causal factors. We are learning that any application of AI for consequential decisions needs to be transparent in the sense that we know why the AI is making recommendations and that those recommendations should be based on causal models rather than simply correlations. Perhaps with clarity about how the algorithm works, biases could be identified and removed.[47]

It will also be useful to develop applications that are attentive to context and developing applications in collaboration with those who will be impacted by the decisions made.

The problem of societal prejudices embedded in AI is perhaps most blatant in criminal justice but can also occur in education, financial decisions, medicine and many other areas. And that is only one of many problems associated with the emergence of AI and robotics. There are growing concerns about the ways AI might facilitate control by authoritarian regimes and can be disruptive to democracy.[48] There also are arguments that AI could be good for sustainability. And there are some arguments that AI could handle the problem of allocating goods and services in an economy. One strong defense of markets and capitalism versus government control of the economy is this problem of allocation of resources, which was often badly, even tragically, mishandled in the Soviet Union. But now AI coupled with ubiquitous sensors (the web of things) may offer a method of controlling resource allocation that avoids those problems. In general, AI opens up a wide variety of serious ethical and political issues and is generating a rapidly growing literature. Those studying decision-making in AI and in sustainability could learn a lot from each other.

## 5.3    Criterion 2: Efficiency

A fascinating contradiction can be found in much environmental and economic thinking.[49] Environmentalists often emphasize scarcity. Given the anticipated increase in human populations and their consumption, such concerns about scarcity are warranted. But environmentalists tend to be skeptical of economics, which is the science of scarcity. Economists partake of a parallel contradiction. While ideas of scarcity drive their discipline, when it comes to thinking about environmental problems, economists are often skeptical about scarcity, arguing that price increases will drive human ingenuity to find substitutes for whatever is scarce.[50]

The problem of scarcity is real. Before the pandemic, about 9 percent of the world's population (~680 million people) subsisted on the equivalent of $1.90 per day or less, and the best estimates indicate that the pandemic has increased this to 10 percent, pushing another 75 million into poverty.[51] So, if for no other reason, given the needs of the poor we should use resources as efficiently as possible. There are a multitude of good things that could be done with the resources we will deploy in any decision, so it is reasonable to find the allocation of resources that does the most good. In utilitarian terms, we want to make decisions that maximize utility.[52] The utilitarian tradition offers a sophisticated repertoire of tools for policy analysis, such as benefit-cost analysis (see Box 5.4), that are based on efficiency as a primary goal, so we are well supplied with efficiency analysis.

Analyzing efficiency can be of immense use in making environmental decisions. However, efficiency analysis implemented via benefit-cost analysis uses market prices or surrogates for them as measures of social value. We should think carefully about the limits of markets and prices in guiding such analyses and about the technical issues that must be resolved with judgment calls or value judgments. We must also take account of the fact that efficiency is only one criterion for making decisions. Since efficiency can often be quantified by benefit-cost and risk analysis and other criteria cannot, we should be careful not to let what we can quantify dominate what we cannot. We should not let "bad numbers drive out good paragraphs" or even let good numbers displace what can only be expressed qualitatively.[53]

Within conservation biology, recognition that resources to protect endangered species and threatened habitats are limited has led to some use of cost-effectiveness analysis, an effort to save "the most butterflies for the buck." It is simpler than benefit-cost analysis in that it is not necessary to put all costs and benefits into a common metric such as market prices. Rather, the analysis assumes a limited budget – for example, for buying land or for implementing programs to protect endangered species – and that there are more possible uses for those funds than the budget will cover. Thus, given the budget and a goal (preserving biodiversity, protecting endangered species), what allocation of the budget across actions gives the best return? Triage is a simple version of this logic: It is simply too expensive to save some species in some habitats and that those species should be "let go" to use resources for species and habitats with better prospects.[54] A subtler approach is to use tools developed in the decision sciences to find out how to optimally allocate resources across decisions to achieve a goal. For example, if conservation of biodiversity is a goal of a land acquisition program, and both the amount of biodiversity on parcels of land and the costs of protecting that biodiversity can be estimated, it is possible to find the sequences of land purchases that will lead to maximum protection within the budget constraint.

Using the idea of efficiency in a different way, we can ask how well nations, US states or other geopolitical units do in providing well-being for their human populations relative to the harm they do to the environment. Figure 2.4 shows the variation across nations in life expectancy, one measure of well-being, and greenhouse gas emissions, one measure of stress on the environment. Clearly, some nations do a very good job of producing well-being without much environmental damage.[55] Many studies have inverted the efficiency ratio into a measure of the "Ecological Intensity of Well-Being" –how much harm is done to produce well-being – and examined how economic growth, inequality, institutions, policies and other factors influence the ability to minimize environmental damage while increasing human well-being.[56] The body of work is mostly quantitative, but one can imagine a fruitful series of case studies making sense of why some nations are very good at producing well-being relative to the amount of environmental damage they do while others perform poorly on this criterion.

## Box 5.4  Benefit-cost analysis

Benefit-cost analysis is one of the most influential methods used to analyze policies. It is mandated as part of decision-making by many governments and international organizations such as the Word Bank and has been central to debates about sustainability issues such as climate change.[57] The ethical argument underpinning benefit-cost analysis is that we ought to make decisions under a utilitarian ethics that provides the greatest good for the greatest number (benefit-cost analysis).[58] In practice, benefit-cost analysis is used to compare a number of alternatives, including "keep things as they are," to determine the ratio of the benefits to the costs. The option that provides the highest benefit-to-cost ratio is preferable on grounds of efficiency.

Benefit-cost analysis was originally introduced to reduce waste from "pork barrel" projects that use public funds in ways that benefit only cronies and supporters of those with the power to authorize the projects. If a benefit-cost analysis indicates public benefits did not exceed public costs, the project should not go forward.[59] Benefit-cost analysis is now required as part of the criteria for making many government decisions in the United States. The logic is that the government should use public funds as efficiently as possible. A short summary will show how the logic of the rational actor model and utility maximization forms the basis of an approach to making collective decisions.

The steps in a benefit-cost analysis look like those in the individual decision process under the rational actor model I outlined in Chapter 3:

(1) List all the alternatives.
(2) For each alternative, list all the possible outcomes, including estimates of the point in the future at which those outcomes would occur – classifying each as a social benefit or a social cost.
(3) For each outcome at each point in time, estimate the value to society of its occurrence.[60]
(4) Estimate the probability of each outcome occurring (see Chapters 2 and 3 on risk analysis).
(5) Assign a weight to each utility so that utilities occurring further in the future count less than those that occur closer to the present (the discount rate).
(6) Multiply the utility of each outcome for each event by the discount rate at the time of occurrence and the probability of occurrence.
(7) Add up all these resulting expected discounted values of benefits and of costs for each choice.
(8) Calculate the ratio of benefit to costs.
(9) Pick the choice that yields the greatest benefit-cost ratio.

This is the basic logic. In practice, benefit-cost analysis is much more complicated and sophisticated.

Benefit-cost analysis applied to environmental problems and sustainability remains controversial for at least four reasons. First, it can be difficult to estimate the value (social value in the language of benefit-cost analysis) of many things we feel are important but that do not have prices that emerge from competitive markets – for example, the value of disease prevention or seeing a bald eagle in the wild. Second, benefit-cost analyses nearly always deploy discounting, and discounting itself is controversial.[61] Third, most applications of benefit-cost analysis do not take account of who gets the benefits and who bears the costs. In principle, a benefit-cost analysis could give greater weight to benefits to low-income or other groups but there is no consensus on how to develop such weights.[62] As a result, equity is usually ignored. Fourth, there remains a debate about whether "existence" values belong in a benefit-cost analysis. Existence values are part of what the Millennium Ecosystem Assessment classifies as cultural services.[63] They account for the fact that I may value the existence of species I have never encountered and places I have never been and probably will never visit. Quantifying such values is challenging and some argue they should not be included in a benefit-cost analysis even if sound estimates for them could be developed.

## 5.4    Criterion 3: Enhance Freedom

Good decisions should enhance individual freedom. This is the essence of the anarchist tradition and its libertarian offshoot. However, simply minimizing the role of government is not adequate to do that. We have to find mechanisms that prevent our lives devolving into a war of all against all, as Hobbes put it.[64] Fukuyama argued that finding successful mechanisms of governance has been one of the major challenges in human history, while Graeber and Wengrow illustrate the many societies that managed to provide good levels of human well-being and substantial personal freedom.[65] The issue of commons discussed in Chapter 3 raises important questions for overly simplistic libertarianism. Most of our actions, thus most of our decisions, have substantial consequences for others. If I put a factory emitting noxious fumes on my property, I have in some substantial way impinged on the freedom of my neighbors – they may need to stay indoors when the factory is running, suffer health problems, spend funds to paint their house more frequently, lose property value and more. For many commons, such as the atmosphere, the oceans or even just a fishery or a forest that is not owned privately, my narrow pursuit of self-interest in the way predicted by the rational actor model can lead to disaster if everyone else does the same. The COVID-19 pandemic is a poignant example – the exercise of individual freedom to not wear masks and not be vaccinated facilitates the spread of the virus, creating risks to those other than the person choosing to exert those freedoms.

The libertarian version of environmental ethics differs from its anarchist roots in that it often suggests that environmental problems, usually labeled externalities because they are outside of what is being captured in market prices, might best be handled by negotiations or law suits.[66] If your actions have an adverse effect on me, then I can sue you. Hypothetically, this might seem a reasonable way to deal with externalities. But in practical decision-making in contemporary societies, an inequitable distribution of power does not make legal action an easy remedy. Those with the most power not only command the greatest legal resources. They also have the greatest influence on what laws, regulations and standards are written and even, via support for elected officials, on which judges get appointed or elected.[67] Simply minimizing the role of government without taking into account other effects is not sufficient for good decision-making. But we can develop effective policies and programs that minimize the burden they place on us. I believe that is the reasonable point to extract from libertarian thinking – maximize freedom while acknowledging there are many problems that require collective rather than purely individual action.[68] A good decision should avoid putting in place rigid and cumbersome procedures and processes. The major implication of this reasoning for day-to-day decision-making is to think through the implications of a decision in terms of how it will affect personal freedom and always ask: "Is there a way of achieving this goal that enhances personal freedom or at least minimizes any adverse effects on it?" "Can we make this an easy policy to follow?" In Chapter 8, I review the idea of design principles that can make programs or policies both effective and minimally intrusive.

In the United States, the libertarian view carries with it not just an emphasis on individual freedom but also a deep skepticism of government. The sense is that government rather than any private concentration of power is the biggest threat to individual liberty. As I noted, the anarchist tradition differs in being skeptical of all large organizations. In identifying enhanced freedom as one of seven xcriteria, I am not arguing that government is inept or dangerous, merely that freedom should be given some consideration. Indeed, as Box 5.5 argues, the stereotypes of inefficient government may be more the result of biased reasoning of the sort described in Chapter 3 than of strong evidence.

---

### Box 5.5  Trust and red tape

In the United States, we have a contradictory assessment of government. On the one hand, we regularly complain about the rigidity of government rules and the slow, cumbersome and expensive way in which governments act. On the other hand, we don't trust government. I have worked directly for state government, have many friends and students who worked for the federal government, have received via my universities government grants and have served on many committees offering advice to federal agencies. And for nearly all of my university education and career (more than 90 percent of that time) I have been at public (state) universities, which are either agencies of the state government or separate bureaucracies. I believe government agencies are generally well managed, but they can have what seem to be odd and arbitrary rules. This so-called red tape usually arises because we don't trust government and want a detailed record of what has been done by government officials.[69] We have these procedures because we don't have sufficient trust. If you would like to see a more efficient government, trust the government bureaucrats to do what is right. And if you don't trust them, it's not logical to complain about the cumbersome mechanisms that allow verification that they are doing the right thing. The one major study I have found comparing government and private sector provision of services found no systematic difference between the two in efficiency or quality.[70]

---

Finally, while I think freedom should certainly be considered in decision-making, most of the theoretical literature in libertarianism tends to ignore all power differentials except that between the individual and government. Inequality is one of the great problems we have faced across human history. Inequality between nations is still immense, inequality within many nations is growing and there can be substantial and destructive inequality even within a household.[71] When thinking about freedom as a criterion and about how to make policies easy to follow, the question of "For whom?" must always be asked. And one of the best ways to design policies so they take account of diverse groups within a society is to engage with those groups in the design and implementation of the policy.[72]

## 5.5    Criterion 4: Competence about Facts and Values

Environmental decisions usually involve a great deal of uncertainty about facts, as detailed in Chapter 3. A good decision should take account of the scientific information available and also attend to the uncertainty in that science. We never know for certain the facts that describe the physical, biological and social processes that determine the outcomes of a course of action. We don't know with certainty what will happen in the future. However, decision processes that take explicit account of uncertain science are rather new and can roughly be traced to the rise of risk analysis in environmental and technological decision-making in the early 1980s (see Chapter 2).[73] Before the use of risk analysis, we have a long history of solving engineering problems in which the science was reasonably certain and a long history of solving economic and other problems involving much uncertainty.[74]

In Chapter 4, I argued that using uncertain science competently in making decisions requires special care. Moving from areas of science with high ostensibility and repeatability and low sensitivity to context (e.g., much of physics) to areas where things are very context-dependent, where results can be hard to "see" and where there are seldom replications within a specific context (e.g., much of the ecological and social sciences), is a great challenge. As I will argue in Chapter 9, while formal risk and benefit-cost analysis are useful, the high degree of uncertainty for many sustainability decisions requires participation from diverse perspectives, including those holding Indigenous and local knowledge.

But beyond scientific (factual) competence, good decisions must also be competent about values. People differ in their values. In addition, when faced with novel problems, we may be uncertain as to how our values apply. In contrast to the substantial effort to refine our ability to deal with scientific or factual uncertainty, relatively little effort has been spent on dealing with value uncertainty.

Value uncertainty arises in two ways. One is because there is no single best way of aggregating from individual values to societal values. In a classic analysis, Arrow considered the very common situation where people have preferences that can be expressed only as rank orderings ("I like policy A better than B but my first choice is C") rather than as "solid" numbers ("I assign a score of 7 to A, 5 to B and 9 to C") that can be compared across persons (your score of 7 reflects the same thing as my score of 7). With only rank orderings, the outcome of any vote depends in part on how votes are taken. For example, we might ask people to rank choices and if no choice gets a majority have a runoff among the two top choices from the first round. Or we might simply take the choice with the most votes in round 1. Suppose the votes come out A = 40 percent, B = 35 percent, C = 25 percent. If we take the one-round approach, A wins. But suppose B is the second choice for most folks who voted for C, say 20 percent of the voters. Then a second round "runoff" vote would have A = 45 percent and B = 55 percent. Arrow showed mathematically that with rank orderings, outcomes are influenced by the rules of the voting system, so that some voting systems can produce different results than other voting systems even if the mix of preferences is the same.[75]

While the problem of moving from individual to collective values has been given much attention, less thought has been devoted to the second form of value uncertainty – uncertainty at the individual level.[76] This problem arises because environmental and sustainability problems are novel and their value implications are unclear when we first become aware of them.[77] When new sustainability problems emerge onto the public agenda, the discussion often draws attention to aspects of human interactions with biophysical systems that are not familiar to most citizens and that are far removed from their everyday life. For example, most people have to think through the wisdom of direct manipulation of the genome to come to a position on the use of genetically modified plants in agriculture. Genetically modified organisms (GMOs) engage more familiar issues as well: safety of food, effects on nonagricultural species, impacts on the political economy of agriculture, and so on. Myriad other emerging problems are equally hard to map into existing values: geoengineering to mitigate climate change, use of autonomous robots in combat, the creation of artificial life, development of artificial intelligence with broad capabilities that exceed those of humans, and many others. The example of ethical choices for autonomous vehicles offered in Box 5.3 may seem a very traditional problem of the good of the many versus the good of the few, or the good of unknown others versus my own interests. But posing it in the form of autonomous vehicles undoubtedly adds complexity as we think it through.

Climate change provides an instructive example. For most people, climate change probably first comes up unexpectedly and in a context that does not encourage careful thinking.[78] It might be mentioned by a coworker or neighbor in passing or be a topic on a television or radio broadcast offering a minute or two of coverage. It might be the subject of a question in a public opinion survey.[79] Often it will be a social media posting on a topic you haven't thought about before. That is, our initial encounter with a new issue like climate change may be in a context that calls for an affective, fast, System I response rather than thinking through the issues and talking about them with others in an open-minded way.[80] Then the heuristics and biases mechanisms described in Chapter 3 come into play. Once an initial reaction is formed quickly and without much reflection, biased assimilation may make it persist and reenforce it.[81] The initial reaction provides the starting point for future thinking and a filter for the credibility of further information. New information that is consistent with the initial view is more likely to be accepted than information discordant with that view. In such circumstances, views of climate change may not reflect a thoughtful assessment of values nor the current state of scientific understanding.

Value uncertainty is often enhanced by the strategic efforts of interested parties to frame the problems with polarizing and very intense images, as discussed in Chapter 4. Such campaigns encourage people to settle on positions prematurely, without having talked through the full implications of them. Campaigns to block action on climate change follow this model to the extent that McCright and Dunlap have labeled the strategy "anti-reflexivity" – they discourage careful reflection on facts and values.[82]

Such premature closure precludes serious value learning. Yet such value learning is essential in dealing with environmental and other emerging problems grounded in science. We need to develop methods of making decisions that are competent regarding both uncertain science and uncertain values. In the last few decades, we have gotten better at estimating and expressing uncertainty about facts and incorporating that uncertainty into decision processes. We need parallel developments for value uncertainty.

## 5.6   Criterion 5: Fairness in Process and Outcome

Fairness in process means that all those having an interest in or affected by a decision have a say in that decision. It further suggests that each person should have equal say, or perhaps a standing with weight proportional to what they stand to gain or lose. This is an ancient democratic principle that is very widely accepted in the contemporary world and has been extensively theorized.[83] It is the core idea of the deliberative tradition.[83] The special question of fairness towards nonhuman species is raised in Box 5.6. Deliberative processes have been at the core of the decision-making process of many Indigenous communities, traditions that can inform and shape the practices we need to evolve to meet our current challenges.[84] I will discuss deliberation in more detail in Chapter 9. Here, I simply raise it as part of the criteria for a good decision.

In the United States, many state and federal agencies have long been required to use "public participation" as part of their decision-making process. Such participation can often be a sham.[85] The phrase "decide, announce, defend" summarizes a cynical view of how many government agencies are perceived to handle public participation. A substantial literature has moved from these theoretical arguments to describe practices that attempt to engage interested and affected parties ("the public" in Dewey's sense), drawing on the deliberative approaches noted in the Introduction.

A comprehensive review of that literature by the US National Research Council, *Public Participation in Environmental Assessment and Decision Making*, concluded that a deliberative process, when done well, can improve decision-making.[86] The review does not claim that such processes are always fair or competent. Rather, our claim in the report is that the scientific understanding is there to support a fair and competent process if the political will exists to do so. When the intent is to make processes fair and competent, there is knowledge that can help in designing processes that work well in achieving those goals.

However, it is not clear how fairness can be implemented in controversies where decisions involve large numbers of people, some highly mobilized and articulate, some not even aware of the controversy. We do know a good bit about how to conduct a process that is competent about facts even at the global level.[87] The many assessments of global environmental processes, such as the Millennium Ecosystem Assessment and those conducted by the Intergovernmental Panel on Climate Change, while not without flaws, do a reasonable job of assessing the state of the science on these issues, see Criterion 6.[88] But fairness in large-scale deliberation remains a major challenge.

Fairness means more than simply a chance to speak or vote. It means a chance to have your views taken seriously, to be given a respectful hearing, to speak without having your voice overwhelmed by the bombast or prestige of others. That is not to say that all views should be given equal weight in decisions but rather that the weight given a position should be proportional to its logic and sincerity, not to catchphrases tested with focus groups. Some arguments are more persuasive than others, but all arguments should have an equal chance to persuade. This is procedural fairness. *Public Participation in Environmental Assessment and Decision Making* demonstrates that we know how to achieve procedural fairness when we can have repeated face-to-face interactions of the interested and affected parties. Achieving procedural fairness for global issues remains a major challenge of governance in the twenty-first century. I will return to this issue in Chapter 9.

Yet procedural fairness, while necessary, is not sufficient. We must also consider fairness in outcomes. In democracies, we usually rely on procedural fairness to assure fairness in outcomes. Most democracies have developed a sense that rules about some things should be hard to change while rules about other things can be easy to change. At any given moment, this seems appropriate. But from an historical perspective, the difficulty in changing some rules can perpetuate situations we later understand to be horrendous. Before the Civil War, slavery was legitimated in the US Constitution.[89] The difficulty of amending the Constitution and procedural rules in

Congress made it difficult to redress this horrible injustice because the "rights" of the minority of Southern slaveholders were protected against those who wanted abolition, but at unconscionable cost to another minority, those in bondage, who had no direct voice in the halls of Congress. One might make the opposite case regarding the persecution of communists, the disabled, gays, Jews, Romani, socialists, unionists and other groups by fascists in the 1930s and 1940s.[90] Rapid rule change devastated their rights. Substantive fairness requires great care in deciding what constitutes procedural fairness – history is filled with horrific unfairness to some in the name of narrow views of procedural fairness.

Issues of environmental justice and fairness are central to sustainability, and climate justice is a growing priority.[91] The benefits, costs and risks of both environmental problems and the measures we use to address them are never evenly distributed. They will usually reflect the distribution of power in society. The powerful will buffer themselves from risks and often find ways to benefit from policies to reduce risk. Indeed, the existence of those environmental risks often reflect decisions that profit some while visiting risks on others. The first empirical analyses of environmental justice properly focused on problems of exposure to pollution in general and to toxic wastes in particular.[92] We now understand that it permeates every type of environmental issue and environmental policy, and we find inequities at every level of analysis, from the local to the global. The call for deliberative approaches is an effort to ensure that we are attentive to justice in our decisions.

---

### Box 5.6  Who will speak for wolf?

Only humans can have "voices" in most mechanisms we deploy for making decisions. If the decision is one that involves talk or voting, the best we can do for other species is to let someone speak for them. In economic analysis, our methods of valuation rely on using human actions, either in the market or in surveys, to assign value to nonhuman species and ecosystems. And even in the legal system of the United States, despite some arguments that we should do otherwise, only human citizens have "standing" – the right to take a dispute to court.[93] A different approach has emerged in New Zealand and Argentina where some legal rights have been granted to our closest genetic kin, the great apes. There has not been comparable progress in the United States, although several court cases attempt to establish rights for chimpanzees.[94] Nonhuman species who may be affected by a decision are excluded from having a direct say either because legal theory is inherently anthropocentric or because even those who give ethical standing to nonhumans aren't sure how to incorporate those voices into deliberations. Hadley has argued that part of the problem can be solved by granting animals some property rights over their habitats.[95] Some courts are experimenting with appointing advocates for animals in abuse cases. My colleague David Favre has argued for respectful use of other species. It is increasingly clear that taking account of the diversity and flexibility in animal decision-making is crucial to building effective policy and programs. Having someone speak for nonhumans harkens back to Iroquoian tradition of having someone "speak for wolf" in making decisions. The argument was anticipated by Carl Barks in *Uncle Scrooge* Issue 18 in 1957. In the story, a Native American leader argues that decisions about the land must be made by "the chiefs of all the brothers [the other species] in a powwow with the seasons."

## 5.7    Criterion 6: Relying on Human Strengths, Not Weaknesses

A good decision process should rely on what humans do well, not presume we can do things we usually can't. We are not very good at doing complex algebra in our head, nor at sitting alone and sorting out the reality that lies behind sound bites and advertising images. As Chapter 3 documents, the shortcuts and biases we deploy lead us to deviate from the calculations of the rational actor model. Over our evolutionary history, these shortcuts may have served us very well when decisions needed to be made quickly, when the consequences of an error were not disastrous and particularly in pre-industrial environments where most of our interactions were with other humans, with other animal species and with ecosystems in which our social group had lived for generations. But they may serve us poorly in dealing with the contemporary world. Now, we often interact with strangers or at least with individuals with whom we have little personal history and limited social network connections and are surrounded by complex technologies that often behave in ways very different from other animals or ecosystems. The kinds of uncertainty, complex trade-offs and potentially catastrophic outcomes that character- ize many sustainability decisions in the twenty-first century are in many ways different in character from those typical of most of human history.

Our strengths lie elsewhere than in formal calculations. Human intelligence is a social or linguistic intelligence, just what we would expect in a species whose primary mode of adaptation is via cultural evolution.[96] We are good at pattern recognition, language processing and learning from each other in discussion. Obviously, there are limits to these skills and many foibles associated with them. This may be why we are so easily taken in by sound bites and campaign rhetoric. We usually listen to what is said with some respect. Our default position for evaluating what is offered in conversation may come from millennia in societies where public deliberation was a key part of decision-making. There, all can speak and be heard and an extreme view will likely be refuted by others. Advertising, tweets and much of what passes for political discussion in the early twenty-first century don't incorporate a broad range of perspec- tives and don't allow extended and thoughtful responses. The views presented are monolithic, polarized and more often intended to entrain the feelings of the listener than provide meaning- ful discourse. The tendency to listen with respect that has been useful for most of human history betrays us when manipulated in this way.[97]

We need processes of decision-making that take account of our strengths and weaknesses. The decision sciences, formal logic and critical thinking help us compensate for these weaknesses.[98] Some of these tools deploy quantitative methods to carry out a version of the rational actor model calculus, including risk, benefit-cost and cost-effectiveness analyses described earlier. Other tools are aids for clarifying our values when they are uncertain and for delineating the nature of value conflicts, and some are designed to facilitate the sorts of group deliberation called for in this chapter and Chapter 9.

In the last few decades, we have developed national and international "assessment" processes to summarize the available scientific information on complex problems such as ozone depletion, climate change and loss of biodiversity.[99] Prominent examples include the reports of the Intergovernmental Panel on Climate Change (www.ipcc.ch), the Intergovernmental Science-

Policy Platform on Biodiversity and Ecosystem Services (www.ipbes.net) and the US National Climate Assessment (www.globalchange.gov/nca5). In these processes, a diverse group of scientists attempt to synthesize what is known in a way that will be useful to decision-making. Often these assessments are coproduced with interested and affected parties using a process that links scientific analysis with public deliberation.[100] In many cases, they use scenarios about the social, economic, political and technological future to help think through the complex interactions that should be considered in making policy decisions. These processes often are quite good at getting the science right. When done well, local and regional processes that link scientific analysis to public deliberation also seem to do a good job of overcoming our cognitive weaknesses around handling facts. We are only beginning to develop approaches to factual competence to public deliberation at the national or global level.[101]

## 5.8    Criterion 7: A Chance to Learn

All good decision processes are social processes. They are social in the sense that they involve many people speaking with many voices. They are also social in that they continue over time. We will never be certain that any particular decision is correct. But we can hope that we will learn from successes and failures and that over time the process of making decisions will improve. Thus a good decision process must involve both social and individual learning.[102]

Social learning is cultural evolution – we learn from experience and by sharing what we learned. A long tradition assumes that we don't know how social programs work and that we must design evaluations into program implementation to make both corrective and summative judgments. But we seldom take this approach for environmental programs, let alone efforts to move towards sustainability. Programmatic efforts to evaluate energy conservation programs started in the 1970s and 1980s.[103] Similar work examines biodiversity protection and sustainability programs. More needs to be done.

Esty posed a question that is still relevant: "Why hasn't anyone done careful environmental measurement before? Businessmen always say, 'what matters gets measured.' Social scientists started quantitative measurement 30 years ago and even political science turned to hard numbers 15 years ago. Yet look at environmental policy and the data are lousy."[104] I suspect that the reason we have been slow to do better analyses of environmental problems is a disciplinary disjuncture. We don't assume that social programs will work because we realize how complex the social world can be. Further, the social sciences have a half a century of trying to understand how to extract information about causation from nonexperimental data on complex systems so we are properly cautious about how to draw conclusions from less than perfect data but still make effective use of the information that is there.[105] In contrast, environmental programs are often grounded in the culture of the physical sciences, where it is possible to have high levels of ostensibility and repeatability around most key issues (see Chapter 4). This leads to great confidence in theory and a concomitant inexperience with causal analysis of messy nonexperimental data. However, environmental policies always involve some aspects of human behavior and the physical and biological systems involved are complex, so the assessment of effects is not simple. Progress will be made as we adapt the methods of the social sciences to the evaluation of environmental policies.

Good decisions will require opportunities for both factual and value learning. In Chapter 4, I argued that science is useful and due respect because it is based on an "evolutionary epistemology" – science is a process that is structured so that we learn from our mistakes. A good decision is one that is scientific in the sense that it allows learning from error. Dewey argued that such learning could engage the public:

But opinion in the sense of beliefs formed and held in the absence of evidence will be reduced in quantity and importance. No longer will views generated in view of special situations be frozen into standards and masquerade as eternal truths.[106]

Current political debates would seem to belie Dewey's hope. The evolution of public views on many issues, such as climate change or the COVID-19 pandemic, is strongly influenced by campaigns promoting views that are out of accord with scientific consensus. The efforts of powerful interests, deploying tools that play to our use of heuristics and biases, especially our tendencies towards BAHP, are overwhelming any tendency towards social learning based on careful scientific analysis and reasoned debate (see Chapters 3 and 4; I will discuss deliberation in the face of polarization in Chapter 9). Here, I am not arguing that the kinds of trends Dewey described are inevitable but rather that in making decisions we should pay attention to how we might learn from the decision.

We hope that provision of information about how policies are working can change public views about not just policy but how the world works.[107] Learning can and must take place around values as well. In Chapter 3, I noted that values come from early socialization but are modified by life experience. A good decision process is one that is value-competent in the sense described in Section 5.5. But a good decision also encourages reflection on values. The decision process should articulate conflicting value positions so these positions can be understood and respected even in the face of disagreement. Most important, the decision process should encourage people to reflect on their own values and thoughtfully modify them and their application as new views and new problems arise. Value learning is as important as factual learning.

Yet while a clear consensus exists that we need to learn as we go, we will have to learn how to do that learning. As Henry put it: "The process of learning is often treated as a black box, and the design of strategies to promote learning are thus based primarily on anecdotal evidence rather than lessons from theoretically-grounded and empirically-based models."[108] As an initial step towards building such a theory, he first emphasizes that there are diverse perspectives on who the "learner" is: individuals, coalitions, policy systems, organizations, societies, the global community. I concur with his argument that if we start with individuals, always being attentive to the context in which they act and learn, we can build to more aggregate levels, but if we start with aggregate levels we may not find our way back to the individual. Henry then defines learning as a "change in … cognitions/behaviors as a result of new information or experience on the part of a focal agent." This includes changes in values and changes in beliefs and even changes in habits that are not subject to reflection. And under this definition, learning may not be towards greater factual accuracy or towards a value consensus – learning may move individuals away from what many sustainability advocates would consider desirable. Given the kinds of conflicts and dynamics that have arisen around issues such as climate change, these dynamics must be given attention in our analysis.[109] Henry identifies four challenges that must be met if learning is to support sustainability (paraphrased here):

(1) Understanding complexity
(2) Attenuating conflict around norms and values
(3) Getting knowledge into the heads of those who take action
(4) Developing new values that reflect sustainability

I have discussed the bases of these challenges in Chapter 3. I will offer thoughts on how we might deal with them in Chapter 9 of the book.

Realizing that we need to learn also suggests that we should be suspicious of irreversible actions. To some extent, all actions are irreversible if they have any consequences. But given uncertainty about how our actions will unfold and how coupled human and natural systems will respond to them, it seems prudent to give some weight to courses of action that, if they prove undesirable, can be changed.

## 5.9    Apologia

I have suggested seven criteria for making a decision that has consequences for sustainability. How can we:

(1) Enhance the well-being of humans, other species and the environment?
(2) Be efficient in allocating resources?
(3) Act to enhance individual freedoms?
(4) Take account of uncertain facts and uncertain and conflicting values in a competent way?
(5) Promote fairness in process and in outcomes?
(6) Rely on our cognitive strengths and compensate for our weaknesses?
(7) Encourage learning from our actions?

For any decision, it is likely that there will be trade-offs across these criteria. If I am trying to decide whether or not I support solar radiation management as a response to climate change, I will have to think through all of them. Solar radiation management might enhance well-being by reducing climate change but it might also have adverse consequences. It is likely to be efficient in the narrow sense that it won't cost much to implement compared to limiting greenhouse gas emissions, but the risks need to be considered to assess efficiency realistically. There will be substantial uncertainty about the facts, and values will almost certainly be in conflict. Fairness in outcomes is crucial and that implies governance processes that are inclusive. The complexity of the analysis requires careful formal analysis, including modeling of outcomes under different scenarios of solar radiation management and such complex analysis, again, should be done in deliberation with those at risk. For most of my criteria, much more information is needed to see how solar radiation management impacts what I value. That is what most proposals call for – substantial research to answer some of these questions before each of us can decide where we stand. More information won't resolve differences in our values and our assessment of the facts but it will clarify what they are. This is why deliberation is crucial – it helps us as individuals to think through what matters in proposals to use solar radiation management to reduce climate change. And it may help us come to a consensus on what to decide. But there will certainly be conflicts. Chapter 6 reviews some of the sources of conflict in sustainability decisions.[110]

Some of these suggested criteria may be based on flawed logic. I am aware that there are large and thoughtful literatures touching on these issues whose wisdom is not reflected in what I have written. Undoubtedly, there are other good criteria for sustainability decisions that I have ignored and that may be more important than the criteria I discuss. But all these flaws may be an advantage if they motivate you to participate in a dialogue about good sustainability decision-making. My hope is simply to encourage further conversation. The dialogue will influence our thinking, help us develop better criteria and better tools to deploy the criteria and ultimately lead to better decisions.

To return to Winky and Wanda, there were clearly trade-offs on the criteria of well-being, efficiency and freedom. Their well-being would be enhanced, given what was known of elephants, but visitors to the zoo would miss an opportunity to see them. Their freedom would be enhanced, but a choice was lost for zoo visitors. And the zoo conceivably lost some revenue. (I don't have a detailed enough knowledge of the decision process to discuss my other criteria.) The Detroit Zoo clearly decided to give strong priority to the outcomes for Winky and Wanda, despite some losses for humans. It is a decision I endorse, and since then the Detroit Zoo has been recognized as a leader in humane education and practices, a perhaps unanticipated benefit.

# 6    Decisions and Conflicts

In the early twentieth century, progressive politicians in California wanted to dam the Hetch Hetchy Valley in Yosemite National Park to provide water and hydroelectric power to San Francisco. Their goal was to displace for-profit utilities with a publicly owned system. As noted in Chapter 2, conservationists including John Muir and the Sierra Club had worked hard to establish Yosemite as a national park. They fought fiercely to prevent the damming of the valley, which some thought the most beautiful in the park.[1]

The fight crystallized an environmental movement focused on wilderness and biodiversity and foreshadowed many conflicts to come. Muir and the Sierrans were committed to leaving as much area as possible "natural," a "wilderness." They saw building a dam in a national park as a travesty. The battle was a fight between protecting a "pristine" area and at least one vision of economic development – the sort of conflict at the center of sustainability.

An earlier conflict around those lands has not been given much attention until recently. The Yosemite and Hetch Hetchy valleys had long been inhabited by Indigenous peoples who were displaced by settler colonists, a pattern seen in establishment of parks around the world.[2] It appears that the Indigenous population of the valleys was decimated by European disease even before direct contact. The introduction of settler economic activities in the valleys exacerbated those impacts. Tragic displacements are part of the history of this beautiful area. Efforts are underway to engage traditional communities in the management of protected areas and to better understand the long coevolution of those cultures and the ecosystems of the region.

The conflict about damming Hetch Hetchy was a prototype for current disputes and those we will see in the future. It takes only a quick glance at current debates about climate to see that some things remain much the same.[3] All sides claim concern with public well-being. Often all sides claim to be concerned about the environment. The process of biased assimilation, homophily and polarization (BAHP) sets in. The claims of the other side are refuted as being naïve, extreme, insincere and/or self-serving. Issues of environmental justice may be at the center of disputes or they may be hidden and largely unarticulated. The conflict is fierce and compromise is hard to envision. Powerful economic interests are arrayed against environmentalists, whose major resource is public support. In the current debate about climate change, arguments about the validity of the scientific basis for projected impacts and about the degree of uncertainty in the science enter the debate in a central way. This seemed to be less of a feature in the Hetch Hetchy debate.

Many environmental professionals are puzzled by the way environmental conflicts develop. I have heard scientists trained in the physical, ecological or engineering sciences complaining of "too much *political* science" – by which they mean too much politicization of science.[4] They seem to feel that decisions should be made based on science alone, and conflict can be explained by the information deficit model. The idea, whether expressed or hidden, that science alone can lead to a decision is deeply incorrect, as I hope the preceding chapters have made clear. In a democracy, science can give clear guidance on what decision to make only if everyone agrees on what values to assign to various possible outcomes, on the weight to give to uncertainty in our understanding of the future and on the degree to which we will discount the future, if at all. If we have agreement on all those points – if we have agreement about our values – then science can suggest the decision that best allows us to achieve our goals. But it is rarely the case that we have agreement on all these points. So, while science is essential to making a good decision, it is not sufficient. And scientists who don't think carefully about the value bases for their views may not be very effective in persuading others to base their assertions of fact on the best available science.[5]

We need a solid understanding of why conflicts emerge and what underpins them, one grounded in consistent theory and disciplined with evidence. Value differences are certainly one source of conflict. So are decisions that could produce winner and losers. Both are features of all policy disputes. But environmental problems also have some features that make them particularly contentious. It is those unusual features I want to emphasize here.[6] If we ignore these special features of sustainability disputes, it will be much more difficult to find reasonable resolutions. My hope is that a better understanding of what happens in environmental conflicts will lead us towards better outcomes.

My interest in environmental problems has its origins in my undergraduate experience. I was first drawn to study human ecology for intellectual reasons (see the Introduction and Chapter 1.) I was fascinated by the ability of ecological anthropologists to integrate knowledge from nearly all the academic disciplines into an understanding of how a society relates to its environment. But as a student at Kent State in the late 1960s and early 1970s, I was profoundly and tragically aware that politics and conflict impose themselves on even the most scholarly pursuits.[7] So an interest in the intersection between science and politics was a natural outgrowth of developing a scientific interest in human ecology at that very special place and time.

Why focus on sustainability conflicts? There are at least two reasons. First, as we move through the twenty-first century we will face more and even sharper sustainability conflicts. We can't know the future with certainty. But reasonable projections suggest that climate change, disruption of major biogeochemical cycles, loss of biodiversity, the ubiquity of many persistent pollutants, land use change, stresses on the water quality and quantity and soil loss all will lead to great stresses on coupled human and natural systems in many parts of the world.[8] Second, as I noted in the Introduction and Chapter 5, sustainability problems are a testbed for dealing with other complicated issues we will face in the twenty-first century.

My observation is that at least eight factors contribute to making environmental problems especially contentious:

(1) Uneven distribution of risks and benefits
(2) A muddling of facts and values
(3) Facts that are uncertain
(4) Values that are unformed
(5) Changes that are concrete and permanent

(6) Harm to innocents and inequities

(7) Confusion of boundaries between the public and the private

(8) A confusion of competences

After discussing each, I will conclude by offering a few thoughts on how we can overcome these obstacles. Disputes over sustainability won't disappear, but a systematic understanding of the sources of conflict can lead to less heat and more light in environmental disputes and ultimately to better decisions.[9]

## 6.1    Problem 1: Unequal Distribution of Risks and Benefits

Most decisions create winners and losers and that is certainly true of decisions about sustainability. In the richest nations, 250 years of releasing greenhouse gases by burning fossil fuels to support economic growth has caused climate change. Those in the least affluent nations and the least affluent in all nations are at greatest risk from climate change, but they have done little to cause the problem and have had the least benefit from growth. The richest 1 percent of people in the world (those with incomes above about $109,000) make decisions that have far more impact on the climate than those of the least affluent 50 percent. There are also inequities along lines of class, race/ethnicity, indigeneity, gender and disability and their intersections.[10]

Even within a community, neighbors facing the same environmental and economic circumstances can be divided on an issue. Brown and Mikkelsen document the sharp conflicts in Woburn, Massachusetts, between those who felt toxic contamination from a local manufacturing plant was causing an outbreak of childhood leukemia and their neighbors who saw them as troublemakers attacking a major employer.[11] Disagreements about growth can split a community. Since the 1960s, scholars have pointed to a conflict between the need for continuous economic growth in contemporary industrial capitalist societies and the stress that growth placed on the environment. Logan and Molotch applied the same argument to the dynamics of the pattern of urban growth deplored by Chrissie Hynde in the epigraph to Chapter 1. Money can be made by expanding economic production or by developing land. Using the environment as a source of raw materials and a dump for waste can be very profitable.[12] Ignoring such environmental costs increases profits. But those costs are sustained by someone. Environmental costs can be direct: exposure to pollution with resulting harm to health. Sometimes the costs seem less tangible – the loss of a viewscape, the knowledge that a species is going extinct, the disruption of the historic conditions of an ecosystem. Sometimes we lose the subtle ways in which ecosystems reduce the risks we face – the buffering effect of coastal wetlands and barrier islands against storm surges from hurricanes.[13]

This problem of costs and risks and benefits going to different people has been part of many human societies, although there also are many examples of egalitarian societies as well.[14] With a division of labor in which some are soldiers, some religious officials, some farmers, some craftspeople, then most group decisions will tend to favor one group or another and conflicts that split along group lines become evident. When property is held privately rather than in common, conflicts between my use of my property and the well-being of others can arise. Those with the most power shape not only the decisions made but also the way we make decisions. For example, in Chapter 4 I noted that we underinvest in understanding environmental impacts and that the powerful often mount active campaigns against science that calls attention to impacts.

Differences in who will bear the risks and costs and who will reap the benefits are usually a fundamental driver of sustainability conflicts. There are ultimately two ways of resolving these conflicts. One, mentioned in Chapter 5, is what economists refer to as "side payments." Hydraulic fracturing – fracking – is being used to extract natural gas in many areas, but there are serious concerns about the environmental impacts.[15] If I want to build a fracking facility, perhaps I should not only pay for leases from land owners where I drill but also contribute to an insurance fund to those at risk from pollution.[16] Such side payments need to be done with the consent of those impacted and with their having a right to say "No" to the project if they feel compensation and protections are not adequate. That leads to a second approach, having an open debate about who will benefit and who will lose as a result of a decision, a topic I will return to in Chapter 9. This can encourage policy that balances the costs, benefits and risks and shapes side payments or insurance funds. We should be skeptical of side payments undertaken without public discussion because it is hard for people to anticipate the risk and costs they may suffer without such debate. Sometimes this process means projects do not go forward or go forward only with profound modification.

The longer-term resolution of this problem may be a move away from narrow self-interest and towards a more altruistic view of what matters in decisions. If I am a natural gas extractor, I may feel an ethical obligation to take account of how my actions will impact the community in which I place my wells. And if the organization supplying energy is a co-op that includes the local community in governance, then profit maximization won't be the only criteria taken seriously. The notion that corporations should take account of more than their profits in making decisions underpins one key theory of sustainability. I will discuss it in some detail in Chapter 7.

## 6.2    Problem 2: Facts and Values Get Muddled

Environmental and sustainability conflicts are usually about both facts and values. We need to address both in making decisions. But we often slip into discussing facts to resolve conflicts about values, thinking a controversy is about facts rather than values. For example, in a study of those actively engaged in the US risk policy systems (see Chapter 2), we found that most policy professionals attributed environmental conflict to a lack of knowledge on the part of the public rather than to conflicting values or uneven distribution of risks and benefits. In the view of these "risk professionals," it was a misunderstanding of the facts by the public that generated environmental conflict rather than some deeper value issue – they were using the information deficit model.[17]

Factual controversies can be resolved by getting better facts. Reasonable people will change their beliefs in the face of new information, although as Chapter 3 makes clear, we are not always very good at doing this. But changing values is more difficult than changing beliefs. Value controversies can be resolved only by compromise that may engender a sense of loss, and we tend to be loss-averse. Indeed, since values are closely related to identity, asking someone to change their values is asking them to change their identity, to change who they are in some fundamental way. Asking for compromise on values is asking for a compromise on those things that a person cares about most deeply. Moving away from long-held values towards a compromise may feel unethical.[18]

It is understandable that we don't focus on value differences. Our cultures evolved around the need to live in cooperative social groups. Following the "tribal hypothesis" of Boyd and Richerson, it may be that we will argue facts with people we see as part of our "tribe" who we assume have a shared set of values. We may not expect to convert those with different values to our view but instead highlight the differences and try to persuade "right thinking" people (people who share our values) to dismiss the views of those from the other groups.[19] This is again the BAHP process. Social media and political strategies may intensify this tendency. Confusing discussion of facts with discussions of values directs attention away from what are often the real sources of conflict.

## 6.3    Problem 3: Uncertain Facts

The facts in sustainability conflicts are always uncertain. The dangers from exposure to a toxic chemical are expressed as a risk. The chances of a species extinction following from a reduction in habitat are expressed as a probability. Risk analysis and decision theory help us deal with these uncertainties in a systematic way by studying both how people process information about uncertainty and how we might make better decisions in the face of uncertainty (see Chapter 4). We need that help because, as we have seen, we have trouble processing information about uncertainty accurately.

Research can both reduce and clarify uncertainty. Weather forecasts are an example. The scientific community has begun to make seasonal weather forecasts with some accuracy two years in advance, drawing in part on our better understanding of the El Niño–La Niña–Southern Oscillation cycle.[20] This cycle has substantial effects on weather patterns that affect droughts, floods and food availability in many places, and the improved forecasts using them show steady scientific progress leading to practical knowledge.

The international climate research program is another excellent example of an effort to reduce uncertainty through research. The first calculation showing that the release of greenhouse gases by burning fossil fuels could lead to warming was published in 1896 by Arrhenius.[21] (His model was very simple but turns out to be roughly correct, just a bit too high.) Since then, models and the data used in them have improved steadily. For about three decades, the United States has invested about $1.5–2 billion per year in research intended to improve our understanding of climate change and related problems, with many other counties also making substantial investments. (This is comparable to what the federal government spends on research on diabetes and digestive and kidney diseases and about half of what it spends on cancer research.) Other nations make comparable investments. The resulting studies have greatly increased our understanding of the climate system and the human impact on it.[22]

Roughly every five years the Intergovernmental Panel on Climate Change (IPCC) writes a report expressing international scientific consensus on what we know about climate from this ongoing research. They take great care to express statements about the state of knowledge and about future events in probabilistic terms.[23] Although talk show hosts and political pundits seem unaware of it, the research summarized by the IPCC has been able to move many statements about climate change from the possible to the probable and from the probable to the category of "beyond a reasonable doubt." There are still many unanswered questions about the future of the planet's climate. But overall the climate change research process of the last few decades has been a triumph of showing how patient investment in research can reduce scientific uncertainty on key problems.

Research helps reduce uncertainty, but underinvestment in key areas of research slows progress. When the US Environmental Protection Agency (EPA) offers a new assessment of risk, environmental groups fear the analysis will underestimate risks. Industry groups fear that risks will be exaggerated. In theory, the conflicting views about errors in analysis should balance each other and the resulting critiques of the EPA analysis will lead to better studies and more certainty about the facts. Remember that in the US risk policy system there are seven to eight PhD scientists working on policy issues for industry for every one scientist working for environmental groups. This leads to a huge imbalance in critiques rather than the diversity needed to advance scientific understanding.[24]

It is important to differentiate scientific uncertainty from public misunderstanding of science. It is certainly true that the average US citizen misunderstands the technical details of many environmental problems. For example, several studies show that people confuse greenhouse warming and ozone depletion.[25] For most day-to-day decisions, ordinary people probably don't need to know the difference. When Dr. Watson was first getting to know Sherlock Holmes, Holmes said: "I consider that a man's [sic] brain originally is like a little empty attic, and you have to stock it with such furniture as you choose. . . . It is a mistake to think that this little room has elastic walls . . . It is of the highest importance, therefore, not to have useless facts elbowing out the useful."[26]

In our busy, information-saturated lives, we all follow Holmes' admonition to some degree, focusing on information that we need to make decisions or information that fascinates us, with little room or framework to retain much else. As detailed in Chapter 3, lots of things other than just the evidence can influence the conclusions we reach about facts, which can lead to at least some members of the public adopting beliefs very much out of line with scientific consensus. Nor is this process of BAHP restricted to the public – it also occurs among policy professionals. But when a community perceives a threat from toxic substances, ordinary citizens can quickly learn enough toxicology and epidemiology to understand, and often dispute, the assertions of experts.[27]

Misunderstandings about facts can have consequences for sustainability. In Chapter 3, I discussed the work by Attari and colleagues showing that most people have incorrect information about how much energy is used by household appliances and their routine use. This makes it difficult for them to reduce energy consumption. A belief that climate change is not happening or that it is not caused by human action will lead to a lack of support for climate policy.[28] A variety of beliefs, some of them out of alignment with scientific consensus, have shaped pandemic responses among both the public and political leaders.[29] For some simple things not strongly linked to values, providing more information can reduce the "information deficit." Chapter 3 notes that providing information about household energy use improved understanding. But when beliefs are strongly linked to values, biased assimilation will engage and new information will have little impact.

The different rules used in journalism and science can increase public confusion. Scientists consider a fact established when there is consensus that the preponderance of solid evidence points in the same direction. Most journalists are trained to cover politics rather than science and use a very different logic.[30] Much of politics is about value disagreements even though we often offer factual arguments when the disagreement is about values. If a dispute is about values, then all reasonable value positions should be heard with roughly equal voice – anything else would be unfair. But when this rule is applied to environmental science, it often gives unwarranted weight to the views of a tiny minority of dissenting scientists. In media coverage of climate change, an overwhelming scientific consensus often is counterbalanced with a handful of "greenhouse skeptics."[31] The public comes away with the feeling that scientists are undecided about an issue where the science is very clear. And, as we saw in Chapter 3, the argument that the science is uncertain can be used to support delays in taking action. A parallel problem exists in judicial proceedings where the adversarial process allows for "dueling experts" and most judges and jury members have too little training in science to separate the wheat from the chaff. And on the web, there are few filters about what is asserted as fact.

For climate change, the BAHP dynamic seems to be very influential. In the United States, about three-quarters of adults believe climate change is happening and would support regulating $CO_2$, the principal greenhouse gas, as a pollutant. The percentages have been relatively stable over the dozen or so years for which we have comparable data.[32] However, there are sharp differences between Democrats and Republicans on the issue, with, for example, 80–90 percent of liberal Democrats supporting regulation of $CO_2$, while only 50 percent of conservative Republicans support such regulation. There is some evidence that the liberal/conservative gap has increased over time and may be larger among those actively engaged in politics than those not engaged and may be larger among those who consider themselves well informed or who have more education.[33]

How should we deal with uncertain facts? We know how to assess uncertainty about facts, how to communicate it effectively and how to use it in decision-making.[34] We know we need to link scientific analysis to public deliberation, what has been called the "analytic deliberative proccess." And we know that we must learn as we proceed (see Chapter 5). This logic has come to be called adaptive risk management. I will have more to say about it in Chapter 9.

In addition to value uncertainty and imbalanced development of science, we also face a kind of uncertainty about values. Values for many aspects of environmental conflicts are unformed. In the next section, I will clarify what I mean by unformed or uncertain values.

## 6.4    Problem 4: Unformed Values and Value Uncertainty

Recall the difference raised in Chapter 3 between the System II, slow, methodical decision-making process (the rational actor model) and the fast, emotional System I decision process. I argued in Chapter 5 that we often use the fast process when confronted with new issues in a news story, a commentary on a website, television or radio, a podcast or a conversation. We need to examine how the new issue fits into our values and beliefs. What are your views about moving elephants from zoos to sanctuaries? Do you think solar radiation management is a good idea? Unless you have already encountered these issues, your first reaction to reading about them was probably to use fast, System I decision processes to come to an initial judgment. Such a quick mapping can be reenforced by biased assimilation of new information unless you take the time to reflect carefully.

In the media and even in casual conversations, issues are framed in a way to map onto our values. Sometimes this framing is inadvertent, but often it is the result of active campaigns to influence us – for example, by advertising. This allows us to simplify the calculation process and generate a quick answer. In the absence of advertising agencies, pundits and spin doctors, quick decision-making probably worked quite well for many issues. But when our decisions have important consequences and when there are active efforts to frame our mapping of a new issue onto our values, quick decision processes can be problematic (see Chapter 3).

How do we make decisions when we aren't under time pressure? While we may sometimes do something like the calculations of the RAM, I believe typical human decision-making is very much a conversational process rather than one of isolated calculation. When we plan to buy a new car or choose a college, we hold internal conversations with ourselves and we nearly always discuss the decisions with others. Often the decisions have consequences for others so we want to get their views. And norms are a powerful influence so we want to check what others are doing and what they think we should do.

For many sustainability issues, the discussions we need to be rational either don't take place, are very abbreviated or confuse a discussion of uncertain facts with a discussion of unformed values. The BAHP process has a huge influence. The media tend to show strongly held opposing positions rather than conversations by intelligent people who are working to form an opinion and who respect and learn from each other's views. The US Congress has grown increasingly polarized, mostly as Republicans have moved to the right over the last few decades and homophily has increased.[35] In everyday life, it takes a good bit of effort or luck to find someone who has different views but with whom one can discuss a sustainability issue in an even-handed way. It is natural to avoid conflict, so our tendency towards homophily leads us to have conversations that reenforce our initial views rather than conversations that encourage us to think through the subtleties of a complex issue.

This dynamic can change if the problem becomes local, such as a local proposed change in land use or concern of toxic contamination, as happened in Flint and Woburn.[36] Then it becomes easier to link the problem to our everyday lives in concrete and specific ways. And our opponents in the debate are often people with whom we have interactions outside of the discussion of the controversy, so we have more basis for finding common ground and respecting the views of those who disagree with us.

Yet, for many sustainability issues, we never have the chance to go through the deliberative conversational process we need to make a reasoned decision. We end up with substantial uncertainty and confusion about what is really at stake. Since value positions are hard to change, this can make conflicts based on value positions that were not carefully developed especially unfortunate.

## 6.5    Problem 5: Permanent Concrete Changes

Many sustainability controversies are about the irrevocable. Talking about them in the language of risk and probability masks that concreteness. Risk analysts think about minimal risks and are aware that the uncertainties in estimates of risk include the possibility that the estimated risk is "lost in the noise" of natural occurrences of adverse health effects and is essentially zero. In many analyses, deaths of less than one person per million per year are seen as too small to matter. But that one in a million who has a terrible outcome because of exposure to toxics might be someone we care about, and that makes the small risk troubling.[37] And, as discussed in Chapter 4, risk estimates become much more uncertain when they have to be applied to specific contexts. Yet it is in these contexts where people suffer harm.

Conflicts about wild places also revolve around the concrete and irrevocable. As the bumper sticker puts it: "Extinction is forever." An extinct species cannot be replaced.[38] An old growth forest, once logged, becomes something very different than it was before. Some marine biologists are worried that our overfishing of top predators, like sharks and tuna, is irrevocably changing the structure of ocean ecosystems. "The rise of slime" is the catchy phrase used to capture this unfortunate possibility – it seems that jellyfish might become the replacement for sharks, tuna and other large predators. Humans have a long history of killing off top predators that compete with them for game animals – for example, in North America wolves and cougars were actively hunted out of many areas. Removing top predators seems to have substantial effects on many ecosystems, and it is not clear if the changes can be reversed by reintroducing predators.[39]

Dealing with irrevocable changes makes compromise difficult. Developers who would use the landscape for immediate economic gain are pitted against preservationists who leave it as free from human influence as possible. For those protecting wild areas or endangered species, or even just open land, every loss may seem permanent, every victory temporary. The slogan of Earth First is "No compromise in defense of Mother Earth!" Their fierce defense of wild places reflects that sense of loss. So does the demoralization of John Muir after the loss of Hetch Hetchy.

Environmentalists are not the only ones who see potential permanent loss. Local communities that have been dependent on resource extraction industries, such as mining, logging and fishing, often feel threatened with a concrete and potentially permanent loss of their jobs and the character of the community that goes with those jobs.[40] For the developer, their chance at profit comes not from the overall pattern of land use but from what happens to a particular parcel they want to develop.[41]

The sense of irretrievable loss comes not just with threats to human health or ecosystems and other species but also with threats to elements of culture and lifestyle. Indigenous people throughout the world worry about continuing threats to ways of life that have historically defined their cultures. They have endured colonialism, forced displacement and genocide, and they increasingly face global environmental change and globalized institutions and culture.[42] Faced with such potential permanent loss of things central to their identities, it can be hard to find compromises.

We seem to care more when identifiable individuals are perceived as at risk. Small risks matter if they are for people or other animals you care about. Save the Children Foundation uses a campaign that links contributors to specific children being helped. Photographers such as Tim Flach, Britta Jaschinski and Joe Zammit-Lucia use animal portraiture rather than traditional nature photography of animals in a landscape to encourage sympathy for and concern with endangered animals. The approach is very effective, perhaps because it generates empathy for the identified individuals and others seen as like them, expanding the scope of altruism.[43]

In sustainability conflicts, some interested and affected parties see the outcomes of a decision on a continuum – an increase in health risks, the loss of some plant or animal populations in particular places, a fluctuation in employment opportunities, a bit more change in a local community. But other participants see a permanent loss of something deeply important to them. It may be possible to reconcile such conflicts but not unless we recognize what is at stake is conceptualized in very different ways by different parties to the decision.

## 6.6     Problem 6: Harm to Innocents and Equity Concerns

Humans seem to be especially attentive to harm to innocents. For most of us, ethical concerns expand beyond immediate kin and community members to include all humans. Many of us include all living things in our scope of concern.[44] Altruism seems particularly engaged when those who are at risk are innocent of generating the impact, have no say in the decisions that produce the impact and receive no benefit from the action generating the impact. It seems unfair and we don't like things that are unfair.[45]

In many sustainability conflicts, those who bear risks seem innocent. In toxic exposure disputes, the innocents include children, those particularly susceptible because their health is otherwise challenged and those who bear risks without gaining any substantial benefits. In disputes about wild lands, the innocents are the members of other species who will be displaced or otherwise suffer harm and the children of future generations who have lost the opportunity to enjoy or use a wild place. A sense of injustice and moral outrage fuels the fire, which can burn with great heat. In environmental justice disputes, communities subject to disproportionate exposures to toxics and other environmental threats often have received little benefit from the processes generating those risk. Environmental injustice is combined with economic injustice and residential segregation.

## 6.7     Problem 7: What Is Public and What Is Private?

In most contemporary societies, some problems are handled by the market. Others are handled by politics. Each realm has its own rules for what is appropriate, for what counts and what doesn't.[46] Environmental disputes often arise when someone attempts to change the rules that are applied to a specific environmental "good." Struggles over pollution are attempts by communities to shift a cost that has been carried by the community back to the private sector. Communities want to make the polluters responsible for the costs of safely handling or cleaning up wastes, rather than continuing with the privately cheap but publicly costly strategy of unsafe dumping. Throughout the 1960s and 1970s, protests and government action forced companies that had been dumping toxic waste into Cuyahoga River to pay for safer waste disposal. In disputes about wild lands, environmentalists argue that there are public costs associated with development because ecosystems services will be lost. Developers emphasize private property rights, private profits and privately controlled jobs.

The mixture of public and private interests puts environmental conflicts at the intersection of two different sets of rules. In the public realm, arguments about the public interest, justice and equity make sense. Democratic procedures are viewed as appropriate means of determining the best course of action. Public opinion is an important resource in political conflicts. But in the realm of markets, the guiding ideas are efficiency and profit. The collective good is not the focus of the debate.[47] Arguments are about private cost, benefits and risks. Public opinion, unless expressed through market transaction – buying and selling – is not a legitimate resource.

In societies such as the United States, where both democratic and market mechanisms are legitimate, problems that invoke both sets of rules simultaneously are bound to generate not only conflict but also misunderstandings. Two corporations operating purely under the rules of profit maximization may be in conflict. So might two nonprofit interest groups who take different sides on the same issue. These disputes can be fierce. Yet within each of these kinds of conflicts a consistent set of rules obtains as to what matters and how to make arguments. Environmental problems are more complicated because they involve not just conflict but conflict that generates simultaneous use of multiple, and contradictory, rule systems regarding the appropriate basis for making decisions.

Defining the boundary between public and private, and thus the rules of decision-making (market processes versus democracy) and the criteria for decisions (profit and economic growth versus measures of well-being of humans, other species and the environment) is a major source of political contention. The tension between private and public arises not just around sustainability but around nearly all collective decisions in contemporary societies.[48] In Chapter 2, I discussed the neoliberal reforms imposed by rich nations and global financial institutions on debtor nations. Neoliberals argued that the private sector would make better decisions about how to allocate resources than the debtor nation government would. The result would be faster economic growth and everyone would be better off. As Chapter 2 notes, that hope has not been realized in many places; neoliberal policies have led to serious problems. But often the basic dimension of political disagreements is often exactly along this axis – how much power does one want to afford to the market and its decision-making mechanisms versus to government and those forms of decision-making?[49]

The politics of defining activities as public or private is evident in the use of the term "socialized" in public discussion. In Europe, while there are certainly fierce conflicts about government programs, terms like "socialist" and "socialized" have some legitimacy and more than a few successful political parties use the term "social" or "socialist" in their names. Since the nineteenth century, in the United States the terms "socialism" and "socialized" have been viewed as negative and often conflated with "communism" and "communist." For decades, government provision of health care or health insurance has been attacked as "socialized medicine." In contrast, government provision of education is usually referred to as "public" education, and while it is the subject of debate and calls for privatization so market forces can shape education, the term "socialized education" is seldom deployed.[50]

## 6.8    Confusions of Competence

"Confusions of competence" occur when someone assumes that an environmental conflict is simpler than it really is or misunderstands or misrepresents what is involved. Nearly everyone tends to do this. These confusions are inherent in environmental conflict because environmental disputes are rarely free from the seven problematic characteristics I have discussed so far: an uneven distribution of risks and benefits; a muddling of facts and values; facts that are uncertain; values that are unformed; changes that are concrete and permanent; harm to innocents and inequities; and confusion of boundaries between the public and the private.

These problems create confusion and difficulty in moving towards a decision. This confusion is not neutral. Treating an environmental problem as one kind of issue rather than another or invoking one set of rules for the conflict rather than another has important consequences. It shapes what counts in the discussion and who has a say in making decisions. Because of this, the confusions sometimes are part of the tactics used to shape environmental policy. A struggle over how the situation should be defined or framed and thus over what rules are appropriate in debating the problem arises in every environmental conflict.[51]

Defining an environmental problem as a scientific problem – a problem of facts rather than values – delegitimates public opinion. Defining the problem as purely scientific lends advantage to private sector interests, who can use money to buy expertise, and disadvantages public interest groups, who have limited funds but much public support. Another confusion arises when we do not acknowledge that environmental disputes involve both private goods that are allocated by the market and commons, such as open space or clean air, that are allocated by politics. Sometimes issues are framed so that the appropriate rules are those of private gain to corporations (and by implication to workers and their communities). This delegitimates the public interests advocated by environmentalists. If a dispute is defined in terms of private interest, then the arguments of environmental groups with the preservation of public goods are transformed into the concerns of a narrow set of private interests. The environmentalists are portrayed as wanting to use the wilderness for backpacking or keeping it undeveloped to protect endangered species valued only by an elite few. The private interest in a collective good seems selfish ("Saving the woods for a few backpackers") while the private interest in private goods is easily understood ("I know what it's like to have my job threatened").

## 6.9    Two Persistent Challenges

In addition to these eight sources of conflict, there are two challenges that underpin every decision about sustainability. They can be sources of conflict even among those who are committed to sustainability as a high priority in decision-making. And they frame not only each decision we make but how we think about moving cultural evolution towards sustainability. However, unlike the previous eight issues they are not primary sources of conflict but rather undercurrents that may lead to unexamined assumptions and misunderstandings.

### 6.9.1  Transforming Political Economies

Many of the arguments I review question whether a capitalist political economy can improve the well-being of humans and other species and reduce human impacts on the environment. I agree with many of these critiques. But I also find the defenders of markets make some useful points. And often opposition to environmental protection and sustainability efforts is based on a concern with increased government control and socialism.

I return to Ostrom's insight that all real political economies are complex hybrids. Thinking about abstract forms of anarchism capitalism, communism, fascism and socialism is sometimes useful. But in making decisions about sustainability, we have to be specific about the problems generated by the current political economy and think about changes towards something better rather than simply contemplating an ideal. In Chapter 7, I will say more about political and economic transformation but want to examine sources of conflict here.

For more than a century, the dynamics of individuals and corporations seeking profit have led to a growth in the scale of the economy. There have been some benefits from this, including technological innovation and growing affluence for many. The material circumstances of most of the world's population are better now than they were a century ago. For example, from 1900 to the present average human life expectancy across the world has roughly doubled, much of that from reduced infant mortality.[52]

Growth in economic activity has also generated problems. Capitalism as practiced in most places in the world in recent history has tended to increase inequality, with the largest corporations coming to dominate markets and with wealth concentrating in the hands of the most affluent. As Figure 2.1 indicates, these changes are not inevitable, they depend on the details of policy; and as policy changes, inequality can increase or decrease. Inequality is problematic for at least three reasons. First, the increased affluence at the top does not balance the difficulties and suffering of those at the bottom. Second, it seems unjust. While some differences in income and wealth resulting from differences in skills and effort might be justified, I don't believe they justify the levels of inequality we observe. For example, the CEOs of the largest corporations in the United States now make more than 350 times as much as the average worker, as compared to 25 times as much in the 1970s.[53] Third, and to me the most pressing issue, is that inequality corrodes the kind of fair and competent deliberative processes needed to make good decisions about the challenges we face.

Most forms of capitalism encourage those engaged in production to ignore the full costs of production. A major source of pollution in the Cuyahoga River in Kent came from factories dumping toxic waste into the river. The corporations doing this believed it was cheaper, more profitable, to do this than to treat the waste to avoid environmental damage. The same logic leads to reduced wages and benefits for workers, to gender and racial discrimination and to the use of political influence to create government subsidies to corporations. There is variation across corporations in the priority they give to the well-being of their workers, of consumers, of communities and to reducing environmental impacts. But there are constant pressures to ignore these costs of economic activities.

Growth in economic activity since the rise of capitalism has increased the amount of stress placed on the environment. Changes in the composition of consumption and the techniques we use to produce goods and services could, and sometimes have, compensated for the growth in the amount we consume. But there is a tendency in capitalism to promote growth, and reductions in the impacts of our economic activity have not kept up with this growth.

All of these concerns support arguments to change the political economy towards forms more compatible with sustainability. In thinking about such changes, a detailed analysis of institutions and their rules, including those encoded in law and those in norms, is crucial. Robinson's backcasting can be useful. If we envision a future we want, we then can ask how we get there from here. Some argue the only way forward comes by destroying current institutions and rebuilding from scratch. But it is not clear that massive social disruption would lead to more sustainable institutions, given current power imbalances. It is more useful to understand how current institutions create selective regimes for laws and norms and find ways to reshape them, starting from where we are. The discourse shaping such changes will need voices from those most disadvantaged by the current institutions as well as those with more privilege who recognize the injustice in them.[54]

For example, the rules structuring many markets exacerbate the problems of capitalism just noted. But it is hard to imagine the coordination of global economic activity via direct control by government or the community without something like a market, some mechanism for coordinating actions. Efforts to displace markets with central planning have often gone awry. All large bureaucracies, whether government or corporate, can favor decisions that are problematic for sustainability. So, the challenge is not to wholly eliminate markets but to reshape them so they can allow true freedom of choice and signals about preference without the distortions that now favor the wealthy and the powerful at the cost of those with little or no power in the market. This may apply especially to markets for ownership of resources, where more community, worker, consumer and public control could help balance the drive for profit with consideration of well-being and the environment.

This in turn suggests that we need to look carefully at a multitude of experiments that can guide us in how to develop a better political economy. How well do co-ops, community-owned business, employee-owned businesses and other alternative forms of corporate ownership perform? What policies are effective at reducing inequality while still allowing or even enhancing freedom of choice? How can the true costs of production, including on communities and the environment, be effectively incorporated into prices? How can the content of consumption and the methods of production be shifted to enhance sustainability while, again, allowing for individual freedom? Imagining solutions is useful; having evidence on how specific policies, programs and initiatives work in specific contexts is even more useful. In Chapter 9, I will consider the ways we make decisions together and revisit these potential sources of conflict, while the Chapter 7 will consider the relationship between reform and transformation.

### 6.9.2   Transforming Ecosystems

Reduction of human impact on the environment is a core element of sustainability. Much of the imagery of the environmental movement, including the imagery that has shaped my thinking, invokes an idea of wilderness.[55] But nearly everywhere labeled wilderness was in some way occupied by Indigenous people, who often recognized some of the areas we now revere as sacred lands. Many pre-European landscapes were the result of human interactions with the ecosystem. So, human impact on the environment has been a part of ecosystem change for many millennia. Even if we ignore human impacts over the last 100,000 years or so, climate change, other changes in biogeochemical cycles, land use change and the widespread dispersal of persistent toxic substances will continue to have impacts for the foreseeable future.[56] The pristine ecosystem may have some use as an ideal, but it is very much a hypothetical place, not one that exists or will exist. As long as humans persist on earth, we will be an active part of the biosphere. So, we need to make decisions taking account not only of our own well-being but of the well-being of other species and of the effects we have on ecosystems.

Just as there are few ecosystems that are not strongly influenced by humans, even the most human-dominated environments are populated by other species. Animal studies scholars emphasize the liminal species, animals that have evolved to live in human-dominated landscapes, including squirrels, mice, rats, pigeons and myriad insect species.[57] Many of us resonate with the ideas of Muir and others who argued for the transformational character of experiences in wilderness. We can reconceptualize wilderness not as romanticized places free from human influence but as places where the current ecosystems reflect a long history of coevolution between humans and other species, where humans do not dominate the landscape in quite the obvious way they do in human settlements and agricultural lands. And, in turn, we can learn to appreciate the presence of other species in our most human-dominated spaces, our neighborhoods, even our homes.

My preference is to make such decisions via deliberative processes. But such processes for ecosystem management need to be especially careful about what voices are engaged. Thinking first of human voices, those who currently live on the landscape should have a voice, but so should those for whom it is a historical home and those "from away" who care about the landscape. Even more challenging is finding ways to represent the voices of nonhumans. We will be able to answer the question "Who will speak for wolf?" only by experimenting with and evaluating ways of deliberating that take account of the well-being of those with whom our species shares the planet (see Chapter 5).

## 6.10   Conclusions

If we are to make sound individual decisions, we must be attentive to how we actually make decisions and compensate for our foibles. The research reviewed in Chapter 3 helps us do that. If we are to make sound collective decisions, then we have to analyze why conflicts arise about sustainability issues, as they almost always do. Most discussions of conflicts I have encountered assume that the conflicts are the result of one of two problems. One is simply that there are winners and losers in every decision. If that were the only source of conflict, and if potential winners did not exert power to their advantage, then some system of "side payments" to compensate the losers from the winners' gains or ways of modifying the decision to make it more acceptable could resolve the conflict. The other major explanation is that not everyone knows the facts, and that if everyone were as well informed as the experts, conflict would dissolve – conflict comes from public ignorance, the information deficit model.

Both are real and serious causes of conflict. But they are only two of the many sources of conflict that can arise when we have a public dispute about a sustainability issue. If we hope to resolve those conflicts, if we hope to make good public decisions about the environment and human well-being, then we must understand the causes of conflict. It is unlikely that conflict resolution mechanisms will work very well if they are designed to address the wrong problems.

I don't think we have very extensive evidence about how common or pernicious each of these problems are in actual conflicts. I offer them as conjectures or hypotheses about why public conflicts arise, in the hope that this will spur both theoretical work to clarify the concepts I have used and empirical work to determine the circumstances under which each of them emerges. Perhaps most important, we need to think through how conflicts driven by each of these mechanisms – and multiple bases of conflict will arise in nearly all public decisions – evolve over time. In Chapter 7, I will discuss the problems of dealing with more than one objective and the potential of reform versus system transformation to move us towards sustainability. The final two chapters will discuss how we might make better decisions as individuals and, finally, the topic we end with here, how to shape the evolution of our collective decision-making processes.

# 7    Reform or Transformation?

In the 1950s, three of my uncles worked as tire builders at Goodyear Tire and Rubber in downtown Akron, Ohio. They were part of a strong union, the United Rubber Workers, so they had good wages and benefits, including health care, pensions and paid vacations. Goodyear was the largest tire manufacturer in the world; three other major tire corporations also built tires in Akron.[1] The rubber industry dominated the city, the "Rubber Capital of the World," and there was always a distinct rubber smell in the air from the factories.

In the late 1960s and 1970s, the major rubber corporations had to decide whether to upgrade their Akron plants to become more efficient and to be capable of building the then new radial tires. (For simplicity, I will discuss corporate decision-making in the same way that I have discussed individual decision-making. Box I.2 discusses how I think about organizations making decisions.) New plants would make manufacturing more efficient and allow relocation to states where unions weren't strong, both factors that could increase profits. The new plants could be built to reduce pollution or they might be located in places where the environmental regulations were less strict. So, environmental impacts could increase or decrease, depending on the details. Workers would either have to move or lose their jobs, and the effect on the Akron economy would be devastating, impacting not only the workers but local businesses and the community overall.[2] Businesses in places where the plants relocated would benefit, as would newly hired workers there. Given these trade-offs, should they move the plants?[3] How should they decide?

Friedman has argued that "the social responsibility of business is to increase its profits." "The business of business is business."[4] If so, the corporations should close the old plants, whatever effect that has on the local community. And for the most part, that is what they did, moving to places with cheaper labor costs and less strict environmental regulations.[5] But arguments for a "triple bottom line" have emerged as part of the larger discourse on sustainability and on the social responsibility of corporations (see Chapter 2). In addition to the bottom line of profits, should corporations also take account of people and the planet? In the case of deciding about the tire plant, this would require weighing the impacts on the community and the environment.

Discussing corporate actions leads to a larger question I introduced in Chapter 6: Can sustainability be achieved by reforms within the existing framework of societal decision-making or is it necessary to radically transform the system in which decisions are made? Can a global capitalist economy based on nation-states reduce human impact on the biosphere sufficiently to prevent catastrophic environmental change? I will discuss reform versus transformation and will try to clarify how we might think about these issues. I will start with corporate decision-making and how profits but also other factors might, and in some cases do, influence decisions. I will then move on to thinking about how we can assess how far reforms might take us and the need for a more substantial transformation in how the political economy shaped decisions.

## 7.1    Corporations and Sustainability

There are at least two common justifications for the argument that only profits should matter.[6] One is the libertarian ethical argument reviewed in Chapter 5: Free market capitalism is a good way to organize a society because it allows maximal individual freedom and because the market is the only effective way to enhance human well-being. This legitimates decisions by owners without any consultation with others who might be impacted by the decision. A company's ethical responsibility is to maximize profits within the constraints of the law. If moving the plant is not illegal and it increases profits, it is the right thing to do.[7] The other argument is based on assumptions about facts. In the long run, plants will move from areas with high labor and environmental protection costs to those with lower costs. A company that doesn't move while competitors do won't be able to compete. Companies that can't compete go bankrupt and the jobs are lost anyway. A closely related argument is that prices give signals about how to most efficiently allocate resources, and efficient allocation is good for society. Society will benefit since tires can be produced at lower prices.[8]

If the tire companies want to look beyond profits, how could they take account of the triple bottom line? Understanding the implications of closing or keeping the old plant requires projecting what will happen under each choice.[9] Since the old plant is inefficient and upgrading it is prohibitively expensive, closing it will increase return on investment, and profits. Assuming that closing the plant will reduce emissions because the newer facilities use more environmentally benign technologies, toxic emissions could be the measure for the planet bottom line.[10] The people bottom line might take account of the well-being of employees and their community, perhaps measured by the subjective well-being of those who live in the communities impacted by the closing of the old plant and the opening of the new one. At the national level, employment will stay the same or decrease slightly because probably not all the workers at the current plant will be needed at the new plant to produce the same amount of product.[11]

The three metrics I have described give a sense of what the company could consider in making its decisions, but they still have to make trade-offs. We don't have a way to compare the impact on well-being with the reduction in toxic emissions and the increase in return on investment. One is in units of lost life satisfaction, one in emissions and one in rate of return on investment. The three metrics by themselves don't point to a decision because we don't know whether the gains in profits or the reduction of greenhouse gas emissions are somehow "worth more" than the loss of jobs. Norman and MacDonald argue that the term "bottom line" implies a way of comparing (commensurating) the three metrics on the same scale.[12] Without a way of translating all three into common units, the three measures don't tell the managers of the company what to do. Often, analyses try to convert all three metrics into monetary units, as in the benefit-cost analysis described in Box 5.4.

Pava emphasizes that: "There is no bottom line nor was there ever a bottom line – only multiple and contingent bottom lines." The trade-offs are left to the company owners and managers who, influenced by tradition, training and incentives, may not give much weight to anything other than profits. In response, triple bottom line advocates argue that simply being aware of the community and environmental "bottom lines" will lead to better decisions than does an exclusive focus on financial measures, such as return on investment.[13]

The lack of commensurability among decision-making criteria is not paralyzing in most organizations. The job of a manager, of a "decision maker," is to make choices with imperfect information. Formal decision analysis tools can be used to clarify the implications of different courses of action, considering multiple criteria.[14] Even in the absence of commensurable measures for multiple decision criteria or formal decision analysis, people informally weigh alternatives and decide. If I follow Friedman's focus on profits as the only basis for decisions, I would move the plant. If I give sufficient weight to community impacts over profits and greenhouse gas emissions, then I might decide not to move the plant, perhaps instead looking for ways to improve efficiencies and reduce emissions at the existing plant, or to build a new plant near the old one to reduce community impacts.[15]

If the triple bottom line approach makes corporate decision makers aware of things that they ignored in the past, how much difference will this awareness make? Efforts to attend to the community date back at least to the utopian schemes of several early industrialists.[16] So, while many corporations have ignored such factors in their decisions, it is not because they are unaware of community impacts.[17] We can contrast the positive example of the pharmaceutical firm Johnson & Johnson, which has adhered to something like a triple bottom line (admittedly with little attention initially to the environment) since the 1940s, with the negative example of Brown & Williamson, a company that offered public reports on some of the domains that would be part of a typical triple bottom line approach while promoting cigarettes – products that are highly deleterious to human health.[18] Companies that are making strong efforts towards sustainability usually advertise that effort, but so do companies that are doing little more than advertising, a practice called "greenwashing."

## 7.2     Can the Triple Bottom Line Save the Planet?

Some corporations seem to be moving towards sustainability. Some corporations are acting in ways that are antithetical to sustainability. With little new federal policy promoting sustainability in the United States, Vandenbergh and Gilligan argue that private environmental governance may be "where the action is." How far can the triple bottom line and private action take us? How many corporations are acting effectively and in good faith? How many are greenwashing by taking credit for sustainability efforts while doing little or nothing? How many oppose efforts for environmental protection? Can sustainability be achieved via reform to the existing system or does sustainability require a transformation of the system?[19] To address these questions, I will start with a key issue about reforms such as private environmental governance – what do we mean by success? I will then review the standard answers that frame the debate about reform versus transformation using "first principles." Such arguments, invoking as they do rather simple models of how decisions are made, can clarify our thinking but are ultimately inadequate. We need to move towards models of variability and evolutionary processes.

To see how far corporate sustainability efforts can take us, we must answer four questions. First, has the approach led to more careful thought and analysis? The widespread adoption of sustainability initiatives would suggest the answer might be yes. Second, has the approach helped some companies do better? Box 7.1 provides examples of substantial reductions in environmental impact by individual corporations, and there are many more, including those documented by ecological modernization scholars. But debate about how much impact corporate action has and how much is greenwashing continues.[20] Third, has the approach improved overall corporate performance enough to have a beneficial impact on the planet? This is a more stringent test. It can be answered in the affirmative only if one can demonstrate that the answer to the first two questions is positive: that more attention is given to issues previously neglected and some corporations are doing better. It also requires a third and higher hurdle – that in the aggregate, or on average, performance is improved. Finally, the issue of reform versus transformation hinges on the hardest question: Will the changes reduce environmental stress enough to lower risks of climate and other environmental changes to acceptable levels? For example, can private governance bring greenhouse gas emissions down enough to keep climate change below a warming of 1.5° or 2°C, the thresholds usually seen as critical, or at least move us substantially in that direction?

---

**Box 7.1  Private sector climate actions**

There are many examples of attention to greenhouse gas emissions by major corporations. Among them:

- Walmart's and other retailers' strong promotion of efficient light bulbs played a major role in reducing US residential electrical consumption (see Section 7.3.1).
- Google has invested more than $7 billion in solar electricity generation across the world, the equivalent of all the electricity it uses.
- More than 300 companies, with $5 trillion in revenues and 14 million employees, have joined the Clean Energy Buyers Association, making commitments to shift to 90 percent clean electricity by 2030. So far, members have committed to about 11 gigawatts of clean electricity. This is about 1 percent of total US electricity generation.
- More than 4,000 organizations, including about 70 percent of the largest corporations in the United States, are members of the Carbon Disclosure Project that publicly reports their greenhouse gas emissions. It is supported by more than 700 institutional investors with about $100 trillion in assets.
- Triple bottom line approaches are included in financial risk analyses by firms that control about half the investments and debt in the world.
- While many insurance companies still issue policies for coal and oil development, more than thirty of the world's largest insurers will no longer cover coal development, thus discouraging further investment in coal.
- When the Trump administration offered new leases for oil and gas in the Arctic National Wildlife Refuge, no major bank was willing to finance such developments.[21]

The third question asks if performance has improved *over and above what would have happened anyway*.[22] New government regulations might reduce greenhouse gas emissions and new programs might reduce unemployment and enhance overall human well-being whether or not a company adopts sustainability goals. On the other hand, if there is no action on the part of government, then corporate action, while perhaps less effective than government action might be, is still better than no action at all.[23] Vandenbergh and Gilligan emphasize that we always must ask, "As compared to what?" The standard of comparison in judging actions, such as corporate environmental actions, should not be a hypothetical government policy but rather what is likely to happen in a given political context. We need to beware of Disney's law – "Wishing will make it so" – and avoid a fascination with the "bright, shiny objects" of an ideal new technology or social change and instead think through alternatives that are possible.[24] Part of that analysis can be understanding why some things are impossible or very difficult and using that knowledge to encourage change.

The dynamics are complex. Anticipated government policy might encourage private action. Private sector actions might block government policy; one motivation for private action by corporations can be to prevent regulation or other government action. The same logic suggests that small steps taken by consumers, such as installing high-efficiency light bulbs, might block further energy conservation actions or even lead to increased consumption. I will discuss these "spillover" effects in Section 7.3.2.

Can private environmental governance "scale up" to make a major contribution to, for example, reducing greenhouse gas emissions? Over time, will practices that reduce emissions spread so that the overall impact becomes substantial? To answer those questions, we have to think about what influences the population of corporations making decisions about emissions.[25] Let us examine what the population looks like and in particular how much variation there is in it.

Zipf observed that in many languages a few words are used with immense frequency, some words are used rarely and others have frequencies between the extremes. He argued that this phenomena of "disproportionality" is common in many human phenomena and may be a general feature of human action.[26] Freudenburg rediscovered Zipf's law in looking at pollution for US industrial plants. The most polluting industrial facility in his analysis was a fertilizer plant that generated 273 times the average amount of pollution from such plants. More telling, it produced more than 1,000 times as much pollution per job created than the national average. There seemed to be nothing in the activities undertaken at that plant that required this much environmental impact. Rather, the disproportionate impact seemed a result of ill-informed, uncaring or inept management. In extensive analyses, Grant, Jorgenson and Longhofer have documented that some electric power plants produce greenhouse gas emission that are vastly larger than is typical and investigated the reasons these plants are outliers.[27] Heede estimated that more than 60 percent of the greenhouse gases emitted since 1854 have come from the ninety largest producers of oil, natural gas, coal and cement. Such outliers producing disproportionate amounts of pollution are the antithesis of sustainability. It would be interesting to conduct the same kind of analysis to find the outliers at the other end of the spectrum: the corporations that rate high on all three domains of the triple bottom line and that are thus exemplars of that approach to sustainability.[28]

Variation of this sort is important for two reasons. First, it implies a different approach to environmental policy than might be appropriate if corporations were more uniform. Policies could be targeted at where they will have the greatest impact. While there is some reason to focus on the behavior of the average firm, a "one-size-fits-all" strategy may not the most effective approach. If the heavily polluting corporations are only marginally profitable, and depend on antiquated processes or equipment to keep costs down, any strategy that raises their costs may cause them to abandon polluting activities.[29]

Variation is also of great theoretical importance. McLaughlin reminds us that some theories tend to explain variation as deviations from a standard pattern or an ideal type.[30] Others see nothing but variation without underlying structure. Neither approach is satisfactory – he encourages us to think in terms of populations of individuals, corporations, organizations and understand both why they vary from one another and what shaped the dynamics of change in the population. This "population" approach I described in the Introduction is at the heart of evolutionary thinking. It moves us from an abstract debate about capitalism or free markets to analysis of ongoing dynamics.[31] In the case of individual corporations, the approach emphasizes that some corporations are sincerely committed to the triple bottom line, some come along reluctantly, some are greenwashing and some reject the idea entirely and will try to block or subvert it.[32] We need to understand why there is variation across corporations and how the selection pressures from the actions of individuals, organizations and social networks favor some corporate strategies and disadvantage others.

Focusing on variation also allows us to rethink in less abstract ways the relationship between the political economy of a nation (and of the globe) and impacts on human well-being and the environment. The institutions of the political economy, including their norms, are selective regimes that shape the response corporations get when they act.[33] Understanding variation across corporations allows us to acknowledge that some corporations are simply trying to maximize profits. It also allows us to recognize that some corporations are "bad actors" – they create a massively disproportionate share of environmental damage and/or try to block efforts to consider the people or planet bottom lines.[34] There is also space for corporations that are working hard to achieve the triple bottom line. McLaughlin's perspective focuses us on how selective regimes in the form of laws and norms (expressed in public opinion and consumer decisions) reward and punish actions by corporations. What decisions are the current forms of laws and norms favoring? What rules will select for the kinds of behavior we want from organizations and individuals? What forms of regulation, law and consumer decision-making will enhance sustainability? How effective are social pressures and norms compared to laws and regulations?[35] And what in turn shapes the pressures, norms and rules that shape corporate behavior?

Both neoclassical economic theory and Marxist theory emphasize the importance of strong returns on investment in a capitalist economy. Profits are a dominant factor in the selective regime that determines whether corporations persist and grow or fail under both lines of theory. In most US states, the law for incorporation of a firm requires a focus on profits.[36] Management will have to justify social and environmental considerations through enhanced profits that flow from them. A firm that is held privately, without publicly traded stock, might seem to have more latitude to pay attention to goals other than profits.[37] So might co-ops. And since most large corporations are owned by a large number of stockholders, and many stockholders own shares of multiple companies, there is pressure to look beyond the profits of a single company (see Box 7.2).

> ## Box 7.2  Common owner theory and collective ownership
>
> Common owner theory argues that stockholders may have broader interests than a single corporation's efforts to maximize profits.[38] Large investment organizations own about 78 percent of stock publicly traded in the United States. These organizations, which include investment firms and pension funds, usually have a broad portfolio of stocks. They are recognizing that climate change puts many of the stocks in their portfolio at risk, so they have a profit motive for addressing climate change. They also have a strong influence on corporate actions. Given their broad interests, they may be motivated to force reductions in greenhouse gas emissions. For example, BlackRock and Vanguard, two investment firms, own about 14 percent of all Exxon stock. BlackRock has calculated that it will lose $6 billion if Exxon rapidly reduces greenhouse gas emissions. But the rest of its portfolio is expected to go up by $9 billion, for a $3 billion overall profit from Exxon decarbonizing. In 2017, BlackRock applied its leverage to bring about changes in Exxon's board of directors to make the company more attentive to climate change, but has since been pressured by Republican legislatures to back away from that stance. Many social justice and sustainability activists also use the ownership of stock as a mechanism to raise ethical issues at stockholders' meetings, hoping to influence corporate behavior.[39]
>
> Common owner theory examines the implications of broad stock ownership by profit-seeking capitalists. Other forms of ownership could lead to more thought about sustainability in corporate decision-making. Since all members own a co-op, the decisions of the co-op can reflect a broader set of values than the financial bottom line. Employee stock ownership plans lead to partial or sometimes full worker ownership of a corporation and might also encourage sustainability.[40] Democratic socialist political platforms argue that, since many corporate decisions have large societal impacts, the public, via government or other mechanisms, should have a say in those decisions.

Logical arguments can be made that corporate social responsibility, and in particular following a triple bottom line approach, will improve profitability and also that it will degrade profitability.[41] What does the evidence show us? A good deal of the literature on corporate social responsibility examines the profitability of corporations that consider social and environmental "bottom lines." My sense of this literature is that the results are very context-specific. Whether the pursuit of sustainability goals by a corporation enhances or degrades profitability seems to depend on the national context, on the industry, on the position of the firm in the industry, on the specific approach to social responsibility and on the measures of financial "bottom line" examined.[42]

Remember that both neoclassical economics and neo-Marxist perspectives argue that individual corporations will seek to maximize profits.[43] If that is so, policy can change the selective regime by making adverse effects on people and the planet costly so that those costs will be included in the profit calculations. Such strategies could include making a firm take account of the costs of pollution by mandating technologies, by limiting emissions or, in the approaches most favored by this line of analysis, via pollution taxes or tradeable permits for pollution. But the neo-Marxist tradition argues that the interests of profit-seeking capitalists are so powerful in shaping the political economy that these reforms will never be sufficient to achieve sustainability and that the need to seek profit produces never-ending growth that, almost inevitably, degrades sustainability. The contrast between reform and transformation lies at the heart of the difference between the neoclassic economic view and the neo-Marxist view. Both see the pursuit of profit as a fundamental driver of decisions. The neoclassical position believes that policy reforms can change selective regimes (e.g., by making pollution part of the costs to be assessed in decisions) to make important moves towards sustainability. The neo-Marxists argue that capitalists will use their vast political power to resist including pollution costs in the bottom line and that, in any event, capitalism requires growth and growth leads to further environmental degradation. I will return to these contrasts in Section 7.3.

In Chapter 3, we saw that in many circumstances the logic of the rational actor model may not be adequate to describe the dynamics of decision-making. So, too, the model that assumes that in the end only profit-maximizing corporations will survive is eloquent but may not be realistic. There is no doubt that some corporate leadership and some investors, perhaps most, are focused almost exclusively on profits and that the ability to generate profits is a strong selection pressure that causes some corporations to grow and others to disappear. It is not clear how strongly real markets select for a narrow focus on profit maximization. There is a lot of variation across corporations in their profitability and many corporations that do not yield the highest short-term return on investment seem to persist.[44] Investors have a diverse set of goals and even when seeking only profits may have different time horizons and views as to what matters for long-term profitability. And sometimes governments intervene to prevent bank-ruptcy. In many industries, rather than fierce competition among many corporations, a few corporations dominate, and their dominance buffers them from competition to a substantial degree, a return to the control of the market by the most powerful last seen in the nineteenth and early twentieth centuries. For example, by some metrics more than 90 percent of web searches are via Google and its subsidiaries (YouTube, Google Maps, etc.); Windows is the operating system on roughly 90 percent of desktop and laptop computers; Walmart makes about one-third of all grocery sales in the United States.[45] With strong dominance in a market, such corporations can have influence that breaks the dynamics of the simple forms of competition that underpin many economic models.[46]

Whatever theoretical arguments are made about corporate behavior, I think the evidence is clear that private environmental governance is leading some corporations to address sustain-ability problems and that some fraction of those efforts is yielding substantial benefits. Then the question becomes how large can that impact become? A very rough estimate is that, globally, corporations could voluntarily reduce emissions by about 1 billion tons, which is about 14 percent of US greenhouse gas emissions or about 3 percent of global emissions.[47] To put this in perspective, the goal of the Biden administration, the most ambitious target ever set by the United States for climate change, was to reduce US greenhouse gas emissions by 50–52 percent by 2030.[48] The promises made by countries at the Climate Summit in Glasgow in 2021, at their most ambitious, would reduce 2030 emissions to about two-thirds of what they are today. So, voluntary US corporate actions could easily be about 5 percent of the global goal or about 25 percent of the Biden administration goal.

We can also consider voluntary action by households and by nonprofits (e.g., churches) as potential sources of reductions in greenhouse gas emissions even in the absence of government action. We estimated "the behavioral wedge" (household behavior as one possible wedge for reducing emissions) could reduce US greenhouse emissions from direct consumption of energy in the household by 20 percent rather quickly. That amounts to more than 7 percent of US total emissions.[49] If we extrapolate to other rich nations and add the household wedge to the corporate voluntary wedge, we have perhaps 10–12 percent of the Glasgow goals. This is not enough to "save the planet," but it is a substantial contribution to addressing the problem.[50] In addition, such actions may push society towards tipping points where reductions are facilitated by positive feedback across types of actions, the spillover effects discussed in Section 7.3.2. Such effects might be more important than the direct impacts of small actions.

Even if private action by corporations is not sufficient to "save the planet," it may be a valuable part of a strategy to address climate change in particular and sustainability in general.[51] Ostrom has decried our tendency towards panacea bias in which any solution that is less than a perfect, total solution is rejected as inadequate.[52] Analyses of ways to reduce greenhouse gas emission use the idea that multiple "wedges" – multiple strategies for reducing emissions – must be deployed together since no one strategy will be adequate to reduce emissions to acceptable levels of risk. Clearly, private environmental governance is not a panacea; rather, it is a wedge in the sense that it can make a substantial contribution to reducing greenhouse gas emissions. So, private action can help move us towards sustainability but is not the only thing required.

The very rough estimate of 10–12 percent of the Glasgow goals assumes a particular mix of technologies and consumption patterns involved in voluntary action. With better technologies and substantial shifts in consumption, perhaps those reductions could be doubled or tripled, driving the world closer to meeting the goals. Pushing for reform in the current political and economic system, for example by establishing a price on greenhouse gas emissions, might be able to address climate change and other sustainability challenges. Still, it is reasonable to argue that even relatively strong policies within the existing system will be too little too late. The drive for economic growth and increased production could overwhelm attempts to achieve sustainability via reform. The triple bottom line reminds us that decisions by corporations have impacts beyond the corporation. Given that, while libertarians object, it seems to me reasonable to ask how we structure the rules of society, including the economy, to promote moves towards sustainability. I emphasize that government already structures the market; the question we must repeatedly ask is what goals we want to achieve with the interplay among government, market and the larger society. In the next section of the chapter, I want to think through arguments about the possibility of whether reform in the rules can save the planet or whether we must have a radical transformation of the current "system."

## 7.3    Reform or Transformation

### 7.3.1    Thinking about Change

What is the boundary between calling changes a transformation versus calling them reform? The conflict over the horror of slavery-shaped US history and is still reflected in US politics.[53] We can certainly interpret the Civil War and the abolition of slavery and the assertion of equal protection under the law for all citizens in the Thirteenth and Fourteenth Amendments to the US Constitution as transformational. We could also call it a reform since the Constitution was amended and the rebelling states were defeated and brought back into the Union. We also could see it as reform, since, while slavery was abolished, crushing discrimination was not, and the status of women and Indigenous people did not improve.[54] The "reform" and "transformation" labels may not be very analytically useful.

Small changes that seem minor can accumulate into larger shifts. The widespread adoption of LED lighting is not much of a transformation in the political economy. It required developing LEDs practical for lighting, introducing a new consumer product that was a close substitute for an existing product, marketing it (including aggressive promotion by Walmart and other large retailers) and its adoption with some consumer adjustment to differing spectra of lighting produced. By one estimate, the use of LED lighting globally reduced greenhouse gas emissions by 1.5 percent and in the United States reduced household electrical demand by about 18 percent below what it would have been.[55] Again, this is not enough to single-handedly "save the planet," but it is a substantial contribution from one simple money-saving technology. On the other hand, shifting entire economies from the use of fossil fuels to renewables will require massive infrastructure changes, could shift the global political economy as some regions are "winners" and some "losers" in the new mix of resource demand and have ripple effects throughout society.[56] Many envision still larger changes in which economic activity is not organized around profit-seeking and in which the consumption of environmentally deleterious goods and services becomes abhorrent. These are all evolutionary changes, some relatively minor, some rather massive, some can happen quite quickly, others seem to require change on a multi-decadal and multigenerational scale.[57] Analyses need to reflect that complexity.

Many discussions of "changing the system" are imprecise about what would be reformed or transformed. Discussions of systems transformation are mostly about transformations of capitalism, but over time and across places the political economies labeled capitalism are highly varied. As I argued in the discussion of the effects of the drive for profit, if the political economy is structured so that most corporations and most investors are primarily interested in profit, if they define profit narrowly in terms of a single firm and if the market is highly competitive, it is hard for corporations that divert resources to care for people and the planet to persist. If investors are not narrowly profit-maximizing, or if the market is not fiercely competitive, or if powerful investors are looking not at single corporations but large portfolios, there could be space for corporations following the triple bottom line.

The actions of individuals and organizations play out in a telecoupled global system.[58] Actions taken in one place often have effects elsewhere in the globe. Greenhouse gases emitted anywhere influence the climate everywhere. The context for decisions in one place may be shaped by international trade with distant countries. For example, Brazil, China and the United States are all tightly linked in the production, processing and consumption of soybeans. Decisions made by consumers, farmers, corporations and governments in each country have effects in the other countries. For large corporations, moves towards sustainability often place requirements on the supply chain of those who sell to the company, and those supply chains are global.

Some lines of theory, notably ecological modernization and environmental Kuznets theory, suggest that contemporary societies are reflexive – they assess risks from environmental change and enact reforms to mitigate these risks.[59] But how general are these phenomena and are they sufficient to be important in reversing overall stress on the environment to acceptable levels of risk? My assessment is that there is reasonable evidence that the environmental Kuznets curve pattern applies when the environmental stressor has substantial local impact, such as air and water pollution. But increasing affluence does not seem to reduce environmental stress when the problem is a global commons, such as climate change caused by greenhouse gas emissions.[60]

In contrast to these theories of reform, many scholars, especially those in the neo-Marxist tradition, argue that environmental stress is inherent in the global capitalist political economy. One of the earliest and still most influential of these arguments is Schnaiberg's idea of the "Treadmill of Production."[61] Schnaiberg's core argument, described in Chapter 2, is that after World War II, in the United States and most other industrial capitalist nations, a compromise was reached with labor that led to an increasing share of profits being allocated to workers and to social welfare. This made it especially important to be able to continue to treat the environment as a source of raw materials and a sink for waste without accounting for the societal costs of such actions. To maintain peace between labor and capitalists, growth in production was essential, leading to a treadmill of growth that could not be slowed down without risk of sharp conflict. Labor is in a contradictory position in this process: Workers are often the most affected by pollution, yet they can also be convinced that they have a common interest with capitalists in resisting environmental reforms.[62] Thus the inherent dynamics of contemporary capitalism will push for growth in the amount of economic activity and will resist efforts to reduce impacts on the environment to the extent that they reduce profits.[63]

There are many important variants of the argument that the contemporary capitalist political economy is incompatible with sustainability.[64] Some emphasize the structure of the global political economy and the ability of the most powerful nations to push adverse environmental consequences onto poorer and less powerful countries and onto the poorest and least powerful groups even in the affluent societies. For example, a lot of tire production was moved from Akron to places with weak labor and environmental laws. Thus the critique of political economy is deeply intertwined with environmental justice. Most analyses also emphasize the need for growth to keep the system stable. Other lines of critique center less on the systematic nature of the contemporary political economy and more on the accumulation of power in the hands of elites who serve their own interests with little attention to impacts on others or the biosphere – a sort of tragedy of the commons with huge disparities in power. It follows that anti-environmental policies are usually associated with the right, since the right tends to accept the accumulation of power in the hands of a few.[65] These theoretical differences are important, but the consensus is that a substantial restructuring in the distribution of power and of the formal and informal rules that guide societal decision-making will be required for a successful move towards sustainability. Reform will not be sufficient.[66]

The ethical stances underpinning policy proposals, including the call for systems transformation, are important. The calls for transformation are generally consistent with altruism since they emphasize inequalities and justice issues.[67] Aspects of the current political economy seem to generate inequalities both within and between nations, in both the distribution of power and in human well-being. Generally, libertarians see these inequalities as either an acceptable outcome of human freedom or a result of constraints on freedom rather than as causes of such constraints. Many utilitarian formulations allow for consideration of inequality, while a central theme of deliberative approaches is a situation in which decisions are made by processes that are fair in the sense of including all interested and affected parties.[68] So, some ethical stances find the contemporary capitalist political economy acceptable or even desirable while others reject it. But most evaluations of capitalism rest more on perceptions of the outcomes of the system – on factual analyses – than on arguments from first principles.

To what degree can reform fix the problems generated by the current system? Some theorists argue against reform on the grounds that every reform legitimates the system, dissipates efforts better spent on moving towards transformation and in the end does more harm than good. This seems to me an empirical question: What happens when reforms are enacted? Looking at changes in the energy system, and in particular, at household energy consumption, gives a sense of the debate about reforms.[69]

## 7.3.2 Spillover Effects, Rebound and Moral Disinhibition

The effects of taking an action might spillover to influence other decisions. For example, there can be "rebound" effects at the individual and household level.[70] If I take an action to reduce my energy consumption, such as installing LED lightbulbs, I may feel that I've "done my part" and become inattentive to other energy uses, perhaps feeling justified to set the thermostat for higher temperatures in winter and cooler ones in summer, or to take longer showers. Recall from Chapter 3 the work of Attari and colleagues demonstrating most people don't have very accurate understandings of energy use. That is one reason a consumer might feel that installing LED bulbs compensates for energy used in heating and cooling even though such uses are far more energy-intensive than lighting. Depending on the size of the increase in use and the amount of efficiency achieved by the more benign technology, the overall impact on the environment could increase because of what York calls "moral disinhibition" of the values that were motivating reduced energy consumption.[71] This spillover will reduce the beneficial impact of the more efficient technology and might even lead to an overall increase in impact. Spillovers might also occur across roles (see Chapter 1). Adopting energy efficiency measures in the home could lead to less interest in or support for policies that support reduction in greenhouse gas emissions.[72] Or perhaps adopting energy efficiency measures makes me less inclined to avoid using pesticides on my lawn.

Yet it is equally plausible that the effect of taking a pro-environmental action could be contagious in encouraging further pro-environmental behavior. Installing LEDs might make me more aware of my overall consumption or make me supportive of government actions to reduce greenhouse gas emissions. Taking an initial action highlights the values, beliefs and norms that support pro-environmental action and could encourage further action.

In a masterful review of the literature on spillover effects, Truelove and colleagues offer a comprehensive theory of how one action might influence another.[73] Their major point is that the importance of spillover will differ between decisions made using a form of the rational actor calculus, even when altruistic values are considered, and quicker decisions that are more based on emotions (System I decisions; see Chapter 3). York's moral disinhibition is a particular form of affect-based decision-making in which taking one action fulfills a moral obligation and can lead to negative spillover. Truelove and colleagues argue that taking one action may invoke an environmentalist identity (see Chapter 3) that could encourage further pro-environmental behaviors. Thus affect-based decisions could lead to either positive or negative spillover effects. Both negative and positive spillover can occur from rational actor calculations as well since the initial action will change the resources available and the ease or difficulty of subsequent decisions. They also note that the reasons for taking an initial decision matter – decisions that are perceived as driven by internal considerations, such as altruism, are more likely to produce positive spillover, while those driven by extrinsic motivations (costs, requirements) are more likely to produce negative spillovers. The ease or difficulty of both the initial decision and the second and subsequent decisions matters, with positive spillover more likely when a hard decision is followed by an easy one and negative spillover more likely when an easy decision is followed by a hard one. Truelove and colleagues' rich analysis makes clear that the factors that influence spillover are complex and need to be carefully specified theoretically. Empirical work on spillover needs to be attentive to alternative mechanisms that might influence it.

One of the most important spillovers might be between citizen action and consumer action, and there is little evidence for negative and some evidence for positive spillover, although it may be that the most impactful household actions reduce policy support.[74] In general, consistent with Truelove and colleagues' argument, the evidence is that spillovers depend on the decision taken. Sun found that purchase of Energy Star certified air conditioners led to further reductions in energy consumption, but consumption increased after the purchase of Energy Star dishwashers. In a meta-analysis of 1,120 estimates of rebound effects on transportation energy use, Dimitropolous and colleagues found that the size of the rebound effect varied with a variety of other factors, including income and gasoline prices, with an overall estimate that the short-term effect is a 10–12 percent increase in driving and the long-term increase is 26–29 percent. That is, in the long term, efficiency efforts achieve about 71–74 percent of the reductions in energy use that would have occurred without a rebound effect. Adua and colleagues find that some household efficiency measures do seem to reduce actual energy consumption but others do not. Overall, it is clear that spillover effects are complex and context-specific, probably have different short-term and long-term effects and will vary across both contexts and types of actions. Clearly, more research is needed and broad generalization are not warranted from what we know now.

Are reforms at the micro-level reducing overall human stress on the environment? That depends not only on the benefits (or lack thereof) of individual actions but also on how the overall political economy is changing. Part of the argument against reform, and especially against consumer action, is that such small changes block the potential for systems transformation. Some corporations and others who do not want large policy changes promote individual action and/or changes in consumption.[75] But it is not clear how prevalent or influential they are. Too often there is an implicit assumption that, for example, encouraging individuals to reduce their personal carbon footprints somehow displaces politics. But we don't know if that is true, and some good evidence suggests the opposite – consumer and citizen action reinforce each other.[76] Further, as Stern argues, those who are promoting system transformation and who dismiss reform may also be contributing to delays in effective action by dismissing, downplaying or ignoring the impacts of reform and individual action. We need much more research to unpack what is actually going on.

Debates about the effectiveness of reform and individual action are based on the implications for large-scale change. What do we know about reforms at the macro-level? Again, strong theoretical arguments need to be disciplined with evidence and detailed analysis.

### 7.3.3    Planetary Change

Have changes at the level of individuals, corporations and governments across the globe cumulated into reductions in stress on the environment? The dynamics of the biosphere ultimately depend on the amount of stress being placed globally and regionally via greenhouse gas emissions, transformation of landscapes, harvesting of ecosystem resources such as trees or fish or groundwater, the release of persistent pollutants and other human actions that transform the ecosystem and even biospheric processes. Identifying individual decisions that lead to reduction of stress on the environment is important and useful. We must also ask how these cumulate into global change.

The debate about reform versus transformation is central to the difference between theories that see progress in continuous reform and theories that argue the only way to avert dire environmental and ultimately human consequences is a radical transformation of the political economy. To engage these arguments, we have to examine what drives stress on the environment. Stress is the product of how many people are consuming, how much they consume per capita and how much stress is placed on the environment for every unit of consumption. The stress is generated both as goods as services are produced and used and as waste is disposed. These three factors are the scale, content and technology of consumption.[77] We can reduce total stress on the environment by reducing the amount of consumption, remembering that the amount of consumption is a product of human population size and per capita consumption. We can also reduce stress by changing what is consumed and by changing the environmental impacts of producing, using and disposing of what is consumed.[78] So, for example, the likely increase in human population from the current 8 billion to 9.8 billion by 2050 will tend to increase stress on the environment.[79] The amount of that increase depends on what the larger population consumes and how goods and services are produced, used and disposed. Population size matters. But how much it matters depends on other things.[80] Smaller population growth or even a decline in the size of the human population could reduce stress on the environment but the amount of reduction depends on consumption and the technology of production. There is a solid understanding of what slows population growth: access to contraception, women's empowerment, social welfare.[81] These forces are powerful, but they act on a time scale of decades and generations, so their contribution to reduced stress on the environment is long term. To avoid further biodiversity loss or very dangerous levels of climate change, we need change over the next quarter-century.

Shifts in what is consumed could reduce impacts even as population grows and can happen much more quickly than population change. For example, shifting away from the consumption of meat towards a more plant-based diet could potentially reduce stress on the environment even as population increases.[82] A shift in technologies could allow the same pattern of consumption with less impact. People could travel as much or more with less impact on climate if transportation emitted fewer greenhouse gases per trip through the use of public transportation, electric vehicles or other low-emissions modes of transport.[83] The discussion of household energy consumption is largely about providing a growing population with the same services from energy (heating, cooling, lighting, running household appliances) with less energy consumption by shifting technologies and how they are used.

Much of the discussion of limiting the magnitude of climate change emphasizes the adoption of technologies, especially solar and wind power, that provide energy with far fewer greenhouse gas emissions.[84] There is clear evidence that in most countries solar and/or wind systems are being installed rapidly and that overall renewable energy with low greenhouse gas emissions is a quickly increasing part of the energy generation portfolio. York and Bell ask the crucial question: Is the deployment of renewable energy technology a *transition* in the energy system away from more polluting forms of generation or are the new technologies an *addition* to older technologies?[85] But even if renewable energy technologies are an addition rather than a substitution, they might still be displacing polluting energy production facilities that would have been built instead. So, while overall energy consumption grows, the growth is less polluting than it might have been. But in the case of climate change, the consensus is that we have to reduce greenhouse gas emissions quickly and massively to avoid very high levels of risk. A slower rate of increase will still entrain unacceptable risk levels.

Some analyses indicate that the growth of renewable energy technologies is more a matter of addition rather than transition.[86] For example, York found that it took 4–13 units of renewable energy to displace 1 unit of fossil fuel energy. York and Bell properly caution against making too much of short-term trends, which, in the case of greenhouse gas emissions, can be influenced by shifts in efficiency and the technology used to generate energy but also by fluctuations in weather and the global economy.[87] From 2010 to 2017, global wind power production more than doubled and solar power production increased by a factor of thirteen. Clearly, great strides are being made in deploying renewables. Overall, fossil fuel use accounts for about three-quarters of greenhouse gas emissions, so it is still the dominant factor; and during that same period, global use of fossil fuels also increased by 14 percent. The very rapid increase in renewables is not keeping up with the demand for energy being produced by increases in the scale (population and affluence) and content of consumption. But total greenhouse gas emissions are also driven by a variety of other human actions, including agriculture, land use change, cement production and the use of fluorinated gases, so changes in demand and production could reduce those sources and contribute to reducing overall human stress on the climate.

Figure 7.1 shows the trajectory of global greenhouse gas emissions for the last three decades. The most important panel is the first one – total emissions. This is what has an impact on the planetary climate system and what must be reduced quickly to levels of risk considered acceptable by most who have analyzed the problem. We have made no progress on what ultimately impacts the planet. But it may be that the curve rises more slowly than it might have had energy efficiency, renewables and other strategies not been deployed. The second panel is emissions per capita. Here, we see a sharply upward trend has begun to flatten out and stabilize. The trajectory we were on has been halted. The third panel is emissions per dollar of gross domestic product. Here, great strides have been made. We generate far fewer emissions per unit of economic activity. The question for the future is how we accelerate the trends seen in the second two panels much more quickly so that, even in the face of some population and economic growth (the scale of human activity), we see substantial declines in total emissions.

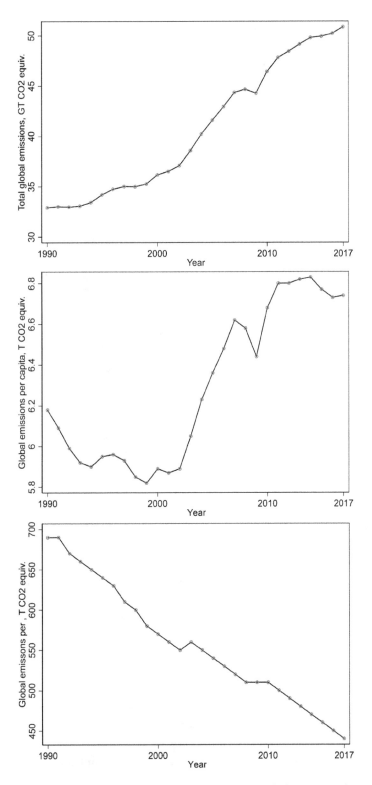

**Figure 7.1** Global total greenhouse gas emissions, emissions per capita and emissions per dollar of gross domestic product (GDP) by year Data from Olivier and Peters (2018).

## 7.4    What Does the Future Hold?

Some major stresses on the environment have been reduced over the fifty years since the first Earth Day. At the first Earth Day, the extinction of bald eagles was invoked as a symbol of the spread of toxic pesticides in the environment. But thanks to the heroic efforts of Rachel Carson and many others, many of the most problematic pesticides have been banned. The bald eagle flying near my home recently is an indication that, overall, they are recovering, although challenged by lead contamination mostly from ammunition used in hunting.[88] Despite the continued production of some banned ozone-depleting substances, the long-term decline in stratospheric ozone is reversing. The amount of the earth's surface in protected areas is increasing. So, reform has had some important impacts.[89] But even with declines in some stresses on the biosphere per person and per unit affluence, many kinds of overall stress are increasing. Greenhouse gas emissions, other shifts in biogeochemical cycles, ocean acidification and biodiversity loss have not been substantially reduced. Reforms so far have helped but not been sufficient.

Ultimately, the debate about reform versus transformation is a debate about what will unfold in the future, and "the future is an undiscovered country."[90] We can "backcast": think about where we would like to be in the future and then analyze what it would take to get there. The wedge approach to climate mitigation is an important application of this approach. Analyzing the risks associated with future atmospheric concentrations of greenhouse gases suggests targets for emissions that hold risks to an acceptable level. Then, changes in current practices can be examined to see what those changes might contribute to emissions reductions over time, acknowledging that some things (household energy efficiency improvements) can happen quite quickly, while others, such as major changes in physical infrastructure for renewable energy or public transport, will take longer. Each strategy is a wedge that contributes to emission reductions. If enough wedges can be implemented, risk reduction goals will be met.

The use of the wedge approach often stops with analyzing the technical potential of a change in consumption or technology. Technical potential (TP) is how much reduction in stress on the environment could be achieved if everyone adopted the practice. Two other factors need to be included in developing assessments of mitigation strategies using the wedge approach: behavioral plasticity (BP) and initiative feasibility (IF).[91] Behavioral plasticity (BP) is the ease or difficulty in getting key actors, including individuals, households, corporations, governments and other groups, to change. Evidence from efforts to implement reforms can give a sense of BP. For example, we know that well-designed programs to encourage home weatherization can produce substantial improvements rather quickly. In contrast, while carpooling can have a substantial impact on energy consumption and emissions when it occurs, the plasticity of driving patterns is relatively low, so it is hard to get a substantial portion of commuters to carpool.

Initiative feasibility (IF) adds an analysis of how easy or hard it will be to put in place effective policies and programs to encourage change. It is an assessment of the politics of making change. Those who profit from the use of fossil fuels have been very effective at blocking many efforts to encourage the use of renewable energies and reductions in fossil fuel use. Because of these efforts, for the last decade there has been little success in implementing a price on greenhouse gas emissions in the United States, despite wide acknowledgment that such prices are an effective and efficient mechanism for reducing emissions and significant efforts to implement them starting in 1994.[92] The IF of a carbon price at the national level has been very low. There has been less resistance to energy efficiency programs and efforts to encourage the use of renewables, so those approaches have higher IF.

Three other factors need to be included when evaluating proposed actions: equity/justice, pace of implementation and spillover effects. Actions should not impose greater inequities and should redress current injustices to the extent possible. Because slowing the pace of greenhouse gas emissions and other stresses on the environment matters, actions that can have quick effects may be preferable to actions that are slower. And actions that have positive rather than negative spillover effects are preferable. These six criteria – TP, BP, IF, equity, pace and spillover – can help find strategies that will bring about change.

Technical potential (TP), behavioral plasticity (BP) and initiative feasibility (IF) are useful in thinking about reform versus transformation. Will the current political economy allow the technologies and actions that can mitigate climate change and other major environmental stresses to develop and be deployed? Or does the structure of politics and the economy limit what we can achieve? Do constraints limit the BP of what individuals, households, communities and organizations can do, and does the culture push against decisions that reduce stress on the environment? IF is largely a matter of political economy, institutional constraints and culture, so how do those limit our ability to reduce environmental stress?

In Chapters 8 and 9, I will address the avenues I see for influencing change. Here, I acknowledge I have no roadmap to "the undiscovered country." Calls for system transformation have been in place for as long as I've thought about environmental issues. The legitimation of environmentalism and the emergences of pro-environmental values, of a robust environmental research community, the growth of environmental organizations, the creation and persistence of many environmental laws and regulations and the organizations to implement them as well as the growing pro-environmental actions of many corporations are hopeful signs. On the other hand, I see little evidence that we are transforming the global political economy towards more democratic and potentially sustainable forms. It is hard to see in the current global political economy the basis for the kind of societal transformations many argue are essential. Indeed, the turn of the last decade or so is away from democracy – but as with the time series of environmental stressors we must be cautious about inferring long-term trends from a few years of data. My judgment, albeit one that I accept is very tentative, is that in the next decade or so we are unlikely to see a radical transformation of the global political economy driven by sustainability.[93] But over that decade, substantial reforms will lay the groundwork for further transformation. Seeing successes, even if they are partial, will facilitate a shift towards improving well-being and reducing stress on the environment as core societal goals.

How far will reforms get us in reducing stress on the environment? So far, we seem to have made progress on some problems, particularly those related to pollution that harms human health. There has also been a lot of progress on sustainability in many local areas and regions. Reforms are doing much less to reduce the drivers that are increasing stress on the global environment. Still, the trends towards more sustainable technologies, production processes, consumption patterns and lifestyles, and towards more pro-environmental decisions, may be accelerating. Perhaps the lack of reduction in greenhouse gas emissions globally might be marking the end of an era. The very rapid increase in renewables, auto manufacturers pledging to go all-electric and the promise of some utilities and even countries to stop using coal are all promising steps. The apparent engagement with climate change by powerful organizations at the core of the capitalist economy may bring about substantial reforms driven by the logic of profit-seeking. We don't know how all this will unfold, and it depends a great deal on the exercise of political power to support or oppose such reforms. The kinds of company-, industry- and community-specific decisions that were in play in Akron in the late twentieth century are still with us. For example, the coal industry and coal-dependent communities in the United States, Germany and throughout the world exert powerful political influence to slow the transition away from fossil fuels. They are worried about the costs, risks and benefits they face under policies to encourage the transition. For them, local and industry-specific concerns outweigh the impacts on the planet.

There seem to be two broad theories about how transformation comes about, paralleling optimism and pessimism about spillover effects and confidence in reform versus calls for transformation. One view is that transformation comes about through the cumulation of reenforcing reforms. Increased democratization leads to increased efforts to reduce inequality that in turn reduce the political power of economic elites and thus allow for policies that reflect broader values and that encourage the spread of altruistic values since the costs of altruism are lower in an egalitarian society. The other view is that reforms produce only minor progress while sapping the political resources needed to bring about larger change. In this view, things have to get worse before they can get better.

We need better theory and empirical evidence on these issues. One might ask what nations, over the time spans for which we have data, have done the most to move towards sustainability – increased human well-being and decreased stress on the environment – and which have done worse (see Figure 2.4). What sorts of dynamics in the political economy have brought about those changes? Have they been revolutionary transformations or accumulated reforms?[94]

Researchers need to redouble efforts to understand the drivers of environmental stress and human well-being, and in particular the factors that influence the decisions of individuals, households, communities, corporations and governments. And for all of us as citizens, we should try to instantiate our values in actions, thinking about not only how our decisions have direct impacts on sustainability but also how they influence the decisions of others as individuals and in shaping organizational decisions. How we might do that is the subject of the final chapters of the book.

# 8 Influencing Decisions

On the first Earth Day in 1970, most talks ended with calls to transform our political and economic systems and our own behaviors to avoid environmental catastrophe. Calls for change continue: "Pathways limiting global warming to 1.5°C with no or limited overshoot would require rapid and far-reaching transitions in energy, land, urban and infrastructure (including transport and buildings), and industrial systems (high confidence). These systems transitions are unprecedented in terms of scale, but not necessarily in terms of speed." A recent global assessment of ecosystem services argued that "urgent transformative change [is needed] that tackles the root causes: the interconnected economic, sociocultural, demographic, political, institutional, and technological indirect drivers behind the direct drivers."[1]

Calling for change is useful, but we have to take the next step and think through how change occurs and what steps will be effective in bringing about change. We have to avoid Disney's law; wishing won't make it so. A call for change without an assessment of how to bring change about is of limited value. Research on social change can help us think through what strategies are likely to be effective in the short run and in the long run and design effective actions.

In this chapter and Chapter 9, I build on what we know about change, including both reform and transformation. Some of the changes we have seen over the last fifty years have been substantial. Norms for many kinds of equality have become widespread, although not universal. The rapid change in norms about rights for nongender-conforming people, including gay marriage, is an important example. So is the broad acceptance of the environment as a crucial issue.[2] Bigotry, discrimination and a rejection of environmental action persist but the changes that have occurred were only imagined by optimists a half-century ago. In addition to cultural change, some key measures of human well-being and the environment have improved. Clark and Harley point out: "By the early twenty-first century more than 80% of the people on Earth had life expectancies higher than those of people in the richest parts of the world as recently as 1950. And the fraction of the world's population living in absolute poverty was lower than it had ever been."[3] They emphasize that these changes have not benefited all; there are huge differences in human well-being across social groups and across countries. Those inequalities likely will be exacerbated by the pandemic, which may increase the global number of people living on less than US$1.90 a day by 80 million or more, reversing much previous progress on poverty reduction. Most of the impact will be in what are already the poorest regions in the world. In many nations, including the United States, income and wealth inequality have increased over the last forty years. The pattern of change towards sustainability has been uneven – some things have gotten much better on average, but those gains have not benefited all. And many of the largest stresses on the biosphere, such as greenhouse gas emissions, continue to increase. So, change is possible, although, as we saw in Chapter 7, we can debate how much change will be sufficient.

How do we promote change? In this chapter, I discuss what we know about influences on individual actions. I begin with decisions made by people in their role as consumers. Those decisions are a good starting point because the literature is well developed and because, while consumer actions alone can never "solve" environmental problems, consumer actions can have a substantial impact in reducing risks and can lay the foundation for further action. Citizen political action is more important than consumer action, so I will discuss that as well. In the next chapter, I will discuss the processes and arrangements that will allow us to make good collective choices about the environment. I am not going to attempt to discuss in detail the immense empirical literature regarding each assertion about how to influence decisions and bring about change. That is a task best left to careful literature reviews and meta-analyses.[4] Rather, I want to examine these approaches at a conceptual level.

The technical potential (TP), behavioral plasticity (BP) and initiative feasibility (IF) framework from Chapter 7 can be helpful in assessing change. Technical potential (TP) is the amount of change in, for example, energy consumption or greenhouse gas emissions that will result if a change occurs in behavior, including switching technologies. Behavioral plasticity (BP) is the proportion of the target audience for a change strategy that will act, for example the proportion of houses that are likely to get weatherized under a particular set of policies, opportunities and constraints, including prices. In our behavioral wedge work (see Chapter 7), we estimated this by looking at what had been accomplished by the most effective programs we could find. Much of what I discuss in this chapter is about mobilizing BP – finding ways to encourage decisions that move towards sustainability.

Finally, initiative feasibility (IF) is how likely it is, given the political realities, that a program or policy will be adopted and implemented. Many economists would argue that a tax on greenhouse gas emissions or a "cap-and-trade" system that places a price on carbon emissions is a very effective and economically efficient way to reduce emissions (see the extended discussion in Section 8.3). They are essentially arguing that BP is high in response to energy prices and would lead to changes in behaviors and adoption of technologies that have a high TP.[5] But in the United States at present, a national carbon pricing mechanism seems to have very low IF. The Clinton administration tried to introduce a carbon price in 1993, and while it had substantial congressional support then, two decades later we still have not implemented such a policy.[6] Looking only at TP and BP justifies an argument for carbon prices, but carbon prices might not be a viable strategy because of political resistance – low IF. I would challenge those who advocate a price on carbon to offer a realistic strategy that would overcome the political resistance to it. It might be possible to increase the IF of carbon taxes by understanding where the blockage points are and finding strategies to overcome resistance. This argument resonates with the tension between reform and transformation discussed in Chapter 7 – transformations may have high TP and BP but often seem to have low IF, at least in the short term. Our best course seems to be a mixed strategy of pursuing options that currently have high TP, BP and IF while at the same time trying to bring about more fundamental change that shifts IF.[7]

My ongoing example for the chapter will be household energy use (see Box 8.1). But it is important to keep in mind that political action shapes IF, and initiatives can change the context in which individuals make decisions and thus their BP. We can make progress with the changes, mostly reforms, that are feasible now. But we also need to change what is feasible so that larger transformations can occur. The next chapter will look at how we change initiative feasibility.

## 8.1    Influencing Sustainability

Tom Heberlein, a founder of environmental sociology, summarized his career in *Navigating Environmental Attitudes*.[8] Much of the book describes a situation familiar to environmental social scientists who engage in interdisciplinary work. In a room with only one or two environmental social scientists among a group of ecologists, wildlife biologists, earth scientists and others, the environmental social scientist is asked, "How can we change people's attitudes (or beliefs or values)?"[9] Tom's book summarizes his career by explaining how he reframed the question into more constructive and useful approaches.

In a sense, the same concerns motivate this chapter. We want to find effective ways to encourage behavior that supports sustainability. I will examine how each of the three schools of thinking about environmental decision-making reviewed in Chapter 3 approach this issue. I will then consider the ethics of taking such actions.

---

### Box 8.1  An example: residential energy efficiency

Household energy consumption may be the most extensively studied of all forms of environmentally significant consumption. The energy crises resulting from the OPEC embargo in the 1970s focused attention on how inefficient energy use was, including energy use by households.[10] This spawned some early collaborations between social scientists and physical scientists and engineers, including active groups at the University of California, Davis, Michigan State University and Yale, foreshadowing interdisciplinary work that has become typical of sustainability research.[11]

A key point of this early research is that no single disciplinary perspective would be adequate for understanding and informing policy about energy use by the household. The physical characteristics of housing units and the kinds of energy systems in them mattered. But so did the economics of consumption and the social psychological factors that shaped understanding of and decisions (or nondecisions) about household energy use. Household decisions are constrained by the physical infrastructure of the dwelling, much of which is out of the control of renters. Those who purchase manufactured housing ("mobile homes") often have had little choice but to accept poor weatherization as part of the package they are purchasing. So, income and social class matter. In addition, the policies and programs of utilities, lenders, developers and local, state and federal governments have tremendous influence on energy consumption and tend to lock in options for decades at a time. Housing discrimination ("redlining"), as discussed in the Introduction, traps some communities in inefficient infrastructure and increases their risks.[12]

From the 1970s into the 1980s, tremendous progress was made in understanding household energy consumption, the factors that influence it and the kinds of policies and programs that would and would not be effective. Lower energy prices combined with an active hostility to energy efficiency by the Reagan administration led to a loss of the funding that was essential to keep the interdisciplinary programs of research active.[13] Over the last decade or so, concern with greenhouse gas emissions from the use of fossil fuels has led to a resurgence of interdisciplinary research on household energy behavior.[14] Throughout this chapter, I will draw on that research for examples.

## 8.2  Information Deficits and Beyond

We can think of many examples of decisions made by individuals that can either facilitate or impede sustainability. For example, we know that household energy consumption in the United States is inefficient – the household could save money and use less energy while still receiving the same benefits from energy use. The same holds true for industry and government. The problem is called the energy efficiency gap – there is a gap between what would make economic and environmental sense and what is happening. Why does the gap exist and what can be done to close it, to change decisions and behavior? This is not a problem unique to sustainability. Nearly every domain of public and private policy includes efforts to change decisions and behavior. Political campaigning and marketing are largely focused on finding ways to influence people's decisions – efforts that are often corrosive to sustainability, although there are also efforts to deploy advertising in support of sustainability.[15]

The information deficit model is likely to be proposed early on in the discussion of how to influence decisions (see Chapters 6): "If members of the public, or other decision makers, knew what I knew, they would make the 'right' decisions, that is the decisions I want them to make." This model is incorrect in several ways I will detail next. Many who want to influence decision-making realize that the information deficit model is inadequate.[16] But often a slightly different form of the standard model applies: change people's attitudes or values or something else to get people to "do the right thing."[17] I am reminded of Strother Martin's character, the Captain, in *Cool Hand Luke*, admonishing Luke to "get your mind right" and noting, "What we got here is failure to communicate." I will turn to those efforts in Section 8.4.

There are some circumstances when a lack of information is indeed a constraint on behavior, as we saw in Chapter 3.[18] A program that provided accurate information about household energy use could have an important impact on the consumption of those who want to save energy[19] But three issues prevent simply providing information from being effective in many circumstances.

First, structural constraints limit decision-making. No matter what I know about the benefits of organic food, I can't buy organic if I can't afford it or if stores near me don't carry it. No matter what I know about the benefits of an electric car, I can't buy one if I can't afford it. Even if I can afford it, if I have to drive trips of several hundred miles such a vehicle is not yet a viable option.[20] These structural constraints not only influence the effectiveness of a policy or program; they also raise concerns about fairness. Some groups are simply left out and in many cases bear higher long-term costs as others adopt more efficient, money-saving practices.

Second, people hold different values, beliefs and norms. Even with a common understanding of the facts, such differences can lead to differences in what actions people feel should be taken and who they feel should take them. Two people may agree about the easily verifiable (ostensible and repeatable evidence in the language of Chapter 4) lower greenhouse gas emission of a hybrid over a conventional vehicle and both may be able to afford the hybrid. But they may differ in beliefs about whether climate change is happening, about whether or not it is largely human-caused and about the impacts it will have. The evidence about each of these is much less ostensible and repeatable than the information about the car. And even if they agree about all that, differences in values and norms may lead to disagreement about whether it is a good idea to reduce emissions.[21]

Further, we know that people prefer to interact with those who have similar views and avoid those who have conflicting views – the problem of biased assimilation, homophily and polarization (BAHP). There is a growing body of evidence on the importance of social network ties on decisions we make as consumers that parallels the literature on how our social networks influence our decisions as citizens.[22] Both descriptive norms (what are others doing?) and prescriptive norms (what do others think I should do?) are based on perceptions of others, so it is not surprising that communication with others directly will have strong effects on behaviors. This in turn can be used to build communication efforts that convey what trusted others are doing. Many science communication efforts could benefit from a better understanding of network structure and evolution.[23]

## 8.3 Getting the Incentives Right

If an economist is present at these discussions, they will usually suggest that the best approach is not providing information or trying to change values, attitudes or norms. Rather, they are likely to make the case for getting the incentives (i.e., the prices) right.[24] There is an ethical logic for this approach based on utilitarianism. In a perfect market, prices reflect the accumulation of individual choices and thus reflect the social value of a good or service. One of the central points of environmental economics is that, for many goods and services, the markets are not perfect and so the prices do not reflect the true social value (which can be a social cost) of a good or service. I will discuss this logic in Chapter 9. But the core idea is that we often damage the environment, and that may be because we have not captured the true social costs of that damage in the prices of goods and services. If we change prices, we can change behavior.

One argument in favor of using prices to change behavior is that price changes are relatively easy to implement compared to directly regulating behavior or technology. When the price of fossil fuels goes up because we have put a price on greenhouse gas emissions, the costs of everything that uses energy will also go up. As a consumer, I pay more for energy and other things and must shift money away from other things that give me utility. I will try to find ways to cut back on energy use.[25] The policy makers don't have to figure out what I should do – that is left, for better or worse, to the consumer. Corporations providing goods and services face the same problem: Their costs for energy have gone up and they will have an incentive to cut their consumption. A change in prices pushes them to find ways to use less energy but leaves to them figuring out how best to do that. There is a presumption in the argument for prices that no one will know better than the energy user how to become more efficient once higher prices encouraged them to do so. There is the additional assumption that the higher prices create a financial incentive for innovation, encouraging the invention of new ways to save energy.[26]

Changing prices is certainly worth considering as a mechanism for shaping decisions. But we need to pay attention to the flaws of price-based policies. First, we know that while prices influence decisions, they are not the only or even the most influential factor in every context. The price elasticity of demand – the amount of change in use that comes from a change in prices – for an environmentally damaging form of consumption can be quite low and can be different in the short term than in the long term. Even for a substantial increase in prices, the consumption might change little.[27] There are several reasons for this.

In a classic study, Stern and colleagues show that programs to encourage home weatherization to save energy had results that differed by a factor of eight even though they all offered the same financial incentives.[28] The way the programs were delivered mattered tremendously. With colleagues, I have argued that substantial reductions in greenhouse gas emissions could be achieved by well-designed programs to encourage energy efficiency but that most programs are not well designed and thus achieve far less than they might. Access to useful information from trusted sources can be far more influential than prices.

Emphasizing incentives and especially prices can also shift how people frame the situation and make decisions. Asenio and Delmas encouraged households to reduce energy consumption.[29] One group in the study was given information about the number of lives saved from reduced pollution. The group significantly reduced their consumption. But providing another group of households with information about cost savings led to *increased* consumption. I suspect this is because the information about lives saved encouraged an altruistic response while information about cost savings encouraged a self-interested response. Since the amount of money saved per month by reduced energy consumption was modest, it seemed to matter little, while perhaps the altruistic appeal of saving even a few lives seemed important.

Second, changing prices has impacts on the distribution of income and wealth, often increasing inequality, as noted in Chapter 7. The impacts on a hypothetical average individual does not capture the impacts on the most vulnerable. A change in energy prices that might motivate households near the median income could place a substantial burden on lower-income households and be ignored by the most affluent households who may be most profligate in their energy use. The most affluent have vastly more impact per household on greenhouse gases and other stresses on the environment than the less wealthy.[30]

As Chen has noted in her work, low-income households tend to spend a higher proportion of their budget on energy, often live in inefficient dwellings and are less likely to have fuel-efficient vehicles.[31] Many energy efficiency measures, while they might be advantageous in an abstract analysis, are simply not feasible for these households. We know that those under financial stress and facing discrimination spend a great deal of time and mental energy dealing with the problems of daily life, as noted in Chapter 3. So, not only do they have less money but they have less opportunity to get the information they need to become more energy-efficient. They may use risk-benefit-cost calculations that evolved under conditions different from those of the more affluent. Increased energy prices could be a substantial extra burden on those already under stress.

There are ways to design a price policy to work around these problems, so that a tax reduces inequality.[32] But we will have to make an effort to do so – a simple tax is likely to have regressive effects. When we examine not just changing prices but also the complementary policies needed to deal with equity issues, the logic of using changing prices to influence decisions may or may not hold up.

Big consumers, in contrast, may see energy costs as such a minor part of their budget that they do not notice the increase in prices. Whether or not it matters in terms of the effectiveness of the policy depends on the degree to which their consumption is disproportionately large. We know that for toxic and greenhouse gas emissions from industrial plants the largest emitters are so disproportionately large that targeting them might prove effective policy (see the discussion in Chapter 7 on disproportional emissions from power plants). But the impact of disproportionally large consumers has been less studied.[33] Since energy costs are a tiny part of their household budget, prices may have less impact on their decisions than prestige and image.

To summarize, the rational actor model perspective suggests that changing incentives and in particular changing prices is an effective way to influence decisions. The ability of markets to coordinate behavior is a major argument in favor of this approach. But we should be careful not to use unrealistic assumptions about theoretical markets in designing policies that will be applied to the complexity of actual markets. As I have emphasized repeatedly and especially in Chapter 4, moving from theoretical arguments to practical applications increases uncertainty and requires careful, contextually sensitive analysis. All policies will play out in complex situations where the logic of markets, government and communities are interacting, and effective policy makes use of those interactions. Not taking account of the complexity can lead to policies that are ineffective and unjust.[34]

## 8.4    Invoking Values, Beliefs and Norms

If the meeting Heberlein describes doesn't end with the discussion of incentives, then there usually will be calls to change people's values and attitudes. These terms are often used without much understanding of what they mean. That can lead to confusion and approaches based on conjecture rather than scientific evidence. Let us consider each of the concepts.

### 8.4.1    Values

Recall from Chapter 3 that in social psychology values are defined as the principles or moral standards of a person or social groups, judgments of what is important. Values are viewed as relatively stable over the life course; they do not change easily. The most important values for sustainability decisions appear to be biospheric altruism, altruism towards other humans, self-interest and sometimes traditionalism and hedonism. People differ in the weight they place on these values, and the resulting conflicts can be hard to resolve because it is difficult and threatening to talk about value disagreements. So, as a short-term solution, I suspect that changing values is not a very effective strategy for changing decisions. But consider three points about changing values.

First, while it is probably hard to change values through a policy intervention or program, it is relatively easy to draw attention to the value implications of a decision. Most people endorse to some degree each of the values that matter for sustainability. The differences across people are in the relative importance assigned to them. The way a decision is framed can change which values come to the fore in making a decision. The example in Section 8.3 of the difference between signaling the monetary value of energy savings versus the human lives saved can be interpreted in this way.

Drawing attention to some values over others is not foolproof. For many issues, any frame offered to influence decision-making will be part of a larger information environment that will often include counter-framing. Framings about climate change that have an effect when presented by themselves have much less effect when paired with the kind of contrary framing that is prevalent in the media.[35] This seems to be part of what has happened in response to the pandemic – any effort to frame a policy or program has to compete with existing framings.

Second, while it can be hard to change values quickly, over the span of generations values change substantially. Unfortunately, we lack consistent measurement of values over long spans of time, so it is hard to assess change directly, but we have indirect evidence from social change. In the United States, the change in civil rights and discrimination against "out" groups over the last century has been massive. Discrimination and prejudice remain, have crushing effects on the lives of many people and are corrosive to politics, but the changes in policy, in what is socially acceptable and in what most people feel they ought to do seem to be very substantial. I suspect some of this change is simply normative change – what is socially acceptable has shifted. But at least part of the change has also been a shift in values. The evidence for such value change may be most evident in the rise of biospheric values. This is an important value to many at present. Before the 1960s, I suspect only a small fraction of the population held biospheric values, although we lack the data to confirm this.

Third, while values are hard to change, we need to be more thoughtful about, and conduct more research on, how values change. The strong moral leadership and direct action of individuals and social movements can sometimes cause the thoughtful reflection that may change values.[36] I suspect that actions that are seen as courageous but not threatening are more likely to encourage reflection on values than more confrontational actions,[37] but we need to know more.

Aside from the sweeping influence of social movements, it may be possible to structure situations that encourage individuals to learn of the values held by others in a nonthreatening way and to reflect on their own values. This is one of the underlying goals of the deliberative processes discussed in the next chapter. The hope is that those who enter the process with different values, through a carefully designed process, can learn about each other's values and by reaching mutual understanding also achieve a consensus on how to move forward.

Finally, while values may be difficult to change, direct engagement via deliberation, civil conversations and increased awareness of the situation of others via media may be very effective at increasing empathy. Then empathy for those who may be adversely impacted can mobilize altruism, since most people seem altruistic to some degree. As noted in previous chapters, portraits of animals may entrain empathy for their species, and courses in animal studies seem very effective at increasing empathy. Exploring mechanisms that change empathy might provide useful guidance on ways to deploy it to bring about change.[38] And I will note in Chapter 9, struggles for social change might give consideration to how actions expand or contract empathy and thus encourage or discourage support.

### 8.4.2  Norms

Changing norms may be one of the most powerful tools available for changing decisions. Norms have a substantial impact on decisions, and they are not difficult to change, at least when compared to values.[39] Descriptive norms, our understanding of what other people are doing, are relatively easy to change by providing information and by offering opportunities to interact with others. Heberlein comes to much the same conclusion; he argues that of all the factors that might be influenced to change behavior, our best leverage point may be norms. Most organizations are more likely to adopt a change if they know that similar organizations have already made the change. Prescriptive norms, our understanding of what other people expect us to do, may be a bit harder to change than descriptive norms but still can be shifted by providing information about what resected others expect. Personal norms are our own view of what we should do. They are probably hardest to change since they are influenced by values and are connected to identity. But they are also influenced by descriptive and prescriptive norms. We take account of what we see others do and what we think others expect into our expectations of ourselves. In Chapter 3, I described studies showing that providing people with information about how much energy neighbors were using along with some positive feedback for low energy use (descriptive and prescriptive norms) increased energy savings.

### 8.4.3    Trust, The Theory of Planned Behavior and Nudges

A lack of trust can be a formidable obstacle to any change in decision-making (see Chapter 3). Biased assimilation, homophily and polarization (BAHP) open us to new information from those we trust and close us to new information from those we don't. In some cases, finding ways to provide information that will engage trust can bring about change. For example, many people are skeptical of home contractors and claims about home improvements. To encourage weatherization, it may help to set up a mechanism by which those wanting to make energy efficiency improvements have access to information about contractors from a source they trust and in a form they can easily use. Transparency and accountability around sustainability labeling on consumer products could also have a beneficial effect.[40] When we move from decisions in the role of consumer to decisions in political realms, trust becomes fundamentally important. Since the mechanisms for developing or restoring political trust involve public deliberation, I will leave discussion of them until the next chapter.

The theory of planned behavior (TPB) is one of the most commonly used approaches to influence decision-making. To review from Chapter 3, TPB targets a behavior with interventions specific to that behavior.[41] Using the TPB to change behavior is likely to influence only the targeted behavior, while appeals to environmental values might impact multiple decisions, although admittedly, as noted in the previous chapter, we are still learning about spillover effects from one environmentally significant action to another (but see the discussion in Chapter 7). If the goal is simply to change a very specific behavior, then the TPB may suggest intervention points. There is a vast literature applying TPB to environmental and sustainability decision-making. If the goal is to achieve broader changes, ultimately leading to value change, then focusing on norms, beliefs or values might serve the larger goal.

The rational actor model still underpins much of national and international policy. But some policy efforts are embracing the idea that in many of the decisions we make we are not fully rational calculators, building on the literature on heuristics and biases described in Chapter 3. This approach, often called "nudges," while sometimes described as innovative, is really a continuation of long-standing efforts by marketers and political campaigners to influence decisions and of social scientists to understand these processes. Professionals in these fields have long known that factors beyond rational choice can be powerful influences on decisions.[42] Certainly, these techniques can be deployed to encourage decisions that reduce human stress on the environment and improve well-being. In a sense, nudges are just designs to make sure that it is easy for people to understand the choices available and to minimize the difficulties of making a "good" choice.[43] But long-standing concern with how decisions are shaped by advertising and political campaigning makes it clear that intervening in decision-making requires thinking about what is ethical.

## 8.5  What Should We Do?

A basic principle for influencing decisions is that programs or policies should be well informed by research on decision-making. Another is that the design of a choice "architecture" for decisions needs to be very attentive to context.[44] There may be some general principles ("norms are powerful and most powerful when they are about peers," "people under-correct for deviations from the starting point anchor," etc.). But the specific context in which the decision will be made matters. An effective way to influence routine purchases such as groceries is not necessarily an effective way to influence purchase of long-lived appliances or transportation decisions or political decisions. What may be effective in reaching affluent members of the middle class may not be helpful when trying to engage those with lower incomes and other constraints.

We ought to design policies and programs so that it will be easy for people to make decisions that match their preferences, and easy to implement those decisions once made. Ostrom suggested that "design principles" could provide a way for making social science useful when processes depend greatly on context.[45] Her goal was to summarize and offer practical advice on how to govern commons. Paul Stern, Kim Wolske and I have argued that design principles, which have emerged in several areas of sustainability, are a useful way to summarize scientific understanding while respecting the intricacies of specific contexts. In Chapter 9, I will discuss design principles for public participation and deliberation. The idea of design principles makes it clear that efforts to influence decisions need to be tailored to the specific context in which they will be applied. There is no "universal" principle or approach.

The design principles for energy efficiency policy in Table 8.1 provide an example of how the idea can be applied to efforts to change individual behavior.[46] First, it is important to target actions that will have the greatest impact on energy consumption (high TP). Second, if actions have nontrivial costs, it is important to provide adequate financial incentives to overcome those cost barriers, especially because if costs are ignored those with the least resources are least likely to benefit from a program, exacerbating existing inequalities. Third, it is important to communicate in ways that will be effective with the target audience. Fourth, while information is rarely sufficient to drive a decision, it is always necessary and is best provided by a source credible to the decision maker and at the time the decision is being made. A long history of bias and discrimination means sources that are trusted by some groups may be viewed skeptically by others. Fifth, hassle matters, so steps should be taken to make it easy to act. Sixth, for many

**Table 8.1 Design principles for household energy efficiency programs**

(1) Prioritize high-impact actions (don't waste people's time and effort on things that don't matter much).
(2) Provide sufficient financial incentives.
(3) Strongly market the program.
(4) Provide valid information from credible sources at the point of decision.
(5) Keep it simple.
(6) Provide quality assurance.

*Sources*: Stern et al. (2010); Vandenbergh et al. (2010).

energy decisions quality is an issue – is a contractor competent? Is the new technology reliable? So, simple mechanisms to assure quality are essential.

The principles in Table 8.1 seem obvious – who would design a program without trying to make sure it is consistent with them? In some cases, programs are very well designed and action is easy. The US federal government's "cash for clunkers" program provided a financial incentive for getting old cars off the road to boost manufacturing, reduce pollution and improve safety and energy efficiency and was very effective.[47] In other cases, such as many programs intended to reduce greenhouse gas emissions by encouraging home energy efficiency upgrades or home solar panels, the policy as implemented seems to negate many of the design principles. Efficiency upgrades and home solar panels certainly have high impact in reducing greenhouse gas emissions. Sometimes the financial incentives offered are adequate, sometimes they are not. Often the programs are not effectively marketed, it can be hard to identify credible sources of information, the paperwork is often very complex and, as with any home improvement, it is hard for homeowners to know if the work is of high quality. Many programs have procedures and paperwork that were designed with deep suspicions about potential fraud and error but don't pay attention to how burdensome that makes the program for potential participants (and for the officials who must implement them). Programs that avoid these problems and align with the design principles provide an opportunity for entrepreneurs.

Individual decision-making is always constrained by context. What might work well for some groups might not work at all or even produce the opposite effect from what is intended with other groups. Further, while we know a lot about how to influence decisions in the short run, far less is known about what matters over the longer term. All of this needs to be addressed when developing a plan to influence behavior. Careful ethical analysis, that is, reflecting on values, is just as important as engaging the science. Once again, engagement with interested and affected parties through deliberation can be an effective way to ensure that the design principles are being applied in a way that is ethical and appropriate to the context.

## 8.6    Do the Ends Justify the Means? Are the Ends Justified?

Each of the traditions described in Chapter 3 offers insights into how to change behaviors. The more difficult issue is deciding when it is appropriate to use those strategies. Let us return to the room described by Heberlein. A group has gathered to determine how to influence decision-making.

I would suggest that the first topic of discussion should not be how to influence the decisions but whether it is appropriate to do so and who has a right to decide whether or not to influence decisions.[48] The ethics of intervention, of means and ends, is a very old issue and clearly I will not resolve it here. But perhaps I can clarify some of the questions that should be raised in trying to decide what is appropriate and what is not.

Is there strong value consensus among those we are trying to influence about desirable ends? That is, do the people who will be subjected to the policy or program tend mostly to agree that decisions should move in the direction being encouraged? Or is there great controversy about the issue? Strong consensus might exist around issues such as reducing infant mortality, about preventing cruelty and coercion to humans and other species and around many other issues. In other cases, such as limiting the magnitude of climate change or protecting endangered species, there may be far less consensus. We should be sensitive to moral consensus changing over time, sometimes as a result of efforts to change people's views. I will return to that in a moment.

Is there strong consensus about appropriate means for influencing behavior? Even if everyone agrees that reducing greenhouse gas emission is a good idea, there can still be very sharp differences about the mechanisms that should be used to do that. Here, I refer to ethical differences, not analyses of what is feasible and effective. But remember, in our typical way of confusing facts and values the arguments about ethics may often be cloaked in arguments about feasibility. For example, even among those who agree that greenhouse gas emission should be limited, some feel the only ethical way to proceeds is via carbon prices since that gives maximum play for free choice in the market. Others may feel that prices are inequitable and prefer mandates. Still others may feel that any government program other than providing information is unwarranted interference in individual decisions.

Imagine a two-dimensional space of strategies. One dimension represents the degree to which there is consensus about the ends – the kinds of decisions that would be made if a program were successful. The other dimension is the degree to which there is agreement about possible means to influence those decisions. This second dimension is, for most people, roughly equivalent to the degree to which the means are transparent and noncoercive. This two-dimensional space roughly maps the questions I have raised about ends and means. Anyone designing a program to influence decisions should try to find strategies that are in the quadrant of high consensus on means and high consensus on ends. Usually the group described by Heberlein has convened because there is a presumed high consensus on ends, at least among the conveners, or because the group is in some way mandated to act as if there is a consensus on ends or the group simply assumes that if they agree on ends that is sufficient.

Who is in the room trying to develop the program? The group might be composed of corporate employees and their consultants. They have a clear mandate about what behavioral changes are required and thus focus on effectiveness and, one hopes, the ethics of the means. The group might be composed of government officials. They may have a mandate via legislation or other forms of policy to achieve a goal and believe that influencing decisions is a good way to do this.[49] It might be a nongovernmental organization such as an environmental group that wants to promote energy efficiency or an animal welfare organization that wants to reduce cruelty to animals. In this case, the group often assumes either that everyone shares their ethical positions or at least that everyone should.

It is reasonable to ask about the basis for the mandate to influence choices. There is always some structure in which decisions are made, so some process will shape that structure. Thus it is probably best if those in the room are aware of the best science, perhaps as summarized in design principles. The process should also be reflective about the ethics of what it is doing. If the mandate was developed by a legitimate political process, then that may suffice. Even then, and especially when the mandate was not the result of a fair and competent democratic process, it seems appropriate to engage in deliberation with those who will be affected by the program. While such engagement is routine practice in public planning, it is much rarer in architecture and engineering. Marketing and political campaigning efforts extract information from target audiences. But such targeted research is not a deliberation that would allow those to be affected by a campaign, policy or program to have input in the design of the program. Such deliberative processes, linked to scientific analysis, are, in my view, not only important in designing contexts for individual choices but essential for influencing the larger, aggregate choices that must be made about societal decisions. I will discuss deliberation further in Chapter 9.

As far back as the first Earth Day, it was clear that individual decisions matter but that they are embedded in larger social processes that shape our values and our beliefs and constrain what we can do. In turn, it is individual decisions that shape the actions of organizations and groups, including social movements, governments, businesses and other organizations. For sustainability, our most important individual decisions are those that, in our various roles, influence organizations. In Chapter 9, I examine how we combine our individual decisions into a group decision, that is, how we come to take action together. The problems with individual decision-making still have to be addressed and lead to new problems as we try to decide together.

# 9    Influencing the Conversation

I served as a member of the Planning Commission of the Town of Grand Isle, Vermont, for a number of years. The role of the Planning Commission was to update the town plan.[1] The plan sets out zoning rules that limit how a property owner could develop and use their land, depending on where the land was located. Libertarians object to the government interfering with a landowner's decision about how to use private property, and many places in the United States do not have zoning.

In Grand Isle, there are concerns about sprawl development, degradation of the environment, the cost of housing, the costs of schools and town services and tax rates. Zoning affects all of these. For example, zoning determines where commercial developments with high traffic flows can and can't be located. So, zoning decisions have to balance differing views about the facts and differing values. Reconciling different values and beliefs is the fundamental problem in trying to come together as a group to make collective decisions. We must have a way of aggregating different and often conflicting individual views into collective decisions.

Land use decisions in Grand Isle are shaped by the three ways of making collective decisions I will discuss in this chapter. The market determines the price of land and what activities are economically viable. The Planning Commission and the Selectboard (the town council) hold hearings where the community discusses how zoning should change, a deliberative process. The citizens of the town vote to elect the Selectboard, who appoint the Planning Commission members, and the citizens also vote to approve or reject changes to the Plan once they are approved by both the Planning Commission and the Selectboard. Individual decision making comes into play as land owners make decisions about how to use their property but with constraints imposed by decisions made by the community as a whole.[2]

The most important decisions we make about sustainability are in our roles as members of groups. All our individual decisions influence and are influenced by networks of families, friends and neighbors and others whose views we consider in assessing facts and norms. But we are also citizens, consumers in markets and members of organizations. We influence the actions of governments, of corporations, of unions, of cooperatives, of social movement groups. Their actions can have great consequences for sustainability both directly and as their actions influence the context for other decisions. To understand decisions and sustainability, we have to understand how we make decisions in groups. That is the subject of this chapter.

Some political forms avoid this problem. Monarchies assume that the decisions of a legitimate monarch reflect the will of God or the gods or the will of heaven. Even without invoking a theological justification, dictatorships are based on the logic that the dictator knows best.[3] The idea of democratic decision-making that has become dominant among nation-states in the later twentieth and early twenty-first centuries has largely displaced this approach (see Chapter 2). The essence of the democratic ideal is that all parties interested in or affected by a decision should be able to influence the decision.[4] But how should individuals exert that influence and how do we aggregate individual preferences into a collective decision? I will review three traditions: aggregating with market prices, with votes and with conversation.

It is important to differentiate ideal types, utopias that perfectly match theoretical arguments, from reality.[5] Remember Ostrom's point: Nearly all real governance systems in the contemporary world are mixtures of markets, government regulation and community control. It is useful to discuss prices, voting and deliberative processes in the abstract. But the performance of actual institutions is more important. Changes in the way we make collective decisions always build on the past, and the past is always a complex hybrid. Even when the constitution of a society is written from scratch, existing institutions and norms usually persist even if they are modified.[6] The evaluation of actual institutions is a complex problem in macro-level analysis. So, for the rest of this chapter, I will work at the edge between the ideal type and reality.

## 9.1    Is the Price Right?

Chapter 8 discussed prices as a way to influence individual decisions. Here, I discuss markets, and the prices that emerge from them, as a way of aggregation across individual differences to reach collective decisions. The core idea is that in a competitive market the prices that emerge from individual decisions are a good way to combine differing views about facts and values. This argument is justified by utilitarian ethics as implemented in micro-economic theory. To review, we can start with the argument that people should be free to make their own decisions and that making such decisions to pursue their own objectives is good for the individual. Utilitarians share this view with libertarians/anarchists, as discussed in Chapter 5. For an anarchist or libertarian, the best policy is one that gives everyone freedom to pursue their own interests, and nothing else matters.[7] But there is an additional argument in utilitarianism that is not present in most libertarian views: that the best policy is one that makes the sum of utility, across all affected individuals, as large as possible.[8] But how do we measure utility in a way that allows us to sum across individuals?

Here, a third argument engages. In a perfect market, prices will reflect social preferences and will lead to the most efficient allocation of resources possible. "Most efficient" means no different allocation of resources would improve the aggregate utility. Under this logic, the workings of the market have allocated resources in a way that is ethically defensible. So, the market itself becomes the way we make decisions as our actions shape and are shaped by prices. Market prices can also be used to influence the other two modes of decision-making, a point I will take up in Sections 9.2 and 9.3.

Most advocates of markets as a mode of decision-making are aware that real markets, shaped as they are by history and the exercise of power, differ substantially from the ideal. I want to emphasize two aspects of these distortions. First, prices don't give much weight to those who have little or no power in the market. Both within countries and across the globe, the voice of the poor is muted while the voice of the affluent is loud. It is sometimes said: "The poor do not create a demand for food." Poor people need food. But because they have little money to purchase food in the market, their need does not impact the market. The result can be food deserts – areas in which there are few opportunities to buy food at all, let alone high-quality food at reasonable prices. Discrimination in the form of redlining (see the Introduction) limits the economic and political power of those communities and limits their ability to create demands through either the market or politics. Nonhumans also don't create any market demand. Ever since Bentham, some utilitarians have argued that the suffering of nonhumans deserves ethical consideration. But the negative utility (suffering) of animals is ignored in a strictly anthropocentric application of aggregating utility via markets.[9]

The second problem is that some things we value are not traded in the market and have no price but cannot be assumed to be of zero value (see the discussion of externalities in Chapter 5). When a bald eagle spent a few minutes soaring near our yard, we enjoyed the experience and knowing that bald eagles exist and are recovering from near extinction in the 1960s. Preserving eagle habitats costs money, so it would be good to have an estimate, in monetary terms, of my preference for having eagles to balance against the costs. Environmental economists have developed rather sophisticated ways to estimate the value people place on aspects of the environment that do not have a price based on market transactions or where the market price is not to be trusted as a reflection of social values.[10] Amuakwa-Mensah and colleagues estimate that in affluent countries the value of eagles is about $60–85 per household, which for the United States as a whole is about $8–11 billion dollars.

Such estimates of nonmarket values in economic terms are key elements in benefit-cost analysis as described in Box 5.4. So, even for government action, prices play a central role in one of the most influential forms of policy analysis. Benefit-cost analysis is structured to follow the norms of science. But, as we have seen, those with political interests in the outcomes of a scientific analysis will participate in debates about how to do the science.

Much of the literature on environmental policy tends to either romanticize or demonize markets. Conservatives, neoliberals and other advocates of the free market feel that the market is the best answer to most problems of collective decision-making. They rely primarily on arguments following an anarchist logic that free choice is a fundamentally good thing, as well as from the belief that markets allocate resources efficiently. They tend to ignore problems of market imperfections and inequality.[11] In contrast, liberals, progressives and other critics of the market emphasize these imperfections, especially the unequal distribution of power that accompanies markets. But they tend to ignore the ability of markets and prices to coordinate complex transactions and the difficulty of doing that by other means. The coordination function of markets, compared to the ineptness of some implementations of state control over the allocation of resources, has long been a central justification for letting markets dominate decision-making.[12]

The idea that markets are efficient assumes a world of rational actors working with perfect information in perfect competition. We have to examine what happens in the real world when we use markets to make decisions. An example comes from the catastrophic energy shortages in Texas in the winter of 2021.[13] The Texas energy system is run largely on market principles. Some suppliers let the price to consumers fluctuate with the overall market price. As a result, some households received energy bills of thousands of dollars as shortages drive the price up. In theory, consumers should respond to the signal of increased prices by reducing their consumption, thus reducing demand. That is the intent of using prices to influence decisions. But in the real world, it can be hard for consumers to monitor rapid changes in prices, there is a time cost of doing so and the only quick response consumers can make is to reduce consumption, which is problematic in the face of record cold weather. The price system "worked" but with the social consequence of wiping out the savings of some consumers and leaving many suffering from the cold.

I think markets and prices can be useful. But an overall structure of rules has to avoid the adverse consequences they can create. Rules shape even the most deregulated market. The challenge is to find rules that will provide some of the efficiency and coordination benefits of markets while also achieving some of the other goals we have for decision-making. In the case of the Texas utilities, perhaps a limit to how quickly consumer costs can rise along with an increasing cost per unit consumed would encourage efficiency while providing a safety net to protect low to moderate income consumers from devastating costs rises. In my own experiences, utilities organized as co-ops of the users do a good job of balancing all the concerns that arise, perhaps because there is ongoing discussion between staff and member/customer owners.

## 9.2    Voting

In the early twenty-first century, democracy has near universal legitimacy as a mechanism for governance.[14] Voting is at the heart of most notions of democracy, and even those who want to sharply limit access to voting argue that they are trying to protect democracy. The origins of Western thinking on democracy, in Mytilene and Athens, involved direct discussion and participation by a small segment of the population. Many historic and Indigenous forms of governance involved deliberation, sometimes with very broad participation. Some remnants of direct deliberative democracy remain in the contemporary world as a supplement to voting – for example, in Vermont town meetings.[15]

Problems of scale preclude using direct deliberation by the public for decision-making in most twenty-first-century democracies.[16] In some jurisdictions, the public can vote directly on ballot measures that enact laws. But most governance is via representation, with citizens electing representatives who then engage in deliberation to enact laws, including allocating budget and forming policy. After the first US Census in 1790, on average each member of the US House of Representatives represented about 35,000 people.[17] At present, since each state is guaranteed at least one member of the House, the lowest population per representative is for Wyoming, with one House member representing a bit less than 600,000 people. The largest states have about 700,000–750,000 people represented by each House member.

One person might be able to assess and reflect the views of a community of 35,000. It is unlikely that they can do this for 700,000. The form of democracy in the United States has changed to one of mass politics and representative democracy, and that increases the importance of funding to finance campaigns since voters have to depend on media rather than personal knowledge to assess candidates. In 2020, more than $20 million was spent on the average campaign for each of the 435 seats in the US House of Representatives.[18] The affluent have an advantage in providing those funds and use them to promote their interests. For example, in

2020 more than 80 percent of donations (more than $60 million) from the fossil fuel industry went to Republicans, who have generally been opposed to action on climate change.

While a substantial fraction of social science research is devoted to governance and politics, a key point was made by Weber in 1919 in his "Politics As Vocation."[19] In large modern democracies, politics has become professionalized. Those practicing this profession include not only elected officials and the employees of government bureaucracies but also many people in the policy system that forms around all branches of government. This network includes lobbyists, analysts, consultants, attorneys and those who work as employees or volunteers for social movement groups.[20] The scale and complexity of contemporary societies, the amount of work to be done, the amount of power wielded by the government and the diversity and depth of expertise needed make such professionalization inevitable. But it also ensures a great distance between a citizen deciding how to vote and the collective decisions made by government.

Voting is a commons dilemma. The likelihood that the results of an election will change because of my vote is very small and there is some time and effort involved in voting.[21] So, a narrow rational actor model might suggest I should not bother to vote. Active campaigns that try to make it easier or harder to vote are aware of this. Groups already facing a lot of challenges from a lack of resources and discrimination can be discouraged from voting if obstacles are placed in their way, and that can skew whose interests are represented in an election, an ongoing theme in this section. Representative democracies are also subject to the principal-agent problem. In most ethical justifications for representative democracy, elected officials (the "agents") are supposed to look out for the best interests of those they represent (the "principals"). It is very difficult for us to be sure that our elected representative is making decisions that represent our interests. The professionalization that comes with the scale and complexity of contemporary societies exacerbates this. Those pursing politics as a vocation are far more likely to have interactions with others pursuing the same vocation than they are with typical citizens. How many of us have had a conversation with our representative in the US Congress or even with someone who represents us in the state legislature?[22]

This means that when we make decisions as citizens, we usually are deciding not what policies we prefer but what individuals will make the policy decisions. They are almost always individuals with whom we have had no meaningful personal contact. What information we have about them has to be extracted from a huge stream of media that is mostly intended to persuade us for or against a candidate, using all the tricks of persuasion discussed in Chapter 3. We need to pick the bundle of policy positions, alliances and ideological stances that come with candidates; we cannot mix and match them to our liking.[23] Recall the complexity of even a fairly simple decision like buying an apple in Chapter 3. Voting decisions are even more complex. Political parties help simplify the decision. If I have a sense of how political parties align with my values, I can substitute that for knowledge of the candidates, assuming that the parties have done a decent job in screening candidates. But here again, the problem of biased assimilation, homophily and polarization (BAHP) has a strong influence on how we make decisions about how to vote.[24]

Over the last few electoral cycles in the United States, legislative districts have been substantially reshaped – gerrymandered – to create "safe" electoral districts for the dominant party in that state.[25] In gerrymandered districts, the nominee of either the Republican or the

Democratic primary has a very high probability of winning the general election. This has at least two adverse effects on voting as a means of aggregating preferences. First, it means the political debate and contestation that influence voting occurs within rather than between parties. The debate will be more ideological than if candidates had to appeal to a wider suite of voters. Second, it effectively disenfranchises many voters who are in a minority in a safe district for the majority party. This happens at the national level in the United States as well. Because every state has two senators, the twenty-six smallest states, with less than 18 percent of the population, are represented by fifty-two senators, a majority. The nine largest states with 51 percent of the population are represented by only eighteen senators.[26]

The literature on voting is substantial, sophisticated and complicated.[27] I do not engage it at more than a superficial level for two reasons. First, how political institutions perform is beyond the scope of what I can cover here. Second, I believe things are in a state of unusually rapid change. In the United States, the loss of the "fairness" doctrine for broadcast media, the deregulation of campaign financing and the rise of the web and social media have altered political campaigns. Mechanisms for voting, including early in-person voting and voting by mail were becoming the norm across the United States. More recently, campaigns oppose these efforts and try to make it more difficult to vote, a continuation of the long, reprehensible tradition of suppressing the rights of African Americans and others.[28] Hundreds of smart and highly motivated people and the organizations where they work are actively combatting each other to gain political power. That contestation may be a routine part of human history since the first stratified societies. But new technologies along with increases in scale and complexity make the current situation very chaotic and very hard to predict.

Scholarship on the political implications of social media, especially around sustainability issues, is evolving rapidly, as are the social media themselves and attempts to use them for political ends.[29] It appears that the sorts of BAHP that characterize other interactions are commonplace on social media. But it is not clear that current political polarization in the United States is driven by social media – the greatest polarization is among those least active on social media. Conventional news coverage can drive activity on social media so traditional forms of political communication are sometimes driving the new forms of communication. There is also some evidence that efforts by social media platforms to curb false content have had some beneficial effects. Overall, the research to date indicates that social media primarily amplify and perhaps accelerate tendencies already observed in political discourse. But I emphasize new research on social media impacts is emerging rapidly, so these tentative conclusions could shift.

Direct democracy is an interesting contrast to representative democracy. In direct democracy, the electorate votes on a law or a constitutional amendment, bypassing the legislature.[30] In Switzerland, direct democracy in some towns dates back to the thirteenth century and was added to the Swiss Constitution in 1847. Over the course of the twentieth century, some degree of direct democracy has emerged in twenty-seven US states to supplement the representative process. The details vary across states but generally the electorate can vote directly on laws, sometimes in the form of amendments to the state constitution. In many states, the legislature has mechanisms for modifying the results of the process.[31] The democracies of the Greek city-states used this kind of direct democracy, as did many Indigenous societies.[32]

Direct democracy avoids the problem of having a body of professionals carry out the task of enacting laws. But it doesn't remove professional specialists from the process of making collective decisions. In nation-states, most laws are quite complex. While the law to extend the national debt passed in 2021 (PL 117–730) is less than fifty words, the Infrastructure Investment and Jobs Act (PL 117–58) passed the same year is more than 1,000 pages long. This complexity comes in part from each law interacting with other laws. It also comes from details added to support the interests of members of Congress who want to see particular issues addressed. The laws passed by direct democracy can sometimes be simpler than what the legislature enacts. But if they are simple, then more effort has to be put into developing the procedures, policies and standards that implement them. The political fight moves to administrative agencies and to the courts. Figuring out what the law means becomes a task for professionals, including lawyers battling in the courts. Decisions about how to implement regulations are a major nexus of power in the policy system.[33] So, direct democracy does not avoid the influence of policy professionals in making collective decisions.

In addition, direct democracy is still mass democracy. The campaigns mounted to support and oppose ballot initiatives use the same tactics and have the same reliance on our cognitive shortcuts as electing representatives. These campaigns encourage fast, affective cognition rather than slow deliberative thinking. Some critics, including some libertarians, fear that direct democracy could be used to trample on individual rights.[34]

Even give these concerns, direct democracy has some features that make it a useful complement to representative democracy in that it can to some degree redress the power of elites and those in the policy system to shape decisions. But it is not deliberative democracy. In deliberative democracy, decisions emerge from a reasoned discussion among interested and affected parties. It is an important alternative to using markets and voting as a means of making decisions, and I will turn to it next.

## 9.3    Deliberation

In Chapter 5, I introduced deliberative approaches as a way to achieve good decisions. By deliberation, I mean processes whereby interested and affected parties engage in reasoned discussion before collectively arriving at a decision. Most visions of democracy assume a public sphere where facts and values can be clarified before voting (see the Introduction). But the changes in scale and complexity discussed in the previous section have required a distinction between democratic processes that rely on voting and deliberative processes that emphasize the process of discussion.

How do deliberation, prices and voting differ as decision-making methods? Recall that most forms of the rational actor model assume fixed preferences – that while consumers may acquire information in the market, they are clear and unwavering in what they want. This is a serious limit of the standard rational actor model offered in Chapter 3 – for sustainability decisions, the key problem is not optimizing utility given the preferences but determining the preferences. In a large representative democracy, citizens may observe political debates in the media and perhaps learn something from them and adjust their views somewhat.[35] More interactive media may blur the lines between passively watching a debate and engaging in a deliberative process. But the nature of such engagement is evolving so quickly that whatever conclusions that might be drawn from past experience may not generalize to new forms of engagement.

In contrast to standard models of voting and making purchases in a market, a key part of the argument for deliberative decision-making is that deliberation may lead to changes in both beliefs and values, something crucial for facing new challenges like those of sustainability. It can be hard to map these new challenges into existing values and norms. How do I assess the prospect of geoengineering to reduce the magnitude of climate change? How do a I develop a position on genetically modifying plants and animals to make them more resilient to climate change? Heuristics and biases may encourage quick and less than thoughtful links between emerging issues and values. But deliberative processes offer the hope that deliberation with other interested and affected parties may help citizens think through their own perspective even as they come to better appreciate the perspective of others. This in turn could facilitate more careful analysis and decision-making and, ultimately, social learning. Can such an approach work in a highly polarized society?

As discussed in Chapter 6, the boundary between the public and the private sphere is often uncertain and contested. Defining that boundary can exclude considerations that are crucial to the well-being of many humans and other species and the state of the biosphere. For example, while research on decision-making often takes the household as a unit of analysis and thus assumes away conflicts within the household, such conflicts not only are the stuff of daily life but can have huge effects on the well-being of women, children and the elderly.[36] Defining such issues as private matters not to be subject to public deliberation thus leaves unchallenged the norms and values that lead to such "private troubles." The definition of what is public and what is private relies on values and norms, and so trying to shift that definition will create resistance. That is not to say that they should not be challenged. By understanding the value and normative basis of private sphere practices, we can help design effective processes for moving them into the public sphere of deliberation and bringing about change. This is making the personal political, acknowledging that power often manifests itself in the routines of daily life.[37]

Decisions about sustainability nearly always require a scientific assessment of facts. Allowing everyone to have a voice is central to deliberation, but good decisions require a factual competence that comes from respecting scientific understanding as well as appreciating its uncertainties. A series of reports by the US National Academy of Sciences call for a linked process of scientific analysis and public deliberation to support environmental and sustainability decision-making. The approach is often called the "analytic deliberative process" or just "analytic deliberation."[38] It is diagrammed in Figure 9.1. Repeated communication between researchers conducting or assessing the scientific analysis and the public is a good way to assess uncertain and context-dependent facts. This helps to get the right science. Consultation with interested and affected parties helps ensure that their views guide the choice of what scientific analysis gets done. It also helps get the science right. Consultation with members of the public who have an understanding of context, including not only about the ecological and social systems that will be affected but also about the politics involved, can help calibrate science so that it can inform decisions.[39] As I argued in Chapter 4, to address environmental and sustainability decision, science that is developed in one context must often be transferred to another. The ongoing

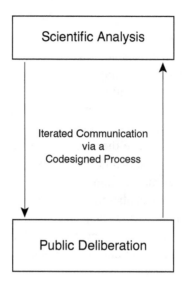

**Figure 9.1** The analytic deliberative process

interaction also helps build trust in the science and an understanding of its strengths and weaknesses.

It is fair to ask if the analytic deliberative approach to environmental and sustainability decision-making produces useful results. *Public Participation in Environmental Assessment and Decision Making* took up this question.[40] A panel of thirteen experts on deliberative processes reviewed more than 1,000 previous studies. We also engaged more than eighty individuals with participation experience from around the United States in workshops and commissioned a series of White Papers, each of which examined the experience with a family of public participation approaches within a particular environmental policy domain (e.g., forest planning, negotiated rulemaking, watershed management). Ten peer reviewers then commented on the report.

As I noted in the Introduction, based on this evidence, the US National Academy of Sciences concluded that: "When done well, public participation improves the quality and legitimacy of decisions and builds the capacity of all involved to engage in the policy process. It can lead to better results in terms of environmental quality and other social objectives. It also can enhance trust and understanding among parties."[41]

Many attempts to engage the public in deliberation around environmental or sustainability decisions fail. In examining success and failures, the report identified fifteen design principles that lead to good outcomes (see Table 9.1). There is no "cookbook"; rather, the design of an analytic deliberative process must be customized to match a variety of contextual factors. As always, context is crucial. Some processes might work well for long-term planning of watershed or forest use in a relatively homogeneous community. Very different processes would be needed to work with a diverse community facing a crisis from exposure to toxics. The report developed a series of diagnostic questions that can guide understanding specific contexts and thus designing processes that are appropriate for those challenges. Table 9.2 presents them.

**Table 9.1 Design principles for public participation**

---

**Agencies should proceed with:**

(1)  Clarity of purpose
(2)  Commitment to use the process to inform actions
(3)  Adequate funding and staff
(4)  Appropriate timing in relation to decisions
(5)  Focus on implementation
(6)  Commitment to self-assessment and process design

---

**The process must be:**

(7)  Inclusive
(8)  Collaborative in problem formation and process design
(9)  Transparent
(10)  Based on good-faith communication

---

**The process must attend to:**

(11)  Ensuring transparency of decision-relevant information and analysis
(12)  Paying explicit attention to both facts and values
(13)  Promoting explicitness about assumptions and uncertainties
(14)  Including independent review of official analysis and/or engaging in a process of collaborative inquiry with interested and affected parties
(15)  Allowing for iteration to reconsider past conclusions on the basis of new information

---

*Source*: US National Research Council (2008).

While the evidence in favor of deliberative processes is strong, it is, not surprisingly, context-specific. *Public Participation in Environmental Assessment and Decision Making* is limited largely to evidence from the United States and to deliberation about environmental issues.[42] Within those limits, the overwhelming majority of evidence comes from deliberation at the local to regional level. That evidence is clear: When done well, deliberation seems to achieve the goals claimed by its advocates, and we know how to do deliberation well, even if practice can fall short of the ideal. But when we move to decisions of national, let alone global, scope, we have far less experience. We thus lack evidence for drawing strong conclusions about the best ways to structure such deliberations or about what can be achieved with well-designed and implemented deliberation.

Approaches for national and even global deliberative processes are an active area of research, with some interesting experiments underway. It took twenty-five years to develop enough experience with deliberation at the regional and local level to establish a research literature that could allow strong conclusions. It would be premature to expect that comparably strong advice can be offered about deliberation at longer scales. Nonetheless, it is worth mentioning some of the issues and opportunities for large-scale deliberation.

I can suggest four principles that might be appropriate for developing fair and competent deliberative processes at the global level, and in particular around existential risks like climate change and responses to them like geoengineering.[43] First, following, any discussion

**Table 9.2  Diagnostic questions for public participation**

---

### Questions about scientific context

(1) What information is currently available on the issues? How adequate is available information for giving a clear understanding of the problem? Do the various parties agree about the adequacy of the information?

(2) Is the uncertainty associated with the information well characterized, interpretable and capable of being incorporated into the assessment or decision?

(3) Is the information accessible to and interpretable by interested and affected parties?

(4) Is the information trustworthy?

---

### Questions about convening and implementing agencies

(5) Where is the decision-making authority? Who would implement any agreements reached? Are there multiple forums in which the issues are being or could be debated and decided?

(6) Are there legal or regulatory mandates or constraints on the convening agency? What laws or policies need to be considered?

---

### Questions about the abilities of and constraints on the participants

(7) Are there interested and affected parties who may have difficulty being adequately represented?

   (a) What does the scale of the problem, especially its geographic scale, imply for the range of affected parties?

   (b) Are there disparities in the attributes of individual potential participants that may affect the likelihood of participation?

   (c) Are there interests that are diffused, unorganized or difficult to reach?

   (d) Are there disparities across groups of participants in terms of their financial, technical or other resources that may influence participation?

(8) What are the differences in values, interests, cultural views and perspectives among the parties? Are the participants polarized on the issue?

(9) Are there substantial disparities across participant groups in their power to influence the process?

(10) To what degree can the individuals at the table act for the parties they are assumed to represent?

(11) Are there significant problems of trust among the agency, the scientists and the interested and affected parties?

   (a) Are there indications that some participants are likely to proceed insincerely or to breach the rules of the process?

   (b) Are some participants concerned that the convening agency will proceed in bad faith?

   (c) Do some participants view the scientists as partisan advocates and so mistrust them?

---

*Source*: US National Research Council (2008: 224).

of large-scale deliberation must acknowledge that any such process can never fully redress the vast inequality that exists within and across nations. Those most vulnerable to the outcomes of collective decisions often have the least resources for effective participation. Nonhumans, who cannot directly participate in a deliberation, also should be given consideration.[44]

Second, deliberation for large-scale decisions needs to be an ongoing process. In dealing with the many risks related to environmental and technological change, the most reasonable strategy seems to be adaptive risk management. Adaptive risk management acknowledges that uncertainty is inevitable and thus we must experiment with approaches to deal with risks, learning from experience as we go. This requires institutions that are flexible and that encourage social learning on networks.[45] We are trying to guide cultural evolution towards the kinds of values embedded in ideas of sustainability. In the process, our ideas of sustainability will continue to evolve. It is a topic that deserves further exploration, taking account of how norms, beliefs and sometimes values can change in the light of new perspectives and new information as well as the obstacles to adaptive change.

Third, there is the issue of who to include in deliberation. Experiments with "mini-publics" use small groups that are selected so as to be representative of the diversity of interested and affected parties, thus allowing some representation of the diversity of values, beliefs, norms and interests while preserving the advantages for deliberation of a group of moderate size. This is one of the most promising areas of research on deliberation in particular and decision-making in general.[46]

Careful thought has to be given to what is to be represented in drawing a sample of people. As I have emphasized several times, in any cultural evolutionary process, including the evolution of values and beliefs in deliberation, it is important to have diversity in the discussion.[47] Mini-publics strive for deliberation with a group that is representative in the same way that a high-quality survey is. That is certainly one appropriate criterion for selecting people to deliberate. But few if any people from groups that are a small part of the population will be in the sample. That can mean that Indigenous people and others who are minorities will not have much voice. As a result, communities that might feel the greatest impact from decisions will not be heard. Sampling can ensure that such voices are represented in the deliberation and more than one process can run in parallel with communication across groups. Important work considers how to incorporate diversity in gender, sexual identity, disability, Indigenous identity and many other important perspectives.[48] Many Indigenous cultures have a tradition of deliberative decision-making that can be a source of insights and also a mechanism for engaging those communities in decision-making. The issue of representing the interests of nonhumans remains.

Fourth, the appropriate goal for deliberation has to be assessed. One might envision a national or even global deliberative body empowered to make decisions. But most deliberative processes remain advisory to those who have the legal authority to make decisions. One of the principles of effective deliberation in Table 9.1 is that decision makers make a commitment to rely substantially on the outcomes of deliberation. But authority is rarely ceded to such processes. We can learn from the experience of processes that conduct scientific assessments, such as the National Climate Assessment in the United States or the Intergovernmental Panel on Climate Change and the Millennium Ecosystem Assessment at the global level. These processes, in trying to produce science that is useful for decision-making, must take account of regional and sectoral variation, and thus are to some degree deliberative processes. There are also evolving examples of co-governance processes, including ones involving Indigenous peoples and national or state/provincial governments.[49]

Who should initiate deliberation and how much deliberation is needed? In theory, anyone can initiate public discussion of an issue. In practice, those with power can easily get a discussion going or suppress it. Social movements can be effective at raising issues even in the face of the opposition of the powerful. Scientists have special responsibilities and opportunities. Because they are developing new understandings, they may be the first to be aware of a problem, although sometimes impacted communities are aware of an issue before there is scientific analysis; the contaminated water in Flint, Michigan, is an example. But in raising an issue for public deliberation, scientists need to reflect carefully on how to frame an issue in ways that reflect uncertainty, that are attentive to the context-dependent nature of our understandings and that are reflective and open about their own values. In my view, scientists should focus on opening the discussion rather than concluding it.

A common criticism of deliberation is that it is a slow, expensive and cumbersome process, especially when conducted under administrative procedures that, while intended to assure a fair and open process, often involve a lot of red tape (see Box 5.5). Not every decision by a government agency requires an extensive deliberative process. Deliberation can shape general principles and procedures that guide specific decisions.[50] Fairness and competence matter in making decisions, but efficiency is an important criterion too.

Finally, I remain concerned that the literature on deliberation remains fragmented. *Public Participation in Environmental Assessment and Decision Making* attempted to bring together the diverse literature then in place to serve as a starting point for future literature reviews. Unfortunately, despite that attempt, work continues to take place in isolated pockets of scholarship. As a result, substantial opportunities for mutual learning and for progress are lost. I hope the field becomes less fragmented and more cumulative, as the insights that would result are badly needed as we face the problems of the twenty-first century.

Despite these challenges, I believe that the deliberative tradition offers important insights about how we can make good decisions together. Unlike markets with their utilitarian and libertarian justifications, deliberation encourages engagement of all the criteria for good decisions I suggest in Chapter 5. And, if done well, it can overcome many of the challenges of mass voting and in particular the tendency towards BAHP. Of course, good deliberation requires work. Even at the small scale of the Planning Commission in Grand Isle, there were always tendencies towards BAHP. The challenge is to learn how to do deliberation well and that will require innovation, experimentation and social learning.

## 9.4    Divisions and Deliberation

All these methods of collective decision-making have flaws. Prices and the markets that generate them produce and reflect inequality, favoring the interests of the powerful. This in turn spills over into voting processes where wealth and power can skew results. Deliberative approaches offer great promise. But they are only beginning to be deployed at the national and global scale, and they have to be expanded to include much more diverse perspectives than is typically the case.

Some conclude that the only way forward is by wholescale transformation of global political economy and governance structure (see Chapter 7). Powerful interests, including some nations, many corporations and many of the wealthiest individuals, have a disproportionate influence on decision-making in most nations and at the global level. Their power came from current geopolitical arrangements, so they tend to resist any radical change in those arrangements that would reduce their power. Some change can come about because their understanding of their interests shifts. Change also comes because those promoting change are able to overcome the opposition of some of the powerful. In particular, grassroots social movements can often be effective at inspiring and leading reforms towards sustainability and deliberative democracy.[51] The struggle between the interests of elites and the interests of others has been an element of human history since the emergence of social stratification. Unfortunately, differences in individual wealth and power have increased in recent decades, reversing a trend towards greater equality.

What can be expected from incremental change and how do we facilitate both incremental and transformational change? For issues like climate change, incremental change reduces risks, reduces impacts and buys time for greater change. And since future decisions depend on the context set by past decisions, even small initial steps can be designed to set the path for greater steps in the future. Much the same can be said around issues of human well-being and social justice. It is always important to be critical of limits to reform. But unless it is clear that reforms block larger transformations, reforms do alleviate some injustices and reduce suffering from those bearing the brunt of such injustice. And reforms may encourage rather than block transformation. In the United States, the progress on civil rights in the last half of the twentieth century certainly did not eliminate racism. But to argue that more needs to be done is not to say that nothing valuable has been accomplished. The struggles of generations have led to important changes. Successful reforms usually don't resolve fully the problems they address. But reforms empower those seeking change, show that change is possible and make clear that more needs to be done. When incremental steps are beneficial, we need to know more about how to take those steps. An ongoing dialogue between researchers and those working to bring about change would inform both science and action.[52]

We also need to better understand what strategies are effective in bringing about transformative change. The study of nonviolent change has been part of scholarship since the mid-twentieth century. The Peace Research Institute Oslo was founded in 1959, the *Journal of Peace Research* in 1964, the Center for Peaceful Change (now the School of Peace and Conflict Studies) at Kent State in 1971, the Institute for Conflict Analysis and Resolution (now the Jimmy and Rosalynn Carter School for Peace and Conflict Resolution) at George Mason University in the 1980s (I helped design the first PhD program there) and the US Institute for Peace was founded in 1984. Many lines of research not labeled peace studies or conflict resolution also make major contributions to our understanding of nonviolent but dramatic social change. Perhaps the unfortunate rise of authoritarian styles of leadership in many parts of the world has inspired a renewed attention to and enthusiasm for this research and for promulgating effective strategies for nonviolent change.[53] Important work is also moving forward on how social innovations can lead to social transformation. All this is consistent with my argument that we must learn by experimentation.

The aftermath of the 2020 US election is unfolding even as I write. Claims were made, without substantiating evidence, of fraud determining the election results. On January 6, 2021, about 2,000 people broke into the US Capitol, vandalizing and looting it and assaulting police officers, in an attempt to stop congressional certification of the election. Some still actively deny the validity of the presidential election. These events, and a decline in some measures of democracy in a number of countries (see Figure 2.2), raise the issue of whether deliberation and peaceful change is possible. Some fear that electoral democracy is losing legitimacy and may cease to be a functional means of addressing societal problems.[54] Given such challenges, calls for deliberation may seem terribly optimistic or even naïve. Here, as always, I think it is useful to think about variation among those engaged in politics. I will portray this variation in terms of ideal types but emphasize these should not be used as stereotypes but simply mark positions in a complex space of values, attitudes, beliefs, norms and actions. My categories may not be correct and are based on the United States. Only careful analysis of solid empirical evidence can provide an accurate map and the contours will certainly differ across countries.

First, there are those whose values, beliefs and norms hold that only a violent overthrow of the current system can achieve what they hope for. For them, violence and terrorism are justified to achieve their goals. There are those who share beliefs with the first group about the current situation but who act based on anger and outrage rather than planning, yielding not large-scale terrorism and insurrection but riots, adventurist mob behavior and tragic events such as the Buffalo mass shooting of Black people by a White supremacist on May 12, 2022. Such uncoordinated actions can provide cover and opportunities for more strategic violence. The BAHP dynamic is at play. So, while some individuals may change their views and move away from these positions, and others may fade away from activism, it can be hard to overcome the processes that exclude their consideration of new information and contrasting views. The likelihood they will take violent action depends in part on the risks they face and the social support (norms) they perceive. Risks and social support can be changed. Governance in the face of organized and disorganized violence has to use a mix of law enforcement, public rejection of violence and strong mobilization of and support for nonviolent direct action.

A third, and larger, group have very strong beliefs but, unlike the first two groups, are not willing to engage in direct violence. Here too, the problem of BAHP makes it very difficult to engage those in this group in effective deliberation. I suspect that little done via mass media or formal institutions can lead to changes in their views. Finally, there are those who may hold strong values and a coherent set of beliefs and norms but are not so locked in by biased assimilation and homophily that they reject other views automatically. And as the work of Haltinner and Sarathchandra suggest, their views may vary across issues – some climate skeptics are concerned about other environmental issues, for example.[55] They can debate beliefs and even values in processes where views can change. This is the group we usually think about as engaging in deliberation.

Despite the impact of those with strong positions on the dynamics of political decision-making, there are several reasons for hope. First, these first three groups probably represent only 20 percent or less of the population, although they have a strong influence on party politics.[56] There may also be ways of generating empathy for those with different views in all but the most polarized. Interpersonal interactions, including but not limited to those that take place in deliberation, may be effective in countering BAHP. In contrast to gerrymandering, competitive voting districts can also reduce the influence of the most ideologically committed on candidate selection. Demographic change via immigration and generational (cohort) succession may also reduce polarization as those holding such entrenched views on a particular set of issues are replaced in the population by those with less entrenched views. These demographic dynamics may have been an important element in shifts in political tolerance, racial prejudice and positions on gay marriage and other LGBTQ issues in the United States, although more research is needed to unpack generational change and changes in views over time across generations.

We need further work on the size, influence and characteristics of the diverse groups that comprise the political landscape. Strategies for effective decision-making depend on that diagnosis. I suspect that a willingness to engage in dialogue with those who differ is strongly linked to values – strong self-interest suggests little motivation to empathize with the views of others while altruists may be more accommodating.[57] Different strategies will be required for dealing with each of these positions. Some of the strategies are large-scale, requiring substantial transformation of laws and institutions, such as preventing gerrymandering and countering tendencies for homophily and biased assimilation in media. Some are more reformist, requiring compromise across those who hold different values and beliefs to produce incremental changes in rules and actions.

As shocking as the January 2021 attack on the US Capitol and the ongoing attempts to delegitimate the election have been, it is also useful to maintain some historical and comparative perspective. Deep, seemingly insurmountable political divides have not been rare in US history. African Americans and others have long had to endure and resist armed, angry mobs using violence for political intimidation. The labor movement has often faced hired thugs sent as strikebreakers.

Positive nonviolent change is also part of US history. The success of the civil rights movement deserves celebration and reflection even if not all of its goals were achieved. The struggles of black and Indigenous and other people of color inspired other social movements, including the environmental movement. Social movements have shown that changes in beliefs and norms can sometimes be very rapid. I am not an expert on comparative history. But a brief look at other nations suggests that many have avoided catastrophic changes and moved forward on seemingly insurmountable problems. Even those that have suffered catastrophes, such as the rise of fascism, eventually, albeit at a horrible cost, recover. There is much to learn about the current situation and the potential for democracy and deliberation by careful analysis not only of the here and now but also of the past and of other experiences.

Coleman, drawing on the literature on conflict, offers two suggestions for moving towards more effective deliberation and a reduction of polarization.[58] He notes that attentive listening by leaders to those most disaffected, especially in times of crisis, can be effective at depolarizing views, as can bridge-building groups that address local problems. Both of these are wholly consistent with the principles of deliberative processes I have outlined in this chapter. Coleman also calls for a strenuous effort to implement these approaches at the scale necessary to bring about change. Some of this work can be initiated by anyone in the role of citizen but some of it requires engagement by those with power. Those who benefit from polarization will resist, but committed effort could allow progress even in the face of those self-interested efforts.[59]

The literature on deliberation environmental policy has demonstrated that well-designed deliberative processes can often overcome deep conflicts. Many of the cases reviewed in *Public Participation in Environmental Assessment and Decision Making* involved many of the sources of conflict discussed in Chapter 6, and in some cases the conflicts verged on violence. But, over time, well-designed processes were able to produce consensus and reduce BAHP. Research is also showing that well-designed deliberation can overcome some of the polarization in American politics.[60]

## 9.5    Looking Ahead

The biophysical environment will continue to shape the context in which we act. Culture will continue to evolve. I think of efforts to bring about transformational and incremental changes as ways of actively shaping the adaptive landscape of culture. We encourage some kinds of decisions and discourage others in an ongoing process. But I also want to highlight technological change, something not adequately integrated into thinking about sustainability.

Some of the earliest debates in the environmental movement circa Earth Day in 1970 were about technological change. The global movement in opposition to nuclear power in the 1970s was a formative element in the environmental movement and, as I have argued in Chapter 4, helped shape our thinking about risk. (The movement drew on the nonviolent direct-action tradition of the civil rights and antiwar movements.) A debate between Barry Commoner on the one hand and Paul Ehrlich and John Holdren on the other was fundamentally about whether choice of technology was the dominant driver of stress on the environment or whether other factors (population, consumption) mattered as well. The "only one thing matters" logic is still found in too much writing on sustainability. And while there is a stereotype that the environmental movement is anti-technology, at least since the 1970s the movement has embraced what were then called appropriate technologies (e.g., solar over nuclear power) and are now called sustainable technologies.[61]

This rich tradition of analysis and debate about technology has not been sufficiently deployed in examination of the technologies that will almost certainly have a transformative impact on the twenty-first century. We know that biotechnology, information technology, nanotechnology, robotics and neurotechnology will produce very rapid changes that are hard to predict. They might enhance the well-being of humans and others and reduce the impact we have on the biosphere. Two motivations are shaping investments in these technologies. One is a drive for profit. The other is a drive for military strength. With these motivations influencing what technologies are developed and how they are deployed, it would be naïve to think that all, or even most, of the technological advances will be in the service of sustainability. Indeed, such motivations raise serious concerns about impacts of impending technological change. How those impacts unfold depends on what technologies we decide to develop, how we deploy them and how we restructure society around the changes that result.

Many applications of information technology and robotics could eliminate large numbers of jobs. Unless policies intervene, those who are unemployed will face tremendous stress as they try to find new jobs and face a loss of income and status. That can generate anger and despair and make reasoned political discourse more difficult. A free market will favor reducing production costs by displacing human workers with technology. But we can imagine a political economy where a reasonable living can be earned by working relatively few hours per week, where a strong social safety net reduces the risk and stress of unemployment, where volunteer work and pursuit of avocations are both financially feasible and socially applauded. We can decide together if new technologies produce massive unemployment and distress or liberate more people to have time for better lives.

It is harder to see how relatively simple policy changes can obviate the potential negative effects of applying the emerging technologies to the military. Weaponized drones are routinely used by the military and have been used by terrorist groups. Robotic weapons systems that can autonomously make "kill" decisions are being developed; some have probably already been used.[62] There are rumors of the use of biotechnology to enhance the capabilities of soldiers. Neurotechnologies can be deployed to the same ends. The dynamics of an arms race will promote increased development and deployment of these technologies. No nation will want to send conventional soldiers into the field to contest with robots and technologically enhanced soldiers. Bans may be the most effective approach. While establishing verifiable and enforceable bans will be a challenge, the world has been quite effective at reducing the use of biological and chemical weapons, slowing the spread of nuclear weapons and limiting the development and testing of ever larger nuclear weapons.

One of the most dauting aspects of some emerging technologies is their potential for use by small groups deeply committed to revolutionary change. Small drones, especially if deployed in number, could be a terribly effective weapon against all but hardened targets. The prevalence of biotechnology means that even groups of modest means could attempt to develop biological weapons. Already many government agencies, private corporations, hospitals and other organizations have had their activities disrupted by cyberattacks. In the case of health care and public safety organizations, those attacks could have deadly consequences.[63]

As noted, the new media are also deployed strategically to influence voting, deliberation and the beliefs and norms of the public. These technologies will have unanticipated consequences as they evolve and interact. Bak-Coleman and colleagues have called for a "crisis science" – the urgent deployment of science to address practical problems – to deal with the impacts of communications technologies.[64]

These emerging technologies will certainly offer possibilities to greatly enhance sustainability if we decide to develop and deploy them to that end. Decisions driven largely by a drive for profit and military strength are unlikely to lead to greater sustainability. But deliberative processes that guide both public and private policy could facilitate decisions that develop and deploy emerging technologies in that direction. We can build on what we are learning about deliberation in the service of sustainability to explore how such processes can shape technological development and deployment. Indeed, such broad deliberation will be essential to examine the ethical implications of emerging technologies.

It took much of the twentieth century to articulate our ethical obligations to other humans, to other species and to the biosphere. That process led to current discussions of sustainability. And, as Rudel has documented, it has also led to some remarkable successes in which societies responded quickly and effectively to major challenges.[65] There have also been catastrophic failures to adapt to change. We can learn from success and failures. The struggle to deploy those insights in decision-making continues.

Such challenges seem daunting, perhaps insurmountable, and it is easy to develop a sense that the future is out of control. It is always the case that the future cannot be controlled. But it can be influenced. Our understanding of how we make decisions evolved over decades and we continue to learn more and find ways to apply that knowledge in the service of better decisions. We need to broaden the scope of our thinking, continuing to deal with problems of violence, inequality and injustice that are millennia-old even as we address sustainability and engage with the emerging technologies. The challenge is daunting and urgent. The world a century hence cannot be accurately predicted; neither catastrophism nor unconstrained optimism is an adequate guide. But we know how to learn – it is a key attribute of our species. We use deliberation about facts and values and their interplay to learn and to make decisions that help shape a world that aligns with what we hope for rather than what we dread.

Each decision we make as individuals matters, as do the decisions we make together. There has been progress – the area of the Cuyahoga that used to catch on fire is now the site of restaurants and music venues, the river is the center of the Cuyahoga River National Park and in Kent the problems we identified in the 1970s have been resolved. Some forms of discrimination have been reduced. On average, across the globe, people have longer life expectancies than a century ago. But we have also become aware of new environmental problems and more subtle but still pernicious forms of bias and inequality, even as the old forms of these problems persist. My hope is that we can learn to make better decisions. That knowledge can shape the process of cultural evolution to encourage decisions that take account of the well-being of humans and other species, reduce stress on the environment and are attentive to the differences in the values and circumstances of those interested in or affected by decisions. The way we make decisions will have to continue to evolve as we face new challenges, but we can build on our success and learn from our mistakes.

# Notes

## Introduction

1. Quoted in Jackson and Gans (2015): 475.
2. Box and Draper (1987): 424.
3. Adler (2002); Stradling and Stradling (2008). For the cohorts strongly influenced by the first Earth Day, the idea of the Cuyahoga as a burning river was iconic. (Social scientists use the term "cohort" to refer to what is commonly called a generation.) *The Lorax*, which seems to have influenced multiple cohorts of children, was published in 1971 (Geisel 1971). Early editions mentioned the pollution in Lake Erie and apparently the problems of the Cuyahoga helped inspire Geisel to write the book (Fortner 2019; I thank Cam Whitley for pointing this out). The baby boom cohort were avid readers of Carl Barks' Uncle Scrooge and Donald Duck stories. Barks often invoked a theme of respect for Indigenous people, "wild" animals and undeveloped ecosystems (see the webpage "The Environmentalist," www.cbarks.dk/theenvironmentalist.htm). Barks in turn drew heavily on *National Geographic*, whose images of animals and non-Western people were also very influential throughout the twentieth century (Kalof and Amthor 2010; see the "Picturing Animals in National Geographic," Michigan State University webpage, https://picturinganimals.msu.edu/). All these may have had an influence on the emergence of the modern environmental movement, although it was Rachel Carson's *Silent Spring* that crystallized key concerns. Images of the earth from space were often used in graphics and are sometimes considered important in influencing public views, but my sense is that they were common primarily because they were easy to access. More work on what images were prevalent and critical analysis of them is needed (Dunaway 2008, 2015). But it is also crucial to understand the impact of images, of reader responses, if that understanding is to be useful (Kalof, Zammit-Lucia and Kelly 2011; Whitley, Kalof and Flach 2021).
4. The cover of James Gang's first album, *Yer Album*, features the dam.
5. Barone et al. (1971). The US National Science Foundation funded "Student Originated Studies" on environmental issues proposed by interdisciplinary teams of undergraduates. The limnologist G. Dennis Cooke was our faculty advisor, but we wrote the proposal and conducted the research.
6. Dietz (2020b).
7. On May 15, police killed students Phillip Lafayette Gibbs and James Earl Green at Jackson State University, so the two tragedies are linked to many of us. Tom Grace's *Kent State: Death and Dissent in the Long Sixties* is the best historical account (Grace 2016: 40). Tom was one of the wounded and is also a professional historian of great skill and diligence. He places the events of spring 1970 in the context of previous civil rights and antiwar protests in Kent. Derf Backderf's graphic novel *Kent State: Four Dead in Ohio* does a stunning job of capturing that time and is the only account I know that mentions the upcoming Project Earth (Backderf 2020). The composite character in panel 2, page 12 is based in part on my announcing Project Earth to the May 1 rally, linking the war and the environment, and on Kerry Blech announcing the Tuesday Night Cinema. At the time, awareness of the devastating environmental effects of the war was just emerging but they are now well documented; see Ehrlich (1969); Hằng (2018);

National Academies of Sciences, Engineering, and Medicine (2018); Stellman et al. (2003); Thuan and Van Ngoc (2018); Thuy and Van Bac (2018). While the social movements of the time are sometimes discussed as if they were distinct, the network of people who were active was strongly interconnected, with nearly everyone in these networks involved in some actions in protest of the Vietnam War. For example, John Barone, Kerry Blech and I organized the activities of the Kent Free University. The Free University provided initial meeting space and publicity for activists in the women's/feminist and gay liberation movements to form their own vibrant organizations. And Kerry, John and I, along with Rolly Brown and later Andy Cohen, helped organize the Kent Folk Festival. In the fall of 1970, I was one of the founders of the Kent Legal Defense Fund (KLDF) formed to resist the Grand Jury indictments of the Kent 25; Tom Grace was also active in KLDF and John and Kerry contributed artwork (see Chapter 6, Note 7).

8. In an early attempt at what would become "Land Acknowledgments," our study was "respectfully dedicated to the Erie peoples who once lived along the Cuyahoga."

9. Endres (2020).

10. Local knowledge was crucial in an informal way. A friend who worked at the plant we suspected of dumping toxics told us where and when to sample to catch the release into the river in the middle of the night.

11. Jorgenson (2015b); Liu et al. (2013).

12. Box was connected to the origins of modern statistics, which in turn was deeply embedded in Darwinian thinking (Dietz and Kalof 2009). Unfortunately, a number of early statisticians were advocates of eugenics, with its many ableist, colonialist, racist and sexist assumptions (Rutherford 2021). These ideas were influential in early US sociology. Paul McLaughlin directed me to the excellent analysis of Box's point by Wimsatt, who argues "Models with false assumptions are commonly and deliberately used to leverage better ones" (Wimsatt and Wimsatt 2007: 40).

13. I have yet to discover where and when Godard said this.

14. Henrich (2015). Learning evolutionary thinking was a crucial part of my education. As an undergraduate, I studied with the biological anthropologist Owen Lovejoy. I then had the good fortune to attend graduate school at the University of California, Davis, where a founder of modern evolutionary thinking, Theodosius Dobzhansky, was still active and Peter Richerson and Rob Boyd were initiating the theory of cultural evolution. Later, I got to know the work of Paul McLaughlin, who continues to explore the implications of Darwinian thinking for environmental sociology; see Chapter 7. The theorist Tom Burns and I advocated an evolutionary approach for sociology (see Burns and Dietz 1992a, 1992b, 1992c; Dietz and Burns 1992; Dietz, Burns and Buttel 1990; McLaughlin 2012b, 2012c; McLaughlin and Dietz 2008). For all his deep insights, Darwin was a Victorian, cis, white male and some of his biases are certainly found in his work; see DeSilva (2021). Richerson, Gavrilets and de Waal (2021) examine his thoughts on human evolution, which offered important insights but also reflected his socialization and the limited evidence available to him. Like all areas of science, evolutionary thinking itself evolves in part by efforts to purge these biases from our understandings – it is an ongoing process.

15. See Burns and Dietz (1992c); Dietz (2005); Dietz and Burns (1992).

16. There are many different terms used for the elements of culture, including "idea" and the neologism "meme." Burns and I used "rules" as the covering term; see Burns et al. (1987); Burns and Dietz (1992c); Ostrom (2005); Smith, Langton and Nisbett (1992).

17. On social learning for sustainability, see Dyball, Brown and Keen (2007); Henrich (2015); Henry (2009, 2020).

18. Some lines of social science research take little account of the effect of others on an individual's decisions. As Robert Frank (2020: 153) put it, "economists and policy analysts doggedly continue to assume that people's assessments of their options are completely independent of the contexts in which they find themselves. Abandonment of that assumption is long overdue."

19. Dietz and Burns (1992: 190). In the social sciences, the ability to exert power, to shape our lives and the larger world, is called "agency" and contrasted with "structure," the larger forces that create possibilities and constraints. I will use the term "power" since "agency" is also a common term for government organizations like the US Environmental Protection Agency.

20. Holland (1975, 1995). I have long thought that we could use evolutionary processes to produce art. An algorithm with adjustable parameters could be used to generate images or objects, initially using a set of random numbers to set the parameters. Presented with a wide variety of these images or objects, you could rank or otherwise select them based on how much you appreciate them. This ranking could be used to favor some values of the parameters and select against others. By repeating the process over time, the algorithm would evolve to produce images or objects that match your preferences.

21. Arnold (1973).

22. Malakoff (2021); Pompeani et al. (2021).

23. Bebber and Eren (2018).

24. An immense literature explicates the nature and conceptual benefits of population thinking. See Darwin (1859); Dietz (2005); Dietz and Burns (1992); Love and Wimsatt (2019); Mayr (1959); McLaughlin (2022); Sober (1980).

25. In the 1950s and early 1960s, theory both in the social sciences and in ecology was dominated by a structural/functional analysis in which the social system or ecosystem was taken as the fundamental reality (Odum 1969; Parsons 1966; Vayda and Rappaport 1968). Explanations focused on how systems maintained homeostasis via feedback loops. Individuals were viewed as more or less programmed to play their roles in the system, with little room for individual exercise of power (Blake and Davis 1964; Parsons 1966). The more sophisticated versions of this approach, such as that of Vayda and Rappaport, provided arguments based on group selection in biological evolution for why the system would be an integrated whole (Vayda and Rappaport 1968). But most approaches were silent on why it was justifiable to treat a social system, an ecosystem, or a coupled social and ecological system, as a unified whole with feedback loops that provide stability. Later Vayda, influenced by the clear thinking of Bonnie McCay, moved from this functionalist view to a position very similar to the one I advocate (McCay and Vayda 1975; Vayda 1988, 2009).

26. I will use the term "corporation" to refer to for-profit business organizations. In the United States, the corporation is granted existence by state governments and in most states corporations must maximize return for the shareholders. But there are provisions for nonprofit corporations and for corporations that pursue goals in addition to profits (see Chapter 7, Note 6). A major rationale for forming a corporation is that the shareholder's liability for the actions of the corporation is limited, but in most states there are also other ways to do that. I prefer the term "corporation" to "business" or "firm" because it implies a large organization with its own internal dynamics that can influence decision-making. Many aspects of modern corporations emerged from the corporations created to build colonial empires, especially the Dutch East India Company and the English East India Company; see Dari-Mattiacci et al. (2017); Gelderblom, De Jong and Jonker (2013); Stern (2015).

27. Coleman (1974).

28. See Chapter 2, Note 39.

29. On policy networks, see Davis, Yoo and Baker (2003); Dietz and Rycroft (1987); Henry (2020); Henry and Vollan (2014); Jenkins-Smith et al. (2018); Weible et al. (2020).

30. Herbert Simon (the first non-economist to win a Nobel Prize in Economics) emphasized the importance of individual decision-making in organizational decisions, an approach now called the Neo-Carnegie perspective after Carnegie-Mellon University (Simon 1947). The individual heuristics and biases discussed in Chapter 3 can have important impacts on organizational risk management, as insightful analyses by Kunreuther, Ussem and Ballestros demonstrate; see Ballesteros and Kunreuther (2018); Kunreuther and Useem (2009, 2018).

31. There is an evolutionary argument for seeing organizations as decision-making units. New organizations are created; existing organizations dissolve, are absorbed into other organizations or split into multiple organizations. The persistence and "reproduction" of an organization depend on both the environment and the rules guiding the organization. So, a group of organizations can be thought of as a population subject to selection pressure. The organizational ecology approach to organizations has made fruitful use of this logic; see Hannan and Freeman (1989); McLaughlin (1996); McLaughlin and Khawaja (2000). A parallel theory in economics is sometimes used to justify the argument that corporations will maximize profits; see Alchian (1950).

32. Della Porta and Diani (2015) offer an overview of the social movements literature, and the journal *Mobilization* is devoted to the topic. Brulle (2000) provides a history of the US environmental movement and Johnson and Burke (2021) a recent assessment. Fisher (2019) shows how contemporary activism has had political impact.

33. See Chapter 3.

34. "Broadly defined, institutions are the prescriptions that humans use to organize all forms of repetitive and structured interactions including those within families, neighborhoods, markets, firms, sports leagues, churches, private associations, and governments at all scales" (Ostrom 2005: 3). These prescriptions can be thought of as norms – what one ought to do (and not do). For Ostrom, the difference between norms and rules was that rules were norms that have clear results if you adhere to them or don't, while the sanctions associated with norms are less precise. I find it useful to include in the idea of an institution not only the norms that guide behavior but also whose behavior is being guided. Thus institutions are strongly related to roles that define what norms are appropriate (see Chapter 3). If the institutional setting is the market, then I am an economic actor – a consumer, a seller. If the institutional setting is the state, then I am a citizen.

35. The work of Elinor Ostrom is central to the arguments I make (Dietz, Ostrom and Stern 2003; Ostrom 2009b). She was the first woman and second non-economist to win a Nobel Prize in Economics. I had the great privilege of working with her, and her influence is everywhere in this book.

36. A similar oversimplification can lead us to misunderstand the rich history of ways people have organized their lives. The common story is that food foragers lived in small egalitarian societies and that agriculture and cities inevitably lead to inequality. But while those may be common patterns, there is immense variation and we can learn a great deal from it; see Graeber and Wengrow (2021). Scholars debate the details of their analysis, but I think the point I draw about variation is robust.

37. This is a central idea in human ecology; see Section I.2.6. My colleague Jack Liu has led the development of conceptual frameworks to clarify our thinking on these issues, including both the idea of coupled human and natural systems (CHANS) and the importance for CHANS of actions at a distance, telecoupling. For a review, see Liu et al. (2007a, 2007b); Liu et al. (2013); Liu et al. (2015); Liu et al. (2021). Burch, Machlis and Force offer a similar and useful conceptual framework (Burch, Machlis and Force 2017).

38. Hutchinson (1965).

39. For example, genetic diversity in reintroduced populations seems to facilitate the success of the reintroduction (Scott et al. 2020).

40. See Economo, Hong and Page (2016); Hong and Page (2004).

41. See Henry (2009). Diversity has been stated as a goal in US colleges and universities since early in the twentieth century. Standardized tests such as the SAT were originally intended to add more social class diversity to elite universities. Affirmative action programs are often justified by the importance of diversity for education. I emphasize the importance of diversity but also agree with Anderson that integration can also be justified as a means of countering racism, including the effects of historical wrongs that still echo in society (Anderson 2010, 2014).

42. McLaughlin (2011).

43. Dietz et al. (2001). In some literatures, the term "pro-social" is used instead of "altruism," but the former often includes behavior motivated by the expectation of reciprocity, so I prefer the term "altruism."

44. Sober and Wilson (1998); Szathmáry and Vladar (2017); Wilson (1983). The work of Vayda and Rappaport referred to in the Introduction, Note 25 argued that local human groups (villages, essentially) are functionally integrated systems because natural selection acting on genes would promote altruism and thus decisions that reflect the interest of the group. They had a logical argument, but as we learned more about what it takes to maintain altruism via selection on genes, the argument seemed increasingly improbable. Many science fiction stories explore the concept of the "hive mind," notably the Borg of *Star Trek*.

45. Analysis of altruism has been a central theme in the literature modeling cultural evolution; see Boyd (2017); Boyd and Richerson (1985, 2005); Davis, Hennes and Raymond (2018); Dietz (2005); Dietz and Whitley (2018); Richerson and Boyd (2005); Richerson, Boyd and Paciotti (2001); Simpson and Willer (2015); Waring et al. (2015); Waring, Goff and Smaldino (2017).

46. Boyd and Richerson (2005); Richerson and Boyd (2001, 2005). Current theories of cultural evolution provide models of altruism towards others based primarily on ideas of multilevel or group selection; see Brooks et al. (2018); Waring et al. (2015). Altruism that extends beyond a local group or beyond those that otherwise seem similar is a crucial topic for research.

47. I will offer a formal definition of values in Chapter 3. Different streams of literature use the term "value" or "values" in slightly different ways, but all have a common theme of things that an individual or group consider important.

48. Schell, Guy et al. (2020).

49. Sinclair (2020). Similarly, Kyle Whyte and Nick Reo, whose work has substantially influenced my thinking, articulate an Indigenous perspective on climate and natural resources. Their work is especially impressive in blending a careful criticism of past and "standard" practices with suggesting ways forward. See Kronk Warner, Lynn and Whyte (2020); Maldonado, Lazrus et al. (2016); Reo et al. (2017); Whyte 2013, 2017a, 2017c, 2018, 2020; Whyte, Brewer and Johnson (2015); Whyte et al. (2017). I was fortunate to read the critiques of colonialism by Frantz Fanon and Chinua Achebe at the same time I was learning evolutionary theory (Achebe [1959] 2017, [1960] 2017, [1964] 2016; Fanon 1969; Wenzel 2017). So, I have always seen arguments for decolonizing knowledge and evolutionary thinking about culture as natural allies and have learned a great deal from scholars working on these issues.

50. Vrla (2019: chap. 2).

51. This perspective is often called "evolutionary epistemology"; see Campbell (1987); Heintz (2018); McLaughlin (2011); Radnitzky and Bartley (1987).

52. There is so much detailed and thoughtful work on ethics by philosophers that my arguments will undoubtedly be rather ill-informed and often naïve. I acknowledge this and the many important ideas, critiques and lines of argument I am not engaging. But I want to adhere to my own admonition, so even if my ethical arguments are flawed, I am at least being clear about them.

53. Berlin ([1953] 2013).

54. Robinson (2020). Young also made important contributions to physics, including the "double slit" experiment showing that light behaves like both a particle and a wave. Especially successful hedgehogs are sometimes called polymaths (Burke 2020). As I note, the Rosetta Stone was stolen by an imperial power from Egypt – controversies about the proper place to locate artifacts now in museums established by colonialists are ongoing.

55. Granovetter (1973); Henry (2009).

56. Bias and prejudice often played a role with women and BIPOC people too often excluded and ignored. For example, the immense contributions of W. E. B. DuBois and his collaborators, and of

many innovative women, were marginalized when sociology was established in the United States, with some of his key insights "rediscovered" by cis, white male sociologists; see Morris (2015).

57. Quoted in Burns (2000) and West (1999). The Grateful Dead had a similar view of their music.

58. Webler (1995) provides a careful and detailed articulation of criteria for deliberation, drawing on the work of Habermas. Brulle (1993, 1994) has examined what Habermasian normative ideas might mean at a societal level, emphasizing the role of social movements. Processes that link scientific analysis with deliberation are a central theme of the book. They are often called transdisciplinary. Renn provides a commanding assessment of transdisciplinarity; see Renn (2021).

59. Graeber and Wengrow (2021).

60. His *Towards a Rational* Society influenced my thinking on social impact assessment, and I went on to explore his other work on deliberative rationality; see Habermas (1970, 1971, 1984, 1987, 1990, 1993).

61. I read Dewey in my first semester of college, so pragmatism has been "running in the background" throughout my intellectual life (Dietz 1987; see also Dewey [1888] 1969, 1923). Menand (2001), points out that pragmatism, like John Dewey himself, has roots in Burlington, Vermont, and at the University of Vermont. He argues that the struggle in the United States over abolition of slavery and the experience of the Civil War had immense influence on key thinkers in this intellectual movement. While the very enjoyable account by Menand is helpful, my current thinking is much influenced by Cheryl Misak and her student Diana Heney (see Heney 2016; Misak 2013) and by conversations with the remarkable Dewey scholar Don Koch. Following Pierce (1878), I want to understand the "upshot" of the idea of sustainability. I am grateful to Ortwin Renn and Carlo Jaeger, who reminded me of the influence of Dewey on Habermas.

62. John Dryzek, John Forester, Margaret Shannon, Ortwin Renn his students Seth Tuler and Tom Webler and I offered similar ideas about theories of deliberation at roughly the same time without being aware of each other until later (Dietz 1984, 1987; Dryzek 1987a, 1987b, 1987c; Forester 1985; Renn et al. 1993; Renn, Webler and Wiedemann 1995; Shannon 1987, 1991; Tuler and Webler 1995). David Bidwell, Ryan Gunderson and Pia-Johanna Schweitzer continue to do important work on the issue (Bidwell 2016; Bidwell and Schweizer 2021; Gunderson 2016; Schweizer et al. 2016). One of the great failings of scholarship in this area is that it remains insular, with very limited cross-citation. This impedes building the cumulative understanding we need. A recent Oxford Handbook brings together a substantial body of scholarship, but there is relatively little cross-citation of the sort that would help build a more cumulative literature on this crucial topic; see Chapter 5, Note 86 and Bächtiger et al. 2018; Curato et al. 2020. Drawing on foundational work by Fiorino (1990) and Stirling (2006, 2008), Renn and colleagues identify six objectives and rationales for deliberative processes, and each implies somewhat different modalities for carrying out deliberations; see Bidwell and Schweizer (2021); Renn (2008); Renn and Klinke (2011); Renn and Schweitzer (2009); Renn and Schweitzer (2020); Rosa, Renn and McCright (2013).

63. US National Research Council (2008: 226). The report is further discussed in Chapter 9. *The Drama of the Commons*, a study synthesizing the literature on commons governance discussed in Chapter 4, led by Elinor Ostrom, was one of the first efforts of the US National Research Council (NRC) Committee on Human Dimensions of Global Change (now the Board on Environmental Change and Society) when I was chair (Dietz, Ostrom and Stern 2003; Ostrom et al. 2002). She told us that until the mid-1980s, research on the commons had been conducted in multiple disciplines in isolation, with each field using its own concepts, terms and methods. In 1986, the NRC held a Conference in Annapolis, Maryland, that went a long way towards creating common concepts and terms and a cumulative interdisciplinary literature (US National Research Council 1986). The NRC public participation report was inspired by her account of the Annapolis meeting. Our goal was to synthesize the public participation literature. I felt that the work on public participation was in the same state as commons research before the Annapolis conference and suggested to Paul Stern, my good friend, frequent collaborator and the

NRC Study Director for the Human Dimensions Committee, that we do a study to bring the literature together. I fondly remember sitting on a bench under a tree on the Indiana University campus near the Workshop in Political Theory and Policy, where the Committee was meeting, discussing the study with Paul. Mike Slimak at the EPA was enthusiastic about the idea and he helped Paul coordinate with a variety of other agencies to find a small pool of funding. The result was *Public Participation in Environmental Assessment and Decision Making* (US National Research Council 2008), which I believe is the broadest synthesis of the literature on public participation presently available. (This is not to deny its limitations. Because all our funding was from US domestic agencies, we didn't have the resources to look in any detail at the extensive literature and experience in other countries and in particular around participation in development projects and programs.)

64. Council of Canadian Academies (2019).
65. Fraser (1992). See also Majewska (2021); Meehan (1995).
66. "Human ecology" seems to me the best covering term for the study of the interactions between humans and the biophysical environment. I was introduced to the idea by Owen Lovejoy, Bud Shane and Gene Wenniger when I was an undergraduate. It was transformational – I decided that this was the area of science I wanted to pursue. My interest in environmental issues followed soon after (Dietz 2020b). In the 1970s, some leading thinkers in Home Economics reconceptualized their field and called their approach human ecology (Bubolz 1996; Bubolz, Eicher and Sontag 1979; Bubolz and Sontag 1988; Hook and Bubolz 1970; Sontag and Bubolz 1993). In sociology, the tradition of human ecology began with links to ideas in biological ecology, but at least one of its leading theorists, Amos Hawley, came to reject those links even while others, such as Otis Dudley Duncan, continued to embrace them; see Duncan (1964); Duncan and Schnore (1959); Hawley (1986). Richerson's (1977) essay on the potential theoretical links between ecology and the social sciences still offers useful insights. Young (1974) provides a detailed history and Dyball and Newell (2014) an overview showing how the concepts of human ecology can be deployed to address sustainability problems. Discussions of these issues continue in the Society for Human Ecology and its journal *Human Ecology Review*. The term is reintroduced periodically with useful new insights but too often with limited attention to the broad scope and theoretical understandings I intend when I use the term, for example Marten (2001); Steiner (2016); Steiner and Steiner (2002). In particular, most formulations don't engage with the concepts of evolution and population thinking I view as essential to a robust human ecology. Liu and colleagues' ideas about coupled human and natural systems (CHANS) and the emergent idea of telecoupling (see Introduction, Note 37) are complementary to human ecology; see Liu et al. (2007a, 2007b); Liu et al. (2013). Different times and contexts in science lead to different terms, and as long as lines of communication allow us to build a cumulative enterprise, little harm is done by multiple terms. However, as I will point out repeatedly, when the terms serve as a barrier to learning across traditions, then progress can be slowed.
67. Key reviews of structural human ecology include Burns and Rudel (2015); Dietz and Jorgenson (2013); Dietz and York (2021). The idea of a theory group is from Mullins (1973, 1983). Gene was a master of acronyms. Others that play a role in this book are STIRPAT (Chapter 2) and HERO (Chapter 4).
68. York and Mancus (2009). Lough (see Chapter 6, Note 7), in a prescient analysis, offered a radical human ecology in which environmental problems are seen as rooted in patriarchy, bias and hierarchical power arrangements (Lough 1999).
69. Jay provides a still useful overview of critical theory in sociology, while Gunderson has explored the implications of key work in the Frankfurt School of Critical Theory for sustainability and our relations with other species (Gunderson 2014a, 2014b, 2015a, 2015b, 2021; Jay 1973). In a sense, critical theory is a scholarly form of consciousness raising, where we try to make visible the structures, assumptions and practices that shape our lives. The environment, other species and sustainability join class, gender, sexualities, race/ethnicity and other social categories in requiring us to break from

"taken for granted" assumptions that influence decisions. A major reason for broad and inclusive deliberative processes is to become aware of what is often hidden from one point of view but evident for another (Dietz 2013c).

70. There has been a recent resurgence of scholarly thinking about utopia, for example Hahnel and Wright (2016); Jacobsen and Tester (2016); Levitas (2013); Wright (2010). And utopian and dystopian thinking have long been a mainstay of science fiction, for example Callenbach (1975, 1981); Le Guin (1969, 1974, 1976, 1987); K. S. Robinson 1984, 1988, 1990).

71. Voltaire (1772). Originally: "The better is the enemy of the good." ("Il meglio è nemico del bene.") Shakespeare has the Duke of Albany express a similar sentiment in *King Lear* (Act 1, Scene 4): "striving to better, oft we mar what's well."

72. J.B. Robinson (1988). The logic of finding what interferes with a desired future plays an important role in "Cause and Effect," an episode of *Star Trek: The Next Generation*, where the number 3, discussed in Section I.4, is important (Rodenberry and Berman 1992).

73. McEvoy and Dietz (1977).

74. Hendry et al. (2004).

75. Renn, Webler and Wiedemann (1995); Tuler and Webler (1995); US National Research Council (1996); Webler (1993). Modeling and simulation can be a tool in deliberative processes; see Hedelin et al. (2021); Schmitt-Olabisi et al. (2020); van den Belt (2004).

76. Dietz and Rycroft (1987); Dietz, Stern and Rycroft (1989); Henry, Dietz and Sweeney (2021).

77. Dietz (2020b).

78. The term "normative" also is used to describe ethical arguments and assertions. I prefer "ethical" to avoid confusion with the psychological concept of norms discussed in Chapter 3. See Box 5.1.

79. Among other things, I am a straight, Anglo, white male, first-generation college student from a union working-class family who grew up in the industrial Midwest of the United States.

80. Henrich, Heine and Norenzayan (2010a, 2010b).

81. Harding (1998, 2015). See also Carrera et al. (2019); Gewin (2022); Sidik (2022b). Infinite Diversity in Infinite Combinations (IDIC) is mentioned in several *Star Trek* episodes: Original Series: "Is There in Truth No Beauty"; *Voyager*: "Gravity"; *Enterprise*: "The Forge," "Awakening" and "kir'Shara."

82. On the antiquity of animal images, see Kalof (2007). On the interplay between humans and other animals across history, see Kalof and Real (2008). On the state of animal studies, see Kalof (2017). Efforts to incorporate an animal studies perspective into sustainability analysis include Dietz and York (2015); York and Longo (2017); York and Mancus (2013), and papers in a special issue of the *International Journal of Sociology* (York and Longo 2017). On ethical issues, see Beauchamp and Frey (2011); Kalof (2017), especially sections 1 and 2. The Animal Studies Bibliography of the Animal Studies Program of Michigan State University provides an extensive curated overview of the literature (https://animalstudies.msu.edu).

83. Garcia's statement is: "Things happen, and we try to figure out what they were." His next sentence is the quote at the top of Prolegomenon.

# 1    Sustainability and Decisions

1. Hynde (2015). Chrissie and I were acquaintances when we were both in Kent in the late 1960s and early 1970s. Some artists are deeply thoughtful and incredibly articulate about politics, for example friends I met at Kent, including Greg Artzner and Terry Leonino (Magpie); Alex Bevan; Kerry Blech; Rolly Brown; Andy Cohen; and Pat Humphries (Emma's Revolution). Musicians, however, are not political analysts and one can enjoy their music but not expect deep insights. There has been a

controversy about conservative talk-show host Rush Limbaugh using a bit of "My City Was Gone" in his theme music. In an interview that touched on this matter, Chrissie indicates that she doesn't care about politics, an odd stance for someone who is outspoken about animal rights (Kozlowski 2018). From what I recall, Chrissie was not very politically active during her time in Kent.

2. Many malls that were developed in the 1960s have fallen into decay (Lange 2022). The Chapel Hill Mall near Kent has faced electrical shutoffs and foreclosures for nonpayment of bills (Goist 2020). Some malls are being repurposed for other uses, others sit abandoned and in decay. Meanwhile many downtown areas that had been in decay are resurging, in part because of public policies intended to revitalize them and the growing desirability of city centers as a place to live. The COVID-19 pandemic, however, may change this trend, as demand for housing in rural areas rises. Of course, many families can't afford to move to rural areas, where local jobs are scarce.

3. Cai (2011).

4. Rapidly growing water consumption in arid regions and the increasing impacts of climate change mean many areas are considering water reuse as a response to serious water shortages. Water reuse requires careful analysis so that policy and practices are grounded in the best available science (Harris-Lovett and Sedlak 2020; US National Research Council 2012). My point about Northern Virginia is that few residents were aware of this consequence of rapid population growth and that reuse was an artifact of how the system had evolved, not an openly discussed policy choice.

5. The conference was organized to reflect the interests of what Logan and Molotch (1987) have called "the growth machine." They use this term to refer to a coalition of developers, politicians and other interests who profit from urban growth and suburbanization. Chapter 2 discusses debates about growth and Chapter 7 examines some of the prevalent theories of growth and sustainability, including the growth machine.

6. Lazo (2021). I thank Tom Grace for making me aware of Hillsboro and Mayor Roger Vance for sharing the experience. It is a fine example of the shifts towards sustainability that can happen via leadership and coalition-building.

7. Manure spreading on farms can create runoff problems that contribute to algal blooms in Lake Champlain. There are ongoing efforts to require best practices in managing manure – the goal is to preserve agriculture while protecting the lake.

8. Centner (2006); Jordan (2009–10). I have often been struck by the contradiction inherent in advocates of the free market who are eager to have the right to sue restricted. The US Supreme Court under Justice Roberts "has been the most pro-business of any since the Second World War" and has made decisions that may sharply limit the ability of citizens, consumers and workers to bring suit for redress (Epstein, Landes and Posner 2012; Surowiecki 2016). Yet the standard free market/libertarian solution to environmental externalities, running back at least to Coase is that those adversely affected by the actions of another, such as pollution, should negotiate a transaction to resolve the dispute, a negotiation often handled via lawsuits and the courts. See Adler (2009); Anderson and Leal (1991); Dolan (2006). So, arguing for little or no government regulation and restricting the right to sue seems to leave no remedy for the harm my activities do to my neighbors. It contradicts the theory that underpins much libertarian thinking about the environment. While logically contradictory, this stance does serve the self-interest of those who might be sued. I will return to the issue of libertarian approaches in Chapter 5. See also Chapter 6, Note 16. (The philosopher Paul Thompson [2010: 295], on first reading Coase's "On the Problem of Social Cost," thought it was a *reductio ad absurdum* argument rather than a serious proposal.)

9. United Nations Department of Economic and Social Affairs (2020).

10. On the acceleration of global environmental change, see Steffen, Broadgate et al. (2015a); Steffen et al. (2018). On planetary boundaries, see Randers et al. (2019); Rockström et al. (2009a, 2009b); Steffen, Richardson et al. (2015).

11. Sage (2020).
12. Seto and Reenberg (2014); Seto et al. (2017).
13. Bush et al. (2021); Koch et al. (2019).
14. Whyte (2017a, 2018).
15. Graeber and Wengrow (2021).
16. Gates (2014); Gilhooley (2020); Gordon-Reed (2018).
17. Azar (2007); Dubrulle (2006); Hochschild (2006).
18. Burns (2012a, 2012b). Such terms are boundary objects spanning across different communities (Pellizzoni 2012).
19. Portney (2015) has thoughtfully engaged the various definitions of the term. The diversity and complexity of views on this issue are evident in the very interesting work *Sustainability Ethics: 5 Questions* (Raffaelle, Robison and Selinger 2010). My own thinking has been strongly influenced by many environmental sociologists and other scholars who have addressed the concepts involved (Burns 2012a, 2012b; Lockie 2012, 2016a, 2016b; Lockie and Wong 2017; Longo et al. 2016; Mitcham 1995; Murphy 2012; Pellizzoni 2012; Robinson 2004). Historians have clarified my understanding. Worster's biographies of John Wesley Powell and John Muir provide useful backdrops to how ideas of sustainability emerged in discourses about environment, natural resources and conservation (Worster 2001, 2008), as do Lear's biography of Rachel Carson (Lear 1998) and Eagan's biography of Barry Commoner (Eagan 2007). Histories of US environmental policy and of the US environmental movement also provide some perspective (Andrews 1999; Brulle 2000). Caradonna and Grober discuss the history of sustainability (Cardonna 2014; Grober 2012). Worster's history of concepts of growth and limits (Worster 2016) and Macekura's history of sustainable development (Macekura 2015) were especially useful. The idea of regenerative development has recently been advocated as a way of moving beyond sustainability, although I agree with Robinson and Cole that the core theoretical issues remain much the same (Dietz 2020d; Robinson and Cole 2015).
20. On greenhouse gas emissions, see "Greenhouse Gas Emissions from a Typical Passenger Vehicle," US Environmental Protection Agency (EPA), web page, www.epa.gov/greenvehicles/greenhouse-gas-emissions-typical-passenger-vehicle. On Davis: Lott, Tardiff and Lott (1977); Lott, Tardiff and Lott (1977); Vine (1981). On current commuting: McKenzie (2014).
21. *Oxford English Dictionary* (*OED*), online edition, accessed March 22, 2013. The *OED* cites Shakespeare in *Henry IV*, Part 2, 4.1.182 in a speech by Westmoreland as one of the earlier uses of the term in English. Shakespeare's plays are largely about decisions, what leads to them and their consequences. In *Two Gentlemen of Verona*, perhaps Shakespeare's first play, the action is initiated by Valentine's decision to travel and his friend Proteus' decision to stay in Verona. *Hamlet* is fundamentally about the difficulty he has in making existential decisions. The end of *The Tempest*, probably Shakespeare's last sole-authored play, is about Prospero's decision not to seek revenge and to give up his powers (in words that many see as Shakespeare's statement about giving up his pen to retire): "I'll break my staff, bury it certain fathoms in the earth, and deeper than did ever plummet sound, I'll drown my book."
22. Social practice theory argues that bundles of habits, "practices," are highly consequential for sustainability and focuses on these practices rather than decisions (Shove, Watson and Spurling 2015). Social practice theory is sometimes posited as in opposition to better established approaches reviewed here and in Chapter 3. I view it as a useful complement and believe progress will best be made by moving towards integrative rather than oppositional approaches. For example, some studies of energy consumption have used quantitative methods to model typical behavior and consumption patterns and then qualitative methods to understand outliers whose consumption is much higher or lower than what might be expected. And if one accepts that habits can be changed, then presumably

they often change as a result of decisions. One insight I draw from social practice theory is that many of our consequential actions as consumers are linked together, and those linkages may either facilitate or retard change (see Chapter 7).

23. See Nielsen, Nicholas et al. (2021); Stern et al. (1999); Stern (2000, 2014). We have elaborated this analysis to look at positions in the supply chain that produce goods and dispose of waste (Stern and Dietz 2020). As consumers, our choices are constrained by the decisions of those who produce what is available to consume and our decisions in turn influence what gets purchased and to a substantial degree what gets produced.

24. Dietz et al. (2009). Vandenbergh and Gilligan also examine in detail the potential contributions of private sector actions on reducing greenhouse gas emissions; see the discussion of their work in Chapter 7 (Gilligan and Vandenbergh 2020; Vandenbergh and Gilligan 2017).

25. We limited our analysis to make it tractable. It took a substantial effort to get solid estimates for electricity and fuel use. Adding food, water and other goods and services is an important topic for further research, and innovative efforts are taking this on (Ivanova et al. 2015; Steen-Olsen and Hertwich 2015).

26. On corporate and supply chain effects, see Vandenbergh and Gilligan (2015); Vandenbergh and Moore (2022). On labeling, see Taufique et al. (2022).

27. The academic literature has segregated substantially into those who study the general public, those who study social movements and social movement activists and those who study policy processes and the policy system (Henry and Dietz 2012). While such a division of labor may increase efficiency, it can also lead to artificial gaps in understanding. Clearly, there are some people who are full-time professional activists and others to whom movement activities are a central part of their identities. They are part of the policy networks noted in the Introduction. There are still others who support a movement in various ways but do not make the movement a major part of their lives. People move along that continuum over the course of their lives. Indeed, a very interesting question that has not been given much attention is how and why people make transitions across these roles, especially the transitions from mild concern to strong concern to activism (Stern et al. 1999).

28. Fischhoff (2007); Shwom (2011); Stern et al. (2016).

29. Coffee (2021); Condon (2020b); Nielsen et al. (2021c, 2021e). On stock ownership, see Chung (2009).

30. Jenkins (2015); Milesi et al. (2005). The National Wildlife Federation (NWF) encourages gardeners, homeowners and others to develop wildlife-friendly landscapes (www.nwf.org/CertifiedWildlifeHabitat), and there are also certification programs for golf courses, cemeteries and other areas. Even small improvements can be helpful. Desiree Di Mauro found that in the Washington, DC metro area the presence of households with NWF certification increased the diversity of butterflies (Di Mauro, Dietz and Rockwood 2007). The study relied on data from butterfly counts conducted by citizens; citizen science can be an important way to link science with local knowledge, engaging those with a passion for some aspect of the environment; see Vohland et al. (2021); Wehn et al. (2021).

31. Large swaths of natural resources are managed by organizations. The US federal government manages about 30 percent of the land in the United States, so the decisions of the agencies managing that land can have immense influence on North American ecosystems. In other cases, a private sector organization or even an individual manages substantial resources. Some land management decisions are made by individuals or organizations behind closed doors. But most resource management, even of privately held land or government land, involves some mix of involvement by the private sector, government and the public (Dietz, Ostrom and Stern 2003). Ranchers lobby US federal agencies about the management of federal rangeland, much of which is leased to them. The US Department of Agriculture provides incentives to farmers to prevent soil erosion and to grow some crops and not others. Communities try to exert pressure on both government and private landowners, for example when small towns resist sprawl development.

32. Paul Stern suggested the term "prosumer." A growing literature examines these decisions (Rai and Henry 2016; Wolske, Stern and Dietz 2017). At our home in Vermont, we have purchased photovoltaic cells through our electrical coop. The cell arrays are not located on our property but are part of a community solar farm a few miles away. I could classify this either as a consumer action or as action in the role of resource manager. We also use firewood in the winter. Most of our wood is from windfalls in our property, which is just over an acre. Again, the boundaries across categories are not rigid.

33. Nielsen et al. (2021d).

34. Lee and Ditko (1962).

35. On the effects of inequality, see Jorgenson (2015a Jorgenson, Schor et al. (2015, 2016); Jorgenson, Schor and Huang (2017); Jorgenson, Dietz and Kelly (2018); Kelly, Thombs and Jorgenson (2021); Knight, Schor and Jorgenson (2017); Mikkelson, Gonzalez and Peterson (2007). The importance of diversity for research and problem-solving is discussed throughout the book and is especially important for research on inequality (Gewin 2022).

36. Stern, Dietz and Vandenbergh (2022). See also Chapter 7.

37. Dietz (2013b). Gene Rosa was an innovative environmental sociologist as well as an artist, and his thinking permeates the book. Context is nearly always shaped by social categories, and in contemporary societies those categories are usually class, race/ethnicity and gender identity, and often geographic location. The contextual factors that shape the adaptive landscape for an individual and community – what is hard, what is easy, what will be facilitated or opposed – are usually intersectional (Carbado et al. 2013; Cho, Crenshaw and McCall 2013; Collins 2019; Crenshaw 1990, 2003). The social categories that shape context are not just the sum of the effects of each social category; rather, together they define a place on the adaptive landscape that reflects all the relevant social categories acting together. Quantitative social science has attempted to model this at least since the 1970s using interaction effects (e.g. allowing the effects of being an African American woman to be different than the simple sum of being a woman and being African American). There were always limitations based on sample size and what was measured, and the growth of intersectionality theory helps refine conceptualization of these analyses. The idea of context is central to my arguments throughout the book, and I always mean it in an intersectional way.

38. The quote is from Mills (1959: 5). The relationship between our personal situation and larger structures is an example of the "population thinking" discussed in the Introduction and Section 1.4.2. It is also the basis of the critical theory I discussed in the Introduction. In Chapter 2, I will use these ideas to look at the emergence of sustainability.

39. See Plumer and Popovich (2020); Squires (2017). Best and Mejia provide an excellent online analysis on how the effects of redlining have persisted over many decades (Best and Meija 2022; see also Zhong and Popovich 2022). Redlining can even influence the distribution and evolution of liminal species (see Chapter 6, Note 57) that live near humans (Schell, Dyson et al. 2020). Not all segregation is a result of exclusionary laws, policies and norms; some segregation can arise from relatively innocent preferences (Clark and Fossett 2008; Schelling 1969, 1971, 2006). If people have a slight preference for having some other people similar to them nearby, over time the distribution of residence can become fairly segregated. This happens even if no one is actively trying to avoid another group or seeking to only have people like them nearby. A very nice online simulation of this is at "Parable of the Polygons," which points out the solution to this problem – people who may want some folks like then nearby but who also want some diversity in their neighborhood ("Parable of the Polygons: A Playable Post on the Shape of Society" website: https://ncase.me/polygons/; accessed June 13, 2022). It often takes a conscious effort to maintain diversity. I emphasize that while some segregation occurs as a result of individual choices, most of the residential patterns that disadvantage some neighborhoods are the result of explicit and biased decisions both in the past and at present.

Segregation is parallel to the system of homophily that shapes individual views and policy debates, a central theme throughout the book (Henry 2020; Henry and Vollan 2014; Klar and Shmargad 2017).

40. On COVID-19, see Perry, Harshbarger and Romer (2020). The idea of multiply deserted areas is from Satcher (2021, 2022).

41. Satcher (2021).

42. Historically, redlining was a mechanism for segregation by race and ethnicity, but the racial and ethnic composition of these communities and the rest of the cities surrounding them has changed over time and now varies tremendously across cities, depending on specific historical trajectories (Perry 2020; Perry and Harshbarger 2019). These trajectories are not often well documented except by case studies. The NAACP and the Brookings Institution have developed a joint Black Assets Index to document and better understand the strengths of African American communities, including majority Black cities in the United States (NAACP Black Progress Assets website: https://naacp.org/cam paigns/black-assets-index).

43. The experiment by Michelson and Morley in Cleveland, Ohio, and in particular the fact that they were unable to detect any variation in the speed of light relative to the earth's motion, was fundamental, underpinning Einstein's thinking in developing special relativity based on the idea that the speed of light is invariant across observers. It is a fact that is not very dependent on context, and that context-independence led to deeper understandings (Michelson and Morley 1887; Wikipedia, s.v. "Michelson–Morley experiment," https://en.wikipedia.org/wiki/Michelson–Morley_ experiment, accessed November 12, 2022).

44. Rivers and Arvai (2007); Stack (1975).

45. Goering and Wienk (1971); Ross and Yinger (2002); Small et al. (2021).

46. The classic study identifying this pattern is Stack (1975). The literature looking at these strategies is now extensive, showing that such strategies are not always possible or useful; see Henly, Danziger and Offer (2005); Frankenhuis and Nettle (2020). See also Chapter 3, Note 100 and Chapter 8.

47. Loan-sharking is an extension of this practice – if friends and kin cannot provide a loan, there may be someone who can, albeit at ruinous interest rates (the vigorish). This is a persistent theme in *The Godfather*, *Wiseguys/Goodfellas* and *The Sopranos*. The idea that organized crime provide services that some communities cannot easily obtain through more conventional means runs through these stories. Recently, the rise of "pay day" loan businesses is legitimizing and commercializing that practice, at least for those who have regular paychecks. Much the same kind of process has led to the displacement of the numbers racket with state lotteries.

48. Coughenour et al. (1985).

49. Goodman and Chokshi (2021).

50. McLaughlin argues that in addition to dealing with structure and agency effectively, Darwinian thinking resolves the apparent conflict between nominalism and essentialism while showing how rather antiquated notions of these concepts still haunt much of our theory (McLaughlin 1998, 2001, 2012a, 2012c; McLaughlin and Dietz 2008).

51. There seem to have been several stages in our approach to unanticipated effects of technology. While technological change has always been a key aspect of social change, widespread acknowledgment of the importance of technological change may have first become prevalent in the late nineteenth and early twentieth century (first Mary Shelley's prescient *Frankenstein* and then the novels of Jules Verne and H. G. Wells are one indication; the celebration of Thomas Edison another). But despite these cautionary stories, the tendency seems to have been to ignore unintended consequences or, in the case of some technologies, like tetraethyl lead, to actively suppress information about those consequences (Kitman 2000). In the late 1960s, with the rise first of concern with nuclear fallout and then the rise of the environmental movement, and especially the emerging emphasis on environmental and social impact assessment, technology assessment and risk assessment, we seem to have acknowledged, tried

to anticipate and struggled to develop strategies to mitigate unintended consequences, or to avoid technologies (e.g. the US SuperSonic Transport) where the unanticipated consequences seemed unacceptable. Now, the heralded search for and claims of "disruptive" technologies seem to be an argument that we value unanticipated consequences. Certainly, ubiquitous computing and communication, the internet of things, artificial intelligence and robots, as well as other technologies, are producing interesting and useful applications that emerge without having been anticipated. But one can speculate that self-driving cars and trucks will displace most people who work by driving, more sophisticated AI and robots will displace a great deal of service work and so on. Then there might be unanticipated consequences: high levels of unemployment in a society where a decent and dignified life, even health, depend on having a job. But other political choices could produce a society where fewer hours of human work are needed to provide a decent income, leaving more time for other pursuits.

52. See Chapter 4.
53. McLaughlin and Dietz (2008); McLaughlin (2012c); Scott-Phillips et al. (2014).
54. Korten (2015).
55. Those with power work very actively to shape the adaptive landscape. For example, the Koch brothers are making substantial investments to block the development of public transit infrastructure in communities around the United States (Tabuchi 2018). Their actions now will have an influence on the choices faced by individuals in those communities for decades to come, making it harder for them to choose public transportation.
56. McLaughlin (2022).
57. Marx ([1851] 1973: 158).
58. Bullard (1983); Burch (1976); Dietz (2020b); Environmental Action (1970); Hare (1970); Mascarenhas (2020).
59. Dietz, Rosa and York (2010), Dietz (2017a); Rosa and Dietz (2012).
60. Jorgenson (2016a, 2016b).
61. Downey (2015); Holifield, Chakraborty and Walker (2017); Mascarenhas (2020); Mohai, Pellow and Roberts (2009); Pellow (2017).
62. See Chapter 2.
63. International Social Science Council, Institute of Development Studies and United Nations Educational Scientific and Cultural Organization (2016); United Nations Development Program (2019).
64. Flint was the subject of Michael Moore's first film *Roger & Me* (1989); the community was facing difficult problems even three decades ago. Jennifer Carrera and other colleagues at Michigan State are conducting research in Flint that is exemplary for how it actively engages the community as partners (Carrera et al. 2019; Carrera and Key 2021; Carrera et al. 2022; Hanna-Attisha et al. 2016; Hanna-Attisha 2017; Hanna-Attisha 2018; Langlois et al. 2017; Michigan Civil Rights Commission 2017; Michigan Legislature Joint Select Committee on the Flint Water Public Health Emergency 2016; Pauli 2020; Ruckart et al. 2019). Collaborations between researchers and those struggling with environmental and sustainability problems are essential to provide the diversity needed to develop useful knowledge, a theme emphasized in Chapters 4 and 9; see also Chapter 6, Note 5.
65. Beck's influential work on risk, usually labeled risk society theory, was troubling to many of us because of its premise that in the late twentieth century risk cut across traditional lines of stratification, especially class. We wondered how he had managed to miss the already very substantial literature on risk and environmental justice (Beck 1986; Dietz, Frey and Rosa 2001; Rosa, Renn and McCright 2013). Even his core example, exposure to radiation from the Chernobyl nuclear accident, produces inequities in risk exposure. Certainly, it is true that the physical and biological processes that distribute radionuclides from Chernobyl across Europe are not driven by

class, race, gender identity, and so on. But the ability to shield oneself from those effects by moving, by being selective in what food to consume, and by otherwise avoiding exposure is directly related to income and power, very traditional lines of stratification. The powerful can make choices to reduce their risk; the disadvantaged cannot. In the end, Beck has some interesting arguments to make but his initial claims certainly led to skepticism in many readers.

66. Fisman et al. (2015).
67. The Berkeley students fell between the Yale Law students and the public with regard to preferences for efficiency over equality but were even more self-interested and less altruistic than the Yale Law students.
68. Cam Whitley and I have found that the degree of altruism and support for policies that promote equality is related to income, with the highest altruism and support for equality in those of middle income (Dietz and Whitley 2018). See also Chapter 3, Note 13 on the effects of economics training on values.
69. Nielsen et al. (2021a).
70. Nielsen et al. (2021d). Decisions we make as groups, whether as a community, a political unit or in organizations, matter as much or more than the decisions of the elite. To address that issue we have to consider the context in which individual decisions are combined into a group decision, that is, we have to consider the political institutions involved. Since one book cannot cover everything, I will not examine political institutions in any detail, although I will briefly discuss arguments about how best to aggregate individual decisions into a group decision in Chapter 9. See also Box I.2 on institutions.
71. Friis and Nielsen (2019); Liu et al. (2013).
72. O'Connor (2013).
73. Turner (1991).

# 2    Sustainability Evolving

1. An earlier version of some of this analysis appeared in Dietz (2015a).
2. This account is based on fallible memory. My father did not talk much about his early life. It was in going through some files after my mother died that I learned about his Bronze Star. His brother Les lost his leg while in the Army in New Guinea. I suspect that many World War II combat veterans dealt with their experiences and trauma in silence.
3. The pandemic killed 20–50 million people worldwide (Johnson and Mueller 2002). Even the low end of this estimate is greater than the total number of fatalities in World War I, which killed 17 million. The population of the world in 1918 was about 1.8 billion; today, the mortality rate of the 1918 flu pandemic would kill about 80–200 million people out of a global population of 7.8 billion. As I write, the COVID-19 pandemic has killed about 6.8 million worldwide.
4. Murray (1982).
5. Endres (2020).
6. The civil rights movement was reshaping the United States during this period. But it was largely absent from my parents' biographies except as national news. The NAACP was active in Kent (Thomas Grace, personal communication, November 2, 2020). But Kent was residentially segregated in fact if not by law, and my parents had little interaction with African American families. I grew up on East Elm St. Two blocks away, West Elm was home to my Irish American grandparents and the Italian American and Polish American grandparents of my friends. The neighborhood had always been the settling point for new migrants to Kent, with children moving to other neighborhoods as they established their own households. By the 1960s, the neighborhood

was transitioning to being predominantly African American as the older generation of Irish, Italian and Polish Americans died out or moved – not so much "white flight" as cohort succession, although I suspect that there may have been discriminatory actions that targeted the neighborhood for African Americans. Our public schools were integrated, but social life centered around churches was largely segregated by denomination and there were only a few African American families in St. Patrick's Catholic Church.

7. The fine scholarship of my friends Bruce Way and Tom Grace has helped me appreciate the historian's craft. I emphasize that I am not trained as an historian or even as an historical sociologist. What follows here is both my reading of some of the primary literature and discussion with a few of the participants and my interpretation of what historians have written. I cede authoritative word on these issues to those who conduct the impressive and detailed historical work I draw upon. However, with some exceptions, most historians strongly prefer detailed accounts that are quite sharply focused in time and space, and for my purposes a longer and broader perspective is required, so I may lose some precision in the interests of that broader perspective. I hope that where I am wrong my errors will encourage trained historians to take up the issues.

8. Hacker (2019); Mills (1959). See the Introduction. The sociological imagination has two components. One is the population thinking: our decisions are shaped by but also shape larger struggles. The second is that when the idea of "personal troubles" is invoked, the sociological imagination also suggests an ethical theory, such as the criteria described in Chapter 5, and can be thought of as critical theory.

9. The focus on income and GDP has more than one justification. For those who are poor, increases in income often lead to increases in well-being: access to potable water, adequate food, safe and secure shelter, education and health care. But increases in GDP and national income do not necessarily change the circumstances of the worst off; that depends on how such increases are distributed. And the interest in economic growth can also be viewed as a manifestation of the need of capitalists to be able to invest for profit. That tension is a major theme in this chapter.

10. The best compilation I've found is on Wikipedia, s.v. "World War II casualties," https://en.wikipedia.org/wiki/World_War_II_casualties (accessed December 14, 2019).

11. The term "capital" is sometimes used to refer to the resources deployed to produce things. Sometimes it is used to refer to the group interests of those who own those resources, particularly physical capital, or just to those who make most of their income from profits from investments rather than from selling their time in labor. I prefer the term "resource" to "capital" since the latter implies that a resource is being used with the intent of profit and that is not always the case (Dietz 2015a). See also Chapter 2, Note 109.

12. See Chapter 2, Note 28.

13. Kapur, Lewis and Webb (1997: 74).

14. Schnaiberg (1980), see especially chap. 5. I will discuss Schnaiberg's and related views of the drivers of environmental stress in some detail in Chapter 7. The period of the great compromise was also a time of continued racial and gender discrimination, and while unions were more legitimate than in the past, there were still important conflicts between them and management.

15. Pilisuk and Hayden (1965).

16. Kuznets (1955, 1979) emphasized that his analysis of the historical experience with declining inequality in England, Germany and the United States might not generalize to future trajectories of inequality. Nearly all of the discussion of growth and inequality in this period, and too much of the discussion more recently, focuses on income inequality. Attention should also be given to wealth inequality and other bases for inequality, such as racism, gender inequality and inequality within the

household (Bennett 2013; Nevena and Giulia 2015). The Kuznets argument has also been applied to the effects of economic growth on the environment, see Section 2.3.2.

17. This shift from competitive to monopoly capitalism was noted by both mainstream economists and the *Monthly Review* school who in turn influenced the environmental sociologists Anderson and Schnaiberg, see Chapter 7, Note 61.

18. Putnam and Garrett (2020).

19. Lepore (2018).

20. McEvoy (1969, 1971).

21. Maxwell and Shields (2019).

22. Gelles (2022).

23. Putnam and Garrett (2020).

24. In Chapter 3, I suggest that unions during this period may have been effective at extending empathy beyond their membership to all workers and even all those facing economic hardship, although even in this period some unions discriminated against women and BIPOC people.

25. Dietz and Whitley (2018).

26. The term "third world" apparently was first used by Sauvy (1952) (*Tiers Monde* in the original) in an essay entitled "Trois monde, une planéte." It was in analogy to the third estate (*le Tiers État*), the population of France not part of the nobility or the clergy. Sauvy argued that, like the third estate at the time of the French Revolution, the third world was looking for a voice in the politics of the time. Over time, the term "third world" came to imply negative stereotypes of poor and dysfunctional countries so we should stop using it (M'ikanatha 2022; Silver 2021). As Note 27 indicates, I have problems with "less developed" as well. We might use non-WEIRD to contrast the majority of the world with the Western, Educated, Industrial, Rich Democracies. Another possibility is Global South, noting that this includes some countries in the north and excludes some in the south. Still another is to group countries by per capita gross domestic product (GDP), so we might have low- and lower-middle-income countries (LMICs) or low-income and middle-income countries (LICs and MICs). We should remember that each nation is unique in its current situation, culture and history, and that every country contains substantial internal variation – the poorest nations have many wealthy people, the most affluent usually have many poor. In the end, the community of these countries should guide us in choice of a collective term to describe them. I thank Jihan Mohammed for guiding me into this discussion.

27. The use of the term "development" reflects the view that the "less developed" nations would follow trajectories similar to those that marked the historical transformations of the "developed" nations (Rostow 1960). This builds on a long and unfortunate history in the social sciences of assuming that social change follows a series of stages, what is best termed an "evolutionist" model since it profoundly misunderstands evolutionary processes (Dietz, Burns and Buttel 1990). A more useful approach is one that embraces evolutionary processes and thus rejects a master narrative, emphasizes contingency and allows a substantial place both for chance and for humans exercising power. See the discussion of Darwinian evolutionary thinking in the Introduction, Chapters 1 and 7, and Burns and Dietz (1992c); Dietz and Burns (1992); McLaughlin (1998); McLaughlin and Dietz (2008); York and Clark (2006).

28. The World Bank was the nexus of development policy in the last half of the twentieth century. The Bank is actually two organizations, the International Bank for Reconstruction and Development (IBRD) and the International Development Association. As the title implies, the IBRD was initially focused on helping European nations recover from World War II (Kapur, Lewis and Webb 1997: 57–84). The World Bank's first loan of $40 million was to Chile in 1946 as a sort of "pilot" on lending to developing nations. But the first big loan, $250 million (about $2.7 billion in today's currency), was to France on June 7, 1947. From 1946 to 1949, 81 percent of Bank loans went to Europe, while

from 1950 to 1959 this dropped to 20 percent. About 53 percent of loans during the 1950s went to Africa and Asia (Kapur, Lewis and Webb 1997: 6). So, even while early efforts were focused on the reconstruction of Europe, the Bank was engaged with lower-income countries from the start.

29. Chase-Dunn (1998); Evans (1979); Jorgenson (2016b).

30. Andrews (1999); Brulle (2000); Dietz (2020b); Worster (2016).

31. "Conservation" is the term most commonly used to cover the several streams of thinking and activism focused on protecting other species, wild places and the biosphere. A more detailed analysis would have to be attentive to the distinctions between conservationists, preservationists and other streams of the overall movement (Andrews 1999; Brulle 2000; Worster 2001, 2008, 2016).

32. Burch (1971). Burch's essay was an early treatment of what we now call environmental justice. The first examination of environmental justice of which I am aware is by Black Studies scholar Nathan Hare (1970) – it is the first paper in the first issue of *The Black Scholar*.

33. Sometimes the environmental movement and the counterculture of the 1960s and 1970s are viewed as "anti-technology." Critiques of mainstream technology, of consumption patterns and of the militarization of technology did emerge during that period. Indeed, the important debate between Commoner on the one hand and Ehrlich and Holdren on the other was one in which both sides acknowledged the importance of technological choice in shaping our impact on the environment but differed on whether or not growing population and affluence mattered (Dietz 1996–1997; see Chapter 2, Note 69). The alternative/appropriate technology movement also emerged during this period, emphasizing new approaches to agriculture, intentional design of communities and renewable energy sources, among other things – what we would now label "sustainable technologies" (Lovins 1976; Schumacher 1973). The *Whole Earth Catalog* (subtitled *Access to Tools*) and the descendent *Whole Earth Review/CoEvolution Quarterly* exemplified this positive engagement with technology (Kirk 2007). Contemporary interest in sustainable/organic agriculture and food systems and renewable energy has deeper historical roots but they flourished in the counterculture. Turner (2006) has argued that the *Whole Earth Catalog* was an influential precursor of the development of personal computing and the web, a point also made by Isaacson (2014). This engagement with technology was not without its critics (Dickson 1975; Pursell 1993; Schnaiberg 1982, 1983).

34. Dietz (2020b); Environmental Action (1970); Hare (1970); Rome (2013).

35. Worster (2008). See also Chapter 6, Note 1. Soukup and Machlis (2021) provide a masterly assessment of the present state and future of the US national parks. The tension between facts and values is central in decision-making about them (Dietz 2017b).

36. See also the discussion in Chapter 6 of a major controversy around the park.

37. Bloom and Duer (2020a); Spence (1999).

38. A rich literature addresses these issues, including important insights from Indigenous perspectives (Balee 1998; Council of Canadian Academies 2019; Dowie 2011; Kimmerer and Lake 2001; Spence 1999; Stevens 2014; Whyte 2017c, 2018, 2020; Whyte, Brewer II and Johnson 2015).

39. While the rhetoric of Western nations contrasted democracy with Communism, and Leninist and Stalinist political theory call for control by a vanguard, the Communist nations of the late twentieth century embraced their own rhetoric of democracy, as, for example, in official national names such as Deutsche Demokratische Republik (German Democratic Republic – East Germany) or the Democratic People's Republic of Korea (North Korea – officially 조선민주주의인민공화국; *Chosŏn Minjujuŭi Inmin Konghwaguk*). These governments were/are hardly democracies by anyone else's standards. But the legitimacy of democracy was so thorough that even these authoritarian regimes cloaked themselves in democratic rhetoric. This is in contrast to, for example, fascist Germany, where a cult of "die Füehrer" (Führerprinzip) was a central part of the political ideology – decisions were justified as "working towards the Füehrer," that is, reflecting

Hitler's will (Kershaw 2008). (Some have argued that Nazi policy was shaped by substantial drug use (Holmes 1984; Ohler and Whiteside 2016)). The modalities of dictatorship are also examined by Lukacs and Dikötter (Dikötter 2019; Lukacs 2011). Much of our understanding of post–World War II history has been filtered by the Cold War and reinterpretations are likely to be ongoing.

40. Liberal has two meanings that can easily be confused. In contemporary politics, especially in the United States, liberal is used to describe a position that is to the left of conservative but not as left as progressives or socialists. In its classical form, especially in the arguments of John Locke, liberals emphasized individual rights and freedom (liberal derives from the Latin *liber* meaning free) over more hierarchical views of proper government. This use of the term "liberal" is based on the idea of autonomous individuals and is closely aligned with stances that support free markets as the appropriate way for societies to allocate resources. Thus liberalism contrasts with views such as pragmatism that emphasize more complex modes of interaction and emergent properties (Menand 2001: 244–245, 304). This contrast will be a central theme in much of the book but especially in Chapters 5 and 6. I use the term "liberal" here in this more classical sense of democracies that are intended to support markets and capitalism, referring to the contemporary form of these arguments as neoliberalism. Neoliberalism places less emphasis on democracy than on markets and capitalism.

41. This essay sparked substantial discussion and was followed by a book elaborating the argument (Fukuyama 1989, 1992). Frank was a colleague when this essay was published, and so I read it then and had the opportunity to discuss it with him, Tom Burns and Mark Jacobs.

42. Graeber and Wengrow (2021).

43. Branch (1988, 1998, 2006); Deloria and Lytle (1998); Fernández-Armesto (2014); Yoo and Azuma (2016).

44. Pinkney (2003).

45. Any index of democracy requires judgments about democratic practices and will be based on data with substantial uncertainty. The V-Dem data sets are among the most extensive, carefully developed and carefully justified. Other indicators from other sources show the same general pattern.

46. The idea that science could help the military stretches back at least to 1863, the height of the US Civil War, when Abraham Lincoln signed the law creating the National Academy of Sciences, charging it to "investigate, examine, experiment, and report upon any subject of science or art" "whenever called upon to do so by any department of the government" (www.nasonline.org/about-nas/mission/, accessed November 17, 2022). The National Academies of Science, Engineering and Medicine, the successor to the original Academy, plays a key role in developing assessments of science around policy issues. The deliberations and reports of the National Academies have strongly influenced my thinking. Note that over time the citations to reports shifts from U.S. National Academy of Sciences, to U.S. National Research Council to National Academies of Science, Engineering and Medicine.

47. Brown (1981); Grober (2012); Meadows et al. (1972); Robinson (2004).

48. Grober (2012). Cardona (2014) suggests that the first use of the concept may have been in John Evelyn's 1662 presentation to the Royal Society later published as a book: *Sylva, or A Discourse of Forest-Trees and the Propagation of Timber in His Majesty's Dominions.*

49. Macekura (2015: 76).

50. World Commission on Environment and Development (1987). Seven years before *Our Common Future*, a similar broad analysis began to address some of the same issues. The independent commission for the report *North–South: A Program for Survival* (Independent Commission on International Development Issues 1980) was chaired by Willy Brandt, a former mayor of West Berlin and Chancellor of Germany. The report discusses energy issues (it was written just after the "energy crisis" of the 1970s) and problems of resource shortages. In an eleven-page chapter on "Population: Growth, Movement and the Environment," about three pages discuss environmental

issues, mentioning, for example, the presumed importance of tropical forests in absorbing carbon dioxide. The chapter "Energy" discusses solar and renewables and identifies the importance of the energy storage problem for solar energy. But while the report was innovative in systematically looking at the situation of the developed and developing countries and its implications, my reading is that *Our Common Future* was the major step in bringing global attention to the interplay of the environment and human well-being. In Google Scholar, *Our Common Future* has about 123,600 citations and *North–South* about 1,500 (May 17, 2020).

51. Robinson (2004).
52. World Commission on Environment and Development (1987: 23).
53. International Union for Conservation of Nature (1980).
54. Independent Commission on International Development Issues (1980). See also Chapter 2, Note 50.
55. Robinson (2004). The sentence after the conventional definition of sustainable development reads: "Far from requiring the cessation of economic growth, it recognizes that the problems of poverty and underdevelopment cannot be solved unless we have a new era of growth in which developing countries play a large role and reap large benefits" (World Commission on Environment and Development 1987: chap. 1, para. 49). Longo et al. (2016) offer a very useful analysis of the concept of sustainability in relation to "taken for granted" assumptions about growth and suggest some alternative framings.
56. The idea that natural resources (often labeled "land") were a factor of production was explicit in the work of Malthus, Smith and Ricardo, the founders of classical economics.
57. See Box I.2 on institutions, Chapter 2, Note 16 for limits of the Kuznets curve argument that growth eventually reduces inequality. The rest of this section will discuss how World Bank and International Monetary Fund (IMF) neoliberal growth policies seem to influence well-being and inequality.
58. McMichael (2008: 59).
59. Bruce (1994); Harvey (2005); Peet (1996); Perkins (2005).
60. For example, Sachs and Warner (1995). The advocates of these policies were influenced by the strong versions of the rational actor model that are sometimes called the "Chicago School." The assumption is that the way people make decisions makes it difficult for government action to do much to ensure economic growth, which is considered nearly identical to human well-being. Unfettered markets are viewed as the secret to growth and thus to development as defined in this line of thinking. The suite of policies that follow from these arguments are usually referred to as neoliberalism and are associated with economists such as Becker and Friedman (see Chapter 3). There is also a strong link to the public choice theory of Buchanan and Tullock and to the Austrian school of economics associated with Hayek and von Mises, and in some strains to the novelist Ayn Rand, see Chapter 5, Note 25. But there are many varieties of these arguments and much disagreement on specific issues. See the discussion in Chapters 3, 5 and 8. On a lighter note, markets are central to Ferengi spiritual life. The universe has "millions of worlds, all with too much of one, and not enough of the other." The "Great Material River" would carry goods from areas of surplus to areas of scarcity, and a good life required successfully navigating the river (see *Star Trek Deep Space 9*: "Progress," "Treachery, Faith and the Great River," "The Dogs of War").
61. The focus on increases in output per worker or per person ignored how the benefits of that production are distributed. This is why the Kuznets assumption is crucial – a reduction of inequality is assumed to come with growth even though most growth policies have no special provisions to reduce inequality or to provide income or well-being to those who are not receiving a share of the increased productivity. Again, Chapter 2, Note 16 points out that Kuznets cautioned against generalizing the historical pattern he saw in the United Kingdom and the United States.
62. The literature examining the environmental Kuznets curve (EKC) and ecological modernization is extensive (Carson 2010; Dietz, Rosa and York 2010, 2012; Dinda 2004; Kaika and Zervas 2013a,

2013b; Mol 1995, 2010; Mol, Spaargaren and Sonnenfeld 2014; Özcan and Öztürk 2019; Sarkodie and Strezov 2019; Selden and Song 1994; Shahbaz and Sinha 2019; Stern 2004; York, Rosa and Dietz 2010). Ecological modernization differs from environmental Kuznets theory in its emphasis on transformational processes that are not inevitable but are the result of action on the part of individuals and organizations, including corporations and governments. Ecological modernization scholars tend to examine cases where there has been success in producing environmental reforms, while the environmental Kuznets literature is mostly statistical analysis. Dependency, world systems and treadmill of production scholars usually focus on notable failures in environmental protection as does work on the anti-reflexivity thesis that examines the efforts of powerful groups to push back against environmental reform efforts based on science. See McLaughlin for insightful critiques of the logic underpinning developmental and especially ecological modernization theories and the problems that a lack of an evolutionary perspective brings (McLaughlin 2012a, 2012b; see also Chapter 7, Note 25). My assessment is that there is reasonable evidence that the EKC pattern produces substantial reductions in environmental stressors that have immediate local impact, such as air and water pollution, but increasing affluence does not reduce environmental stress when the problem is one of a global commons, such as greenhouse gas emissions (Dietz 2017a; Dietz, Rosa and York 2012). I will return to these issues in Chapter 7.

63. Mann (2005); Menjívar and Rodriguez (2009). The pattern of loans, debts and demands when loan payments are not made reminds me of how loans are handled in *Goodfellas/Wiseguy* and *The Sopranos* (Patterson 2000; Pileggi 1985; Scorsese 1990). I am also reminded of Eddie Murphy's character Valentine in *Trading Places* assessing the strategy of brokerage firms: "Sounds to me like you guys are a couple of bookies" (Landis 1983).

64. Longo et al. (2016). There are exceptions. It seems clear that the policies and strategies pursued in China over the last few decades deviate in significant ways from the core neoliberal model even if there are also some resonances and the same might be said for other "emerging" economies (Harvey 2005: chap. 4; So 2014; So and Chu 2012). What constitutes neoliberalism and how it manifests in national systems is quite varied (Kyung-Sup, Fine and Weiss 2012; Ong 2006). As my colleague Xuefei Ren points out, these "variation schools," by seeing each political/social/economic formation as variations on a theme, run the risk of undertheorizing them and thus miss a unique opportunity to advance understanding by more thorough comparative analysis. Fukuyama offers a fuller comparative analysis (Fukuyama 2011, 2014) as does Ren's own work on urbanization (Ren 2011, 2018, 2020; Weinstein and Ren 2009). We need more such work on variations in policy to understand how policy impacts economic growth, human well-being and the environment. Such natural experiments are crucial for social learning for sustainability. Bob Fri, a clear thinker on energy and climate policy, always emphasized the importance of variation across US states for learning what works and what doesn't, calling the states a "Jeffersonian laboratory."

65. Again the literature is extensive (Austin and McCarthy 2016; Clapp 2002; Clapp and Dauvergne 2005; Coburn, Restivo and Shandra 2015a, 2015b; Coburn et al. 2016; Glover 1995; Pfeiffer and Chapman 2010; Restivo, Shandra and Sommer 2020; Shandra, Shircliff and London 2011; Shandra, Shor and London 2008; Shandra et al. 2008; Shandra, Rademacher and Coburn 2016; Sommer et al. 2016; Sommer et al. 2019; Sommer, Restivo and Shandra 2020).

66. Longo et al. (2016); Robinson (2004).

67. Ehrlich (1968); Meadows et al. (1972). Heated debates about population and resources run back well before Malthus wrote his famous essay responding in part to Godwin's anarchist/utopian visions (Dietz and Rosa 1994). However, there was surprisingly little empirical or theoretical work compared to the amount of argument about this issue. My impression is that Coale and Hoover's (1958) analysis of population and economic growth was highly influential in suggesting that while population growth might not create a "Malthusian" disaster, it would slow the pace of growth in per

capita affluence. In 1970, the rate of global population growth was a bit more than 2 percent, implying that the human population would double in thirty-five years, reaching 7.4 billion. But growth slowed, and by 2005 the world human population was 6.5 billion and the growth rate about 1.2 percent. This slowing of growth was the hope of many concerned with population. See Chapter 2, Note 69.

68. Barney (1980a, 1980b, 1981); Speth (2008). Starting in the late 1960s, there were many other simulation models to address the interplay of population, consumption, resource use and so on (Glass and Watt 1971; Mesorvic and Pestel 1974; Watt 1974, 1977). They were part of the larger effort to deploy tools of systems analysis and modeling developed in the space program, the military defense system and industry to complex social problems. In the United States, the effort was funded in large part by the Research Applied to National Needs program of the National Science Foundation (NSF) (David and Lilly 2006; Donlan et al. 2006; McEvoy 1972). The NSF has been attentive to the societal value of the research it funds for half a century, although the approaches shift as does the language used to describe it. When advocates of these approaches found social and environmental problems intractable, in frustration they labeled them "wicked" problems; see Chapter 4, Note 72.

69. The critiques include Boyd (1972); Cole et al. (1973); Nordhaus, Stavins and Weitzman (1992); Simon and Herman (1984); Solow (1974); Weissman (1970). I am never sure what to make of the label "neo-Malthusian." Malthus' original argument was that the growth in human population would outstrip the ability to produce food, leading to poverty and malnutrition (Malthus [1803] 1992). So, the term might refer to an argument that human population growth will outstrip our ability to provide for human well-being. When my own work on the STIRPAT model with Richard York and Gene Rosa (see the discussion in this chapter and Note 83) has been labeled "neo-Malthusian," it seems that simply means that we view the effects of population size on the environment as a research problem. However, the term seems to be used pejoratively, as if those to whom it is attached are ignoring everything except population. When "Malthusian" is used that way, it often shows a lack of careful reading of the arguments being criticized. I am aware of very few serious scholars who argue that population is the only thing that matters. In the original Commoner versus Ehrlich and Holdren debate, Ehrlich and Holdren were not arguing that politics did not matter but that population might as well (Chapter 2, Note 77). A key argument of the STIRPAT approach is that it is not useful to talk of the effects of any one driver of environmental change – population, affluence, technology, composition of consumption, choice of technology, institutions, cultures and so on – without taking the others into account (Dietz and York 2021). Indeed, one of my papers using the STIRPAT models emphasizes the importance of politics and the environmental movement in shaping human impacts on the environment (Dietz et al. 2015). But it also estimates the effects of population. I am not sure if that makes it a "neo-Malthusian" analysis. We would probably be well served by dropping the term "neo-Malthusian" from our discussion since it seems devoid of meaning. See Chapter 5, Note 50 for studies assessing the accuracy of Limits to Growth projections, and Chapter 2, Note 113 for a discussion of concerns with slow population growth.

70. Boulding (1966); Daly (1973). Daly was inspired by Georgescu-Roegen, who argued that entropy laws provided limits to economic progress (Georgescu-Roegen 1971). But, as Cardonna points out, there are strains of no-growth economics even in Adam Smith and John Stuart Mill and more recently Keynes, among others (Cardonna 2014). Contemporary debates about the effects of growth are focused on the reasonably near-term future, not ultimate limits.

71. Daly and Cobb (1989); Hecht (2005).

72. See Chapter 7, Note 66.

73. It is not surprising that many of those concerned with population growth were ecologists, for example Ehrlich and Hardin. Hardin's (1968) "Tragedy of the Commons" is largely an essay on population growth. Population dynamics, including the factors that lead to "crashes" in the populations being studied, are central to biological ecology (Hutchinson 1978; Worster 1977).

74. Cohen (1995) provides a remarkably thorough and insightful examination of the concept of carrying capacity to humans. He argues that while the concept can be difficult to operationalize, current human population now exceeds the majority of estimates of carrying capacity of the earth, and he reached that conclusion more than twenty years ago, when the human population was about 5.7 billion, approximately 1.8 billion (one-quarter) less than it is today.

75. Lade et al. (2020); O'Neill et al. (2018); Rockström et al. (2009a, 2009b). The idea of planetary boundaries is often represented with a circle for the boundaries, and with the space inside the circle representing society functioning without exceeding ecological boundaries. This suggests the center of a doughnut, and inspired Raworth to advocate for Doughnut Economics, a clever image to motivate discussion of operating with ecological limits (Raworth 2017).

76. More recent work in ecology has been able to show in both models and in the field how evolutionary change in adaptive characteristics of species can take place rapidly enough to interact with ecological processes and shape ecosystems (Schoener 2011). Often these processes are caused by environmental stress generated by humans (Alberti, Marzluff and Hunt 2017; Haddad et al. 2015).

77. The debate stretched across several venues (Commoner 1972a, 1972b; Commoner, Corr and Stamler 1971; Ehrlich and Holdren 1970, 1971, 1972a, 1972b). The history of IPAT and its stirps is reviewed by Dietz and Rosa (1994) and Chertow (2001). The Presidential Commission on Population Growth and the American Future (US Commission on Population Growth and the American Future 1972) produced a series of research volumes that were among the first methodologically serious explorations of the effects of population growth on the environment. The Nixon administration did its best to keep the resulting report from gaining much attention. One round of the Commoner/Ehrlich–Holdren debate (see Chapter 2, Note 69) was published there. Unfortunately, there has not been a parallel growth in analysis of the social and psychological effects of population size and density. As noted, development economists have long acknowledged that rapid population growth slows growth in per capita income and thus can be a hindrance to economic development as conventionally defined (Coale and Hoover 1958; McNicoll 1984; US National Academy of Sciences 1971). There is also a small literature on the effects of population size and growth on democratic governance; see Chapter 9. The publicity around John Calhoun's famous experiments with high-density rat populations, however nuanced his intentions were, may well have stigmatized the investigation of the effects of human population density (Calhoun 1957, 1962, 1966; Ramsden and Adams 2009). (In the summer of 1970, I was one of a small group of students who visited Calhoun and his National Institute of Mental Health [NIMH] laboratory in the Maryland suburbs of Washington, DC.) After Calhoun was forced to abandon his research as NIMH shifted to an exclusive focus on drug development, some of the more positive aspects of Calhoun's work were captured in the children's book *Mrs. Frisby and the Rats of NIMH* (O'Brien 1971) and the movie *The Secret of NIHM*.

78. Dietz, Rosa and York (2010). Usually this is just the number of people, but for some kinds of environmental stressors, the number of households may matter more than the number of people (Cramer 1997, 1998; Dietz and Rosa 1994; Liu et al. 2003). It is important to differentiate the rate of population growth from the size of the population. In some contexts, it may be possible for human population to increase without adverse effects if it happens slowly but not if it happens quickly.

79. "Inventory of U.S. Greenhouse Gas Emissions and Sinks," United States Environmental Protection Agency (EPA) website, www.epa.gov/ghgemissions/inventory-us-greenhouse-gas-emissions-and-si nks, accessed November 18, 2022; "2019 U.S. Population Estimates Continue to Show the Nation's

Growth Is Slowing," Press Release Number CB19-198, December 30, 2019, United States Census Bureau website, www.census.gov/newsroom/press-releases/2019/popest-nation.html, accessed November 18, 2022; "GDP per Capita (Current US$)," World Bank data, https://data.world bank.org/indicator/NY.GDP.PCAP.CD?end=2020&start=2019, accessed November 18, 2022.

80. Kaya (1990); Kaya and Yokobori (1997).
81. Dietz (2017a); Dietz and Rosa (1994).
82. Dietz, Rosa and York (2010); Jorgenson et al. (2019).
83. STIRPAT also means "Stochastic Impacts by Regression on Population, Affluence and Technology." STIRPAT posits the model:

$$I=aP^bA^cT^e e$$

where P, A and T are each vectors that can include variables to capture the complexity of the drivers. Then b, c and d are functions linking drivers to I. If each of these is simply a parameter, then the coefficients are elasticities that tell us what percentage change in I results from a 1 percent change in a driver, all other things being equal. The intercept term "a" scales the model, while "e" is a stochastic error term in a regression analysis. The form is very flexible and can allow tests of theories calling for any type of driver on which we have data and also allows for the link between the driver and the impact to take any functional form desired. In particular, STIRPAT allows exploration of everything included in IPAT and Kaya without the simplifying assumptions of strict proportionality but also allows assessment of the impacts of policy, institutions and other factors key to climate policy. Usually, STIRPAT models are estimated with data on nation states or subnational units such as provinces or cities. A Google Scholar (January 20, 2022) search on STIRPAT revealed more than 10,000 papers using the term.

84. Increased electrification is a goal of nearly every development strategy and most analyses find it more closely related to human well-being than energy consumption overall (Cabraal, Barnes and Agarwal 2005; Mazur 2013a, 2013b; UN-Energy 2005). For those of us who have lived our lives with readily available electricity, it takes some imagination to realize the improvements in well-being that come with electricity.

85. Solar photovoltaics do not directly emit greenhouse gases in generating electricity. But a full "life cycle" accounting for the impacts of the photovoltaic generating system on greenhouse gas emissions should take account of the shading of some land that would otherwise support more photosynthesis that might capture $CO_2$, the production, transport and eventual disposal of the materials in the solar arrays and the transmission lines that get the electricity into the grid and so on (Dietz 2017a). While these emissions per kilowatt hour of electricity generated are much smaller than the emissions from coal (which should also be subject to life cycle analysis), they are not zero. As Nugest and Sovacool (2014) emphasize, careful life cycle assessment can identify steps in the life cycle where it is feasible to reduce impacts.

86. Dietz and Hawley (1983). Solar and alternative energy systems are discussed further in Chapters 7 and 8.

87. Grant et al. (2012). The switch to LED lightbulbs produced the first downturn in US per capita electricity consumption since World War II (Davis 2017). While overall consumption increased because of population growth, this is still a substantial impact (see Chapter 7).

88. Parson offers an excellent analysis of the success with protecting the ozone layer (Parson 2003), while Canan provides sociological insights (Canan et al. 2015). Richard Benedick was a lead ambassador in the negotiations that led to these changes (Benedick 1991). I once had dinner with Benedick and Parson and listened to them discuss the history – a fascinating engagement of a scholar who had also

worked in policy at the White House and an ambassador who had also held university positions. The ozone treaty was one of the few environmental policies supported by the Reagan administration.

89. Warren (2001).

90. Ciais et al. (2014); Intergovernmental Panel on Climate Change (2013); US National Research Council (2010a, 2010d).

91. Colt and Knapp (2016); Gaylord et al. (2015); Hönisch et al. (2012); US National Research Council (2010a: 285–86).

92. Dirzo et al. (2014); Pimm et al. (2014); Stork (2010).

93. Norse et al. (2012); Pinsky et al. (2011); Dakos et al. (2015).

94. York (2013).

95. Classic economic development theory noted that rapid population growth could slow increases in per capita affluence; see Chapter 2, Note 67. Research on demographic transition theory demonstrated that empowerment of women, access to contraception and reduced infant and child mortality tended to slow population growth (Bongaarts 2009; Lesthaeghe 2014; Wilkins 2019).

96. J. B. Robinson (1982, 1988). His approach is now a part of many planning efforts, using participatory approaches of the sort that will be discussed in Chapter 9 (Brunner, Huber and Grêt-Regamey 2016; Neuvonen and Ache 2017; Olsson et al. 2015; van Vliet and Kok 2015).

97. Dietz (2013c); Rosa (1998b); York (2013).

98. Finding ways to detect impending tipping points in which a system changes rapidly and radically is an important focus for research in ecology and kindred fields (Carpenter et al. 2011; Dakos et al. 2015; De Zeeuw 2014). The environmental social sciences have not paid much attention to this critical issue. Rosa repeatedly emphasized the need for us to learn from our colleagues in ecology and probe the concept of tipping points and their detection in the environmental social sciences, and Shwom is providing important insights on this issue (Shwom 2020). Long-standing sociological interest in revolution and other rapid social transformations as well as recent work on tipping points in public opinion could form a useful starting point for such investigations (Burns and Dietz 2001; Centola et al. 2018; Frank 2020; Goldstone 1991; Paige 1978; Skocpol 1979; Tilly 2017).

99. Mullon, Fréon and Cury (2005); see also Fogarty, Gamble and Perretti (2016).

100. Ciais et al. (2014); Lenton et al. (2019); Möllmann et al. (2015).

101. While ecologists have mostly worried about nonlinearities that have what most of us would see as adverse consequences, some theories suggest that there are nonlinearities that are beneficial. The environmental Kuznets curve in economics and ecological modernization theory in sociology discussed in Chapter 3, Note 62 have this character.

102. Regens, Dietz and Rycroft (1983).

103. Dietz, Frey and Rosa (2001); Rosa, Renn and McCright (2013).

104. Ruckelshaus (1985).

105. See discussions of uncertainty in Chapters 4 and 6.

106. John Elkington (1997, 2004) is attributed with labeling the "profits, people, planet" approach as the "triple bottom line."

107. Dietz, Rosa and York (2009); Dietz (2015a).

108. The capitals approach has been most thoroughly developed in economics (Neumayer 2010). It gets rather technical rather quickly. There are important conceptual issues to be addressed, for example the difference between capital and resources, and how to handle nonhuman animals in thinking about capital, resources and well-being (Dietz 2015a; Dietz and York 2015). A detailed treatment of these important issues is certainly warranted but will have to be deferred since the issues require a more extensive development of macro-level theory than I can offer here. See also Chapter 2, Note 11.

109. Much of the literature assumes that economic growth is all that matters and never offers a detailed justification for that view. It is also common to hear economic growth criticized without much

consideration about the implications of no growth for the least affluent. As my colleague Jinhua Zhao once said, one would not want to make a broad and unsubtle argument against growth to farmers living near subsistence in a rural area.

110. Support for or opposition to theories in policy debates entrains the interests of the powerful. Growth as the sole goal – the message of much conventional development theory and neoliberal theory – supports those who want to see the scope of relatively unfettered capitalism expanded as well as the strongly overlapping group who see their interests served by a strong military and national security system supported by substantial government spending. Sustainable development theory might be seen as an adjustment to that view by those who either took seriously environmental issues or at least saw that the growing strength of the environmental movement in the last quarter of the twentieth century required some response. As climate change became a central issue, those who saw their economic interests linked to the use of fossil fuels rejected climate change as a serious threat, deploying arguments that had long been used to resist other health and environmental policies (see also Chapter 5, Note 82 on anti-reflexivity). This resistance to environmental policies built on earlier libertarian arguments whose members saw their use of land, extraction of forest resources and mining activities threatened by regulations that set up protected areas and by policies such as the Endangered Species Act that governed actions on public and private lands (see Chapter 6). It also made use of arguments about scientific uncertainty as a rationale for taking no action that can be traced back at least to the controversy about the use of lead additives in gasoline and continued through debates about the risk of smoking, ozone depletion, acid precipitation and other environmental and public health issues, an unfortunate history that I will discuss in several contexts in the rest of the book (Kitman 2000; Michaels and Monforton 2005; Michaels 2006, 2008, 2020; Oreskes and Conway 2010). Each position in these debates has some serious intellectual underpinnings that deserve careful assessment even if in the end they are rejected. But we also have to be aware that the public dynamics of debates on these issues can be strongly influenced by the actions of powerful interests.

111. One approach to utilitarian ethical theory, with its goal of the greatest good for the greatest number, might argue for increased human population size assuming the sum of individual utility increases with population growth (more people being satisfied). There are strong counterarguments to this view (Dietz, Bell and Leshko 2014).

112. As population growth has slowed in the developed nations, the age structure of the population has changed so that a larger fraction of the population is older than has been the case in the past. This has led to arguments about a "crisis" of aging populations. The usual solution offered by pundits is a move towards pronatalist policies to increase the birth rate. They sometimes echo past arguments raised about birth rates and military strength, such as those in France between the Franco-Prussian War and World War II (Gauthier 1998). Now, the arguments are that the size of the labor force is too small to support the population in dependent-age categories (typically those under eighteen or so and those over sixty-five or so), that economic growth cannot be sustained without a growing labor force and that there will not be sufficient caregivers for the elderly. The issue is being discussed with regard to China, the European Union, Japan and the United States (Asian Development Bank Institute 2019; S. P. Morgan 2003). Pundits who advocate a rise in the birth rate seldom mention the adverse effects of population growth, in particular the impacts on other species. Changing age structure in a society is certainly worthy of policy attention but calls for pronatalist policy seem to me as overly simplistic and should be viewed cautiously for several reasons. First, as the STIRPAT body of literature points out, increased population growth increases stress on the environment, with most studies finding an elasticity of 1–1.5 – each 1 percent increase in population produces a 1–1.5 percent increase in stress, controlling for other drivers (Jorgenson and Clark 2010). Second, simple increases in economic activity (GDP per capita) rather than a focus on human well-being may

not be the appropriate goal for affluent nations where population growth is slowing. Third, population growth is a blunt instrument to solve subtle problems of the provision of funds and labor to support the dependent population, problems that could be addressed more directly with policy instruments and new technology. Arguments about a shrinking labor force seem not to be aware of arguments that artificial intelligence and robots will displace large numbers of jobs. Fourth, pronatalist policies have often been entrained with anti-feminist and racist views, and while those connections are not necessary, the history requires such proposals be viewed critically. One wonders, for example, why, when a pundit worries about too small a labor force, they advocate increasing the birth rate rather than increasing immigration. Granted immigration entrains complex issues too, but it should be discussed, and when it is not the motivations for ignoring it need to be examined.

113. Anderson (1976); Boulding (1966); Daly (1973); Schnaiberg (1980). I believe this is an important shift from previous socialist and Marxist theory where the drive for profit was often questioned but where most theorists envisioned a world in which economic growth of a rather conventional sort would continue but under the control of the public (or the workers) rather than under the control of capitalists seeking profit. Much hinges on defining growth in a way that is useful and, as I have argued, making a distinction between capitals and resources; see also Chapter 2, Note 11 and Dietz (2015a).

114. Cosme, Santos and O'Neill (2017); Gunderson (2018); Kallis et al. (2018); Washington and Twomey (2016).

115. Büchs and Koch (2019).

116. "We Can End Poverty: Millennium Development Goals and Beyond 2015," United Nations website, www.un.org/millenniumgoals/bkgd.shtml (accessed April 21, 2022).

117. Hulme (2009).

118. Brolan (2016); International Council for Science and International Social Science Council (2015); Lockie (2012); Yap and Watene (2019).

119. The issue of synergies will be addressed in Chapter 7.

120. Xu, Chau et al. (2020). We were working with Chinese data, so our analysis uses the official regional units of the Chinese government. There is controversy about some territorial claims made by China.

121. Xu, Li et al. (2020).

122. Work on tradeoffs is emerging rapidly; see Barbier and Burgess (2019); Griggs et al. (2017); Pradhan et al. (2017); Scherer et al. (2018); Yang et al. (2022). A review of more than 3,000 studies suggests that the SDGs have had some impact on policy discussions but have not yet transformed decision-making (Biermann et al. 2022). I would expect such larger cultural changes would take more time.

123. There are differences between GDP and gross national product (GNP) but they are not important for this discussion.

124. Kenessey (1994).

125. Kuznets (1934: 7). In a section entitled "Uses and Abuses of National Income Measurements," Kuznets raises a prescient series of cautions about the limits of GNP and related measures when used for decision-making. It is unfortunate that his advice has not been given more attention in policy and research over the following ninety years.

126. Daly and Cobb (1989); Fox and Erickson (2018); Stiglitz, Fitoussi and Durand (2018); US National Research Council (1999b).

127. Barrett, Garg and McBride (2016); Dietz (2015a); Dolan, Peasgood and White (2008); Easterlin (2015); Kahneman and Deaton (2010).

128. Easterlin (1974).

129. Diener, Lucas and Oishi (2018); Organisation for Economic Co-operation and Development (2013); Stiglitz, Fitoussi and Durand (2018); Stiglitz, Sen and Fitoussi (2009). On consideration of nonhumans, see Kalof (2017), especially sections 1 and 2, and Beauchamp and Frey (2011).

130. A recently proposed well-being measure, Years of Good Life, combines life expectancy with being out of absolute poverty, achieving minimal levels of health and subjective life satisfaction (Lutz et al. 2021).
131. Dietz, Rosa and York (2009, 2012).
132. Roberts et al. (2020).
133. Goldemberg et al. (1985); Mazur and Rosa (1974).
134. Jorgenson et al. (2016); Jorgenson, Dietz and Kelly (2018); Jorgenson, Schor and Huang (2017).
135. Dietz (2015a); Yang et al. (2015).
136. "Environmental concern" and "environmentalism" are covering terms for the complex of values, beliefs, norms and attitudes discussed in Chapter 3. "Environmental cognition" is a more precise but less common covering term (Henry and Dietz 2012).

# 3    How We Make Decisions

1. Dietz et al. (2009). There is a debate about how consumer decisions influence decisions intended to influence policy, such as voting. I will discuss spillover effects in Chapter 7.
2. Jaeger et al. (2001). My colleagues Carlo Jaeger, Ortwin Renn, Gene Rosa and Tom Webler prefer the phrase "rational actor paradigm" (RAP). Here, I use "rational actor model" (RAM), but we mean the same thing. This chapter is strongly influenced by their work . It also draws on some of my work with Paul Stern (Dietz and Stern 1995).
3. The RAM is essentially the same as the subjective expected utility model (SEU). The term "SEU" is used in some fields rather than "RAM." Schoemaker and Moscati discuss the history of these concepts (Moscati 2016; Schoemaker 1982). Utility in the RAM is tightly linked to utility in utilitarian ethics. While the history is complex, von Neumann and Morgenstern are usually credited with establishing the ethical theory of expected utility in their *Theory of Games and Economic Behavior* (von Neumann and Morgenstern 1944). They show that if one accepts five rather reasonable (but rather technical) assumptions (axioms in the language of mathematics) about what constitutes a good decision, then the decisions that follow those rules will maximize the utility that results from the choices made. Savage developed the rigorous formal theory that is the starting point for most work today (Savage 1954). Marshak went one step further to *define* such decision-making as rational (Marshak 1950). Even from the start of its popularity in research on decision-making, the RAM as a scientific theory telling us how we *do* make decisions is entangled with an ethical theory telling us how we *ought to* make decisions.
4. For example, Dietz (2020a); Frank (2020).
5. "Economists normally do not try to explain people's tastes because tastes are based on historical and psychological forces that are beyond the realm of economics" (Mankiv 2018: 70). Becker is quite clear on this point: "Since economists generally have had little to contribute, especially in recent times, to the understanding of how preferences are formed, preferences are assumed not to change substantially over time, nor to be very different between wealthy and poor persons, or even between persons in different societies and cultures" (Becker 1976a: 5).
6. For example, preferences are assumed to be transitive. If I prefer A to B and B to C, then I would rather have A than C. Von Neumann and Morgenstern develop these arguments, which are carefully elaborated in any standard microeconomics text (Mas-Colell, Whinston and Green 1995; von Neumann and Morgenstern 1944).
7. RAM-based work nearly always posits a mathematical model of the decision-making process, that is, of utility maximization under constraints. This builds a barrier between those who use the RAM

and those who use other approaches. Even if you have the math background, following the quantitative theory in a RAM analysis is still heavy-going. On the other hand, I suspect many users of the RAM view the other two traditions I will describe as imprecise and even unscientific and are not inclined to pay much attention to them. On the nature of models and their strengths and limits, see Chapter 3, Note 12.

8. Satcher (2021, 2022).

9. Economic analysis is criticized on the grounds that "only dollars matter." But economic analysis is more subtle. Utilitarian analyses require a common metric for all outcomes to make trade-offs. Most economic analysis assumes that, in a "perfect" market, prices are a reflection of collective social values, so prices are one way to assess utility across all the individuals in a society – price reflects social value. (In this section of the chapter, I use the term "value" the way economists do. In Section 3.3, I will talk about values the way psychologists do (Dietz 2015b).) Recall from Chapter 2 the criticism of GDP per capita as a focus of policy: assuming that GDP per capita, which is a measure of economic activity, can be interpreted as a measure of well-being. GDP per capita is based on prices, so the logic of using it as a measure of well-being depends on the idea that prices indicate social values. As I mentioned in Chapter 2, Kuznets, who helped establish the measurement of GDP, warned against equating it with welfare, or in my terms, well-being or utility.

10. Discounting raises the interesting question of what to do with individual discount rates when the time period for effects runs past the expected lifetime of the decision maker. One can handle this with probabilities. I can think about legacy effects on my children and grandchildren, although this moves past the narrowest view of the RAM in which I care only about my own utility. There is evidence people care a great deal about legacy effects (Vandenbergh and Gilligan 2017: chap. 7; Vandenbergh and Raimi 2015). Analyses done for policy decision-making can consider the society or the organization making the decision immortal, so this problem would not arise. Box 5.4 discusses discounting in formal benefit-cost analysis. In those analyses, the value of the discount rate applied to future outcomes has immense importance in shaping the conclusions reached. Economic analyses that come to different conclusions about the amount of action we should take to limit climate change often differ primarily in the discount rates they use (Nordhaus 2008; Stern 2007; US National Research Council 2010b: 408–13; Weyant 2008). Some of the most sophisticated thinking on this issue acknowledges that we do not know the proper discount rate to use for the future and suggests we might want to use discount rates that decline over time (Arrow et al. 2013; Arrow et al. 2014). A further complexity is that, in experiments, people seem to discount future environmental impacts little if at all. Matousek et al. (2021) review research on individual discount rates. The issue of discount rates is very complex with reasonable arguments about not only what discount rates to apply to future costs and benefits but also on whether to discount at all (that is, to pick a discount rate of zero).

11. Benjamin Franklin advocated something like this approach for big decisions, calling it moral algebra (Brands 2010). Apparently, Darwin used this approach in deciding to marry (see Darwin's memorandum on marriage at Darwin Online: darwin-online.org.uk/content/frameset?viewtype=side&itemID=CUL-DAR210.8.2&pageseq=1, accessed November 19, 2022). As in so many other areas, Franklin was in the forefront of thinking in what became decision sciences. After expressing troubling prejudices against BIPOC people and many Europeans, he also acknowledged that he might be subject to what we would today call biased assimilation (see Sections 3.3 and 3.4 and Chapter 3, Note 47) in developing those views: "But perhaps I am partial to the complexion of my Country, for such kind of partiality is natural to Mankind" (Franklin [1755] 1918: 224). His thinking evolved over his life – he held people enslaved, carried advertising in his newspaper about escapees and the sale of those enslaved and wrote defenses of slavery. But late in life he supported abolition (Isaacson 2003: 463–67; E. S. Morgan 2003; Nash 2006). Stephen Jay Gould, in examining the

thinking of historical figures, always tried to incorporate a critique of their views from a contemporary perspective and an understanding of the contexts in which they worked. I endorse this approach as I believe we learn the most from considering both perspectives. It means that figures like Franklin and John Muir (see Chapter 6, Note 1) express both ideas we admire and ideas we deplore; Franklin is especially interesting in the ways he changed his thinking.

12. Chapter 3, Note 7 points out that RAM research nearly always starts with a formal mathematical model of the decision-making process, usually a model of maximization under constraints. This is in contrast to the approaches I will discuss next. The distinction reminds me of Levins' important arguments about models (Levins 1966, 1993; Orzack and Sober 1993). Levins points out that we would like models of the world to have three features: generalizability, realism and precision. But he argues that a model can do well on only two out of three of these goals. The RAM is highly generalizable and very precise, but in emphasizing those qualities does it give away too much in realism? The other systematic approaches I review enhance realism while preserving generality and in doing so sacrifice precision in the sense that they cannot be easily represented by a set of equations that yield precise predictions. Historical, ethnographic and biographical accounts of decision-making may be precise (in details even if not quantified) and realistic but it is not clear how they generalize. I will return to this issue in Chapter 4. I suspect some of the appeal of the RAM is that it is often seen as a universal theory that applies to all decisions and because it is generalizable and precise. Its link to an ethical theory also makes it easy to use in support of decision-making.

13. It appears that education that focuses on the RAM can encourage selfishness in students in part because they don't expect others to treat them fairly, that is, they have lower trust; see Section 3.3 (Frank, Gilovich and Regan 1996; Gerlach 2017).

14. McGann (2018).

15. Bonanno (2017); Carrigan and Coglianese (2015); Harvey (2005); Laurance et al. (2004).

16. For example, Becker (1976b, [1981] 1991). This approach was labeled "human capital theory," the "Chicago school" (confusing because there is also an early twentieth-century Chicago school of sociology with that label) and the "new home economics." It is quite different from the human ecology that arose from home economics at about the same time; see Introduction, Note 66.

17. Buchanan (1954); Buchanan and Tullock (1962).

18. On law, see Dunleavy (2014). MacLean argues that Buchanan's concerns were not just with government bureaucracy but with the ability of a democratic majority to impose its will on individuals (MacLean 2017). The implications are that the richest and most powerful members of society should have the right to exercise their power as they choose, free of constraints imposed by a majority through political processes. This harkens back to social Darwinism (see the discussion of early US sociology in Chapter 5, Note 11) and other efforts to legitimate inequality. It also resonates with the ideas of Ayn Rand (Chapter 5, Note 25).

19. Becker and Barro reformulated the theory, arguing that parents are altruistic towards their offspring and therefore take account of the utility of their children in making decisions (see Becker 1974; Becker and Barro 1986).

20. Smith ([1804] 1976: 446). Smith did not ignore altruism as a motivation (see Chapter 5, Note 32), but most forms of the RAM that have evolved from his work include only self-interest as a motivation.

21. Becker (1976a: 5). I would argue that Walter White in *Breaking Bad* follows this model. He cares deeply about his wife and children. As he changes over the course of the series, it appears he cares about no one else except perhaps Jesse Pinkman. And he fixates on accumulating wealth as his main modality for ensuring his family's future. As the story progresses, he also enjoys (derives utility from) how effective and powerful he is in the identity he has created as "Heisenberg."

22. See Chapter 3, Note 32.

23. Unfortunately, in this case national groups opposed to climate policy poured money into the campaign and the pro-climate policy candidate, who was the incumbent, lost by 21 votes out of about 5,300. The major public complaint about her was that she was "hard to reach" and didn't return phone calls, a claim made based on anecdotal evidence, a case of a story of unknown relevance carrying weight in an important decision; see Box 3.1.

24. The "Tragedy of the Commons" term is usually associated with Hardin's (1968) immensely popular essay. I hope those who read Hardin's essay or who hear arguments based on it also learn what we actually know about commons from decades of research, including the important work of Berkes, McCay, Ostrom and many others (Berkes et al. 1989; Feeny et al. 1990; Ostrom 2009b, 2010a, 2010c; Ostrom et al. 2002). Hardin had it mostly wrong. The argument he offers is based on the RAM, but he seemed to have been unaware of the very substantial theoretical literature in resource economics and game theory addressing the problem he posed. And his example is ironic in that communities around the world have often been very successful in managing commons, including grazing lands, for decades or centuries. In contrast, privatization or control by central government – Hardin's solutions – has often led to collapse. The general lesson of commons research is that what works and what fails depends on many details of the common resource, the social and cultural context in which it is managed and especially the institutional design of the commons management strategy (Dietz and Henry 2008; Dietz, Ostrom and Stern 2003; Ostrom et al. 2002). I had a chance to engage in discussions with Hardin when he was invited to visit University of California, Davis by the ecology graduate students in the 1970s. I came away with the conjecture that there is a style of intellectual engagement that might be called "controversialist": someone is primarily interested in being provocative. For controversialists, accurately reflecting existing theory and empirical evidence is secondary to, and often gets in the way of, getting attention and creating turmoil. The idea that markets are the best way to manage resources is part of the neoliberal policies mentioned in Chapter 2 (Adams and McShane 1996; Anderson and Grove 1987; Peluso 1992; Peluso and Vandergeest 2001).

25. Carol Rose, Bonnie McCay and A. C. Loux have suggested we might refer to the comedy of the commons (Loux 2003; McCay 1995; Rose 1986). And since much of our understanding is based on historical analyses, we have the three forms of classical drama: tragedy, comedy and history. Thus the drama of the commons (Dietz et al. 2002). But in some cases, the term "tragedy" is certainly appropriate as in the "tragedy of the commodity," an insightful analysis of fisheries (Longo, Clausen and Clark 2015).

26. It is gratifying to know that these conceptual frameworks, which Ostrom did so much to clarify (Dietz, Ostrom and Stern 2003; Ostrom 2009b, 2010a), are part of the required curriculum for the entrance exams for the Vulcan Science Academy in the twenty-third century; see the film *Star Trek* (2009).

27. Barbed wire been used extensively to control populations of humans as well as other animals (Hornbeck 2010; Krell 2002; Netz 2004; Razac 2002).

28. Linda Kalof and I experienced this at Johnston Canyon in Banff National Park. A sign suggested that ~1 million people a year hike the trail. It was a gorgeous place (pun intended) but a continuous stream of people on a September day made it a less than ideal hike.

29. Dietz, Ostrom and Stern (2003); Dietz and Zhao (2011); Ostrom (2010b, 2010c); Young (2002).

30. Ostrom (2009a). The literature in the debate about weak versus strong sustainability is about whether or not substitutions of one form of resource for another are feasible and could leave the future better off (Neumayer 2010). See Chapter 2.

31. This situation is called a two-person Prisoner's Dilemma, but my colleague Tom Burns points out that the situation does not exist without at least one other person in the interaction, the jailer/prosecutor, in this case Harvey. During World War II, the work of von Neumann and Morgenstern

generated interest in situations in which the costs and benefits to an individual depend on what other people do (von Neumann and Morgenstern 1944). Their *Theory of Games and Economic Behavior* elaborated on an earlier paper by von Neumann, "Zur Theorie der Gesellschaftsspiele," published in 1928 that showed how the tools of set theory could be used to analyze games; see also Leonard (2010); von Neumann (1928); for the English translation: von Neumann (1959). The book was also central to utility theory; see Chapter 2, Note 3. John Nash followed their approach to game-like interactions in his twenty-seven-page doctoral dissertation that led to his Nobel Prize in Economics (Nash 1950). Nash's life and struggle with schizophrenia are described in the popular biography and the film *A Beautiful Mind* (Nassar 1999). Sadly, in May 2015 Nash and his wife Alicia were killed in a car accident when returning home after Nash received the Abel Prize in mathematics for his work in differential geometry and the theory of differential equations (Goode 2015). He is the only person to have been awarded both a Nobel and an Abel, which is the rough equivalent of the Nobel for mathematics. See also Chapter 3, Notes 56 and 62.

32. As noted in Chapter 3, Note 20, RAM tradition has acknowledged the potential importance of altruism at least since Adam Smith, although there are debates about Smith's views (Coase 1976; Khalil 1990; Smith [1804] 1976). Edgeworth's mathematical work was highly influential in developing maximization of self-interest as the underpinning of microeconomic analysis of decisions, although he too addressed altruism and argued for narrow self-interest primarily in decisions in war and around contracts (Collard 1975; Edgeworth 1881). Sen reviews these issues eloquently in his essay "Rational Fools" (Sen 1977), arguing that Samuelson sees the use of the RAM as the core difference between sociology and economics (Samuelson 1947). There is now extensive use of the RAM in sociology; see, for example, the journal *Rationality and Society*. Ongoing efforts expand the RAM to incorporate the utility gained by others one cares about (Falk, Fehr and Fischbacher 2002; Fehr and Fischbacher 2003; Fehr and Gintis 2007; Rotemberg 2014). Załuski (2016) discusses how various views of rational actors can, and cannot, accommodate moral decision-making. Simpson and Willer (2015) examine how the individual-level approach that is central to the RAM relates to structural (aggregate) influences on altruism. I emphasize a cultural evolutionary perspective because it moves us towards reconciling across levels of analysis and between structure and power; see the discussion in the Introduction and Chapter 1.

33. Stern, Dietz and Black (1986); Stern, Dietz and Kalof (1993). I will use "humanistic" and "biospheric altruism" to describe these two values. Sometimes "humanistic altruism" is simply called "altruism" and "biospheric altruism" just "biospheric values."

34. The literature on values in environmental decision-making continues to grow. Our 1993 paper has been cited more than 4,200 times (Google Scholar, February 12, 2022). Several reviews summarize the environmental values literature, for example Bouman and Steg (2019); Dietz (2015b); Dietz, Fitzgerald and Shwom (2005); Steg (2016); Steg and de Groot (2012). My goal is to show the place of values in decision-making and so I will not go into the details of this literature; those are provided in the reviews.

35. This definition is from Dietz, Fitzgerald and Shwom (2005). In social psychology, values are often defined as: "(a) concepts or beliefs, (b) about desirable end states or behaviors, (c) that transcend specific situations, (d) guide selection or evaluation of behavior and events, and (e) are ordered by relative importance" (Schwartz and Bilsky 1987: 551). Philosophers and economists use the term "values" in ways that, while not wholly inconsistent with use in social psychology and sociology, can still lead to some confusion (Elliott 2017). But philosophers refer to the kinds of values discussed here as non-epistemic values. This is in contrast with epistemic values, which are related to truth, knowledge and understanding. I will discuss these in Chapter 4. More problematic is the tendency to use the term "values" as an undefined catchall for any concepts that might be thought of as influencing decisions. "Values" is often used by those who do not know the research literature to

mean not only values as defined here but also beliefs, preferences, norms and attitudes, among other things. Martin and Lembo (2020) argue that there is some confusion and inconsistency about how the idea of values is deployed in the sociological literature. I respect their critique and have learned from it but believe that the problems they engage arise largely from the lack of a cultural evolutionary perspective in sociology. The tradition I describe here, which stretches from Dewey through Rokeach to Schwartz and on to work on individual environmental decision-making seems to me robust with regard to their arguments. Vaisey (2021) offers a very insightful assessment of their arguments and the current state of thinking about values.

36. Dewey ([1939] 1988) argued that values are how we resolve conflicts among our preferences; that is, that values drive preferences. As Williams (1979: 16) put it: "Values serve as criteria for selection in action." Dewey ([1939] 1988) and Mead (1934) both emphasized the fundamental link between values and identity. All this seems consistent with, and to my mind not troubled by, Martin and Lembo's (2020) argument that values do not perfectly predict actions, that values might be thought of as a sort of averaging of preferences or interests and that values seem rather like aspects of personality.

37. Schwartz builds on the work of Rokeach (1968, 1973, 1979a, 1979b). Rokeach identified the difference between instrumental and terminal values. Terminal values are ends; instrumental values are means to those ends. I focus on terminal values because those are the ones that have the closest connections to the larger theory of self-interest and altruism and that have the longest history of being applied to environmental decision-making (Dunlap, Grieneeks and Rokeach 1983). Inglehart has argued that much of the political dynamics in the Western world since World War II can be explained by shifts in instrumental values, with older cohorts adhering more to materialist values because of their experience in the Great Depression and World War II and younger cohorts holding more "post-materialist" values (Baker 2006; Inglehart 1977, 1990; Inglehart and Baker 2000). His argument parallels ecological modernization and environmental Kuznets theory – as things get better economically, environmental issues are addressed. This has led to a substantial research literature (Brechin 1999; Brechin and Kempton 1997; Dunlap and Mertig 1995, 1997; Fischer, Milfont and Gouveia 2011; Gökşen, Adaman and Zengínobuz 2002; Inglehart 1995; Kidd and Lee 1997; Lee and Kidd 1997; Marquart-Pyatt 2008, 2012; Mostafa 2013; Oreg and Katz-Gerro 2006; Pierce 1997). My reading is that in general the terminal values yield better predictions of environmental beliefs and pro-environmental action, and they fit much more coherently into a general theory of decision-making with their emphasis on self-interest versus altruism, so I will not review the work on Rokeach's instrumental values further. Baker has built on Inglehart's use of Rokeach's values and added to them items to reflect aspects of US culture (Baker 2006, 2012, 2013, 2022; Inglehart and Baker 2000). Interestingly, he notes that libertarians, political-religious conservatives and young liberals stand out as distinct groups in terms of the values he analyzed. Research on moral judgments made by the public is quite similar to values in many ways (Graham et al. 2013; Haidt 2001, 2012). Efforts to integrate these traditions, especially one using a cultural evolutionary perspective, would be beneficial; see the proposal of Kaasa (2021). The "cultural theory" approach operationalized by Dake and deployed by Kahan captures some mixture of terminal values, instrumental values and current rhetoric in American political culture (Dake 1991, 1992; Kahan 2012). Since it is not connected with any standard theorizing in environmental decision-making and has been heavily critiqued, I also will not discuss it further (Abel 1985; Stern 2016; van der Linden 2016).

38. Schwartz labels what I am calling traditional values as "conservation" – conserving the status quo or traditions. Using the term "conservation" in that way in work on environment and sustainability would be very confusing, so my colleagues and I have relabeled this pole in the values space "traditional."

39. In many studies, humanistic and biospheric altruism load on the same factor in exploratory and confirmatory factor analyses. My conjecture is that they tend to separate into distinct, albeit positively correlated, factors in populations that have given thought to environmental issues. Schwartz prefers to use smallest space analysis, which displays the detailed value types at the core of his work in a two-dimensional space. The altruism/self-interest and openness to change/traditionalism dimensions define this space. I believe the use of values in the environmental and sustainability decision-making literature is consistent with and respectful of the impressive body of work around Schwartz's approach. The difference is largely one of emphasis, and in particular the central importance of altruism versus self-interest around questions of the environment and sustainability.

40. Dietz (2005, 2015b); Dietz, Fitzgerald and Shwom (2005); Steg (2016); Stern, Dietz and Kalof (1993). Sanderson has used value theory to examine decision-making among farmers and shown how values and norms can be incorporated into hydro-ecological models (Lauer et al. 2018; Roobavannan et al. 2018; Sanderson et al. 2018).

41. Dietz, Kalof and Stern (2002). In an important emerging line of work, Bowers, Whitley and others are examining the relationship between values and the identity of oppressed groups, an extension of both the arguments presented here and the feminist ethics that inspired the current use of values to explain environmental decision-making (Whitley and Bowers 2020).

42. The literature on the political correlates of environmental concern is extensive (Brulle 2000; Dietz 2020b; Kirk 2007; McCright 2000; McCright and Dunlap 2003; McCright, Dunlap and Marquart-Pyatt 2016; McLaughlin and Khawaja 2000; Turner 2006).

43. Shwom et al. (2010); Whitfield et al. (2009).

44. Lind et al. (2015); Steg, Perlaviciute et al. (2014). We have some preliminary evidence that concern with the well-being of nonhuman animals and a desire to interact with them is a separate value from the five described here (Dietz, Allen and McCright 2017; Suchyta 2020b).

45. Heberlein brought the Schwartz norm activation model and the idea of altruism into environmental sociology (Black, Stern and Elsworth 1985; Dunlap and Van Liere 1977; Heberlein 1977, 2012; Schwartz 1968a, 1968b, 1970, 1973, 1977; Van Liere and Dunlap 1978). I will discuss his work in Chapter 8. I worked with Heberlein's student Stan Black and my long-term collaborator Paul Stern in expanding the "ascription of responsibility" concept from personal responsibility to act to include viewing corporations or government as responsible for action (Stern, Dietz and Black 1986). At roughly the same time VBN theory was emerging, Paul Sabatier and other political scientists developed a very similar theory about those active in policy networks, albeit using different terms, as part of the Advocacy Coalition Framework (Henry and Dietz 2012; Weible et al. 2020). I took perhaps the first graduate course Paul taught, but we were not aware of each other's work until years later.

46. Bouman and Steg (2019); Bouman, Steg and Perlaviciute (2021); Steg (2016).

47. Other common terms are "motivated reasoning," "confirmation and disconfirmation bias" and "myside bias" – there are technical distinctions among them that need not concern us. The literature is extensive and is not well integrated (Bayes and Druckman 2021; Druckman, Leeper and Slothuus 2018; Druckman and McGrath 2019; Druckman and Nelson 2003; Henry 2011; Henry and Dietz 2011; Henry and Vollan 2014; Lord, Ross and Lepper 1979; Munro and Ditto 1997; Munro et al. 2002; Stanovich 2021). Everyone, including experts, are subject to such biases; the norms of science are in part intended to overcome them (see Chapter 4). While biased assimilation has often been invoked as an explanation for why conservatives in the anglophone countries reject climate change, Druckman and McGrath (2019) suggest that an alternative explanation may be differing criteria about what is credible evidence, an issue related to the problem of how we handle scientific uncertainty discussed in Sections 3.4 and 3.5. A recent review is somewhat more optimistic than

initial assessments of citizens' reasoning (Bolsen and Palm 2019). Some intriguing evidence suggests that sharing personal experiences about issues, especially experiences that involved harm, rather than factual arguments based on objective evidence, may overcome biased assimilation and facilitate dialogue (Bavel et al. 2021; Kubin et al. 2021). Such stories may deviate substantially from scientific consensus (see Box 3.1), but they also point to the importance of the deliberative processes, discussed in the Introduction and Chapter 9, that allow for both personal narratives and scientific information to be assessed.

48. There are many examples of how small tendencies can lead to large aggregate effects. Schelling's model of residential segregation described in Chapter 1, Note 39 is an example. Henry and colleagues have shown that small preferences in who to talk to and who to avoid can lead to a difficult situation where networks become fragmented with little sharing of information or other connections across the clusters (Henry, Prałat and Zhang 2011). The effects of networks on decision-making will be revisited in Chapter 8.

49. Cialdini and Jacobson (2021); Farrow, Grolleau and Ibanez (2017); Nyborg (2018); Ostrom (2000); Steg (2016).

50. Learning that there is a strong scientific consensus that the climate is changing and largely as a result of human activity can have strong effects on climate beliefs (Goldberg, van der Linden, Ballew et al. 2019; Goldberg, van der Linden, Maibach and Leiserowitz 2019; van der Linden, Maibach and Leiserowitz 2019). Here, the descriptive norm is about what scientists believe rather than what other citizens believe.

51. Sparkman, Howe and Walton (2021); Sparkman and Walton (2017).

52. Schultz et al. (2007). In this case, the problem posed is that people who receive feedback that their behavior is "better" than the descriptive norm will ease back to the norm, or at least will have no incentive to get any better. Many scholars assume this is true without carefully evaluating the evidence. While a rebound effect has been found in some studies, far more work is needed to understand how general this is, under what circumstances it occurs and, as in the work of Schultz and colleagues, what can be done to counter it (Azevedo 2014; Sparkman, Attari and Weber 2021; Truelove et al. 2014). The issue also arises in recent studies that show that renewal energy sources are less than 100 percent effective in displacing fossil fuels. I will return to this important issue in Chapter 7.

53. Cialdini's *Influence: The Psychology of Persuasion*, discussed in Section 3.4, reviews many examples as well as how often sound evidence of how to make normative appeals was ignored in program design (Cialdini [1984] 2007; Dietz 2011). For example, Cialdini and collaborators have shown that a message indicating that previous occupants of a hotel room have reused towels was far more effective than any other appeal for towel reuse (Goldstein, Cialdini and Griskevicius 2008; Goldstein, Griskevicius and Cialdini 2007). Despite that, I have only once stayed in a hotel that used that appeal, a hotel in Montreal about where Suzanne's place by the river in Leonard Cohen's song was located.

54. I thank Cam Whitley for directing me towards the literature on empathy. Extensive reviews of the literature include Cuff et al. (2016) and Hall and Schwartz (2019). Davidson (2022) provides a useful integration of theories of empathy in the context of climate change. Important work focuses on how empathy is extended to other species and probably reenforces empathy for other humans (Whitley et al. under review; Young, Khalil and Wharton 2018). The generation of empathy is probably why animal portraiture is so effective at eliciting concern with the well-being of other species and the environment; see Chapter 5.

55. Coleman (1988, 1990); Fukuyama (1995); Sztompka (1999). If we could fully trust those we deal with, we might not need government. One work-around for a lack of trust is a contract, where there are ways of enforcing defections from agreed-upon behavior. The 2016 Nobel Prize in Economics was awarded to Hart and Holmström for work that emphasizes that it is usually impossible to write

a contract that covers all contingencies (Committee for the Prize in Economic Sciences in Memory of Alfred Nobel 2016). Every contract, and every market, requires methods of adjudication to resolve disputes. Usually this adjudication is by government. In general, as Ostrom emphasized, there are no markets without governments. My colleague Joe Hamm has done excellent work on trust, including on the measurement of public trust in government (Hamm, Smidt and Mayer 2019), and how trust relates to a variety of sustainability issues, including water management in Uganda (Hamm et al. 2020), dioxin contamination in Michigan (Hamm et al. 2019), land owner behavior in Nebraska (Hamm et al. 2016) and hunter decisions in Michigan (Hamm 2017).

56. Recall from Chapter 3, Note 31 that there is a third party involved in the Prisoner's Dilemma, the police officer or prosecutor making the offer of a lighter sentence in exchange for a confession. The prisoners may or may not trust those making the offer, and they also have to anticipate the actions of those who might be affected by a confession who are not part of the deal. Contracts comes up in some stories of Prisoner's Dilemma – the contracts for murder placed on those who violate the code of silence is a contract enforced by those outside of the usual Prisoner's Dilemma calculation.

57. Fehr (2009).

58. My limited foray into the general literature on trust and on networks is in collaboration with Adam Douglas Henry (Henry 2020; Henry and Dietz 2011; Henry and Vollan 2014) and is also informed by the work of my friend Ken Frank (Frank et al. 2012; Leonard et al. 2011). Economists have been paying more attention to networks (Frank 2020). Recent work is also examining how perception of society-wide norms influences behavior (Bouman et al. 2021; Wang et al. 2021).

59. Siegrist (2019); Uslaner (2018) Whitfield et al (2009).

60. Whitfield et al. (2009). As a sociologist reading the magnificent and disturbing *Watchmen* by Alan Moore, Dave Gibbons and John Higgins (1987), I am struck by the absence of institutions other than the media. Indeed, that may characterize the universes inhabited by most superheroes – the corporate sector is often there (Stark Enterprises, Ferris Corporation, the holdings of the Wayne Foundation), as is government (S.H.I.E.L.D.). The press is sometimes part of the world (The Daily Planet, The Daily Bugle). But we seldom see social movements save in rather caricatured form. Yet social movements are often the watchers of the watchmen in contemporary society (and hopefully free of Juvenal's sexist context).

61. On VBN: Dietz and Stern (1995). On values and identity: Hitlin (2003); Hitlin (2011). One approach to measuring values, called the Portrait Values Questionnaire, describes the values of hypothetical individuals and asks respondents, "how much each person is or is not like you" (Schwartz et al. 2001; Schwartz et al. 2012). This approach seems to be tapping exactly the identity question of who is similar to me.

62. There is relatively little work linking values and identity to trust. From a game theory perspective, if I know someone's values then I can predict their behavior and make decisions accordingly. And to the extent that I am altruistic, I will prefer people who are also altruistic because that will allow me to develop cooperative strategies with them. If I am purely self-interested, I also would prefer to interact with altruists because then I can develop strategies that take advantage of their altruism. Scholars of game theory have examined how these interactions might unfold over time both in theoretical models and in experiments (Colman 1982; Myerson 2013; Uslaner 2018: part IV). Smaldino (2019) has argued for the importance of identity in the cultural evolution of large-scale societies.

63. On identity and nature, see Clayton (2003); Schultz (2000, 2002); Schultz et al. (2004). Clayton (2003, 2012) provides useful overviews of the literature on identity as it applies to the environment, while other studies examine the effects of identity on decisions in the role of consumer and as citizen (Dunlap and McCright 2008; McCright and Dunlap 2008, 2015; Gatersleben, Murtagh and Abrahamse 2014; Van der Werff, Steg and Keizer 2014).

64. Dietz (2005).

65. Brosch (2021); van Valkengoed and Steg (2019). Norgaard has explored how the magnitude of climate change and the difficulty in mobilizing can lead to denial. She uses the term in a more classic psychological sense of ignoring an overwhelming problem rather than the more common use of climate denial to describe those who reject the scientific consensus (Norgaard 2011, 2019b). Davidson and Kecinski (2021) offer a useful review and emphasize the need for more attention to diversity in research on emotions and sustainability.

66. Cole et al. 2023 and Judge et al. 2023 review polarization in environmental decision making.

67. See Dias and Lelkes (2021); Druckman and Levendusky (2019); Druckman et al. (2021a, 2021b); Iyengar, Sood and Lelkes (2012); Iyengar et al. (2019); Munro and Ditto (1997); Brady et al. (2017); Finkel et al. (2020). This is similar to the "devil shift" in Advocacy Coalition Framework (ACF) theory; see Chapter 6, Note 19.

68. The literature is extensive and growing rapidly (Bonikowski, Feinstein and Bock 2021; Johnson and Schwadel 2019; Jost, Baldassari and Druckman 2022; Lord, Ross and Lepper 1979; McCright and Dunlap 2011b; McCright, Xiao and Dunlap 2014).

69. Krupnikov and Ryan (2022).

70. Muthukrishna and Henrich (2019).

71. Kim Wolske, Paul Stern and I found it very useful to combine VBN theory, the theory of planned behavior (TPB) and the theory of adoption of innovation to understand the decision of individuals to acquire residential photovoltaics (RPV) (Wolske and Stern 2018; Wolske, Stern and Dietz 2017). Muthukrishna and Henrich (2019) suggest that cultural evolution models can help integrate theory. Kennedy's (2022) proposal of eco-types based on one's environmental interests is an example of the potential value of theoretical integration. She sometimes frames this approach as in opposition to VBN theory, but I think the two approaches can be complementary. Interests reflect context and experience, and shape but are also shaped by values, beliefs, norms and identity, so an integration allows for better understanding of short- and long-term dynamics. VBN theory provides a way to link ideas of interests to larger theoretical discussions of cultural evolution and, through population thinking, of structure and agency. In particular, VBN theory's long emphasis on empathy, the experiences of those oppressed and social movements could link the idea of interests and eco-types to broader concerns with power and social change.

72. Core statements are Ajzen (1985, 1991). Sniehotta, Presseau and Araújo-Soares (2014) provide a critical assessment of TPB in the context of health behaviors and Volume 9, Issue Number 2 of *Health Psychology Review* includes a baker's dozen of papers responding to their critiques; reading through this discussion provides an excellent overview of the current state of the theory. Reciprocal causation of the sort just discussed may be at play in TPB (Kroesen and Chorus 2018).

73. Ajzen (2012: 36–37).

74. Klöckner (2013). I thank Kristian Nielsen for noting that, even in this strong review, most of the studies are based on surveys and not experiments so there are always challenges to establishing causal order. This is one more example of the need for multiple methods complementing each other. The issue is further explored in Kroesen and Chorus (2018). Nielsen also notes that the best models still leave a lot of unexplained variation in human behaviors, something I attribute in part to not having an integrated theory that takes account of contexts. One of my graduate advisors, Tim Tardiff, argued persuasively that individual-level models with even modest levels of predictive ability can be useful for policy.

75. Nielsen (2017); Nielsen and Hofmann (2021).

76. Bouman, Steg and Perlaviciute (2021); Guagnano, Stern and Dietz (1995).

77. Kahneman (2011).

78. Dietz and Stern (1995).

79. Brown (2004); Simon (1947, 1972, 1982, 1986). Simon was the first non-economist to win the Nobel Prize in Economics, one of four given for work that is critical of or expands on the RAM: Simon, Kahneman, Ostrom, Smith. Of these Nobel laureates, only one, my former colleague, Vern Smith, is an economist by training. It is wonderful that the committee convened by the Royal Swedish Academy takes seriously the term "Economic Sciences" in the formal name of the prize (Sveriges Riksbank Prize in Economic Sciences in Memory of Alfred Nobel; in Swedish: *Sveriges riksbanks pris i ekonomisk vetenskap till Alfred Nobels mine*) and has given the prize to important work done by those who are not economists per se. Simon's interests were diverse, including early forays into causal analysis of nonexperimental data and foundational work on artificial intelligence (AI) (Simon 1991). His work emphasizing the importance of individual decisions in understanding organizations was noted in the Introduction.

80. Simon (1972) argued that we cannot be universal in our analysis because there are uncertainties in what the outcomes of our actions will be and we don't fully understand or even know about all the alternatives we face.

81. Tversky (1972).

82. A major theory of ethics articulated by Kant ([1781] 1998, [1785] 2002) suggests that ethical decisions are made by adhering to strong rules, "categorical imperatives" that preclude some courses of action and require others; see Box 5.2. The use of such rules would look a bit like elimination by aspects. The set of strong rules to guide ethical decisions is similar to the status of norms discussed in this section. This kind of logic is implemented in the "Three Laws of Robotics"; see Note 83.

83. Gigerenzer (2008); Hammond, Keeney and Raiffa (1999); Morgan and Henrion (1990); Van Leuven et al. (2022). An interesting new line of research examines how AI and robots should make decisions (Gershman, Horvitz and Tenenbaum 2015; Lin, Abney and Jenkins 2017; Parkes and Wellman 2015; see also many papers in the *International Journal of Social Robotics*). At one level, decision-making by AI and robots seems novel and entertaining and undoubtedly will produce some changes most of us will view as improvements. Indeed, the suggestions about websites, products and media we routinely receive on the web, even the autocorrect that comes when typing, are trivial examples of decision-making by AI, albeit with only modest ethical implications. (Granted suggesting products without taking account of their consequences for sustainability and justice or suggesting websites that encourage BAHP can have deleterious effects on society.) As AI and robots become more prevalent, and more involved in actions that can have dire consequences (e.g. combat robots, self-driving cars, surgical robots), it is also a matter with serious social consequences. Asimov offered a provocative solution to this problem with his "three laws of robotics" sixty years ago (from the "*Handbook of Robotics*, 56th Edition, 2058 A.D." as quoted in Asimov 1956). But not only do roboticists not have a way to build the three laws as absolutes in robot decision-making; some of the most active areas of research, such as combat robots, seem to be direct violations of the first and dominant of the three laws: "A robot may not injure a human being or, through inaction, allow a human being to come to harm." I have heard roboticists speak of the Asimov laws with disdain. I find that puzzling and even disturbing given the growing concern with the possible adverse impacts of robots and AI and the very modest progress towards resolution of those issues. While the three laws may not make any sense in the context of how AI and robots are actually developed at present, they are at least an inspiration and a reminder that those working in these fields have an obligation to engage with the societal and ethical implications of their work. (Asimov's treatment of women both in person and in his novels, where they are largely absent, is troubling.) I will return to the issue of AI and ethics in Chapters 4 and 5.

84. Kahneman (2011).

85. Kahneman, Slovic and Tversky (1982). It is widely believed that Tversky would have been awarded the prize as well but he died in 1996 and the Nobel is only given to living scientists. Lewis (2016)

provides a useful history of the development of the heuristics and biases literature in a joint biography of Kahneman and Tversky.

86. One of my biases, and I think a valuable heuristic, is that our academic disciplines often are as much barriers to better science as they are facilitators of it. All disciplines read more of their own literature than the literature from other fields, and too many researchers read only in their own field. As a result, problems that are well resolved in one field are still seen as difficulties in other fields. I suspect this tendency towards intellectual involution varies across disciplines and it would be interesting to examine which disciplines are the most narcissistic and which the most open to building on innovations in other fields. One version of this inward-looking tendency is to take approaches, theories and findings from one field, relabel them with some new term and then proceed as if work in the establishing fields did not exist. A much healthier approach is to actively draw on ongoing research in multiple fields to create a synthetic and more robust understanding. This is the approach that Berkes, McCay, Ostrom and many others established for work on commons (Berkes et al. 1989; McCay 2002; McCay and Acheson 1990; McCay and Svein 2010; Ostrom et al. 2002). One measure of how well I have done in wrestling with questions of sustainability and decision-making in this book will be the diversity of literature from which I have learned.

87. Bruch and Feinberg (2017); Sniderman, Brody and Tetlock (1991). For example, when presented with a novel topic, rather than thinking through the implications via the RAM, citizens may note the stand of their favored political party or a respected public figure and take the same position. Analysis of this tendency provides important insights into political decision-making, especially when combined with other perspectives (Lupia 2015; Lupia and McCubbins 1998). Some have even invoked the same kind of arguments that are offered by evolutionary psychologists discussed later in the chapter – that genetic evolution during life in small groups has "hard wired" certain heuristics (Petersen 2015). However, this explanation seems to give too little credit to cultural evolution. But as Druckman, Kuklinski and Sigelman (2009) point out, the political heuristics argument is not framed in contrast to the RAM but rather as a theory of how citizens who seem to know very little about politics make decisions. I think the insights of the heuristics literature can be well captured in thinking about framing effects, a topic I will address in Chapters 6, 7 and 8. There is some evidence that humans have heuristics and biases that make them especially attentive not just to other humans (see Henrich 2015) but also to other species (New, Cosmides and Tooby 2007).

88. Attari (2014); Attari et al. (2009); Attari et al. (2010, 2011); Dietz (2010, 2014); Dietz, Leshko and McCright (2013). They also have done some very interesting work comparing the perceived difficulty of various household energy conservation actions with the estimates of how much energy can be saved by those actions (the estimates of actual savings were developed by my colleagues Gerry Gardner and Paul Stern) (Attari et al. 2011; Gardner and Stern 2008). This allows the identification of the things that are both perceived as easy and have substantial impact: using more energy-efficient light bulbs and keeping one's car tuned.

89. Attari (2014); Dietz (2014).

90. On experts: Kantenbacher and Attari (2021). On multiple anchors: Marghetis, Attari and Landy (2019). On labeling: Camilleri et al. (2019); Taufique et al. (2022).

91. Cialdini ([1984] 2007); Dietz (2011); Thaler and Sunstein (2009). The difference in tone across the two books is interesting. Cialdini explicitly says he hopes his work will help us protect ourselves from those who would manipulate us. Thaler and Sunstein advocate "libertarian paternalism" in which "choice architects" design decision contexts so as to encourage choices that are good for the chooser. While Thaler and Sunstein discuss ethical issues, they do not seem nearly as concerned by manipulations in the private sector as Cialdini, while Cialdini places less emphasis on the possibility of designing choice contexts for the good. Sunstein's (2014) subsequent book seems to be more measured about the problems of design of choice architecture, although it mostly reads as if

the problem of anchoring effects and related heuristics and biases were discovered within economics. Thaler (2018) has decried the use of nudges for "less beneficial purposes" and labeled them "sludge" while Sunstein has begun to explore further some of the ethical and distributional implications of nudges (Sunstein 2021; Sunstein and Reisch 2019). Selinger and Whyte (2010, 2011, 2012) provide thoughtful analysis of the ethics and practicality of "nudges." There are suggestions for "boosting" rather than "nudging" where insights from research on decision-making are used to enhance cognitive capacity and thus produce better decisions (Harrison and Ross 2017). The general message of this body of research has had some influence at the highest levels of policy. On September 15, 2015, President Obama issued an Executive Order "Using Behavioral Science Insights to Better Serve the American People," calling for federal agencies to make use of behavioral science in designing policies (The White House 2015). The team was dissolved under the Trump administration (Stillman 2017). A similar unit in the British government has been reformed as a "social purpose company," which is partly owned by the Cabinet but not formally part of the government (www.bi.team/; accessed November 19, 2022). See Chapter 8 for discussion of ends versus means in sustainability decisions.

92. Halberstam and Montagnes (2015); Madariaga and Ozen (2015); Stoll (2015).

93. Siegrist and Árvai (2020). While I focus here on environmental and technological risks, it is clear that in general humans have a great deal of difficulty in handling uncertainty and probabilities. For example, many areas of physical and biological science advanced more quickly than did statistics, which is substantially a product of the twentieth century (Bernstein 1998; Dietz and Kalof 2009; Salsburg 2001). Anyone who has taken or especially who has taught an introductory statistics course will appreciate the challenges we face in handling uncertainty.

94. Exact numbers of shark attack and bee sting fatalities are hard to obtain but it seems clear that bee stings kill far more people than shark attacks. One estimate suggests that in 2014 there were two fatal unprovoked shark attacks worldwide (Florida Museum International Shark Attack Files, www.flmnh.ufl.edu/fish/sharks/isaf/2014summary.html, accessed February 9, 2020), while in the United States alone there seem to be about forty fatal bee stings per year (Graft 2006).

95. Fischhoff and Kadvany (2011).

96. US National Academies of Science (2016: chap. 3).

97. A growing literature addresses how perceived scientific uncertainty influences public opinion (Bolsen and Druckman 2018; Kerr and Wilson 2018; Visschers 2018). The results so far suggest the effects are complex. It appears that perceived lack of scientific consensus has different effects than, for example, perceived uncertainty in forecasts. And, as with many environmental issues, those with different values and political ideologies are differently influenced by communications about consensus.

98. Criteria for decisions and processes will be the subject of Chapter 5.

99. Cialdini ([1984] 2007); Cosmides and Tooby (1996); Gigerenzer (1998).

100. Desmond (2012, 2016); Desmond and Gershenson (2016). The television series *Maid* is filled with examples where what would be small challenges or even just annoyances for someone with some savings and predictable income can be potentially catastrophic for someone with no financial resources (Land 2019; Metzler 2021). The difficulties encountered by low-income people are sometimes attributed to their psychology, including an inability to make long-term plans. But long-term plans and deferred gratification only make sense in predictable environments (Kidd, Palmeri and Aslin 2013; Moffett, Flannagan and Shah 2020). For low-income people and those subject to discrimination, the environment can be quite unpredictable. In my own family history, if my grandfather's family had funds to buffer his job loss via programs later promoted by unions, my father might have finished high school and been on a different life trajectory. A social "safety net" of unemployment and health insurance can allow people to make decisions that are less risk-averse and closer to the RAM. See Chapter 1, Note 46 and Chapter 8.

101. Bruch and Feinberg (2017); Rivers and Arvai (2007); Whyte 2012a, 2012b; Whyte, Brewer and Johnson (2015).
102. Edwards, Lee and Esposito (2019).
103. Weaver and Prowse (2020) provide a valuable overview of research on the prevalance of violence, especially police violence, in African American and other BIPOC communities in the United States.
104. Cojean, Combalbert and Taillandier-Schmitt (2020); Mears et al. (2017).
105. Fischhoff et al. (1978); Fischhoff et al. (1981). For a recent review, see Siegrist and Árvai (2020). Rosa used this method in an eloquent cross-cultural comparison between the United States and Japan, two nations with relatively similar technologies but very different cultures and histories (Kleinhesselink and Rosa 1991, 1994; Rosa and Matsuda 2005; Rosa, Matsuda and Kleinhesselink 2000). A key element of that history was that Japan was the only nation that has been attacked with nuclear weapons and the United States the only nation to use them in war. Note that a comparison of shark attacks and bee stings invokes multiple heuristics: dread, a sense of control and dramatic events that are more cognitively available.
106. Personal control or dread might be a factor that influences the utility associated with one course of action versus another. Then these considerations could be incorporated into the RAM as an elaboration. It is entirely reasonable that people have strong preferences about risks based on things like dread. The point of the risk perception literature is not to deny those preferences but to show that they influence not just what risks are disliked but the estimates of the underlying risk itself. As noted in Chapter 2, public concerns that deviate from the RAM are often dismissed as "irrational."
107. Siegrist and Árvai (2020). There is a challenging methodological problem in the literature on this issue. In most surveys, we ask people a number of questions about a single topic, for example about their values. We have two dimensions – questions and people. We have very well-developed methods for analyzing these two-dimensional data – factor analysis and structural equation modeling. But the risk work has three dimensions: people (the respondents), risk objects to be assessed (car accidents, airplane accidents, shark attacks, drowning, etc.) and the dimensions on which the respondents rate the risk (the survey items to get at dread, control, probability, etc.). To the best of my knowledge, we have no well-developed methods for handling such three-dimensional data. In the original studies, Fischhoff, Slovic, Lichtenstein and colleagues averaged scores across respondents, thus eliminating one dimension (Fischhoff et al. 1978). Most of the statistical analysis in their papers is based not on individuals' responses but on the average response across all individuals in the study. If people differ substantially in how they think about risk, this approach may miss something since it is difficult to use in trying to understand contextual differences.
108. Starr (1969).
109. Renn (2008); Rosa, Renn and McCright (2013); Stern (2013); US National Research Council (1996, 2008).
110. Lewis (2016).
111. Dietz and Stern (1995).
112. In an impressive series of papers, my colleague Ken Frank and his collaborators have argued persuasively that the issue is not whether an analysis of an experiment or observational analysis is "right" or "wrong" (Frank 2000; Frank and Min 2007; Frank et al. 2013). Rather, they provide methods for quantifying the degree to which the conclusion a researcher might draw from a study is vulnerable to alternative explanations – that the experimental results are not generalizable or the causal conclusions about observational data are spurious. The importance of multi-methods is well established in the literature on commons (Pottete, Janssen and Ostrom 2010).
113. Guagnano, Stern and Dietz (1995); Peterson et al. (2021). And there is variation across people even within a context. For example, while in general a lack of concern with climate change aligns with a

pattern of values, beliefs and norms that minimizes environmental concerns, there are exceptions. In a very insightful study, Haltinner and Sarathchandra (2022) demonstrate that many skeptical about climate change still have concerns with habitat preservation and other environmental issues. This can open a space for the kinds of deliberation I will emphasize in Chapter 9 as a way of dealing with the BAHP.

114. Bouman and Steg (2021); Pedersen and Favero (2020).

115. Barrios and Hochberg (2020); Bouman, Steg and Dietz (2021); Bouman and Steg (2021); Geiger, Gore et al. (2021); Hamilton, Hartter and Saito (2015); Painter and Qiu (2020).

116. That is we would like to occupy what Stokes referred to as Pasteur's Quadrant, where our work contributes both to fundamental understanding and to solving practical problems (Stokes 1997). Stokes uses as an example Louis Pasteur, who developed key aspects of microbiology while trying to fight infectious disease and improve wine and cheese. I prefer to refer to the intellectual space where one meets both goals as Ostrom's Quadrant, after Elinor Ostrom. A recent discussion about the balance between theory and application in environmental psychology elaborates on the issue (Lange et al. 2021; Nielsen, Cologna et al. 2021; van Valkengoed et al. 2021). See also the Introduction.

# 4    Facts and Values

1. We are learning how tropical forests recover after being cut, and while there are some grounds for optimism it appears that important features like biodiversity and biomass may take more than a century to return to precut levels (Poorter et al. 2021). Before Europeans arrived, many landscapes in the tropics and elsewhere had been shaped by centuries of sophisticated management practices by Indigenous people. But the issue is complicated, in part because we may have the most data from the places with the greatest human engagement in the landscape (McMichael et al. 2017; Roberts et al. 2017). In Chapter 1, I noted that recent work suggests that the "great dying" of Indigenous peoples in the Americas was so massive that the afforestation that resulted absorbed so much carbon dioxide that it contributed to the "little ice age" that in turn had substantial impacts on human political and economic systems (Koch et al. 2019). This tragedy is also an example of the complex interplay of coupled human and natural systems.

2. These are not exact quotes but a pastiche of this and a number of similar discussions I have heard. I am oversimplifying a bit for the sake of pointing out the divergence of facts and values.

3. The ecologist was endorsing strong sustainability in which all forms of resources warrant protection, the economist weak sustainability in which one resource is traded off (biodiversity) for another (revenue to invest in other things); see Chapter 2.

4. The importance of science to public policy decisions has certainly grown over time but has a long history. The US National Academy of Sciences was founded by Abraham Lincoln to provide science advice; see Chapter 2, Note 46. Dewey, writing in 1923, emphasized the important scientific content of some of the public controversies of the time and speaks to issues that arise in linking analysis and deliberation (Dewey 1923); see Chapter 9. Science and estimates of risk were at the center of the controversy about nuclear fallout and the above-ground testing of nuclear weapons in the 1950s and 1960s that was a precursor to the environmental movement of the 1960s (Commoner 1966; Eagan 2007; Pauling 1958). In 1956, Hubbert argued that the world would soon reach "peak oil" and that production would decline with disastrous consequences for the economy (Hubbert 1956). All this was background to the developments described in Chapter 2.

5. See Plato, *Meno* 70a (Perseus Digital Library, www.perseus.tufts.edu/hopper/text?doc=Perseus%3Atext%3A1999.01.0178%3Atext%3DMeno).

6. Our interaction with companion animals may be one of the few stable modes of information flow across human history. While our family and friends may communicate via Twitter and Facebook, our dogs and other companion animals interact with us in more or less the same way their ancestors interacted with our ancestors 15,000 or more years ago. Barking to let us know there's a stranger nearby is probably much the same today as it was then.

7. As the scale of society increased, markets and states often, but not always, became more important ways of structuring social interactions (Graeber and Wengrow 2021). That meant more interactions with strangers. With strangers, being able to make assumptions based on roles rather than detailed knowledge of the individual becomes important. One goal of democracy is to develop a "public sphere" in which people can engage as individuals not just in roles and carry out discourse to develop shared values, beliefs and norms (see the Introduction). In a sense, the public sphere is a return to modes of interaction and collective decision-making that characterized most of human history. An important caveat is that in deliberative theory the norms about the nature of the discourse are intended to be egalitarian, and that has not always been the case in earlier forms of deliberative decision-making – some were allowed to speak, other voices were silent. One of the major challenges of the twenty-first century is conceptualizing and implementing a public sphere that can function effectively not only in very large states but globally (Gunderson 2016; Gunderson and Dietz 2018). See also the further discussion of deliberation in Chapters 5 and 8.

8. The most useful and compelling statements of this position may come not from the social constructionists in the social sciences and Western philosophy but from the Buddhists.

9. For example, Carnap ([1928] 1967). Sometimes this view is labeled "positivist." But usually when a position is called "positivist" it seems to mean an epistemological view that I have not encountered among scientists, at least not since I lived in a dorm filled with first-year physical science and engineering majors who were in many ways prototypes of the male leads on *The Big Bang Theory*. This seems to be another case of critics using a label to dismiss the position of a group whose actual position is not well understood by the critics. Criticisms are far more useful if they are based on a careful reading of what is being criticized.

10. Like any substantial community of scholars, the "Vienna Circle" varied in its views across individuals and over time. The logical positivists held very strong views, and so did the "Austrian economists" whose work underpins public choice and libertarian theories (see Chapters 3 and 5). Both were part of the same social network. Perhaps there was something about those Viennese coffeehouses that led to rather strong and systematic assertions in theory.

11. For example, Kuhn (1962, 1977); Popper (1974, 1987).

12. Bruno Latour, a major constructionist scholar, frames his arguments about climate change as follows: "[B]oth sides agree that policy should *follow* scientific expertise and that we cannot make decisions based on uncertain science. Part one: science is about incontrovertible and indisputable facts; part two: policy follows science" (Latour 2015: 148). As Latour points out, the view that we cannot make decisions based on uncertain science is indeed an argument made by those who oppose climate policy. (He does not cite the scholars who have done the research to establish this; see Chapter 5, Note 82. Nor does he cite the literature on how perception of scientific consensus influences the views of members of the public; see Chapter 3.) But his emphasis on certainty is hardly the view of those who research climate change. The US National Academy of Science, in the largest study they have done on climate, calls for adaptive risk management linked with analytic deliberative processes as the best approach to addressing climate change (US National Research Council 2010a, 2011). The use of the phrase "risk management" should make clear that there is no expectation that the science that will be used for decision-making will be certain. Many National Academies reports call for processes that link scientific analysis and public deliberation and thus acknowledge that science alone is not sufficient for decision-making (Dietz 2013a; US National Research Council 2010a); see Chapter 9.

The Intergovernmental Panel on Climate Change (IPCC) works hard to incorporate the Moss–Schneider guidance that all statements about facts and all projections of the future should be accompanied by language that describes the uncertainty in them (Moss 2004; Moss and Schneider 2000); see Chapter 6, Note 23. Part of the problem may be in Latour's framing of the issue as facts *versus* values. I see the issue as facts *and* values, while admitting the two are often conflated in public debate. In contrast, Latour's argument about "Science its View-from-Nowhere" (p. 148) suggests he is unaware of the nuanced arguments by Rosa that I will review in Section 4.3 on when science is highly certain and not context-specific (applies everywhere and thus I suppose could be called "from nowhere") and when science is highly uncertain and highly context-specific. In the end, by calling the IPCC a lobby, Latour seems to shift back to a constructivist position and suggests that the resolution of climate change is a "territorial war." In that sense, his argument seems not all that different from that of Douglas and Wildavsky in their view that environmental disputes are about tribal battles (Douglas and Wildavsky 1982). A strong constructionist stance was also offered in some of the earliest sociological commentary on climate change (Buttel and Taylor 1994; Taylor and Buttel 1992), a position Rosa and I rebutted using an early version of the position I am taking here (Rosa and Dietz 1998). I can only conclude that the policy debates and scholarly literature Latour is observing are far different from those I know and have participated in. In my experience and reading, the characterization of uncertainty in scientific knowledge is a central theme of discussion as are the appropriate ways to make decisions in the face of uncertainty. I readily acknowledge that I may misunderstand his positions since I cannot read him in French, and even when he is kind enough to write in English I have trouble following his arguments.

13. Haraway (1989, 2016); Rosa (1998b). My thinking has also been influenced by my colleague Kevin Elliott's excellent and accessible discussion of the philosophy of science literature on values in science (Elliott 2017) and by Heather Douglas' important work (Douglas 2009). I will elaborate on Elliott's work in Section 4.2.

14. I use the term "evolves" intentionally – I view science as an example of cultural evolution, what is often called "evolutionary epistemology"; see Introduction, Note 51.

15. This mode of communication seems to have begun when the Royal Society in 1752 established a "Committee on Papers" to provide reviews, but some scholars point out that the Royal Society of Edinburgh had something like a peer-review process as early as 1731, and like most major ideas, there are antecedents in the ancient world (Fitzpatrick 2011; Spier 2002).

16. While the details differ across government agencies and foundations, most organizations that fund science also use a peer-review process to select the projects to support.

17. Allowing the prestige of a claimant to have some weight in assessing the strength of a claim is not irrational. If a scholar has a history of producing claims that turn out to be seen as correct when given thorough examination, it is a reasonable expectation that new claims might also work out. But the norms of science suggest that the "benefit of the doubt" should in the end be given only very modest weight and should always be overturned based on evidence.

18. Huber et al. (2022); Merton (1968). A biological scientist I know defended the single-blind review: "I need to know what lab did the work to know if they are capable of doing it right." My response is that the evidence presented in the paper should be the basis of that judgment, not a reputation. Debates about the best way to handle peer-review continue (De Silva and Vance 2017; Siler and Strang 2017).

19. Kean (2021).

20. Max Planck's *Scientific Autobiography* contains a famous statement on this point: "A new scientific truth does not triumph by convincing its opponents and making them see the light, but rather because its opponents eventually die, and a new generation grows up that is familiar with it" (Planck 1949: 33–34). (He makes a similar statement later in the book.) It has been quoted by Thomas Kuhn and Paul Feyerabend, who I believe would have benefited from a modern view of cultural evolution in thinking through the implications of this idea. Many scholars do change their

minds in response to debate. I am impressed by C. Vann Woodward's gracious acknowledgment of his critics and the mistakes they pointed out in his important *The Strange Career of Jim Crow* (Woodward 1955, 1988). While the debate clarified the history of segregation in the United States, many key ideas he raised about the economic consequences of segregation, including its negative impact on poor whites as well as on African Americans, were on target and heavily influenced the thinking of the civil rights movement (King 1968). Some of Benjamin Franklin's biased statements about race can be to some degree tempered by his willingness to change his mind and eventually advocate for abolition; see Chapter 3, Note 11.

21. Sagan (1996).
22. A growing body of research disaggregates a general idea of public trust in science into trust in particular types of scientists, especially as defined by who employs them, what they work on and what they say or don't say about both their values and their conclusions; see Chapter 6.
23. For journals, the open access to data requirement is usually at time of publication. For research funding agencies, it is usually at some modest time interval after the research project closes. Access is through various online archives usually supported by universities or research institutes. For many decades, the social science community has had a norm of storing major data sets in repositories such as the Inter-University Consortium for Political and Social Research. As with open access publishing, there are still a lot of issues around how best to make data available and how to pay for the process of setting up the data in a useable form and curating them over decades. There is also a growing norm and often a formal requirement that the computer code used to analyze the data be made available. In the United States, there are restrictions to accessing data that could be traced back to a specific individual with protocols required to maintain anonymity and privacy – for example, under the US Health Insurance Portability and Accountability Act 1996.
24. Du Bois ([1935] 2014); Morris (2015).
25. Fanon (1969); Freire ([1968] 1972).
26. Cook, Grillos and Andersson (2019); Gay-Antaki and Liverman (2018); Harding (2015); Hofstra et al. (2020); Mindt et al. (2018); Schell, Guy et al. (2020); Vollan and Henry (2019).
27. Once again, we run into the problem of terms having different meanings in different fields. Most philosophers of science use the term "values" for what would be called "norms" in VBN theory described in Chapter 3. Since the term "epistemic values" is strongly embedded in philosophy of science, I will use it in discussing Elliott's taxonomy in Section 4.2, keeping in mind that values shape norms. When I turn to my own approach, I will shift back to norms. It would be interesting to try to differentiate norms about scientific practice and epistemic values in the scientific community. It may be that, in some communities, and in some subcultures, especially around professions, values and norms are so tightly linked that it is hard to differentiate them, while in larger more diverse groups, such as the US public, there is sufficient variation and only modest selective pressures to be consistent so that norms and values can be more readily distinguished.
28. Elliott (2017). For clarity, I stick with his typology but note that there is an excellent ongoing discussion about it (Brown 2018; Douglas 2018; Elliott 2018; Kourany 2018).
29. Baralt (2010) has shown that the dominant nonprofits supporting research on breast cancer focus almost exclusively on a "cure" while ignoring environmental carcinogens that may cause breast cancer and research that might lead to cancer prevention.
30. Thompson (2015, 2017) offers very clear and balanced accounts of the diverse ethical issues that arise when we think about food and agriculture.
31. Levins (1966, 1993); Orzack and Sober (1993). See Chapter 3, Note 12.
32. Levins' criteria apply most cleanly to simulation models where we create an artificial world using mathematics and computer code and then use the behavior of the model to better understand and predict the observable world. But similar issues arise in the choice of methods for collecting and

analyzing empirical data. The traditional distinctions between the physical, biological and social sciences substantially reflect historical traditions that in turn are instantiated in the structures of professional societies and disciplines. These distinctions can be misleading. I find more useful the distinction between the experimental and the nonexperimental sciences. This gets at the norms for how best to collect and analyze data, given the constraints regarding the degree to which the scientists can actively intervene in the systems being studied. Within the social sciences, there has also been a tendency to make much of a "quantitative/qualitative" split that I also feel has more to do with the history of the field than with careful thought about real methods as they are applied. But Elliott's point applies here too. Scientists must make choices about what sort of methods they will deploy. Every method when carefully deployed has strengths and weaknesses. Every scientist has a set of skills and experiences that makes them facile with some methods and naïve about others. So, the choice of methods for collection and analysis of empirical data depends in part on values.

33. This issue became prominent in US science after the Manhattan Project, where those involved had very different views about what should be done and how they should convey their views to decision makers and the public (Reed 2014, 2019).

34. The gender difference here is notable.

35. After the publication of our article "The Struggle to Govern the Commons," Elinor Ostrom, Paul Stern and I were approached by a producer for John Stossel asking us to be interviewed for the ABC television show *20/20*. All three of us declined. Our sense was that Stossel would take a strongly libertarian stand while our view was that government, markets and communities all sometimes fail and sometimes succeed in managing commons. The science on commons is complicated and subtle. An "interview" with a media figure who has a strong stance didn't seem to us a good way to convey such complexity.

36. There are horrible exceptions where the scientific process has been dominated by prejudice and ideology, as in "scientific" justifications of racism and sexism, see Section 4.4. Harding is compelling in her arguments that science is impeded by a lack of diversity in the standpoints represented in scientific discussions (Harding 1998, 2015). The exclusion of DuBois and his colleagues noted in Section 4.1 is an example of what we lose from a lack of diversity. I will return to this point in Chapter 8; see also the Introduction.

37. McCright and Dunlap (2010); Michaels (2020).

38. Schnaiberg (1977). Every discipline has something to contribute to both the production sciences and the impact sciences. The examples simply give a flavor of the dominant orientation of a few disciplines.

39. One hopeful development is deploying the goals and values of sustainability in the design of new products, promoting the sort of sustainable or appropriate technology mentioned in Chapter 2, Note 33. See also the discussion in Chapter 7.

40. The Toolbox Dialogue Initiative offers resources for facilitating interdisciplinary collaboration (Hubbs, O'Rourke and Orzack 2020; see also the Toolbox Dialogue Initiative website, https://tdi.m su.edu/). Design principles for communicating scientific evidence to the public are useful (Blastland et al. 2020; Van der Bles et al. 2019).

41. National Academies of Sciences, Engineering, and Medicine (2016).

42. Bidwell, Dietz and Scavia (2013); Briley, Brown and Kalafatis (2015). The Regional Integrated Science and Assessments centers of the US National Oceanographic and Atmospheric Administration have been very effective at using this model to support climate adaptation ("Climate Adaptation Partnerships," Climate Program Office website, https://cpo.noaa.gov/Divisions-Programs/Climate-and-Societal-Intera ctions/RISA/About-RISA). The excellent work being done by my Michigan State colleagues in collaboration with the community in Flint, Michigan, is another example; see Chapter 1, Note 64.

43. Haraway (1988, 1989, 2013, 2016). Since Rosa was interested in the same set of problems that I am, his work is a useful way to frame the discussion. But many others have influenced me. I perhaps feel an especial affinity for Donna Haraway since she has long been a supporter of the Animal Studies Program at Michigan State and was a student of the innovative ecological theorist G. Evelyn Hutchinson. From early on, my work on deliberative processes for melding scientific analysis and public engagement has been influenced by the arguments of Sandra Harding (1998, 2015), who has frequently engaged with the Michigan State Philosophy Department. Gould's writings have also been part of my thinking because of their grounding in an evolutionary perspective (Gould 1965, 1997, 2000, 2011; York and Clark 2011).

44. His thinking evolved over time in conversation with others, in particular with Ortwin Renn, with whom he coauthored his last book (Aven and Renn 2009, 2010; Aven, Renn and Rosa 2011; Ravetz and Functowicz 1998; Rosa 1998a, 1998b, 2010; Rosa, Renn and McCright 2013). He framed his work in terms of realism. My sense is that most of his arguments hold if one is not a realist but an empiricist. While the distinction is important and made in much more nuanced ways in the philosophy of science, it is seldom raised in human ecology and kindred fields like environmental sociology, and I don't think the distinctions matter much here.

45. Rosa engaged the work of Functowitz and Ravetz (1993) to argue that we should move beyond the dichotomy of logical positivism and social construction of science; see Chapter 4, Note 9. He was informed by Marxism but was by no means a traditional Marxist and I don't recall him being much impressed by Hegel. But it is interesting that he has taken two contradictory and opposed views and created a synthesis in a way that could certainly be labeled dialectic.

46. The Rosa quote is from Rosa (1998a: 34–35). One can think of research methodology as ways of establishing what are stronger and weaker claims in the conversation. See the discussion of the important work of Frank and colleagues in Chapter 3, Note 112. He sometimes calls this a "Habermasian" approach to statistics in the sense that his approach is embedded in the idea of science as an ongoing deliberation. His sensitivity analysis techniques facilitate more nuanced discussion than those that usually emerge if we focus on conventional hypothesis tests alone.

47. Those who teach introductory social science courses often refer to the "I know a guy who …" argument (apologies for the gendered form). Students, when encountering scientific generalizations derived from the social sciences, will point to a counterexample from their personal experience – a story. As I sometimes say, "Data is not the plural of anecdote." (The origins of this statement are hard to trace. Indeed, one sometimes hears it expressed the opposite way: "The plural of anecdote is data" (Nguyen 2015).)

48. I thank John Barone for this example.

49. Newton established that the force of attraction between two objects is proportional to the product of their masses, so in fact the gravitational force on the heavier ball is greater. But in our part of the universe, it appears that gravitational mass and inertial mass are equal, so the resistance to motion of the heavier ball is also greater by exactly the same amount as the force exerted on it is greater.

50. Suppose the average high school in the United States has twenty students per physics class and lab teams of two and offers two physics classes per year. There are about 28,000 high schools in the United States. So, in US high schools alone this experiment might be replicated $20/2 * 2 * 28,000 = 560,000$ times per year. If we expand to non-US high schools, colleges and universities around the world, and take into account that this experiment has probably been common at least since the post-Sputnik emphasis on science in the 1960s, it is likely that this experiment has been replicated tens of millions of times. My "Fermi" (i.e., "back of the envelope") estimate is 42 million times. Any of my assumptions may be off, but clearly this is a frequently repeated experiment.

51. Studies like those that led to the confirmation of the existence of gravity waves are not things that will be done even dozens of times with current technology, and they certainly can't be replicated in the

high school physics lab with any technology we will have in the near future. In those cases, the argument for repeatability comes from the strength in each line of reasoning in the argument that leads to the conclusion that the wave has been detected. For the detection to be credible, each part of the argument must be based on facts that have been well accepted in the community of researchers. The ostensibility comes because anyone interested in the outcomes of a study can follow the logic and observe the results, and/or because they trust those carrying out the research. In the case of the dropping balls of different densities from the Tower of Pisa or rolling them down an inclined plane, the logic is simple and anyone standing by can observe the results. In the case of detection of gravity waves, while the logic is magnificently complex, there is a high degree of trust in the team that undertook the experiment and in the physics community in general. No one but a specialist can follow all the details of how the team came to its conclusion. Most of us trust that highly expert specialists have looked over the design of the gravity wave experiments for the years during which it was developed and implemented and have carefully vetted the results reported. We trust the consensus of the scientific community that has emerged after decades of active discussion. Again, the importance of invariance principles is clear. If each assumption that leads to conclusions had to be tested for each new experiment, progress would be very, very slow. But because large-scale experiments can rely on what has been established in the past to remain true, it is easier to build a cumulative body of results.

52. One of the justifications for calling the current geological epoch the Anthropocene is that human-created compounds less common or absent in the previous history of the earth will become evident for the first time in geological strata. The emerging consensus seems to be that these changes become visible in the 1950s, although social changes such as the rise of colonialism and of capitalism and industrialization that drive it started earlier (Crutzen and Stoermer 2000; Steffen et al. 2011; Voosen 2022; Waters et al. 2016).

53. The narrative is based on a variety of press accounts and blogs (Boucher 2014; Kroh 2014; Trip 2014).

54. Research on the effects of the spill not only will help us understand what happened but will help assess risks of future spills of this sort, although each toxic spill or other exposure is unique and requires attention to context (Cozzarelli et al. 2017; Guilfoos et al. 2017; Horzmann et al. 2017; Thomasson et al. 2017).

55. Hanna-Attisha et al. (2016); Sadler, LaChance and Hanna-Attisha (2017). See Chapter 1, Note 64 for citations to the excellent work being done by researchers in collaboration with the Flint community.

56. We found that beliefs that minorities have received unfair advantage, often termed "symbolic racism" in the political science literature, predicts a lack of support for contaminated communities. Others also have found a strong link between symbolic racism and a lack of environmental concern (Benegal 2018; Chanin 2018; Dietz et al. 2018).

57. Dietz, Frey and Rosa (2002).

58. The gendered language is telling. The old tradition of testing only on one sex and assuming there is a simple extrapolation to the other is deeply flawed. We are moving into an era when we recognize that genetic and developmental diversity has implications for the efficacy and toxicity of the drugs we use and the toxicity of the compounds to which we are exposed. However, this diversity makes testing for effects that much more challenging since more testing and modeling must be done to account for the diversity in response across different individuals.

59. Rollin (1989, 2017). Substantial efforts are underway to improve the quality of toxicity analysis based on computer modeling and in vitro tests. While it is a major challenge because of complex interactions in the biochemistry and biology of the toxics, advances can both reduce the suffering of the animals used for testing and reduce cost and increase the speed of testing so better information is available on a wider array of potential toxins.

60. As noted in Chapter 1, Rosa argued that the essence of sociology, his chosen discipline, was "Context matters" (Dietz 2013b).

61. He drew the term from the work of Funtowitz and Ravetz (1993); Ravetz and Functowicz (1998); Redclift (1996); Rosa (1998a).

62. Gould (1965). We are more aware of gender, ethnicity and ableness biases in science but still struggle to purge them. In a very interesting study, Handley et al. (2015) show that there are gender biases in accepting research that shows gender bias in science.

63. In the science fiction series *Remembrance of Earth's Past*, Liu Cixin makes the fascinating argument that a civilization's ability to make technological advances and thus its military strength depend on the ability to do high energy physics. This is just one of a cornucopia of provocative ideas in this trilogy.

64. Successful corporations are nimble and deploy multiple strategies. It should not be surprising that a corporation that invests heavily in supporting critiques of the scientific consensus on climate change will also invest in shifting its business away from fossil fuels. Diversifying in the face of risks is a basic investment strategy; see Chapter 7.

65. An extensive literature documents these efforts across many technological risks (Kitman 2000; McCright 2000; McCright and Dunlap 2003, 2010; McCright et al. 2013; McCright, Marquart-Pyatt et al. 2016; Michaels 2006, 2008, 2020; Michaels and Monforton 2005; Oreskes and Conway 2010). The same individuals are often engaged across controversies. Thomas Midgley, a famous industrial chemist, was central to the development of tetraethyl lead as an anti-knock additive to gasoline, and thus perhaps to one of the most serious exposures to toxic compounds in human history (McGrayne 2001). He also was central in the development of chlorofluorocarbons (CFCs) for industrial use. CFCs were later found to be the major cause of stratospheric ozone depletion and are a potent greenhouse gas.

66. See Chapter 4, Note 65 and Chapter 2, Note 110. Lear (1998) provides an excellent biography of Carson, while Emma's Revolution commemorates her struggle in the song "Silent Spring" (for the song and lyrics, see the Emma's Revolution website, https://emmasrevolution.com/track/1287089/si lent-spring) and Magpie's *Songs for the Earth* is a tribute to her (Magpie Discography webpage, htt ps://magpiemusic.com/discography.html).

67. Busch (2011); Shwom (2011).

68. My friend John Barone worked for a time for a consulting firm that helped companies meet regulations regarding air quality when a new facility was built or an existing facility modified. The permitting process required simulation of the air quality impacts, using computer models accepted by the US Environmental Protection Agency. It was common for him to have to explain key aspects of the models to the state environmental regulators who were assessing whether or not the proposed changes met the rules. His sense was that when a state regulator had the scientific expertise to be deeply familiar with these models, they were often hired away by the private sector at much higher salaries than state governments can pay. John is a committed environmentalist so he worked hard to be sure his firm's corporate clients met the regulations. But the pressure to cut corners is constant. He left the private sector to teach high school science, thus his suggestion about the prevalence of the inclined plane experiment discussed in Section 4.3. John was the lead author on my first peer-reviewed publication (Barone et al. 1978) and on the Cuyahoga River Project (see the Introduction).

69. The knowledge needed can be very field-specific. I rarely have difficulty engaging in discussions with climatologists and ecologists even when the discussion is filled with jargon. But when I gave a talk at a meeting on public views of and decision-making about food, I had trouble following perhaps 20 percent of the discussion because most participants were using shorthand phrases, especially around laws and regulations, that were well known to them but not to me. Sometimes it is important to cut out the jargon, but there is a cost, usually in the amount that has to be said. In many of my research papers, I describe the statistical analysis in a paragraph or two, using language common within the field. I can also explain those methods to a general audience. Indeed, I have often

taught a one-semester course that does so and have written with Linda Kalof a 500-plus-page text to explain them (Dietz and Kalof 2009). While jargon can be hard to disentangle when you are new to a field, and thus is a barrier to broad communication, it is efficient for communicating with others with similar backgrounds. We must constantly balance efficiency and clarity for a broader audience.

70. Dietz and Rycroft (1987).

71. When the powerful can substantially control the legislature, judicial and/or the executive branches of government, they can act with less nuance and negotiate less with environmentalists and sustainability advocates. They can write the laws, eliminate regulations and defund the parts of government that enforce them. Shwom has argued that we need theories that examine the political dynamics of how power works in a particular place and time to supplement grand theories (Dietz et al. 2015; Shwom 2011).

72. It is popular to label complex problems as "wicked." I dislike the term in part because it seems to have lost precise meaning and in part because it implies someone is creating the problem. I prefer the term "moiling." I find it telling that the first use of the term "wicked problems" by Horst Rittel seemed to emerge when systems scientists (including engineers, architects and management scientists) who had achieved great success in the defense and space programs felt they could turn their tools of systems analysis to social problems such as the environment and poverty (Churchman 1967; Rittel and Webber 1973). I think the label "wicked" emerged out of a sense of frustration that the tools that worked well in space and defense analysis weren't very useful in examining the complex adaptive systems that generate environmental degradation and poverty. In the original discussion, "wicked" problems are contrasted with "tame" ones. Logically, the contrast with wicked should be benign and the contrast for tame would be wild.

73. Drummond and Fischhoff (2017).

74. McCright and Dunlap (2011a, 2011b); McCright, Marquart-Pyatt et al. (2016).

75. I will discuss public opinion on climate change in more detail in Chapter 6.

76. Rosa (1998b); Rosa, Renn and McCright (2013). I have selected a few areas of research and roughly estimated the ostensibility and repeatability of each and the degree to which powerful interests are interested in the consensus about facts. The numbers are illustrative; more extensive analysis might revise them.

77. Scientists who overgeneralize about the confidence that is warranted in context-specific assessments used in environmental and sustainability decision-making often assume an information deficit model of public decision-making. See Chapters 6 and 8.

78. Rosa (1998b).

79. Nor is industry the only powerful actor involved. I suspect our understanding of the risks of radioactive fallout from above-ground testing of nuclear weapons was slowed by resistance on the part of those branches of national governments that favored testing.

80. Dietz (2013a, 2013c).

81. Nelson and Shilling (2018); Whyte (2013); Whyte, Brewer and Johnson (2015).

82. The Advocacy Coalition Framework (ACF) makes a similar argument; see Chapter 3, Note 45.

83. Under this hypothesis, the pattern we might expect in data would be a bit complex. Where the science has low ostensibility and repeatability and matters to the powerful, the beliefs of most individuals about a risk, such as climate change, would be strongly shaped by their values and general beliefs. Where ostensibility and repeatability are higher and where the results are of less interest to the powerful, most people will move to the consensus view and there will be less variance in beliefs about risks to explain. But we would expect that those who reject the consensus would still be influenced by their values and general beliefs. Even when the science has high ostensibility and repeatability, some people may reside in subcultures whose beliefs reject that consensus – for

example, those who reject evolution, the safety and efficacy of vaccinations or the fact that the earth is not flat (Landrum, Olshansky and Richards 2019).

84. As yet we probably have little or no influence on the deep ocean thermal vent communities but eventually warming of the oceans now occurring closer to the surface will also reach the deep ocean. We are altering the chemistry of the ocean but I suspect that mixing to the depth at which these vent ecosystem occur will be slow and that water chemistry there is dominated by emissions from the vents. Over human history, predictions that an ecosystem is independent of human action have always proved wrong, and so it's possible that this one will as well. There are the deep lakes under the Antarctic ice, such as Lake Vostok, that we are trying to keep free from human influence even as we investigate them. We also know that extremophiles live in fairly deep geologic strata. But the generalization still holds – for the most part, humans now affect every ecosystem on the surface of the earth and in all but the deepest layers of the oceans.

85. This is another case where the lack of adequate funding for environmental social science research precludes us from assessing value change over time. The ideas underpinning biospheric values stretch back at least to Fromm (Fromm 1964; Gunderson 2014b), but we don't have consistent data to know how values being deployed have changed. Biospheric values are discussed in Section 3.3 and Chapter 5, Note 41.

86. Recall that Dewey ([1939] 1988) argued that we use values when our preferences are in conflict.

# 5    What Is a Good Decision?

1. My understanding is based on both published accounts ("Winky and Wanda: A Tale of Two Elephants," Detroit Zoo website, https://detroitzoo.org/about/your-detroit-zoo/) and personal communication with Linda Kalof, who served on an advisory panel to the zoo. For more information on the Detroit Zoological Society, see https://humane.detroitzoo.org/.

2. The literature on both scientific and ethical questions and their interplay is growing rapidly (Aldy et al. 2021; Corner and Pidgeon 2010; Cummings, Lin and Trump 2017; Gunderson and Dietz 2018; Gunderson, Stuart and Petersen 2018; Keith 2021; National Academies of Sciences, Engineering, and Medicine 2021; Parson 2021; Pidgeon et al. 2013; Raimi et al. 2019).

3. The animal studies literature is quite sophisticated in this regard – most scholars I read seem to be aware of the complexity of the ethical issues involved in human–nonhuman interactions (Beauchamp and Frey 2011; Kalof 2017). Many ethicists, including several colleagues from whom I have learned a great deal, have written wisely and extensively on ethical theories applied to the environment and sustainability (Thompson 2010, 2017; Whyte, Brewer and Johnson 2015; Whyte and Cuomo 2016). My concern is that most environmental and sustainability scientists, whether from the biological, engineering, health, physical or social sciences, seem unaware of the ethical complexities that should be addressed in discussing policy decisions. I often hear strong advocacy for courses of action without much discussion of the ethical justification for that choice and little engagement with the ethics literature.

4. An earlier version of this discussion focused on environmental decision-making appeared in Dietz (2003). The use of the term "pillars" reflects Lawrence's *Seven Pillars of Wisdom*, a book I recognize as anachronistic at best but that fascinated me as an early teen (Lawrence [1926] 1962). As I came to know people from Palestine and other parts of the region where Lawrence worked, their insights helped me reflect on Lawrence's imperialist and "orientalist" assumptions, as did biographies reflected on his gender identity in its historical context. Thomas Merton has also been a major influence on my thinking and one of the best biographies is *The Seven Mountains of Thomas Merton*,

building on Merton's autobiographical *The Seven Story Mountain*, reinforcing the trope of seven (Merton 1948; Mott 1984).

5. Ethicists often make the distinction between consequentialist theories and deontological theories. A consequentialist ethics looks to the outcomes of our decisions to judge them; a deontological ethics looks at criteria for the decisions themselves. So, my first three criteria could be viewed consequentialist and the last four deontological.

6. Keynes ([1917] 1999): 18).

7. The use of the term "normative" in both ethics and psychology can be confusing. In ethics, a normative theory or statement is a statement about what we ought to do. In psychology, norms are statements about what we or others think we should do or what we think others are doing. Statements about what we think others think we should do are prescriptive norms while our views about what we think we should do are personal norms. So, the two uses are related but in psychology we are often making descriptive (positive in Keynes' terms) statements rather than the prescriptive ones of ethics.

8. Hume ([1738] 1978); Moore ([1903] 1993) . Scott Frey introduced me to Moore's analysis some years ago. Scott was one of a handful of early environmental sociologists who thought deeply about ethical theories and his work will be noted elsewhere in the chapter (Freeman and Frey 1986, 1990–91; Frey and Said 1988).

9. Like all other evaluations of fact, our beliefs about the past are filtered through our values. Those who advocate the US Constitution as the fundamental guide to good policy don't seem to pay much attention to disenfranchisement of much of the population in its rules or that compromises about slavery were fundamental to the framing of it. See Chapter 1.

10. For example, a proposal to restore a vast area of the Great Plains of the United States to a "buffalo commons" – essentially the ecosystem that existed there before European domination – has been debated for decades (Popper and Popper 1987). Early on, the proposal met with great opposition and skepticism (Umberger 2002), but gradually the idea has become more respectable as a way of adapting to the Plains ecosystem (Kansas City Star 2010; Ochsner 2009). Some have gone further back in time to suggest that megafauna from around the world should be introduced to North America to restore something resembling the Pleistocene (Donlan et al. 2006; Martin 2007). It is not clear how this might be done and what the implications would be (Svenning et al. 2016). The issue of rewilding is a complex one ecologically, socially and ethically (Ginsburg 2019). Perhaps these discussions should be led by people from the cultures who inhabited these ecosystems for many generations and coevolved with them, especially given the history of displacing Indigenous people to create "protected areas" raised in Chapter 2 and the beginning of Chapter 7. How we might engage with nonhuman species is also worthy of serious analysis in this context; Celermajer calls for a multispecies justice (Celermajer 2020; see also Box 5.6).

11. Laissez-faire, the view that government should not intervene in the market and that reforms are futile or even harmful, is prominent in policy debates. The arguments for nonintervention often rely on some sense of a natural order to decisions guided by market forces. This debate was prominent in the late nineteenth century, when it was linked to social "Darwinism" (a profound misunderstanding of Darwin's thinking). American sociology was founded in part around the debate about markets and the state. William Graham Sumner, who is usually credited with teaching the first sociology course in the United States, titled an essay "The Absurd Effort to Make the World Over" to express his contempt for the efforts to improve the lot of workers and regulate industrial capitalism:

Nine-tenths of the socialistic and semi-socialistic, and sentimental or ethical, suggestions by which we are overwhelmed come from failure to understand the phenomena of the industrial organization and its expansion. It controls us all because we are all in it. It creates the conditions of our existence, sets the limits of our social activity, regulates the bonds of our social relations, determines our conceptions of good and evil, suggests our life-philosophy, molds our inherited political institutions, and reforms the oldest and toughest customs, like marriage and property. (Sumner 1883b: 197; see also Sumner 1883a)

His argument, in essence, is that it is foolish to interfere in the "natural law" of "survival of the fittest" in the market. In contrast, Lester Ward, a cofounder of the *American Journal of Sociology* who is usually credited with writing the first US sociology textbook, *Dynamic Sociology*, was an opponent of laissez-faire. His essay "Mind As a Social Factor" (Ward 1884) presages contemporary interest in cultural evolution as a force that often overwhelms selection acting on genes. It also anticipated the focus on altruism as a key factor in human societies:

The truth thus comes forth from a rational study of nature and human society that social progress has been due only in very slight degree to natural evolution as accomplished through the survival of the fittest, and its chief success has resulted from the reduction of competition in the struggle for existence and the protection of the weaker members. (Ward 1884: 572)

So, arguments about the relative importance of cultural evolution and genetic evolution and of altruism versus self-interest, which are central to contemporary theories of sustainability decision-making, were central to the emergence of American sociology (Dietz 2015b).

12. Drawing on John Neville Keynes, Friedman said of economics:

Normative economics and the art of economics, on the other hand, cannot be independent of positive economics. Any policy conclusion necessarily rests on a prediction about the consequences of doing one thing rather than another, a prediction that must be based – implicitly or explicitly – on positive economics. The relationship between policy conclusions and the conclusions of positive economics is not perfect; if there were, there would be no separate normative analysis. Two individuals may agree on the consequences of a particular piece of legislation. One may regard them as desirable on balance and so favor the legislation; the other, as undesirable and so oppose the legislation. (Friedman 1953: 4)

Roscoe (2015) provides a useful discussion of the links between positive and normative theory in economics, the assumptions underlying economic models for policy and the problems that arise from nonreflective use of simple models.

13. My colleague Paul Thompson's exceptionally clear writing about ethical theories as they apply to food and agriculture is a great starting point if you wish to delve further (Thompson 2015, 2017).

14. Beauchamp (2011); Korsgaard (2011); Johnson and Cureton (2022); Rawls (2001). See also Chapter 3, Note 82.

15. Aristotle [350 BCE] 2014. On including nature and the environment, see Jordan and Kristjánsson (2017); Van Wensveen (2001). On other species, see Hursthouse (2011).

16. Thompson (2015). Aristotle emphasizes that practicing virtues can lead to happiness, thus laying a precursor to both utilitarianism and the measurement of subjective well-being; see Chapter 2.

17. The core approach is described in Nussbaum (2000, 2006); Nussbaum and Sen (1993); Sen (1999). Extensions are described in Bockstael and Watene (2016); Nussbaum (2006, 2018); Van Jaarsveld (2020). A journal is devoted to the approach: *The Journal of Human Development and Capabilities* published by the Human Development & Capabilities Association (hd-ca.org/).

18. Dietz (1994). As I write, it appears that a fourth approach, a strong man (*sic*) nationalism is also on the rise, with many democracies seeing successful candidates for national office who propose a mix of nationalist and nativist policies, and moves towards greater democracy are stalled in other countries in favor of centralized leadership; see Figure 2.2. In the traditional democracies, these leaders usually deploy some rhetoric and policy proposals that appeal to a libertarian/anarchist logic even though many of their positions, such as strong security and state surveillance, contradict the libertarian/anarchist view. There seems to be little explicit ethical theory behind these views, and in

any event, as Renton has pointed out, the actions of strong state regimes often have relatively little to do with the theory that attempts to justify them (Renton 1999). On the strategies and logic of emerging authoritarianism, see also Guriev and Treisman (2022); Naím (2022). Ben-Ghiat is particularly useful in examining the gendered logic of authoritarianism (Ben-Ghiat 2020).

19. There are also interesting hybrids. A series of essays in *The Economist* traces the foundations of classical liberalism (related to but not the same as the liberal stance associated with the Democratic Party in the United States; see Chapter 2, Note 40) to a diverse set of thinkers, including Mill, de Tocqueville, Keynes, Schumpeter, Popper, Hayek, Berlin, Rawls and Nozick (*The Economist*, August 4 to September 8, 2018). Note that these are all white men. More diverse perspectives are needed.

20. Values are strongly correlated with contemporary political ideologies (Caprara et al. 2006; Caprara et al. 2017; Roccas, Schwartz and Amit 2010; Schwartz et al. 2014; Vecchione et al. 2014). I focus on the underpinning ideas that might be guides in decision-making and not on contemporary political dynamics. In politics, ideas about what is ethically correct and desirable can be motivating. But they are also deployed tactically as means to garner support for positions held for other reasons, and especially to acquire power. Perhaps we should take advocates of these positions seriously. Those who hold that all individuals are narrowly self-interested may be wholly self-interested and their motivation in advocating policies is to advance their own interest, while those who argue that altruism is not rare are perhaps rather altruistic.

21. Broadman et al. (2000); Hanley and Spash (1993); Jaeger et al. (2001).

22. The foundational works are Bentham (1776); Mill (1879). The quote is from Bentham (1776: preface, para 2), available online at http://socserv.mcmaster.ca/~econ/ugcm/3ll3/bentham/govern ment.html (accessed May 13, 2016). It is worth noting that in that same year Bentham published a strong critique of the American Declaration of Independence, which appeared as a chapter in John Lind's book on the Declaration (Lind 1776). The full set of ideas of brilliant and prolific writers is seldom accurately captured in a terse summary. It is ironic that many who hold the Declaration of Independence to be an almost sacred document also adhere to an ethical theory developed by a critic of the Declaration. Some scholars have argued that if the then thirteen colonies had not gained independence, slavery would have ended sooner and the state that would have evolved instead of the United States and Canada might be more progressive than the United States is now (Gopnik 2017).

23. Frey (2011); Singer (1995).

24. See, however, US National Research Council (2008). Benefit-cost analysis, risk analysis and other forms of technical policy analysis can be inputs to a deliberative process; see Box 5.4 (Dietz 1994). The literature on deliberation emphasizes the importance of linking scientific analysis with public deliberation, a process called analytic deliberation that will be discussed in Chapter 9. There have been some efforts to use deliberative processes to assess monetary values as inputs into benefit-cost analyses; see Chapter 5, Note 53.

25. Libertarianism grew out of the work of the economists Hayek and von Mises (Hayek [1944] 2014, 1948; von Mises [1949] 1998). A Nietzschean frame sometimes aligns with libertarianism in emphasizing not the freedom of all but the freedom of "special people," the *Übermensch* of *The Gay Science* (Nietzsche [1887] 2001) and *Thus Spoke Zarathustra* (Nietzsche [1883–91] 1961). This is most evident in the views of Ayn Rand, the popularizer of libertarianism. Rand's life and influence are critically assessed by Duggan (Duggan 2019). I am sympathetic with a point made by Sunstein in his review of Duggan's book – any serious assessment of libertarianism as a philosophy requires reading Hayek, von Mises, Friedman and scholars rather than Rand (Sunstein 2020), but I would add that her views are central to understanding libertarianism in politics. Her work inspires a populist libertarianism that remains influential among many American conservatives, including the comic book creators

Steve Ditko (cocreator of Spider-Man, Dr. Strange and the Question) and Frank Miller (writer of *Sin City*, *300*, *Dark Knight*), the economist Alan Greenspan (the former Chairman of the Federal Reserve), John Mackey (the founder of Whole Foods) and the politicians Rand Paul, his father Ron Paul and Paul Ryan. The history of the twentieth century makes clear the danger of political theory that asserts the actions of an elite carry special ethical justification, whether one looks at fascism or Leninism/Stalinism. Some very conservative theorists have been critical of von Mises and Rand. See, for example, Friedman's critique of intolerance in their work and his admonition that von Mises felt government was essential for liberty, contrary to much libertarian thinking (Friedman 1991). Lest we romanticize Friedman, remember that perhaps the first application of his libertarian idea of school vouchers blocked access of Black children to public education in the South after the *Brown* v. *Board of Education* desegregation decision. Although there is ongoing debate about where Friedman stood on segregation, it seems clear that school choice, justified by libertarian theoretical arguments, has often been deployed for segregation and can perpetuate and exacerbate inequality (Currie-Knight 2019; Friedman 1955; Hale 2021; MacLean 2017; McKluskey 2019; Minow 2010; Ravitch 2016; Suitts 2019).

26. Marshall (2008); Woodcock (2004).
27. A good friend was arrested during an anti–Vietnam War protest for carrying a black flag, the anarchist symbol. The case was dropped since the very old law against displaying a black flag would almost certainly be seen as an unconstitutional restraint of free speech. Such laws were enacted in substantial degree in response to efforts by anarchists, including the Industrial Workers of the World (IWW, the Wobblies) to organize unions. Black flags are also associated with pirates and with some jihadists.
28. Anarchism is a negative trope in literature as diverse as Conrad's *The Secret Agent* (Conrad [1907] 1963) and perhaps Yeats' "The Second Coming" (Yeats [1921] 1997). "The Second Coming" is not about the anarchist movement, but its images and oft-quoted lines are often invoked as if it were. Among contemporary writers, anarchism/libertarianism is viewed favorably in works by Robert Heinlein (*The Moon Is a Harsh Mistress*), Ursula Le Guin (*The Dispossessed*) and Alan Moore (*V for Vendetta*; *Watchmen*).
29. Key thinkers include Godwin, Kropotkin, Goodman and Bookchin; Bakunin is an exception in advocating violence. Franks and colleagues provide a contemporary overview (Franks, Jun and Williams 2018).
30. Skocpol and Williamson (2012). For example, the platform of the Libertarian Party included the following statement:

### 2.6  Monopolies and Corporations
We defend the right of individuals to form corporations, cooperatives and other types of companies based on voluntary association. We seek to divest government of all functions that can be provided by non-governmental organizations or private individuals. We oppose government subsidies to business, labor, or any other special interest. Industries should be governed by free markets. (www.lp.org/platform, accessed July 12, 2011)

Since it is labeled with the term "monopoly," I would interpret the statement as indicating that the Libertarian Party is not worried about monopoly power as long as it is not shaped by government. As the discussion in Chapter 5, Note 11 indicates, the debate about whether or not it is appropriate to intervene in the workings of the market is not new. The late nineteenth century was the period when near monopolies ("combines") began to dominate the US economy and this concentration of power was a central focus of the Progressive movement. The argument that monopolies could prevent free markets from improving human well-being was raised by Adam Smith (Salvadori and Signorino 2014).

31. The founders of utilitarianism, Bentham and Mill, can be interpreted as favoring socialism (Hansson 2013; McCabe 2015) while some libertarians draw on utilitarian arguments to support their position (Friedman and Friedman 1980).

32. Edwards (2015: 4, 14) Friedman argues that owners of sole proprietorships are free to do what they want, since the company is their private property. He also holds that only individuals have values – corporations and governments do not. It would seem to follow from this that he would argue that corporations should not be involved in politics, since they are not "persons" who can hold values and thus ethical stances. But, under US law, corporations are usually treated as persons; see the Introduction and Chapter 7, Note 6 on the implications of this. The line of reasoning from Friedman and other conservative theorists could be seen as a form of sustainability theory where only markets have the necessary information to allow solid choices about how to allocate resources and how to adequately take into account obligations for the future. The ethical obligations of the private sector is a major theme in Chapter 7.

33. See Box 5.5; Downs and Larkey (1986).

34. Anderson and Leal (1991).

35. The literature on environmental conflict resolution has offered criteria for resolving such conflicts (Crowfoot and Wondolleck 1990; Lewicki, Gray and Elliot 2003). Shutkin (2000) and Clark and Dickson (2001) have some suggestions about components of good environmental policy. Webler (1995) provides detailed criteria for deliberative practice as does the US National Research Council report on public participation (US National Research Council 2008; see Chapter 9). But there has been little extended discussion of what constitutes a good decision.

36. I use the term "well-being" rather than "welfare" as the latter term suggests a utilitarian view of how to make ethical judgments. "Health" is an alternative but "human health" has a narrower connotation than I want to imply. "Security" is used in some discussions but too easily invokes the idea of national security in the sense of military and diplomatic strength. Here, as elsewhere, I am following the precedent of the Millennium Ecosystem Assessment (Alcalmo et al. 2003; Reid et al. 2005).

37. Caldicott (1992); Kalof (2017: section V); Regan (2004).

38. US National Research Council (2013). This happens primarily in areas where cougars, a predator of horses and burros, are no longer present. Predators are usually key parts of ecosystems, and when they are removed, things change.

39. See Chapter 3 on the social psychology of environmental concern for the distinctions between concern with humans and with the rest of the biosphere. In some discussions, the term "anthropocentrism" refers not to ethics but to the attribution of human characteristics to other species (Calarco 2015; De Waal 1999). From both an evolutionary perspective and the stance of many Indigenous cultures, the distinction between humans and others is not a categorical one and allows for more subtle thinking about humans and others.

40. The pure anthropocentric position should be differentiated from a weaker, "methodological" anthropocentrism that acknowledges the intrinsic value of environmental well-being but notes that all efforts to assign value or importance to the environment depend on humans assigning that value or importance. One can be a nomothetic ecocentrist but an anthropocentric methodologist.

41. A long line of argument supports this view. John Muir and Aldo Leopold have been highly influential. Erich Fromm, a member of the Frankfurt school of critical theory and a sometime lecturer at Michigan State University, invoked the idea of biophilia twenty years before E. O. Wilson who is often credited with the concept (Fromm 1964; Gunderson 2014b, 2014c; Wilson 1984). Growing evidence suggests that carrying out pro-environmental behaviors enhances personal

well-being, providing an anthropocentric justification for actions that otherwise do not impact human well-being (Schmitt et al. 2018, Venhoeven, Bolderdijk and Steg 2013, 2016; Venhoeven, Steg and Bolderdijk 2017).

42. Grignon and Kimmerer (2017); Norgaard and Reed (2017); Sinclair (2020).

43. To some degree the problem of trade-offs is simplified for libertarians who hold that the only criterion on which to assess a decision is the impact it has on freedom of choice. But, even from that standpoint, complexities arise. For example, imposing a price on greenhouse gas emissions is generally seen as inappropriate by libertarians. Their view, going back to Coase, is that the price should be set by market forces without government interference (Black et al. 2014; Coase 1937, 1960, 1988; Dawson 2011). But substantial climate change will alter ecosystems in ways that will restrict the choices of others, including those who have made minimal contributions to atmospheric greenhouse gas concentrations. Freedom of choice for contemporary fossil fuel users may substantially constrain choices for those who live in low-lying coastal areas now and in the future. Decision-making is never easy, whatever criteria you think are appropriate.

44. Habermas considers a political process technocratic if the kind of analysis I am describing dominates, with politics largely used to legitimate the outcome of the formal analysis (Habermas 1970). The term seems to apply to the arguments of Starr and others discussed in Chapter 3. Although largely forgotten, there was an effort to promote technocracy as a way of implementing democratic governance, starting at least with Veblen (1933 [1954]). The early arguments for technocracy emphasized energy as a fundamental unit of analysis in making decisions, an approach that would reemerge with the work of H. T. Odum, among others (Berndt 1982; Odum 1996). Foster and Holleman offer an interesting interpretation of Odum's ideas in the context of international power dynamics of unequal exchange (Foster and Holleman 2014).

45. That is not to say that this is not happening. I'm sure there are many efforts already deployed for just this kind of technocratic decision-making within private sector and political contexts.

46. Awad et al. (2018); Awad et al. (2020); Bonnefon, Shariff and Rahwan (2016); Fleetwood (2017) (one can view the scenarios and participate in surveys at the Moral Machine platform, www.moralmachine.net/, accessed January 29, 2022).

47. Slobogin (2021); Villasenor and Foggo (2020). The science fiction writer Philip K. Dick anticipated these issues in his short story "The Minority Report" in which people are eliminated based on a prediction that they will commit a crime in the future (Dick [1956] 2002), which is a bit like the idea of a "thought crime" that George Orwell introduced in *1984* (Orwell [1949] 1977).

48. On democracy, see Feldstein (2019). On sustainability, see Herweijer (2018); Taddeo and Floridi (2018). On resource allocation, see *The Economist* (2019). Examples of the growing literature include Boddington (2017); Cath (2018); Wischmeyer and Rademacher (2020). Signé and Dooley describe the special opportunities and challenges that come with the emergence of the metaverse (Signé and Dooley 2022).

49. The tendency for antagonism between economic and environmental thinking is a central theme in most discussions of environmental decision-making. Perhaps, as discussed in Chapter 2, one reason the idea of sustainability became popular is that discussions of sustainability and sustainable development try to reconcile environmental, economic and social goals.

50. When this contradiction is recognized and articulated, fruitful work can follow. Much of the careful thinking about sustainability in economics emerged as economists responded to the "Limits to Growth" and related studies reviewed in Chapter 2 (Meadows et al. 1972; Pezzey and Toman 2002; Worster 2016). While this literature was often sharply critical of studies arguing for limits to growth, my sense is that they were provoked by it. In the conversation that is science, productive work can flow even from analyses that are, in the end, seen as flawed, as noted in the Introduction. There are arguments about whether or not the predictions of the Limits to Growth studies are reasonably

matched by historical trends since the 1972 "Limits to Growth" study was released (Castro 2012; Herrington 2021; Johnson 2014; Turner 2012, 2013).

51. See the World Bank database "Poverty 2000–2021" at https://data.worldbank.org/topic/poverty (accessed January 30, 2022). This is the usual $2 per day figure adjusted for price differences across countries. On the effects of the pandemic, see Sidik (2022a).

52. The rational actor model of Chapter 3 assumes that this is how we do in fact make decisions. As the first part of this chapter argued, we can differentiate that descriptive theory from the normative argument that this is how we should make decisions. But in application, some of the justification for using prices as measures of social value comes from assumptions that those in the market are following the rational actor model to maximize their utility. So, while we can logically distinguish the rational actor model from utilitarianism as a normative theory, the two are intertwined in most utilitarian policy analyses.

53. While I have framed the discussion in terms of risk-benefit-cost analysis, much the same framing is used in risk analysis, where alternative choices are assessed based on their potential impact on human, or sometimes ecosystem, health; see the discussion in Chapter 3 and Dietz, Frey and Rosa (2002). The two are intimately related as both are motivated by the rational actor paradigm that underpins economics and much of the rest of the social sciences (Jaeger et al. 2001). As with the use of benefit-cost analysis, when risk analysis is deployed debate tends to focus on the risk numbers and the assumptions, data and analysis that led to them. Considerations that are not quantified have little influence. In addition, both benefit-cost analysis and risk analysis encourage framing a decision as a technical one in which the discourse is primarily scientific and public views and value issues not captured in the quantification are left aside. Chapter 3 suggested this can advantage some groups – those with the resources to deploy substantial analytical strength – and disadvantage others – those who lack expensive analytical resources but who may be advocating widely held public concerns. O'Brien (2000) highlights this problem. As Silbergeld (2001: 68) eloquently put it: "We cannot escape the burden of trying to incorporate what we know into what we feel, to find a common path to deciding what is harmful, what is good, and, finally, how we can accept the necessary compromises among all our goals." Fischhoff (2015) makes the point that risk analysis and benefit-cost analysis, and the integration of the two in risk-benefit-cost analysis can and should be embedded in a process that links scientific analysis with public deliberation. Science informs the deliberation but the deliberation raises questions about the science and especially about the values and assumptions that underpin the risk-benefit-cost analysis. The process allows both public perceptions and science to evolve. See Chapter 9.

54. Bottrill et al. (2008); Cornwall (2018); Gerber (2016); Jenkins et al. 2015; Moilanen, Wilson and Possingham (2009); Wilson et al. (2006).

55. The "Happy Planet Index," a ratio of human well-being to environmental stress, uses this logic (Friends of the Earth and New Economics Foundation 2006; New Economics Foundation 2009; Happy Planet Index, happyplanetindex.org/).

56. Richard York, Gene Rosa and I proposed a "production function" in which use of the environment is one input into the production of well-being (Dietz, Rosa and York 2009; Dietz 2015a). We then suggested examining the ratio of well-being to environmental stress, the approach of the Happy Planet Index. Jorgenson and other scholars have produced a rich and nuanced literature extending that approach (Dietz, Rosa and York 2009, 2012; Jorgenson 2014, 2015a; Jorgenson and Dietz 2015; Jorgenson, Dietz and Kelly 2018; Jorgenson et al. 2019; Kelly, Thombs and Jorgenson 2021; Knight and Rosa 2011).

57. The literature on benefit-cost analysis is vast, for example Adler and Posner (2006); Arrow et al. (1996), Atkinson and Mourato (2008); Fischhoff (2015); Graves (2007); Hanley and Spash (1993); Prest and Turvey (1965); Shaffer (2010); White and VanLandingham (2015). A professional society

devoted to it was founded in 2007 followed in 2009 by a journal devoted to research on benefit-cost analysis; see the Society for Benefit-Cost Analysis website, benefitcostanalysis.org (accessed November 7, 2021).

58. Shaffer (2010). Technically, benefit-cost analysis is looking for Pareto optimality, a situation in which there is no change in policy that would leave someone better off without making someone else worse off. The idea of Pareto optimality motivates the suggestion that some conflicts between those who gain and those who lose from a decision could be balanced by a "side payment" from the winners to the losers, something discussed in Chapters 5 and 6. Side payments are discussed in theory more often than they are implemented. However, "Payment for Ecosystem Services" where the affluent pay the less affluent to not disrupt ecosystem services can be seen as an implementation of this logic (Costanza 2020).

59. Hanley and Spash (1993); Prest and Turvey (1965).

60. A particularly contentious part of assessing economic values is assigning a monetary value to the loss of a human life or the prevention of such loss (Friedman 2020; Murphy 2017). Such valuations also are made in court cases where damages have to be decided. If the valuation is based on things such as earnings, then social inequalities shape the analysis. The same kind of problems arises when loss of nonhuman life is a possible outcome. The argument in favor of such valuations in policy analysis is that the resources used to prevent a death could be used for other purposes. Suppose a strict inspection routine might reduce toxic chemical releases and thus prevent some cancers. But if the cost of such inspections is in the hundreds of millions of dollars per life saved, might society be better off using those resources for other worthy actions? As we have seen throughout the discussion, dealing with trade-offs is rarely simple and the right choice is not obvious.

61. See Chapter 3 and Box 5.4 for further discussion of the issues involved in discounting.

62. See, for example, Adler (2016); McDermott, Mahanty and Schreckenberg (2013); Pascual et al. (2014); Robinson, Hammitt and Zeckhauser (2016). The issue of equity arises in all policies based on prices and payments, including payments made for efforts to preserve ecosystem services that are not priced in the market (McDermott, Mahanty and Schreckenberg 2013, Pascual et al. 2014). From the 1970s, benefit-cost analysis guidance for US federal agencies called for differentiating between national-level benefits and costs and those that accrue at the regional level as a way of bringing in equity across regions (Mann 1972). A project that might make sense in terms of regional flows of costs and benefits might not make sense at the national level and vice versa. Hird (1991) shows equity and efficiency considerations do influence project decision-making even in the face of pork barrel politics. And the way utility is aggregated across individuals and groups matters. Typically, using the utilitarian logic of the greatest good to the greatest number, the sum or, equivalently, the average is used. But that may lead to different decisions than would result if one took, for example, the median or took special account of the most disadvantaged (Dietz, Bell and Leshko 2014). In nearly all economic policy analysis, the sum of utilities, which is the average multiplied by the population size, is used as the criterion.

63. Reid et al. (2005).

64. In *De Cive*, Hobbes writes: "the state of men without civil society (which we may properly call the state of nature) is nothing else but a mere warre of all against all" (Hobbes 1651: 34). Parallel phrases are used in *Leviathan*. It is interesting that Hobbes invokes population size and the pressure on resources as part of his rationale for the "warre of all against all" ("bellum omnium contra omnes"). See Chapter 8 on the lack of empirical work on population and democracy. Population growth is also at the center of Hardin's famous but deeply flawed "Tragedy of the Commons" essay; see Chapter 3.

65. Fukuyama (2011, 2014); Graeber and Wengrow (2021).

66. Coase (1960); Medema (2017). See Chapter 1, Notes 8 and 28 and Chapter 6, Note 16.

67. Dietz and Whitley (2018).

68. A major point of debate will be determining when some collective action is necessary and when individual free choices, uncoordinated with the choices of others, will be sufficient. For some, only individual free choice is acceptable. Many theorists associated with libertarian views acknowledge the need for some rules to structure society and our interactions. So, the issue is not one of absolutes but of where to draw the line and can be argued around specific issues rather than in the abstract. As Box 5.5 points out, we often rely on preconceptions about the actions of government, a problem of heuristics, biases and prior beliefs shaping how we handle new information. While we know a good bit about how to evaluate programs, we don't apply those tools comparatively to find out what works and what doesn't (see Criterion 7 in Section 5.8).

69. Red tape refers to the ribbons that were used to hold together documents being handled in the bureaucracy. I once saw such "tape" holding together papers on the desk of the Minister of Health of Trinidad and Tobago.

70. Downs and Larkey (1986).

71. Alvaredo et al. (2018); Jorda and Alonso (2020).

72. See Chapter 9; see also Maldonado, Lazrus et al. (2016); Reo et al. (2017); Whyte (2012a); Whyte et al. (2017).

73. Dietz, Frey and Rosa (2002). Taking explicit account of risk in financial decision-making is much older and is intimately linked to the rational actor model (Jaeger et al. 2001). Bernstein (1998) has argued that the ability to adequately handle risk was a major driver of economic growth. Analyses in engineering and the physical sciences have long included hedges against uncertainty in such design standards as "the 100-year flood" – design to withstand the largest flood seen in the last 100 years – and by adding "margins of safety." But it was not until the 1980s that risk analysis became a common tool in environmental and technological decision-making; see Chapter 2. Most discussions of sustainability don't connect with the risk literature except around the debates about discounting the future. This may be changing through discussions of adaptive risk management in the face of climate change; see Lockie and Wong (2017); US National Research Council (2011).

74. Sophisticated methods of incorporating uncertainty into financial analysis became an important field of both research and practice in the late twentieth century. Myron Scholes and Robert C. Merton (the son of the sociologist Robert K. Merton) won the Nobel Prize in Economics in 1997 for work in this area (Royal Swedish Academy of Sciences 1997). Models of uncertainty drive a great deal of stock market trading, especially via hedge funds that have come to have substantial impacts on financial markets and, ultimately, may influence ecosystems (Galaz et al. 2015; Lo, Getmansky and Lee 2015).

75. Arrow (1951). A huge literature flows from Arrow's analysis. Sen's (2002) thinking on social choice is another key contribution to understanding the move from the individual to the collectivity. He and others have begun the task of linking the social choice tradition with ideas of deliberative rationality that flow from Habermas (Dryzek and List 2003; Habermas 1979; List 2018; List et al. 2012; Van Aaken and List 2017). A number of jurisdictions, including Maine and Alaska and several US cities, have adopted preferential or "instant runoff" voting, as have nineteen countries, including Denmark, Italy, the Netherlands, Poland and Sweden. In this system, rather than picking one from candidates A, B or C, voters rank them. Then, if no majority emerges from first choices, the lowest ranking candidate is dropped and the second choices of voters who gave that candidate top ranking votes are counted as votes for that candidate. The process continues until one candidate has a majority. While many favor this approach as it allows votes for third parties without "throwing away" a vote in a tightly contested election with two major candidates, some libertarians oppose it (von Spakovsky and Adams 2019).

76. In part, this may be because standard versions of the rational actor model of decision-making in economics and other disciplines, as described in Chapter 3, take preferences as "given" in the sense that they assume people have clear preferences. This has left the study of preference formation and even the nature of preferences to other disciplines, yet relatively little communication takes place between economics and the other social sciences. It is often the case that the ability of our disciplines to form walls around themselves and ignore issues that fall between those walls, focusing instead on what is currently in vogue within a discipline, leads to large and important gaps in our knowledge. Campbell discussed this in his "fishscale" model of knowledge – the most interesting ideas emerge where fields overlap (Campbell 1969). But those are exactly the questions most likely to be ignored. The push to focus on the "core" of a field often yields woeful ignorance about relevant theory, methods and results in related fields. In some cases, this can lead to great hubris, such as Becker's efforts to reduce the social sciences to economics and sociobiology discussed in Chapter 3. It can also lead to addressing stereotypes of disciplines rather than the current core of thinking in the field. Too often I hear sociologists critiquing the economics I was taught in graduate school rather than engaging contemporary thinking in economics.

77. Dietz and Stern (1995); Stern et al. (1995).

78. As noted in Chapter 1, Whyte has eloquently argued that climate change and apocalyptic environmental change are part of the history and lived experience of many Indigenous peoples, usually as a result of actions of settler colonists and imperialist states (Whyte 2017a, 2018). This is a very different perspective from that of most members of the public.

79. A long-standing criticism of survey research argues that the values, beliefs, norms and other measures in surveys are constructed by individuals in response to the question (e.g., Blumer 1948). But the process of social construction in response to being asked a survey question models the process by which values, beliefs, norms, attitudes and so on are evoked in everyday life and thus is a fair assessment of how they may influence decision-making.

80. I am thinking of conversation to achieve value competence in terms of Habermas' sense of communicative rationality (Habermas 1984), although his ideas need elaboration via a more informed social psychology and by taking account of various critiques. For example, Kompridis' ideas about critical visioning (Kompridis 2006) and about technology(Kompridis 2009) may be important in thinking about how communicative rationality applies to sustainability, which is very much about visions of the future.

81. See Chapter 3; see also Lord, Ross and Lepper (1979); Munro and Ditto (1997); Munro et al. (2002).

82. The anti-reflexivity thesis counters the ecological modernization and environmental Kuznets arguments arguing from the long history of active efforts to resist acknowledging technological risks in the interest of protecting corporate profits (see Chapter 2, Notes 62 and 110 and Chapter 4, Note 65). Anti-reflexivity scholarship has examined both large-scale political dynamics and public opinion (Givens et al. 2020; McCright 2016; McCright and Dunlap 2010; McCright, Marquart-Pyatt et al. 2016).

83. The Dewey/Habermas tradition and Habermas' arguments in particular are often compared to those of Rawls. The standard distinction is to suggest that Rawls offers a theory of what we ought to accept as a just state of affairs. I can crudely summarize his view as arguing that we should make decisions as if you don't know where you will be in society and thus how the decision will affect you, that is, decisions are made behind a "veil of ignorance" (Rawls 1971). Habermas, in contrast, emphasizes a process of decision-making and the criteria for the process rather than the criteria for the decision. But with two such prolific writers and deep thinkers this is an oversimplification. In particular, later Rawls (1993) is more focused on process. Hedrick's (2010) comparison of Rawls and Habermas is very useful. I find Habermas' arguments more compelling in thinking about decision-making for sustainability.

84. Ani (2013, 2014, 2018); Graeber and Wengrow (2021); Hébert (2018).

85. Arnstein (1969). The controversy over the meaning and implementation of the phrase "maximum feasible participation" in the US Economic Opportunity Act 1964 is indicative of the conflicts that can arise in bureaucratic implementation of a participatory ideal (Moynihan 1969; Rubin 1969).

86. US National Research Council (2008: 226). See also the Introduction and Chapter 9. However, the literature remains highly fragmented, with new contributions seemingly unaware of much previous work and many scholars working in small communities not connected with other communities; see the Introduction, Notes 62 and 63. As I have argued in several places, I believe this homophily slows our intellectual process – it is as problematic in scholarship as it is in policy processes.

87. Ryan Gunderson and I take up this problem in examining how deliberation might be used to address catastrophic risks (Gunderson 2016; Gunderson and Dietz 2018). Smith (2018) provides a useful overview of large-scale processes.

88. US National Research Council (2007); National Academies of Sciences, Engineering, and Medicine (2017a); InterAcademy Council (2010).

89. That is, article IV, section 2.

90. Kershaw (2008). While many states have persecuted some groups defined as "others," the particular horror of the Holocaust is the large scale of the genocide committed with the intent of eliminating all Jews and other targeted groups.

91. Malin and Ryder's (2018) introduction to a special issue of *Environmental Sociology* on environmental justice is a good entry point to the literature as are the books by Mascarenhas (2020) and Pellow (2017). Early and ongoing scholarship documents injustices by race/ethnicity, class and gender (Brulle and Pellow 2006; Bullard 1983; Bullard and Johnson 2000; Burch 1971; Downey 2015; Mascarenhas 2016, 2020; Mohai, Pellow and Roberts 2009; Pellow 2002, 2007, Pellow 2016; Taylor 2000). More recent work demonstrates inequities across lines of Indigenous identity (Maldonado, Colombi and Pandya 2016; Mascarenhas 2016; Norgaard 2019a; Whyte 2012a, 2017b), sexuality and queerness (Butler 2017; Mortimer-Sandilands and Erickson 2010; Seymour 2013) and disability (Gaskin et al. 2017; Ray and Sibara 2019) and especially their intersections. Climate justice cuts across all these lines of discrimination and points to global inequities (Dietz, Shwom and Whitley 2020; Leach et al. 2018; Lockie 2016a; Roberts and Parks 2006). Scott Frey demonstrated that such international inequities also occur in exposure to toxics (Frey 1994, 1995, 1997a, 1997b, 1998a, 1998b, 2003, 2006).

92. Bullard (1983); Burch (1976); Taylor (2000).

93. Stone (1972, 1985).

94. Herald (2014); Lubinski (2002); *The Nonhuman Rights Project, Inc. on behalf of Tommy, Petitioners, v. Patrick C. Lavery, individually and as an officer of Circle L Trailer Sales, Inc., Diane Lavery, and Circle L Trailer Sales, Inc., Respondents* (Supreme Court Appellate Division Third Department New York 2014).

95. Favre (2018); Hadley (2015). On advocates, see Rojas (2017). On the need to take account of diversity in policy, see Edelblutte (2022); Edelblutte, Krithivasan and Hayek (2022). On "Speaking for Wolf," see Underwood and Howell (1983). Vrla offers the most comprehensive review of including animal voices, especially in his chapter 3 (Vrla 2019).

96. Henrich (2015); Leacock and Lee (1982, especially pt. I).

97. To argue that current discourse is problematic is not to romanticize the past. One need only review Branch's history of the civil rights movement in the twentieth century to see that these problems existed before television and the Internet (Branch 1988, 1998, 2006). Unfortunately, distorted communication and political violence have a long history. It is a common trope in many of

Shakespeare's Histories and Tragedies. Biased assimilation of information about collective choices is probably as old as the state as a form of governance. But we also seem capable of assessing complex arguments given the right context. Reading speeches around the struggle for abolition and the US Civil War is instructive. There were certainly "sound bites" meant to play on biased assimilation. But political speeches, such as those of Lincoln and Douglas, went on for hours, were attended by huge audiences and were often printed word for word in newspapers, suggesting public engagement in complex arguments, although the debates also included appeals based on biased assimilation (Brands 2020; Jaffa 2012; Zarefsky 1986, 1993).

98. Arvai, Gregory and McDaniels (2001); Bessette, Arvai and Campbell-Arvai (2014); Gigerenzer (2008); Morgan (2017); Morgan and Cohon (2017); Morgan and Henrion (1990); Stern and Kalof (1996); von Winterfeldt (2013).

99. Morgan et al. (2005); US National Research Council (2007).

100. Ford et al. (2016); Peterson et al. (2018); Tengö et al. (2017); US National Research Council (2008).

101. Gunderson (2016); Gunderson and Dietz (2018).

102. Henry (2009, 2020); Henry and Vollan (2014). Frey and colleagues argued for avoiding decisions that polarized conflict and that limited future options in important early work on criteria for decision-making that has influenced my thinking (Freeman and Frey 1986, 1990–91; Frey and Said 1988). I see these as part of allowing us to learn from experience.

103. Dietz and Vine (1982); Harris and Blumstein (1984); Kowalczyk et al. (1983); Stern et al. (1986); Vine and Crawley (1991); Vine, Crawley and Centolella (1991). On biodiversity program evaluations, see Börner et al. (2016); Liu and Yang (2013); McKinnon et al. (2015); Sills et al. (2015); Tuanmu et al. (2016); Yang, McKinnon and Turner (2015).

104. Daniel Esty, personal communication, December 12, 2022; see also Esty and Emerson (2018).

105. Frank (2000); Frank and Min (2007); Frank et al. (2013).

106. The Dewey quote is from Dewey (1923: 202–03). See Radnitzky and Bartley (1987) on these issues.

107. A century ago, Dewey foresaw the special problem associated with technological change:

In reality, the trouble springs rather from the ideas and absence of ideas in connection with which technological factors operate. Mental and moral beliefs and ideals change more slowly than outward conditions. If the ideals associated with the higher life in our cultural past have been impaired, the fault is primarily with them. Ideals and standards formed without regard to the means by which they are to be achieved and incarnated in flesh are bound to be thin and wavering. Since the aims, desires and purposes created by a machine age do not connect with tradition, there are two sets of rival ideals and those which have actual instrumentalities at their disposal have the advantage. Because the two are rivals and because the older ones retain their glamour and sentimental prestige in literature and religions, the newer ones are perforce harsh and narrow. (Dewey 1923: 141–42)

108. Henry (2009: 131, 133).

109. See the discussion of anti-reflexivity in Chapter 6, Note 82; see also Chapter 2, Notes 62 and 110 and Chapter 4, Note 65.

110. I leave thinking through how my seven criteria might apply to the decision about whether or not to move Winky and Wanda to a sanctuary as an exercise for the reader.

# 6    Decisions and Conflict

1. Muir is a central figure in the history of environmentalism. He had changing and often contradictory views about the Indigenous people who had long inhabited and respected the landscapes Muir revered and who were displaced to make way for the parks; see Introduction and Fleck (1978);

Robbins and Moore (2019). From our perspective, some of Muir's statements about people of color are troubling and he apparently was comfortable in friendships with advocates of scientific racism (Purdy 2015). So, his legacy is problematic – an articulate advocate for wilderness with other views highly problematic from our perspective; see Chapter 3, Note 11 for a similar discussion of Benjamin Franklin's views. Environmental justice has long been part of the environmental movement focused on human health but has been less central to the conservation wing of the movement. Even the health-focused movement has sometimes displaced community engagement in favor of a more "professional" and risk-focused approach to environmentalism, in part a result of the dynamics of foundation funding (Brulle 2000; Dietz 2020b; Purdy 2017). But the problem is being recognized and analyzed, and efforts are underway to incorporate environmental justice concerns into both ecological and wildlife science and to protect relatively undisturbed ecosystems. Cassandra Johnson pioneered these efforts (Johnson 1998); see also Bourgin (2020); Lagin (2020); Schell, Guy et al. (2020).

2. Colchester (2004); Fletcher et al. (2021). On displacement in the Yosemite Valley, see Hull (2009). On the ecosystem effects, see Bloom and Deur (2020b).

3. In the United States, environmental policies and conflicts date to the colonial period. By the mid-nineteenth century, several US groups that could be considered environmental organizations had formed. Andrews (1999) describes the history of US environmental policy and Brulle (2000) the history of the US environmental movement. The ongoing controversies over the Glen Canyon dam that created Lake Powell, which is now at troublingly low levels because of climate change, are a parallel controversy to Hetch Hetchy. Because my father's unionized job allowed him long vacations, we once took a family trip to the West, bringing along his father. We stayed in Page, Arizona, and saw the dam under construction, and I read about the goal of providing water for irrigation and urban development in the Desert Southwest. Later, Eliot Porter's *The Place No One Knew: Glen Canyon on the Colorado* made me aware of the environmental issues around dams (Porter 1968). Still later, via Worster's biography of John Wesley Powell, I became aware of the irony of naming the lake after Powell, since he had long argued that human use of the Southwestern United States must attend to drought (Worster 2001). In 1981, Earth First with Edward Abbey dropped a plastic "crack" down the dam ("The Cracking of Glen Canyon Damn with Edward Abbey and Earth First!" (1982) Energy History Online video: https://energyhistory.yale.edu/library-item/video-cracking-glen-canyon-dam n-edward-abbey-and-earth-first-1982). A few years ago, with some of my family I visited the site and took a boat tour of the canyon, with low water levels revealing some of Porter had photographed.

4. The subtext in such a remark is a denigration of social science, which is ironic since in such circumstances it is social science that can lend insights into what is going on, why and what might be done about it.

5. Dietz (2013a); Sidik (2022b). Whyte and colleagues have pointed out that this is a major problem for scientists attempting to work with Indigenous communities (Reo et al. 2017; Whyte 2013, 2020; Whyte, Brewer and Johnson 2015). Scientists usually pride themselves on their neutrality and their independence from political control and often assume others acknowledge that. But to a community that has generations of troubling and often tragic experience dealing with the federal government and other outside groups, a reasonable starting assumption is to view a scientist not as a neutral party but as someone who represents the power and interests of those outside groups. So, for an outside scientist to work effectively with these communities they first have to understand how the community views scientists.. The importance of diverse views in science and deliberation are discussed in Chapter 4. I use the issue of Indigenous communities as an example but the same logic applies to most communities struggling with environmental justice issues. The historical trajectory and current conditions will differ in detail from community to community but the challenge of how

to engage science in the face of historical injustice and differential power is nearly universal. See also Chapter 1, Note 64 on community engagement in research.

6. As noted in the Introduction, my work, and thus my assessment of conflicts, has been focused on the United States. The arguments I make here should be treated as hypotheses about what may or may not obtain in other nations and cultures.

7. One of the most important influences on my thinking at that time was Tom Lough, a creative environmental sociologist who in the late 1960s was doing research on the ways in which organizational form (more hierarchical or flatter, larger or smaller) influenced the energy use of businesses and on the political economy of energy and developing the views I have labeled "radical human ecology" in the Introduction. He, along with Owen Lovejoy (who did the biomechanics of Lucy's knee, among other things) and Eugene Wenninger (who was holding seminars in sustainability science before that term existed), formed my thinking. Tom was politically active and was the one faculty member indicted as part of the Kent 25 (see Introduction, Note 7). As a result, his research was sidetracked for many years, with publications on his very original ideas appearing only years later (Lough 1996, 1999).

8. US National Research Council (1999a).

9. By "better," I mean doing well along the criteria described in Chapter 5.

10. On the affluent, see Nielsen, Nicholas et al. (2021) . See also Chapter 5, Note 91.

11. On Woburn, see Brown and Mikkelsen (1990). On urban development conflicts, see Logan and Molotch (1987). Chapter 7 engages growth conflicts in some detail.

12. This is a point where the environmental sociologists I have cited agree with neoclassical environmental economists. In environmental economics, the environmental damage that is not captured in the costs of production are called externalities. Sociologists see the process as "socializing" the costs of production in the sense that the profits are captured privately but everyone bears some of the costs. See Chapter 5.

13. The Millennium Ecosystem Assessment and subsequent literature refer to these as regulating and supporting services (Reid et al. 2005). Many of us argue against a purely anthropocentric view – harm to nonhumans should be considered in making decisions even though those harms have to be articulated in the decision process by humans. See Box 5.6 and Chapter 5, Notes 39, 40 and 41.

14. Graeber and Wengrow (2021); von Rueden (2020).

15. The literature on the environmental, health and social impacts of fracking is extensive; see Black et al. (2021); Brasier et al. (2015); Ladd (2018); Mayer (2017); Suchyta (2020a); Suchyta and Kelsey (2018); Whitley (2019).

16. One response to this kind of "externality" problem is traced back to Coase. The usual argument is that the legal system allows me to sue the fracker if my groundwater is harmed. But powerful interests can shape the laws, regulations and standards to their advantage while the average homeowner relying on groundwater may not even be aware of this complex set of rules. Further, lawsuits are expensive and so that system of redress favors those with financial resources. See also Chapter 1, Note 8 and Chapter 5.

17. Dietz, Stern and Rycroft (1989). The film *Anonymous* asserts that Shakespeare did not write Shakespeare's plays and develops an outrageous conspiracy theory to make that claim, part of a long line of arguments that reject Shakespeare as the author of the works we attribute to him (Emmerich 2011). I see this as another case of arguing about facts when the disagreement is about values and letting broad general beliefs block acceptance of contrary evidence. The detailed facts are very hard to tease out given the limited evidence we have about the life of an actor and playwright in the late sixteenth and early seventeenth centuries. The general beliefs involved may be about elitism versus egalitarianism, with the latter allowing that genius can come from humble origins. The denialists always seem to claim that someone from the English middle class who didn't attend

Oxford or Cambridge couldn't possibly have written some of the most brilliant works in the English language. This is a class bias, a broad generalization that elites are the source of all good things that leads to biased assimilation of detailed facts. Bryson's (2007) marvelous and funny *Shakespeare* provides a useful counterpoint to these conspiracy theories, as does a wealth of scholarship. Put simply, all the hard evidence we have points to Shakespeare as author of the plays and no serious evidence, as opposed to conjecture, indicates anything else. As Carl Sagan once said, expressing a key logic of science, extraordinary claims require extraordinary evidence. (The source for Sagan and other versions of this logic are at Garson O'Toole's website: https://quoteinvestigator.com/20 21/12/05/extraordinary/.) The Shakespeare denialists have yet to produce any reasonable evidence, let alone any extraordinary evidence. The existence of the dispute points to two unfortunate human tendencies. One is class bias. The other is a desire to be part of an in-group that holds special knowledge that is not widely available because of an assumed conspiracy. When these tendencies produce a dispute about who wrote Shakespeare's work, it is annoying. When they produce disputes about climate change, vaccinations or the outcomes of an election, they are corrosive and dangerous.

18. In some circumstances, the idea of compromise is seen as offensive as it threatens identity and what have been called "sacred values" (Atran and Axelrod 2008; Atran and Ginges 2012).

19. Boyd and Richerson (2005); Richerson and Boyd (2001, 2005). At least since Richard Nixon invoked the "silent majority" in 1969, this has been a standard trope in US politics. The Advocacy Coalition Framework (ACF) identifies the "devil shift" in policy networks in which opponents are seen as beyond the pale of reason and even as ethically suspect, a strong version of BAHP involving affective polarization; see Chapter 3; see also Sabatier, Hunter and McLaughlin (1987). When opponents are perceived this way, efforts to develop empathy for them may be precluded, although as I will discuss in later chapters, deliberative processes can sometimes reduce polarization. For a recent discussion, see Wilson, Parker and Feinberg (2020) and Chapter 9.

20. Bauer, Thorpe and Brunet (2015); Robertson et al. (2015). Thanks to my colleague Jeff Andresen, Michigan's State Climatologist, for his patience in guiding me in this literature.

21. Arrhenius (1896) is the original publication. The history of the idea is clearly presented by Weart (2004). Uppenbrink (1997) offers a sort commentary on the 100th anniversary of the publication.

22. National Academies of Sciences, Engineering, and Medicine (2017a); InterAcademy Council (2010).

23. Intergovernmental Panel on Climate Change (2021). On uncertainty, see Budescu, Broomwell and Por (2009); Ha-Duong, Swart and Bernstein (2007); Moss (2004); Moss and Schneider (2000). The move towards more careful statements about probability has come with the support and hard work of many people, but without doubt the emphasis on assessing uncertainty was led by the deep insights and very hard work of Richard Moss and Steve Schneider. See Schneider's autobiographical (and sadly last) book for a description of some of their struggles (Schneider 2009). It has been one of the privileges of my career to learn from both Richard and Steve.

24. See Chapter 5. The distinction between impact and production sciences described in Chapter 4 also seems to play out in the mind of the public. Conservatives trust production scientists more than impact scientists, while liberals trust impact scientists more than production scientists (McCright et al. 2013).

25. Kempton (1991) and Henry (2000) give examples of this misunderstanding. The confusion is perhaps understandable. Ozone depletion is caused primarily by chlorofluorocarbons (CFCs). CFCs are also a contributor to the greenhouse effect.

26. Doyle ([1887] 1967: 154). But Holmes engaged in many areas of knowledge not directly relevant to his craft, and many commentators suggest he may have been pulling Watson's leg; see the discussion in the notes on *A Study in Scarlet* in Baring-Gould (1967).

27. On BAHP among risk professionals, see Henry, Dietz and Sweeney (2021). On the public's folk ecology, see Stern et al. (1995). On popular epidemiology, see Brown and Mikkelsen (1990); Brown et al. (2004); Brown et al. (2006); McCormick (2007). And on the history of citizens raising the alarm in the Flint water crisis, see Chapter 1, Note 64. As I argue throughout the book, getting the facts right and getting the right facts often requires ongoing deliberation between scientists and those who have intimate knowledge of the local situation.

28. Dietz, Dan and Shwom (2007); Ding et al. (2011); Givens et al. (2020).

29. See Box 3.3 and Chapter 9, Note 7 for consideration of these processes around the pandemic.

30. Bennett (2016); Nisbet, Brossard and Kroepsch (2003); National Academies of Sciences, Engineering, and Medicine (2016).

31. Boykoff and Boykoff (2007); Brüggemann and Engesser (2017).

32. Data from Yale Program on Climate Control Communication, https://climatecommunication.yale.edu/ (accessed February 21, 2022).

33. A substantial and rapidly growing literature examines public opinion on climate change in the United States, and increasingly around the globe, and deploys a variety of theoretical and conceptual frames. My overall reading is that the general ideas of VBN theory and of the BAHP dynamic apply. Some useful entry points to the literature include Bayes and Druckman (2021); Dietz (2020c); Druckman and McGrath (2019); Hamilton (2021); Leiserowitz et al. (2021); McCright, Marquart-Pyatt et al. (2016); Poortinga et al. (2019); Shwom et al. (2015). Climate change may have become such a dominant issue that it encourages broader environmentalism, rather than vice versa, a finding that is different than the typical argument in VBN theory that general beliefs shape more specific ones; see Egan, Konisky and Mullin (2022). Some who are skeptical about climate change do hold other environmental concerns – there is variation within the overall pattern; see Haltinner and Sarathchandra (2022). This can be important in thinking about how we make collective decisions as deliberative processes can build on this variation in views, an idea I will revisit in Chapter 9.

34. Blastland et al. (2020); Van der Bles et al. (2019).

35. DeSilver (2022); Neal (2020); Neal, Domagalski and Yan (2022).

36. See Chapter 6, Note 27 and Chapter 1, Note 64.

37. It may be that this disjuncture between thinking about probabilities and thinking about specific cases is very deep in our cognitive processing. But if information is presented in terms of frequencies rather than probabilities, people seem to do a much better job of handling uncertainty (Cosmides and Tooby 1996; Gigerenzer and Gaissmaier 2011). The classic studies that established fast, System I cognitive processing usually presented the information in the form of probabilities.

38. There are proposals to reintroduce extinct species by using "fossil" DNA. However, these "revived" species usually would be introduced into ecosystems that are very different from their historical ecosystems so it is not clear that this is really a restoration but rather the introduction of a novel species. See Chapter 5, Note 10 on rewilding.

39. Estes et al. (2011); Paine (1966); Winnie and Creel (2017).

40. We do tend to overgeneralize from recent history following the availability heuristic; see Chapter 3. For example, the fierce conflict over preserving habitat for the spotted owl centered in large part around claims that these protected areas would devastate the logging industry and thus local economies. But the historical record suggests that resource-dependent communities have a long history of boom and bust cycles in employment that cannot be attributed to environmental protection (Force, Machlis and Zhang 2000; Freudenburg, Wilson and O'Leary 1998; Machlis and Force 2019). That is not to say that such regulations are without impacts (Charmley, Donoghue and Moseley 2008; Helvoigt, Adams and Ayre 2003) but rather that we must calibrate our discussions of the consequences of decisions based on careful analysis and not suppositions. And here again, the

general pattern (most workers end up with only short periods of unemployment) does not displace the strong feelings of the particular individual ("I haven't been able to find steady work in two years").

41. I once heard a local developer admit in a hearing that his real profits came not from building and selling houses but from getting changes in zoning and getting exemptions in permits that allowed him to develop extra lots. Those extra lots made the land worth more than he paid for it. In one case, he got the local town to break a no-subdivision covenant placed on a 100-plus-acre parcel of pasture, allowing him to split it into ten lots, worth in total far more to him than the swath of pasture he had bought. But there were costs to the community not captured in the transaction – externalities – including increases in the costs of services beyond what would be captured in increased property taxes, degradation of viewscape and rising costs of pasture for those who wished to farm.

42. Whyte (2017c, 2018, 2020).

43. Their work can be viewed online: Tim Flach (www.timflach.com); Britta Jaschinski (www.brittaphotography.com); Joe Zammit-Lucia (jzlimages.com). On the effectiveness of their approach, see Kalof, Zammit-Lucia and Kelly (2011); Kalof et al. (2016); Whitley, Kalof and Flach (2021). Empathy is discussed in Chapter 3.

44. The idea of scope of concern in environmental values was developed independently by Merchant (1992) and by Stern, Dietz and Kalof (1993). Emerging research shows that humans can show empathic and other subtle reactions to even rather simple robots (Broadbent 2017; Darling, Nandy and Breazeal 2015; Horstmann et al. 2018).

45. Perceptions of injustice produce an emotional response but emotions also influence what is seen as fair (Fehr 2009; Mullen 2016). Many other species have a strong sense of justice and fairness (Frans de Waal, "Moral Behavior in Animals," TED-ed video (2013), www.youtube.com/watch?v=PnnSjdpoBVw&t=781s).

46. Some economists argue that politics and even family life can be understood by using the same logic that applies to the rules of the market, as we have seen in Chapter 3 (Becker 1976b; Buchanan 1954). For them, there is only one realm of decision-making. Habermas (1984, 1987) offers a very different and more critical assessment of the use of market logic in nonmarket social contexts.

47. Recall the discussion of utilitarianism and libertarianism/anarchism in Chapter 5. An emphasis on efficiency and utility maximization is aligned with a belief that perfect markets allocate resources efficiently and that values are reflected in prices. Even Robert Frank (2020: 254), while extolling other economists to move beyond the assumption that decisions are made by individuals in isolation, also admits that "efficiency is in fact my deepest passion."

48. In public discourse, there seems to be an association made between arguments based on "hard" scientific analysis (e.g., "hard facts") and the "hard" pursuit of economic efficiency (e.g., "hard reality"); see Box 4.3. At the same time, the "soft" evocation of values, emotion and equity is linked to the "soft" pursuit of collective interest. I see no necessary connection between scientific analysis and market logic. Rather, the language is tactical – intended to make one line of argumentation seem more valid than another. I use the terms "hard" and "soft" intentionally. The hard/soft distinction evokes a gendered language, and the debates are themselves often gendered.

49. Private political donations in the contemporary United States exemplify this conflict. Many feel that such donations are public actions and should be openly documented. But when the Supreme Court became much more conservative it decided many such donations are private actions and can be kept secret from the public. As a result, a large portion of the money used for political purposes in the United States comes from sources that cannot be identified. Such "dark money" from corporations and the richest families can skew policy in their favor (Gilens, Patterson and Haines 2021). It also contributes to polarization (Kujala 2020; Lu, Gao and Szymanski 2019). See also Chapter 9 on voting.

50. See Chapter 5, Note 25 and Chapter 7, Note 31 for a discussion of the political theories that underpin the language.
51. Dietz, Stern and Rycroft (1989). See discussion in Chapter 3.
52. Bruckner (2016).
53. Mishel and Kandra (2021).
54. I am thinking here of feminist and other counterpublics discussed in the Introduction (Fraser 1992; Majewska 2021) and the "new class" articulated by Gouldner (1979), whose ideas warrant reassessment in light of our understanding of current societal dynamics and with an intersectional lens. Much of what I suggest falls within the scope of what many mean by democratic socialism, but again, I want to emphasize the need for context-specific analyses and proposals over a broad covering term, especially since the covering terms have different meanings in different countries.
55. My early experiences were not with wilderness but with wooded lots and with fields embedded near my home in Kent, with walks along the Cuyahoga River with my father and with fishing from a rowboat in small lakes with my grandfather. In the 1960s, I discovered the invocations of the wild in the writings of Gary Snyder and Matsuo Basho and the photographs of Eliot Porter and Ansel Adams.
56. McKibben (1989).
57. O'Connor (2013, 2017); Owens and Wolch (2017). As I write, I see every day a few Boxelder beetles (*Boisea trivittatus*) in our house. They are harmless, not in such large numbers as to be a nuisance and a reminder that we share this space with other species.

# 7    Reform or Transformation

1. Love and Giffels (1999).
2. As noted in Chapter 2, my father chose to stay in Ohio when Goodyear wanted him to move to Arizona. By then, my uncles had retired or died. A younger worker would have had to trade off job loss with a move that would be very disruptive to family. The effects of such plant closing and of unemployment in general can be substantial and long-lasting (Brand 2015). Many countries have laws that require analysis of and compensation for the impacts closing plants have on workers and on the community.
3. I am simplifying the history to make a clear example. There were multiple companies, multiple plants for each, different kinds of tires and options for factories near enough to Akron that community impacts would be modest.
4. Friedman (1970). This assertion is usually attributed to Alfred P. Sloan, the long-time CEO of General Motors. It is ironic given the resources major corporations spend on influencing policy. The logic is often deployed selectively – corporations should not become advocates for or implementors of social reforms since that is not "business." But shaping government action is seen as part of business. As discussed in Chapter 2, from the 1940s through the 1970s, US corporations, government and labor were involved in the "Great Compromise" in which this strict profits-only logic was not strictly followed. But the rise of neoliberal ideology, Reaganism and a profits-only style of corporate leadership led to rising inequality, increased concentration of power and a lack of action on many emerging environmental issues.
5. Only Goodyear now has a manufacturing facility in Akron. The decline is reflected in the innovative punk rock of Akron (Backderf 2010), inspired in part by Devo, a band created in reaction to the shootings at Kent State. The Black Keys album *Rubber Factory* was recorded in the abandoned General Tire factory.

6. In a corporation, profit maximization is often the dominant goal. Indeed, under the law in most US states, corporations owned by stockholders have a legal obligation to maximize profits. If management fails to do this, by, for example, taking steps to protect the environment or improve the local community at the expense of maximum profits, they can be sued by the stockholders. In response, a growing number of governments, including many US states, have created the opportunity for publicly held companies to be incorporated as Benefit Corporations or "B Corporations," using laws that allow the management to pursue goals other than strict profit maximization (Ciepley 2019; Collart 2014; Cummings 2012; Ho 2015a; Loewenstein 2013; Reiser 2011; Robson 2015). Time horizons and discounting matter: If a company maximizes quarterly or annual profits, it might make decisions that are detrimental to profits in the long run. But executives can leave and investors sell out before the long run occurs. For example, a senior manager at HSBC Asset Management argued that climate change doesn't matter because its effects are beyond the time horizon of investment payouts (Wagner 2022). See Chapter 3, especially Note 10 on discounting.

7. What is legal and illegal will depend on the exercise of power in the past to shape the law.

8. The efficiency argument is used in defense of the stores of Genericville, such as Walmart, Costco, Ikea and Home Depot and with online retailers especially Amazon. They are criticized for displacing small businesses that cannot compete. The low prices at these huge retailers come because they have cheap labor costs, often sell goods that are manufactured outside the United States and have efficiencies due to their size. They are also oligopsonies (a buyer who dominates the market just as a monopoly is a seller who dominates) who have so much market power that they can make demands on suppliers that smaller buyers cannot. Sometimes this power is used to set sustainability standards, an approach discussed in this chapter and Chapter 9. The argument in favor of them is that in providing goods more efficiently, the consumer's dollar goes further, and that overall society is better off as a result. This contrasts with the standard justification for competition as a mechanism for ensuring that markets are allocating resources efficiently.

9. The triple bottom line is part of a broader and older movement advocating for "corporate social responsibility" (Carroll 2008). Norman and MacDonald argue that the triple bottom line makes five claims:

- (Measurement Claim) The components of "social performance" or "social impact" can be measured in relatively objective ways on the basis of standard indicators ... These data can then be audited and reported.
- (Aggregation Claim) A social "bottom line" – that is, something analogous to a net social "profit/loss" – can be calculated using data from these indicators and a relatively uncontroversial formula that could be used for any firm.
- (Convergence Claim) Measuring social performance helps improve social performance, and firms with better social performance tend to be more profitable in the long-run.
- (Strong Social-Obligation Claim) Firms have an obligation to maximize (or weaker: to improve) their social bottom line – their net positive social impact – and accurate measurement is necessary to judge how well they have fulfilled this obligation.
- (Transparency Claim) The firm has obligations to stakeholders to disclose information about how well it performs with respect to all stakeholders. (Norman and MacDonald 2004: 246; see also MacDonald and Norman 2007)

They further argue that "what's sound about the 3BL project is not novel, and what is novel is not sound." Their view is that much of the argument for the triple bottom line is essentially equivalent to the argument that corporations have "stakeholders" other than shareholders. See also Freeman (1984). The arguments about the triple bottom line are part of a large ongoing debate about corporate social responsibility.

10. John Barone pointed out to me that many of the toxics emitted in manufacturing start as chemicals that are expensive to buy. So, there can be profit-based incentives to reduce emissions.

11. Any analysis of this sort must make assumptions about scope or scale. In the example, I am focusing on the adverse impacts on the community where the old plant might be closed. The literature on benefit-cost analysis has long recognized the need to keep track of separate "accounts" for regional- and national-level economic impacts; see Chapter 5, Note 62. If your scope of concern does not end at national borders, you might also want a global account. Jobs "off-shored" from the United States may decrease well-being in communities within the United States but it may create employment elsewhere in the globe. But often the new plant will have much looser safety and environmental standards and worse labor practices than the old plant, so comparisons have to take account of a complex set of impacts (Frey 1998a; Frey, Gellert and Dahms 2018). I won't review the literature here but point out that the example I am using is simplified compared to real sustainability decisions. At the national level, consumers might be able to buy more environmentally friendly products at a lower price if the plant moves.

12. MacDonald and Norman (2007); Norman and MacDonald (2004: 246).

13. Pava (2007: 108). Much of environmental economics tries to commensurate multiple outcomes from decisions using the idea that in a competitive market prices reflect social values and that when prices are absent or not accurate reflections of values then it may be possible to develop reasonable surrogates for prices. Then, it is possible to look at profitability, job losses in the community and reduced greenhouse gas emissions in a common metric. See Section 5.3.

14. Garcia et al. (2016); Kumar et al. (2017); Morgan and Cohon (2017); Thabrew et al. (2018).

15. Looking for improvements at the existing plant or rebuilding nearby is changing the set of options, and might include good strategies, but I want to keep the example simple.

16. Perhaps the most notable example is the history of the Pullman district in Chicago. Worried about labor strife, in 1880 the railroad millionaire George Pullman built a community for his workers. (He was worth about $500 million in today's dollars.) The district was praised for the high quality of the houses and amenities such as gas and indoor plumbing, not common at the time. At the Prague International Hygienic and Pharmaceutical Exposition in 1896, Pullman was declared "the world's most perfect town" ("The History of Pullman," Historic Pullman Foundation website, www.pullmanil.org/the-history-of-pullman/, accessed November 22, 2022). But Pullman was also paternalistic, exerting control over what stores could open, limiting churches to his favored one, even limiting what books could be in the library and spying on the workers' lives in the community. During the recession of 1893–94, Pullman cut his workers' wages but refused to cut the rents he charged them. Most of his workers joined the American Railway Union led by Eugene V. Debs and went on strike. The strike was tumultuous and violent and led to Debs being sent to federal prison. (Key sources include the Historic Pullman Foundation (www.pullmanil.org/); and work by Lindsey and Wish (Lindsey 1942; Wish 1939).) The famed social reformer Jane Addams, who influenced John Dewey, wrote an essay on the strike, comparing Pullman and others who felt aggrieved, despite their power, to King Lear (Addams 1912). The town of Pullman was only one of many efforts by industrialists to develop planned communities, usually based on a logic that the owners of capital knew better than the workers what the workers needed. (Pullman, Washington, was named for George Pullman but had no direct connection with him and was not a planned community.) Among them: Bessbrook, Northern Ireland, developed by John Richardson (1846); Saltaire, Britain, developed by Titus Salt (1851); Bournville, Britain, developed by George Cadbury (1879); Port Sunlight, Britain, developed by William Lever (1888) and Gary, Indiana, developed by US Steel (1906). In Akron, the tire companies built some segregated neighborhoods for workers (Love and Giffels 1999). The history of these "company towns" with their paternalistic logic is an interesting contrast to that of Reston, Virginia, discussed in Chapter 1. They were part of a general effort by corporations to provide for

workers' welfare, motivated by both good intentions and a desire to stave off union organizing (Brandes 1976). (I thank Rachel Kelly for her fine summary of the history of company towns and Alex Fleet for his insights on corporate welfare activities and company unions – yet another example of variation in motivations and outcomes on the part of corporations.)

17. The story of tetraethyl lead in the United States gives clear evidence that senior executives were, in this case, well aware of the health effects of lead and worked actively to suppress public and scientific awareness of those issues (Kitman 2000; McGrayne 2001). Similar stories of decisions to ignore all except the financial bottom line emerge across the twentieth and twenty-first centuries, from lead through pesticides to climate change (Michaels 2020). The focus on only one bottom line can happen in government, too – it is what underpins the tragedy in Flint, Michigan; see Chapter 1, Note 64. And often government and corporations are influencing each other in these tragedies. Some of the worst disasters have occurred outside the United States all too often with similar dynamics of malfeasance (Deb 2020, 2021).

18. MacDonald and Norman (2007); Norman and MacDonald (2004); Pava (2007). On greenwashing, see Jones (2019).

19. Gilligan and Vandenbergh (2020); Vandenbergh (2017); Vandenbergh and Gilligan (2017). I have been involved in debates about reform versus transformation for many years. During the emergence of the "new" environmental movement around the first Earth Day in 1970, some on the left saw the movement as a "distraction" from the real cause of overthrowing capitalism. Some went so far as to try to disrupt meetings of our campus environmental group at Kent State, arguing that "there is no pollution in Mao's China." I still know some of those folks and they now embrace a progressive environmentalism that is not very far from the stance of many of us in the campus environmental movement around Earth Day. As noted in Chapter 1, the environmental movement of the time called for government and consumer action but also for radical transformation of the consumerist and capitalist economy, criticized the military industrial complex and the Vietnam War and strongly emphasized issues of environmental justice (Dietz 2020b; Environmental Action 1970; Rome 2013). While our understandings have evolved over the last fifty years, these themes were all present in the movement in 1970 but apparently missed by some on the left.

20. See Vandenbergh (2017); Vandenbergh and Gilligan (2017: chap. 2). For example, corporations might only act on their own operations while ignoring the larger environmental impacts of their supply chain or simply be vague about what they are doing to achieve publicized goals (Tollefson 2022). Assessing what is going on requires careful analysis of the variation in action across corporations, considering best, worst and typical examples. Vandenbergh and Moore provide careful analysis around the issue of supply chain contracting, which is becoming an important commitment by many corporations (Vandenbergh and Moore 2022).

21. On Walmart, see Gilligan and Vandenbergh (2020). On Google: Ambrose (2019). On Clean Energy Buyers: https://cebuyers.org/. On Carbon Disclosure Project: www.cdp.net/en. On financial risk assessments: Ho (2015b). On insurance: Insure Our Future (2021). On development in the Arctic National Wildlife Refuge: Butler (2020). See Chapter 7, Note 39 on the pushback against divestiture campaigns.

22. This is the idea of the counterfactual – what would have happened to the things we are interested in if a particular event, program, policy and so on had not occurred? There is a very sophisticated literature in statistical methodology on what can and cannot be said about causal effects given various types of data (Frank et al. 2013; Morgan and Winship 2014; Pearl and Mackenzie 2018). For a discussion, see Chapter 3, Note 112. In this case, the issue is what would have happened if a company had not adopted a triple bottom line approach.

23. Stern, Dietz and Vandenbergh (2021); Vandenbergh and Gilligan (2017).

24. Stern, Dietz and Vandenbergh (2022). The term "Disney's law" seems to have originated with John Gibbons, Science Advisor to President Bill Clinton (Gibbons 1998).

25. The distinction between "populational" approaches discussed in this section and case studies is an important rift between the literature on ecological modernization theory (EMT) and its critics (McLaughlin 2012a; Mol 2010; York, Rosa and Dietz 2010). Most EMT literature is based on case studies. They provide evidence about processes of change and a proof that some corporations, industries or nations have dealt with environmental problems. The more important claim is about aggregate effects. Overall, as affluence increases, do we see a decline in stress placed on the environment? For the most part, EMT research has not addressed this question while research that has is, overall, less than supportive of the EMT argument.

26. Zipf (1932, [1949] 2016); Freudenburg (2005, 2006). Zipf's logic was later expanded by Mandelbrot (1982) in his ideas about fractals.

27. Grant, Jorgenson and Longhofer (2016, 2020), Jorgenson, Longhofer and Grant (2016); Heede (2014). Grant and colleagues' detailed analysis also notes that increased fuel prices do tend to reduce emissions, as expected by economic theory, and that there can be rebound effects where increased efficiency ultimately leads to higher rather than lower emissions.

28. Case study scholarship identifies corporations that seem to be doing an exemplary job (Vandenbergh and Gilligan 2017). I know of no analysis that uses the kind of methodology deployed by Freudenburg to first identify corporations that are outstanding in this regard and then examine their characteristics, although Jorgenson and colleagues are beginning this work. Statistical analyses are often misunderstood in this context. Freudenburg (2005) correctly argues that typical analyses such as ordinary least squares methods (mean, variance, regression) are heavily influenced by outliers and that wise practice is to look at those outliers for what they are telling us. But the matter is more subtle (Dietz, Frey and Kalof 1987; Dietz, Kalof and Frey 1991). Statisticians have developed methods that are resistant to outliers and would be a better starting point in looking for outliers. Further, there are methods for focusing not on the center of the data, such as the mean or median, but on any point in the distribution. These "quantile regression" methods can, for example, focus on predicting the 75th or the 90th percentile and thus are well suited to extending the kind of analysis Freudenburg initiated (Hao and Naiman 2007; Koenker 2017; Koenker and Hallock 2001). At least one study uses this approach in examining corporate sustainability efforts (Gallego-Álvarez and Ortas 2017). The founders of modern statistical analysis were heavily influenced by Darwinian thinking and saw the task of science to be, to a large extent, explaining variation, which they viewed as "normal" rather than deviation from an ideal (Bennett 1998; Dietz and Kalof 2009).

29. Pollution taxes or permits for pollution that can be bought and sold in a market are among the most frequently recommended environmental policies (Schmalensee and Stavins 2017; Tietenberg 2002, 2013). The idea is usually attributed to Pigou (1920). The logic assumes that market transactions lead to the efficient allocation of resources. The government creates a "market" in pollution by putting a price on pollution through taxes or limiting the amount of pollution through tradeable permits (cap and trade) that become costly. Then the ability of the market to process information is deployed to protect the environment. A thoughtful review by Goulder and Schein (2013) clarifies the advantages and disadvantages of taxes versus cap and trade and reviews the impressive body of scholarship that has tried to work through the details not of an abstract price on emissions in a perfect market but of the implications of various forms of policy.

30. McLaughlin (1998, 2001, 2012b, 2012c); see also Sober (1980).

31. There seem to be no terms to describe forms of economic organization since the industrial revolution that don't have strong normative connotations. "Capitalism" is the term most favored by scholars and especially by Marxists critical of the system. "Free markets" is the term favored by most advocates of the current system. These terms all need to be unpacked. The economic systems that currently dominate

in nearly all nations are a complex hybrid of institutional arrangements and configurations of organizations. The key issue is how social structure and norms, including those codified in law and policy, influence the distribution of power in a particular social formation, that is, whose interests are served by individual, corporate and government decisions and how these change over time.

32. Vandenbergh (2017); Vandenbergh and Gilligan (2017).

33. One strategy is to act to change the landscape by changing laws and norms. A great advantage of the population approach is that it explicitly examines the interplay between structure and power; see Dietz and Burns (1992); McLaughlin (2012b, 2012c); McLaughlin and Dietz (2008).

34. Malm (2021) argues that the fossil fuel industry has many and unfortunate connections with racist actions and with ultra-right and fascist policies.

35. The variations we observe across current and historical political economies are all, at least for the last century or two, embedded in and shaped by a global capitalist economy. For some theorists, it follows that the variation we observe is of little value in understanding what would be possible absent that world system. This claim has some credibility, but it also seems to imply that empirical evidence is irrelevant in understanding what is possible outside the current global system. Here, Vandenbergh and Gilligan's question "Compared to what?" is answered with a hypothetical world in which there is no capitalist global political economy.

36. See Chapter 7, Note 6.

37. Like everyone else, corporate leaders can have seemingly contradictory views. John Mackey, the former CEO of Whole Foods, is an interesting case. Under his management, Whole Foods was attentive to the treatment of animals in their supply chain, was routinely listed by Fortune as one of the 100 "best places to work" in the United States, emphasized sustainable and organic products and limited executive salaries to nineteen times that of the average employee. On the other hand, Mackey, who is influenced by Ayn Rand (see Chapter 5, Note 25) is profoundly anti-union and is a climate change denier (Apple 2002; Little 2004; Paumgarten 2010).

38. Azar et al. (2021); Condon (2020a).

39. Efforts to get universities, pension funds and other large holders of stock to take account of the triple bottom line in choosing investments for their portfolios are an example. Divestiture was a major strategy in the campaign against apartheid in South Africa. Currently, there are comparable campaigns to decarbonize investment portfolios. The potential impact has led state legislatures in some fossil fuel–producing states to try to block state governments from doing business with companies that divest (Buchele 2022). Vandenbergh points out that this is evidence that these efforts are seen as consequential by those who support the fossil fuel industry (Michael Vandenbergh, personal communication, March 16, 2022). Corporate commitments are likely to be volatile in response to political and profit pressures. Some corporations are backing away from prior commitments even as others are making new commitments (Sadasivam 2022).

40. I am not aware of extensive research on sustainability in decision-making by co-ops and employee-owned companies but there is some evidence that worker involvement in decisions has a beneficial effect on moves towards sustainability (Farooq, Farooq and Reynaud 2019). The exception is the large body of work on co-ops of agricultural producers, where there is some evidence for support for sustainability (Candemir, Duvaleix and Latruffe 2021).

41. Again, Vandenbergh and Gilligan (2017) provide an excellent review of these arguments.

42. The performance of publicly held versus privately held corporations has been the subject of scholarly debate at least since Berle and Means ([1933] 2009). In their overview of the literature, Wang et al. (2016) identify more than thirty papers examining the impacts of corporate social responsibility; of those, more than half examine financial outcomes. McGuire, Holtmaat and Prakash (2022) look at the impacts of large fines on British Petroleum (BP) for the *Deepwater Horizon* oil spill and find that there was a short-term impact (~2 months) on BP stock prices and an intermediate-term impact on

BP's reputation (~2 years). But there was little long-term impact on either BP or the industry as a whole. Part of the complexity in assessing these impacts is estimating how long a period of adverse effects is needed to change corporate decision-making and how long those changes persist.

43. See Chapter 2 and earlier discussions in this chapter.

44. Corporations that were part of the "Great Compromise" discussed in Chapter 2 were probably sacrificing short-term profits in order to achieve broader goals, while a return to a focus on profits alone seemed to emerge after 1980.

45. On searches, see Desjardins (2018). On operating systems: www.netmarketshare.com (accessed November 28, 2018). On Walmart: Howard (2016).

46. Here again, there is some convergence between neoclassical economics and Marxist theory in that both approaches have examined how concentration in buying power or selling power leads the dynamics of the market and the behavior of corporations to deviate from the hypothetical forms that provide much of the justification of markets as an efficient way to organize collective decision-making. Howard (2016, especially chap. 1) provides a nice overview of the Marxist perspective.

47. The estimate for the corporate sector and the extrapolation from our US-based behavioral wedge work to other affluent nations is from a personal communication with Jonathan Gilligan (December 2, 2018). These further extrapolations from our published estimates for US households are very rough estimates. More work needs to be done to develop realistic estimates of what can be done. In the behavioral wedge papers, we argue that there is a tendency to look only at technical potential (TP) of an emission reductions action – what would happen if all companies or all households took the action. That is very unrealistic. We have estimated behavioral plasticity (BP) – the likelihood that a household will take the action, based on what has been accomplished given the record of the best efforts to encourage those actions. A third factor must be included in policy discussions – the initiative feasibility (IF). IF is the likelihood that a policy to encourage emission reductions will be adopted and effectively implemented (Stern, Dietz and Vandenbergh 2022). One motivation for Mike Vandenbergh and Jonathan to write *Beyond Politics* (Vandenbergh and Gilligan 2017) is that, while carbon taxes, cap and trade (see Chapter 8, Note 6) or even direct limits on emission or technology mandates could have substantial TP and high BP as households and corporations respond to prices or mandates, these approaches have low IF in the United States. TP, BP and IF will be discussed in Chapter 8.

48. The White House (2021).

49. Dietz et al. (2009). The behavioral wedge example was developed around direct emissions of greenhouse gases by US households. Subsequent work is expanding the approach to indirect emissions (e.g., through consumption of food and other consumer goods), decisions by actors other than households (e.g., organizations of many sorts) and beyond greenhouse gas emission to other environmentally consequential actions (e.g., water consumption).

50. These are very rough "Fermi" calculations and are only intended to demonstrate that quick and cost-effective actions contribute substantially but are not sufficient. Note that calculating what pledges mean is complicated and that even the most optimistic interpretation of pledges made to date still entrains what many experts see as a dangerous level of climate change. For more details on pledges and their implications for climate change, see the Climate Action Tracker (climateactiontracker.org/). On tipping points: Moore et al. (2022).

51. I am reminded of the glass that is described by an optimist as half full, by a pessimist as half empty and by an engineer as a poorly designed glass.

52. Ostrom (2007). This is another example of the "best is the enemy of the good." See the Introduction. On wedges, see Pacala and Socolow (2004).

53. Webber (2008).

54. As Lapore reminds us, the Amendments themselves were used to justify personhood for corporations and restrictions on the rights of many Americans (Lepore 2018). Some, but by no means all, staunch

abolitionist held what we would now see as racist views – they could be fierce in their opposition to slavery but not acknowledge the fundamental equality of those in bondage (Brands 2020).

55. Gilligan and Vandenbergh (2020); IHS Markit (2017).

56. The shift in power across corporations, nations and regions depends on what strategies are followed. Corporations focused on fossil fuels could invest elsewhere and may be forced to by shareholders worried about the vulnerability of their portfolios to climate change; see Box 7.2. A transition will be more difficult for regions and nations who depend on fossil fuel production as a major source of revenue and will require creative, forward-looking strategies. It is likely to be resisted by petrostates whose interests are strongly aligned with those of the fossil fuel industry (Davidson and Gismondi 2011; Haluza-Delay 2012) as well as political interests traditionally aligned with those industries (Malm 2021). To date, the most visible reaction of such corporations, regions and nations is to actively resist the idea that the climate is changing, that such change is caused by humans and that it is feasible to shift to other sources of energy rather than adapting to changes that would come from addressing the climate problem.

57. There is nothing inherent in evolutionary thinking that suggests that changes will usually be incremental or slow. That is one common pattern in cultural evolution. Rapid and massive changes also occur, what Gould and Eldridge called "punctuated equilibrium" (Burns and Dietz 1992c; Dietz, Burns and Buttel 1990; Gould and Eldredge 1993; McLaughlin 2012a, 2012b).

58. Friis and Nielsen (2019); Liu et al. (2013); Liu et al. (2015); Liu et al. (2018); Jorgenson (2015b); Xu, Li et al. (2020). On soybeans, see Silva et al. (2017). On supply chains: Vandenbergh and Gilligan (2017).

59. See also Chapter 3, especially Note 24.

60. Dietz (2017a); Dietz, Rosa and York (2012).

61. Gould, Pellow and Schnaiberg (2008); Oliver (2005); Schnaiberg (1980, 1994). Schnaiberg's analysis was anticipated by Anderson, whose *The Sociology of Survival* is a classic that is too little read (Anderson 1976). The neo-Marxist underpinning of this work is largely the *Monthly Review* school's arguments about the nature of monopoly capital in the mid to late twentieth century (Baran 1957; Baran and Sweezy 1966; Braverman 1974; Foster 2013; Mamdami 1973; Sweezy [1942] 1968; Sweezy and Magdoff 1972). I recall a conversation with Schnaiberg where he mentioned that his move towards the *Monthly Review* school was strongly influenced by Anderson. Major publications on metabolic rift and related theory often appear in *Monthly Review* publications, strengthening the links among these lines of analysis (Foster 1994; Foster, Clark and York 2010). Chapter 9 in Foster, Clark and York (2010) provides a thoughtful explication of the relationship between Schnaiberg's analysis and the *Monthly Review* school.

62. We are only beginning careful assessment of the relationship between the labor movement and the environment (Alvarez, McGee and York 2019). The US labor movement was a strong supporter of the first Earth Day in 1970 (Environmental Action 1970; Rome 2013; Van Alstyne 2015). As an undergraduate, I was at a public hearing in Cleveland on the Clean Air Act. Police blocked our entry to the room saying it was too crowded. We students couldn't change their mind. But when we were joined by members of the United Steelworkers, whose neighborhoods suffered from air pollution, the police opened the hearing room. Splits between the labor movement and environmentalists came later and the ongoing dynamic is complex (Felli 2014; Räthzel and Uzzell 2011; Stevis 2002, 2011).

63. As discussed in Chapters 2 and 6, Molotch and Logan developed a very parallel argument about urban development (Adua and Lobao 2021; Logan and Molotch 1987; Molotch 1976). Urban growth, including expansion into previously undeveloped areas and redevelopment of areas already urban, is pushed by a growth machine coalition. Developers who stand to profit directly are at the core of the coalition and they frequently find allies in businesses, politicians and workers who feel they will also reap benefits from growth. The idea that growth had problematic social and environmental impacts but was promoted by a political coalition that benefited from it was anticipated by Applebaum, Molotch

and colleagues in a series of papers that preceded the Logan and Molotch idea of a growth machine (Appelbaum 1978; Appelbaum et al. 1976; Molotch 1976). Such coalitions drove the development in Northeast Ohio and Northern Virginia that is discussed in Chapter 1. They also played a part on a very small scale in the deliberations of the Planning Commission of Grand Isle, Vermont, mentioned in Chapter 9. The treadmill is a very useful framework that has been modified to examine not just land use but also the dynamics of the military industrial complex (Clark, Jorgenson and Kentor 2010; Hooks, Lengefeld and Smith 2021; Hooks and Smith 2004, 2005, Jorgenson and Clark 2016). Sanderson and Hughes (2019) combine the treadmill logic with the Jevons paradox (see Chapter 7, Note 78) to explain the dynamics of groundwater depletion, an increasingly crucial global problem.

64. Arguments about capitalism and growth were a central theme in the work of Commoner and were part of his debate with Holdren and Ehrlich (see Chapter 2). Anderson (1976) provided the first sociological articulation of the issue, while Schnaiberg's analysis made the issue central in environmental sociology (Schnaiberg 1980). Foster reminded us of Marx's analysis of what we would now consider environmental issues (Foster 1999). Meanwhile, development scholars were articulating the effects of differential power across nations on the environment (Frey 1994, 1995; Jorgenson 2003, 2004). These threads have become intertwined, leading to important elaborations and syntheses (Downey 2015; Foster, Clark and York 2010; Jorgenson and Givens 2014; White, Rudy and Gareau 2016). Rudel offers an especially important assessment, including a contrast between defensive (i.e., self-interested) and altruistic environmentalism (Rudel 2013, 2019a). See also Chapter 7, Note 61.

65. Anti-environmentalism also seems to be aligned with racism, and perhaps fascism (Chanin 2018; Dietz et al. 2018; Malm 2021; Mascarenhas 2016; Satcher 2021).

66. Calls for "degrowth" build on these arguments, asserting that we must reduce energy and resource use. Degrowth can mean simply reduced use of energy and resources to accomplish that end, or it can mean reductions in economic activity or human population in order to reduce energy and resources use. It is clear that there are multiple types of change that can reduce human stress on the environment, and I will discuss them in Section 7.3.3 (Cosme, Santos and O'Neill 2017; Gunderson 2018; Kallis et al. 2018; Washington and Twomey 2016; Weiss and Cattaneo 2017).

67. On inequality, see Alderson and Pandian (2018); Piketty (2020, 2022). On the libertarian view: Tanner (2018). Proponents of capitalism are usually rather explicit in their invocation of utilitarian or libertarian ethics. While I disagree with them on many points, I respect that they are often clear about the values they emphasize and the ethical traditions they invoke. (Many proponents of capitalism do not offer detailed arguments; here, I am thinking of the most careful analysts.) I am often frustrated that those arguing for societal transformation are often mute or vague on the ethical theory that underpins their position. Early in the development of social impact assessment, a few of us argued that if we were to engage in policy analysis we needed to have those analyses based in ethical theory (Dietz 1984, 1987; Freeman 1992; Freeman and Frey 1986, 1990–91). Those arguments have had little influence and normative theory is badly underdeveloped in the environmental social sciences, with the exception of the routine use of utilitarianism in economics. Chapter 5 is my attempt to encourage discussion of ethical theories.

68. A key theme in critiques of capitalism is that the ability to influence decisions is a function of income and wealth (Dietz and Whitley 2018). That is true when the decisions are made in the market, and it is also true when the power of wealth spills into political decision-making. In addition to the poor having very little voice in these decision processes, other species who enter the market only as commodities or as a form of labor have no voice. Finding a way to incorporate the voices, needs and interests of nonhumans is a problem for all ethical systems. See Box 5.6.

69. I have had the good fortune to be friends and frequent collaborators with major thinkers on both sides of this debate, in particular Richard York and Andrew Jorgenson on the transformation side and Michael Vandenbergh and Jonathan Gilligan on the reform side. Having learned an immense

amount not only from their writing but also from conversations with them, I have deep respect for the subtlety of their views and their ability to learn from each other. Unfortunately, some in this debate have taken rather rigid and antagonistic stances. There seems to be an intellectual hubris that assumes that one's own position is so obviously correct that those who disagree are ill-informed, are not thinking clearly or have questionable motives. In the larger society, this is the BAHP dynamic and it can occur in scholarly debates. Such rhetorical strategies are not new; see Chapter 7, Note 19. I have even seen some from the "only transformation will work" camp call advocates of individual actions "climate deniers." I know of no one who thinks that individual consumer actions are sufficient to solve problems like climate change. The argument as outlined earlier in this section is that individual actions can make a contribution. One could easily turn this denunciation around and argue that those who argue individual actions are irrelevant are just "apologists for profligate consumption." The issues around reform and transformation are complex and difficult; to make progress, we need to engage each other with respect and humility. Some exciting new syntheses are emerging (Fisher and Jorgenson 2019). There is evidence that the credibility of those who advocate for action on climate policy is influenced by the amount of greenhouse gases they emit in their work and personal life (Attari, Krantz and Weber 2019; Sparkman and Attari 2020).

70. The names used for this phenomena: spillover effects, rebound effects, moral licensing, moral disinhibition, gateway effects and single action bias; see also Chapter 7, Note 73 and Truelove et al. (2014). I will stick with the first three. Vandenbergh and Gilligan (2017) note that the greater prevalence of labels that imply such negative effects rather than positive ones is a bias in the literature. In the telecoupling framework, the term "spillover system" is used to mean systems whose link to "sending" and "receiving" systems is indirect, a meaning not inconsistent with but distinct from how the term "spillover" is used in the literature I am reviewing (Liu et al. 2013; Liu et al. 2018).

71. York (2017a). York introduces the interesting concept of the "consequence elasticity of demand," arguing that the demand for a good is in part driven by perceived consequences. If the perceived consequences are reduced, then demand may increase in analogous fashion to a reduction in prices leading to an increase in demand.

72. Chapter 7, Note 19 recounts an extreme view of this – that environmentalism is a distraction from the "real" issue, the transformation of the capitalist political economy. Unfortunately, this tendency towards ideological purism and a less than careful reading of the arguments actually being made still occurs in the scholarly literature. Ironically, some conservatives now feel that the environmental movement is not a source of legitimation for capitalism – a view taken by some leftists in the 1960s – but rather a major threat to it.

73. Truelove et al. (2014). They draw careful distinctions among, and examine the literature on, negative spillovers, rebound effects, single action biases, moral licensing, positive spillover, consistency effect and identity effects. These distinctions are important for conceptualizing empirical work and for program and policy design but need not concern us here.

74. On policy support and consumer action, see Geiger (2022); Geiger, Brick et al. (2021); Maki et al. (2019); Sun (2018); Werfel (2017). On road transit: Dimitropoulos, Oueslati and Sintek (2018). On household measures: Adua et al. (2019).

75. Lamb et al. (2020). Again, Schnaiberg argued the "Great Compromise" discussed in Chapter 2 and Chapter 7, Note 4 was intended to forestall larger reforms of capitalism.

76. Sparkman, Attari and Weber (2021); Stern (2020).

77. One version of this decomposition is the I=P*A*T equation, which is essentially the Kaya identity used in climate scenarios. It is the focus of the STIRPAT research program I initiated with Gene Rosa and Richard York discussed in Chapter 2. In this discussion I refer to consumption rather than affluence, and include in consumption not just the actions of individuals but also those of organizations, such as the military, whose consumption and environmental impact are often huge.

78. Over the last thirty years the amount of energy used and greenhouse gases emitted per unit economic activity in the United States and globally have decreased substantially; see Figure 7.1 (Olivier and Peters 2018). Sometimes increased efficiency in energy-using technologies encourages further use of the technology and leads to increased energy consumptions. In the nineteenth century, William Stanley Jevons identified what we now call the Jevons paradox (Rolimeni, Mayumi and Giampietro 2008; York 2006; York, Adua and Clark 2022). He observed that in England, as technological improvements made the use of coal more efficient (less coal was needed to produce a quantity of work thus lowering the fuel costs of that work), the total amount of coal used increased because it became economically feasible to use coal energy more extensively. York has initiated discussions examining the idea that while increased use of renewable energy sources displaces use of fossil fuels to some degree, the substitution is not perfect and so increasing the use of renewables is also associated with increased energy use (Jorgenson 2012; York 2012, 2017b; York, Adua and Clark 2022; York and Bell 2019; York and McGee 2016, 2017).

79. See the United Nations Department of Public Information press release "World Population Projected to Reach 9.8 Billion in 2050, and 11.2 Billion in 2100 – Says UN" (www.un.org/en/development/desa/population/events/pdf/other/21/21June_FINAL%20PRESS%20RELEASE_WPP17.pdf) and the US Census Bureau press release "Census Bureau Projects U.S. and World Populations on New Year's Day" (www.census.gov/newsroom/press-releases/2019/new-years-population.html) (accessed February 3, 2019).

80. A major goal of the STIRPAT research program is to move past the rather pointless debates about "Malthusianism" to actually assess how changes in human population size change stress on the environment in a formulation that explicitly takes the effect of population to always be a product of consumption. See Chapter 2, Notes 67 and 69.

81. See Chapter 2, Note 95.

82. The impacts of animal agriculture, consumption of animal products, organic agriculture, alternative dietary choices and a variety of related issues are being examined via life cycle assessment. Recent work shows the very substantial variation that exists both in how food is produced and in the consumption patterns of individuals and social groups (Boehm et al. 2018; Lacour et al. 2018; Marques, Fuinhas and Pais 2018; Rosi et al. 2017). While much more work is needed, it does appear that a shift away from consumption of meat and towards organically produced food tends to substantially reduce impacts on both the environment and the well-being of other species.

83. Rapid progress is being made towards low-emissions modes of transportation in all modes but air travel, where it has been difficult to find a substitute for the high energy density of fossil fuels. This is troubling as the amount of air travel is projected to rise substantially (Hasan et al. 2021; Lai et al. 2022).

84. Geothermal, tidal, biomass, hydroelectric and nuclear power all generate energy with far fewer emissions than fossil fuels. Geothermal power makes important contributions in some parts of the world but is limited in geographic scope, as is tidal power. Expanding biomass requires either putting new land into agriculture or using land currently producing food, thus putting pressure on the food system. While hydroelectric power is expanding in many parts of the world, in those areas with a long history of hydro, there is a movement towards decommissioning dams to restore natural flows and growing concerns with how hydro facilities will operate under a shifting climate. And new hydro facilities often have substantial social and environmental impacts. The problem of the long-term (centuries to millennia) management of nuclear waste has not been resolved despite half a century of efforts to find an acceptable approach; every decade or so catastrophic accidents raise questions about claims of safety, and it does not appear that the economics of nuclear power make it a desirable investment. Fusion remains a distant possibility whose possible social and environmental impacts are only beginning to be studied (Banacloche et al. 2020; Lukacs and Williams 2020). Each of these

technologies undoubtedly has something to contribute to a transition to a climate-safe energy system. While things may change, at present wind, solar and efficiency seem to be the major components of that transition.

85. York and Bell (2019).

86. Jorgenson (2012); York (2012); York and McGee (2017).

87. In a careful analysis that shows the importance of unpacking trends, Greiner, York and McGee (2022) find that renewables tend to displace nuclear power but that recently the displacement has shifted towards displacing fossil fuels.

88. On bald eagles, see Slabe et al. (2022). On ozone depletion: World Meteorological Organization (2019). On protected areas: Maxwell et al. (2020).

89. A substantial, sophisticated and growing literature flowing from the STIRPAT approach is unpacking differences across countries and subnational units within countries in both environmental stress and human well-being and examining the political, economic and social structural factors shaping those dynamics (Alvarez, McGee and York 2019; Givens 2018; Huang and Jorgenson 2018; Jorgenson et al. 2019; Kelly, Thombs and Jorgenson 2021; Kick and McKinney 2014). A key finding is that inequality within and between nations is deleterious to sustainability; see Chapter 1, Note 35.

90. Chancellor Gorkon refers to the future as an undiscovered country, taking a liberty with Hamlet's reference to the afterlife as an undiscovered country (see *Star Trek VI: The Undiscovered Country*). But Gorkon says that he prefers Shakespeare in the "original" Klingon so perhaps that is the source of the difference in interpretation. It is interesting that the "undiscovered country" is not in the "bad Quarto" versions of the soliloquy. On backcasting, see Chapter 6 and J. B. Robinson (1988).

91. Dietz et al. (2009); Nielsen et al. (2020); Vandenbergh et al. (2011); Vandenbergh and Gilligan (2017). See also the discussion of TP, BP and IF in Chapter 8. In some discussions of these issues, we refer to mitigation potential rather than TP since that is common in the literature. We also sometimes refer to response plasticity rather than BP to emphasize that some of the most important targets for change are not individuals, as the term behavior might imply, but organizations; see Stern, Dietz and Vandenbergh (2022). While we have developed these ideas in the context of mitigating environmental stresses, the same logic could be applied to any policy domain – for example, gun safety or poverty reduction. As I have noted repeatedly, settling on common language for these concepts will facilitate cumulative understanding.

92. US National Research Council (2010d). Some of the resistance to carbon prices comes from an important argument that such prices might be inequitable, causing substantial hardship for low-income households (Carattini, Carvalho and Fankhauser 2018; Maestre-Andrés, Drews and van den Bergh 2019; Reed, O'Reilly and Hall 2019). Any policy that changes prices can have substantial equity impacts that need to be considered. There are policy designs that make increased energy prices neutral or even progressive with regard to income distribution but it is still unclear whether or not such efforts will increase IF (Klenert et al. 2018; Mildenberger et al. 2022). This may be because energy prices are a substantial and highly visible (highly available cognitively) part of most household budgets. I will return to these issues in Chapter 9.

93. Technological change based on advances in biotechnology, information technology and robotics and neurotechnology is likely to have huge influences at every level from individual decision-making to the global political economy. It is very difficult to predict those changes. Indeed, while we certainly need more interdisciplinary work on the traditional idea of sustainability (see Chapter 2), we desperately need more interdisciplinary work on the unfolding impacts and possibilities of these technological changes. Technological change is no more "natural" than the human impact on the biosphere; rather, it is an unfolding of decisions and both the intended and the unintended consequences of those decisions.

94. The examples of revolutionary transformation from the twentieth century are hard to summarize, and there are too many factors in play to allow any clear generalizations. The Russian and Chinese revolutions led to a great deal of violence and suppression. They also led to substantial economic growth and perhaps improved well-being for the average citizen – it is hard to balance the effects of repression and economic growth. Some revolutionary transformations, such as the decolonization in India and many other countries, produced substantial violence but perhaps less than other revolutions, and in some cases led to stable democracies while in other cases little political stability followed decolonization. But teasing out causality is difficult. Colonial and imperial regimes usually suppress a great deal of Indigenous knowledge, norms and practices making it hard to create a new social and political order. Armed revolutionary processes probably select for leaders who are particularly focused and willing to deploy violence for "the greater good." The trajectory of the Soviet Union and China was certainly influenced by great hostility from capitalist nations and by the bureaucratic politics of authoritarian regimes. While we may be able to learn from these important histories, any robust conclusions will require careful attention to counterfactuals and assessment of competing explanations. In the end, it may be that we simply do not have enough information (degrees of freedom in the language of statistics) to draw any robust conclusions from the most profound transformations in recent history.

# 8     Influencing Decisions

1. Dietz (2020b). Quotes are from Intergovernmental Panel on Climate Change (2018: 15) and Díaz et al. (2018).
2. Frank (2020); Silver (2015). In looking at change over time, it is important to differentiate the effects of time periods, cohorts (generations) and age. For example, a change in values, beliefs and norms might come about because while older cohorts don't change they are gradually replaced by younger cohorts – this is the model of scientific change via funerals noted in Chapter 4, Note 20. Lagos (2022) shows that although there are nuanced complexities identification as transgender began increasing with cohorts born after 1984. It appears that change in at least some views on gender-nonconforming people in the United States has happened in all cohorts (Twenge and Blake 2021). As I write in 2022, there is concern with a growing pushback against gay and especially trans rights. Important work is examining support for these rights, including the effects of general beliefs and of biased assimilation, homophily and polarization (BAHP) (Bishin, Freebourn and Teten 2021; Bowers and Whitley 2018, 2020; Lewis et al. 2022). Change in environmental concern is complex, with little change over time or across cohorts for conservatives but substantial cohort differences for others (Pampel and Hunter 2012).
3. Clark and Harley (2020: 333). On pandemic impacts: Sumner, Hoy and Ortiz-Juarez (2020). On income inequality: Alvaredo et al. (2018); Piketty (2020); and Figure 2.1.
4. Comprehensive reviews focused on individual action include the important book by Gardner and Stern (2002) and review papers that try to engage the broad literature, especially around energy consumption; for example, Dietz (2015b); Klöckner (2013); Nielsen et al. (2020); Steg and de Groot (2012); Steg (2016); Steg, Bolderdijk et al. (2014); Steg, Shwom and Dietz (2018); Stern (2002, 2008, 2011b, 2014); Stern and Wolske (2017); Wolske and Stern (2018). There are also a number of meta-analyses that cover important portions of the literature in ways useful for thinking about influencing decision: Abrahamse and Steg (2013); Brons et al. (2008); Espey and Espey (2004); Hawcroft and Milfont (2010); Stern et al. (2016). One problem with several of these is a tendency to view the literature as a battle of the bands rather than as a symphony; see the discussion of the theory of

planned behavior in Chapter 3. For example, some analyses dismiss the importance of values because the effects of values are reduced (mediated to use the technical term) when other variables are controlled. But too often these analyses don't look at the total (indirect plus direct) effect of values. When one controls for norms, values might have little net effect. But values may have a substantial effect on norms and thus a substantial effect acting through norms, an indirect effect. For most purposes, we would want to know the total effect. Many reviews and summary statements also do not differentiate short- versus long-term change. For household energy efficiency, where the most important changes come with weatherization and replacement of appliances, the long term is very important. But it is harder to study. Finally, there has been a tendency in the social psychological literature to focus on behaviors that are easy to study rather than those that are most consequential and a lack of integration across studies that examine behavior in the role of consumer and that in other roles, including that of citizen.

5. See Chapter 7, Notes 47 and 91. Price elasticity is the economic approach to behavioral plasticity – it is the percent change in consumption that occurs in response to a 1 percent change in prices. There is an immense body of scholarship on the price elasticity of demand for energy: Brons et al. (2008); Espey and Espey (2004); Goodwin, Dargay and Hanly (2004); Stern (2010). As discussed in Chapter 3, microeconomics provides assessment of what influences decision-making if the rational actor model is accurate, and in particular if consumers know their preferences. Social psychological theories give us a better sense of what those preferences are and what influences them, while the heuristics and biases literature shows how actual decisions often deviate from what is expected under the rational actor model. Because I want to consider more than is usually incorporated into rational actor models, I use the term "behavioral plasticity" rather than "elasticity."

6. Michael Vandenbergh, personal communication, November 12, 2021. The "social costs of carbon" is a monetary estimate of how much damage can be expected from climate change translated back into the costs of emitting greenhouse gases (National Academies of Sciences, Engineering, and Medicine 2017b; Neumann et al. 2020). The number matters because it not only gives a general sense of how much harm will come from climate change but also can be used to determine how stringent policies should be, and in particular how big a tax should be put on fossil fuels to discourage their use; see Voosen (2021). The Obama administration estimated the cost of damages from the release of a ton of greenhouse gas emissions at $53. In a survey of economists, more than 60 percent thought this figure was too low (Peter and Derek 2015). The Trump administration set the cost at $1–$7, in part by only including damages within the United States and by sharply discounting future impacts (Plumer 2018). The Biden administration estimates the cost at $51 (Chemnick 2021). A carbon tax of $50 a ton would increase gasoline prices in the United States by a bit more than $0.40 per gallon. For comparison, gas prices have fluctuated by $2–$4 dollars a gallon over the last two decades as oil prices shifted.

7. Trying to pursue both strategies does split resources across the two approaches, and Chapter 7 discusses the argument that promoting reform blocks transformation. To repeat, while there is a logic to a "transformation only" argument, the empirical evidence is mixed and outcomes seem to depend on context. Pursuing only one strategy is like an investor placing all their resources in one form of asset, which is not an effective way to deal with risk. It seems to reflect a level of self-assurance in one's analysis that I find problematic.

8. Heberlein (2012). As noted in Chapter 3, he laid the groundwork for coherent work on the social psychology of the environment that initiated thinking about altruism that is a foundation for VBN theory. In a too rare collaboration between economists and sociologists, he also did foundational studies in methods for assessing the value of things for which there is no market price, an issue I have noted repeatedly around economic policy analysis (Bishop and Heberlein 1979; Bishop, Heberlein and Kealy 1983; Heberlein and Bishop 1986; Heberlein et al. 2005). He also did important work (much of it unpublished but influential at the time) using experiments to influence household energy

consumption (Heberlein and Warriner 1983) and did some of the first systematic analyses of public participation processes (Gundry and Heberlein 1984; Heberlein 1976).

9. Some environmental social scientists feel that we should avoid such rooms because the views coming from environmental social science will have to be explained to scholars from other disciplines. Indeed, some seem to feel that they should participate only if their discipline dominates. (In my experience, scholars who are dismissive of other disciplines often lack much understanding of the disciplines being dismissed.) I believe environmental social science has evidence and arguments that can be persuasive and that by engaging with other disciplines we learn a great deal. It is true that thirty years ago I once or twice had the experience of having those from other disciplines objecting to the presence of an environmental social scientist (me) at the table for high-level discussions. But those days seem to have passed, to the point that when the US National Academies briefed the president's Science Advisor and the White House Office of Science and Technology on the *Advancing the Science of Climate Change* study, an environmental social scientist led the briefing on the science of climate change (US National Research Council 2010a).

10. The energy crisis of the 1970s was an important part of a major shift in environmental politics in the United States (Dietz 2020b). It was also crucial in shaping an energy social science that remains robust and is the basis for much of the social science work on climate change (Rosa, Machlis and Keating 1988). The embargo shows how sustainability is entangled with other issues – a key motivation for the embargo was the oil-importing nations' support for Israel in the war with Egypt and Syria.

11. Paul Stern and Heberlein's student Stan Black were at Yale. Craig Harris, Willett Kempton and Bonnie Morrison at Michigan State. The Davis group included Jim Cramer, Paul Craig, Ed Vine, Bruce Hackett and me; the energy sociologist Loren Lutzenhiser continued this work under Bruce's guidance but after the formal group had broken up for lack of funding during the Reagan administration.

12. Chen, Dietz et al. (2022).

13. Some organizations such as the American Council for an Energy Efficient Economy (ACEEE) (aceee.org) and the Energy Modeling Forum (emf.stanford.edu/) and leaders such as Art Rosenfeld and Ed Vine at Lawrence Berkeley Lab and Jim Sweeney and John Weyant at Stanford, inter alia, kept the field alive and moving forward. The ACEEE is vibrant, the annual Behavior, Energy and Climate Change meetings bring together practitioners and researchers from across many disciplines and the journal *Energy Research and Social Science* is filled with excellent studies in the tradition of the early household energy groups.

14. Steg, Shwom and Dietz (2018).

15. Lunde (2018); Nyamnjoh (2018). While I appreciate the fine acting, writing and directing in *Mad Men*, my overall take on the series is that the moral ambiguity and narcissism of most of the characters might be seen as a comment on how the creators view the ad industry. The "Mad Men" are essentially unreflective of the ethics or social value of what they do save for the episode "Blowing Smoke" that raises issues about the ethics of promoting cigarette smoking, and even then, ethical issues are raised after the firm loses the tobacco account. Such small exceptions highlight the overall absence of ethical considerations. I find the contrast with the roughly contemporary *Breaking Bad* telling. *Breaking Bad* is primarily about ethical (or unethical choices) choices. See Chapter 3, Note 21 on Walter White as a self-interested rational actor.

16. The information deficit model is still very common. The committee that wrote a National Academies report on the science of science communication felt the information deficit model was still sufficiently influential that it went to some length to point out the problems with this default model of obstacles to science communication (National Academies of Sciences, Engineering, and Medicine 2016).

17. Often terms like "attitudes" and "values" are invoked without any real understanding of what is meant by social scientists who use those terms analytically. "Attitudes" and "values" in many of these

conversations are just placeholders for elements of Henry's "cognitive soup" – the terms are used without any specificity or clarity (Henry and Dietz 2012). Social scientists must share some responsibility for this imprecision in that we don't have a standard covering term for the factors that may influence sustainability decision-making, what Henry and I have called environmental cognition; see Chapter 2, Note 137.

18. The work of Kempton and colleagues also identified problems in consumer understanding of energy systems (Kempton and Montgomery 1982; Kempton 1986; Kempton et al. 1985). As discussed in Chapter 3 around the work of Attari and colleagues, the problem of inadequate understanding is not limited to energy consumption; it applies to water and probably to other kinds of household decisions and undoubtedly to organizational decisions as well, and affects experts as well as consumers.

19. Marghetis, Attari and Landy (2019); Taufique et al. (2022). A great deal of effort is going into "smart metering" of electricity to provide detailed information on consumption, although those programs are usually linked to other kinds of feedback to householders, such as time of day pricing that favors shifting electricity use to times of day when demand is low. The overall effects are likely complex and the subject of ongoing research around the developed world (Carroll, Lyons and Denny 2014; McCoy and Lyons 2016).

20. On food deserts, see Satcher (2021). As I write, it appears that the best range on a single charge for a vehicle costing less than $100,000 is 358 miles, the $55,000 Model 3 Tesla. By the time you read this, the top mileage will have increased and the cost of a high-mileage vehicle will have decreased. There are a number of vehicles that can go more than 200 miles on a charge and cost less than $40,000. The Inflation Recovery Act of 2022 intends to provide a national grid of charging stations that will make long distance travel with electric vehicles easier.

21. Jansson (2011); Jansson, Marell and Nordlund (2010); Lane and Potter (2007). These differences in perspective can occur within a family, a topic that has not been sufficiently studied. A large body of research demonstrates gender differences in environmentalism but far less explores the implications for sustainability decisions of those differences and what is typically a gendered division of decision-making within the household (Grønhøj and Ölander 2007). There is also evidence of generational differences in perspectives on the environment and sustainability that may influence household dynamics (Grønhøj and Thøgersen 2011). In general, more work on the internal dynamics of household decision-making in the developed world is badly needed to expand on the bulk of studies who take one member of a household as "representative" (Kleinschafer and Morrison 2014; Scott, Oates and Young 2015).

22. Abrahamse and Steg (2013); Noll, Dawes and Rai (2014); Rai and Henry (2016); Rai and Robinson (2013).

23. Abrahamse and Steg (2013); Allcott (2011); Nolan et al. (2008); Staats, Harland and Wilke (2004). An intriguing study of views about vaccination presented on Facebook pages shows that those opposed to vaccination have extensive connections to those who are neutral and to those who may engage in discussions about vaccinations, for example school board Facebook pages (Johnson et al. 2020). In contrast, the pages advocating the science of vaccinations are isolated from the "undecideds" and thus unlikely to have much influence on them.

24. For the rational actor model, most policies are seen as changes in incentives (or disincentives). Fines, prison sentences and public shaming are all forms of disincentives. Even providing information can be seen as lowering the costs of getting the information and thus changing incentives facing decision makers. But most policy proposals grounded in the rational actor model emphasize prices, probably because of the belief in ease of implementation discussed next.

25. In rational actor model theory, the increased costs of energy will shift my budget constraint by making goods and services with a high energy content more expensive, so the bundle of goods and services that is tangent to the indifference curve with highest utility will have less energy in it than if energy prices were lower, *ceteris paribus*.

26. Ostrom's point that there is no pure market-based policy is important. Details of even market-based policies depend on a structure of government regulation and the details of those regulations matter to powerful actors. Keefe (2017) documents the strenuous efforts of the billionaire Carl Icahn to change the federal rules regarding a detail of the mechanism, essentially a cap-and-trade system, to ensure a minimum ethanol content in gasoline. Details about who in the gasoline supply chain was responsible for having the permits were worth hundreds of millions of dollars to Icahn. On influences in shaping regulations, see Busch (2011); Shwom (2011).

27. For example, Garnett et al. (2021) found that changing prices had only a modest effect on student purchases of meat versus vegetarian meal options. In a review of more than 100 studies, Zhu et al. (2018) conclude that residential electricity demand has almost no price elasticity in the short run and that elasticity in the long run depends on context. See Chapter 8, Note 5 for further discussion of price elasticity.

28. Stern et al. (1986). On program design, see Carrico et al. (2011); Dietz et al. (2009); Stern et al. (2010); Vandenbergh et al. (2011); and the discussion of nudges in Chapters 3 and 8.

29. Asenio and Delmas (2015); Dietz (2015c). In a much-cited study, Gneezy and Rustichini (2000) found that imposing a fine for parents who came late to pick up their children at a day care center increased rather than decreased that behavior, probably by shifting the social construction of what it meant to be late. A fee may have been redefined as a service that could be purchased rather than a violation of a social norm. Parents shifted roles from that of a member of the community of day care users with mutual responsibilities to that of a consumer with an ability to spend money to compensate for violating a rule. Other studies find that an appeal to economic self-interest may have less impact than appeals to altruism (Bolderdijk et al. 2013; Sloot, Jans and Steg 2019).

30. Nielsen, Nicholas et al. (2021); Otto et al. (2019).

31. Chen, Dietz et al. (2022); Chen, Grieg et al. (2022); Chen, Xu and Day (2017); Chen, Xu et al. (2022); Xu and Chen (2019). On benefit-risk calculations in financially stressed groups, see Chapter 1, Note 46 and Chapter 3, Note 100. Often the neighborhoods in which these households are located suffer from the effects of historic redlining, making access to programs and services more difficult.

32. Maestre-Andrés, Drews and van den Bergh (2019). Some of the resistance in the United States and in France – the giletes juanes ("yellow vests") protests – are from workers and consumers opposed to higher prices (Carattini, Kallbekken and Orlov 2019; Falcao 2019). Carbon taxes could be designed to compensate for those costs. But other opposition comes from powerful individuals and organizations who profit from fossil fuels. Strategies to overcome their resistance need to be analyzed as well.

33. Galli Robertson and Collins (2019); Kennedy, Krahn and Krogman (2014); Nielsen, Nicholas et al. (2021); Dietz (2020a); Frank (2010, 2020).

34. See the discussion of the possible link between segregation and giving parents "school choice" as a market-based approach to education in Chapter 5, Note 25 and the discussion in Chapter 2 of the problems that flowed from many neoliberal strategies to reform the political economy of developing countries.

35. McCright, Charters et al. (2016). We found that an experimental stimulus that had a substantial effect for an issue like the health effects of the chemical BPA (bisphenol A) had little effect when used with climate change. We suspect that this is because the debates about climate change have become so prevalent that most members of the public have formed views that are very hard to change. The framings and counter-framings are "locked in" for many people in the United States.

36. Effective leaders of civil rights movements offer persuasive theories of why nonviolent change is effective as well as transformational examples of its impacts (King 1963; Sharp 1973, 2012). We need research to refine their insights and experience and learn how to generalize across contexts. Such research was underway as early as the 1960s; see Chapter 9.

37. Alfoqahaa and Jones (2020); Orazani and Leidner (2019); Selvanathan and Jetten (2020). Many of those whose actions are the target of even nonviolent activists may feel threatened. But others will not be. In a violent confrontation, the violence itself becomes the focus for many in assessing the situation. I suspect nonviolence leaves open the possibility of empathy towards taking action while violence precludes it.

38. Cuff et al. (2016); Hall and Schwartz (2019); Young, Khalil and Wharton (2018).

39. Dietz (2020a); Frank (2020).

40. Taufique et al. (2022); Vandenbergh, Dietz and Stern (2011). I emphasize again that much of the benefit from sustainability labeling will likely come from changing corporate behavior, not just consumer behavior.

41. Ajzen (1991, 1985); De Groot and Steg (2007).

42. Given the tendency to highlight what is new without understanding the origins of the supposedly new ideas, a lot of attention has been given to nudges as something inspired by behavioral economics; see Chapter 3, especially Note 91. In behavioral economics, there may be a tendency to view the cognitive heuristics and biases we use to make decisions as "mistakes" that are preventing our inner rational actor from guiding us, what Infante, Lecouteux and Sugden (2016) argue is a dualistic model. The idea of nudge is a popularization of two related points long prevalent in the literature on decision-making and how to influence it. The first is that, because of the cognitive shortcuts we use for many decisions, we are subject to manipulations. The second is that how we actually make decisions should be a prominent aspect of the design of programs and policies so as to make it as easy as possible for people to understand their options and the implications of those options and implement the decision they make. In some cases, what is described as a nudge is simply substituting a well-designed modality for a poorly designed one. For example, in one prominent study the nudge to encourage people to appear in court is primarily a redesign of communications materials to make them more effective (Fishbane, Ouss and Shah 2020). This seems a normal part of honing policies and practices to make them more user-friendly. It appears that the original communications and forms were designed with little thought to the needs of those who would have to understand and respond to them. Given inequities and racism in the US criminal justice system, while such changes seem useful, there are much larger issues that warrant attention, issues that almost certainly would have emerged if interested and affected parties were engaged in the design of the nudge policies, as I suggest below (Kohler-Hausmann 2020).

43. Marteau and colleagues offer a useful typology of the kinds of nudge interventions that have been used to influence some health-related behaviors in the hopes of encouraging a more cumulative literature (Hollands et al. 2017; Marteau et al. 2021). They have proposed ways of developing interventions for sustainability issues that could be implemented at a large enough scale to have significant impacts.

44. I use the term "choice architecture" since it seems to be stuck in the literature. But "choice engineering" would be a better choice. The term is trying to describe a situation in which people use scientific information to design a practical solution to a problem. That is what engineers do. Architects often have a strong, even dominant, intent to build a work of art, and it is common to hear architects dismiss concerns with how the building is used once constructed. This is not what we want of those who are designing policies, programs and campaigns. I suspect the term "architecture" was chosen over "engineering" because there would be more resistance to choice engineering. But perhaps that resistance is appropriate.

45. Design principles have to be adapted to the context in which a program or policy will have impact. Ostrom proposed diagnostic questions to understand the context and guide the use of design principles to suggest ways of taking effect action that are sensitive to context (Dietz, Ostrom and Stern 2003; Ostrom 2007, 2009a, 2010b, 2010c; Pottete, Janssen and Ostrom 2010; Stern, Dietz and Ostrom 2002).

These diagnostic questions and design principles are ways to deploy scientific analysis, and as I argued in Chapter 4, often require input from many forms of expertise, not just science. Ostrom's strategy for creating useful generalizations from complex and context-sensitive science inspired the approach we have used in looking at energy consumption and greenhouse gas emissions mitigation. For recent work on design principles, see Stern, Wolske and Dietz (2021); Wolske, Stern and Dietz (2020). See also International Expert Panel on Behavioral Science for Design (2019). Archetype analysis is coherent with the design principles perspective, including the point that generalizations like design principles must be coupled with context-specific knowledge. See Oberlack et al. (2019).

46. Carrico et al. (2011); Stern (2011a); Stern et al. (2010); Vandenbergh, Dietz and Stern (2011); Vandenbergh et al. (2010), (2011).

47. Lenski, Keoleian and Bolon (2012); Tyrrell and Dernbach (2010). The Vermont Electric Co-op has a very well-designed program to encourage efficiency upgrades and the purchase of solar panels (https://vermontelectric.coop/), as do many other co-ops, government agencies and private corporations.

48. Cialdini focuses on this issue, and the nudge arguments of Thaler and Sunstein and especially Sunstein's more recent work engages it; see Cialdini ([1984] 2007); Dietz (2011); Sunstein (2014); Sunstein and Reisch (2019); Thaler and Sunstein (2009).

49. One might argue that all policy is about decisions. When Michigan State University's School of Criminal Justice decided to partner with the Environmental Science and Policy Program to hire a decision scientist, Ed McGarrel, the very insightful director of the School, said: "We need someone who knows decision science. A lot of our profession deals with people making bad decisions."

# 9    Influencing the Conversation

1. Grand Isle Select Board (2017).

2. Adua and Labao (2021) offer an insightful analysis of how the politics of land use regulation and growth promotion play out in the United States, drawing on the growth machine arguments noted in Chapters 2 and 7. My experienced in Grand Isle differs a bit in that in so small a community growth policy is almost exclusively land use policy.

3. Fukuyama and Graeber and Rengrow document the mechanisms of legitimating decision-making across a broad swath of history (Fukuyama 2011, 2014; Graeber and Wengrow 2021). As I write, some less democratic regimes are quick to point to trouble in democracies, arguing that democracies lack stability and are less than ideal. And within many democracies, there are those who seem to prefer "strong man" (*sic*) authoritarianism over traditional democracy. But despite some dissent I believe that most people would prefer to live in a democracy than in any of the current alternatives. See Chapter 2.

4. A common way to express this is that everyone should "have a say," a conversational metaphor.

5. Weber ([1949] 2017) deployed the idea of an ideal type as an abstraction (a "mental image") based on observation of many individual instances. He and social scientists since have found this a useful tool for linking observation and theory. Like all prolific thinkers, his views evolved over time. Rosenberg provides a useful assessment of the approach (Rosenberg 2016).

6. Elinor Ostrom's work was strongly influenced by her husband Vincent, who was a very important theorist of how constitutional arrangements influence the evolution of institutions. While I worked with Lin and only met Vincent a few times, I see their work as a joint theoretical school with a strong evolutionary trope (Dietz 2005). Vincent was an important influence on the way the Constitution of Alaska defines natural resources as a public trust.

7. The limit of this logic is evident in managing commons: individuals acting from narrow self-interest will have trouble preventing the collapse of a commons. The usual libertarian solution is one of the options offered by Hardin and frequently advocated in policy circles (see discussion in Chapter 5): make the resource private property. The problems that come from narrow self-interest action have certainly been evident in the COVID-19 pandemic. But it appears in the early stages of the pandemic in many places that altruistic personal norms overcame narrow self-interest in shaping decisions (Bouman and Steg 2021). How this changed deserves careful analysis.

8. See Box 5.4 for a discussion of the problems in aggregating utilities.

9. Bentham (1823: chap. 4; Frey (2011).

10. Kling, Phaneuf and Zhao (2012); Rietbergen-McCracken and Abaza (2013); US National Research Council (1999b). On bald eagles: Amuakwa-Mensah, Bärenbold and Riemer (2018). One interesting approach is to use a deliberative process, rather than isolated individuals' responses, to develop a price for changes in the state of the environment; see Bartkowski and Lienhoop (2018, 2019); Bunse, Rendon and Luque (2015); Dietz, Stern and Dan (2009); Howarth and Wilson (2006); Kenter et al. (2016); Kentor (2016); Lienhoop, Bartkowski and Hansjürgens (2015); Lliso et al. (2020); Lo (2013); Lo and Spash (2013); Raymond et al. (2014); Spash (2007); Vargas et al. (2016); Wilson and Howarth (2002); Witt (2019). These efforts attempt to combine the arguments that humans do well at deliberation rather than abstract calculation with the power of having a quantitative metric that allows assessment of trade-offs. My view is that economic analyses of the sort routinely conducted by deploying utilitarian logic to policy analysis can be a very useful input to deliberative processes of the sort discussed in Section 9.3 but must also be guided by such practices to avoid the problems in generalizing in the face of uncertainty discussed in Chapter 4.

11. Economics gives a great deal of attention to market imperfections; many Nobel Prizes have been awarded for working on the issue. See Stiglitz (2019) for a critical view that respects conventional economics. But neoliberal and libertarian policy analysis tends to brush the issues aside as, in the end, not consequential. And those who benefit from current economic institutions deploy their resources to promote exactly those analyses that support the institutions that give them power.

12. See also Chapters 3 and 5 on the arguments for the benefits of markets.

13. Chen, Dietz et al. (2022); Monroe (2022), Nieto del Rio, Bogel-Burroughs and Penn (2021).

14. See Chapter 1. Remember that my discussion of political processes is very US-centric and so much of what I say may not apply to other democratic traditions. Even in the tumult of the 2020 US election, there were relatively few who argued that elections were not the proper way to make decisions; rather, the extreme claims accepted the legitimacy of the idea of elections but disputed the fairness of the 2020 process. Support for electoral processes is not universal. Some elements of the US Constitution, such as the electoral college, were intended to allow elites to moderate the outcomes of popular voting. See also Chapter 9, Note 3 and Chapter 2.

15. On Indigenous systems, see Graeber and Wengrow (2021). In the traditional town meeting, votes are taken after open discussion by all citizens who show up for town meeting on the first Tuesday in March. In my town, the town budget is very detailed, and each line item, down to a few hundred dollars for membership in regional associations, is subject to a yes or no vote. However, in most towns, including mine, because of problems of scale and participation, town meeting is now a place for town and school officials to present the budget and other issues, and for all who show up to engage in discussion of them at some length. The vote is then taken by Australian ballot (i.e., by secret ballot of the sort typical in US elections) the next day. About one-third of Vermont towns use floor votes at town meeting rather than Australian ballots for decision-making, while about half use both (Bryan 2010; Zimmerman 1999).

16. I continue to be surprised at how little scholarship examines issues of scale and democracy even though the issue was raised as early as the seventeenth century by Hobbes; see Chapter 5, Note 64; but see Dahl and Tufte (1973); Dietz (1996–97); Frey and Al-Mansour (1995); Frey et al. (1999).

17. At that point, the plan was for the size of the House to increase with the overall population. If we had kept to one representative per 35,000 people, then the current House would have about 8,800 members, based on the most recent Census at the time I am writing. Initially, only property-owning white males, perhaps a third of the adult population, could vote. (Historians continue to work on understanding who was enfranchised and who was not, as each state had different, and changing, rules; see Ratcliffe 2013). In the original US Constitution, those in bondage, who had no ability to vote, were counted as 60 percent of a person for the purposes of allocating House seats (Article I, Section 2, Clause 3). There were just under 700,000 in bondage in 1790 out of a population of 3.9 million ("Statistics on Slavery," https://faculty.weber.edu/kmackay/statistics_on_slavery.htm; accessed November 26, 2022). So, about 13 percent of the House seats were allocated based on them. Native Americans were counted only if they were taxed. They could not vote. Women were counted in the population but could not vote. In a remnant of these older manifestations of discrimination, the 700,000 citizens of the District of Columbia, 64 percent of whom are nonwhite, have only a nonvoting "delegate" in the US House and no representation in the Senate. So, while there are certainly some things to admire about the ideas that were foundational to US democracy, there are also very troubling elements of racism, sexism, ableism and class bias. The distinction between the views of Franklin and Washington on these matters gives some insight into the conflicts involved in forming the country (Larson 2020).

18. On affluence and political power, see Dietz and Whitley (2018). On donations and the costs of elections, see "Cost of Election," Open Secrets, www.opensecrets.org/elections-overview/cost-of-election (accessed February 15, 2022).

19. I originally read this in the Mills and Gerth volume (Mills and Gerth 1958: 77–127) but have benefited from the new translation by Waters and Waters (Weber [1919] 2015).

20. In our 1984 study of the US risk policy system, we found that only about 41 percent of the risk professionals were employed by federal, state or local government, including the executive, legislative and judicial branches (Dietz and Rycroft 1987: table 2).

21. Many people are happy to take long odds if the outcomes are important. For voters in some states, the chances of a single vote determining a presidential election are as high as 1 in 10 million (Gelman, Silver and Edlin 2012). For the average American, the odds that their vote will determine the election are 1 in 60 million. For comparison, the odds of winning the Powerball lottery are about 1 in 185 million. While the number of Powerball tickets sold increases with the size of the jackpot, typically at least 200 million tickets are sold. Many people buy multiple tickets while other people pool their money in buying tickets, so it is not clear how many individuals are playing. By contrast, recent presidential elections have turned out roughly 130–160 million voters out of about 240 million potential voters; in the 2020 presidential election, the turnout was a record high of 67 percent of those eligible (Fabina 2021). So, while the odds for having a decisive influence via voting appear to be larger than those of winning Powerball, relatively few people vote. Of course, this analysis is oversimplified. One usually votes for multiple candidates and often ballot propositions, not just for president, and since those elections are at the state and local level, the chances of having a deciding influence are larger. At the same time, Powerball and other lotteries have multiple payoffs, which makes the odds and return on ticket purchase more complex.

22. Because of the small scale of democracy in Vermont, it is not hard to be in a small group meeting with your US senators or member of the House, and interactions with members of the state legislature are quite common. I suspect this ease of interaction tends to keep Vermont politics fairly civil. If you care about an issue, you can discuss it with the person who represents you, and in the case of state legislators, it is common to have them only a step or two distant in your social network.

23. Even if we could, it is hard to evaluate the implications of policies for what we value. How will a treaty opening up relatively unrestricted ("free") trade with a bloc of other nations affect me? Jobs might be

offshored, prices of some consumer goods may decline, some industries will prosper and some will decline, the balance of trade and exchange rates may shift resulting in ripples through the economy, and so on. Again, the decision process for the individual is very complex and fraught with uncertainty. Indeed, it has been recognized at least since Stolper and Samuelson's (1941) analysis eighty years ago that, while the average impact of free trade may be beneficial, the effects vary vastly across contexts, in this case, nations, regions, communities, industries and individuals. I am again surprised at how little attention is given by advocates of "free trade" to mechanisms for compensating those who suffer real costs and risks under such policies. Stolper and Samuelson called for just such compensation: "or if effects on the terms of trade can be disregarded, it has been shown that the harm which free trade inflicts upon one factor of production is necessarily less than the gain to the other. Hence, it is always possible to bribe the suffering factor by subsidy or other redistributive devices so as to leave all factors better off as a result of trade" (p. 73). A recent analysis suggests that current patterns of trade helped developed countries and hindered developing countries in achieving the UN Sustainable Development Goals (Xu, Li et al. 2020).

24. On biased assimilation, homophily and polarization (BAHP), see Lupia (2015). And when politicians deviate from the party line, it is hard for voters to monitor their actual behavior, and there is some evidence that strong partisans among the electorate may be more misinformed than others (Dancey and Sheagley 2013).

25. McGann et al. (2016) and Keena et al. (2021) provide reviews. Cho and Cain (2020) suggest ways in which artificial intelligence could help to create districts that better reflect democratic values. King and Browning (2017) have offered a thoughtful op-ed piece on how we might more reasonably draw district boundaries. Engstrom (2014) demonstrated that the problem is not a new one. Efforts are underway in many states to make redistricting a bipartisan process to avoid gerrymandering. For example, as a result of a ballot initiative, in Michigan redistricting now will be done by an independent commission chosen at random from volunteers. No one holding elected office, or their families or their employees, is eligible to serve. As I write, fierce battles over redistricting under the new population estimates from the 2020 Census are underway.

26. See Chapter 9, Note 17.

27. For sociological perspectives, see the special issue of *Sociological Quarterly* on voting behavior (Vol. 55, No. 4, 2014). For many decades, a substantial fraction of political scientists have pursued voting behavior as a key research topic, so the literature is immense. I have found a few relatively recent reviews helpful: Dewan and Shepsle (2011); Fiorina and Abrams (2008); Jacobson and Carson (2015); Lupia (2015); Prior (2013). One of the first social science texts I read was Marty Lipset's (1963) *Political Man*, an important treatise in the field. Years later, Marty would be a colleague at George Mason University.

28. Abrams et al. (2020); Anderson (2018); Epperly et al. (2020); Hajnal, Lajevardi and Nielson (2017); Montoya (2020).

29. Anderson (2017); Bail (2021); Boykoff (2020); Gentzkow (2017); O'Neill and Boykoff (2012); O'Neill et al. (2015); Pearce et al. (2019). On the least active: Boxell, Gentzkow and Shapiro (2017). On traditional media and new media: Gentzkow (2017); King, Schneer and White (2017). On science communication online: Brossard and Scheufele (2022); and the special section in *Science*, March 25, 2022.

30. LeDuc (2020).

31. For example, in Michigan the state legislature used a loophole that forbids ballot initiatives from modifying legislation that includes a budget to block two initiatives that would have prevented the hunting of wolves.

32. While the typical claim is that Athens was the first democracy, history is rarely simple. There is evidence that Gilgamesh in ancient Sumer shared authority with a council, and some form of

democratic influence probably existed in the earliest city-states in India. Many societies that have not been included in the standard Western narrative had egalitarian methods of making decisions (Graeber and Wengrow 2021).

33. Busch (2011); Shwom (2011).

34. Haskell (2018). Arguments about individual rights and in particular about states' rights have long been used to protect discrimination.

35. Benoit, Hansen and Verser (2003); Cho and Ha (2012); Druckman and Lupia (2016).

36. Abayomi, Gelman and Srebotnjak (2002); Bennett (2013); Himmelweit et al. (2013); Nevena and Giulia (2015). During the 1970s, my major professor, Jim Cramer, was doing innovative work on how childbirth influenced the division of labor within the household (Cramer 1979, 1980). Since then I have been attentive to the division of labor within the household and intra-household conflicts in decision-making. Perhaps half of all households in the WEIRD nations include nonhumans as part of the social dynamic (Irvine and Cilia 2017). Amy Fitzgerald has done pathbreaking work showing how ignoring the importance of companion animals can have dire consequences when abusive situations occur (Fitzgerald 2005; Fitzgerald et al. 2019; Fitzgerald et al. 2020). See also Irvine (2008).

37. The phrase "the personal is political" was a rallying cry in the emerging discourse of the women's/feminist movement in the late 1960s (Hanisch 1969). See the discussion of counterpublics in the Introduction.

38. US National Research Council (1996; 1999a, 2008, 2010a, 2013). (Note that studies are in the voice of the US National Academy of Sciences but cited as by the US National Research Council.) It is also sometimes called "co-production" (Voorberg, Bekkers and Tummers 2015). The public in these discussions is defined as Dewey did: those interested in and/or affected by the decision (Dewey 1923).

39. Dietz (2013c).

40. US National Research Council (2008). See the discussion in Chapter 5.

41. US National Research Council (2008: 226). See also Chapter 5.

42. See Introduction, Note 63 on the origins of the study.

43. On existential threats, see Gunderson (2016); Gunderson and Dietz (2018); Payne, Shwom and Heaton (2015). On global deliberation in general: Downey (2015); Gould (2014).

44. See Box 5.6.

45. Dyball, Brown and Keen (2007); Henry (2009, 2020).

46. Curato, et al. (2021); O'Grady (2020). The approach is closely related to deliberative polling in which there is discussion before responding to a survey (Fishkin 2021; Fishkin and Luskin 2005). The literature is evolving very rapidly, including frequent papers in the *Journal of Deliberative Democracy*.

47. Dietz (2013c); Harding (2015); Vollan and Henry (2019).

48. Afsahi (2017, 2020, 2021); Barvosa (2018); Karpowitz and Raphael (2016). On Indigenous traditions, see Ani (2018); Ani (2013, 2014); Hébert (2018).

49. See Chapter 5. Council of Canadian Academies (2019).

50. Chess, Dietz and Shannon (1998).

51. Della Porta (2020a, 2020b); Majewska (2021).

52. Bidwell (2016); Bidwell, Dietz and Scavia (2013); Dilling et al. (2019).

53. Chenoweth, Hendrix and Hunter (2019); Chenoweth and Stephan (2011). See also the US Institute of Peace's Nonviolent Action issue areas: www.usip.org/issue-areas/nonviolent-action. On social innovations: Pel et al. (2020); Rudel (2019a, 2019b); see also the Seeds of Good Anthropocenes website: https://goodanthropocenes.net/.

54. Majewska reviews the debate about whether to call these trends fascism or to differentiate them from previous forms by calling them neo-fascism (Majewska 2021). We can learn a great deal, and be cautioned by, historical examples, but we should not overgeneralize as every evolving governance form has unique features.

55. Haltinner and Sarathchandra (2022).

56. On the proportion polarized, see Krupnikov and Ryan (2022). The civil rights and other movements have dealt with fierce opposition and BAHP; see Chapter 8, Note 36. A substantial but not well-integrated literature shows that deliberative processes and simply conversation can overcome the "lock in" that comes from BAHP (Caluwaerts et al. 2021; Fishkin et al. 2021). Integration, synthesis and more studies in "real-world" field settings are badly needed. On rapid shifts in public views, see Eisenstein, Clark and Jelen (2017); Gorodzeisky and Semyonov (2018); Schwadel and Garneau (2017).

57. If this conjecture is correct, it implies that deliberative processes have to be structured in ways that hinder the ability of the self-interested to manipulate the process to their own advantage. The concept of the free rider is central to the commons and game theory literature and may provide useful insights for process design. An important study by Bidwell and Schweizer (2021) shows that altruism and self-interest influence what goals members of the US public favor for deliberative processes.

58. Coleman (2021b).

59. Coleman (2021a, 2021b); Ripley (2021).

60. Bago, Rand and Pennycook (2020); Druckman (2004); Druckman and Nelson (2003); Dryzek et al. (2019); Fishkin (2018); Gastil (2018); Harrison and Michelson (2017); Himmelroos and Christensen (2020); Leeper and Slothuus (2018); Neblo, Esterling and Lazer (2018).

61. See Chapter 2, Note 33.

62. Fryer-Biggs (2019, 2021); Walker-Munro (2022).

63. Frisch et al. (2022); Goodwin et al. (2022); Stowman, Cacciatore et al. (2022); Stowman, Frisch et al. (2022).

64. Bak-Coleman et al. (2021).

65. Rudel (2019b). On failures: Butzer and Endfield (2012); Costanza, Graumlich and Steffen (2007); Diamond (2005).

# References

Abayomi, K. A., A. Gelman, and T. Srebotnjak. 2002. "Imputing Missing Values." Pp. 51–55 in *2002 Environmental Sustainability Index*, edited by World Economic Forum, Yale Center for Environmental Law and Policy and Center for International Earth Science Information Network. Geneva: Global Leaders of Tomorrow World Economic Forum, pp. 51–55.

Abel, R. L. 1985. "Blaming Victims." *Law and Social Inquiry* 10(2): 401–17.

Abrahamse, W. and L. Steg. 2013. "Social Influence Approaches to Encourage Resource Conservation: A Meta-Analysis." *Global Environmental Change* 23(6): 1773–85.

Abrams, S., C. Anderson, K. M. Kruse, H. C. Richardson and H. A. Thompson. 2020. *Voter Suppression in US Elections*. Athens: University of Georgia Press.

Achebe, C. [1959] 2017. *Things Fall Apart*. New York: Penguin.

Achebe, C. [1960] 2017. *No Longer at Ease*. New York: Penguin.

Achebe, C. [1964] 2016. *Arrow of God*. New York: Penguin.

Adams, J. S. and T. McShane. 1996. *The Myth of Wild Africa: Conservation without Illusion*. Berkeley: University of California Press.

Addams, J. 1912. "A Modern Lear." *Survey* 29 (5): 131–37.

Adler, J. H. 2002. "Fables of the Cuyahoga: Reconstructing a History of Environmental Protection." *Fordham Environmental Law Review* 14: 89–146.

Adler, J. H. 2009. "Taking Property Rights Seriously: The Case of Climate Change." *Social Policy and Philosophy* 26(2): 296–316.

Adler, M. D. 2016. "Benefit–Cost Analysis and Distributional Weights: An Overview." *Review of Environmental Economics and Policy* 10(2): 264–85.

Adler, M. D. and E. A. Posner. 2006. *New Foundation of Cost-Benefit Analysis*. Cambridge, MA: Harvard University Press.

Adua, L., B. Clark, R. York and C.-f. Chen. 2019. "Modernizing Our Way Out or Digging Ourselves In? Reconsidering the Impacts of Efficiency Innovations and Affluence on Residential Energy Consumption, 2005–2015." *Journal of Environmental Management* 252: 109659.

Adua, L. and L. Lobao. 2021. "The Political-Economy of Local Land-Use Policy: Place-Making and the Relative Power of Business, Civil Society, and Government." *The Sociological Quarterly* 62(3): 413–38.

Afsahi, A. 2017. "Talking Across Diversity: Deliberative Capital and Facilitating Discourse Quality." Paper presented at the Western Political Science Association Conference, April 13–15, Vancouver, British Columbia.

Afsahi, A. 2020. "Disabled Lives in Deliberative Systems." *Political Theory* 48(6): 751–76.

Afsahi, A. 2021. "Gender Difference in Willingness and Capacity for Deliberation." *Social Politics: International Studies in Gender, State and Society* 28(4): 1046–72.

Ajzen, I. 1985. "From Intentions to Actions: A Theory of Planned Behavior." Pp. 11–39 in *Action Control*, edited by J. Kuhl and J. Beckmann. SSSP Springer Series in Social Psychology. Berlin: Springer.

Ajzen, I. 1991. "The Theory of Planned Behavior." *Organizational Behavior and Human Decision Processes* 50: 172–211.

Ajzen, I. 2012. "Values, Attitudes, and Behavior." Pp. 33–38 in *Methods, Theories, and Empirical Applications in the Social Sciences: Festschrift for Peter Schmidt*, edited by S. Salzborn, E. Davidov and J. Reinecke. Berlin: Springer.

Alberti, M., J. Marzluff and V. M. Hunt. 2017. "Urban Driven Phenotypic Changes: Empirical Observations and Theoretical Implications for Eco-evolutionary Feedback." *Philosophical Transactions of the Royal Society B* 372(1712): 20160029.

Alcalmo, J., N. J. Ash, C. D. Butler et al. 2003. *Ecosystems and Human Well-being: A Framework for Analysis*. Washington, DC: Island Press.

Alchian, A. 1950. "Uncertainty, Evolution and Economic Theory." *Journal of Political Economy* 58(3): 211–21.

Alderson, A. S. and R. K. Pandian. 2018. "What Is Really Happening with Global Inequality?" *Sociology of Development* 4(3): 261–81.

Aldy, J. E., T. Felgenhauer, W. A. Pizer et al. 2021. "Social Science Research to Inform Solar Geoengineering." *Science* 374(6569): 815–18.

Alfoqahaa, S. and E. Jones. 2020. "Leading at the Edge of Chaos: Historical Perspectives on the Qualities of Leadership for Cultural Diversity and Conflict Resolution." *International Journal of Public Leadership* 16 (2): 217–48.

Allcott, H. 2011. "Social Norms and Energy Conservation." *Journal of Public Economics* 95(9): 1082–95.

Alvaredo, F., L. Chancel, T. Piketty, E. Saez and G. Zucman. 2018. *World Inequality Report 2018*. Cambridge, MA: Belknap Press of Harvard University Press.

Alvarez, C. H., J. A. McGee and R. York. 2019. "Is Labor Green?: A Cross-National Panel Analysis of Unionization and Carbon Dioxide Emissions." *Nature and Culture* 14 (1): 17–38.

Ambrose, J. 2019. "Google Signs Up to $2bn Wind and Solar Investment." *The Guardian*, September 20. www.theguardian.com/tech nology/2019/sep/20/google-says-its-energy-deals-will-lead-to-2bn-wind-and-solar-investment.

Amuakwa-Mensah, F., R. Bärenbold and O. Riemer. 2018. "Deriving a Benefit Transfer Function for Threatened and Endangered Species in Interaction with Their Level of Charisma." *Environments* 5(2): 31.

Anderson, A. A. 2017. "Effects of Social Media Use on Climate Change Opinion, Knowledge, and Behavior" in *Oxford Research Encyclopedia*, edited by H. Von Storch. Oxford: Oxford University Press. https://doi.org/10.1093/acrefore/978019022862 0.013.369.

Anderson, C. 2018. *One Person, No Vote: How Voter Suppression Is Destroying Our Democracy*. New York: Bloomsbury Publishing USA.

Anderson, C. H. 1976. *The Sociology of Survival: Social Problems of Growth*. Homewood, IL: Dorsey Press.

Anderson, D. and R. Grove, eds. 1987. *Conservation in Africa: Peoples, Policies and Practice*. Cambridge: Cambridge University Press.

Anderson, E. 2010. *The Imperative of Integration*. Princeton, NJ: Princeton University Press.

Anderson, E. 2014. "Reply to Critics of the Imperative of Integration." *Political Studies Review* 12(3): 376–82.

Anderson, T. L. and D. R. Leal. 1991. *Free Market Environmentalism*. San Francisco, CA: Pacific Institute for Public Policy.

Andrews, R. N. L. 1999. *Managing the Environment, Managing Ourselves: A History of American Environmental Policy*. New Haven, CT: Yale University Press.

Ani, E. 2018. "Africa and Deliberative Politics." Pp. 819–28 in *The Oxford Handbook of Deliberative Democracy*, edited by A. Bächtiger, J. S. Dryzek, J. Mansbridge and M. E. Warren. Oxford: Oxford University Press.

Ani, E. I. 2013. "Africa and the Prospects of Deliberative Democracy." *South African Journal of Philosophy* 32(3): 207–19.

Ani, E. I. 2014. "On Traditional African Consensual Rationality." *Journal of Political Philosophy* 22(3): 342–65.

Appelbaum, R. P. 1978. *Size, Growth and U.S. Cities*. New York: Praeger Publishers.

Appelbaum, R. P., J. Bigelow, H. P. Kramer, H. Molotch and P. M. Relis. 1976. *The Effects of Urban Growth: A Population Impact Analysis*. New York: Praeger Publishers.

Apple, L. 2002. "The Whole Foods Cure for Herpes: Whole Foods Market Lays Off a Group of Low-Wage Employees." The Austin Chronicle, October 25.

Aristotle. [350 BCE] 2014. *Nicomachean Ethics*. Cambridge: Cambridge University Press.

Arnold, J. 1973. *The Cook and the Carpenter: A Novel by the Carpenter*. New York: New York University Press.

Arnstein, S. R. 1969. "A Ladder of Citizen Participation." *American Institute of Planners Journal* 35(4): 216–24.

Arrhenius, S. 1896. "On the Influences of Carbonic Acid in the Air upon the Temperature of the Ground." *The London, Edinburgh and Dublin Philosophical Magazine and Journal of Science* Series 5 41 (251): 237–76.

Arrow, K. 1951. *Social Choice and Individual Values*. New York: John Wiley & Sons.

Arrow, K., M. Cropper, C. Gollier et al. 2013. "Determining Benefits and Costs for Future Generations." *Science* 341(6144): 349–50.

Arrow, K. J., M. L. Cropper, G. C. Eads et al. 1996. "Is There a Role for Benefit-Cost Analysis in Environmental, Health and Safety Regulation?" *Science* 272(5259): 221–22.

Arrow, K. J., M. L. Cropper, C. Gollier et al. 2014. "Should Governments Use a Declining Discount Rate in Project Analysis?" *Review of Environmental Economics and Policy* 8(2): 145–63.

Arvai, J. L., R. Gregory and T. McDaniels. 2001. "Testing a Structured Decision Approach: Value-Focused Thinking for Deliberative Risk Communication." *Risk Analysis* 21(6): 1065–76.

Asenio, O. I. and M. A. Delmas. 2015. "Non-Price Incentives and Energy Conservation." *Proceedings of the National Academy of Sciences* 112(6): E510–15.

Asian Development Bank Institute, ed. 2019. *Aging Societies: Policies and Perspectives*. Tokyo: Asian Development Bank Institute.

Asimov, I. 1956. *I, Robot*. New York: Signet.

Atkinson, G. and S. Mourato. 2008. "Environmental Cost-Benefit Analysis." *Annual Review of Environment and Resources* 33: 317–44.

Atran, S. and R. Axelrod. 2008. "Reframing Sacred Values." *Negotiation Journal* 24(3): 221–46.

Atran, S. and J. Ginges. 2012. "Religious and Sacred Imperatives in Human Conflict." *Science* 336(6083): 855–57.

Attari, S. Z. 2014. "Perceptions of Water Use." *Proceedings of the National Academy of Sciences* 111(14): 5129–34. www.pnas.org/cg i/doi/10.1073/pnas.1316402111.

Attari, S. Z., M. L. DeKay, C. I. Davidson and W. Bruine de Bruin. 2010. "Public Perceptions of Energy Consumption and Savings." *Proceedings of the National Academy of Sciences, USA* 107(37): 16054–59.

Attari, S. Z., M. DeKay, C. I. Davidson and W. Bruine de Bruin. 2011. "Changing Household Behaviors to Curb Climate Change: How Hard Can It Be?" *Sustainability* 4(1): 9–11.

Attari, S. Z., D. H. Krantz and E. U. Weber. 2019. "Climate Change Communicators' Carbon Footprints Affect Their Audience's Policy Support." *Climatic Change* 154(3): 529–45.

Attari, S. Z., M. Schoen, C. I. Davidson et al. 2009. "Preferences for Change: Do Individuals Prefer Voluntary Actions, Soft Regulations, or Hard Regulations to Decrease Fossil Fuel Consumption?" *Ecological Economics* 68(6): 1701–10.

Austin, K. F. and K. McCarthy. 2016. "Choking on Structural Adjustment: Dependency and Exposure to Indoor Air Pollution in Developing Countries." *World*

*Journal of Social Science Research* 3(2): 161–84.

Aven, T. and O. Renn. 2009. "On Risk Defined As an Event Where the Outcome Is Uncertain." *Journal of Risk Research* 12(1): 1–11.

Aven, T. and O. Renn. 2010. "Response to Professor Eugene Rosa's Viewpoint to Our Paper." *Journal of Risk Research* 13(3): 255–59.

Aven, T., O. Renn and E. A. Rosa. 2011. "On the Ontological Status of the Concept of Risk." *Safety Science* 49(8): 1074–79.

Awad, E., S. Dsouza, R. Kim et al. 2018. "The Moral Machine Experiment." *Nature* 563 (7729): 59–64. https://doi.org/10.1038/s4158 6-018-0637-6.

Awad, E., S. Dsouza, A. Shariff, I. Rahwan and J.-F. Bonnefon. 2020. "Universals and Variations in Moral Decisions Made in 42 Countries by 70,000 Participants." *Proceedings of the National Academy of Sciences* 117(5): 2332–37.

Azar, C. 2007. "Bury the Chains and the Carbon Dioxide." *Climatic Change* 85(3): 473–75.

Azar, J., M. Duro, I. Kadach and G. Ormazabal. 2021. "The Big Three and Corporate Carbon Emissions around the World." *Journal of Financial Economics* 142 (2): 674–96.

Azevedo, I. M. 2014. "Consumer End-Use Energy Efficiency and Rebound Effects." *Annual Review of Environment and Resources* 39: 393–418.

Bächtiger, A., J. S. Dryzek, J. Mansbridge and M. E. Warren, eds. 2018. *The Oxford Handbook of Deliberative Democracy.* Oxford: Oxford University Press.

Backderf, D. 2010. *Punk Rock and Trailer Parks.* San Jose, CA: SLG Publishing.

Backderf, D. 2020. *Kent State: Four Dead in Ohio.* New York: Abrams Comicarts.

Bago, B., D. G. Rand and G. Pennycook. 2020. "Fake News, Fast and Slow: Deliberation Reduces Belief in False (but Not True) News Headlines." *Journal of Experimental Psychology: General* 149(8): 1608–13.

Bail, C. A. 2021. *Breaking the Social Media Prism: How to Make Our Platforms Less Polarizing.* Princeton, NJ: Princeton University Press.

Bak-Coleman, J. B., M. Alfano, W. Barfuss et al. 2021. "Stewardship of Global Collective Behavior." *Proceedings of the National Academy of Science, USA* 118(27): e2025764118.

Baker, W. E. 2006. *America's Crisis of Values: Reality and Perception.* Princeton, NJ: Princeton University Press.

Baker, W. E. 2012. "Are There Core American Values?" *Social Science Research Network.* http://dx.doi.org/10.2139/ssrn.3961608.

Baker, W. E. 2013. *America's Crisis of Values.* Princeton, NJ: Princeton University Press.

Baker, W. E. 2022. "Our COVID Morality Play." *Read the Spirit,* January 17. https://re adthespirit.com/explore/dr-wayne-baker-our-covid-morality-play/.

Balee, W. L., ed. 1998. *Advances in Historical Ecology.* New York: Columbia University Press.

Ballesteros, L. and H. Kunreuther. 2018. "Organizational Decision Making Under Uncertainty Shocks." National Bureau of Economic Research, Working Paper No. 24924.

Banacloche, S., A. R. Gamarra, Y. Lechon and C. Bustreo. 2020. "Socioeconomic and Environmental Impacts of Bringing the Sun to Earth: A Sustainability Analysis of a Fusion Power Plant Deployment." *Energy* 209(C): 118460.

Baralt, L. 2010. "Biomedical and Environmental Health Perspectives: The Example of Confronting Breast Cancer." Pp. 139–56 in *Health and Environment: Social Science Perspectives,* edited by H. Kopnina and H. Keune. New York: Nova Science Publishers.

Baran, P. A. 1957. *The Political Economy of Growth.* New York: Monthly Review Press.

Baran, P. A. and P. M. Sweezy. 1966. *Monopoly Capital: An Essay on the American Economic and Social Order.* New York: Monthly Review Press.

Barbier, E. B. and J. C. Burgess. 2019. "Sustainable Development Goal

Indicators: Analyzing Trade-Offs and Complementarities." *World Development* 122: 295–305.

Baring-Gould, W. S., ed. 1967. *The Annotated Sherlock Holmes*. New York: Clarkson N. Potter.

Barney, G. O. 1980a. *The Global 2000 Report to the President: Entering the Twenty-First Century*, Vol. 1. Washington, DC: US Government Printing Office.

Barney, G. O. 1980b. *The Global 200 Report to the President: The Technical Report*, Vol. 2. Washington, DC: Government Printing Office.

Barney, G. O. 1981. *The Global 2000 Report to the President: Documentation on the Government's Global Sectoral Models: The Government's "Global Model,"* Vol. 3. Washington, DC: Government Printing Office.

Barone, J., R. Buller, T. Carrothers et al. 1971. *An Interdisciplinary Study of Some Environmental, Social and Economic Factors Affecting a Section of the Cuyahoga River Watershed*. Kent, OH: Center for Urban Regionalism, Kent State University.

Barone, J., T. Cahill, R. Eldred et al. 1978. "A Multivariate Statistical Analysis of Visibility Degradation at Four California Cities." *Atmospheric Environment (1967)* 12 (11): 2213–21.

Barrett, C. B., T. Garg and L. McBride. 2016. "Well-Being Dynamics and Poverty Traps." *Annual Review of Resource Economics* 8: 303–27.

Barrios, J. M. and Y. Hochberg. 2020. "Risk Perception through the Lens of Politics in the Time of the Covid-19 Pandemic." National Bureau of Economic Research, Working Paper No. 27008.

Bartkowski, B. and N. Lienhoop. 2018. "Beyond Rationality, Towards Reasonableness: Enriching the Theoretical Foundation of Deliberative Monetary Valuation." *Ecological Economics* 143: 97–104.

Bartkowski, B. and N. Lienhoop. 2019. "Deliberative Monetary Valuation." *Oxford Research Encyclopedia of Environmental Science*. https://doi.org/10.1093/acrefore/978 0199389414.013.595.

Barvosa, E. 2018. *Deliberative Democracy Now: LGBT Equality and the Emergence of Large-Scale Deliberative Systems*. Cambridge: Cambridge University Press.

Bauer, P., A. Thorpe and G. Brunet. 2015. "The Quiet Revolution of Numerical Weather Prediction." *Nature* 525(7567): 47–55.

Bavel, J. J. V., D. A. Reinero, V. Spring, E. A. Harris and A. Duke. 2021. "Speaking My Truth: Why Personal Experiences Can Bridge Divides but Mislead." *Proceedings of the National Academy of Sciences* 118(8): e2100280118. https://doi.org/10.1073/pnas .2100280118.

Bayes, R. and J. N. Druckman. 2021. "Motivated Reasoning and Climate Change." *Current Opinion in Behavioral Sciences* 42: 27–35. https://doi.org/10.1016/j .cobeha.2021.02.009.

Beauchamp, T. L. 2011. "Rights Theory and Animal Rights." Pp. 198–227 in *The Oxford Handbook of Animal Ethics*, edited by T. L. Beauchamp and R. G. Frey. Oxford: Oxford University Press.

Beauchamp, T. L. and R. G. Frey, eds. 2011. *The Oxford Handbook of Animal Ethics*. Oxford: Oxford University Press.

Bebber, M. R. and M. I. Eren. 2018. "Toward a Functional Understanding of the North American Old Copper Culture 'Technomic Devolution'." *Journal of Archaeological Science* 98: 34–44. https://doi.org/10.1016/j .jas.2018.08.001.

Beck, U. 1986. *Risk Society: Towards a New Modernity*. Thousand Oaks, CA: Sage.

Becker, G. S. 1974. "A Theory of Social Interactions." *Journal of Political Economy* 82(6): 1063–93.

Becker, G. S. 1976a. "Altruism, Egoism and Genetic Fitness: Economics and Sociobiology." *Journal of Economic Literature* 14(3): 817–26.

Becker, G. S. 1976b. *The Economic Approach to Human Behavior*. Chicago, IL: University of Chicago Press.

Becker, G. S. [1981] 1991. *A Treatise on the Family: Enlarged Edition*. Cambridge, MA: Harvard University Press.

Becker, G. S. and R. J. Barro. 1986. "Altruism and the Economic Theory of Fertility." *Population and Development Review* 12 (Suppl.): 69–76.

Ben-Ghiat, R. 2020. *Strongmen: Mussolini to the Present*. New York: W. W. Norton & Company.

Benedick, R. E. 1991. *Ozone Diplomacy*. Cambridge, MA: Harvard University Press.

Benegal, S. D. 2018. "The Spillover of Race and Racial Attitudes into Public Opinion about Climate Change." *Environmental Politics* 27 (4): 733–56.

Bennett, D. J. 1998. *Randomness*. Cambridge, MA: Harvard University Press.

Bennett, F. 2013. "Researching Within-Household Distribution: Overview, Developments, Debates, and Methodological Challenges." *Journal of Marriage and Family* 75(3): 582–97.

Bennett, W. L. 2016. *News: The Politics of Illusion*. Chicago, IL: University of Chicago Press.

Benoit, W. L., G. J. Hansen and R. M. Verser. 2003. "A Meta-analysis of the Effects of Viewing US Presidential Debates." *Communication Monographs* 70(4): 335–50.

Bentham, J. 1776. *A Fragment on Government; Being an Examination of What Is Delivered, on the Subject of Government in General in the Introduction to Sir William Blackstone's Commentaries*. London: T. Payne, P. Emily and E. Brooks.

Bentham, J. 1823. *An Introduction to the Principles of Morals and Legislation: A New Edition Corrected by the Author*. Oxford: Clarendon Press.

Berkes, F., D. Feeny, B. J. McCay and J. M. Acheson. 1989. "The Benefits of the Commons." *Nature* 340(6229): 91–93.

Berle, A. A. and G. C. Means. [1933] 2009. *The Modern Corporation and Private Property*. New Brunswick, NJ: Transaction Publishers.

Berlin, I. [1953] 2013. *The Hedgehog and the Fox: An Essay on Tolstoy's View of History*. Princeton, NJ: Princeton University Press.

Berndt, E. R. 1982. "From Technocracy to Net Energy Analysis: Engineers, Economists and Recurring Energy Theories of Value." Massachusetts Institute of Technology Studies in Energy and the American Economy Discussion Paper No. 1353-82.

Bernstein, P. L. 1998. *Against the Gods: The Remarkable Story of Risk*. New York: John Wiley & Sons.

Bessette, D. L., J. Arvai and V. Campbell-Arvai. 2014. "Decision Support Framework for Developing Regional Energy Strategies." *Environmental Science and Technology* 48(3): 1401–08.

Best, R. and E. Meija. 2022, "The Lasting Legacy of Redlining," FiveThirtyEight website, February 10. https://projects .fivethirtyeight.com/redlining/.

Bidwell, D. 2016. "Thinking through Participation in Renewable Energy Decisions." *Nature Energy* 1(5): 16051.

Bidwell, D., T. Dietz and D. Scavia. 2013. "Fostering Knowledge Networks for Climate Adaptation." *Nature Climate Change* 3(7): 610–11.

Bidwell, D. and P.J. Schweizer. 2021. "Public Values and Goals for Public Participation." *Environmental Policy and Governance* 31(4): 257–69.

Biermann, F., T. Hickmann, C.-A. Sénit et al. 2022. "Scientific Evidence on the Political Impact of the Sustainable Development Goals." *Nature Sustainability* 5(9): 795–800. https://doi.org/10.1038/s41893-022-00909-5.

Bishin, B.G., J. Freebourn and P. Teten. 2021. "The Power of Equality? Polarization and Collective Mis-representation on Gay Rights in Congress, 1989–2019." *Political Research Quarterly* 74(4): 1009–23.

Bishop, R.C. and T.A. Heberlein. 1979. "Measuring Values of Extramarket Goods: Are Indirect Measures Biased?". *American Journal of Agricultural Economics* 61(5): 926–30.

Bishop, R.C., T.A. Heberlein and M.J. Kealy. 1983. "Contingent Valuation of Environmental Assets: Comparison with a Stimulated Market." *Natural Resources Journal* 23(3): 619–33.

Black, G., D.A. Dalton, S. Islam and A. Batteen. 2014. "The Coasean Framework of the New York City Watershed Agreement." *Cato Journal* 34(1): 1–32.

Black, J.S., P.C. Stern and J.T. Elsworth. 1985. "Personal and Contextual Influences on Household Energy Adaptations." *Journal of Applied Psychology* 70(1): 3–21.

Black, K.J., A.J. Boslett, E.L. Hill, L. Ma and S. J. McCoy. 2021. "Economic, Environmental, and Health Impacts of the Fracking Boom." *Annual Review of Resource Economics* 13: 311–34. https://doi.org/10.1146/annurev-resource-110320-092648.

Blake, J. and K. Davis. 1964. "Norms, Values and Sanctions." Pp. 456–84 in *Handbook of Modern Sociology*, edited by R. E. L. Faris. New York: Rand McNally.

Blastland, M., A. L. Freeman, S. van der Linden, T. M. Marteau and D. Spiegelhalter. 2020. "Five Rules for Evidence Communication." *Nature* 587: 362–64. https://doi.org/10.1038/d41586-020-03189-1.

Bloom, R. and D. Deur. 2020a. "Reframing Native Knowledge, Co-Managing Native Landscapes: Ethnographic Data and Tribal Engagement at Yosemite National Park." *Land* 9(9): 335.

Bloom, R. and D. Duer. 2020b. "'Through a Forest Wilderness': Native American Environmental Management at Yosemite and Contested Conservation Values in America's National Parks." Pp. 151–73 in *Public Lands in the Western US: Place and Politics in the Clash between Public and Private*, edited by K. M. Sullivan and J. H. McDonald. Lanham, MD: Lexington Books.

Blumer, H. 1948. "Public Opinion and Public Opinion Polling." *American Sociological Review* 13(5): 542–49.

Bockstael, E. and K. Watene. 2016. "Indigenous Peoples and the Capability Approach: Taking Stock." *Oxford Development Studies* 44(3): 265–70.

Boddington, P. 2017. *Towards a Code of Ethics for Artificial Intelligence*. Cham: Springer.

Boehm, R., P. E. Wilde, M. Ver Ploeg, C. Costello and S. B. Cash. 2018. "A Comprehensive Life Cycle Assessment of Greenhouse Gas Emissions from US Household Food Choices." *Food Policy* 79: 67–76. https://doi.org/10.1016/j.foodpol.2018.05.004.

Bolderdijk, J. W., L. Steg, E. S. Geller, P. K. Lehman and T. Postmes. 2013. "Comparing the Effectiveness of Monetary versus Moral Motives in Environmental Campaigning." *Nature Climate Change* 3(4): 413–16.

Bolsen, T. and J. N. Druckman. 2018. "Do Partisanship and Politicization Undermine the Impact of a Scientific Consensus Message about Climate Change?" *Group Processes and Intergroup Relations* 21(3): 389–402.

Bolsen, T. and R. Palm. 2019. "Motivated Reasoning and Political Decision Making." *Oxford Research Encyclopedia of Politics*, edited by W. R. Thompson. Oxford: Oxford University Press. https://doi.org/10.1093/acrefore/9780190228637.013.923.

Bonanno, A. 2017. *The Legitimation Crisis of Neoliberalism: The State, Will-Formation, and Resistance*. Cham: Springer.

Bongaarts, J. 2009. "Human Population Growth and the Demographic Transition." *Philosophical Transactions of the Royal Society B: Biological Sciences* 364(1532): 2985–90.

Bonikowski, B., Y. Feinstein and S. Bock. 2021. "The Partisan Sorting of 'America': How Nationalist Cleavages Shaped the 2016 U.S. Presidential Election." *American Journal of Sociology* 127(2): 492–561. https://doi.org/10.1086/717103.

Bonnefon, J.-F., A. Shariff and I. Rahwan. 2016. "The Social Dilemma of Autonomous Vehicles." *Science* 352(6293): 1573–76.

Börner, J., K. Baylis, E. Corbera et al. 2016. "Emerging Evidence on the Effectiveness of

Tropical Forest Conservation." *PloS One* 11 (11): e0159152.

Bottrill, M. C., L. N. Joseph, J. Carwardine et al. 2008. "Is Conservation Triage Just Smart Decision Making?" *Trends in Ecology and Evolution* 23(12): 649–54.

Boucher, D. 2014. "Marshall University Scientist Says Formaldehyde in Charleston Water Likely Was from Spill." *Pittsburgh Post-Gazette*, January 29.

Boulding, K. E. 1966. "The Economics of the Coming Spaceship Earth." Pp. 3–14 in *Environmental Quality in a Growing Economy*, edited by H. Jarrett. Baltimore, MD: Johns Hopkins Press.

Bouman, T. and L. Steg. 2019. "Motivating Society-Wide Pro-environmental Change." *One Earth* 1(1): 27–30.

Bouman, T. and L. Steg. 2021. "Worrying about the Consequences of COVID-19 for Distant Others Relates to Mitigative Actions." *Health Communication*: 1–11. https://doi.org /10.1080/10410236.2021.1981564.

Bouman, T., L. Steg and T. Dietz. 2021. "Insights from Early COVID-19 Responses about Promoting Sustainable Action." *Nature Sustainability* 4(3): 194–200.

Bouman, T., L. Steg and G. Perlaviciute. 2021. "From Values to Climate Action." *Current Opinion in Psychology* 42: 102–07.

Bouman, T., E. van der Werff, G. Perlaviciute and L. Steg. 2021. "Environmental Values and Identities at the Personal and Group Level." *Current Opinion in Behavioral Sciences* 42: 47–53.

Bourgin, C. 2020. "It's Past Time to Dismantle Racism in the Outdoors." *Sierra Club*, June 16. www.sierraclub.org/articles/2020/0 6/it-s-past-time-dismantle-racism-outdoors.

Bowers, M. M. and C. T. Whitley. 2018. "Assessing Voter Registration among Transgender and Gender Non-conforming Individuals." *Political Behavior* 42: 143–64. https://doi.org/10.1007/s11109-018-9489-x.

Bowers, M. M. and C. T. Whitley. 2020. "What Drives Support for Transgender Rights? Assessing the Effects of Biological Attribution on US Public Opinion of

Transgender Rights." *Sex Roles* 83(7): 399–411.

Box, G. E. and N. R. Draper. 1987. *Empirical Model-Building and Response Surfaces*. New York: John Wiley & Sons.

Boxell, L., M. Gentzkow and J. M. Shapiro. 2017. "Greater Internet Use Is Not Associated with Faster Growth in Political Polarization among US Demographic Groups." *Proceedings of the National Academy of Sciences* 114(4): 10612–17.

Boyd, R. 1972. "World Dynamics: A Note." *Science* 177(4048): 516–19.

Boyd, R. 2017. *A Different Kind of Animal: How Culture Transformed Our Species*. Princeton, NJ: Princeton University Press.

Boyd, R. and P. J. Richerson. 1985. *Culture and the Evolutionary Process*. Chicago, IL: University of Chicago Press.

Boyd, R. and P. J. Richerson. 2005. *The Origin and Evolution of Cultures*. Oxford: Oxford University Press.

Boykoff, M. 2020. "Digital Cultures and Climate Change: 'Here and Now'." *Journal of Environmental Media* 1(1): 21–25.

Boykoff, M. T. and J. M. Boykoff. 2007. "Climate Change and Journalistic Norms: A Case-Study of US Mass-Media Coverage." *Geoforum* 38(6): 1190–204.

Brady, W. J., J. A. Wills, J. T. Jost, J. A. Tucker and J. J. V. Bavel. 2017. "Emotion Shapes the Diffusion of Moralized Content in Social Networks." *Proceedings of the National Academy of Sciences* 114(28): 7313–18. https://doi.org/10.1073/pnas .1618923114.

Branch, T. 1988. *Parting the Waters: America in the King Years 1954–1963*. New York: Simon & Schuster.

Branch, T. 1998. *Pillar of Fire: America in the King Years 1963–65*. New York: Simon & Schuster.

Branch, T. 2006. *At Canann's Edge: American in the King Years 1965–68*. New York: Simon & Schuster.

Brand, J. E. 2015. "The Far-Reaching Impact of Job Loss and Unemployment." *Annual Review of Sociology* 41: 359–75.

Brandes, S. D. 1976. *American Welfare Capitalism, 1880–1940*. Chicago, IL: University of Chicago Press.

Brands, H. W. 2010. *The First American: The Life and Times of Benjamin Franklin*. New York: Anchor Books.

Brands, H. W. 2020. *The Zealot and the Emancipator: John Brown, Abraham Lincoln, and the Struggle for American Freedom*. New York: Doubleday.

Brasier, K. J., L. Davis, L. Glenna et al. 2015. "Communities Experiencing Shale Gas Development." Pp. 149–78 in *Economics of Unconventional Shale Gas Development*, edited by W. E. Hefley and Y. Wany. New York: Springer.

Braverman, H. 1974. *Labor and Monopoly Capital*. New York: Monthly Review Press.

Brechin, S. R. 1999. "Objective Problems, Subjective Values, and Global Environmentalism: Evaluating the Postmaterialist Argument and Challenging a New Explanation." *Social Science Quarterly* 80(4): 783–809.

Brechin, S. R. and W. Kempton. 1997. "Beyond Postmaterialist Values: National versus Individual Explanations of Global Environmentalism." *Social Science Quarterly* 78(1): 16–20.

Briley, L., D. Brown and S. E. Kalafatis. 2015. "Overcoming Barriers during the Co-production of Climate Information for Decision-Making." *Climate Risk Management* 9: 41–49. https://doi.org/10.1016/j.crm.2015.04.004.

Broadbent, E. 2017. "Interactions with Robots: The Truths We Reveal about Ourselves." *Annual Review of Psychology* 68: 627–52.

Broadman, A. E., D. H. Greenberg, A. Vining and D. Weimer. 2000. *Cost-Benefit Analysis: Concepts and Practices*. Upper Saddle River, NJ: Pearson Education.

Brolan, C. E. 2016. "A Word of Caution: Human Rights, Disability, and Implementation of the Post-2015 Sustainable Development Goals." *Laws* 5(2): 22.

Brons, M., P. Nijkamp, E. Pels and P. Rietveld. 2008. "A Meta-analysis of the Price Elasticity of Gasoline Demand: A SUR Approach." *Energy Economics* 30(5): 2105–22.

Brooks, J. S., T. M. Waring, M. B. Mulder and P. J. Richerson. 2018. "Applying Cultural Evolution to Sustainability Challenges: An Introduction to the Special Issue." *Sustainability Science* 13(1): 1–8.

Brosch, T. 2021. "Affect and Emotions As Drivers of Climate Change Perception and Action: A Review." *Current Opinion in Behavioral Sciences* 42: 15–21. https://doi.org/10.1016/j.cobeha.2021.02.001.

Brossard, D. and D. A. Scheufele. 2022. "The Chronic Growing Pains of Communicating Science Online." *Science* 375(6581): 613–14.

Brown, L. 1981. *Building a Sustainable Society*. New York: W. W. Norton.

Brown, M. J. 2018. "Weaving Value Judgment into the Tapestry of Science." *Philosophy, Theory, and Practice in Biology* 10(10). https://philpapers.org/rec/BROWVJ.

Brown, P., S. McCormick, B. Mayer et al. 2006. "'A Lab of Our Own': Environmental Causation of Breast Cancer and Challenges to the Dominant Epidemiological Paradigm." *Science, Technology and Human Values* 31(5): 499–536.

Brown, P. and E. J. Mikkelsen. 1990. *No Safe Place: Toxic Waste, Leukemia and Community Action*. Berkeley: University of California Press.

Brown, P., S. Zavestoski, S. McCormick et al. 2004. "Embodied Health Movements: New Approaches to Social Movements in Health." *Sociology of Health and Illness* 26(1): 50–80.

Brown, R. 2004. "Consideration of the Origin of Herbert Simon's Theory of 'Satisficing' (1933–1947)." *Management Decision* 42(10): 1240–56.

Bruce, R. 1994. *Mortgaging the Earth*. Boston, MA: Beacon Press.

Bruch, E. and F. Feinberg. 2017. "Decision-Making Processes in Social Contexts." *Annual Review of Sociology* 43: 207–27.

Bruckner, T. A. 2016. "Life Expectancy." Pp. 1–4 in *The Blackwell Encyclopedia of*

*Sociology*, edited by G. Ritzer. London: Blackwell.

Brüggemann, M. and S. Engesser. 2017. "Beyond False Balance: How Interpretive Journalism Shapes Media Coverage of Climate Change." *Global Environmental Change* 42: 58–67. https://doi.org/10.1016/j.gloenvcha.2016.11.004.

Brulle, R. 2000. *Agency, Democracy and Nature: The U.S. Environmental Movement from a Critical Theory Perspective*. Cambridge, MA: MIT Press.

Brulle, R. J. 1993. "Environmentalism and Human Emancipation." Pp. 2–12 in *Human Ecology: Crossing Boundaries*, edited by S. D. Wright, T. Dietz, R. Borden, G. Young and G. Guagnano. Ft. Collins, CO: Society for Human Ecology.

Brulle, R. J. 1994. "Power, Discourse and Social Problems: Social Problems from a Rhetorical Perspective." *Current Perspectives in Social Problems* 5: 95–121.

Brulle, R. J. and D. N. Pellow. 2006. "Environmental Justice: Human Health and Environmental Inequalities." *Annual Review of Public Health* 27: 103–24.

Brunner, S. H., R. Huber and A. Grêt-Regamey. 2016. "A Backcasting Approach for Matching Regional Ecosystem Services Supply and Demand." *Environmental Modelling and Software* 75: 439–58. https://doi.org/10.1016/j.envsoft.2015.10.018.

Bryan, F. M. 2010. *Real Democracy: The New England Town Meeting and How It Works*. Chicago, IL: University of Chicago Press.

Bryson, B. 2007. *Shakespeare: The World As State*. New York: HarperCollins.

Bubolz, M. M. 1996. *Home Economics to Human Ecology: 100 years at Michigan State University*. East Lansing: College of Human Ecology, Michigan State University.

Bubolz, M. M., J. B. Eicher and M. S. Sontag. 1979. "The Human Ecosystem: A Model." *Journal of Home Economics* 71(1): 28–31.

Bubolz, M. M. and M. S. Sontag. 1988. "Integration in Home Economics and Human Ecology." *Journal of Consumer Studies and Home Economics* 12(1): 1–14.

Buchanan, J. M. 1954. "Individual Choice in Voting and the Market." *Journal of Political Economy* 62(4): 334–43.

Buchanan, J. M. and G. Tullock. 1962. *The Calculus of Consent: Logical Foundations of Constitutional Democracy*. Ann Arbor: University of Michigan Press.

Buchele, M. 2022. "Texas and Other States Want to Punish Fossil Fuel Divestment." Houston Public Media (A Service of the University of Houston), March 16. www.houstonpublicmedia.org/npr/2022/03/16/1086764072/texas-and-other-states-want-to-punish-fossil-fuel-divestment/.

Büchs, M. and M. Koch. 2019. "Challenges for the Degrowth Transition: The Debate about Wellbeing." *Futures* 105: 155–65. https://doi.org/10.1016/j.futures.2018.09.002.

Budescu, D. V., S. Broomwell and H.-H. Por. 2009. "Improving Communication of Uncertainty in the Reports of the Intergovernmental Panel on Climate Change." *Psychological Science* 20(3): 299–308.

Bullard, R. D. 1983. "Solid Waste Sites and the Black Houston Community." *Sociological Inquiry* 53(2–3): 273–88.

Bullard, R. D. and G. S. Johnson. 2000. "Environmentalism and Public Policy: Environmental Justice: Grassroots Activism and Its Impact on Public Policy Decision Making." *Journal of Social Issues* 56(3): 555–78.

Bunse, L., O. Rendon and S. Luque. 2015. "What Can Deliberative Approaches Bring to the Monetary Valuation of Ecosystem Services? A Literature Review." *Ecosystem Services* 14: 88–97. https://doi.org/10.1016/j.ecoser.2015.05.004.

Burch, W. R. 1971. "The Peregrine Falcon and the Urban Poor. Some Sociological Interrelations." Revised version of paper presented at American Sociological Association annual meeting, Denver, CO, August.

Burch, W. R. 1976. "The Peregrine Falcon and the Urban Poor." Pp. 308–16 in *Human Ecology: An Environmental Approach*, edited by P. J. Richerson and J. McEvoy, III. North Scituate, MA: Duxbury.

Burch, W. R., G. E. Machlis and J. E. Force. 2017. *The Structure and Dynamics of Human Ecosystems: Toward a Model for Understanding and Action*. New Haven, CT: Yale University Press.

Burke, P. 2020. *The Polymath: A Cultural History from Leonardo da Vinci to Susan Sontag*. New Haven, CT: Yale University Press.

Burns, K. 2000. *Jazz*. Studio Hamburg Fernseh Allianz.

Burns, T. J. and T. K. Rudel. 2015. "Metatheorizing Structural Human Ecology at the Dawn of the Third Millennium." *Human Ecology Review* 22(1): 13–34.

Burns, T. R. 2012a. "The Sustainability Revolution: A Societal Paradigm Shift." *Sustainability* 4(6): 1118–34.

Burns, T. R. 2012b. "Sustainable Development: A Comment." *Sociologica* 6(2). https://doi.org/10.2383/38272.

Burns, T. R. and T. Dietz. 1992a. "Technology, Sociotechnical Systems, Technological Development: An Evolutionary Perspective." Pp. 206–38 in *New Technology at the Outset: Social Forces in the Shaping of Technological Innovation*, edited by M. Dierkes and U. Hoffmann. Frankfurt am Main: Campus Verlag.

Burns, T. R. and T. Dietz. 1992b. "Institutionelle Dynamik: Ein Evolutionarer Ansatz." *Journal fur Sozialforschung* 32(3/4): 283–306.

Burns, T. R. and T. Dietz. 1992c. "Socio-cultural Evolution: Social Rule Systems, Selection and Agency." *International Sociology* 7(3): 259–83.

Burns, T. R. and T. Dietz. 2001. "Revolution: An Evolutionary Perspective." *International Sociology* 16(4): 531–55.

Burns, T. R., H. Flam, R. de Man et al. 1987. *The Shaping of Social Organization: Social Rule Systems Theory with Applications*. London: Sage Publications.

Busch, L. 2011. *Standards: Recipes for Reality*. Cambridge, MA: MIT Press.

Bush, M., M. Nascimento, C. Åkesson et al. 2021. "Widespread Reforestation before European Influence on Amazonia." *Science* 372(6541): 484–87.

Butler, C. 2017. "A Fruitless Endeavour: Confronting the Heteronormativity of Environmentalism." Pp. 270–84 in *Routledge Handbook of Gender and Environment*, edited by S. MacGregor. Abingdon and New York: Routledge.

Butler, R. A. 2020. "Top 10 Environmental News Stories of 2020." *Mongabay*, December 22. www.news.mongabay.com/2020/12/top-10-environmental-news-stories-of-2020.

Buttel, F. and P. Taylor. 1994. "Environmental Sociology and Global Environmental Change: A Critical Assessment." in *Social Theory and the Global Environment*, edited by M. Redclift and T. Benton. London: Routledge.

Butzer, K. W. and G. H. Endfield. 2012. "Critical Perspectives on Historical Collapse." *Proceedings of the National Academy of Science, USA* 109(10): 3628–31.

Cabraal, R. A., D. F. Barnes and S. G. Agarwal. 2005. "Productive Uses of Energy for Rural Development." *Annual Review of Environment and Resources* 30: 117–44.

Cai, Q. 2011. "A Decade of Change in Virginia's Population." *The Virginia News Letter* 87(4): 1–6.

Calarco, M. 2015. *Thinking through Animals: Identity, Difference, Indistinction*. Stanford, CA: Stanford University Press.

Caldicott, J. B. 1992. "Animal Liberation and Environmental Ethics: Back Together Again." Pp. 249–61 in *Animal Rights/Environmental Ethics Debate: The Environmental Perspective*, edited by E. C. Hargrove. Albany, NY: SUNY Press.

Calhoun, J. B. 1957. "Social Welfare As a Variable in Population Dynamics." *Cold*

*Spring Harbor Symposium on Quantitative Biology* 22: 339–56.

Calhoun, J. B. 1962. "Population Density and Social Pathology." *Scientific American* 206 (2): 139–50.

Calhoun, J. B. 1966. "The Role of Space in Animal Sociology." *Journal of Social Issues* 22(4): 46–58. https://doi.org/10.1111/j.1540-4560.1966.tb00548.x.

Callenbach, E. 1975. *Ecotopia: The Notebooks and Reports of William Weston*. New York: Bantam.

Callenbach, E. 1981. *Ecotopia Emerging*. Berkeley, CA: Heyday Books.

Caluwaerts, D., K. Bernaerts, R. Kesberg, B. Spruyt and F. Turner-Zwinkels. 2021. "Deliberation and Polarization: A Multi-disciplinary Review." Paper presented at the 2021 ECPR General Conference, August 30 to September 3 (virtual event). https://researchportal.vub.be/en/publications/deliberation-and-polarization-a-multi-disciplinary-review.

Camilleri, A. R., R. P. Larrick, S. Hossain and D. Patino-Echeverri. 2019. "Consumers Underestimate the Emissions Associated with Food but Are Aided by Labels." *Nature Climate Change* 9(1): 53–58.

Campbell, D. T. 1969. "Ethnocentrism of Disciplines and the Fish-Scale Model of Omniscience." Pp. 328–48 in *Interdisciplinary Relationships in the Social Sciences*, edited by M. Sherif and C. W. Sherif. Chicago, IL: Aldine.

Campbell, D. T. 1987. "Evolutionary Epistemology." Pp. 47–89 in *Evolutionary Epistemology, Rationality and the Sociology of Knowledge*, edited by G. Radnitzky and W. W. I. Bartley. La Salle, IL: Open Court.

Canan, P., S. O. Andersen, N. Reichman and B. Gareau. 2015. "Introduction to the Special Issue on Ozone Layer Protection and Climate Change: The Extraordinary Experience of Building the Montreal Protocol, Lessons Learned, and Hopes for Future Climate Change Efforts." *Journal of Environmental Studies and Sciences* 5(2): 111–21.

Candemir, A., S. Duvaleix and L. Latruffe. 2021. "Agricultural Cooperatives and Farm Sustainability: A Literature Review." *Journal of Economic Surveys* 35(4): 1118–44.

Caprara, G. V., S. Schwartz, C. Capanna, M. Vecchione and C. Barbaranelli. 2006. "Personality and Politics: Values, Traits, and Political Choice." *Political Psychology* 27(1): 1–28.

Caprara, G. V., M. Vecchione, S. H. Schwartz et al. 2017. "Basic Values, Ideological Self-Placement, and Voting: A Cross-Cultural Study." *Cross-Cultural Research* 51(4): 388–411.

Carattini, S., M. Carvalho and S. Fankhauser. 2018. "Overcoming Public Resistance to Carbon Taxes." *Wiley Interdisciplinary Reviews: Climate Change* 9(5): e531.

Carattini, S., S. Kallbekken and A. Orlov. 2019. "How to Win Public Support for a Global Carbon Tax." *Nature* 565: 289–91. https://doi.org/10.1038/d41586-019-00124-x.

Carbado, D. W., K. W. Crenshaw, V. M. Mays and B. Tomlinson. 2013. "Intersectionality: Mapping the Movements of a Theory." *Du Bois Review: Social Science Research on Race* 10(2): 303–12.

Cardonna, J. L. 2014. *Sustainability: A History*. New York: Oxford University Press.

Carnap, R. [1928] 1967. *The Logical Structure of the World*, translated by R. A. George. Berkeley: University of California Press.

Carpenter, S. R., J. J. Cole, M. L. Pace et al. 2011. "Early Warnings of Regime Shifts: A Whole-Ecosystem Experiment." *Science* 332 (6033): 1079–82.

Carrera, J. S., S. Bailey, R. Wiggins et al. 2022. "Community Science As Resistance to Neoliberal Scientific Praxis." *Environmental Justice* [Preprint]. https://doi.org/10.1089/env.2021.0099.

Carrera, J. S. and K. Key. 2021. "Troubling Heroes: Reframing the Environmental Justice Contributions of the Flint Water Crisis." *Wiley Interdisciplinary Reviews: Water* 8(4): e1524.

Carrera, J. S., K. Key, S. Bailey et al. 2019. "Community Science As a Pathway for

Resilience in Response to a Public Health Crisis in Flint, Michigan." *Social Sciences* 8 (3): 94.

Carrico, A., M. P. Vandenbergh, P. C. Stern et al. 2011. "Energy and Climate Change: Key Lessons for Implementing the Behavioral Wedge." *George Washington Journal of Energy and Environmental Law* 2 (Winter): 61–67.

Carrigan, C. and C. Coglianese. 2015. "George J. Stigler, 'The Theory of Economic Regulation'." Pp. 292–93 in *The Oxford Handbook of Classics in Public Policy and Administration*, edited by S. J. Balla, M. Lodge and E. C. Page. Oxford: Oxford University Press.

Carroll, A. B. 2008. "A History of Corporate Social Responsibility: Concepts and Practices." Pp. 19–46 in *The Oxford Handbook of Corporate Social Responsibility*, edited by A. Crane, D. Matten, A. McWilliams, J. Moon and D. S. Siegel. Oxford: Oxford University Press.

Carroll, J., S. Lyons and E. Denny. 2014. "Reducing Household Electricity Demand through Smart Metering: The Role of Improved Information about Energy Saving." *Energy Economics* 45: 234–43. https://doi.org/10.1016/j .eneco.2014.07.007.

Carson, R. T. 2010. "The Environmental Kuznets Curve: Seeking Empirical Regularity and Theoretical Structure." *Review of Environmental Economics and Policy* 4(1): 3–23.

Castro, R. 2012. "Arguments on the Imminence of Global Collapse Are Premature When Based on Simulation Models." *GAIA-Ecological Perspectives for Science and Society* 21(4): 271–73.

Cath, C. 2018. "Governing Artificial Intelligence: Ethical, Legal and Technical Opportunities and Challenges." *Philosophical Transactions of the Royal Society A: Mathematical, Physical and Engineering Sciences* 376: 20180080. http://d oi.org/10.1098/rsta.2018.0080.

Celermajer, D. 2020. "Rethinking Rewilding through Multispecies Justice." *Animal Sentience* 5(28): 12.

Centner, T.J. 2006. "Governments and Unconstitutional Takings: When Do Right-to-Farm Laws Go Too Far." *Boston College Environmental Affairs Law Review* 33 (1): 87–148.

Centola, D., J. Becker, D. Brackbill and A. Baronchelli. 2018. "Experimental Evidence for Tipping Points in Social Convention." *Science* 360(6393): 1116–19.

Chanin, J. 2018. "The Effect of Symbolic Racism on Environmental Concern and Environmental Action." *Environmental Sociology* 4(3): 1–13.

Charmley, S., E. M. Donoghue and C. Moseley. 2008. "Forest Management Policy and Community Well-Being in the Pacific Northwest." *Journal of Forestry* 106(8): 440–47.

Chase-Dunn, C. 1998. *Global Formation: Structures of the World-Economy*. Lanham, MD: Rowman & Littlefield.

Chemnick, J. 2021. "Cost of Carbon Pollution Pegged at $51 a Ton," *E&E News*, March 1.

Chen, C.-f., T. Dietz, N. H. Fefferman et al. 2022. "Extreme Events, Energy Security and Equality through Micro- and Macro-Levels: Concepts, Challenges and Methods." *Energy Research and Social Science* 85: 102401. http s://doi.org/10.1016/j.erss.2021.102401.

Chen, C.-f., J. Greig, H. Nelson and F. Li. 2022. "When Disadvantage Collides: The Concentrated Effects of Energy Insecurity and Internet Burdens in the United States." *Energy Research and Social Science* 91: 102713. https://doi.org/10.1016/j .erss.2022.102713.

Chen, C.-f., X. Xu, L. Adua, M. Briggs and H. Nelson. 2022. "Exploring the Factors That Influence Energy Use Intensity across Low-, Middle-, and High-Income Households in the United States." *Energy Policy* 168: 113071. https://doi.org/10.1016/j .enpol.2022.113071.

Chen, C.-f., X. Xu and J. K. Day. 2017. "Thermal Comfort or Money Saving?

Exploring Intentions to Conserve Energy among Low-Income Households in the United States." *Energy Research and Social Science* 26: 61–71. https://doi.org/10.1016/j.erss.2017.01.009.

Chenoweth, E. and M. J. Stephan. 2011. *Why Civil Resistance Works: The Strategic Logic of Nonviolent Conflict*. New York: Columbia University Press.

Chenoweth, E., C. S. Hendrix and K. Hunter. 2019. "Introducing the Nonviolent Action in Violent Contexts (NVAVC) Dataset." *Journal of Peace Research* 56(2): 295–305.

Chertow, M. 2001. "The IPAT Equation and Its Variants: Changing Views of Technology and Environmental Impact." *Journal of Industrial Ecology* 4(4): 13–29.

Chess, C., T. Dietz and M. Shannon. 1998. "Who Should Deliberate When?" *Human Ecology Review* 5(1): 45–48.

Cho, J. and Y. Ha. 2012. "On the Communicative Underpinnings of Campaign Effects: Presidential Debates, Citizen Communication, and Polarization in Evaluations of Candidates." *Political Communication* 29(2): 184–204.

Cho, S., K. W. Crenshaw and L. McCall. 2013. "Toward a Field of Intersectionality Studies: Theory, Applications, and Praxis." *Signs: Journal of Women in Culture and Society* 38 (4): 785–810.

Cho, W. K. T. and B. E. Cain. 2020. "Human-Centered Redistricting Automation in the Age of AI." *Science* 369(6508): 1179–81.

Chung, H. 2009. "The Richest 1% Own 50% of Stocks Held by American Households." *Yahoo Finance*, January 17. https://finance.yahoo.com/news/the-richest-1-own-50-of-stocks-held-by-american-households-150758595.html?fr=sycsrp_catchall&guccounter=1.

Churchman, C. W. 1967. "Guest Editorial: Wicked Problems." *Management Science* 14 (4, Application Series): B141–42.

Ciais, P., C. Sabine, G. Bala et al. 2014. "Carbon and Other Biogeochemical Cycles." Pp. 465–570 in *Climate Change 2013: The Physical Science Basis. Contribution of Working Group I to the Fifth Assessment Report of the Intergovernmental Panel on Climate Change*, edited by T. F. Stocker, G.-K. Plattner, M. Tignor et al. Cambridge: Cambridge University Press.

Cialdini, R. B. [1984] 2007. *Influence: The Psychology of Persuasion*. New York: HarperCollins.

Cialdini, R. B. and R. P. Jacobson. 2021. "Influences of Social Norms on Climate Change-Related Behaviors." *Current Opinion in Behavioral Sciences* 42: 1–8. https://doi.org/10.1016/j.cobeha.2021.01.005.

Ciepley, D. 2019. "Can Corporations Be Held to the Public Interest, or Even to the Law?". *Journal of Business Ethics* 154(4): 1003–18.

Clapp, J. and P. Dauvergne. 2005. *Paths to a Green World: The Political Economy of the Global Environment*. Cambridge, MA: MIT Press.

Clapp, R. W. 2002. "Popular Epidemiology in Three Contaminated Communities." *The Annals of the American Academy of Political and Social Science* 584(1): 35–46.

Clark, B., A. K. Jorgenson and J. Kentor. 2010. "Militarization and Energy Consumption: A Test of Treadmill of Destruction Theory in Comparative Perspective." *International Journal of Sociology* 20(2): 23–43.

Clark, W. A. and M. Fossett. 2008. "Understanding the Social Context of the Schelling Segregation Model." *Proceedings of the National Academy of Sciences* 105(11): 4109–14.

Clark, W. C. and N. Dickson. 2001. "Civic Science: America's Encounter with Global Environmental Risks." Pp. 259–94 in *Learning to Manage Global Environmental Risks: A Comparative History of Social Responses to Climate Change, Ozone Depletion and Acid Rain*, Vol. 2, edited by The Social Learning Group. Cambridge, MA: MIT Press.

Clark, W. C. and A. G. Harley. 2020. "Sustainability Science: Toward a Synthesis." *Annual Review of Environment and Resources* 45: 331–86.

Clayton, S. D. 2003. *Identity and the Natural Environment: The Psychological Significance of Nature*. Cambridge, MA: MIT Press.

Clayton, S. D. 2012. " Environment and Identity." Pp. 164–80 in *The Oxford Handbook of Environmental and Conservation Psychology*, edited by S. Clayton. Oxford: Oxford University Press.

Coale, A. J. and E. M. Hoover. 1958. *Population Growth and Economic Development in Low-Income Countries*. Princeton, NJ: Princeton University Press.

Coase, R. H. 1937. "The Nature of the Firm." *Economica* 4(16): 386–405.

Coase, R. H. 1960. "The Problem of Social Costs." *Journal of Law and Economics* 3(1): 1–44.

Coase, R. H. 1976. "Adam Smith's View of Man." *The Journal of Law and Economics* 19 (3): 529–46.

Coase, R. H. 1988. "The Nature of the Firm: Influence." *Journal of Law, Economics and Organization* 4(1): 33–47.

Coburn, C., H. E. Reed, M. Restivo and J. M. Shandra. 2016. "The World Bank, Organized Hypocrisy, and Women's Health: A Cross-National Analysis of Maternal Mortality in Sub-Saharan Africa." *Sociological Forum* 32(1): 50–71. https://doi.org/10.1111/socf.12320.

Coburn, C., M. Restivo and J. M. Shandra. 2015a. "The African Development Bank and Women's Health: A Cross-National Analysis of Structural Adjustment and Maternal Mortality." *Social Science Research* 51: 307–21. https://doi.org/10.1016/j.ssresearch.2014.09.007.

Coburn, C., M. Restivo and J. M. Shandra. 2015b. "The African Development Bank and Infant Mortality: A Cross-National Analysis of Structural Adjustment and Investment Lending from 1990 to 2006." *International Journal of Comparative Sociology* 56(3–4): 275–96.

Coffee, J. C. 2021. "The Future of Disclosure: ESG, Common Ownership, and Systematic Risk." *Colombia Business Law Review* 2021 (2): 601–50.

Cohen, J. E. 1995. *How Many People Can the Earth Support?* New York: W. W. Norton & Company.

Cojean, S., N. Combalbert and A. Taillandier-Schmitt. 2020. "Psychological and Sociological Factors Influencing Police Officers' Decisions to Use Force: A Systematic Literature Review." *International Journal of Law and Psychiatry* 70: 101569. https://doi.org/10.1016/j.ijlp.2020.101569.

Colchester, M. 2004. "Conservation Policy and Indigenous Peoples." *Environmental Science and Policy* 7(3): 145–53.

Cole, H. S. D., C. Freeman, M. Jahoda and K. L. R. Pavitt, eds. 1973. *Models of Doom: A Critique of the Limits to Growth*. New York: Universe Books.

Cole JC, Gillis AJ, Van Der Linden S, Cohen MA, Vandenbergh MP. 2023. "Social Psychological Perspectives on Political Polarization: Insights and Implications for Climate Change." PsyArXiv. https://doi.org/10.31234/osf.io/xz6wk

Coleman, J. S. 1974. *Power and the Structure of Society*. New York: W. W. Norton.

Coleman, J. S. 1988. "Social Capital in the Creation of Human Capital." *American Journal of Sociology* 94: S95–S120.

Coleman, J. S. 1990. *Foundations of Social Theory* Cambridge, MA: Belknap Press of Harvard University Press.

Coleman, P. T. 2021a. *The Way Out: How to Overcome Toxic Polarization*. New York: Columbia University Press.

Coleman, P. T. 2021b. "Data-Driven Solutions to U.S. Polarization." *Science* 371(6526): 244.

Collard, D. 1975. "Edgeworth's Propositions on Altruism." *The Economic Journal* 85(338): 355–60.

Collart, A. 2014. "Benefit Corporations: A Corporation Structure to Align Corporate Personhood with Societal Responsibility." *Seton Hall Law Review* 44(4): 1160–94.

Collins, P. H. 2019. *Intersectionality As Critical Social Theory*. Durham, NC: Duke University Press.

Colman, A. M. 1982. *Game Theory and Experimental Games: The Study of Strategic Interaction*. New York: Pergammon.

Colt, S. G. and G. P. Knapp. 2016. "Economic Effects of an Ocean Acidification Catastrophe." *American Economic Review* 106(5): 615–19.

Committee for the Prize in Economic Sciences in Memory of Alfred Nobel. 2016. "The Sveriges Riksbank Prize in Economic Sciences in Memory of Alfred Nobel 2016." www.nobelprize.org/prizes/economic-sciences/2016/summary.

Commoner, B. 1966. *Science and Survival*. New York: Viking.

Commoner, B. 1972a. "A Bulletin Dialogue on 'The Closing Circle': Response." *Bulletin of the Atomic Scientists* 28(5): 17, 42–56.

Commoner, B. 1972b. "The Environmental Cost of Economic Growth." Pp. 339–63 in *Population, Resources and the Environment*, edited by R. G. Ridker. Washington, DC: Government Printing Office.

Commoner, B., M. Corr and P. J. Stamler. 1971. "The Causes of Pollution." *Environment* 13 (3): 2–19.

Condon, M. 2020a. "Climate Change's New Ally: Big Finance." *Boston Review*, July 28.

Condon, M. 2020b. "Externalities and the Common Owner." *Washington Law Review* 95(1): 1–59.

Conrad, J. [1907] 1963. *The Secret Agent: A Simple Tale*. London: Penguin.

Cook, N. J., T. Grillos and K. P. Andersson. 2019. "Gender Quotas Increase the Equality and Effectiveness of Climate Policy Interventions." *Nature Climate Change* 9(4): 330–34. https://doi.org/10.1038/s41558-019-0438-4.

Corner, A. and N. Pidgeon. 2010. "Geoengineering the Climate: The Social and Ethical Implications." *Environment* 52(1): 24–37. https://doi.org/10.1080/00139150903479563.

Cornwall, W. 2018. "Should It Be Saved?" *Science* 361(6406): 962–65.

Cosme, I., R. Santos and D. W. O'Neill. 2017. "Assessing the Degrowth Discourse: A Review and Analysis of Academic Degrowth Policy Proposals." *Journal of Cleaner Production* 149: 321–34. https://doi.org/10.1016/j.jclepro.2017.02.016.

Cosmides, L. and J. Tooby. 1996. "Are Humans Good Intuitive Statisticians After All? Rethinking Some Conclusions from the Literature on Judgment under Uncertainty." *Cognition* 58(1): 1–73.

Costanza, R. 2020. "Valuing Natural Capital and Ecosystem Services toward the Goals of Efficiency, Fairness, and Sustainability." *Ecosystem Services* 43: 101096. https://doi.org/10.1016/j.ecoser.2020.101096.

Costanza, R., L. J. Graumlich and W. Steffen, eds. 2007. *Sustainability or Collapse? An Integrated History and Future of People on Earth*. Cambridge, MA: MIT Press.

Coughenour, M. B., J. E. Ellis, D. M. Swift et al. 1985. "Energy Extraction and Use in a Nomadic Pastoral Ecosystem." *Science* 230 (4726): 619–25.

Council of Canadian Academies. 2019. *Greater Than the Sum of Its Parts: Toward Integrated Natural Resource Management in Canada*. Ottawa: Council of Canadian Academies.

Cozzarelli, I. M., D. M. Akob, M. J. Baedecker et al. 2017. "Degradation of Crude 4-MCHM (4-Methylcyclohexanemethanol) in Sediments from Elk River, West Virginia." *Environmental Science and Technology* 51 (21): 12139–45.

Cramer, J. C. 1979. "Employment Trends of Young Mothers and the Opportunity Cost of Babies in the United States." *Demography* 16 (2): 177–97.

Cramer, J. C. 1980. "The Effects of Fertility on Husbands' Economic Activity: Evidence from Static Dynamic and Nonrecursive Models." *Research in Population Economics* 2: 151–82.

Cramer, J. C. 1997. "A Demographic Perspective on Air Quality: Conceptual Issues Surrounding Environmental Impacts of Population Growth." *Human Ecology Review* 3(2): 191–96.

Cramer, J. C. 1998. "Population Growth and Air Quality in California." *Demography* 35 (1): 45–56.

Crenshaw, K. 1990. "Mapping the Margins: Intersectionality, Identity Politics, and Violence against Women of Color." *Stanford Law Review* 43(6): 1241–99.

Crenshaw, K. 2003. "Traffic at the Crossroads: Multiple Oppressions." Pp. 43–57 in *Sisterhood Is Forever: The Women's Anthology for a New Millennium*, edited by R. Morgan. New York: Washington Square Press.

Crowfoot, J. and J. Wondolleck. 1990. *Environmental Disputes: Community Involvement in Conflict Resolution*. Washington, DC: Island Press.

Crutzen, P. J. and E. F. Stoermer. 2000. "The Anthropocene." *Global Change Newsletters* No. 41: 17–18.

Cuff, B. M., S. J. Brown, L. Taylor and D. J. Howat. 2016. "Empathy: A Review of the Concept." *Emotion Review* 8(2): 144–53.

Cummings, B. 2012. "Benefit Corporations: How to Enforce a Mandate to Promote the Public Interest." *Columbia Law Review* 112 (3): 578–627.

Cummings, C. L., S. H. Lin and B. D. Trump. 2017. "Public Perceptions of Climate Geoengineering: A Systematic Review of the Literature." *Climate Research* 73(3): 247–64.

Curato, N., D. Farrell, B. Geissel et al. 2021. *Deliberative Mini-Publics: Core Design Features*. Bristol, UK: Policy Press.

Curato, N., J. Sass, S. A. Ercan and S. Niemeyer. 2020. "Deliberative Democracy in the Age of Serial Crisis." *International Political Science Review* 43(1): 55–66.

Currie-Knight, K. 2019. "The Libertarian Pioneers of School Choice." *Cato Policy Report* 41(4): 1, 6–8.

Dahl, R. A. and E. R. Tufte. 1973. *Size and Democracy*. Stanford, CA: Stanford University Press.

Dake, K. 1991. "Orienting Dispositions in the Perception of Risk: An Analysis of Contemporary Worldviews and Cultural Biases." *Journal of Cross-Cultural Psychology* 22(1): 61–82.

Dake, K. 1992. "Myths of Nature: Culture and the Social Construction of Risk." *Journal of Social Issues* 48(4): 21–37.

Dakos, V., S. R. Carpenter, E. H. van Nes and M. Scheffer. 2015. "Resilience Indicators: Prospects and Limitations for Early Warnings of Regime Shifts." *Philosophical Transactions of the Royal Society B: Biological Sciences* 370(1659): 20130263.

Daly, H.E. 1973. *Toward a Steady-State Economy*. San Francisco, CA: Freeman.

Daly, H. E. and J. B. Cobb, Jr. 1989. *For the Common Good: Redirecting the Economy Toward Community, the Environment and a Sustainable Future*. Boston, MA: Beacon Press.

Dancey, L. and G. Sheagley. 2013. "Heuristics Behaving Badly: Party Cues and Voter Knowledge." *American Journal of Political Science* 57(2): 312–25.

Dari-Mattiacci, G., O. Gelderblom, J. Jonker and E. C. Perotti. 2017. "The Emergence of the Corporate Form." *The Journal of Law, Economics, and Organization* 33(2): 193–236.

Darling, K., P. Nandy and C. Breazeal. 2015. "Empathic Concern and the Effect of Stories in Human–Robot Interaction." Pp. 770–75 in *2015 24th IEEE International Symposium on Robot and Human Interactive Communication (RO-MAN)*. IEEE. https://doi.org/10.1109/ROMAN .2015.7333675.

Darwin, C. 1859. *On the Origin of Species by Means of Natural Selection, or the Preservation of Favoured Races in the Struggle for Life*. London: John Murray.

David, E. and D. Lilly. 2006. "Remembering RANN." *Issues in Science and Technology* 22 (3): 11–14.

Davidson, D. J. 2022. "Can Empathy Save Us? Human Predispositions, Social Manifestations, and Climate Futures." Paper presented at the Annual Meetings of the American Sociological Association. August 6, Los Angeles, CA.

Davidson, D. J. and M. Gismondi. 2011. *Challenging Legitimacy at the Precipice of Energy Calamity*. New York: Springer Science & Business Media.

Davidson, D. J. and M. Kecinski. 2021. "Emotional Pathways to Climate Change

Responses." *Wiley Interdisciplinary Reviews: Climate Change* 13(2): e751.

Davis, G. F., M. Yoo and W. E. Baker. 2003. "The Small World of the American Corporate Elite, 1982–2001." *Strategic Organization* 1(3): 301–26.

Davis, L. W. 2017. "Evidence of a Decline in Electricity Use by US households." *Economics Bulletin* 37(2): 1098–105.

Davis, T., E. P. Hennes and L. Raymond. 2018. "Cultural Evolution of Normative Motivations for Sustainable Behaviour." *Nature Sustainability* 1(5): 218–24.

Dawson, G. 2011. "Free Markets, Property Rights and Climate Change: How to Privatize Climate Policy." *Libertarian Papers* 3(10): 1–29.

De Groot, J. and L. Steg. 2007. "General Beliefs and the Theory of Planned Behavior: The Role of Environmental Concerns in the TPB." *Journal of Applied Social Psychology* 37(8): 1817–36.

De Silva, P. U. K. and C. K. Vance. 2017. "Preserving the Quality of Scientific Research: Peer Review of Research Articles." Pp. 73–99 in *Scientific Scholarly Communication: The Changing Landscape*, edited by P. U. K. De Silva and C. K. Vance. Cham: Springer.

De Waal, F. B. 1999. "Anthropomorphism and Anthropodenial: Consistency in Our Thinking about Humans and Other Animals." *Philosophical Topics* 27(1): 255–80.

De Zeeuw, A. 2014. "Regime Shifts in Resource Management." *Annual Review of Resource Economics* 6(1): 85–104.

Deb, N. 2020. "Law and Corporate Malfeasance in Neoliberal India." *Critical Sociology* 46(7–8): 1157–71.

Deb, N. 2021. "Slow Violence and the Gas Peedit in Neoliberal India." *Social Problems.* https://doi.org/10.1093/socpro/spab058.

Della Porta, D. 2020a. *How Social Movements Can Save Democracy: Democratic Innovations from Below.* New York: John Wiley & Sons.

Della Porta, D. 2020b. "How Progressive Social Movements Can Save Democracy in Pandemic Times." *Interface: A Journal for and About Social Movements* 12(1): 355–58.

Della Porta, D. and M. Diani, eds. 2015. *The Oxford Handbook of Social Movements.* Oxford: Oxford University Press.

Deloria, V. and C. M. Lytle. 1998. *The Nations Within: The Past and Future of American Indian Sovereignty.* Austin: University of Texas Press.

DeSilver, D. 2022. *The Polarization in Today's Congress Has Roots That Go Back Decades.* Washington, DC: Pew Research Center. https://pewrsr.ch/3tMrxsF.

DeSilva, J., ed. 2021. *A Most Interesting Problem: What Darwin's Descent of Man Got Right and Wrong about Human Evolution.* Princeton, NJ: Princeton University Press.

Desjardins, J. 2018, "What Market Domination Looks Like." www.visualcapitalist.com/this-chart-reveals-googles-true-dominance-over-the-web/.

Desmond, M. 2012. "Eviction and the Reproduction of Urban Poverty." *American Journal of Sociology* 118(1): 88–133.

Desmond, M. 2016. *Evicted: Poverty and Profit in the American City.* New York: Crown.

Desmond, M. and C. Gershenson. 2016. "Housing and Employment Insecurity among the Working Poor." *Social Problems* 63(1): 46–67. https://doi.org/10.1093/socpro/spv025.

Dewan, T. and K. A. Shepsle. 2011. "Political Economy Models of Elections." *Annual Review of Political Science* 14: 311–30.

Dewey, J. [1888] 1969. "The Ethics of Democracy." Pp. 227–49 in *The Early Works of John Dewey, 1882–1898*, Vol. 1, edited by J. A. Boydston. Carbondale, IL: Southern Illinois University Press.

Dewey, J. 1923. *The Public and Its Problems.* New York: Henry Holt.

Dewey, J. [1939] 1988. "Theory of Valuation." Pp. 189–251 in *Later Works*, Vol. 13. Carbondale: Southern Illinois University Press.

Di Mauro, D., T. Dietz and L. Rockwood. 2007. "Determining the Effect of Urbanization on Generalist Butterfly Species Diversity in Butterfly Gardens." *Urban Ecosystems* 10(4): 427–39.

Diamond, J. 2005. *Collapse: How Societies Choose to Fail or Succeed.* New York: Viking.

Dias, N. and Y. Lelkes. 2021. "The Nature of Affective Polarization: Disentangling Policy Disagreement from Partisan Identity." *American Journal of Political Science* 66(3): 775–90.

Díaz, S., U. Pascual, M. Stenseke et al. 2018. "Assessing Nature's Contributions to People." *Science* 359(6373): 270–72.

Dick, P. K. [1956] 2002. "The Minority Report." Pp. 71–102 in *The Minority Report and Other Classic Stories By Philip K. Dick.* New York: Kensington Publishing Corporation.

Dickson, D. 1975. *Politics of Alternative Technology.* New York: Universe Books.

Diener, E., R. E. Lucas and S. Oishi. 2018. "Advances and Open Questions in the Science of Subjective Well-Being." *Collabra: Psychology* 4(1): 15. https://doi.org/10.1525/collabra.115.

Dietz, T. 1984. "Social Impact Assessment As a Tool for Rangelands Management." Pp. 1613–34 in *Developing Strategies for Rangelands Management*, edited by National Research Council. Boulder, CO: Westview.

Dietz, T. 1987. "Theory and Method in Social Impact Assessment." *Sociological Inquiry* 57 (1): 54–69.

Dietz, T. 1994. "'What Should We Do?' Human Ecology and Collective Decision Making." *Human Ecology Review* 1(2): 301–09.

Dietz, T. 1996–97. "The Human Ecology of Population and Environment: From Utopia to Topia." *Human Ecology Review* 3(2): 168–71.

Dietz, T. 2003. "What Is a Good Decision? Criteria for Environmental Decision Making." *Human Ecology Review* 10(1): 60–67.

Dietz, T. 2005. "The Darwinian Trope in the Drama of the Commons: Variations on Some Themes by the Ostroms." *Journal of Economic Behavior and Organization* 57(2): 205–25.

Dietz, T. 2010. "Narrowing the US Energy Efficiency Gap." *Proceedings of the National Academy of Sciences, USA* 107(37): 16007–08.

Dietz, T. 2011. "The Art of Influence." *Nature* 479(7372): 176.

Dietz, T. 2013a. "Bringing Values and Deliberation to Science Communication." *Proceedings of the National Academy of Sciences* 110(10): 14081–87.

Dietz, T. 2013b. "Context Matters: Eugene A. Rosa's Lessons for Structural Human Ecology." Pp. 189–215 in *Structural Human Ecology: Essays in Risk, Energy, and Sustainability*, edited by T. Dietz and A. K. Jorgenson. Pullman: Washington State University Press.

Dietz, T. 2013c. "Epistemology, Ontology, and the Practice of Structural Human Ecology." Pp. 31–52 in *Structural Human Ecology: Essays in Risk, Energy, and Sustainability*, edited by T. Dietz and A. K. Jorgenson. Pullman, WA: Washington State University Press.

Dietz, T. 2014. "Understanding Environmentally Significant Consumption." *Proceedings of the National Academy of Sciences* 111(14): 5067–68. www.pnas.org/cgi/doi/10.1073/pnas.1403169111.

Dietz, T. 2015a. "Prolegomenon to a Structural Human Ecology of Human Well-Being." *Sociology of Development* 1(1): 123–48.

Dietz, T. 2015b. "Environmental Values." Pp. 329–49 in *The Oxford Handbook of Values*, edited by T. Brosch and D. Sander. Oxford: Oxford University Press.

Dietz, T. 2015c. "Altruism, Self-Interest, and Energy Consumption." *Proceedings of the National Academy of Sciences* 112(6): 1654–55. https://doi.org/10.1073/pnas.1423686112.

Dietz, T. 2017a. "Drivers of Environmental Stress in the Twenty-First Century." *Annual Review of Environment and Resources* 42: 189–213.

Dietz, T. 2017b. "Science, Values, and Conflict in the National Parks." Pp. 247–74 in *Science, Conservation, and National Parks*, edited by S. R. Beissinger, D. B. Ackerly, H. Doremus and G. E. Machlis. Chicago, IL: University of Chicago Press.

Dietz, T. 2020a. "Levering Change: The Power of Peer Pressure." *Nature* 577(7791): 468–69. https://doi.org/10.1038/d41586-020-00111-7.

Dietz, T. 2020b. "Earth Day: Fifty Years of Continuity and Change in

Environmentalism." *One Earth* 2(4): 306–08. https://doi.org/10.1016/j.oneear.2020.04.003.

Dietz, T. 2020c. "Political Events and Public Views on Climate Change." *Climatic Change* 161(1): 1–8. https://doi.org/10.1007/s10584-020-02791-6.

Dietz, T. 2020d. "Governing Regenerative Development." Pp. 93–114 in *Regenerative Development: Urbanization, Climate Change and the Common Good*, edited by B. S. Caniglia, B. Frank, J. Knott, K. Sagendorf and E. Wilkerson. Abingdon: Taylor & Francis.

Dietz, T., S. Allen and A. McCright. 2017. "Integrating Concern for Animals into Personal Values." *Anthrozoös* 30(1): 109–22.

Dietz, T., J. Bell and C. Leshko. 2014. "Population Growth." Pp. 1515–21 in *Encyclopedia of Food and Agricultural Ethics*, edited by D. M. Kaplan and P. B. Thompson. Heidelberg: Springer.

Dietz, T. and T. R. Burns. 1992. "Human Agency and the Evolutionary Dynamics of Culture." *Acta Sociologica* 35(3): 187–200.

Dietz, T., T. R. Burns and F. H. Buttel. 1990. "Evolutionary Theory in Sociology: An Examination of Current Thinking." *Sociological Forum* 5(2): 155–71.

Dietz, T., A. Dan and R. Shwom. 2007. "Support for Climate Change Policy: Social Psychological and Social Structural Influences." *Rural Sociology* 72(2): 185–214.

Dietz, T., N. Dolšak, E. Ostrom and P. C. Stern. 2002. "The Drama of the Commons." Pp. 3–35 in *The Drama of the Commons*, edited by E. Ostrom, T. Dietz, N. Dolšak, P. C. Stern, S. Stonich and E. Weber. Washington, DC: National Academy Press.

Dietz, T., R. Duan, J. Nalley and A. Van Witsen. 2018. "Social Support for Water Quality: The Influence of Values and Symbolic Racism." *Human Ecology Review* 24(1): 51–70.

Dietz, T., A. Fitzgerald and R. Shwom. 2005. "Environmental Values." *Annual Review of Environment and Resources* 30: 335–72.

Dietz, T., K. A. Frank, C. Whitley, J. Kelly and R. Kelly. 2015. "Political Influences on Greenhouse Gas Emissions from US states." *Proceedings of the National Academy of Sciences* 112(27): 8254–59. https://doi.org/10.1073/pnas.1417806112.

Dietz, T., R. S. Frey and L. Kalof. 1987. "Estimation with Cross-National Data: Robust and Nonparametric Methods." *American Sociological Review* 52(3): 380–90.

Dietz, T., R. S. Frey and E. Rosa. 2002. "Risk, Technology and Society." Pp. 562–629 in *Handbook of Environmental Sociology*, edited by R. E. Dunlap and W. Michelson. Westport, CT: Greenwood Press.

Dietz, T., R. S. Frey and E. A. Rosa. 2001. "Risk Assessment and Management." Pp. 272–99 in *The Environment and Society Reader*, edited by R. S. Frey. New York: Allyn and Bacon.

Dietz, T., G. T. Gardner, J. Gilligan, P. C. Stern and M. P. Vandenbergh. 2009. "Household Actions Can Provide a Behavioral Wedge to Rapidly Reduce U.S. Carbon Emissions." *Proceedings of the National Academy of Sciences* 106(44): 18452–56.

Dietz, T. and J. Hawley. 1983. "The Impact of Market Structure and Economic Concentration on the Diffusion of Alternative Technologies: The Photovoltaics Case." Pp. 17–38 in *The Social Constraints on Energy Policy Implementation*, edited by M. Nieman and B. Burt. Lexington, MA: D. C. Heath.

Dietz, T. and A. D. Henry. 2008. "Context and the Commons." *Proceedings of the National Academy of Sciences* 105(36): 13189–90.

Dietz, T. and A. K. Jorgenson, eds. 2013. *Structural Human Ecology: New Essays in Risk, Energy, and Sustainability*. Pullman: Washington State University Press.

Dietz, T. and L. Kalof. 2009. *Introduction to Social Statistics: The Logic of Statistical Reasoning*. New York: Wiley-Blackwell.

Dietz, T., L. Kalof and R. S. Frey. 1991. "On the Utility of Robust and Resampling Procedures." *Rural Sociology* 56(3): 461–74.

Dietz, T., L. Kalof and P. C. Stern. 2002. "Gender, Values and Environmentalism." *Social Science Quarterly* 83(1): 353–65.

Dietz, T., C. Leshko and A. M. McCright. 2013. "Politics Shapes Individual Choices about Energy Efficiency." *Proceedings of the National Academy of Sciences* 110(23): 9191–92.

Dietz, T., E. Ostrom, N. Dolšak and P. C. Stern. 2001. "The Drama of the Commons." Pp. 3–35 in *The Drama of the Commons*, edited by E. Ostrom, T. Dietz, N. Dolšak, P. C. Stern, S. Stonich and E. Weber. Washington, DC: National Academy Press.

Dietz, T., E. Ostrom and P. C. Stern. 2003. "The Struggle to Govern the Commons." *Science* 301(5652): 1907–12.

Dietz, T. and E. A. Rosa. 1994. "Rethinking the Environmental Impacts of Population, Affluence and Technology." *Human Ecology Review* 1(2): 277–300.

Dietz, T., E. A. Rosa and R. York. 2009. "Environmentally Efficient Well-Being: Rethinking Sustainability As the Relationship between Human Well-Being and Environmental Impacts." *Human Ecology Review* 16(1): 113–22.

Dietz, T., E. A. Rosa and R. York. 2010. "Human Driving Forces of Global Change: Examining Current Theories." Pp. 83–134 in *Human Footprints on the Global Environment: Threats to Sustainability*, edited by E. A. Rosa, A. Diekmann, T. Dietz and C. Jaeger. Cambridge, MA: MIT Press.

Dietz, T., E. A. Rosa and R. York. 2012. "Environmentally Efficient Well-Being: Is There a Kuznets Curve?" *Journal of Applied Geography* 32(1): 21–28.

Dietz, T. and R. W. Rycroft. 1987. *The Risk Professionals*. New York: Russell Sage Foundation.

Dietz, T., R. L. Shwom and C. T. Whitley. 2020. "Climate Change and Society." *Annual Review of Sociology* 46: 135–58.

Dietz, T. and P. C. Stern. 1995. "Toward a Theory of Choice: Socially Embedded Preference Construction." *Journal of Socio-Economics* 24(2): 261–79.

Dietz, T., P. C. Stern and A. Dan. 2009. "How Deliberation Affects Stated Willingness to Pay for Mitigation of Carbon Dioxide Emissions: An Experiment." *Land Economics* 85(2): 329–47.

Dietz, T., P. C. Stern and R. W. Rycroft. 1989. "Definitions of Conflict and the Legitimation of Resources: The Case of Environmental Risk." *Sociological Forum* 4(1): 47–70.

Dietz, T. and E. Vine. 1982. "Energy Impacts of a Municipal Conservation Policy." *Energy* 7 (9): 755–58.

Dietz, T. and C. T. Whitley. 2018. "Inequality, Decisions, and Altruism." *Sociology of Development* 4(3): 282–303.

Dietz, T. and R. York. 2015. "Animals, Capital and Sustainability." *Human Ecology Review* 22(1): 35–53.

Dietz, T. and R. York. 2021. "Structural Human Ecology." Pp. 439–56 in *Handbook of Environmental Sociology*, edited by B. S. Caniglia, A. Jorgenson, S. A. Malin, L. Peek, D. N. Pellow and X. Huang. Cham: Springer.

Dietz, T. and J. Zhao. 2011. "Paths to Climate Cooperation." *Proceedings of the National Academy of Science, USA* 108(38): 15671–72.

Dikötter, F. 2019. *How to Be a Dictator: The Cult of Personality in the Twentieth Century*. New York: Bloomsbury Publishing USA.

Dilling, L., A. Prakash, Z. Zommers et al. 2019. "Is Adaptation Success a Flawed Concept?" *Nature Climate Change* 9(8): 572–74.

Dimitropoulos, A., W. Oueslati and C. Sintek. 2018. "The Rebound Effect in Road Transport: A Meta-analysis of Empirical Studies." *Energy Economics* 75: 163–79. https://doi.org/10.1016/j.eneco.2018.07.021.

Dinda, S. 2004. "Environmental Kuznets Curve Hypothesis: A Survey." *Ecological Economics* 49(4): 431–55.

Ding, D., E. Maibach, X. Zhao, C. Roser-Renouf and A. Leiserowitz. 2011. "Support for Climate Policy and Societal Action Are Linked to Perceptions about Scientific Agreement." *Nature Climate Change* 1(9): 462–66.

Dirzo, R., H. S. Young, M. Galetti et al. 2014. "Defaunation in the Anthropocene." *Science* 345(6195): 401–06.

Dolan, E. G. 2006. "Science, Public Policy, and Global Warming: Rethinking the

Market-Liberal Position." *Cato Journal* 26 (3): 445–68.

Dolan, P., T. Peasgood and M. White. 2008. "Do We Really Know What Makes Us Happy? A Review of the Economic Literature on the Factors Associated with Subjective Well-Being." *Journal of Economic Psychology* 29(1): 94–122.

Donlan, C. J., J. Berger, C. E. Bock et al. 2006. "Pleistocene Rewilding: An Optimistic Agenda for Twenty-First Century Conservation." *American Naturalist* 168(5): 660–81.

Douglas, H. 2009. *Science, Policy, and the Value-Free Ideal*. Pittsburgh, PA: University of Pittsburgh Press.

Douglas, H. 2018. "From Tapestry to Loom: Broadening the Perspective on Values in Science." *Philosophy, Theory, and Practice in Biology* 10(8). https://doi.org/10.3998/ptpbio .16039257.0010.008.

Douglas, M. and A. Wildavsky. 1982. *Risk and Culture: An Essay on the Selection of Technological and Environmental Dangers*. Berkeley: University of California Press.

Dowie, M. 2011. *Conservation Refugees: The Hundred-Year Conflict between Global Conservation and Native Peoples*. Cambridge, MA: MIT Press.

Downey, L. 2015. *Inequality, Democracy, and the Environment*. New York: NYU Press.

Downs, G. W. and P. D. Larkey. 1986. *The Search for Government Efficiency: From Hubris to Helplessness*. Philadelphia, PA: Temple University Press.

Doyle, S. A. C. [1887] 1967. "A Study in Scarlet." Pp. 143–234 in *The Annotated Sherlock Holmes*, Vol. 1, edited by W. S. Baring-Gould. New York: Clarkson N. Potter.

Druckman, J. N. 2004. "Political Preference Formation: Competition, Deliberation, and the (Ir)relevance of Framing Effects." *American Political Science Review* 98(4): 671–86.

Druckman, J. N., S. Klar, Y. Krupnikov, M. Levendusky and J. B. Ryan. 2021a. "Affective Polarization, Local Contexts and Public Opinion in America." *Nature Human Behaviour* 5(1): 28–38.

Druckman, J. N., S. Klar, Y. Krupnikov, M. Levendusky and J. B. Ryan. 2021b. "How Affective Polarization Shapes Americans' Political Beliefs: A Study of Response to the COVID-19 Pandemic." *Journal of Experimental Political Science* 8(3): 223–34.

Druckman, J. N., J. H. Kuklinski and L. Sigelman. 2009. "The Unmet Potential of Interdisciplinary Research: Political Psychological Approaches to Voting and Public Opinion." *Political Behavior* 31(4): 485–510.

Druckman, J. N. and A. Lupia. 2016. "Preference Change in Competitive Political Environments." *Annual Review of Political Science* 19: 13–31.

Druckman, J. N., T. J. Leeper and R. Slothuus. 2018. "Motivated Responses to Political Communications." Pp. 125–50 in *The Feeling, Thinking Citizen: Essays in Honor of Milton Lodge*, edited by H. Lavine and C. S. Taber. New York: Routledge.

Druckman, J. N. and M. S. Levendusky. 2019. "What Do We Measure When We Measure Affective Polarization?" *Public Opinion Quarterly* 83(1): 114–22.

Druckman, J. N. and M. C. McGrath. 2019. "The Evidence for Motivated Reasoning in Climate Change Preference Formation." *Nature Climate Change* 9(2): 111–19.

Druckman, J. N. and K. R. Nelson. 2003. "Framing and Deliberation: How Citizens' Conversations Limit Elite Influence." *American Journal of Political Science* 47(4): 729–45.

Drummond, C. and B. Fischhoff. 2017. "Individuals with Greater Science Literacy and Education Have More Polarized Beliefs on Controversial Science Topics." *Proceedings of the National Academy of Sciences* 114(36): 9587–92.

Dryzek, J. S. 1987a. "Complexity and Rationality in Public Life." *Political Studies* 35(3): 424–42.

Dryzek, J. S. 1987b. "Discursive Designs: Critical Theory and Political Institutions."

*American Journal of Political Science* 31(3): 656–79.

Dryzek, J. S. 1987c. *Rational Ecology: Environment and Political Economy*. Oxford: Oxford University Press.

Dryzek, J. S., A. Bächtiger, S. Chambers et al. 2019. "The Crisis of Democracy and the Science of Deliberation." *Science* 363(6432): 1144–46.

Dryzek, J. S. and C. List. 2003. "Social Choice Theory and Deliberative Democracy: A Reconciliation." *British Journal of Political Science* 33(1): 1–28.

Du Bois, W. E. B. [1935] 2014. *Black Reconstruction in America: An Essay Toward a History of the Part Which Black Folk Played in the Attempt to Reconstruct Democracy in America, 1860–1880*. The Oxford W. E. B. Du Bois. Oxford: Oxford University Press.

Dubrulle, H. 2006. "Review of Adam Hochschild. Bury the Chains: Prophets and Rebels in the Fight to Free an Empire's Slaves. Boston: Houghton Mifflin, 2005. Pp. 468. $26.95." *Journal of British Studies* 45(1): 179–81.

Duggan, L. 2019. *Mean Girl: Ayn Rand and the Culture of Greed*. Berkeley: University of California Press.

Dunaway, F. 2008. "Gas Masks, Pogo, and the Ecological Indian: Earth Day and the Visual Politics of American Environmentalism." *American Quarterly* 60(1): 67–99.

Dunaway, F. 2015. *Seeing Green: The Use and Abuse of American Environmental Images*. Chicago: University of Chicago Press.

Duncan, O. D. 1964. "From Social System to Ecosystem." *Sociological Inquiry* 31(2): 140–49.

Duncan, O. D. and L. F. Schnore. 1959. "Cultural, Behavioral and Ecological Perspectives in the Study of Social Organization." *American Journal of Sociology* 65(2): 132–46.

Dunlap, R. E., J. K. Grieneeks and M. Rokeach. 1983. "Human Values and Pro-Environmental Behavior." Pp. 145–68 in *Energy and Mineral Resources: Attitudes, Values and Public Policy*, edited by D. W. Conn. Washington, DC: American Association for the Advancement of Science.

Dunlap, R. E. and A. G. Mertig. 1995. "Global Concern for the Environment: Is Affluence a Prerequisite?" *Journal of Social Issues* 51(4): 121–37.

Dunlap, R. E. and A. G. Mertig. 1997. "Global Environmental Concern: An Anomaly for Postmaterialism." *Social Science Quarterly* 78(1): 24–29.

Dunlap, R. E. and A. M. McCright. 2008. "Social Movement Identity: Validating a Measure of Identification with the Environmental Movement." *Social Science Quarterly* 89(5): 1045–65. https://doi.org/10.1111/j.1540-6237.2008.00573.x.

Dunlap, R. E. and K. D. Van Liere. 1977. "Land Ethic or Golden Rule." *Journal of Social Issues* 33(3): 200–07.

Dunleavy, P. 2014. *Democracy, Bureaucracy and Public Choice: Economic Approaches in Political Science*. London: Routledge.

Dyball, R., V. A. Brown and M. Keen. 2007. "Towards Sustainability: Five Strands of Social Learning." Pp. 181–95 in *Social Learning towards a Sustainable World*, edited by A. E. J. Wahls. Wagenigen: Wagenigen Academic Publishers.

Dyball, R. and B. Newell. 2014. *Understanding Human Ecology: A Systems Approach to Sustainability*. London: Routledge.

Eagan, M. 2007. *Barry Commoner and the Science of Survival: The Remaking of American Environmentalism*. Cambridge, MA: MIT Press.

Easterlin, R. A. 1974. "Does Economic Growth Improve the Human Lot? Some Empirical Evidence." Pp. 89–125 in *Nations and Households in Economic Growth: Essays in Honor of Moses Abramovitz*, edited by P. A. David and M. W. Reder. New York: Academic Press.

Easterlin, R. A. 2015. "Happiness and Economic Growth: The Evidence." Pp. 283–99 in *Global Handbook of Quality of Life*, edited by W. Glatzer, L. Camfield, V. Moller and M. Rojas. Dordrecht: Springer.

The Economist. 2019. "Beware the Borg." *The Economist*, December 21.

Economo, E., L. Hong and S. E. Page. 2016. "Social Structure, Endogenous Diversity, and Collective Accuracy." *Journal of Economic Behavior and Organization* 125: 212–31. https://doi.org/10.1016/j.jebo.2016.01.003.

Edelblutte, É. 2022. "The Secret to Wildlife Conservation Might Be the 'Animal Agency' Approach: Giving Creatures a Role in Their Own Preservation." *The Brink*, March 9.

Edelblutte, É., R. Krithivasan and M. N. Hayek. 2022. "Animal Agency in Wildlife Conservation and Management." *Conservation Biology*: e13853. https://doi.org/10.1111/cobi.13853.

Edgeworth, F. Y. 1881. *Mathematical Psychics: An Essay on the Application of Mathematics to the Moral Sciences*. London: Kegan Paul.

Edwards, C. 2015. "Why the Federal Government Fails." Cato Institute Policy Analysis No. 777, July.

Edwards, F., H. Lee and M. Esposito. 2019. "Risk of Being Killed by Police Use of Force in the United States by Age, Race–Ethnicity, and Sex." *Proceedings of the National Academy of Sciences* 116(34): 16793–98.

Egan, P. J., D. M. Konisky and M. Mullin. 2022. "Ascendant Public Opinion: The Rising Influence of Climate Change on Americans' Attitudes about the Environment." *Public Opinion Quarterly* 86 (1): 134–48. https://doi.org/10.1093/poq/nfab071.

Ehrlich, P. R. 1968. *The Population Bomb*. New York: Ballantine.

Ehrlich, P. R. 1969. "Eco-Catastrophe." *Ramparts* (September–October): 24–28.

Ehrlich, P. R. and J. P. Holdren. 1970. "Hidden Effects of Overpopulation." *Saturday Review* 53(31): 52.

Ehrlich, P. R. and J. P. Holdren. 1971. "Impact of Population Growth." *Science* 171(3977): 1212–17.

Ehrlich, P. R. and J. P. Holdren. 1972a. "Impact of Population Growth." Pp. 365–77 in *Population, Resources and the Environment*, edited by R. G. Ridker. Washington, DC: US Government Printing Office.

Ehrlich, P. R. and J. P. Holdren. 1972b. "A Bulletin Dialogue on 'The Closing Circle': Critique." *Bulletin of the Atomic Scientists* 28(5): 16, 18–27.

Eisenstein, M. A., A. K. Clark and T. G. Jelen. 2017. "Political Tolerance and Religion: An Age-Period-Cohort Analysis, 1984–2014." *Review of Religious Research* 59(3): 395–418.

Elkington, J. 1997. *Cannibals with Forks: Triple Bottom Line of 21st Century Business*. Gabriola Island, BC: New Society Publishers.

Elkington, J. 2004. "Enter the Triple Bottom Line." Pp. 1–16 in *The Triple Bottom Line, Does It All Add Up? Assessing the Sustainability of Business and CSR*, edited by A. Henriques and J. Richardson. London: Earthscan.

Elliott, K. C. 2017. *A Tapestry of Values: An Introduction to Values in Science*. New York: Oxford University Press.

Elliott, K. C. 2018. "A Tapestry of Values: Response to My Critics." *Philosophy, Theory, and Practice in Biology* 10(11). https://doi.org/10.3998/ptpbio.16039257.0010.011.

Emmerich, R. 2011. *Anonymous*. Sony Pictures.

Endres, F., ed. 2020. *Under Fire, Under Siege: Strikebreakers in Kent, Ohio*. Kent, OH: PBS Western Reserve.

Engstrom, E. J. 2014. *Partisan Gerrymandering and the Construction of American Democracy*. Ann Arbor: University of Michigan Press.

Environmental Action, ed. 1970. *Earth Day: The Beginning*. New York: Bantam Books.

Epperly, B., C. Witko, R. Strickler and P. White. 2020. "Rule by Violence, Rule by Law: Lynching, Jim Crow, and the Continuing Evolution of Voter Suppression in the US." *Perspectives on Politics* 18(3): 756–69.

Epstein, L., W. M. Landes and R. A. Posner. 2012. "How Business Fares in the Supreme Court." *Minnesota Law Review* 97: 1431–73. https://scholarship.law.umn.edu/mlr/359.

Espey, J. A. and M. Espey. 2004. "Turning On the Lights: A Meta-analysis of Residential

Electricity Demand Elasticities." *Journal of Agricultural and Applied Economics* 36(1): 65–81.

Estes, J. A., J. Terborgh, J. S. Brashares et al. 2011. "Trophic Downgrading of Planet Earth." *Science* 333(6040): 301–06.

Esty, D. C. and J. W. Emerson. 2018. "From Crises and Gurus to Science and Metrics: Yale's Environmental Performance Index and the Rise of Data-Driven Policymaking." Pp. 93–102 in *Routledge Handbook of Sustainability Indicators*, edited by S. Bell and S. Morse. New York: Routledge.

Evans, P. 1979. *Dependent Development: The Alliance of State, Local and Multinational Capital in Brazil*. Princeton, NJ: Princeton University Press.

Fabina, J. 2021. "Despite Pandemic Challenges, 2020 Election Had Largest Increase in Voting between Presidential Elections on Record." *America Counts* (US Census Bureau), April 29. www.census.gov/library/s tories/2021/04/record-high-turnout-in-2020-general-election.html.

Falcao, T. 2019. "Yellow Vests and Young Greens: Searching for Equity and Public Acceptance in Carbon Taxation." *Tax Notes International* 95(3). https://ssrn.com /abstract=3827543.

Falk, A., E. Fehr and U. Fischbacher. 2002. "Appropriating the Commons: A Theoretical Explanation." Pp. 157–91 in *The Drama of the Commons*, edited by E. Ostrom, T. Dietz, N. Dolšak, P. C. Stern, S. Stonich and E. Weber. Washington, DC: National Academy Press.

Fanon, F. 1969. *The Wretched of the Earth*, translated by Constance Farrington. London: Penguin Books.

Farooq, O., M. Farooq and E. Reynaud. 2019. "Does Employees' Participation in Decision Making Increase the Level of Corporate Social and Environmental Sustainability? An Investigation in South Asia." *Sustainability* 11(2): 511.

Farrow, K., G. Grolleau and L. Ibanez. 2017. "Social Norms and Pro-environmental Behavior: A Review of the Evidence."
*Ecological Economics* 140: 1–13. https://doi .org/10.1016/j.ecolecon.2017.04.017.

Favre, D.S. 2018. *Respecting Animals: A Balanced Approach to Our Relationship with Pets, Food, and Wildlife*. Amherst, NY: Prometheus Books.

Feeny, D., F. Berkes, B. J. McCay and J. M. Acheson. 1990. "The Tragedy of the Commons: Twenty-Two Years Later." *Human Ecology* 18(1): 1–19.

Fehr, E. 2009. "On the Economics and Biology of Trust." *Journal of the European Economics Association* 7(2–3): 235–66.

Fehr, E. and U. Fischbacher. 2003. "The Nature of Human Altruism." *Nature* 425(6690): 785–91.

Fehr, E. and H. Gintis. 2007. "Human Motivation and Social Cooperation: Experimental and Analytical Foundations." *Annual Review of Sociology* 33: 43–64.

Feldstein, S. 2019. "The Road to Digital Unfreedom: How Artificial Intelligence Is Reshaping Repression." *Journal of Democracy* 30(1): 40–52.

Felli, R. 2014. "An Alternative Socio-ecological Strategy? International Trade Unions' Engagement with Climate Change." *Review of International Political Economy* 21(2): 372–98.

Fernández-Armesto, F. 2014. *Our America: A Hispanic History of the United States*. New York: W. W. Norton & Company.

Finkel, E. J., C. A. Bail, M. Cikara et al. 2020. "Political Sectarianism in America." *Science* 370(6516): 533–36.

Fiorino, D. J. 1990. "Citizen Participation and Environmental Risk: A Survey of Institutional Mechanisms." *Science, Technology and Human Values* 15(2): 226–43.

Fiorina, M. P. and S. J. Abrams. 2008. "Political Polarization in the American Public." *Annual Review of Political Science* 11: 563–88.

Fischer, R., T. L. Milfont and V. V. Gouveia. 2011. "Does Social Context Affect Value Structures? Testing the Within-Country Stability of Value Structures with a Functional Theory of Values." *Journal of Cross-Cultural Psychology* 42(2): 253–70. ht tps://doi.org/10.1177/0022022110396888.

Fischhoff, B. 2015. "The Realities of Risk-Cost-Benefit Analysis." *Science* 350(6260): aaa6516.

Fischhoff, B. and J. Kadvany. 2011. *Risk: A Very Short Introduction*. Oxford: Oxford University Press.

Fischhoff, B., S. Lichtenstein, P. Slovic, S. L. Derby and R. H. Keeney. 1981. *Acceptable Risk*. Cambridge: Cambridge University Press.

Fischhoff, B., P. Slovic, S. Lichtenstein, S. Read and B. Combs. 1978. "How Safe Is Safe Enough? A Psychometric Study of Attitudes towards Technological Risks and Benefits." *Policy Sciences* 9(2): 127–52.

Fischhoff, M. E. 2007. "Electricity Company Managers' Views of Environmental Issues: Implications for Environmental Groups and Government." *Energy Policy* 35(7): 3868–78.

Fishbane, A., A. Ouss and A. K. Shah. 2020. "Behavioral Nudges Reduce Failure to Appear for Court." *Science* 370(6517): 658–59. https://doi.org/10.1126/science.abb6591.

Fisher, D. and A. K. Jorgenson. 2019. "Ending the Stalemate: Toward a Theory of the Anthro-Shift." *Sociological Theory* 37(4): 342–62.

Fisher, D. R. 2019. *American Resistance*. New York: Columbia University Press.

Fishkin, J., A. Siu, L. Diamond and N. Bradburn. 2021. "Is Deliberation an Antidote to Extreme Partisan Polarization? Reflections on 'America in One Room'." *American Political Science Review* 115(4): 1464–81.

Fishkin, J. S. 2018. *Democracy When the People Are Thinking: Revitalizing Our Politics through Public Deliberation*. Oxford: Oxford University Press.

Fishkin, J. S. 2021. "Deliberative Public Consultation via Deliberative Polling: Criteria and Methods." *The Hastings Center Report* 51(S2): S19–S24.

Fishkin, J. S. and R. C. Luskin. 2005. "Experimenting with a Democratic Ideal: Deliberative Polling and Public Opinion." *Acta Politica* 40(3): 284–98.

Fisman, R., P. Jakiela, S. Kariv and D. Markovits. 2015. "The Distributional Preferences of an Elite." *Science* 349(6254): aab0096.

Fitzgerald, A. J. 2005. *Animal Abuse and Family Violence*. Lewiston, NY: Edwin Mellen Press.

Fitzgerald, A. J., B. J. Barrett, R. Stevenson and C. H. Cheung. 2019. "Animal Maltreatment in the Context of Intimate Partner Violence: A Manifestation of Power and Control?" *Violence against Women* 25(15): 1806–28.

Fitzgerald, A. J., B. J. Barrett, D. Mcphee, P. T. Fritz and R. Stevenson. 2020. "People in Abusive Relationships Face Many Barriers to Leaving – Pets Should Not Be One." *The Conversation*, June 16. https://the conversation.com/people-in-abusive-relationships-face-many-barriers-to-leaving-pets-should-not-be-one-139540.

Fitzpatrick, K. 2011. *Planned Obsolescence: Publishing, Technology, and the Future of the Academy*. New York: NYU Press.

Fleck, R. F. 1978. "John Muir's Evolving Attitudes toward Native American Cultures." *American Indian Quarterly* 4(1): 19–31.

Fleetwood, J. 2017. "Public Health, Ethics, and Autonomous Vehicles." *American Journal of Public Health* 107(4): 532–37.

Fletcher, M.-S., R. Hamilton, W. Dressler and L. Palmer. 2021. "Indigenous Knowledge and the Shackles of Wilderness." *Proceedings of the National Academy of Sciences* 118(40): e2022218118. https://doi.org/10.1073/pnas.2022218118.

Fogarty, M. J., R. Gamble and C. T. Perretti. 2016. "Dynamic Complexity in Exploited Marine Ecosystems." *Frontiers in Ecology and Evolution* 4: 68. https://doi.org/10.3389/fevo.2016.00068.

Force, J. E., G. E. Machlis and L. Zhang. 2000. "The Engines of Change in Resource-Dependent Communities." *Forest Science* 46(3): 410–22.

Ford, J. D., L. Cameron, J. Rubis et al. 2016. "Including Indigenous Knowledge and Experience in IPCC Assessment Reports." *Nature Climate Change* 6(4): 349.

Forester, J., ed. 1985. *Critical Theory and Public Life*. Cambridge, MA: MIT Press.

Fortner, R., 2019. "There's Nothing Smeary about Lake Erie Anymore," Ohio Sea Grant website article, March 2. https://ohioseagrant.osu.edu/news/2019/abfir/lorax-lake-erie.

Foster, J. B. 1994. *The Vulnerable Planet*. New York: Monthly Review Press.

Foster, J. B. 1999. "Marx's Theory of Metabolic Rift: Classical Foundations for Environmental Sociology." *American Journal of Sociology* 105(2): 366–405.

Foster, J. B. 2013. *The Theory of Monopoly Capitalism*. New York: Monthly Review Press.

Foster, J. B., B. Clark and R. York. 2010. *The Ecological Rift: Capitalism's War on the Earth*. New York: Monthly Review Press.

Foster, J. B. and H. Holleman. 2014. "The Theory of Unequal Ecological Exchange: A Marx-Odum Dialectic." *Journal of Peasant Studies* 41(2): 199–233.

Fox, M.-J. V. and J. D. Erickson. 2018. "Genuine Economic Progress in the United States: A Fifty State Study and Comparative Assessment." *Ecological Economics* 147: 29–35. https://doi.org/10.1016/j.ecolecon.2018.01.002.

Frank, K., I.-C. Chen, Y. Lee et al. 2012. "Network Location and Policy-Oriented Behavior: An Analysis of Two-Mode Networks of Coauthored Documents Concerning Climate Change in the Great Lakes Region." *Policy Studies Journal* 40(3): 492–515.

Frank, K. A. 2000. "The Impact of a Confounding Variable on a Regression Coefficient." *Sociological Methods and Research* 29(2): 147–94.

Frank, K. A., S. Maroulis, M. Q. Duong and B. Kelcey. 2013. "What Would It Take to Change an Inference? Using Rubin's Causal Model to Interpret the Robustness of Causal Inferences." *Educational Evaluation and Policy Analysis* 35(4): 437–60.

Frank, K. A. and K.-S. Min. 2007. "Indices of Robustness for Sample Representation." *Sociological Methodology* 37(1): 349–92.

Frank, R. H. 2010. *Luxury Fever: Weighing the Cost Of Excess*. Princeton, NJ: Princeton University Press.

Frank, R. H. 2020. *Under the Influence: Putting Peer Pressure to Work*. Princeton, NJ: Princeton University Press.

Frank, R. H., T. D. Gilovich and D. T. Regan. 1996. "Do Economists Make Bad Citizens?" *Journal of Economic Perspectives* 10(1): 187–92.

Frankenhuis, W. E. and D. Nettle. 2020. "The Strengths of People in Poverty." *Current Directions in Psychological Science* 29(1): 16–21.

Franklin, B. [1755] 1918. *Observations Concerning the Increase of Mankind, Peopling of Countries, &c*. Tarrytown, NY: W. Abbatt.

Franks, B., N. Jun and L. Williams. 2018. *Anarchism: A Conceptual Approach*. New York: Routledge.

Fraser, N. 1992. "Rethinking the Public Sphere: A Contribution to the Critique of Actually Existing Democracy." Pp. 109–42 in *Habermas and the Public Sphere*, edited by C. Calhoun. Cambridge, MA: MIT Press.

Freeman, D. M. 1992. *Choice Against Chance: Constructing a Policy-Assessing Sociology for Social Development*. Niwot: University Press of Colorado.

Freeman, D. M. and R. S. Frey. 1986. "A Method for Assessing the Social Impacts of Natural Resource Policies." *Journal of Environmental Management* 23(3): 229–45.

Freeman, D. M. and R. S. Frey. 1990–91. "A Modest Proposal for Assessing Social Impacts of Natural Resource Policies." *Journal of Environmental Systems* 20(4): 375–404.

Freeman, R. E. 1984. *Strategic Management: A Stakeholder Approach*. Boston, MA: Pitman.

Freire, P. [1968] 1972. *Pedagogy of the Oppressed*, translated by M. B. Ramos. New York: Harper.

Freudenburg, W. R. 2005. "Privileged Access, Privileged Accounts: Toward a Socially Structured Theory of Resources and Discourses." *Social Forces* 84(1): 89–114.

Freudenburg, W. R. 2006. "Environmental Degradation, Disproportionality, and the Double Diversion: Reaching Out, Reaching Ahead, and Reaching Beyond." *Rural Sociology* 71(1): 3–32.

Freudenburg, W. R., L. J. Wilson and D. J. O'Leary. 1998. "Forty Years of Spotted Owls? A Longitudinal Analysis of Logging Industry Job Losses." *Sociological Perspectives* 41(1): 1–26.

Frey, R. G. 2011. "Utilitarianism and Animals." Pp. 172–97 in *The Oxford Handbook of Animal Ethics*, edited by T. L. Beauchamp and R. G. Frey. Oxford: Oxford University Press.

Frey, R. S. 1994. "The International Traffic in Hazardous Wastes." *Journal of Environmental Systems* 23(2): 165–77.

Frey, R. S. 1995. "The International Traffic in Pesticides." *Technological Forecasting and Social Change* 50(2): 151–69.

Frey, R. S. 1997a. "The International Traffic in Tobacco." *Third World Quarterly* 18(2): 303–17.

Frey, R. S. 1997b. "The Export of Asbestos to the Peripheral Zones of the World Economy." Paper presented at the Annual Meeting of the American Sociological Association. Toronto.

Frey, R. S. 1998a. "The Export of Hazardous Industries to the Peripheral Zones of the World-System." *Journal of Developing Societies* 14(1): 66–81.

Frey, R. S. 1998b. "The Hazardous Waste Flow in the World-System." Pp. 84–103 in *Space and Transport in the World System*, edited by P. Ciccantell and S. G. Bunker. Westport, CT: Greenwood Press.

Frey, R. S. 2003. "The Transfer of Core-Based Hazardous Production Processes to the Export Processing Zones of the Periphery: The Maquiladora Centers of Northern Mexico." *Journal of World-Systems Research* 9(2): 317–54.

Frey, R. S. 2006. "The Flow of Hazardous Exports in the World System." Pp. 133–49 in *Globalization and the Environment*, edited by A. Jorgenson and E. Kick. Leiden: Brill Academic Press.

Frey, R. S. and I. Al-Mansour. 1995. "The Effects of Development, Dependence and Population Pressure on Democracy: The Cross-National Evidence." *Sociological Spectrum* 15(2): 181–208.

Frey, R. S., K. Al-Sharideh, K. Bausman et al. 1999. "Development, Dependence, Population Pressure, and Human Rights: The Cross-National Evidence." *Human Ecology Review* 6(1): 49–56.

Frey, R. S., P. K. Gellert and H. F. Dahms, eds. 2018. *Ecologically Unequal Exchange: Environmental Injustice in Comparative and Historical Perspective*. New York: Springer.

Frey, R. S. and I. Said. 1988. "A Social Assessment of Alternative Water Management Policies in Southwestern Kansas." *Journal of Environmental Systems* 18(2): 173–82.

Friedman, H. S. 2020. *Ultimate Price: The Value We Place on Life*. Berkeley: University of California Press.

Friedman, M. 1953. *Essays in Positive Economics*. Chicago, IL: University of Chicago Press.

Friedman, M. 1955. "The Role of Government in Education in Economics and the Public Interest." In *Economics and the Public Interest*, edited by R. A. Solo. New Brunswick, NJ: Rutgers University Press. https://la.utexas.edu/users/hcleaver/330T/350kPEEFriedmanRoleOfGovttable.pdf.

Friedman, M. 1970. "The Social Responsibility of Business Is to Increase Its Profits." *New York Times Magazine*, September 13, pp. 32–33, 122, 124, 126.

Friedman, M. 1991. "Say 'No' to Intolerance." *Liberty Magazine* 4(6): 17–20.

Friedman, M. and R. D. Friedman. 1980. *Free to Choose: A Personal Statement*. Orlando, FL: Harcourt.

Friends of the Earth and New Economics Foundation. 2006. *The (un)Happy Planet Index*. London: New Economics Foundation.

Friis, C. and J. Ø. Nielsen, eds. 2019. *Telecoupling: Exploring Land-Use Change in a Globalised World.* Cham: Palgrave Macmillan.

Frisch, N. K., P. C. Gibson, A. M. Stowman et al. 2022. "Anatomy of a Cyberattack: Part 4: Quality Assurance and Error Reduction, Billing and Compliance, Transition to Uptime." *American Journal of Clinical Pathology* 158(1): 18–26.

Fromm, E. 1964. *The Heart of Man.* New York: Harper & Row.

Fryer-Biggs, Z. 2019. "Coming Soon to a Battlefield: Robots That Can Kill." *Atlantic*, September 3. www.theatlantic.com/technology/archive/2019/09/killer-robots-and-new-era-machine-driven-warfare/597130/.

Fryer-Biggs, Z. 2021. "Can Computer Algorithms Learn to Fight Wars Ethically?" *Washington Post Magazine*, February 17. www.washingtonpost.com/magazine/2021/02/17/pentagon-funds-killer-robots-but-ethics-are-under-debate/.

Fukuyama, F. 1989. "The End of History?" *The National Interest* (Summer): 3–18.

Fukuyama, F. 1992. *The End of History and the Last Man.* New York: Free Press.

Fukuyama, F. 1995. *Trust: The Social Virtues and the Creation of Prosperity.* New York: Free Press.

Fukuyama, F. 2011. *The Origins of Political Order: From Prehuman Times to the French Revolution.* New York: Farrar, Straus & Giroux.

Fukuyama, F. 2014. *Political Order and Political Decay: From the Industrial Revolution to the Globalization of Democracy.* New York: Macmillan.

Funtowitz, S. and J. Ravetz. 1993. "Science in the Postnormal Age." *Futures* 25(7): 739–55.

Galaz, V., J. Gars, F. Moberg, B. Nykvist and C. Repinski. 2015. "Why Ecologists Should Care about Financial Markets." *Trends in Ecology and Evolution* 30(10): 571–80.

Gallego-Álvarez, I. and E. Ortas. 2017. "Corporate Environmental Sustainability Reporting in the Context of National Cultures: A Quantile Regression Approach." *International Business Review* 26(2): 337–53.

Galli Robertson, A. M. and M. B. Collins. 2019. "Super Emitters in the United States Coal-Fired Electric Utility Industry: Comparing Disproportionate Emissions across Facilities and Parent Companies." *Environmental Sociology* 5(1): 70–81.

Garcia, S., Y. Cintra, S. Rita de Cássia and F. G. Lima. 2016. "Corporate Sustainability Management: A Proposed Multi-criteria Model to Support Balanced Decision-Making." *Journal of Cleaner Production* 136: 181–96. https://doi.org/10.1016/j.jclepro.2016.01.110.

Gardner, G. T. and P. C. Stern. 2002. *Environmental Problems and Human Behavior.* Boston, MA: Pearson Custom Publishing.

Gardner, G. T. and P. C. Stern. 2008. "The Short List: The Most Effective Actions U.S. Households Can Take to Curb Climate Change." *Environment* 50(5): 13–24.

Garnett, E. E., A. Balmford, T. M. Marteau, M. A. Pilling and C. Sandbrook. 2021. "Price of Change: Does a Small Alteration to the Price of Meat and Vegetarian Options Affect Their Sales?" *Journal of Environmental Psychology* 75: 101589. https://doi.org/10.1016/j.jenvp.2021.101589.

Gaskin, C. J., D. Taylor, S. Kinnear et al. 2017. "Factors Associated with the Climate Change Vulnerability and the Adaptive Capacity of People with Disability: A Systematic Review." *Weather, Climate, and Society* 9(4): 801–14.

Gastil, J. 2018. "The Lessons and Limitations of Experiments in Democratic Deliberation." *Annual Review of Law and Social Science* 14: 271–91.

Gatersleben, B., N. Murtagh and W. Abrahamse. 2014. "Values, Identity and Pro-environmental Behaviour." *Contemporary Social Science* 9(4): 374–92. https://doi.org/10.1080/21582041.2012.682086.

Gates, H. L. J. 2014. "Slavery, by the Numbers." *The Root.* www.theroot.com/slavery-by-the-numbers-1790874492.

Gauthier, A. H. 1998. "The State and the Family: A Comparative Analysis of Family Policies in Industrialized Countries." Oxford: Clarendon Press.

Gay-Antaki, M. and D. Liverman. 2018. "Climate for Women in Climate Science: Women Scientists and the Intergovernmental Panel on Climate Change." *Proceedings of the National Academy of Sciences* 115(9): 2060–65.

Gaylord, B., K. J. Kroeker, J. M. Sunday et al. 2015. "Ocean Acidification through the Lens of Ecological Theory." *Ecology* 96(1): 3–15.

Geiger, S. J., C. Brick, L. Nalborczyk, A. Bosshard and N. B. Jostmann. 2021. "More Green Than Gray? Toward a Sustainable Overview of Environmental Spillover Effects: A Bayesian Meta-analysis." *Journal of Environmental Psychology* 78: 101694. https://doi.org/10.1016/j.jenvp.2021.101694.

Geiger, N., A. Gore, C. V. Squire and S. Z. Attari. 2021. "Investigating Similarities and Differences in Individual Reactions to the COVID-19 Pandemic and the Climate Crisis." *Climatic Change* 167(1): 1–20.

Geiger, S. J. 2022. "Proenvironmental Behaviour Spillover." *Nature Reviews Psychology* 1: 191. https://doi.org/10.1038/s44159-022-00043-1.

Geisel, T. S. 1971. *The Lorax*. New York: Random House Books for Young Readers.

Gelderblom, O., A. De Jong and J. Jonker. 2013. "The Formative Years of the Modern Corporation: The Dutch East India Company VOC, 1602–1623." *The Journal of Economic History* 73(4): 1050–76.

Gelles, D. 2022. *The Man Who Broke Capitalism: How Jack Welch Gutted the Heartland and Crushed the Soul of Corporate America – and How to Undo His Legacy*. New York: Simon & Schuster.

Gelman, A., N. Silver and A. Edlin. 2012. "What Is the Probability Your Vote Will Make a Difference?" *Economic Inquiry* 50(2): 321–26.

Gentzkow, M. 2017. "Small Media, Big Impact." *Science* 358(6364): 726–27.

Georgescu-Roegen, N. 1971. *The Entropy Law and Economic Progress*. Cambridge, MA: Harvard University Press.

Gerber, L. R. 2016. "Conservation Triage or Injurious Neglect in Endangered Species Recovery." *Proceedings of the National Academy of Science* 113(13): 3563–66.

Gerlach, P. 2017. "The Games Economists Play: Why Economics Students Behave More Selfishly Than Other Students." *PloS one* 12 (9): e0183814. https://doi.org/10.1371/journal.pone.0183814.

Gershman, S. J., E. J. Horvitz and J. B. Tenenbaum. 2015. "Computational Rationality: A Converging Paradigm for Intelligence in Brains, Minds, and Machines." *Science* 349(6245): 273–78.

Gewin, V. 2022. "The Rise of Inequality Research: Can Spanning Disciplines Help Tackle Injustice?" *Nature* 606(7915): 827–29. https://doi.org/10.1038/d41586-022-01684-1.

Gibbons, J. H. 1998. "Sustainable Growth: Fantasy or Vision?" Paper presented at the Compton Lecture at the Massachusetts Institute of Technology, April 26, Cambridge, MA.

Gigerenzer, G. 1998. "Ecological Rationality: An Adaptation for Frequencies." Pp. 9–29 in *The Evolution of Mind*, edited by D. D. Cummins and C. Allen. New York: Oxford University Press.

Gigerenzer, G. 2008. *Rationality for Mortals: How People Cope with Uncertainty*. Oxford: Oxford University Press.

Gigerenzer, G. and W. Gaissmaier. 2011. "Heuristic Decision Making." *Annual Review of Psychology* 62: 451–82.

Gilens, M., S. Patterson and P. Haines. 2021. "Campaign Finance Regulations and Public Policy." *American Political Science Review* 115(3): 1074–81.

Gilhooley, S. J. 2020. *The Antebellum Origins of the Modern Constitution: Slavery and the Spirit of the American Founding*. Cambridge: Cambridge University Press.

Gilligan, J. M. and M. P. Vandenbergh. 2020. "A Framework for Assessing the Impact of Private Climate Governance." *Energy Research and Social Science* 60: 101400. https://doi.org/10.1016/j.erss.2019.101400.

Ginsburg, B. 2019. "Wilding the World through the Practice of Ethology." Working Paper. Department of Philosophy, Michigan State University.

Givens, J. E. 2018. "Ecologically Unequal Exchange and the Carbon Intensity of Well-Being, 1990–2011." *Environmental Sociology* 4(3): 311–24.

Givens, J. E., S. O. Hazboun, M. D. Briscoe and R. S. Krannich. 2020. "Climate Change Views, Energy Policy Support, and Personal Action in the Intermountain West: The Anti-Reflexivity Effect." *Society and Natural Resources*: 1–23. https://doi.org/10.1080/089 41920.2020.1769782.

Glass, N. R. and K. E. F. Watt. 1971. *Land Use, Energy, Agriculture, and Decision-Making: A Report to the National Science Foundation, Office of Interdisciplinary Research*. Davis, CA: Institute of Ecology.

Glover, D. 1995. "Structural Adjustment and the Environment." *Journal of International Development* 7(2): 285–89.

Gneezy, U. and A. Rustichini. 2000. "A Fine Is a Price." *Journal of Legal Studies* 29(1): 1–17.

Goering, J. and R. Wienk, eds. 1971. *Mortgage Lending, Racial Discrimination and Federal Policy*. Farnham: Ashgate.

Goist, R. 2020. "Akron's Chapel Hill Mall Avoids Closing Friday with Partial Utility Payment by Owner." *Cleveland.com*, January 3. www.cleveland.com/business/202 0/01/akrons-chapel-hill-mall-avoids-closing-friday-with-partial-utility-payment-by-owner.html.

Gökşen, F., F. Adaman and E. Ü. Zengínobuz. 2002. "On Environmental Concern, Willingness to Pay and Postmaterialist Values: Evidence from Istanbul." *Enviornment and Behavior* 34(5): 616–33.

Goldberg, M. H., S. van der Linden, M. T. Ballew, S. A. Rosenthal and A. Leiserowitz. 2019a. "The Role of Anchoring in Judgments About Expert Consensus." *Journal of Applied Social Psychology* 49(3): 192–200.

Goldberg, M. H., S. van der Linden, E. Maibach and A. Leiserowitz. 2019b. "Discussing Global Warming Leads to Greater Acceptance of Climate Science." *Proceedings of the National Academy of Sciences* 116(30): 14804–05.

Goldemberg, J., T. B. Johansson, A. K. Reddy and R. H. Williams. 1985. "Basic Needs and Much More with One Kilowatt per Capita." *Ambio* 14(4–5): 190–200.

Goldstein, N. J., R. B. Cialdini and V. Griskevicius. 2008. "A Room with a Viewpoint: Using Social Norms to Motivate Environmental Conservation in Hotels." *Journal of Consumer Research* 35(3): 472–82.

Goldstein, N. J., V. Griskevicius and R. B. Cialdini. 2007. "Invoking Social Norms: A Social Psychology Perspective on Improving Hotels' Linen-Reuse Programs." *Cornell Hotel and Restaurant Administration Quarterly* 48(2): 145–50.

Goldstone, J. A. 1991. *Revolution and Rebellion in the Early Modern World*. Berkeley: University of California Press.

Goode, E. 2015. "John F. Nash Jr., Math Genius Defined by a 'Beautiful Mind,' Dies at 86." *New York Times*, May 24.

Goodman, P. S. and N. Chokshi. 2021. "How the World Ran Out of Everything." *New York Times*, July 1.

Goodwin, A., C. Wilburn, C. Wojewoda et al. 2022. "Anatomy of a Cyberattack: Part 2: Managing a Clinical Pathology Laboratory During 25 Days of Downtime." *American Journal of Clinical Pathology* 157(5): 653–63.

Goodwin, P., J. Dargay and M. Hanly. 2004. "Elasticities of Road Traffic and Fuel Consumption with Respect to Price and Income: A Review." *Transport Reviews* 24(3): 275–92.

Gopnik, A. 2017. "We Could Have Been Canadian: Was the American Revolution Such a Good Idea?" *The New Yorker*,

May 15. www.newyorker.com/magazine/201 7/05/15/we-could-have-been-canada.

Gordon-Reed, A. 2018. "America's Original Sin: Slavery and the Legacy of White Supremacy." *Foreign Affairs* 97: 2–7.

Gorodzeisky, A. and M. Semyonov. 2018. "Competitive Threat and Temporal Change in Anti-immigrant Sentiment: Insights from a Hierarchical Age-Period-Cohort Model." *Social Science Research* 73: 31–44. https://doi .org/10.1016/j.ssresearch.2018.03.013.

Gould, C. C. 2014. *Interactive Democracy: The Social Roots of Global Justice.* Cambridge: Cambridge University Press.

Gould, K. A., D. N. Pellow and A. Schnaiberg. 2008. *The Treadmill of Production: Injustice and Unsustainability in the Global Economy.* Boulder, CO: Paradigm Publishers.

Gould, S. J. 1965. *The Mismeasure of Man.* New York: W. W. Norton & Company.

Gould, S. J. 1997. "Nonoverlapping Magisteria." *Natural history* 106(2): 16–22.

Gould, S. J. 2000, "Deconstructing the 'Science Wars' by Reconstructing an Old Mold." *Science* 287(5451): 252–61.

Gould, S. J. 2011. *Rocks of Ages: Science and Religion in the Fullness of Life.* New York: Random House.

Gould, S. J. and N. Eldredge. 1993. "Punctuated Equilibrium Comes of Age." *Nature* 366(6452): 223.

Goulder, L. H. and A. R. Schein. 2013. "Carbon Taxes versus Cap and Trade: A Critical Review." *Climate Change Economics* 4(03): 1350010.

Gouldner, A. 1979. *The Future of Intellectuals and the Rise of the New Class: A Frame of Reference, Theses, Conjectures, Arguments, and an Historical Perspective on the Role of Intellectuals and Intelligentsia in the International Class Contest of the Modern Era.* New York: Seabury.

Grace, T. M. 2016. *Kent State: Death and Dissent in the Long Sixties.* Amherst: University of Massachusetts Press.

Graeber, D. and D. Wengrow. 2021. *The Dawn of Everything: A New History of Humanity.* London: Penguin.

Graft, D. F. 2006. "Insect Sting Allergy." *Medical Clinics of North America* 90(1): 211–32.

Graham, J., J. Haidt, S. Koleva et al. 2013. "Moral Foundations Theory: The Pragmatic Validity of Moral Pluralism." Pp. 55–130 in *Advances in Experimental Social Psychology*, Vol. 47, edited by P. Devine and A. Plant. Amsterdam: Elsevier.

Grand Isle Select Board. 2017. *Grand Isle Town Plan.* Grand Isle, VT: Grand Isle Select Board. www.grandislevt.org/wp-content/upl oads/2022/04/Grand-Isle-Town-Plan.pdf.

Granovetter, M. S. 1973. "The Strength of Weak Ties." *American Journal of Sociology* 78(6): 1360–80.

Grant, D., A. K. Jorgenson and W. Longhofer. 2016. "How Organizational and Global Factors Condition the Effects of Energy Efficiency on $CO_2$ Emission Rebounds among the World's Power Plants." *Energy Policy* 94: 89–93. https://doi.org/10.1016/j .enpol.2016.03.053.

Grant, D., A. Jorgenson and W. Longhofer. 2020. *Super Polluters: Tackling the World's Largest Sources of Climate-Disrupting Emissions.* New York: Columbia University Press.

Grant, S. B., J.-D. Saphores, D. L. Feldman et al. 2012. "Taking the 'Waste' Out of 'Wastewater' for Human Water Security and Ecosystem Sustainability." *Science* 337 (6095): 681–86.

Graves, P. E. 2007. *Environmental Economics: A Critique of Benefit-Cost Analysis.* Lanham, MD: Rowman & Littlefield.

Greiner, P. T., R. York and J. A. McGee. 2022. "When Are Fossil Fuels Displaced? An Exploratory Inquiry into the Role of Nuclear Electricity Production in the Displacement of Fossil Fuels." *Heliyon*: e08795. https://doi .org/10.1016/j.heliyon.2022.e08795.

Griggs, D., M. Nilsson, A. Stevance and D. McCollum, eds. 2017. *A Guide to SDG Interactions: From Science to Implementation.* Paris: International Council for Science.

Grignon, J. and R. W. Kimmerer. 2017. "Listening to the Forest." Pp. 67–74 in

*Wildness: Relations of People and Place*, edited by G. Van Horn and J. Hausdoeffer. Chicago, IL: University of Chicago Press.

Grober, U. 2012. *Sustainability: A Cultural History*, translated by R. Cunningham. Devon, UK: Green Books.

Grønhøj, A. and F. Ölander. 2007. "A Gender Perspective on Environmentally Related Family Consumption." *Journal of Consumer Behaviour* 6(4): 218–35.

Grønhøj, A. and J. Thøgersen. 2011. "Feedback on Household Electricity Consumption: Learning and Social Influence Processes." *International Journal of Consumer Studies* 35 (2): 138–45.

Guagnano, G. A., P. C. Stern and T. Dietz. 1995. "Influences on Attitude-Behavior Relationships: A Natural Experiment with Curbside Recycling." *Environment and Behavior* 27(5): 699–718.

Guilfoos, T., D. Kell, A. Boslett and E. L. Hill. 2017. "The Economic and Health Effects of the 2014 Chemical Spill in the Elk River, West Virginia." *American Journal of Agricultural Economics* 100(2): 609–24.

Gunderson, R. 2014a. "The First-Generation Frankfurt School on the Animal Question: Foundations for a Normative Sociological Animal Studies." *Sociological Perspectives* 57(3). https://doi.org/10.1177 /0731121414523393.

Gunderson, R. 2014b. "Erich Fromm's Ecological Messianism: The First Biophilia Hypothesis As Humanistic Social Theory." *Humanity and Society* 38(2). https://doi.org/ 10.1177/0160597614529112.

Gunderson, R. 2014c. "Social Barriers to Biophilia: Merging Structural and Ideational Explanations for Environmental Degradation." *The Social Science Journal* 51 (4): 681–85.

Gunderson, R. 2015a. "Environmental Sociology and the Frankfurt School 2: Ideology, Techno-Science, Reconciliation." *Environmental Sociology* 2(1): 64–76.

Gunderson, R. 2015b. "Environmental Sociology and the Frankfurt School 1:

Reason and Capital." *Environmental Sociology* 1(3): 224–35.

Gunderson, R. 2016. "Why Global Environmental Governance Should Be Participatory: Empirical and Theoretical Justifications and the Problem of Scale." *International Sociology* 33(6): 715–37.

Gunderson, R. 2018. "Degrowth and Other Quiescent Futures: Pioneering Proponents of an Idler Society." *Journal of Cleaner Production* 198: 1574–82. https://doi.org/10 .1016/j.jclepro.2018.07.039.

Gunderson, R. 2021. *Hothouse Utopia: What Is to Be Done When the Future's Already Ablaze?* Winchester: Zer0 Books.

Gunderson, R. and T. Dietz. 2018. "Deliberation and Catastrophic Risks." Pp. 768–89 in *The Oxford Handbook of Deliberative Democracy*, edited by A. Bächtiger, J. Mansbridge, M. E. Warren and J. Dryzek. Oxford: Oxford University Press.

Gunderson, R., D. Stuart and B. Petersen. 2018. "The Political Economy of Geoengineering as Plan B: Technological Rationality, Moral Hazard, and New Technology." *New Political Economy* 24(5): 696–715.

Gundry, K. G. and T. A. Heberlein. 1984. "Research Report: Do Public Meetings Represent the Public?" *Journal of the American Planning Association* 50(2): 175–82.

Guriev, S. and D. Treisman. 2022. *Spin Dictators: The Changing Face of Tyranny in the 21st Century*. Princeton, NJ: Princeton University Press.

Ha-Duong, M., R. Swart and L. Bernstein. 2007. "Uncertainty Management in the IPCC: Agreeing to Disagree." *Global Environmental Change* 17(1): 8–11.

Habermas, J. 1970. *Towards a Rational Society*. Boston, MA: Beacon Press.

Habermas, J. 1971. *Knowledge and Human Interests*. Boston, MA: Beacon Press.

Habermas, J. 1979. *Theory and Practice*. Boston, MA: Beacon Press.

Habermas, J. 1984. *The Theory of Communicative Action, Vol 1: Reason and the*

*Rationalization of Society*. Boston, MA: Beacon Press.

Habermas, J. 1987. *The Theory of Communicative Action, Vol. 2: System and Lifeworld. A Critique of Functionalist Reasoning*. Boston, MA: Beacon Press.

Habermas, J. 1990. *Moral Consciousness and Communicative Action*. Boston, MA: Beacon Press.

Habermas, J. 1993. *Justification and Application: Remarks on Discourse Ethics*. Cambridge, MA: MIT. Press.

Hacker, J. S. 2019. *The Great Risk Shift: The New Economic Insecurity and the Decline of the American Dream*. Oxford: Oxford University Press.

Haddad, N. M., L. A. Brudvig, J. Clobert et al. 2015. "Habitat Fragmentation and Its Lasting Impact on Earth's Ecosystems." *Science Advances* 1(2): e1500052.

Hadley, J. 2015. *Animal Property Rights: A Theory of Habitat Rights for Wild Animals*. Lanham, MD: Lexington Books.

Hahnel, R. and E. O. Wright. 2016. *Alternatives to Capitalism: Proposals for a Democratic Economy*. London: Verso Books.

Haidt, J. 2001. "The Emotional Dog and Its Rational Tail: A Social Intuitionist Approach to Moral Judgment." *Psychological Review* 108(4): 814.

Haidt, J. 2012. *The Righteous Mind: Why Good People Are Divided by Politics and Religion*. New York: Vintage.

Hajnal, Z., N. Lajevardi and L. Nielson. 2017. "Voter Identification Laws and the Suppression of Minority Votes." *The Journal of Politics* 79(2): 363–79.

Halberstam, Y. and B. P. Montagnes. 2015. "Presidential Coattails versus the Median Voter: Senator Selection in US Elections." *Journal of Public Economics* 121: 40–51. https://doi.org/10.1016/j.jpubeco.2014.10.002.

Hale, J. 2021. *The Choice We Face: How Segregation, Race, and Power Have Shaped America's Most Controversial Education Reform Movement*. Boston, MA: Beacon Press.

Hall, J. A. and R. Schwartz. 2019. "Empathy Present and Future." *The Journal of Social Psychology* 159(3): 225–43. https://doi.org/10.1080/00224545.2018.1477442.

Haltinner, K. and D. Sarathchandra. 2022. *Inside the World of Climate Change Skeptics*. Seattle: University of Washington Press.

Haluza-Delay, R. 2012. "Giving Consent in the Petrostate: Hegemony and Alberta Oil Sands." *Journal for Activist Science and Technology Education* 4(1): 1–6.

Hamilton, L. C. 2021. "The Slow Dawn of Climate-Change Awareness, and Its Challenge for a Sustainable Planet." The Carsey School of Public Policy. https://dx.doi.org/10.34051/p/2021.19.

Hamilton, L. C., J. Hartter and K. Saito. 2015. "Trust in Scientists on Climate Change and Vaccines." *Sage Open* 5(3): https://doi.org/10.1177/2158244015602752.

Hamm, J. A. 2017. "Trust, Trustworthiness, and Motivation in the Natural Resource Management Context." *Society and Natural Resources* 30(8): 919–33.

Hamm, J. A., J. G. Cox, A. Zwickle et al. 2019. "Trust in Whom? Dioxin, Organizations, Risk Perception, and Fish Consumption in Michigan's Saginaw Bay Watershed." *Journal of Risk Research* 22(12): 1624–37.

Hamm, J. A., L. Hoffman, A. J. Tomkins and B. H. Bornstein. 2016. "On the Influence of Trust in Predicting Rural Land Owner Cooperation with Natural Resource Management Institutions." *Journal of Trust Research* 6(1): 37–62.

Hamm, J. A., A. L. Pearson, J. Namanya and M. L. Gore. 2020. "Vulnerability, Trustworthiness, and Motivation As Emergent Themes in Cooperation With Community-Based Water Management in Southwestern Uganda." *Frontiers in Environmental Science* 8: 47. https://doi.org/10.3389/fenvs.2020.00047.

Hamm, J. A., C. Smidt and R. C. Mayer. 2019. "Understanding the Psychological Nature and Mechanisms of Political Trust." *PloS One* 14(5): e0215835.

Hammond, J. S., R. L. Keeney and H. Raiffa. 1999. *Smart Choices: A Practical Guide to Making Better Decisions*. Boston, MA: Harvard Business School.

Handley, I. M., E. R. Brown, C. A. Moss-Racusin and J. L. Smith. 2015. "Quality of Evidence Revealing Subtle Gender Biases in Science Is in the Eye of the Beholder." *Proceedings of the National Academy of Sciences* 112(43): 13201–06.

Hằng, N. T. T. 2018. "Effects of Warfare on Social Environments: The Exposure of Vietnamese Veterans to Agent Orange and Other Herbicides." Pp. 123–40 in *Armed Conflict and Environment*, edited by D. Briesen. Baden-Baden: Nomos Verlagsgesellschaft.

Hanisch, C. 1969. "The Personal Is Political." Pp. 76–78 in *Notes from the Second Year: Women's Liberation* edited by S. Firestone and A. Koedt. New York: Radical Feminism.

Hanley, N. and C. L. Spash. 1993. *Cost-Benefit Analysis and the Environment*. Cheltenham: Edward Elgar.

Hanna-Attisha, M. 2017. "Flint Kids: Tragic, Resilient, and Exemplary." *American Journal of Public Health* 107(5): 651–52. https://doi.org/10.2105/AJPH.2017.303732.

Hanna-Attisha, M. 2018. *What the Eyes Don't See: A Story of Crisis, Resistance, and Hope in an American City* New York: Random House.

Hanna-Attisha, M., J. LaChance, R. C. Sadler and A. Champney Schnepp. 2016. "Elevated Blood Lead Levels in Children Associated with the Flint Drinking Water Crisis: A Spatial Analysis of Risk and Public Health Response." *American Journal of Public Health* 106(2): 283–90.

Hannan, M. T. and J. Freeman. 1989. *Organizational Ecology*. Cambridge, MA: Harvard University Press.

Hansson, S. O. 2013. "John Stuart Mill's Political Self-Identifications." *Journal of Political Ideologies* 18(3): 348–57.

Hao, L. and D. Q. Naiman. 2007. *Quantile Regression*. Thousand Oaks, CA: Sage Publications.

Haraway, D. 1988. "Situated Knowledge: The Science Question in Feminism and the Privilege of Partial Perspective." *Feminist Studies* 14(3): 575–99.

Haraway, D. 2013. *Simians, Cyborgs, and Women: The Reinvention of Nature*. London: Routledge.

Haraway, D. J. 1989. *Primate Visions: Gender, Race, and Nature in the World of Modern Science*. New York: Routledge.

Haraway, D. J. 2016. *Staying with the Trouble: Making Kin in the Chthulucene*. Durham, NC: Duke University Press.

Hardin, G. 1968. "The Tragedy of the Commons." *Science* 162(3859): 1243–48.

Harding, S. 1998. *Is Science Multi-cultural? Postcolonialisms, Feminisms and Epistemologies*. Bloomington: Indiana University Press.

Harding, S. 2015. *Objectivity and Diversity: Another Logic of Scientific Research*. Chicago, IL: University of Chicago Press.

Hare, N. 1970. "Black Ecology." *The Black Scholar* 1(6): 2–8.

Harris, J. and C. Blumstein, eds. 1984. *What Works: Documenting Energy Conservation in Buildings*. Washington, DC: American Council for an Energy-Efficient Economy.

Harris-Lovett, S. and D. Sedlak. 2020. "Protecting the Sewershed." *Science* 369 (6510): 1429–30.

Harrison, B. F. and M. R. Michelson. 2017. *Listen, We Need to Talk: How to Change Attitudes about LGBT Rights*. Oxford: Oxford University Press.

Harrison, G. W. and D. Ross. 2017. "Varieties of Paternalism and the Heterogeneity of Utility Structures." *Journal of Economic Methodology* 25(1): 42–67.

Harvey, D. 2005. *A Brief History of Neoliberalism*. Oxford: Oxford University Press.

Hasan, M. A., A. A. Mamun, S. M. Rahman et al. 2021. "Climate Change Mitigation Pathways for the Aviation Sector." *Sustainability* 13(7): 3656.

Haskell, J. 2018. *Direct Democracy or Representative Government? Dispelling the Populist Myth*. New York: Routledge.

Hawcroft, L. J. and T. L. Milfont. 2010. "The Use (and Abuse) of the New Environmental Paradigm Scale Over the Last 30 Years: A Meta-analysis." *Journal of Environmental Psychology* 30(2): 143–58.

Hawley, A. H. 1986. *Human Ecology: A Theoretical Essay*. Chicago, IL: University of Chicago Press.

Hayek, F. A. 1948. *Individualism and Economic Order*. Chicago, IL: University of Chicago Press.

Hayek, F. A. [1944] 2014. *The Road to Serfdom: Text and Documents: The Definitive Edition*. New York: Routledge.

Heberlein, T. A. 1976. "Some Observations on Alternative Mechanisms for Public Involvement: The Hearing, Public Opinion Poll, the Workshop and the Quasi-Experiment." *Natural Resources Journal* 16(1): 197–212.

Heberlein, T. A. 1977. "Norm Activation and Environmental Action." *Journal of Social Issues* 33(3): 79–87.

Heberlein, T. A. 2012. *Navigating Environmental Attitudes*. Oxford: Oxford University Press.

Heberlein, T. A. and R. C. Bishop. 1986. "Assessing the Validity of Contingent Valuation: Three Field Experiments." *Science of the Total Environment* 56: 99–107. https://doi.org/10.1016/0048-9697(86)90317-7.

Heberlein, T. A. and G. K. Warriner. 1983. "The Influence of Price and Attitude on Shifting Residential Electricity Consumption from On-to Off-Peak Periods." *Journal of Economic Psychology* 4(1): 107–30.

Heberlein, T. A., M. A. Wilson, R. C. Bishop and N. C. Schaeffer. 2005. "Rethinking the Scope Test As a Criterion for Validity in Contingent Valuation." *Journal of Environmental Economics and Management* 50(1): 1–22.

Hébert, M. 2018. "Indigenous Spheres of Deliberation." Pp. 100–09 in *The Oxford Handbook of Deliberative Democracy*, edited by A. Bächtiger, J. S. Dryzek, J. Mansbridge and M. E. Warren. Oxford: Oxford University Press.

Hecht, J. E. 2005. *National Environmental Accounting: Bridging the Gap between Ecology and Economy*. Washington, DC: Resources for the Future.

Hedelin, B., S. Gray, S. Woehlke et al. 2021. "What's Left before Participatory Modeling Can Fully Support Real-World Environmental Planning Processes: A Case Study Review." *Environmental Modelling and Software* 143: 105073. https://doi.org/10.1016/j.envsoft.2021.105073.

Hedrick, T. 2010. *Rawls and Habermas: Reason, Pluralism and the Claims of Political Philosophy*. Stanford, CA: Stanford University Press.

Heede, R. 2014. "Tracing Anthropogenic Carbon Dioxide and Methane Emissions to Fossil Fuel and Cement Producers, 1854–2010." *Climatic Change* 122(1): 229–41.

Heintz, C. 2018. "Updating Evolutionary Epistemology." Pp. 195–222 in *Perspectives on Science and Culture*, edited by K. Rutten, S. Blancke and R. Soetaert. West Lafayette, IN: Purdue University Press.

Helvoigt, T. L., D. M. Adams and A. L. Ayre. 2003. "Employment Transitions in Oregon's Wood Products Sector During the 1990s." *Journal of Forestry* 101(4): 42–46.

Hendry, J., S. Depoe, J. Delicath and M. Elsenbeer. 2004. *Decide, Announce, Defend: Turning the NEPA Process into an Advocacy Tool Rather Than a Decision-Making Tool*. Albany, NY: SUNY Press.

Heney, D. B. 2016. *Toward a Pragmatist Metaethics*. New York: Routledge.

Henly, J. R., S. K. Danziger and S. Offer. 2005. "The Contribution of Social Support to the Material Well-Being of Low-Income Families." *Journal of Marriage and Family* 67(1): 122–40.

Henrich, J. 2015. *The Secret of Our Success: How Culture Is Driving Human Evolution, Domesticating Our Species, and Making Us Smarter*. Princeton, NJ: Princeton University Press.

Henrich, J., S. J. Heine and A. Norenzayan. 2010a. "Most People Are Not WEIRD." *Nature* 466(7302): 29.

Henrich, J., S. J. Heine and A. Norenzayan. 2010b. "Beyond WEIRD: Towards a Broad-Based Behavioral Science." *Behavioral and Brain Sciences* 33(2–3): 111.

Henry, A.D. and B. Vollan. 2014. "Networks and the Challenge of Sustainable Development." *Annual Review of Environment and Resources* 39: 583–610.

Henry, A. D. 2000. "Public Perceptions of Global Warming." *Human Ecology Review* 7 (1): 25–30.

Henry, A. D. 2009. "The Challenge of Learning for Sustainability: A Prolegomenon to Theory." *Human Ecology Review* 16(2): 131–40.

Henry, A. D. 2011. "Ideology, Power, and the Structure of Policy Networks." *Policy Studies Journal* 39(3): 361–83.

Henry, A. D. 2020. "Meeting the Challenge of Learning for Sustainability through Policy Networks." *Human Ecology Review* 26(2): 171–93.

Henry, A. D. and T. Dietz. 2011. "Information, Networks, and the Complexity of Trust in Commons Governance." *International Journal of the Commons* 5(2): 188–212.

Henry, A. D. and T. Dietz. 2012. "Understanding Environmental Cognition." *Organization and Environment* 25(3): 238–58.

Henry, A. D., T. Dietz and R.L. Sweeney. 2021. "Coevolution of Networks and Beliefs in US Environmental Risk Policy." *Policy Studies Journal* 49(3): 675–702. https://doi.org/10.1111/psj.12407.

Henry, A. D., P. Prałat and C.-Q. Zhang. 2011. "Emergence of Segregation in Evolving Social Networks." *Proceedings of the National Academy of Science, USA* 108(21): 8605–10.

Herald, N. Z. 2014. "Orangutan Granted Legal Rights in Argentina." *New Zealand Herald*, December 21.

Herrington, G. 2021. "Update to Limits to Growth: Comparing the World3 Model with Empirical Data." *Journal of Industrial Ecology* 25(3): 614–26.

Herweijer, C. 2018. "Ways AI Can Help Save the Planet." *World Economic Forum*. January 24. www.weforum.org/agenda/2018/01/8-ways-ai-can-help-save-the-planet/.

Himmelroos, S. and H. S. Christensen. 2020. "The Potential of Deliberative Reasoning: Patterns of Attitude Change and Consistency in Cross-Cutting and Like-Minded Deliberation." *Acta Politica* 55(2): 135–55.

Himmelweit, S., C. Santos, A. Sevilla and C. Sofer. 2013. "Sharing of Resources within the Family and the Economics of Household Decision Making." *Journal of Marriage and Family* 75(3): 625–39.

Hird, J. A. 1991. "The Political Economy of Pork: Project Selection at The US Army Corps of Engineers." *American Political Science Review* 85(02): 429–56.

Hitlin, S. 2003. "Values As the Core of Personal Identity: Drawing Links between Two Theories of Self." *Social Psychology Quarterly* 66(2): 118–37.

Hitlin, S. 2011. "Values, Personal Identity, and the Moral Self." Pp. 515–29 in *Handbook of Identity Theory and Research*, Vol. 4, edited by S. J. Schwartz, K. Luyclx and V. L. Vignoles. New York: Springer.

Ho, T. H. 2015a. "Social Purpose Corporations: The Next Targets for Greenwashing Practices and Crowdfunding Scams." *Seattle Journal for Social Justice* 13(3): 14.

Ho, V. H. 2015b. "Risk-Related Activism: The Business Case for Monitoring Nonfinancial Risk." *Journal of Corporate Law* 41(3): 647–705.

Hobbes, T. 1651. *De Cive: containing the elements of civill politie in the argreement which it hath both with naturall and divine lawes in which is demonstrated, both what the origine of justice is, and wherein the essence of Christian religion doth consiste together with the nature, limits and qualifications of regiment and subjection.* Oxford: University of Oxford Text Archive.

Hochschild, A. 2006. *Bury the Chains: Prophets and Rebels in the Fight to Free an Empire's Slaves.* New York: Houghton Mifflin Harcourt.

Hofstra, B., V. V. Kulkarni, S. M.-N. Galvez et al. 2020. "The Diversity–Innovation Paradox in Science." *Proceedings of the National Academy of Sciences* 117(17): 9284–91.

Holifield, R., J. Chakraborty and G. Walker. 2017. *The Routledge Handbook of Environmental Justice*. New York: Routledge.

Holland, J. H. 1975. *Adaptation in Natural and Artificial Systems*. Ann Arbor: University of Michigan Press.

Holland, J. H. 1995. *Hidden Order: How Adaptation Builds Complexity*. Reading, MA: Addison-Wesley.

Hollands, G. J., G. Bignardi, M. Johnston et al. 2017. "The TIPPME Intervention Typology for Changing Environments to Change Behaviour." *Nature Human Behaviour* 1(8): 1–9.

Holmes, R. 1984. *Herold Hedd: Hitler's Cocaine*. Princeton, WI: Kitchen Sink Publishers.

Hong, L. and S. E. Page. 2004. "Groups of Diverse Problem Solvers Can Outperform Groups of High-Ability Problem Solvers." *Proceedings of the National Academy of Sciences* 101(46): 16385–89.

Hönisch, B., A. Ridgwell, D. N. Schmidt et al. 2012. "The Geological Record of Ocean Acidification." *Science* 335(6072): 1058–63.

Hook, N. C. and M. M. Bubolz. 1970. "The Family As an Ecosystem." *Journal of Home Economics* 62(5): 10–13.

Hooks, G., M. Lengefeld and C. L. Smith. 2021. "Recasting the Treadmills of Production and Destruction: New Theoretical Directions." *Sociology of Development* 7(1): 52–76. https://doi.org/10.1525/sod.2021.7.1.52.

Hooks, G. and C. Smith. 2004. "The Treadmill of Destruction: National Sacrifice Areas and Native Americans." *American Sociological Review* 69(4): 558–75.

Hooks, G. and C. Smith. 2005. "Treadmills of Production and Destruction: Threats to the Environment Posed by Militarism." *Organization and Environment* 18(1): 19–37.

Hornbeck, R. 2010. "Barbed Wire: Property Rights and Agricultural Development." *The Quarterly Journal of Economics* 125(2): 767–810.

Horstmann, A. C., N. Bock, E. Linhuber et al. 2018. "Do a Robot's Social Skills and Its Objection Discourage Interactants from Switching the Robot Off?" *PloS One* 13(7): e0201581.

Horzmann, K. A., C. de Perre, L. S. Lee, A. J. Whelton and J. L. Freeman. 2017. "Comparative Analytical and Toxicological Assessment of Methylcyclohexanemethanol (MCHM) Mixtures Associated with the Elk River Chemical Spill." *Chemosphere* 188: 599–607. https://doi.org/10.1016/j.chemosphere.2017.09.026.

Howard, P. H. 2016. *Concentration and Power in the Food System: Who Controls What We Eat?* London: Bloomsbury Academic.

Howarth, R. B. and M. A. Wilson. 2006. "A Theoretical Approach to Deliberative Valuation: Aggregation by Mutual Consent." *Land Economics* 82(1): 1–16.

Huang, X. and A. K. Jorgenson. 2018. "The Asymmetrical Effects of Economic Development on Consumption-Based and Production-Based Carbon Dioxide Emissions, 1990 to 2014." *Socius* 4. https://doi.org/10.1177/2378023118773626.

Hubbert, M. K. 1956. *Nuclear Energy and the Fossil Fuels*. Houston, TX: Shell Development Company.

Hubbs, G., M. O'Rourke and S. H. Orzack. 2020. *The Toolbox Dialogue Initiative: The Power of Cross-Disciplinary Practice*. New York: CRC Press.

Huber, J., S. Inoua, R. Kerschbamer et al. 2022. "Nobel and Novice: Author Prominence Affects Peer Review." *Proceedings of the National Academy of Sciences* 119(41): e2205779119.

Hull, K. L. 2009. *Pestilence and Persistence: Yosemite Indian Demography and Culture in Colonial California*. Berkeley: University of California Press.

Hulme, D. 2009. "The Millennium Development Goals (MDGs): A Short

History of the World's Biggest Promise." Brooks World Poverty Institute, Working Paper No. 100. https://ssrn.com/abstract=1544271 or http://dx.doi.org/10.2139/ssrn.1544271.

Hume, D. [1738] 1978. *A Treatise of Human Nature*, edited by L. A. Selby-Biggs and P. H. Nidditch. Oxford: Oxford University Press.

Hursthouse, R. 2011. "Virtue Ethics and the Treatment of Animals." Pp. 119–43 in *The Oxford Handbook of Animal Ethics*, edited by T. L. Beauchamp and R. G. Frey. Oxford: Oxford University Press.

Hutchinson, G. E. 1965. *The Ecological Theater and the Evolutionary Play*. New Haven, CT: Yale University Press.

Hutchinson, G. E. 1978. *An Introduction to Population Ecology*. New Haven, CT: Yale University Press.

Hynde, C. 2015. *Reckless: My Life As a Pretender*. New York: Penguin Random House.

IHS Markit. 2017. "LEDs Took Half a Billion Tons of Carbon Dioxide from the Sky in 2017, IHS Markit Says." IHS Markit News Release, December 21. https://news.ihsmarkit.com/press-release/energy/leds-took-half-billion-tons-carbon-dioxide-sky-2017-ihs-markit-says.

Independent Commission on International Development Issues. 1980. *North–South: A Program for Survival*. Cambridge, MA: MIT Press.

Infante, G., G. Lecouteux and R. Sugden. 2016. "Preference Purification and the Inner Rational Agent: A Critique of the Conventional Wisdom of Behavioural Welfare Economics." *Journal of Economic Methodology* 23(1): 1–25.

Inglehart, R. 1977. *The Silent Revolution: Changing Values and Political Styles among Western Publics*. Princeton, NJ: Princeton University Press.

Inglehart, R. 1990. *Culture Shift in Advanced Industrial Society*. Princeton, NJ: Princeton University Press.

Inglehart, R. 1995. "Public Support for Environmental Protection: Objective Problems and Subjective Values in 43 Societies." *PS: Political Science and Politics* 28(1): 57–71.

Inglehart, R. and W. E. Baker. 2000. "Modernization, Cultural Change, and the Persistence of Traditional Values." *American Sociological Review* 65(1): 19–51.

Insure Our Future. 2021. "NEW REPORT: U.S. Insurance Companies Undermine Climate Targets by Supporting Oil & Gas Expansion and Providing a Last Lifeline to Coal." Insure Our Future, Press Release report, November 3. www.insureourfuture.us/updates/2021/11/2/new-report-us-insurance-companies-undermine-climate-targets-scorecard.

InterAcademy Council. 2010. *Climate Change Assessments: Review of the Processes and Procedures of the IPCC*. Amsterdam: InterAcademy Council. www.interacademies.org/publication/climate-change-assessments-review-processes-procedures-ipcc.

Intergovernmental Panel on Climate Change. 2013. *Climate Change 2013: The Physical Science Basis. Contribution of Working Group I to the Fifth Assessment Report of the Intergovernmental Panel on Climate Change*. Cambridge: Cambridge University Press.

Intergovernmental Panel on Climate Change. 2018. *Global Warming of 1.5°C*. Geneva: World Meteorological Organization.

Intergovernmental Panel on Climate Change. 2021. *Climate Change 2021: The Physical Science Basis. Contribution of Working Group I to the Sixth Assessment Report of the Intergovernmental Panel on Climate Change*. Cambridge: Cambridge University Press.

International Council for Science and International Social Science Council. 2015. *Review of the Sustainable Development Goals: The Science Perspective*. Paris: International Council for Science.

International Expert Panel on Behavioral Science for Design. 2019. *Twenty Questions about Design Behavior for Sustainability*. New York: Nature Sustainability.

International Social Science Council, Institute of Development Studies and United Nations Educational Scientific and Cultural Organization, eds. 2016. *Word Social Science Report 2016: Challenging Inequalities: Pathways to a Just World*. Paris: UNESCO Publishing.

International Union for Conservation of Nature. 1980. *World Conservation Strategy*. Gland: International Union for Conservation of Nature.

Irvine, L. 2008. *If You Tame Me: Understanding Our Connection with Animals*. Philadelphia, PA: Temple University Press.

Irvine, L. and L. Cilia. 2017. "More-Than-Human Families: Pets, People, and Practices in Multispecies Households." *Sociology Compass* 11(2): e12455.

Isaacson, W. 2003. *Benjamin Franklin: An American Life*. New York: Simon & Schuster.

Isaacson, W. 2014. *The Innovators: How a Group of Hackers, Geniuses, and Geeks Created the Digital Revolution*. New York: Simon & Schuster.

Ivanova, D., K. Stadler, K. Steen-Olsen et al. 2015. "Environmental Impact Assessment of Household Consumption." *Journal of Industrial Ecology* 20(3): 526–36.

Iyengar, S., Y. Lelkes, M. Levendusky, N. Malhotra and S. J. Westwood. 2019. "The Origins and Consequences of Affective Polarization in the United States." *Annual Review of Political Science* 22: 129–46.

Iyengar, S., G. Sood and Y. Lelkes. 2012. "Affect, Not Ideology: A Social Identity Perspective on Polarization." *Public Opinion Quarterly* 76(3): 405–31.

Jackson, B. and D. Gans. 2015. *This Is All a Dream We Dreamed: An Oral History of the Grateful Dead*. New York: Flatiron Books.

Jacobsen, M. H. and K. Tester, eds. 2016. *Utopia: Social Theory and the Future*. London: Routledge.

Jacobson, G. C. and J. L. Carson. 2015. *The Politics of Congressional Elections*. Lanham, MD: Rowman & Littlefield.

Jaeger, C., O. Renn, E. A. Rosa and T. Webler. 2001. *Risk, Uncertainly and Rational Action*. London: Earthscan.

Jaffa, H. V. 2012. *Crisis of the House Divided: An Interpretation of the Issues in the Lincoln–Douglas Debates*. Chicago, IL: University of Chicago Press.

Jansson, J. 2011. "Consumer Eco-Innovation Adoption: Assessing Attitudinal Factors and Perceived Product Characteristics." *Business Strategy and the Environment* 20(3): 192–210.

Jansson, J., A. Marell and A. Nordlund. 2010. "Green Consumer Behavior: Determinants of Curtailment and Eco-Innovation Adoption." *Journal of Consumer Marketing* 27(4): 358–70.

Jay, M. 1973. *The Dialectical Imagination: A History of the Frankfurt School and the Institute for Social Research*. Berkeley: University of California Press.

Jenkins, C. N., K. S. Van Houtan, S. L. Pimm and J. O. Sexton. 2015. "US Protected Lands Mismatch Biodiversity Priorities." *Proceedings of the National Academy of Sciences* 112(16): 5081–86.

Jenkins, V. 2015. *The Lawn: A History of an American Obsession*. Washington, DC: Smithsonian Books.

Jenkins-Smith, H. C., D. Nohrstedt, C. M. Weible and K. Ingold. 2018. "The Advocacy Coalition Framework: An Overview of the Research Program." Pp. 135–71 in *Theories of the Policy Process*, edited by C. M. Weible and P. A. Sabatier. New York: Routledge.

Johnson, C. Y. 1998. "A Consideration of Collective Memory in African American Attachment to Wildland Recreation Places." *Human Ecology Review* 5(1): 5–15.

Johnson, E. W. and J. Burke. 2021. "Environmental Movements in the United States." Pp. 495–515 in *Handbook of Environmental Sociology*, edited by B. S. Caniglia, A. Jorgenson, S. A. Malin et al. Cham: Springer.

Johnson, E. W. and P. Schwadel. 2019. "Political Polarization and Long-Term Change in Public Support for Environmental Spending." *Social Forces* 98(2): 915–41.

Johnson, I. 2014. "Towards a Contemporary Understanding of The Limits to Growth." Pp. 79–103 in *Is the Planet Full?*, edited by I. Goldin. Oxford: Oxford University Press.

Johnson, N. F., N. Velásquez, N. J. Restrepo et al. 2020. "The Online Competition between Pro-and Anti-vaccination Views." *Nature* 582(7811): 230–33.

Johnson, N. P. and J. Mueller. 2002. "Updating the Accounts: Global Mortality of the 1918–1920 'Spanish' Influenza Pandemic." *Bulletin of the History of Medicine* 76(1): 105–15.

Johnson, R. and A. Cureton. 2022. "Kant's Moral Philosophy." in *The Stanford Encyclopedia of Philosophy*, edited by E. N. Zalta. Stanford, CA: Stanford University. https://plato.stanford.edu/archives/fall2022/entries/kant-moral/.

Jones, E. 2019. "Rethinking Greenwashing: Corporate Discourse, Unethical Practice, and the Unmet Potential of Ethical Consumerism." *Sociological Perspectives* 62 (5): 728–54.

Jorda, V. and J. M. Alonso. 2020. "What Works to Mitigate and Reduce Relative (and Absolute) Inequality? A Systematic Review." United Nations University World Institute for Development Economics Research, Working Paper No. 152/2020. https://doi.org/10.35188/UNU-WIDER/2020/909-9.

Jordan, J. 2009–10. "A Pig in the Parlor or Food on the Table: Is Texas's Right to Farm Act an Unconstitutional Mechanism to Perpetuate Nuisances or Sound Public Policy Ensuring Sustainable Growth?" *Texas Tech Law Review* 42: 943–85.

Jordan, K. and K. Kristjánsson. 2017. "Sustainability, Virtue Ethics, and the Virtue of Harmony with Nature." *Environmental Education Research* 23(9): 1205–29.

Jorgenson, A. K. 2003. "Consumption and Environmental Degradation: A Cross-National Analysis of the Ecological Footprint." *Social Problems* 50(3): 374–94.

Jorgenson, A. K. 2004. "Uneven Processes and Environmental Degradation in the World-Economy." *Human Ecology Review* 11(2): 103–17.

Jorgenson, A. K. 2012. "Energy: Analyzing Fossil Fuel Displacement." *Nature Climate Change* 2(6): 398–99.

Jorgenson, A. K. 2014. "Economic Development and the Carbon Intensity of Human Well-Being." *Nature Climate Change* 4(3): 186–89. https://doi.org/10.1038/nclimate2110.

Jorgenson, A. K. 2015a. "Inequality and the Carbon Intensity of Human Well-Being." *Journal of Environmental Studies and Sciences* 5(3): 277–82.

Jorgenson, A. K. 2015b. "Five Points on Sociology, PEWS and Climate Change." *Journal of World-Systems Research* 21(2): 270–75.

Jorgenson, A. K. 2016a. "The Sociology of Ecologically Unequal Exchange, Foreign Investment Dependence and Environmental Load Displacement: Summary of the Literature and Implications for Sustainability." *Journal of Political Ecology* 23(1): 334–49.

Jorgenson, A. K. 2016b. "Environment, Development, and Ecologically Unequal Exchange." *Sustainability* 8(3): 227.

Jorgenson, A. K. and B. clark. 2010 "Assessing the Temporal Stability of the Population/Environment Relationship in Comparative Perspective: A Cross-National Panel Study of Carbon Dioxide Emissions, 1960–2005." Population and Environment 32(1): 27–41.

Jorgenson, A. K. and B. Clark. 2016. "The Temporal Stability and Developmental Differences in the Environmental Impacts of Militarism: The Treadmill of Destruction and Consumption-Based Carbon Emissions." *Sustainability Science* 11: 505–514.

Jorgenson, A. K., T. Dietz and O. Kelly. 2018. "Inequality, Poverty, and the Carbon Intensity of Human Well-Being in the United States: A Sex-Specific Analysis." *Sustainability Science* 13(4): 1167–74.

Jorgenson, A. K., S. Fiske, K. Hubacek et al. 2019. "Social Science Perspectives on Drivers of and Responses to Global Climate Change." *Wiley Interdisciplinary Reviews: Climate Change* 10(1): e554.

Jorgenson, A. K. and J. Givens. 2014. "The Emergence of New World-Systems Perspectives on Global Environmental Change." Pp. 31–44 in *The Routledge International Handbook of Social and Environmental Change*, edited by S. Lockie, D. A. Sonnenfeld and D. Fisher. New York: Routledge.

Jorgenson, A. K., W. Longhofer and D. Grant. 2016. "Disproportionality in Power Plants' Carbon Emissions: A Cross-National Study." *Scientific Reports* 6. https://doi.org/10.1038/srep28661.

Jorgenson, A. K., J. Schor and X. Huang. 2017. "Income Inequality and Carbon Emissions in the United States: A State-Level Analysis, 1997–2012." *Ecological Economics* 134: 40–48. https://doi.org/10.1016/j.ecolecon.2016.12.016.

Jorgenson, A. K., J. B. Schor, X. Huang and J. Fitzgerald. 2015. "Income Inequality and Residential Carbon Emissions in the United States: A Preliminary Analysis." *Human Ecology Review* 22(1): 93–106.

Jorgenson, A. K., J. B. Schor, K. W. Knight and X. Huang. 2016. "Domestic Inequality and Carbon Emissions in Comparative Perspective." *Sociological Forum* 31(S1): 770–86. https://doi.org/10.1111/socf.12272.

Jost, J. T., D. S. Baldassari and J. N. Druckman. 2022. "Social and Cognitive-Motivational Mechanisms of Political Polarization." *Nature Reviews Psychology*: 1–17. https://doi.org/10.1038/s44159-022-00093-5.

Judge, M. A.T., Y. Kashima, L. Steg and T. Dietz. 2023. "Environmental Decision Making in Times of Polarization." *Annual Review of Environment and Resources*: 48: in press.

Kaasa, A. 2021. "Merging Hofstede, Schwartz, and Inglehart into a Single System." *Journal of Cross-Cultural Psychology* 52(4): 339–53.

Kahan, D. M. 2012. "Cultural Cognition As a Conception of the Cultural Theory of Risk." Pp. 725–59 in *Handbook of Risk Theory*, edited by S. Roeser. Berlin: Springer.

Kahneman, D. 2011. *Thinking Fast and Slow*. New York: Farrar, Straus & Giroux.

Kahneman, D. and A. Deaton. 2010. "High Income Improves Evaluation of Life but Not Emotional Well-Being." *Proceedings of the National Academy of Sciences* 107(38): 16489–93.

Kahneman, D., P. Slovic and A. Tversky, eds. 1982. *Judgement under Uncertainty: Heuristics and Biases*. Cambridge: Cambridge University Press.

Kaika, D. and E. Zervas. 2013a. "The Environmental Kuznets Curve (EKC) Theory: Part A: Concept, Causes and the $CO_2$ Emissions Case." *Energy Policy* 62: 1392–402. http://dx.doi.org/10.1016/j.enpol.2013.07.131.

Kaika, D. and E. Zervas. 2013b. "The Environmental Kuznets Curve (EKC) Theory: Part B: Critical Issues." *Energy Policy* 62: 1403–11. http://dx.doi.org/10.1016/j.enpol.2013.07.130.

Kallis, G., V. Kostakis, S. Lange et al. 2018. "Research on Degrowth." *Annual Review of Environment and Resources* 43(1): 291–316. https://doi.org/10.1146/annurev-environ-102017-025941.

Kalof, L. 2007. *Looking at Animals in Human History*. London: Reaktion Books.

Kalof, L., ed. 2017. *The Oxford Handbook of Animal Studies*. New York: Oxford University Press.

Kalof, L. and R. F. Amthor. 2010. "Cultural Representation of Problem Animals in National Geographic." *Études rurales* 185: 165–80. https://doi.org/10.4000/etudesrurales.9134.

Kalof, L. and B. Real, eds. 2008. *A Cultural History of Animals*. London: Bloomsbury.

Kalof, L., J. Zammit-Lucia, J. Bell and G. Granter. 2016. "Fostering Kinship with Animals: Animal Portraiture in Humane Education." *Environmental Education Research* 22(2): 203–28.

Kalof, L., J. Zammit-Lucia and J. R. Kelly. 2011. "The Meaning of Animal Portraiture in a Museum Setting: Implications for Conservation." *Organization and Environment* 24(2): 150–74.

Kansas City Star. 2010. "Mr. President, Kansas Needs a National Park." *Kansas City Star*, June 6.

Kant, I. [1781] 1998. *Critique of Pure Reason*. Cambridge: Cambridge University Press.

Kant, I. [1785] 2002. *Groundwork for the Metaphysics of Morals*. New Haven, CT: Yale University Press.

Kantenbacher, J. and S. Z. Attari. 2021. "Better Rules for Judging Joules: Exploring How Experts Make Decisions about Household Energy Use." *Energy Research and Social Science* 73: 101911. https://doi.org/10.1016/j.erss.2021.101911.

Kapur, D., J. P. Lewis and R. Webb. 1997. *The World Bank: Its First Half Century, Vol. 1: History*. Washington, DC: Brookings Institution.

Karpowitz, C. F. and C. Raphael. 2016. "Ideals of Inclusion in Deliberation." *Journal of Public Deliberation* 12(2). https://doi.org/10.16997/jdd.255.

Kaya, Y. 1990. "Impact of Carbon Dioxide Emission Control on GNP Growth: Interpretation of Proposed Scenarios." Paper Presented to the IPCC Energy and Industry Subgroup, Response Strategies Working Group, Paris, May 9.

Kaya, Y. and K. Yokobori. 1997. *Environment, Energy, and Economy: Strategies for Sustainability*. Tokyo and New York: United Nations University Press.

Kean, S. 2021. *The Icepick Surgeon: Murder, Fraud, Sabotage, Piracy and Otherly Dastardly Deeds Perpetrated in the Name of Science*. New York: Little, Brown.

Keefe, P. R. 2017. "Carl Icahn's Failed Raid on Washington: Was President Trump's richest adviser focussed on helping the Country – or his own Bottom line?" *The New Yorker*, August 21.

Keena, A., M. Latner, A. J. M. McGann and C. A. Smith. 2021. *Gerrymandering the States: Partisanship, Race, and the Transformation of American Federalism*. Cambridge: Cambridge University Press.

Keith, D. W. 2021. "Toward Constructive Disagreement about Geoengineering." *Science* 374(6569): 812–15.

Kelly, O., R. P. Thombs and A. Jorgenson. 2021. "The Unsustainable State: Greenhouse Gas Emissions, Inequality, and Human Well-Being in the United States, 1913 to 2017." *Socius* 7: https://doi.org/10.1177/23780231211020536.

Kempton, W. 1991. "Lay Perspectives on Global Climate Change." Pp. 29–69 in *Energy Efficiency and the Environment: Forging the Link*, edited by E. L. Vine, D. Crawley and P. Centolella. Washington, DC: American Council for an Energy-Efficient Economy.

Kempton, W. and L. Montgomery. 1982. "Folk Quantification of Energy." *Energy* 7(10): 817–28.

Kempton, W., C. Harris, J. Keith and J. Weihl. 1985. "Do Customers Know 'What Works' in Energy Conservation?" *Marriage and Family Review* 9(1–2): 115–33. https://doi.org/10.1300/J002v09n01_07.

Kempton, W. 1986. "Two Theories of Home Heat Control." *Cognitive Science* 10(1): 75–90.

Kenessey, Z. 1994. "The Genesis of National Accounts: An Overview." Pp. 1–15 in *The Accounts of Nations*, edited by Z. Kenessey. Amsterdam: IOS Press.

Kennedy, E. H., H. Krahn and N. T. Krogman. 2014. "Egregious Emitters: Disproportionality in Household Carbon Footprints." *Environment and Behavior* 46(5): 535–55.

Kennedy, E. H. 2022. *Eco-Types: Five Ways of Caring about the Environment*. Princeton, NJ: Princeton University Press.

Kenter, J. O., R. Bryce, M. Christie et al. 2016. "Shared Values and Deliberative Valuation: Future Directions." *Ecosystem Services* 21: 358–71. https://doi.org/10.1016/j.ecoser.2016.10.006.

Kentor, J. 2016. "Shared, Plural and Cultural Values." *Ecosystem Services* 21: 175–183.

Kerr, J. R. and M. S. Wilson. 2018. "Changes in Perceived Scientific Consensus Shift Beliefs about Climate Change and GM Food Safety." *PloS One* 13(7): e0200295.

Kershaw, I. 2008. *Hitler: A Biography*. New York: W. W. Norton.

Keynes, J. N. [1917] 1999. *The Scope and Method of Political Economy*. Kitchener, ON: Batoche Books.

Khalil, E. L. 1990. "Beyond Self-Interest and Altruism: A Reconstruction of Adam Smith's Theory of Human Conduct." *Economics and Philosophy* 6(2): 255–73.

Kick, E. L. and L. A. McKinney. 2014. "Global Context, National Interdependencies, and the Ecological Footprint: A Structural Equation Analysis." *Sociological Perspectives* 57(2): 256–79.

Kidd, C., H. Palmeri and R. N. Aslin. 2013. "Rational Snacking: Young Children's Decision-Making on the Marshmallow Task Is Moderated by Beliefs about Environmental Reliability." *Cognition* 126 (1): 109–14.

Kidd, Q. and A.-R. Lee. 1997. "Postmaterialist Values and the Environment: A Critique and Reappraisal." *Social Science Quarterly* 78(1): 1–15.

Kimmerer, R. W. and F. K. Lake. 2001. "The Role of Indigenous Burning in Land Management." *Journal of Forestry* 99(11): 36–41. https://doi.org/10.1093/jof/99 .11.36.

King, G. and R. X. Browning. 2017. "How to Conquer Partisan Gerrymandering." *Boston Globe* 46(1161): 303–41.

King, G., B. Schneer and A. White. 2017. "How the News Media Activate Public Expression and Influence National Agendas." *Science* 358(6364): 776–80.

King, M. L., Jr. 1963. "Letter from Birmingham Jail." *Liberation: An Independent Monthly* 8 (4): 10–16, 23.

King, M. L., Jr. 1968. *Where Do We Go from Here: Chaos or Community?* Boston: Beacon Press.

Kirk, A. G. 2007. *Counterculture Green: The Whole Earth Catalog and American Environmentalism.* Lawrence: University Press of Kansas.

Kitman, J. L. 2000. "The Secret History of Lead." *The Nation* 270(11): 11–44.

Klar, S. and Y. Shmargad. 2017. "The Effect of Network Structure on Preference Formation." *The Journal of Politics* 79(2): 717–21.

Kleinhesselink, R. R. and E. A. Rosa. 1991. "Cognitive Representation of Risk Perceptions: A Comparison of Japan and the United States." *Journal of Cross-Cultural Psychology* 22(1): 11–28.

Kleinhesselink, R. R. and E. A. Rosa. 1994. "Nuclear Trees in a Forest of Hazards: A Comparison of Risk Perceptions Between American and Japanese University Students." Pp. 109–19 in *Nuclear Power at the Crossroads*, edited by G. W. Hinman, S. Kondo, T. C. Lowinger and K. Matsui. Boulder, CO: International Research Center for Energy and Economic Development.

Kleinschafer, J. and M. Morrison. 2014. "Household Norms and Their Role in Reducing Household Electricity Consumption." *International Journal of Consumer Studies* 38(1): 75–81.

Klenert, D., L. Mattauch, E. Combet et al. 2018. "Making Carbon Pricing Work for Citizens." *Nature Climate Change* 8(8): 669– 77.

Kling, C. L., D. J. Phaneuf and J. Zhao. 2012. "From Exxon to BP: Has Some Number Become Better Than No Number?" *Journal of Economic Perspectives* 26(4): 3–26.

Klöckner, C. A. 2013. "A Comprehensive Model of the Psychology of Environmental Behaviour: A Meta-Analysis." *Global Environmental Change* 23(5): 1028–38.

Knight, K. and E. A. Rosa. 2011. "The Environmental Efficiency of Well-Being: A Cross-National Analysis." *Social Science Research* 40(3): 931–49.

Knight, K. W., J. B. Schor and A. K. Jorgenson. 2017. "Wealth Inequality and Carbon Emissions in High-income Countries." *Social Currents* 4(5): 403–12. https://doi.org/ 10.1177/2329496517704872.

Koch, A., C. Brierley, M. M. Maslin and S. L. Lewis. 2019. "Earth System Impacts of the European Arrival and Great Dying in the Americas after 1492." *Quaternary Science Reviews* 207: 13–36. https://doi.org/10.1016/j .quascirev.2018.12.004.

Koenker, R. 2017. "Quantile Regression: 40 Years On." *Annual Review of Economics* 9: 155–76.

Koenker, R. and K. F. Hallock. 2001. "Quantile Regression." *Journal of Economic Perspectives* 15(4): 143–56.

Kohler-Hausmann, I. 2020. "Nudging People to Court." *Science* 370(6517): 658–59.

Kompridis, N. 2006. *Critique and Disclosure: Critical Theory between Past and Future.* Cambridge, MA: MIT Press.

Kompridis, N. 2009. "Technology's Challenge to Democracy: What of the Human?" *Parrhesia* 8(1): 20–30.

Korsgaard, C. M. 2011. "Interacting with Animals: A Kantian Account." Pp. 91–118 in *The Oxford Handbook of Animal Ethics*, edited by T. L. Beauchamp and R. G. Frey. Oxford: Oxford University Press.

Korten, T. 2015. "In Florida, Officials Ban Term 'Climate Change'." Florida Center for Investigative Reporting. News Release, March 8. http://fcir.org/2015/03/08/in-florida-officials-ban-term-climate-change/.

Kourany, J.A. 2018. "Adding to the Tapestry." *Philosophy, Theory, and Practice in Biology* 10(9). https://doi.org/10.3998/ptpbio .16039257.0010.009.

Kowalczyk, D., J. C. Cramer, B. Hackett et al. 1983. "Evaluation of a Community-Based Electricity Load Management Program." *Energy* 8(3): 253–43.

Kozlowski, C. 2018, "Chrissie Hynde: 'My Dad Loved Rush Limbaugh'." *Hollywood in Toto*, July 19. www.hollywoodintoto.com/chrissie-hynde-rush-limbaugh/.

Krell, A. 2002. *The Devil's Rope: A Cultural History of Barbed Wire.* London: Reaktion Books.

Kroesen, M. and C. Chorus. 2018. "The Role of General and Specific Attitudes in Predicting Travel Behavior: A Fatal Dilemma?" *Travel Behaviour and Society* 10: 33–41. https://doi .org/10.1016/j.tbs.2017.09.004.

Kroh, K. 2014. "The Complete Guide to Everything That's Happened Since the Massive Chemical Spill in West Virginia." ClimateProgress, February 9.

Kronk Warner, E. A., K. Lynn and K. Whyte. 2020. "Changing Consultation." *UC Davis Law Review* 54: 1127–83. http://dx.doi.org/10 .2139/ssrn.3544240.

Krupnikov, Y. and J. B. Ryan. 2022. *The Other Divide: Polarization and Disengagement in American Politics.* Cambridge: Cambridge University Press.

Kubin, E., C. Puryear, C. Schein and K. Gray. 2021. "Personal Experiences Bridge Moral and Political Divides Better Than Facts." *Proceedings of the National Academy of Sciences* 118(6): e2008389118. https://doi.org /10.1073/pnas.2008389118.

Kuhn, T. S. 1962. *The Structure of Scientific Revolutions.* Chicago, IL: University of Chicago Press.

Kuhn, T. S. 1977. *The Essential Tension: Selected Studies in Scientific Tradition and Change.* Chicago, IL: University of Chicago Press.

Kujala, J. 2020. "Donors, Primary Elections, and Polarization in the United States." *American Journal of Political Science* 64(3): 587–602.

Kumar, A., B. Sah, A. R. Singh et al. 2017. "A Review of Multi Criteria Decision Making (MCDM) towards Sustainable Renewable Energy Development." *Renewable and Sustainable Energy Reviews* 69: 596–609. https://doi.org/10.1016/j .rser.2016.11.191.

Kunreuther, H. and M. Useem. 2009. *Learning from Catastrophes: Strategies for Reaction and Response.* Hoboken, NJ: Pearson Prentice Hall.

Kunreuther, H. and M. Useem. 2018. *Mastering Catastrophic Risk: How Companies Are Coping with Disruption.* Oxford: Oxford University Press.

Kuznets, S. 1934. "National Income, 1929–1932." *National Bureau of Economic Research Bulletins* 49: 1–12. www.nber.org/ books/kuzn34-1.

Kuznets, S. 1955. "Economic Growth and Income Inequality." *American Economic Review* 45(1): 1–28.

Kuznets, S. 1979. *Growth, Population and Income Distribution: Selected Essays*. New York: Norton.

Kyung-Sup, C., B. Fine and L. Weiss. 2012. *Developmental Politics in Transition: The Neoliberal Era and Beyond*. New York: Palgrave Macmillan.

Lacour, C., L. Seconda, B. Allès et al. 2018. "Environmental Impacts of Plant-Based Diets: How Does Organic Food Consumption Contribute to Environmental Sustainability?" *Frontiers in Nutrition* 5: 8. https://doi.org/10.3389/fnut.2018.00008.

Ladd, A. E., ed. 2018. *Fractured Communities: Risk, Impacts, and Protest against Hydraulic Fracking in US Shale Regions*. New Brunswick, NJ: Rutgers University Press.

Lade, S. J., W. Steffen, W. De Vries et al. 2020. "Human Impacts on Planetary Boundaries Amplified by Earth System Interactions." *Nature Sustainability* 3(2): 119–28.

Lagin, K. 2020. "'I Can't Even Enjoy This': #BlackBirdersWeek Organizer Shares Her Struggles As a Black Scientist." *Science*, June 5. https://doi.org/10.3389/fnut.2018.00008.

Lagos, D. 2022. "Has There Been a Transgender Tipping Point? Gender Identification Differences in US Cohorts Born between 1935 and 2001." *American Journal of Sociology* 128(1): 94–143.

Lai, Y. Y., E. Christley, A. Kulanovic et al. 2022. "Analysing the Opportunities and Challenges for Mitigating the Climate Impact of Aviation: A Narrative Review." *Renewable and Sustainable Energy Reviews* 156: 111972. https://doi.org/10.1016/j.rser.2021.111972.

Lamb, W. F., G. Mattioli, S. Levi et al. 2020. "Discourses of Climate Delay." *Global Sustainability* 3: e17. https://doi.org/10.1017/sus.2020.13.

Land, S. 2019. *Maid: Hard Work, Low Pay and a Mother's Will to Survive*. New York: Hachette Books.

Landis, J. 1983. *Trading Places*. Dir. John Landis. Paramount Pictures.

Landrum, A. R., A. Olshansky and O. Richards. 2019. "Differential Susceptibility to Misleading Flat Earth Arguments on YouTube." *Media Psychology* 24(1): 136–65.

Lane, B. and S. Potter. 2007. "The Adoption of Cleaner Vehicles in the UK: Exploring the Consumer Attitude–Action Gap." *Journal of Cleaner Production* 15(11): 1085–92.

Lange, A. 2022. *Meet Me by the Fountain: An Inside Story of the Mall*. New York: Bloomsbury.

Lange, F., K. S. Nielsen, V. Cologna, C. Brick and P. C. Stern. 2021. "Making Theory Useful for Understanding High-Impact Behavior: A Response to van Valkengoed et al. (2021)." *Journal of Environmental Psychology* 75: 101611. https://doi.org/10.1016/j.jenvp.2021.101611.

Langlois, D. K., J. B. Kaneene, V. Yuzbasiyan-Gurkan et al. 2017. "Investigation of Blood Lead Concentrations in Dogs Living in Flint, Michigan." *Journal of the American Veterinary Medical Association* 251(8): 912–21.

Larson, E. J. 2020. *Franklin and Washington: The Founding Partnership*. New York: William Morrow.

Latour, B. 2015. "Telling Friends from Foes in the Time of the Anthropocene." Pp. 145–55 in *The Anthropocene and the Global Environmental Crisis: Rethinking Modernity in a New Epoch*, edited by C. Hamilton, C. Bonneuil and F. Gemenne. London: Routledge.

Lauer, S., M. Sanderson, D. Manning et al. 2018. "Values and Groundwater Management in the Ogallala Aquifer Region." *Journal of Soil and Water Conservation* 73(5): 593–600.

Laurance, W. F., A. K. Albernaz, P. M. Fearnside, H. L. Vasconcelos and L. V. Ferreira. 2004. "Deforestation in Amazonia." *Science* 304(5674): 1109–11.

Lawrence, T. E. [1926] 1962. *Seven Pillars of Wisdom: A Triumph*. New York: Dell Books.

Lazo, L. 2021. "As Infrastructure Debate Lingers, $34 Million and a New Sidewalk Are Bringing Life to a Small Virginia Town." The Washington Post, July 23.

Le Guin, U. K. 1969. *The Left Hand of Darkness*. New York: Ace.

Le Guin, U. K. 1974. *The Dispossessed: An Ambiguous Utopia*. New York: Harper & Row.

Le Guin, U. K. 1976. *The Word for World Is Forest*. New York: Berkeley Books.

Le Guin, U. K. 1987. "Buffalo Gals, Won't You Come Out Tonight." *The Magazine of Fantasy and Science Fiction* 73(5): 131–58.

Leach, M., B. Reyers, X. Bai et al. 2018. "Equity and Sustainability in the Anthropocene: A Social–Ecological Systems Perspective on Their Intertwined Futures." *Global Sustainability* 1(e13): 1–13.

Leacock, E. and R. Lee, eds. 1982. *Politics and History in Band Societies*. Cambridge: Cambridge University Press.

Lear, L. 1998. *Rachel Carson: Witness for Nature*. New York: Macmillan.

LeDuc, L. 2020. *The Politics of Direct Democracy*. Toronto, ON: University of Toronto Press.

Lee, A.-R. and Q. Kidd. 1997. "More on Postmaterialist Values and the Environment." *Social Science Quarterly* 78 (1): 36–43.

Lee, S. and S. Ditko. 1962. "Spider-Man." *Amazing Fantasy* 15: 1–11.

Leeper, T. and R. Slothuus. 2018. "Deliberation and Framing." Pp. 555–72 in *The Oxford Handbook of Deliberative Democracy*, edited by A. Bächtiger, J. S. Dryzek, J. Mansbridge and M. E. Warren. Oxford: Oxford University Press.

Leiserowitz, A., C. Roser-Renouf, J. Marlon and E. Maibach. 2021. "Global Warming's Six Americas: A Review and Recommendations for Climate Change Communication." *Current Opinion in Behavioral Sciences* 42: 97–103. https://doi.org/10.1016/j.cobeha.2021.04.007.

Lenski, S., G. A. Keoleian and K. M. Bolon. 2012. "The Impact of 'Cash for Clunkers' on Greenhouse Gas Emissions: A Life Cycle Perspective." *Environmental Research Letters* 5(4): 044003. https://doi.org/10.1088/1748-9326/5/4/044003.

Lenton, T. M., J. Rockström, O. Gaffney et al. 2019. "Climate Tipping Points: Too risky to Bet Against." *Nature* 575(27): 592–95. https://doi.org/10.1038/d41586-019-03595-0.

Leonard, N. J., W. W. Taylor, C. I. Goddard et al. 2011. "Information Flow within the Social Network Structure of a Joint Strategic Plan for Management of Great Lakes Fisheries." *North American Journal of Fisheries Management* 31(4): 629–55.

Leonard, R. 2010. *Von Neumann, Morgenstern, and the Creation of Game Theory*. Cambridge: Cambridge University Press.

Lepore, J. 2018. *These Truths: A History of the United States*. New York: W. W. Norton.

Lesthaeghe, R. 2014. "The Second Demographic Transition: A Concise Overview of Its Development." *Proceedings of the National Academy of Sciences* 111(51): 18112–15. https://doi.org/10.1073/pnas.1420441111.

Levins, R. 1966. "The Strategy of Model Building in Population Biology." *American Scientist* 54(4): 421–31.

Levins, R. 1993. "A Response to Orzack and Sober: Formal Analysis and Fluidity of Science." *Quarterly Review of Biology* 68(4): 547–55.

Levitas, R. 2013. *Utopia As Method: The Imaginary Reconstitution of Society*. New York: Palgrave Macmillan.

Lewicki, R. J., B. Gray and M. Elliot, eds. 2003. *Making Sense of Intractable Environmental Conflicts: Concepts and Cases*. Washington, DC: Island Press.

Lewis, D. C., A. R. Flores, D. P. Haider-Markel, P. R. Miller and J. K. Taylor. 2022. "Transitioning Opinion?: Assessing the Dynamics of Public Attitudes Toward transgender Rights." *Public Opinion Quarterly* 86(2): 343–68. https://doi.org/10.1093/poq/nfac014.

Lewis, M. 2016. *The Undoing Project: A Friendship That Changed Our Minds*. New York: W. W. Norton.

Lienhoop, N., B. Bartkowski and B. Hansjürgens. 2015. "Informing Biodiversity Policy: The Role of Economic Valuation, Deliberative Institutions and

Deliberative Monetary Valuation." *Environmental Science and Policy* 54: 522–32. https://doi.org/10.1016/j.envsci.2015.01.007.

Lin, P., K. Abney and R. Jenkins. 2017. *Robot Ethics 2.0: From Autonomous Cars to Artificial Intelligence*. Oxford: Oxford University Press.

Lind, H. B., T. Nordfjærn, S. H. Jørgensen and T. Rundmo. 2015. "The Value-Belief-Norm Theory, Personal Norms and Sustainable Travel Mode Choice in Urban Areas." *Journal of Environmental Psychology* 44: 119–25. https://doi.org/10.1016/j .jenvp.2015.06.001.

Lind, J. 1776. *An Answer to the Declaration of the American Congress*. London: T. Cadell in the Strand; J. Walter, Charing-cross; and T. Sewell, near the Royal Exchange.

Lindsey, A. 1942. *The Pullman Strike: The Story of a Unique Experiment and of a Great Labor Upheaval*. Chicago, IL: University of Chicago Press.

Lipset, S. M. 1963. *Political Man: The Social Bases of Politics*. New York: Anchor Books.

List, C. 2018. " Democratic Deliberation and Social Choice: A Review." Pp. 463–89 in *The Oxford Handbook of Deliberative Democracy*, edited by A. Bächtiger, J. Dryzek, J. Mansbridge and M. E. Warren. Oxford: Oxford University Press.

List, C., R. C. Luskin, J. S. Fishkin and I. McLean. 2012. "Deliberation, Single-Peakedness, and the Possibility of Meaningful Democracy: Evidence from Deliberative Polls." *The Journal of Politics* 75 (1): 80–95.

Little, A. 2004. "The Whole Foods Shebang: An interview with John Mackey, founder of Whole Foods." *Grist*, December 18.

Liu, J., G. C. Daily, P. R. Ehrlich and G. W. Luck. 2003. "Effects of Household Dynamics on Resource Consumption and Biodiversity." *Nature* 421(6922): 530–33.

Liu, J., T. Dietz, S.R. Carpenter et al. 2007a. "Complexity of Coupled Human and Natural Systems." *Science* 317(5844): 1513–16.

Liu, J., T. Dietz, S.R. Carpenter et al. 2007b. "Coupled Human and Natural Systems." *Ambio* 36(8): 639–49.

Liu, J., T. Dietz, S.R. Carpenter et al. 2021. "Coupled Human and Natural Systems: The Evolution and Applications of an Integrated Framework." *Ambio* 50(10): 1778–83.

Liu, J., Y. Dou, M. Batistella et al. 2018. "Spillover Systems in a Telecoupled Anthropocene: Typology, Methods, and Governance for Global Sustainability." *Current Opinion in Environmental Sustainability* 33: 58–69. https://doi.org/10 .1016/j.cosust.2018.04.009.

Liu, J., V. Hull, M. Batistella et al. 2013. "Framing Sustainability in a Telecoupled World." *Ecology and Society* 18(2): 26.

Liu, J., V. Hull, J. Luo et al. 2015. "Multiple Telecouplings and Their Complex Interrelationships." *Ecology and Society* 20 (3): 44.

Liu, J. and W. Yang. 2013. "Integrated Assessments of Payments for Ecosystem Services Programs." *Proceedings of the National Academy of Sciences* 110(41): 16297–98.

Lliso, B., U. Pascual, S. Engel and P. Mariel. 2020. "Payments for Ecosystem Services or Collective Stewardship of Mother Earth? Applying Deliberative Valuation in an Indigenous Community in Colombia." *Ecological Economics* 169: 106499. https://d oi.org/10.1016/j.ecolecon.2019.106499.

Lo, A. W., M. Getmansky and P. A. Lee. 2015. "Hedge Funds: A Dynamic Industry In Transition." *Annual Review of Financial Economics* 7: 483–577. https://doi.org/10 .1146/annurev-financial-110311-101741.

Lo, A. Y. 2013. "Agreeing to Pay Under Value Disagreement: Reconceptualizing Preference Transformation in Terms of Pluralism with Evidence from Small-Group Deliberations on Climate Change." *Ecological Economics* 87: 84–94. https://doi.org/10.1016/j .ecolecon.2012.12.014.

Lo, A. Y. and C. L. Spash. 2013. "Deliberative Monetary Valuation: In Search of a Democratic and Value Plural Approach to

Environmental Policy." *Journal of Economic Surveys* 27(4): 768–89.

Lockie, S. 2012. "Sustainability and a Sociology of Monsters." *Sociologica* 6(2). https://doi.org/10.2383/38273.

Lockie, S. 2016a. "Beyond Resilience and Systems Theory: Reclaiming Justice in Sustainability Discourse." *Environmental Sociology* 2(2): 115–17.

Lockie, S. 2016b. "Sustainability and the Future of Environmental Sociology." *Environmental Sociology* 2(1): 1–4.

Lockie, S. and C. M. L. Wong. 2017. "Risk, Sustainability and Time: Sociological Perspectives." Pp. 187–98 in *Sustainability: Social Science Contributions*, edited by H. Schandl and I. Walker. Clayton, Australia: CSIRO Publishing.

Loewenstein, M. J. 2013. "Benefit Corporations: A Challenge in Corporate Governance." *The Business Lawyer* 68: 1007–38. https://scholar.law.colorado.edu/faculty-articles/441.

Logan, J. R. and H. L. Molotch. 1987. *Urban Fortunes: The Political Economy of Place*. Berkeley: University of California Press.

Longo, S. B., B. Clark, T. E. Shriver and R. Clausen. 2016. "Sustainability and Environmental Sociology: Putting the Economy in Its Place and Moving Toward an Integrative Socio-Ecology." *Sustainability* 8(5): 437.

Longo, S. B., R. Clausen and B. Clark. 2015. *The Tragedy of the Commodity: Oceans, Fisheries, and Aquaculture*. New Brunswick, NJ: Rutgers University Press.

Lord, C. G., L. Ross and M. R. Lepper. 1979. "Biased Assimilation and Attitude Polarization: The Effects of Prior Theories on Subsequently Considered Evidence." *Journal of Personality and Social Psychology* 37(11): 2098–109.

Lott, D. Y., T. J. Tardiff and D. F. Lott. 1977. "Bicycle Transportation for Downtown Work Trips: A Case Study in Davis, California." *Transportation Research Record* 629: 30–37.

Lough, T. S. 1996. "Energy Analysis of the Structures of Industrial Organizations." *Energy* 21(2): 131–39.

Lough, T. S. 1999. "Energy, Agriculture, Patriarchy and Ecocide." *Human Ecology Review* 6(2): 100–11.

Loux, A. C. 2003. "A 'Comedy of the Commons'? Custom, Community and Rights of Public Access to the Links of St Andrews." *Liverpool Law Review* 22(2–3): 123–55.

Love, A. C. and W. Wimsatt. 2019. *Beyond the Meme: Development and Structure in Cultural Evolution*. Minneapolis: University of Minnesota Press.

Love, S. and D. Giffels. 1999. *Wheels of Fortune: The Story of Rubber in Akron*. Akron, OH: University of Akron Press.

Lovins, A. B. 1976. "Energy Strategy: The Road Not Taken." *Foreign Affairs* 55(1): 65–96.

Lu, X., J. Gao and B. K. Szymanski. 2019. "The Evolution of Polarization in the Legislative Branch of Government." *Journal of the Royal Society Interface* 16(156): 20190010. https://doi.org/10.1098/rsif.2019.0010.

Lubinski, J. 2002, "Legal Overview of Animal Rights": Animal Legal and Historical Center, Detroit College of Law, Michigan State University. www.animallaw.info/article/overview-animal-rights.

Lukacs, J. 2011. *The Hitler of History*. New York: Vintage.

Lukacs, M. and L. G. Williams. 2020. "Nuclear Safety Issues for Fusion Power Plants." *Fusion Engineering and Design* 150: 111377. https://doi.org/10.1016/j.fusengdes.2019.111377.

Lunde, M. B. 2018. "Sustainability in Marketing: A Systematic Review Unifying 20 Years of Theoretical and Substantive Contributions (1997–2016)." *AMS Review* 8 (3–4): 85–110.

Lupia, A. 2015. *Uninformed: Why People Seem to Know So Little about Politics and What We Can Do about It*. Oxford: Oxford University Press.

Lupia, A. and M. D. McCubbins. 1998. *The Democratic Dilemma: Can Citizens Learn*

*What They Need to Know?* Cambridge: Cambridge University Press.

Lutz, W., E. Striessnig, A. Dimitrova et al. 2021. "Years of Good Life Is a Well-Being Indicator Designed to Serve Research on Sustainability." *Proceedings of the National Academy of Sciences* 118(12): e1907351118.

MacDonald, C. and W. Norman. 2007. "Rescuing the Baby from the Triple-Bottom-Line Bathwater: A Reply to Pava." *Business Ethics Quarterly* 17(1): 111–14.

Macekura, S. J. 2015. *Of Limits and Growth: The Rise of Global Sustainable Development in the Twentieth Century*. New York: Cambridge University Press.

Machlis, G. E. and J. E. Force. 2019. "Community Stability and Timber-Dependent Communities: Future Research." Pp. 259–76 in *Community and Forestry*, edited by R. G. Lee. New York: Routledge.

MacLean, N. 2017. *Democracy in Chains: The Deep History of the Radical Right's Stealth Plan for America*. London: Penguin.

Madariaga, A. G. and H. E. Ozen. 2015. "Looking for Two-Sided Coattail Effects: Integrated Parties and Multilevel Elections in the US." *Electoral Studies* 40: 66–75. https://doi.org/10.1016/j.electstud.2015.06.006.

Maestre-Andrés, S., S. Drews and J. van den Bergh. 2019. "Perceived Fairness and Public Acceptability of Carbon Pricing: A Review of the Literature." *Climate Policy* 19(9): 1186–204.

Majewska, E. 2021. *Feminist Antifascism: Counterpublics of the Common*. London: Verso Books.

Maki, A., A. R. Carrico, K. T. Raimi et al. 2019. "Meta-analysis of Pro-environmental Behaviour Spillover." *Nature Sustainability* 2(4): 307.

Malakoff, D. 2021. "Great Lakes People among First Coppersmiths." *Science* 371(6536): 1299.

Maldonado, J., H. Lazrus, S.-K. Bennett et al. 2016. "The Story of Rising Voices: Facilitating Collaboration between Indigenous and Western Ways of Knowing." Pp. 15–26 in *Responses to Disasters and Climate Change: Understanding Vulnerability and Fostering Resilience*, edited by M. Companion and M. Chaiken. Boca Raton, FL: CRC Press.

Maldonado, J. K., B. Colombi and R. Pandya. 2016. *Climate Change and Indigenous Peoples in the United States*. Cham: Springer.

Malin, S. A. and S. S. Ryder. 2018. "Developing Deeply Intersectional Environmental Justice Scholarship." *Environmental Sociology* 4(1): 1–7.

Malm, A. 2021. *White Skin, Black Fuel: On the Danger of Fossil Fascism*. New York: Verso Books.

Malthus, T. R. [1803] 1992. *An Essay on the Principle of Population*. Cambridge: Cambridge University Press.

Mamdami, M. 1973. *The Myth of Population Control: Family, Caste and Class in an Indian Village*. New York: Monthly Review Press.

Mandelbrot, B. B. 1982. *The Fractal Geometry of Nature*. New York: W. H. Freeman.

Mankiv, N. G. 2018. *Principles of Microeconomics*. Boston, MA: Cengage Learning.

Mann, D. E. 1972. "Social Objectives of Water Resources Development in the United States." *Water Resources Bulletin* 8(3): 553–60.

Mann, M. 2005. *Incoherent Empire*. London: Verso.

Marghetis, T., S. Z. Attari and D. Landy. 2019. "Simple Interventions Can Correct Misperceptions of Home Energy Use." *Nature Energy* 4(10): 874–81.

Marquart-Pyatt, S. T. 2008. "Are There Similar Sources of Environmental Concern? Comparing Industrialized Countries." *Social Science Quarterly* 89(5): 1312–35.

Marquart-Pyatt, S. T. 2012. "Contextual Influences on Environmental Concern Cross-Nationally: A Multilevel Investigation." *Social Science Research* 41: 1085–99. https://doi.org/10.1016/j.ssresearch.2012.04.003.

Marques, A. C., J. A. Fuinhas and D. Pais. 2018. "Economic Growth, Sustainable Development and Food Consumption: Evidence across Different Income Groups of

Countries." *Journal of Cleaner Production* 196: 245–58. https://doi.org/10.1016/j .jclepro.2018.06.011.

Marshak, J. 1950. "Rational Behavior, Uncertain Prospects, and Measurable Utility." *Econometrica* 18(2): 111–41.

Marshall, P. 2008. *Demanding the Impossible: A History of Anarchism.* Oakland, CA: PM Publishers.

Marteau, T. M., P. C. Fletcher, M. R. Munafò and G. J. Hollands. 2021. "Beyond Choice Architecture: Advancing the Science of Changing Behaviour at Scale." *BMC Public Health* 21(1): 1–7.

Marten, G. G. 2001. *Human Ecology: Basic Concepts for Sustainable Development.* London: Earthscan.

Martin, J. L. and A. Lembo. 2020. "On the Other Side of Values." *American Journal of Sociology* 126(1): 52–98.

Martin, P. S. 2007. *Twilight of the Mammoths: Ice Age Extinctions and the Rewilding of America.* Berkeley: University of California Press.

Marx, K. [1851] 1973. "The 18th Brumaire of Louis Bonaparte." Pp. 143–249 in Marx, *Surveys from Exile*, edited by D. Fernbach. New York: Penguin.

Mascarenhas, M., ed. 2020. *Lessons in Environmental Justice: From Civil Rights to Black Lives Matter and Idle No More.* Thousand Oak, CA: Sage Publishing.

Mascarenhas, M. J. 2016. "Where the Waters Divide: Neoliberal Racism, White Privilege and Environmental Injustice." *Race, Gender and Class* 23(3/4): 6–25.

Mas-Colell, A., M. D. Whinston and J. R. Green. 1995. *Microeconomic Theory.* New York: Oxford University Press.

Matousek, J., T. Havranek and Z. Irsova. 2021. "Individual Discount Rates: A Meta-Analysis of Experimental Evidence." *Experimental Economics* 1–41. https://doi .org/10.1007/s10683-021-09716-9.

Maxwell, A. and T. Shields. 2019. *The Long Southern Strategy: How Chasing White Voters in the South Changed American Politics.* New York: Oxford University Press.

Maxwell, S .L., V. Cazalis, N. Dudley et al. 2020. "Area-Based Conservation in the Twenty-First Century." *Nature* 586(7828): 217–27. https://doi.org/10.1038/s41586-020-2773-z.

Mayer, A. 2017. "Quality of Life and Unconventional Oil and Gas Development: Towards a Comprehensive Impact Model for Host Communities." *The Extractive Industries and Society* 4(4): 923–30. https://d oi.org/10.1016/j.exis.2017.10.009.

Mayr, E. 1959. "Typological versus Population Thinking." Pp. 409–12 in *Evolution and Anthropology: A Centennial Appraisal*, edited by B. J. Meggers. Washington, DC: Anthropological Society of Washington.

Mazur, A. 2013a. "Energy and Electricity in Industrial Nations." Pp. 121–38 in *Structural Human Ecology: New Essays in Risk, Energy and Sustainability*, edited by T. Dietz and A. K. Jorgenson. Pullman: Washington State University Press.

Mazur, A. 2013b. *Energy and Electricity in Industrial Nations: The Sociology and Technology of Energy.* Oxford: Earthscan.

Mazur, A. and E. Rosa. 1974. "Energy and Life-Style: Massive Energy Consumption May Not Be Necessary to Maintain Current Living Standards in America." *Science* 186 (4164): 607–10.

McCabe, H. 2015. "John Stuart Mill's Analysis of Capitalism and the Road to Socialism." Pp. 8–22 in *A New Social Question: Capitalism, Socialism and Utopia*, edited by C. Harrison. Newcastle upon Tyne: Cambridge Scholars Publishing.

McCay, B. 1995. "Common and Private Concerns." *Advances in Human Ecology* 4: 89–116.

McCay, B. J. 2002. "Emergence of Institutions for the Commons: Contexts, Situations and Events." Pp. 361–402 in *The Drama of the Commons*, edited by E. Ostrom, T. Dietz, N. Dolšak, P. C. Stern, S. Stonich and E. Weber. Washington, DC: National Academy Press.

McCay, B. J. and J. M. Acheson. 1990. *The Question of the Commons: The Culture and*

*Ecology of Communal Resources.* Tucson: University of Arizona Press.

McCay, B. J. and J. Svein. 2010. "Uncommon Ground: Critical Perspectives on Common Property." Pp. 203–30 in *Human Footprints on the Global Environment: Threats to Sustainability*, edited by E. A. Rosa, A. Diekmann, T. Dietz and C. Jaeger. Cambridge, MA: MIT Press.

McCay, B. J. and A. P. Vayda. 1975. "New Directions in Ecology and Ecological Anthropology." *Annual Review of Anthropology* 4: 293–306.

McCormick, S. 2007. "Democratizing Science Movements: A New Framework for Contestation." *Social Studies of Science* 37 (4): 1–15.

McCoy, D. and S. Lyons. 2016. "Unintended Outcomes of Electricity Smart-Metering: Trading-off Consumption and Investment Behaviour." *Energy Efficiency*: 1–20. https://doi.org/10.1007/s12053-016-9452-9.

McCright, A. M. 2000. "Challenging Global Warming As a Social Problem: An Analysis of the Conservative Movement's Counter-Claims." *Social Problems* 47(4): 499–522.

McCright, A. M. 2016. "Anti-reflexivity and Climate Change Skepticism in the US General Public." *Human Ecology Review* 22 (2): 77–108.

McCright, A. M., M. Charters, K. Dentzman and T. Dietz. 2016. "Examining the Effectiveness of Climate Change Frames in the Face of a Climate Change Denial Counter-Frame." *topiCS: Topics in Cognitive Science* 8(1): 76–97. https://doi.org/10.1111/tops.12171.

McCright, A. M., K. Dentzman, M. Charters and T. Dietz. 2013. "The Influence of Political Ideology on Trust in Science." *Environmental Research Letters* 8: 044029. https://doi.org/10.1088/1748-9326/8/4/044029.

McCright, A. M. and R. E. Dunlap. 2003. "Defeating Kyoto: The Conservative Movement's Impact on U.S. Climate Change Policy." *Social Problems* 50(3): 348–73.

McCright, A. M. and R. E. Dunlap. 2008. "Social Movement Identity and Belief Systems An Examination of Beliefs about Environmental Problems within the American Public." *Public Opinion Quarterly* 72(4): 651–76.

McCright, A. M. and R. E. Dunlap. 2010. "Anti-reflexivity: The American Conservative Movement's Success in Undermining Climate Science and Policy." *Theory, Culture, and Society* 27(2–3): 100–33.

McCright, A. M. and R. E. Dunlap. 2011a. "Cool Dudes: The Denial of Climate Change among Conservative White Males in the United States." *Global Environmental Change* 21(4): 1163–72.

McCright, A. M. and R. E. Dunlap. 2011b. "The Politicization of Climate Change and Polarization in the American Public's Views of Global Warming, 2001–2010." *Sociological Quarterly* 52(2): 155–94.

McCright, A. M. and R. E. Dunlap. 2015. "Comparing Two Measures of Social Movement Identity: The Environmental Movement as an Example." *Social Science Quarterly* 96(2): 400–16.

McCright, A. M., R. E. Dunlap and S. T. Marquart-Pyatt. 2016. "Political Ideology and Views about Climate Change in the European Union." *Environmental Politics* 25(2): 338–58.

McCright, A. M., S. T. Marquart-Pyatt, R. L. Shwom, S. R. Brechin and S. Allen. 2016. "Ideology, Capitalism, and Climate: Explaining Public Views about Climate Change in the United States." *Energy Research & Social Science* 21: 180–89. https://doi.org/10.1016/j.erss.2016.08.003.

McCright, A. M., C. Xiao and R. E. Dunlap. 2014. "Political Polarization on Support for Government Spending on Environmental Protection in the USA, 1974–2012." *Social Science Research* 48: 251–60. https://doi.org/10.1016/j.ssresearch.2014.06.008.

McDermott, M., S. Mahanty and K. Schreckenberg. 2013. "Examining Equity: A Multidimensional Framework for Assessing Equity in Payments for Ecosystem Services." *Environmental Science and Policy*

33: 416–27. https://doi.org/10.1016/j.envsci.2012.10.006.

McEvoy, J., III. 1972. "Multi- and Interdisciplinary Research: Problems of Initiation, Control, Integration and Reward." *Policy Sciences* 3(2): 201–08.

McEvoy, J. I. 1969. "Conservatism or Extremism: Goldwater Supporters in the 1964 Presidential Election." Pp. 241–79 in *The American Right Wing: Readings in Political Behavior*, edited by R. A. Schoenberger. New York: Holt, Rinehart and Winston.

McEvoy, J. I. 1971. *Radicals or Conservatives? The Contemporary American Right*. Chicago: Rand McNally.

McEvoy, J. I. and T. Dietz, eds. 1977. *Handbook of Environmental Planning: The Social Consequences of Environmental Change*. New York: Wiley Intersciences.

McGann, A. J., C. A. Smith, M. Latner and A. Keena. 2016. *Gerrymandering in America: The House of Representatives, the Supreme Court, and the Future of Popular Sovereignty*. Cambridge: Cambridge University Press.

McGann, J. G., ed. 2018. *Think Tanks and Emerging Power Policy Networks*. Cham: Springer.

McGhee, E. 2020. "Partisan Gerrymandering and Political Science." *Annual Review of Political Science* 23: 171–85.

McGrayne, S. B. 2001. "Leaded Gasoline, Safe Refrigeration, and Thomas Midgley, Jr.: May 18, 1889–November 3, 1944." Pp. 79–105 in McGrayne, *Prometheans in the Lab: Chemistry and the Making of the Modern World*. New York: McGraw-Hill.

McGuire, W., E. A. Holtmaat and A. Prakash. 2022. "Penalties for Industrial Accidents: The Impact of the Deepwater Horizon Accident on BP's Reputation and Stock Market Returns." *PloS One* 17(6): e0268743.

McKenzie, B. 2014. "Modes Less Traveled: Bicycling and Walking to Work in the United States: 2008–2012." United States Census Bureau, Report Number Acs-25, May 8. www.census.gov/library/publications/2014/acs/acs-25.html?#.

McKibben, W. 1989. *The End of Nature*. New York: Anchor Books.

McKinnon, M. C., M. B. Mascia, W. Yang, W. R. Turner and C. Bonham. 2015. "Impact Evaluation to Communicate and Improve Conservation Non-governmental Organization Performance: The Case of Conservation International." *Philosophical Transactions of the Royal Society B* 370 (1681): 20140282.

McKluskey, N. 2019. "Segregation and the School Choice Movement." *Education Next*. www.educationnext.org/segregation-and-school-choice-movement/.

McLaughlin, P. 1996. "Resource Mobilization and Density Dependence in Cooperative Purchasing Associations in Saskatchewan, Canada." *Rural Sociology* 61(2): 326–48.

McLaughlin, P. 1998. "Rethinking the Agrarian Question: The Limits of Essentialism and the Promise of Evolutionism." *Human Ecology Review* 5(2): 25–39.

McLaughlin, P. 2001. "Towards an Ecology of Social Action: Merging the Ecological and Constructivist Traditions." *Human Ecology Review* 8(2): 12–28.

McLaughlin, P. 2011. "Climate Change, Adaptation, and Vulnerability: Reconceptualizing Societal–Environment Interaction Within a Socially Constructed Adaptive Landscape." *Organization and Environment* 24(3): 269–91.

McLaughlin, P. 2012a. "Ecological Modernization in Evolutionary Perspective." *Organization and Environment* 25(2): 178–96.

McLaughlin, P. 2012b. "The Second Darwinian Revolution: Steps Toward a New Evolutionary Environmental Sociology." *Nature and Culture* 7(3): 231–58.

McLaughlin, P. 2012c. "Climate Change, Adaptation, and Vulnerability: Reconceptualizing Societal–Environment Interaction Within a Socially Constructed Adaptive Landscape." *Organization and Environment* 24(3): 269–91.

McLaughlin, P. 2022. "Durkheim's Failed Darwinian Encounter: Missed Opportunities on the Path to a Post-exemptionalist Environmental Sociology." *Sociological Perspectives* [Preprint]. https://doi.org/10.1177/07311214221121164.

McLaughlin, P. and T. Dietz. 2008. "Structure, Agency and Environment: Toward an Integrated Perspective on Vulnerability." *Global Environmental Change* 18(1): 99–111.

McLaughlin, P. and M. Khawaja. 2000. "The Organization Dynamics of the U.S. Environmental Movement: Legitimation, Resource Mobilization, and Political Opportunity." *Rural Sociology* 65(3): 422–39.

McMichael, C. N., F. Matthews-Bird, W. Farfan-Rios and K. J. Feeley. 2017. "Ancient Human Disturbances May Be Skewing Our Understanding of Amazonian Forests." *Proceedings of the National Academy of Sciences* 114(3): 522–27.

McMichael, P. 2008. *Development and Social Change: A Global Perspective*. Los Angeles: Pine Forge Press.

McNicoll, G. 1984. "Consequences of Rapid Population Growth: An Overview and Assessment." *Population and Development Review* 10(2): 177–240.

Mead, G. H. 1934. *Mind, Self and Society*. Chicago, IL: University of Chicago Press.

Meadows, D. H., D. L. Meadows, J. Randers and W. I. Behrens. 1972. *The Limits to Growth*. New York: Potomac Associates.

Mears, D. P., M. O. Craig, E. A. Stewart and P. Y. Warren. 2017. "Thinking Fast, Not Slow: How Cognitive Biases May Contribute to Racial Disparities in the Use of Force in Police–Citizen Encounters." *Journal of Criminal Justice* 53: 12–24. https://doi.org/10.1016/j.jcrimjus.2017.09.001.

Medema, S. G. 2017. "The Coase Theorem at Sixty." *Journal of Economic Literature*. 58(4): 1045–1128.

Meehan, J., ed. 1995. *Feminists Read Habermas: Gendering the Subject of Discourse*. New York: Routledge.

Menand, L. 2001. *The Metaphysical Club: A Story of Ideas in America*. New York: Farrar, Straus & Giroux.

Menjívar, C. and N. Rodriguez. 2009. *When States Kill: Latin America, the US, and Technologies of Terror*. Austin: University of Texas Press.

Merchant, C. 1992. *Radical Ecology: The Search for a Livable World*. New York: Routledge.

Merton, T. 1948. *The Seven Story Mountain*. New York: Signet.

Merton, R. K. 1968. "The Matthew Effect in Science." *Science* 159(3810): 56–63.

Mesorvic, M. and E. Pestel. 1974. *Mankind at the Turning Point*. New York: E. P. Dutton.

Metzler, M. S. 2021. *Maid*. Netflix.

Michaels, D. 2006. "Manufactured Uncertainty: Protecting Public Health in the Age of Contested Science and Product Defense." *Annals of the New York Academy of Sciences* 1076(1): 149–62. https://doi.org/10.1196/annals.1371.058.

Michaels, D. 2008. *Doubt Is Their Product: How Industry's Assault on Science Threatens Your Health*. New York: Oxford University Press.

Michaels, D. 2020. *The Triumph of Doubt: Dark Money and the Science of Deception*. Oxford: Oxford University Press.

Michaels, D. and C. Monforton. 2005. "Manufacturing Uncertainty: Contested Science and the Protection of the Public's Health and Environment." *American Journal of Public Health* 95(S1): S39–S48.

Michelson, A. A. and E. W. Morley. 1887. "On the Relative Motion of the Earth and the Luminiferous Ether." *American Journal of Science* 34(203): 333–45.

Michigan Civil Rights Commission. 2017. *The Flint Water Crisis: Systemic Racism through the Lens of Flint*. Report, Michigan Civil Rights Commission, Lansing, MI, February 17.

Michigan Legislature Joint Select Committee on the Flint Water Public Health Emergency. 2016. *FLINT WATER CRISIS: Report of the Joint Select Committee on the Flint Water Emergency*. Report, Michigan Legislature

Joint Select Committee on the Flint Water Public Health Emergency, Lansing, MI.

M'ikanatha, N. M. 2022. "The Trouble with Labels." *Science* 375(6586): 1306.

Mikkelson, G. M., A. Gonzalez and G. D. Peterson. 2007. "Economic Inequality Predicts Biodiversity Loss." *PloS One* 2(5): e444.

Mildenberger, M., E. Lachapelle, K. Harrison and I. Stadelmann-Steffen. 2022. "Limited Evidence That Carbon Tax Rebates Have Increased Public Support for Carbon Pricing." *Nature Climate Change* 12(2): 121–22. https://doi.org/10.1038/s41558-021-01270-9.

Milesi, C., C. Elvidge, J. Dietz et al. 2005. "A Strategy for Mapping and Modeling the Ecological Effects of US Lawns." *J. Turfgrass Manage* 1(1): 83–97.

Mill, J. S. 1879. *Utilitarianism*. London: Longmans, Green, and Co.

Mills, C. W. 1959. *The Sociological Imagination*. New York: Oxford University Press.

Mills, C. W. and H. H. Gerth. 1958. *From Max Weber: Essays in sociology*. Oxford: Oxford University Press.

Mindt, M. R., R. C. Hilsabeck, J. P. Olsen et al. 2018. "Advancing Science through Diversity and Inclusion in the Editorial Process: A Case Study." *Science Editor* 41(3): 93–96.

Minow, M. 2010. *In Brown's Wake: Legacies of America's Educational Landmark*. Oxford: Oxford University Press.

Misak, C. 2013. *The American Pragmatists*. New York: Oxford University Press.

Mishel, L. and J. Kandra. 2021. "CEO Pay Has Skyrocketed 1,322% since 1978." Economic Policy Institute, August 10. www.epi.org/publication/ceo-pay-in-2020/.

Mitcham, C. 1995. "The Concept of Sustainable Development: Its Origins and Ambivalence." *Technology in Society* 17(3): 311–26. http://dx.doi.org/10.1016/0160-791X(95)00008-F.

Moffett, L., C. Flannagan and P. Shah. 2020. "The Influence of Environmental Reliability in the Marshmallow Task: An Extension Study." *Journal of Experimental Child Psychology* 194: 104821. www.epi.org/publication/ceo-pay-in-2020/.

Mohai, P., D. Pellow and J. T. Roberts. 2009. "Environmental Justice." *Annual Review of Environment and Resources* 34: 405–30.

Moilanen, A., K. A. Wilson and H. Possingham. 2009. *Spatial Conservation Prioritization: Quantitative Methods and Computational Tools*. Oxford: Oxford University Press.

Mol, A. 1995. *The Refinement of Production: Ecological Modernization Theory and the Chemical Industry*. Utrecht: Van Arkel.

Mol, A. P. J. 2010. "Ecological Modernization As Social Theory of Environmental Reform." Pp. 63–76 in *The International Handbook of Environmental Sociology, Second Edition*, edited by M. R. Redclift and G. Woodgate. Cheltenham: Edward Elgar.

Mol, A. P. J., G. Spaargaren and D. A. Sonnenfeld. 2014. "Ecological Modernization Theory: Taking Stock, Moving Forward." Pp. 15–30 in *Routledge International Handbook of Social and Environmental Change*, edited by S. Lockie, D. A. Sonnenfeld and D. Fisher. New York: Routledge.

Möllmann, C., C. Folke, M. Edwards and A. Conversi. 2015. "Marine Regime Shifts around the Globe: Theory, Drivers and Impacts." *Philosophical Transactions of the Royal Society B: Biological Sciences* 370(1659). https://doi.org/10.1098/rstb.2013.0260.

Molotch, H. 1976. "The City As a Growth Machine: Toward a Political Economy of Place." *American Journal of Sociology* 82(2): 309–32.

Monroe, R. 2022. "Why Texas's Power Grid Still Hasn't Been Fixed." *The New Yorker*, 9 February.

Montoya, C. 2020. "Intersectionality and Voting Rights." *PS: Political Science and Politics* 53(3): 484–89.

Moore, A., D. Gibbons and J. Higgins. 1987. *Watchmen*. New York: DC Comics.

Moore, F. C., K. Lacasse, K. J. Mach et al. 2022. "Determinants of Emissions Pathways in the Coupled Climate–Social System."

*Nature* 603(7899): 103–11. https://doi.org/10 .1038/s41586-022-04423-8.

Moore, G. E. [1903] 1993. *Principia Ethica*. Cambridge: Cambridge University Press.

Morgan, E. S. 2003. *Benjamin Franklin*. New Haven, CT: Yale University Press.

Morgan, M. G. 2017. *Theory and Practice in Policy Analysis*: Cambridge: Cambridge University Press.

Morgan, M. G., R. Cantor, W. C. Clark et al. 2005. "Learning from the U.S. National Assessment of Climate Change Impacts." *Environmental Science and Technology* 39 (23): 9023–32. https://doi.org/10.1021 /es050865i.

Morgan, M. G. and J. L. Cohon. 2017. "Multi-Attribute Utility Theory and Multi-Criteria Decision Making." Pp. 155–84 in *Theory and Practice in Policy Analysis: Including Applications in Science and Technology*, edited by M. G. Morgan. Cambridge: Cambridge University Press.

Morgan, M. G. and M. Henrion. 1990. *Uncertainty: A Guide to Dealing with Uncertainty in Quantitative Risk and Policy Analysis*. New York: Cambridge University Press.

Morgan, S. L. and C. Winship. 2014. *Counterfactuals and Causal Inference*. Cambridge: Cambridge University Press.

Morgan, S. P. 2003. "Is Low Fertility a Twenty-First-Century Demographic Crisis?" *Demography* 40(4): 589–603.

Morris, A. 2015. *The Scholar Denied*. Berkeley: University of California Press.

Mortimer-Sandilands, C. and B. Erickson, eds. 2010. *Queer Ecologies: Sex, Nature, Politics, Desire*. Bloomington: Indiana University Press.

Moscati, I. 2016. "Retrospectives: How Economists Came to Accept Expected Utility Theory: The Case of Samuelson and Savage." *Journal of Economic Perspectives* 30 (2): 219–36.

Moss, R. H. 2004. "Improving Information for Managing an Uncertain Future Climate." *Global Environmental Change* 17(1): 4–7.

Moss, R. H. and S. H. Schneider. 2000. "Uncertainties in the IPCC TAR: Recommendations to Lead Authors for More Consistent Assessment and Reporting." Pp. 33–51 in *Guidance Papers on the Cross-Cutting Issues of the Third Assessment Report of the IPCC*, edited by R. Pachauri, T. Taniguchi and K. Tanaka. Geneva: World Meteorological Organization.

Mostafa, M. M. 2013. "Wealth, Post-materialism and Consumers' Pro-environmental Intentions: A Multilevel Analysis across 25 Nations." *Sustainable Development* 21(6): 385–99.

Mott, M. 1984. *The Seven Mountains of Thomas Merton*. New York: Houghton Mifflin.

Moynihan, D. P. 1969. *Maximum Feasible Misunderstanding: Community Action in the War on Poverty*. New York: Macmillan-Free Press.

Mullen, E. 2016. "The Reciprocal Relationship between Affect and Perceptions of Fairness." Pp. 31–54 in *Distributive and Procedural Justice*, edited by K. Törnblom and R. Vermunt. Abingdon: Routledge.

Mullins, N. C. 1973. *Theories and Theory Groups in Contemporary American Sociology*. New York: Harper & Row.

Mullins, N. C. 1983. "Theories and Theory Groups Revisited." *Sociological Theory* 1: 319–37. https://doi.org/10.2307/202056.

Mullon, C., P. Fréon and P. Cury. 2005. "The Dynamics of Collapse in World Fisheries." *Fish and Fisheries* 6(2): 111–20.

Munro, G. D. and P. H. Ditto. 1997. "Biased Assimilation, Attitude Polarization, and Affect in Reactions to Stereotype-Relevant Scientific Information." *Personality and Social Psychology Bulletin* 23(6): 636–53.

Munro, G. D., P. H. Ditto, L. K. Lockhart et al. 2002. "Biased Assimilation of Sociopolitical Arguments: Evaluating the 1996 U.S. Presidential Debate." *Basic and Applied Social Psychology* 24(1): 15–26.

Murphy, M. 2017. *The Economization of Life*. Durham, NC: Duke University Press.

Murphy, R. 2012. "Sustainability: A Wicked Problem." *Sociologia* (2). https://doi.org/10.2383/38274.

Murray, D. L. 1982. "The Abolition of El Cortito, the Short-Handled Hoe: A Case Study in Social Conflict and State Policy in California Agriculture." *Social Problems* 30 (1): 26–39.

Muthukrishna, M. and J. Henrich. 2019. "A Problem in Theory." *Nature Human Behaviour* 3(3): 221–29.

Myerson, R. B. 2013. *Game Theory*. Cambridge, MA: Harvard University Press.

Naím, M. 2022. *The Revenge of Power: How Autocrats Are Reinventing Politics for the 21st Century*. New York: St. Martin's Press.

Nash, G. B. 2006. "Franklin and Slavery." *Proceedings of the American Philosophical Society* 150(4): 618–35.

Nash, J. F. 1950. "Equilibrium Points in n-Person Games." *Proceedings of the National Academy of Sciences* 36(1): 48–49.

Nassar, S. 1999. *A Beautiful Mind: A Biography of John Forbes Nash, Jr*. New York: Touchstone Books.

National Academies of Sciences, Engineering, and Medicine. 2016. *Communicating Science Effectively: A Research Agenda*. Washington, DC: National Academies Press.

National Academies of Sciences, Engineering, and Medicine. 2017a. *Accomplishments of the US Global Change Research Program*. Washington, DC: National Academies Press.

National Academies of Sciences, Engineering, and Medicine. 2017b. *Valuing Climate Damages: Updating Estimation of the Social Cost of Carbon Dioxide*. Washington, DC: National Academies Press.

National Academies of Sciences, Engineering, and Medicine. 2018. *Veterans and Agent Orange: Update 11*. Washington, DC: The National Academies Press.

National Academies of Sciences, Engineering, and Medicine. 2021. *Reflecting Sunlight: Recommendations for Solar Geoengineering Research and Research Governance*. Washington, DC: National Academies Press.

Neal, Z. P. 2020. "A Sign of the Times? Weak and Strong Polarization in the US Congress, 1973–2016." *Social Networks* 60: 103–12. https://doi.org/10.1016/j.socnet.2018.07.007.

Neal, Z. P., R. Domagalski and X. Yan. 2022. "Homophily in Collaborations among US House Representatives, 1981–2018." *Social Networks* 68: 97–106. https://doi.org/10.1016/j.socnet.2021.04.007.

Neblo, M. A., K. M. Esterling and D. M. Lazer. 2018. *Politics with the People: Building a Directly Representative Democracy*. Cambridge: Cambridge University Press.

Nelson, M. K. and D. Shilling. 2018. *Traditional Ecological Knowledge: Learning from Indigenous Practices for Environmental Sustainability*. Cambridge: Cambridge University Press.

Netz, R. 2004. *Barbed Wire: An Ecology of Modernity*. Middletown, CT: Wesleyan University Press.

Neumann, J. E., J. Willwerth, J. Martinich et al. 2020. "Climate Damage Functions for Estimating the Economic Impacts of Climate Change in the United States." *Review of Environmental Economics and Policy* 14(1): 25–43.

Neumayer, E. 2010. *Weak versus Strong Sustainability: Exploring the Limits of Two Opposing Paradigms*. Cheltenham: Edward Elgar.

Neuvonen, A. and P. Ache. 2017. "Metropolitan Vision Making: Using Backcasting As a Strategic Learning Process to Shape Metropolitan Futures." *Futures* 86: 73–83. https://doi.org/10.1016/j.futures.2016.10.003.

Nevena, K. and D. S. Giulia. 2015. "Intra-Household Sharing of Financial Resources: A Non-technical Review of the Research Field and Its Historical Development." European University Institute, Working Paper. https://mpra.ub.uni-muenchen.de/68420/.

New Economics Foundation. 2009. *The Happy Planet Index*. London: New Economics Foundation.

New, J., L. Cosmides and J. Tooby. 2007. "Category-Specific Attention for Animals Reflects Ancestral Priorities, Not Expertise." *Proceedings of the National Academy of Sciences* 104(42): 16598–603.

Nguyen, D. 2015. "Don't Forget: The Plural of Anecdote Is Data," blog, September 10. http://blog.danwin.com/don-t-forget-the-plural-of-anecdote-is-data/#: ~: text=You%2 0may%20have%20heard%20the%20phrase%20the%20plural,sense%3A%20Data%20does%20not%20have%20a%20virgin%20birth.

Nielsen, K. S. 2017. "From Prediction to Process: A Self-Regulation Account of Environmental Behavior Change." *Journal of Environmental Psychology* 51: 189–98. https://doi.org/10.1016/j.jenvp.2017.04.002.

Nielsen, K. S., S. Clayton, P. C. Stern et al. 2020. "How Psychology Can Help Limit Climate Change." *American Psychologist*. https://doi.org/10.1037/amp0000624.

Nielsen, K. S., V. Cologna, F. Lange, C. Brick and P. Stern. 2021. "The Case for Impact-Focused Environmental Psychology." *Journal of Environmental Psychology* 74. https://doi.org/10.1016/j.jenvp.2021.101559.

Nielsen, K. S. and W. Hofmann. 2021. "Motivating Sustainability through Morality: A Daily Diary Study on the Link between Moral Self-Control and Clothing Consumption." *Journal of Environmental Psychology* 73: 101551. https://doi.org/10.1016/j.jenvp.2021.101551.

Nielsen, K. S., T. M. Marteau, J. M. Bauer et al. 2021. "Biodiversity Conservation As a Promising Frontier for Behavioural Science." *Nature Human Behaviour* 5(5): 550–56.

Nielsen, K. S., K. A. Nicholas, F. Creutzig, T. Dietz and P. C. Stern. 2021. "The Role of High Socioeconomic-Status People in Locking In or Rapidly Reducing Energy-Driven Greenhouse Gas Emissions." *Nature Energy* 6(11): 1011–16. https://doi.org/10.1038/s41560-021-00900-y.

Nieto del Rio, G. M., N. Bogel-Burroughs and I. Penn. 2021. "His Lights Stayed on During Texas' Storm: Now He Owes $16,752." *New York Times*, February 20 (updated March 1).

Nietzesche, F. [1883–91] 1961. *Thus Spoke Zarathustra*, translated by R. J. Hollingdale. Harmondsworth: Penguin Books.

Nietzesche, F. [1887] 2001. *The Gay Science*, translated by J. Nauckhoff. Cambridge: Cambridge University Press.

Nisbet, M. C., D. Brossard and A. Kroepsch. 2003. "Framing Science: The Stem Cell Controversy in an Age of Press/Politics." *Harvard International Journal of Press/Politics* 8(2): 36–70.

Nolan, J. M., P. W. Schultz, R. B. Cialdini, N. J. Goldstein and V. Griskevicius. 2008. "Normative Social Influence Is Underdetected." *Personality and Social Psychology Bulletin* 34(7): 913–23.

Noll, D., C. Dawes and V. Rai. 2014. "Solar Community Organizations and Active Peer Effects in the Adoption of Residential PV." *Energy Policy* 67: 330–43. https://doi.org/10.1016/j.enpol.2013.12.050.

Nordhaus, W. 2008. *A Question of Balance: Weighing the Options on Global Warming Policies*. New Haven, CT: Yale University Press.

Nordhaus, W. D., R. N. Stavins and M. L. Weitzman. 1992. "Lethal Model 2: The Limits to Growth Revisited." *Brookings Papers on Economic Activity* 1992(2): 1–59. https://doi.org/10.2307/2534581.

Norgaard, K. M. 2011. *Living in Denial: Climate Change, Emotions, and Everyday Life*. Cambridge, MA: MIT Press.

Norgaard, K. M. 2019a. *Salmon and Acorns Feed Our People: Colonialism, Nature and Social Action*. New Brunswick, NJ: Rutgers University Press.

Norgaard, K. M. 2019b. "Making Sense of the Spectrum of Climate Denial." *Critical Policy Studies* 13(4): 437–41.

Norgaard, K. M. and R. Reed. 2017. "Emotional Impacts of Environmental Decline: What Can Native Cosmologies Teach Sociology about Emotions and Environmental Justice?" *Theory and Society* 46(6): 463–95.

Norman, W. and C. MacDonald. 2004. "Getting to the Bottom of 'Triple Bottom Line'." *Business Ethics Quarterly* 14(2): 243–62.

Norse, E. A., S. Brooke, W. W. Cheung et al. 2012. "Sustainability of Deep-Sea Fisheries." *Marine Policy* 36(2): 307–20.

Nugent, D. and B. K. Sovacool. 2014. "Assessing the Lifecycle Greenhouse Gas Emissions from Solar PV and Wind Energy: A Critical Meta-Survey." *Energy Policy* 65: 229–44. https://doi.org/10.1016/j.enpol.2013.10.048.

Nussbaum, M. C. 2000. *Women and Human Development: The Capabilities Approach.* Cambridge: Cambridge University Press.

Nussbaum, M. C. 2006. *Frontiers of Justice: Disability, Nationality, Species Membership.* Cambridge, MA: Belknap Press of Harvard University Press.

Nussbaum, M. C. 2018. "Working With and For Animals: Getting the Theoretical Framework Right." *Journal of Human Development and Capabilities* 19(1): 2–18.

Nussbaum, M. C. and A. Sen. 1993. *The Quality of Life.* New York: Oxford University Press.

Nyamnjoh, F. B. 2018. *The Rational Consumer: Bad for Business and Politics: Democracy at the Crossroads of Nature and Culture.* Bamenda: Langaa Research & Publishing Common Initiative Group.

Nyborg, K. 2018. "Social Norms and the Environment." *Annual Review of Resource Economics* 10: 405–23.

Oberlack, C., D. Sietz, E. Bürgi Bonanomi et al. 2019. "Archetype Analysis in Sustainability Research: Meanings, Motivations, and Evidence-Based Policy Making." *Ecology and Society* 24(2). https://doi.org/10.5751/ES-10747-240226.

O'Brien, M. 2000. *Making Better Environmental Decisions: An Alternative to Risk Assessment.* Cambridge, MA: MIT Press.

O'Brien, R. C. 1971. *Mrs. Frisby and the Rats of NIMH.* New York: Atheneum.

Ochsner, C. 2009. "A New Park to Save the Plains." *Kansas City Star*, November 14.

O'Connor, T. 2013. *Animals As Neighbors: The Past and Present of Commensal Animals.* East Lansing: Michigan State University Press.

O'Connor, T. 2017. "Commensual Species." Pp. 525–41 in *The Oxford Handbook of Animal Studies*, edited by L. Kalof. Oxford: Oxford University Press.

Odum, E. P. 1969. "The Strategy of Ecosystem Development." *Science* 164(3877): 262–70.

Odum, H. T. 1996. *Environmental Accounting: EMERGY and Environmental Decison Making.* New York: John Wiley & Sons.

O'Grady, C. 2020. "Power to the People." *Science* 270(6516): 518–21.

Ohler, N. and S. Whiteside. 2016. *Blitzed: Drugs in Nazi Germany.* Boston: Houghton Mifflin Harcourt.

Oliver, C. 2005. "The Treadmill of Production Under NAFTA." *Organization and Environment* 18(1): 55–71.

Olivier, J. G. J. and J. A. H. W. Peters. 2018. *Trends in Global CO2 and Total Greenhouse Gas Emissions: 2018 Report.* The Hague: PBL Netherlands Environmental Assessment Agency.

Olsson, L., L. Hjalmarsson, M. Wikström and M. Larsson. 2015. "Bridging the Implementation Gap: Combining Backcasting and Policy Analysis to Study Renewable Energy in Urban Road Transport." *Transport Policy* 37: 72–82. https://doi.org/10.1016/j.tranpol.2014.10.014.

Ong, A. 2006. *Neoliberalism As Exception: Mutations in Citizenship and Sovereignty.* Durham, NC: Duke University Press.

O'Neill, C. S. and M. Boykoff. 2012. "The Role of New Media in Engaging the Public with Climate Change." Pp. 259–77 in *Engaging the public with Climate Change*, edited by L. Whitmarsh, S. O'Neill and I. Lorenzi. Abingdon: Routledge.

O'Neill, D. W., A. L. Fanning, W. F. Lamb and J. K. Steinberger. 2018. "A Good Life for All within Planetary Boundaries." *Nature Sustainability* 1(2): 88–95.

O'Neill, S., H. T. Williams, T. Kurz, B. Wiersma and M. Boykoff. 2015. "Dominant Frames in Legacy and Social Media Coverage of the

IPCC Fifth Assessment Report." *Nature Climate Change* 5(4): 380–85.

Orazani, S. N. and B. Leidner. 2019. "The Power of Nonviolence: Confirming and Explaining the Success of Nonviolent (Rather Than Violent) Political Movements." *European Journal of Social Psychology* 49(4): 688–704.

Oreg, S. and T. Katz-Gerro. 2006. "Predicting Proenvironmental Behavior Cross-Nationally: Values, the Theory of Planned Behavior, and Value-Belief-Norm Theory." *Environment and Behavior* 38(4): 462–83.

Oreskes, N. and E. M. Conway. 2010. *Merchants of Doubt: How a Handful of Scientists Obscured the Truth on Issues from Tobacco Smoke to Global Warming.* New York: Bloomsbury.

Organisation for Economic Co-operation and Development. 2013. *OECD Guidelines on Measuring Subjective Well-Being.* Paris: Organisation for Economic Co-operation and Development.

Orwell, G. [1949] 1977. *Nineteen Eighty-Four* New York: Signet Classics.

Orzack, S. H. and E. Sober. 1993. "A Critical Assessment of Levins: The Strategy of Model Building (1966)." *Quarterly Review of Biology* 68(4): 534–46.

Ostrom, E. 2000. "Collective Actions and the Evolution of Norms." *Journal of Economic Perspectives* 14(3): 137–58.

Ostrom, E. 2005. *Understanding Institutional Diversity.* Princeton, NJ: Princeton University Press.

Ostrom, E. 2007. "A Diagnostic Approach for Going Beyond Panaceas." *Proceedings of the National Academy of Sciences, USA* 104(39): 15181–87.

Ostrom, E. 2009a. "A General Framework for Analyzing Sustainability of Social-Ecological Systems." *Science* 325 (5939): 419–22.

Ostrom, E. 2009b. "Beyond Markets and States: Polycentric Governance of Complex Economic Systems." Paper presented at the Nobel Lecture, December 8, Stockholm, Sweden. http://nobelprize.org/nobel_prizes/economics/laureates/2009/ostrom_lecture.pdf.

Ostrom, E. 2010a. "A Long Polycentric Journey." *Annual Review of Political Science* 13: 1–23.

Ostrom, E. 2010b. "Polycentric Systems for Coping with Collective Action and Global Environmental Change." *Global Environmental Change* 20(4): 550–57.

Ostrom, E. 2010c. "A Multi-Scale Approach to Coping with Climate Change and Other Collective Action Problems." *Solutions* 1(2): 27–36.

Ostrom, E., T. Dietz, N. Dolšak, P.C. Stern, S. Stonich and E. Weber, eds. 2002. *The Drama of the Commons.* Washington, DC: National Academy Press.

Otto, I. M., K. M. Kim, N. Dubrovsky and W. Lucht. 2019. "Shift the Focus from the Super-Poor to the Super-Rich." *Nature Climate Change* 9(2): 82–84.

Owens, M. and J. Wolch. 2017. "Lively Cities." Pp. 542–70 in *The Oxford Handbook of Animal Studies*, edited by L. Kalof. Oxford: Oxford University Press.

Özcan, B. and I. Öztürk. 2019. *Environmental Kuznets Curve (EKC): A Manual.* Cambridge, MA: Academic Press.

Pacala, S. and R. Socolow. 2004. "Stablization Wedges: Solving the Climate Problem for the Next 50 Years with Current Technologies." *Science* 305(5685): 968–72.

Paige, J. M. 1978. *Agrarian Revolution.* New York: Simon & Schuster.

Paine, R. T. 1966. "Food Web Complexity and Species Diversity." *American Naturalist* 100 (910): 65–75.

Painter, M. and T. Qiu. 2020. "Political Beliefs Affect Compliance with Covid-19 Social Distancing Orders." *Covid Economics* 4: 103–23. https://cepr.org/publications/covid-economics-issue-4.

Pampel, F. C. and L. M. Hunter. 2012. "Cohort Change, Diffusion, and Support for Environmental Spending in the United States." *American Journal of Sociology* 118 (2): 420–48.

Parkes, D. C. and M. P. Wellman. 2015. "Economic Reasoning and Artificial Intelligence." *Science* 349(6245): 267–72.

Parson, E. A. 2003. *Protecting the Ozone Layer: Science and Strategy*. New York: Oxford University Press.

Parson, E. A. 2021. "Geoengineering: Symmetric Precaution." *Science* 374(6569): 795.

Parsons, T. 1966. *Societies: Evolutionary and Comparative Perspectives*. Englewood Cliffs, NJ: Prentice Hall.

Pascual, U., J. Phelps, E. Garmendia et al. 2014. "Social Equity Matters in Payments for Ecosystem Services." *BioScience* 64(11): 1027–36.

Patterson, J. (Dir.) 2000. *Bust-Out*. HBO.

Pauli, B. J. 2020. "The Flint Water Crisis." *Wiley Interdisciplinary Reviews: Water* 7(3): e1420.

Pauling, L. 1958. *No More War!* New York: Dodd, Mead.

Paumgarten, N. 2010. "Food Fighter: Does Whole Foods C.E.O. Know What's Best for You?" *The New Yorker*, January 4.

Pava, M. A. 2007. "A Response to 'Getting to the Bottom of "Triple Bottom Line"'." *Business Ethics Quarterly* 17(1): 105–10.

Payne, C. R., R. Shwom and S. Heaton. 2015. "Public Participation and Norm Formation for Risky Technology: Adaptive Governance of Solar-Radiation Management." *Climate Law* 5(2–4): 210–51.

Pearce, W., S. Niederer, S. M. Özkula and N. Sánchez Querubín. 2019. "The Social Media Life of Climate Change: Platforms, Publics, and Future Imaginaries." *Wiley Interdisciplinary Reviews: Climate Change* 10 (2): e569.

Pearl, J. and D. Mackenzie. 2018. *The Book of Why: The New Science of Cause and Effect*. New York: Basic Books.

Pedersen, M. J. and N. Favero. 2020. "Social Distancing during the COVID-19 Pandemic: Who Are the Present and Future Non-compliers?" *Public Administration Review* 8 (5): 805–14.

Peet, R. 1996. *The Unholy Trinity: The World Bank, International Monetary Fund, and World Trade Organization*. London: Zed Books.

Peirce, C. S. 1878. "How to Make Our Ideas Clear." *Popular Science Monthly* 12: 286–302.

Pel, B., A. Haxeltine, F. Avelino et al. 2020. "Towards a Theory of Transformative Social Innovation: A Relational Framework and 12 Propositions." *Research Policy* 49(8): 104080.

Pellizzoni, L. 2012. "Reassessing Sustainability." *Sociologica* 2. https://doi.org/10.2383/38266.

Pellow, D. N. 2002. *Garbage Wars: The Struggle for Environmental Justice in Chicago*. Cambridge, MA: MIT Press.

Pellow, D. N. 2007. *Resisting Global Toxics: Transnational Movements for Environmental Justice*. Cambridge, MA: MIT Press.

Pellow, D. N. 2016. "Toward a Critical Environmental Justice Studies: Black Lives Matter As an Environmental Justice Challenge." *Du Bois Review: Social Science Research on Race* 13(2): 221–36.

Pellow, D. N. 2017. *What Is Critical Environmental Justice?* New York: John Wiley & Sons.

Peluso, N. L. 1992. *Rich Forests, Poor People: Resource Control and Resistance*. Berkeley: University of California Press.

Peluso, N. L. and P. Vandergeest. 2001. "Genealogies of the Political Forest and Customary Rights in Indonesia, Malaysia, and Thailand." *The Journal of Asian Studies* 60(3): 761–812.

Perkins, J. 2005. *Confessions of an Economic Hit Man*. New York: Penguin.

Perry, A. M. 2020. *Know Your Price: Valuing Black lives and Property in America's Black Cities*. Washington, DC: Brookings Institution Press.

Perry, A. M. and D. Harshbarger. 2019. America's Formerly Redlined *Neighborhoods Have Changed, and So Must*

*Solutions to Rectify Them.* Brookings Institution, Washington, DC, October 14.

Perry, A. M., D. Harshbarger and C. Romer. 2020. "Mapping Racial Inequity Amid COVID-19 Underscores Policy Discriminations against Black Americans." *The Avenue* (Brookings Institution, Washington, DC), April 16.

Peter, H. and S. Derek. 2015. *Expert Consensus on the Economics of Climate Change.* New York: Institute for Policy Integrity at New York University School of Law.

Petersen, M. B. 2015. "Evolutionary Political Psychology: On the Origin and Structure of Heuristics and Biases in Politics." *Political Psychology* 36: 45–78. https://doi.org/10 .1111/pops.12237.

Peterson, G. D., Z. V. Harmáčková, M. Meacham et al. 2018. "Welcoming Different Perspectives in IPBES." *Ecology and Society* 23(1). www.jstor.org/stable/ 26799030.

Peterson, J. C., D. D. Bourgin, M. Agrawal, D. Reichman and T. L. Griffiths. 2021. "Using Large-Scale Experiments and Machine Learning to Discover Theories of Human Decision-Making." *Science* 372 (6547): 1209–14.

Pezzey, J. C. V. and M. Toman. 2002. "The Economics of Sustainability: A Review of Journal Articles." Discussion Paper No. 02-03. Resources for the Future, Washington, DC.

Pfeiffer, J. and R. Chapman. 2010. "Anthropological Perspectives on Structural Adjustment and Public Health." *Annual Review of Anthropology* 39: 149–65.

Pidgeon, N., K. Parkhill, A. Corner and N. Vaughan. 2013. "Deliberating Stratospheric Aerosols for Climate Geoengineering and the SPICE Project." *Nature Climate Change* 3(5): 451–57.

Pierce, J. C. 1997. "The Hidden Layer of Political Culture: A Comment on 'Postmaterialist Values and the Environment: A Critique and Reappraisal'." *Social Science Quarterly* 78(1): 30–35.

Pigou, A. C. 1920. *The Economics of Welfare.* London: Macmillan.

Piketty, T. 2020. *Capital and Ideology.* Cambridge, MA: Harvard University Press.

Piketty, T. 2022. *A Brief History of Equality.* Cambridge, MA: Harvard University Press.

Pileggi, N. 1985. *Wiseguy: Life in a Mafia Family.* New York: Simon & Schuster.

Pilisuk, M. and T. Hayden. 1965. "Is There a Military Industrial Complex Which Prevents Peace? Consensus and Countervailing Power in Pluralistic Systems." *Journal of Social Issues* 21(3): 61–117.

Pimm, S., C. Jenkins, R. Abell et al. 2014. "The Biodiversity of Species and Their Rates of Extinction, Distribution, and Protection." *Science* 344(6187): 1246752.

Pinkney, R. 2003. *Democracy in the Third World.* Boulder, CO: Lynne Rienner Publishers.

Pinsky, M. L., O. P. Jensen, D. Ricard and S. R. Palumbi. 2011. "Unexpected Patterns of Fisheries Collapse in the World's Oceans." *Proceedings of the National Academy of Sciences* 108(20): 8317–22.

Planck, M. 1949. *Scientific Autobiography and Other Papers*, translated by F. Gaynor. New York: F. Gaynor.

Plumer, B. 2018. "Trump Put a Low Cost on Carbon Emissions. Here's Why It Matters." *New York Times*, August 23.

Plumer, B. and N. Popovich. 2020. "How Decades of Racist Housing Policy Left Neighborhoods Sweltering." *New York Times*, August 24.

Pompeani, D. P., B. A. Steinman, M. B. Abbott et al. 2021. "On the Timing of the Old Copper Complex in North America: A Comparison of Radiocarbon Dates from Different Archaeological Contexts." *Radiocarbon* 63(2): 513–31.

Poorter, L., D. Craven, C. C. Jakovac et al. 2021. "Multidimensional Tropical Forest Recovery." *Science* 374(6573): 1370–76.

Poortinga, W., L. Whitmarsh, L. Steg, G. Böhm and S. Fisher. 2019. "Climate Change Perceptions and Their Individual-Level Determinants: A Cross-European Analysis." *Global*

*Environmental Change* 55: 25–35. https://doi.org/10.1016/j.gloenvcha.2019.01.007.

Popper, D. E. and F. J. Popper. 1987. "The Great Plains: From Dust to Dust. A Daring Proposal for Dealing with an Inevitable Disaster." *Planning* (December): 12–18. www.planning.org/planning/2018/oct/the greatplains/.

Popper, K. R. 1974. "Scientific Reduction and the Essential Incompleteness of All Science." Pp. 259–84 in *Studies in the Philosophy of Biology*, edited by F. J. Ayala and T. Dobzhansky. London: Macmillan.

Popper, K. R. 1987. "Campbell on the Evolutionary Theory of Knowledge." Pp. 115–20 in *Evolutionary Epistemology, Rationality and the Sociology of Knowledge*, edited by G. Radnitzky and W. W. I. Bartley. La Salle, IL: Open Court.

Porter, E. 1968. *The Place No One Knew: Glen Canyon on the Colorado*. New York: Ballantine.

Portney, K. E. 2015. *Sustainability*. Cambridge: MIT Press.

Pottete, A. R., M. A. Janssen and E. Ostrom. 2010. *Working Together: Collective Action, the Commons, and Multiple Methods in Practice* Princeton, NJ: Princeton University Press.

Pradhan, P., L. Costa, D. Rybski, W. Lucht and J. P. Kropp. 2017. "A Systematic Study of Sustainable Development Goal (SDG) Interactions." *Earth's Future* 5(11): 1169–79.

Prest, A. R. and R. Turvey. 1965. "Cost-Benefit Analysis: A Survey." *The Economic Journal* 75(300): 683–735.

Prior, M. 2013. "Media and Political Polarization." *Annual Review of Political Science* 16: 101–27.

Purdy, J. 2015. "Environmentalism's Racist History." *The New Yorker*, August 13.

Purdy, J. 2017. "The Long Environmental Justice Movement." *Ecology Law Quarterly* 44(4): 809–64.

Pursell, C. 1993. "The Rise and Fall of the Appropriate Technology Movement in the United States, 1965–1985." *Technology and Culture* 34(3): 629–37.

Putnam, R. D. and S. R. Garrett. 2020. *How America Came Together a Century Ago and How We Can Do It Again*. New York: Simon & Schuster.

Radnitzky, G. and W. W. I. Bartley, eds. 1987. *Evolutionary Epistemology, Rationality, and the Sociology of Knowledge*. La Salle, IL: Open Court.

Raffaelle, R., W. Robison and E. Selinger, eds. 2010. *Sustainability Ethics: 5 Questions*. Copenhagen: Automatic Press.

Rai, V. and S. A. Robinson. 2013. "Effective Information Channels for Reducing Costs of Environmentally-Friendly Technologies: Evidence from Residential PV Markets." *Environmental Research Letters* 8(1): 014044.

Rai, V. and A. D. Henry. 2016. "Agent-Based Modelling of Consumer Energy Choices." *Nature Climate Change* 6(6): 556–62.

Raimi, K. T., A. Maki, D. Dana and M. P. Vandenbergh. 2019. "Framing of Geoengineering Affects Support for Climate Change Mitigation." *Environmental Communication* 13(3): 300–19.

Ramsden, E. and J. Adams. 2009. "Escaping the Laboratory: The Rodent Experiments of John B. Calhoun and Their Cultural Influence." *Journal of Social History* 42(3): 761–92.

Randers, J., J. Rockström, P.-E. Stoknes et al. 2019. "Achieving the 17 Sustainable Development Goals within 9 Planetary Boundaries." *Global Sustainability* 2: e24. https://doi.org/10.1017/sus.2019.22.

Ratcliffe, D. 2013. "The Right to Vote and the Rise of Democracy, 1787–1828." *Journal of the Early Republic* 33(2): 219–54.

Räthzel, N. and D. Uzzell. 2011. "Trade Unions and Climate Change: The Jobs versus Environment Dilemma." *Global Environmental Change* 21(4): 1215–23.

Ravetz, J. and S. Functowicz. 1998. "Commentary." *Journal of Risk Research* 1 (1): 45–48.

Ravitch, D. 2016. *The Death and Life of the Great American School System: How Testing and Choice Are Undermining Education*. New York: Basic Books.

Rawls, J. 1971. *A Theory of Justice*. Cambridge, MA: Belknap Press of Harvard University Press.

Rawls, J. 1993. *Political Liberalism*. New York: Columbia University Press.

Rawls, J. 2001. *Justice As Fairness: A Restatement*. Cambridge, MA: Harvard University Press.

Raworth, K. 2017. *Doughnut Economics: Seven Ways to Think Like a 21st-Century Economist*. White River Junction, VT: Chelsea Green Publishing.

Ray, S. J. and J. Sibara, eds. 2019. *Disability Studies and the Environmental Humanities: Toward an Eco-Crip Theory*. Lincoln: University of Nebraska Press.

Raymond, C. M., J. O. Kenter, T. Plieninger, N. J. Turner and K. A. Alexander. 2014. "Comparing Instrumental and Deliberative Paradigms Underpinning the Assessment of Social Values for Cultural Ecosystem Services." *Ecological Economics* 107: 145–56. https://doi.org/10.1016/j.ecolecon.2014.07.033.

Razac, O. 2002. *Barbed Wire: A Political History*. New York: New Press.

Redclift, M. 1996. *Wasted: Counting the Costs of Consumption*. London: Earthscan Publications.

Reed, B. C. 2014. *The History and Science of the Manhattan Project*. Cham: Springer.

Reed, B. C. 2019. *Manhattan Project: The Story of the Century*. Cham: Springer.

Reed, M., P. O'Reilly and J. Hall. 2019. "The Economics and Politics of Carbon Taxes and Regulations: Evidence from Voting on Washington State's Initiative 732." *Sustainability* 11(13): 3667. https://doi.org/10.3390/su11133667.

Regan, T. 2004. *The Case for Animal Rights*. Berkeley: University of California Press.

Regens, J. L., T. M. Dietz and R. W. Rycroft. 1983. "Risk Assessment in the Policy-Making Process: Environmental Health and Safety Protection." *Public Administration Review* 43(2): 137–45.

Reid, W. V., H. A. Mooney, A. Cropper et al. 2005. *Ecosystems and Human Well-Being: Synthesis*. Washington, DC: Island Press.

Reiser, D. B. 2011. "Benefit Corporations: A Sustainable Form of Organization." *Wake Forest Law Review*. 46: 591.

Ren, X. 2011. *Building Globalization: Transnational Architecture Production in Urban China*. Chicago, IL: University of Chicago Press.

Ren, X. 2018. "From Chicago to China and India: Studying the City in the Twenty-First Century." *Annual Review of Sociology* 44: 497–513.

Ren, X. 2020. *Governing the Urban in China and India: Land Grabs, Slum Clearance, and the War on Air Pollution*: Princeton, NJ: Princeton University Press.

Renn, O. 2008. *Risk Governance: Coping with Uncertainty in a Complex World*. London: Earthscan.

Renn, O. 2021. "Transdisciplinarity: Synthesis towards a Modular Approach." *Futures* 130: 102744. https://doi.org/10.1016/j.futures.2021.102744.

Renn, O. and A. Klinke. 2011. "Complexity, Uncertainty and Ambiguity in Inclusive Risk Governance." Pp. 53–70 in *Risk and Social Theory in Environmental Management*, edited by S. Lockie and T. Measham. Collingwood, Victoria, Australia: CSIRO Publishing.

Renn, O. and P.-J. Schweitzer. 2009. "Inclusive Risk Governance: Concepts and Application to Environmental Policy Making." *Environmental Policy and Governance* 19(3): 174–85.

Renn, O. and P.-J. Schweizer. 2020. "Inclusive Governance for Energy Policy Making: Conceptual Foundations, Applications, and Lessons Learned." Pp. 39–79 in *The Role of Public Participation in Energy Transitions*, edited by O. Renn, F. Ulmer and A. Deckert. Amsterdam: Elsevier.

Renn, O., T. Webler, H. Rakel, B. Johnson and P. Dienel. 1993. "A Three-Step Procedure for Public Participation in Decision Making."

*Policy Sciences* 26: 189–214. https://doi.org/10.1007/BF00999716.

Renn, O., T. Webler and P. Wiedemann, eds. 1995. *Fairness and Competence in Citizen Participation: Evaluating Models for Environmental Discourse*. Dordrecht: Kluwer Academic Publishers.

Renton, D. 1999. *Fascism: Theory and Practice*. London: Pluto Press.

Reo, N. J., K. P. Whyte, D. McGregor, M. Smith and J. F. Jenkins. 2017. "Factors That Support Indigenous Involvement in Multi-actor Environmental Stewardship." *AlterNative: An International Journal of Indigenous Peoples* 13(2): 58–68.

Restivo, M., J. M. Shandra and J. M. Sommer. 2020. "Exporting Forest Loss? A Cross-National Analysis of the United States Export–Import Bank Financing in Low-and Middle-Income Nations." *The Journal of Environment and Development* 29(2): 245–69.

Richerson, P. J. 1977. "Ecology and Human Ecology: A Comparison of Theories in the Biological and Social Sciences." *American Ethnologist* 4(1): 1–26.

Richerson, P. J. and R. Boyd. 2001. "The Biology of Subjective Commitment to Groups: A Tribal Social Instincts Hypothesis." Pp. 186–220 in *Evolution and the Capacity for Commitment*, edited by R. M. Neese. New York: Russell Sage Foundation.

Richerson, P. J. and R. Boyd. 2005. *Not by Genes Alone: How Culture Transformed Human Evolution*. Chicago, IL: University of Chicago Press.

Richerson, P. J., R. Boyd and B. Paciotti. 2001. "An Evolutionary Theory of Commons Management." Pp. 403–42 in *The Drama of the Commons*, edited by E. Ostrom, T. Dietz, N. Dolsak, P. C. Stern, S. Stonich and E. Weber. Washington, DC: National Academy Press.

Richerson, P. J., S. Gavrilets and F. B. de Waal. 2021. "Modern Theories of Human Evolution Foreshadowed by Darwin's Descent of Man." *Science* 372(6544): eaba3776. https://doi.org/10.1126/science.aba3776.

Rietbergen-McCracken, J. and H. Abaza. 2013. *Environmental Valuation: A Worldwide Compendium of Case Studies*. New York: Routledge.

Ripley, A. 2021. *High Conflict: Why We Get Trapped and How We Get Out*. New York: Simon & Schuster.

Rittel, H. W. and M. M. Webber. 1973. "Dilemmas in a General Theory of Planning." *Policy Sciences* 4(2): 155–69.

Rivers, L. I. and J. Arvai. 2007. "Win Some, Lose Some: The Effect of Chronic Losses on Decision Making Under Risk." *Journal of Risk Research* 10(8): 1085–99.

Robbins, P. and S. A. Moore. 2019. "Return of the Repressed: Native Presence and American Memory in John Muir's Boyhood and Youth." *Annals of the American Association of Geographers* 109(6): 1748–57.

Roberts, J. T. and B. C. Parks. 2006. *A Climate of Injustice: Global Inequality, North–South Politics, and Climate Policy*. Cambridge, MA: MIT Press.

Roberts, J. T., J. K. Steinberger, T. Dietz et al. 2020. "Four Agendas for Research and Policy on Emissions and Well-Being." *Global Sustainability* 3(e3): 1–7. https://doi.org/10.1017/sus.2019.25.

Roberts, P., C. Hunt, M. Arroyo-Kalin, D. Evans and N. Boivin. 2017. "The Deep Human Prehistory of Global Tropical Forests and Its Relevance for Modern Conservation." *Nature Plants* 3(8): 17093.

Robertson, A. W., A. Kumar, M. Peña and F. Vitart. 2015. "Improving and Promoting Subseasonal to Seasonal Prediction." *Bulletin of the American Meteorological Society* 96(3): ES49–ES53.

Robinson, A. 2020. "The Race to Decipher Egyptian Hieroglyphs." *Science* 369(651): 1574.

Robinson, J. B. 1982. "Energy Backcasting: A Proposed Method of Policy Analysis." *Energy Policy* 10(4): 337–44.

Robinson, J. B. 1988. "Unlearning and Backcasting: Rethinking Some of the Questions We Ask about the Future." *Technological Forecasting and Social Change*

33: 325–38. https://doi.org/10.1016/0040-162 5(88)90029-7.

Robinson, J. B. 2004. "Squaring the Circle? Some Thoughts on the Idea of Sustainable Development." *Ecological Economics* 48(4): 369–84. https://doi.org/ 10.1016/j.ecolecon.2003.10.017.

Robinson, J. B. and R. J. Cole. 2015. "Theoretical Underpinnings of Regenerative Sustainability." *Building Research and Information* 43(2): 133–43.

Robinson, K. S. 1984. *The Wild Shore.* New York: Ace.

Robinson, K. S. 1988. *The Gold Coast.* New York: St. Martin's Press.

Robinson, K. S. 1990. *Pacific Edge.* New York: Tor.

Robinson, L. A., J. K. Hammitt and R. J. Zeckhauser. 2016. "Attention to Distribution in US Regulatory Analyses." *Review of Environmental Economics and Policy* 10(2): 308–28.

Robson, R. 2015. "A New Look at Benefit Corporations: Game Theory and Game Changer." *American Business Law Journal* 52 (3): 501–57.

Roccas, S., S. H. Schwartz and A. Amit. 2010. "Personal Value Priorities and National Identification." *Political Psychology* 31(3): 393–419. https://doi.org/10.1111/j.1467-9221 .2010.00763.x.

Rockström, J., W. Steffen, K. Noone et al. 2009a. "Planetary Boundaries: Exploring the Safe Operating Space for Humanity." *Ecology and Society* 14(2). www.jstor.org/st able/26268316.

Rockström, J., W. Steffen, K. Noone et al. 2009b. "A Safe Operating Space for Humanity." *Nature* 461(282): 472–75.

Rodenberry, G. and R. Berman. 1992. "Cause and Effect." *Star Trek: The Next Generation.* Dir. J. Frakes. Paramount Studios.

Rojas, R. 2017. "Abused Dogs and Cats Now Have a (Human) Voice in Connecticut Courts." *New York Times*, August 27.

Rokeach, M. 1968. *Beliefs, Attitudes and Values: A Theory of Organization and Change.* San Francisco, CA: Jossey-Bass.

Rokeach, M. 1973. *The Nature of Human Values.* New York: The Free Press.

Rokeach, M. 1979a. *Understanding Human Values: Individual and Societal.* New York: The Free Press.

Rokeach, M. 1979b. "From Individual to Institutional Values: With Special Reference to the Values of Science." Pp. 47–70 in *Understanding Human Values* edited by M. Rokeach. New York: The Free Press.

Rolimeni, J. M., K. Mayumi and M. Giampietro, eds. 2008. *The Jevons Paradox and the Myth of Resource Efficiency Improvements.* London: Earthscan.

Rollin, B. E. 1989. *The Unheeded Cry: Animal Consciousness, Animal Pain and Science.* Oxford: Oxford University Press.

Rollin, B. E. 2017. "The Ethics of Animal Research." Pp. 345–63 in *The Oxford Handbook of Animal Studies*, edited by L. E. Kalof. Oxford: Oxford University Press.

Rome, A. 2013. *The Genius of Earth Day: How a 1970 Teach-In Unexpectedly Made the First Green Generation.* New York: Macmillan.

Roobavannan, M., T. H. Van Emmerik, Y. Elshafei et al. 2018. "Norms and Values in Sociohydrological Models." *Hydrology and Earth System Sciences* 22(2): 1337–49.

Rosa, E. A. 1998a. "Comments on Commentary by Ravetz and Funtowicz: 'Old Fashioned Hypertext'." *Journal of Risk Research* 1(2): 111–15.

Rosa, E. A. 1998b. "Metatheoretical Foundations for Post-Normal Risk." *Journal of Risk Research* 1(1): 15–44.

Rosa, E. A. 2010. "The Logical Status of Risk: To Burnish or to Dull." *Journal of Risk Research* 13(3): 239–53.

Rosa, E. A. and T. Dietz. 1998. "Climate Change and Society: Speculation, Construction and Scientific Investigation." *International Sociology* 13(4): 421–55.

Rosa, E. A. and T. Dietz. 2012. "Human Drivers of National Greenhouse Gas Emissions." *Nature Climate Change* 2(8): 581–86.

Rosa, E. A., G. E. Machlis and K. M. Keating. 1988. "Energy and Society." *Annual Review of Sociology* 14: 149–72.

Rosa, E. A. and N. Matsuda. 2005. "Risk Perceptions in the Risk Society: The Cognitive Architecture of Risk between Americans and Japanese." Pp. 113–30 in *Peace, Security, and Kyosei*, edited by Y. Murakami, N. Kawamura and S. Chiba. Pullman: Washington State University Press.

Rosa, E. A., N. Matsuda and R. R. Kleinhesselink. 2000. "The Cognitive Architecture of Risk: Pancultural Unity or Cultural Shaping?" Pp. 185–210 in *Comparative Risk Perception*, edited by O. Renn and B. Rohrmann. Dordrecht: Kluwer.

Rosa, E. A., O. Renn and A. M. McCright. 2013. *The Risk Society Revisited: Social Theory and Governance*. Philadelphia, PA: Temple University Press.

Roscoe, P. 2015. *A Richer Life: How Economics Can Change the Way We Think and Feel*. New York: Penguin.

Rose, C. 1986. "The Comedy of the Commons: Custom, Commerce, and Inherently Public Property." *The University of Chicago Law Review* 53(3): 711–81.

Rosenberg, M. M. 2016. "The Conceptual Articulation of the Reality of Life: Max Weber's Theoretical Constitution of Sociological Ideal Types." *Journal of Classical Sociology* 16(1): 84–101.

Rosi, A., P. Mena, N. Pellegrini et al. 2017. "Environmental Impact of Omnivorous, Ovo-lacto-vegetarian, and Vegan Diet." *Scientific Reports* 7(1): 6105.

Ross, S. L. and J. Yinger. 2002. *The Color of Credit: Mortgage Discrimination, Research Methodology, and Fair-Lending Enforcement*. Cambridge, MA: MIT Press.

Rostow, W. W. 1960. *The Stages of Economic Growth: A Non-Communist Manifesto*. London: Cambridge University Press.

Rotemberg, J. J. 2014. "Models of Caring, or Acting As If One Cared, about the Welfare of Others." *Annual Review of Economics* 6(1): 129–54.

Royal Swedish Academy of Sciences. 1997, "Advanced Information: Additional Background Material on the Bank of Sweden Prize in Economic Sciences in Memory of Alfred Nobel 1997", October 14. www.nobelprize.org/nobel_prizes/economic-sciences/laureates/1997/advanced.html.

Rubin, L. 1969. "Maximum Feasible Participation: The Origins, Implications, and Present Status." *The Annals of the American Academy of Political and Social Science* 385(1): 14–29.

Ruckart, P. Z., A. S. Ettinger, M. Hanna-Attisha et al. 2019. "The Flint Water Crisis: A Coordinated Public Health Emergency Response and Recovery Initiative." *Journal of Public Health Management and Practice* 25 (Suppl. 1): S84–S90. https://doi.org/10.1097/PHH.0000000000000871.

Ruckelshaus, W. W. 1985. "Risk, Science and Democracy." *Issues in Science and Technology* 1(3): 19–38.

Rudel, T. 2013. *Defensive Environmentalists and the Dynamics of Global Reform*. Cambridge: Cambridge University Press.

Rudel, T. K. 2019a. "Shocks, States, and Societal Corporatism: A Shorter Path to Sustainability?" *Journal of Environmental Studies and Sciences* 9(4): 429–36.

Rudel, T. K. 2019b. *Shocks, States, and Sustainability: The Origins of Radical Environmental Reforms*. Oxford: Oxford University Press.

Rutherford, A. 2021. "A Cautionary History of Eugenics." *Science* 373(6562): 1419.

Sabatier, P., S. Hunter and S. McLaughlin. 1987. "The Devil Shift: Perceptions and Misperceptions of Opponents." *Western Political Quarterly* 40(3): 449–76.

Sachs, J. D. and A. Warner. 1995. "Economic Reform and the Process of Global Integration." *Brookings Papers on Economic Activity* 1: 1–118. https://doi.org/10.2307/2534573.

Sadasivam, N. 2022. "Wall Street's biggest names are backing off their climate commitments." *Grist* 9 December.

Sagan, C. 1996. *The Demon-Haunted World: Science As a Candle in the Dark*. New York: Ballantine Books.

Sage, R. F. 2020. "Global Change Biology: A Primer." *Global Change Biology* 26(1): 3–30.

Salsburg, D. 2001. *The Lady Tasting Tea: How Statistics Revolutionized Science in the Twentieth Century*. New York: W. H. Freeman and Company.

Salvadori, N. and R. Signorino. 2014. "Adam Smith on Monopoly Theory: Making Good a Lacuna." *Scottish Journal of Political Economy* 61(2): 178–95.

Samuelson, P. A. 1947. *The Foundations of Economic Analysis*. Cambridge, MA: Harvard University Press.

Sanderson, M. R., J. S. Bergtold, J. L. Heier Stamm et al. 2018. "Climate Change Beliefs in an Agricultural Context: What Is the Role of Values Held by Farming and Non-farming Groups?" *Climatic Change* 150(3): 259–72.

Sanderson, M. R. and V. Hughes. 2019. "Race to the Bottom (of the Well): Groundwater in an Agricultural Production Treadmill." *Social Problems* 66(3): 392–410.

Sarkodie, S. A. and V. Strezov. 2019. "A Review on Environmental Kuznets Curve Hypothesis Using Bibliometric and Meta-Analysis." *Science of the Total Environment* 649: 128–45. https://doi.org/10.1016/j.scitotenv.2018.08.276.

Satcher, L. 2021. "(Un)Just Deserts: Examining the Consequences of Economic, Social, and Environmental Disinvestment in the Urban South." PhD thesis, Vanderbilt University. http://hdl.handle.net/1803/16650.

Satcher, L. A. 2022. "Multiply-Deserted Areas: Environmental Racism and Food, Pharmacy, and Greenspace Access in the Urban South." *Environmental Sociology* 8 (3): 279–91. https://doi.org/10.1080/23251042.2022.2031513.

Sauvy, A. 1952. "Trois mondes, une planète." *L'Observateur*, August 14.

Savage, L. J. 1954. *The Foundations of Statistics*. New York: John Wiley & Sons.

Schell, C. J., K. Dyson, T. L. Fuentes et al. 2020. "The Ecological and Evolutionary Consequences of Systemic Racism in Urban Environments." *Science* 369(6510). https://doi.org/10.1126/science.aay4497.

Schell, C. J., C. Guy, D. S. Shelton et al. 2020. "Recreating Wakanda by Promoting Black Excellence in Ecology and Evolution." *Nature Ecology and Evolution* 4: 1285–87. https://doi.org/10.1038/s41559-020-1266-7.

Schelling, T. C. 1969. "Models of Segregation." *American Economic Review* 59(2): 488–93.

Schelling, T. C. 1971. "Dynamic Models of Segregation." *Journal of Mathematical Sociology* 1(2): 143–86.

Schelling, T. C. 2006. "Some Fun, Thirty-Five Years Ago." Pp. 1639–44 in *Handbook of Computational Economics*, Vol. 2, edited by L. Tefatsion and K. J. Judd. Amsterdam: North-Holland. https://doi.org/10.1016/S1574-0021(05)02037-X.

Scherer, L., P. Behrens, A. de Koning et al. 2018. "Trade-Offs between Social and Environmental Sustainable Development Goals." *Environmental Science and Policy* 90: 65–72. https://doi.org/10.1016/j.envsci.2018.10.002.

Schmalensee, R. and R. Stavins. 2017. "Lessons Learned from Three Decades of Experience with Cap-and-Trade." *Review of Environmental Economics and Policy* 11(1): 59–79.

Schmitt-Olabisi, L., M. McNall, W. Porter and J. Zhao. 2020. *Innovations in Collaborative Modeling*. East Lansing: Michigan State University Press.

Schmitt, M. T., L. B. Aknin, J. Axsen and R. L. Shwom. 2018. "Unpacking the Relationships between Pro-environmental Behavior, Life Satisfaction, and Perceived Ecological Threat." *Ecological Economics* 143: 130–40. https://doi.org/10.1016/j.ecolecon.2017.07.007.

Schnaiberg, A. 1977. "Obstacles to Environmental Research by Scientists and Technologists: A Social Structural Analysis." *Social Problems* 24(5): 500–20.

Schnaiberg, A. 1980. *The Environment: From Surplus to Scarcity*. New York: Oxford University Press.

Schnaiberg, A. 1982. "Did You Ever Meet a Payroll? Contradictions in the Structure of the Appropriate Technology Movement."

*Humboldt Journal of Social Relations* 9(2): 38–62. https://doi.org/10.2307/23261947.

Schnaiberg, A. 1983. "Redistributive Goals versus Distributive Politics: Social Equity Limits in Environmental and Appropriate Technology Movements." *Sociological Inquiry* 53(2–3): 200–15. https://doi.org/10.1111/j.1475-682X.1983.tb00034.x.

Schnaiberg, A. 1994. "The Political Economy of Environmental Problems and Policies: Consciousness, Conflict and Control Capacity." *Advances in Human Ecology* 3: 23–64.

Schneider, S. H. 2009. *Science As a Contact Sport.* Washington, DC: National Geographic.

Schoemaker, P. J. H. 1982. "The Expected Utility Model: Its Variants, Purposes, Evidence and Limitations." *Journal of Economic Literature* 20(2): 529–63.

Schoener, T. W. 2011. "The Newest Synthesis: Understanding the Interplay of Evolutionary and Ecological Dynamics." *Science* 331 (6016): 426–29.

Schultz, P. W. 2000. "Empathizing with Nature: The Effects of Perspective Taking of Concern for Environmental Issues." *Journal of Social Issues* 56(3): 391–406.

Schultz, P. W. 2002. "Inclusion with Nature: The Psychology of Human–Nature Relations." Pp. 61–78 in *The Psychology of Sustainable Development*, edited by P. W. Schultz. New York: Kluwer.

Schultz, P. W., J. M. Nolan, R. B. Cialdini, N. J. Goldstein and V. Griskevicius. 2007. "The Constructive, Destructive, and Reconstructive Power of Social Norms." *Psychological Science* 18(5): 429–34.

Schultz, P. W., C. Shriver, J. J. Tabanico and A. M. Khazian. 2004. "Implicit Connections with Nature." *Journal of Environmental Psychology* 24(1): 31–42.

Schumacher, E. F. 1973. *Small Is Beautiful: Economics As If People Mattered.* New York: Perennial Library.

Schwadel, P. and C. R. Garneau. 2017. "The Diffusion of Tolerance: Birth Cohort Changes in the Effects of Education and Income on Political Tolerance." *Sociological Forum* 32(4): 748–69.

Schwartz, S. H. 1968a. "Words, Deeds and the Perception of Consequences and Responsibility in Action Situations." *Journal of Personality and Social Psychology* 10(3): 232–42.

Schwartz, S. H. 1968b. "Awareness of Consequences and the Influence of Moral Norms on Interpersonal Behavior." *Sociometry* 31(4): 355–69.

Schwartz, S. H. 1970. "Moral Decision Making and Behavior." Pp. 127–41 in *Altruism and Helping Behavior*, edited by J. Macauley and L. Berkowitz. New York: Academic Press.

Schwartz, S. H. 1973. "Normative Explanations of Helping Behavior: A Critique, Proposal and Empirical Test." *Journal of Experimental Social Psychology* 9(4): 349–64.

Schwartz, S. H. 1977. "Normative Influences on Altruism." Pp. 221–79 in *Advances in Experimental Social Psychology*, Vol. 10, edited by L. Berkowitz. Orlando, FL: Academic.

Schwartz, S. H. and W. Bilsky. 1987. "Toward a Universal Psychological Structure of Human Values." *Journal of Personality and Social Psychology* 53(3): 550–62.

Schwartz, S. H., G. V. Caprara, M. Vecchione et al. 2014. "Basic Personal Values Underlie and Give Coherence to Political Values: A Cross National Study in 15 Countries." *Political Behavior* 36(4): 899–930.

Schwartz, S. H., G. Melech, A. Lehmann et al. 2001. "Extending the Cross-Cultural Validity of the Theory of Basic Human Values with a Different Method of Measurement." *Journal of Cross-Cultural Psychology* 32(5): 519–42.

Schwartz, S. H., M. Vecchione, R. Fischer et al. 2012. "Refining the Theory of Basic Individual Values." *Journal of Personality and Social Psychology* 103(4): 663–88.

Schweizer, P.-J., O. Renn, W. Köck et al. 2016. "Public Participation for Infrastructure Planning in the Context of the German 'Energiewende'." *Utilities Policy* 43: 206–09. https://doi.org/10.1016/j.jup.2014.07.005.

Scorsese, M. (Dir.) 1990. *Goodfellas*. Warner Brothers.

Scott, A., C. Oates and W. Young. 2015. "A Conceptual Framework of the Adoption and Practice of Environmental Actions in Households." *Sustainability* 7(5): 5793–818.

Scott, P. A., L. J. Allison, K. J. Field, R. C. Averill-Murray and H. B. Shaffer. 2020. "Individual Heterozygosity Predicts Translocation Success in Threatened Desert Tortoises." *Science* 370(6520): 1086–89.

Scott-Phillips, T. C., K. N. Laland, D. M. Shuker, T. E. Dickins and S. A. West. 2014. "The Niche Construction Perspective: A Critical Appraisal." *Evolution* 68(5): 1231–43.

Selden, T. M. and D. Song. 1994. "Environmental Quality and Development: Is There a Kuznets Curve for Air Pollution Emissions?" *Journal of Environmental Economics and Management* 27(2): 147–62.

Selinger, E. and K. P. Whyte. 2010. "Competence and Trust in Choice Architecture." *Knowledge, Technology and Policy* 23(3–4): 461–82.

Selinger, E. and K. Whyte. 2011. "Is There a Right Way to Nudge? The Practice and Ethics of Choice Architecture." *Sociology Compass* 5(10): 923–35.

Selinger, E. and K. Whyte. 2012. "Nudging Cannot Solve Complex Policy Problems." *European Journal of Risk Regulation* 1(1): 26–31.

Selvanathan, H. P. and J. Jetten. 2020. "From Marches to Movements: Building and Sustaining a Social Movement Following Collective Action." *Current Opinion in Psychology* 35: 81–85. https://doi.org/10.1016/j.copsyc.2020.04.004.

Sen, A. K. 1977. "Rational Fools: A Critique of the Behavioral Foundations of Economic Theory." *Philosophy and Public Affairs* 6(4): 317–44.

Sen, A. K. 1999. *Development As Freedom*. New York: Random House.

Sen, A. K. 2002. "Environmental Evaluation and Social Choice." Pp. 531–52 in *Rationality and Freedom*, edited by A. Sen.

Cambridge, MA: Belknap Press of Harvard University Press.

Seto, K. C., J. S. Golden, M. Alberti and B. L. Turner. 2017. "Sustainability in an Urbanizing Planet." *Proceedings of the National Academy of Sciences* 114(34): 8935–38.

Seto, K. C. and A. Reenberg. 2014. *Rethinking Global Land Use in an Urban Era*. Cambridge, MA: MIT Press.

Seymour, N. 2013. *Strange Natures: Futurity, Empathy, and the Queer Ecological Imagination*. Urbana: University of Illinois Press.

Shaffer, M. 2010. *Multiple Account Benefit-Cost Analysis: A Practical Guide for the Systematic Evaluation of Project and Policy Alternatives*. Toronto, ON: University of Toronto Press.

Shahbaz, M. and A. Sinha. 2019. "Environmental Kuznets Curve for $CO_2$ Emissions: A Literature Survey." *Journal of Economic Studies* 46(1): 106–68. https://doi.org/10.1108/JES-09-2017-0249.

Shandra, J., E. Shircliff and B. London. 2011. "The International Monetary Fund, World Bank and Structural Adjustment: A Cross-National Analysis of Forest Loss." *Social Science Research* 40(1): 210–25.

Shandra, J. M., H. Rademacher and C. Coburn. 2016. "The World Bank and Organized Hypocrisy? A Cross-National Analysis of Structural Adjustment and Forest Loss." *Environmental Sociology* 2(2): 192–207.

Shandra, J. M., E. Shor and B. London. 2008. "Debt, Structural Adjustment, and Organic Water Pollution: A Cross-National Analysis." *Organization and Environment* 21(1): 38–55. https://doi.org/10.1177/1086026608314759.

Shandra, J. M., E. Shor, G. Maynard and B. London. 2008. "Debt, Structural Adjustment, and Deforestation: A Cross-National Study." *Journal of World-Systems Research* 14(1). https://doi.org/10.5195/jwsr.2008.345.

Shannon, M. 1987. "Forest Planning: Learning with People." Pp. 233–52 in *Social Science in Natural Resource*

*Management Systems*, edited by M. L. Miller, R. P. Gale and P. J. Brown. Boulder, CO: Westview.

Shannon, M. A. 1991. *Building Public Decisions: Learning through Planning*. Washington, DC: Office of Technology Assessment.

Sharp, G. 1973. *The Politics of Nonviolent Action: The Dynamics of Nonviolent Action*. Boston, MA: Extending Horizons Books.

Sharp, G. 2012. *From Dictatorship to Democracy: A Conceptual Framework for Liberation*. New York: The New Press.

Shove, E., M. Watson and N. Spurling. 2015. "Conceptualizing Connections: Energy Demand, Infrastructures and Social Practices." *European Journal of Social Theory* 18(3): 274–87.

Shutkin, W. A. 2000. *The Land That Could Be*. Cambridge, MA: MIT Press.

Shwom, R. L. 2011. "A Middle Range Theorization of Energy Politics: The U.S. Struggle for Energy Efficient Appliances." *Environmental Politics* 20(5): 705–26.

Shwom, R. L. 2020. "Social Tipping Points in the Climate System: Theorizing Conditions and Mechanisms of Rapid Social Change." Rutgers Energy Institute, Working Paper.

Shwom, R. L., D. Bidwell, A. Dan and T. Dietz. 2010. "Understanding U.S. Public Support for Domestic Climate Change Policies." *Global Environmental Change* 20 (3): 472–82.

Shwom, R. L., A. M. McCright, S. T. Marquart-Pyatt and L. C. Hamilton. 2015. "Public Opinion on Climate Change." Pp. 269–99 in *Climate Change and Society: Sociological Perspectives*, edited by R. E. Dunlap and R. J. Brulle. Oxford: Oxford University Press.

Sidik, S. M. 2022a. "How COVID Has Deepened Inequality – in Six Stark Graphics." *Nature* 606(7915): 638–39.

Sidik, S. M. 2022b. "Weaving Indigenous Knowledge into the Scientific Method." *Nature* 601(7892): 285–87.

Siegrist, M. 2019. "Trust and Risk Perception: A Critical Review of the Literature." *Risk Analysis* 41(3): 480–90.

Siegrist, M. and J. Árvai. 2020. "Risk Perception: Reflections on 40 Years of Research." *Risk Analysis* 40(S1): 2191–206.

Signé, L. and H. Dooley. 2022. "A Proactive Approach towards Addressing the Challenges of the Metaverse." *TechStream* (Brookings Institution), July 21. www.brookings.edu/techstream/a-proactive-approach-toward-addressing-the-challenges-of-the-metaverse/.

Silbergeld, E. 2001. "Review of Mary O'Brien's *Making Better Environmental Decisions*." *Public Health Reports* 116(1): 66–68.

Siler, K. and D. Strang. 2017. "Peer Review and Scholarly Originality: Let 1,000 Flowers Bloom, but Don't Step on Any." *Science, Technology, and Human Values* 42 (1): 29–61. https://doi.org/10.1177/0162243916656919.

Sills, E. O., D. Herrera, A. J. Kirkpatrick et al. 2015. "Estimating the Impacts of Local Policy Innovation: The Synthetic Control Method Applied to Tropical Deforestation." *PloS One* 10(7): e0132590.

Silva, R., M. Batistella, Y. Dou et al. 2017. "The Sino-Brazilian Telecoupled Soybean System and Cascading Effects for the Exporting Country." *Land* 6(3): 53.

Silver, M. 2021. "Memo to People of Earth: 'Third World' Is an Offensive Term!" Goats and Soda: Stories of Life in a Changing World (blog), National Public Radio, January 8. www.npr.org/sections/goatsandsoda/2021/01/08/954820328/memo-to-people-of-earth-third-world-is-an-offensive-term.

Silver, N. 2015. "Change Doesn't Usually Come This Fast." *FiveThirtyeight.com*, June 26. https://fivethirtyeight.com/features/change-doesnt-usually-come-this-fast/.

Simon, H. A. 1947. *Administrative Behavior*. New York: Macmillan.

Simon, H. A. 1972. "Theories of Bounded Rationality." *Decision and Organization* 1(1): 161–76.

Simon, H. A. 1982. *Models of Bounded Rationality*, Vols. 1 & 2. Cambridge, MA: MIT Press.

Simon, H. A. 1986. "Rationality in Psychology and Economics." Pp. 25–40 in *Rational Choice: The Contrast between Economics and Psychology*, edited by R. M. Hogarth and M. W. Reder. Chicago, IL: University of Chicago Press.

Simon, H. A. 1991. *Models of My Life*. New York: Basic Books.

Simon, J. L. and K. Herman. 1984. *Resourceful Earth: A Response to Global 2000*. New York: Basil Blackwell.

Simpson, B. and R. Willer. 2015. "Beyond Altruism: Sociological Foundations of Cooperation and Prosocial Behavior." *Annual Review of Sociology* 41: 43–63.

Sinclair, R. 2020. "Exploding Individuals: Engaging Indigenous Logic and Decolonizing Science." *Hypatia* 35(1): 58–74.

Singer, P. 1995. *Animal Liberation*. New York: Random House.

Skocpol, T. 1979. *States and Social Revolutions: A Comparative Analysis of France, Russia and China*. Cambridge: Cambridge University Press.

Skocpol, T. and V. Williamson. 2012. *The Tea Party and the Remaking of Republican Conservatism*. New York: Oxford University Press.

Slabe, V. A., J. T. Anderson, B. A. Millsap et al. 2022. "Demographic Implications of Lead Poisoning for Eagles across North America." *Science* 375(6582): 779–82.

Slobogin, C. 2021. *Just Algorithms: Using Science to Reduce Incarceration and Inform a Jurisprudence of Risk*. Cambridge: Cambridge University Press.

Sloot, D., L. Jans and L. Steg. 2019. "In It for the Money, the Environment, or the Community? Motives for Being Involved in Community Energy Initiatives." *Global Environmental Change* 57: 101936. https://doi.org/10.1016/j.gloenvcha.2019.101936.

Smaldino, P. E. 2019. "Social Identity and Cooperation in Cultural Evolution." *Behavioural Processes* 161: 108–16. https://doi.org/10.1016/j.beproc.2017.11.015.

Small, M. L., A. Akhavan, M. Torres and Q. Wang. 2021. "Banks, Alternative Institutions and the Spatial–Temporal Ecology of Racial Inequality in US Cities." *Nature Human Behaviour* 5(12): 1622–28.

Smith, A. [1804] 1976. *A Theory of Moral Sentiments*. New York: Oxford University Press.

Smith, E. E., C. Langton and R. E. Nisbett. 1992. "The Case for Rules in Reasoning." *Cognitive Sciences* 16(1): 1–40.

Smith, W. 2018. "Transnational and Global Deliberation." Pp. 856–68 in *The Oxford Handbook of Deliberative Democracy*, edited by A. Bächtiger, J. Mansbridge, M. E. Warren and J. Dryzek. Oxford: Oxford University Press.

Sniderman, P. M., R. A. Brody and P. E. Tetlock. 1991. *Reasoning and Choice: Explorations in Social Psychology*. Cambridge: Cambridge University Press.

Sniehotta, F. F., J. Presseau and V. Araújo-Soares. 2014. "Time to Retire the Theory of Planned Behaviour." *Health Psychology Review* 8(1): 1–7.

So, A. Y. 2014. "The Chinese Model of Development: Characteristics, Interpretations, Implications." *Perspectives on Global Development and Technology* 13(4): 444–64.

So, A. Y. and Y.-w. Chu. 2012. "The Transition from Neoliberalism to State Neoliberalism in China at the Turn of the Twenty-First Century." Pp. 166–87 in *Developmental Politics in Transition: The Neoliberal Era and Beyond*, edited by C. Kyung-Sup, B. Fine and L. Weiss. New York: Palgrave Macmillan.

Sober, E. 1980. "Evolution, Population Thinking, and Essentialism." *Philosophy of Science* 47(3): 350–83.

Sober, E. and D. S. Wilson. 1998. *Unto Others: The Evolution and Psychology of Unselfish Behavior*. Cambridge, MA: Harvard University Press.

Solow, R. M. 1974. "The Economics of Resources or the Resources of Economics." *American Economic Review* 64(2): 1–14.

Sommer, J. M., M. Restivo and J. M. Shandra. 2020. "The United States, Bilateral Debt-for-Nature Swaps, and Forest Loss: A

Cross-National Analysis." *The Journal of Development Studies* 56(4): 748–64.

Sommer, J. M., J. M. Shandra, M. Restivo and C. Coburn. 2016. "Water, Sanitation, and Health in Sub-Saharan Africa: A Cross-National Analysis of Maternal and Neo-natal Mortality." *Human Ecology Review* 22(1): 129.

Sommer, J. M., J. M. Shandra, M. Restivo and H. E. Reed. 2019. "The African Development Bank, Organized Hypocrisy, and Maternal Mortality: A Cross-National Analysis of Sub-Saharan Africa." *Sociology of Development* 5(1): 31–49.

Sontag, M. S. and M. M. Bubolz. 1993. "Human Ecology Theory." Pp. 419–48 in *Sourcebook of Family Theories and Methods: A Contextual Approach*, edited by P. G. Boss, W. J. Doherty, R. LaRossa, W. R. Schumm and S. K. Steinmetz. New York: Plenum.

Soukup, M. A. and G. E. Machlis. 2021. *American Covenant: National Parks, Their Promise, and Our Nation's Future*. New Haven, CT: Yale University Press.

Sparkman, G. and S. Z. Attari. 2020. "Credibility, Communication, and Climate Change: How Lifestyle Inconsistency and Do-Gooder Derogation Impact Decarbonization Advocacy." *Energy Research and Social Science* 59: 101290. https://doi.org/10.1016/j.erss.2019.101290.

Sparkman, G., S. Z. Attari and E. U. Weber. 2021. "Moderating Spillover: Focusing on Personal Sustainable Behavior Rarely Hinders and Can Boost Climate Policy Support." *Energy Research and Social Science* 78: 102150. https://doi.org/10.1016/j.erss.2021.102150.

Sparkman, G., L. Howe and G. Walton. 2021. "How Social Norms Are Often a Barrier to Addressing Climate Change but Can Be Part of the Solution." *Behavioural Public Policy* 5(4): 528–55.

Sparkman, G. and G. M. Walton. 2017. "Dynamic Norms Promote Sustainable Behavior, Even If It Is Counternormative." *Psychological Science* 28(11): 1663–74.

Spash, C. 2007. "Deliberative Monetary Valuation (DMV): Issues in Combining Economic and Political Processes to Value Environmental Change." *Ecological Economics* 63(4): 690–99.

Spence, M. D. 1999. *Dispossessing the Wilderness: Indian Removal and the Making of the National Parks*. Oxford: Oxford University Press.

Speth, J. G. 2008. "The *Global 2000 Report* and Its Aftermath." Pp. 47–50 in *Foundations of Environmental Sustainability*, edited by L. L. Rockwood, R. E. Stewart and T. Dietz. Oxford: Oxford University Press.

Spier, R. 2002. "The History of the Peer-Review Process." *Trends in Biotechnology* 20(8): 357–58.

Squires, G. D. 2017. *The Fight for Fair Housing: Causes, Consequences, and Future Implications of the 1968 Federal Fair Housing Act*. New York: Routledge.

Staats, H., P. Harland and H. A. Wilke. 2004. "Effecting Durable Change: A Team Approach to Improve Environmental Behavior in the Household." *Environment and Behavior* 36(3): 341–67.

Stack, C. B. 1975. *All Our Kin: Strategies for Survival in a Black Community*. New York: Harper & Row.

Stanovich, K. E. 2021. *The Bias That Divides Us: The Science and Politics of Myside Thinking*. Cambridge, MA: MIT Press.

Starr, C. 1969. "Societal Benefit Versus Technological Risk." *Science* 165(3899): 1232–38.

Steen-Olsen, K. and E. G. Hertwich. 2015. "Life Cycle Assessment As a Means to Identify the Most Effective Action for Sustainable Consumption." Pp. 131–44 in *Handbook of Research on Sustainable Consumption*. Edited by L. A. Reisch and J. Thøgersen. Cheltenham: Edward Elgar.

Steffen, W., W. Broadgate, L. Deutsch, O. Gaffney and C. Ludwig. 2015. "The Trajectory of the Anthropocene: The Great Acceleration." *The Anthropocene Review* 2(1): 81–98.

Steffen, W., J. Grinevald, P. Crutzen and J. McNeill. 2011. "The Anthropocene: Conceptual and Historical Perspectives." *Philosophical Transactions of the Royal Society A* 369(1938): 842–67.

Steffen, W., K. Richardson, J. Rockström et al. 2015. "Planetary Boundaries: Guiding Human Development on a Changing Planet." *Science* 347(6223): 1259855.

Steffen, W., J. Rockström, K. Richardson et al. 2018. "Trajectories of the Earth System in the Anthropocene." *Proceedings of the National Academy of Sciences* 115(33): 8252–59.

Steg, L. 2016. "Values, Norms, and Intrinsic Motivation to Act Pro-environmentally." *Annual Review of Environment and Resources* 41: 277–92.

Steg, L., J. W. Bolderdijk, K. Keizer and G. Perlaviciute. 2014. "An Integrated Framework for Encouraging Pro-environmental Behaviour: The Role of Values, Situational Factors and Goals." *Journal of Environmental Psychology* 38: 104–15. https://doi.org/10.1016/j.jenvp.2014.01.002.

Steg, L. and J. I. M. de Groot. 2012. "Environmental Values." Pp. 81–92 in *The Oxford Handbook of Environmental and Conservation Psychology*, edited by S. Clayton. New York: Oxford University Press.

Steg, L., G. Perlaviciute, E. van der Werff and J. Lurvink. 2014. "The Significance of Hedonic Values for Environmentally Relevant Attitudes, Preferences, and Actions." *Environment and Behavior* 46(2): 163–92.

Steg, L., R. Shwom and T. Dietz. 2018. "What Drives Energy Consumers? Engaging People in a Sustainable Energy Transition." *IEEE Power and Energy Magazine* 16(1): 20–28.

Steiner, F. R. 2016. *Human Ecology: How Nature and Culture Shape Our World*. Washington, DC: Island Press.

Steiner, F. R. and F. Steiner. 2002. *Human Ecology: Following Nature's Lead*. Washington, DC: Island Press.

Stellman, J. M., S. D. Stellman, R. Christian, T. Weber and C. Tomasallo. 2003. "The Extent and Patterns of Usage of Agent Orange and Other Herbicides in Vietnam." *Nature* 422(6933): 681–87.

Stern, D. I. 2004. "The Rise and Fall of the Environmental Kuznets Curve." *World Development* 32(8): 1419–39.

Stern, D. I. 2010. "Between Estimates of the Emissions-Income Elasticity." *Ecological Economics* 69(11): 2173–82.

Stern, N. 2007. *The Economics of Climate Change: The Stern Review*. Cambridge: Cambridge University Press.

Stern, P. C. 2000. "Toward a Coherent Theory of Environmentally Significant Behavior." *Journal of Social Issues* 56(3): 407–24.

Stern, P. C. 2002. "Changing Behavior in Households and Communities: What Have We Learned?" Pp. 201–11 in *New Tools for Environmental Protection: Education, Information and Voluntary Measures*, edited by T. Dietz and P. C. Stern. Washington, DC: National Academy Press.

Stern, P. C. 2008. "Environmentally Significant Behavior in the Home." Pp. 363–82 in *The Cambridge Handbook of Psychology and Economic Behaviour*, edited by A. Lewis. Cambridge: Cambridge University Press.

Stern, P. C. 2011a. "Design Principles for Global Commons: Natural Resources and Emerging Technologies." *International Journal of the Commons* 5(2): 213–32.

Stern, P. C. 2011b. "Contributions of Psychology to Limiting Climate Change." *American Psychologist* 66(4): 303–14.

Stern, P. C. 2013. "Design Principles for Governing Risks from Emerging Technologies." Pp. 91–118 in *Structural Human Ecology: New Essays in Risk, Energy and Sustainability*, edited by T. Dietz and A. K. Jorgenson. Pullman: Washington State University Press.

Stern, P. C. 2014. "Individual and Household Interactions with Energy Systems: Toward Integrated Understanding." *Energy Research and Social Science* 1: 41–48. https://doi.org/10.1016/j.erss.2014.03.003.

Stern, P. C. 2016. "Sociology: Impacts on Climate Change Views." *Nature Climate Change* 6(4): 341–42.

Stern, P. C. 2020. "Well-Meaning Discourses of Climate Delay." *Global Sustainability* 3(e35): 1–3.

Stern, P. C., E. Aronson, J. Darley et al. 1986. "The Effectiveness of Incentives for Residential Energy Conservation." *Evaluation Review* 10(2): 147–76.

Stern, P. C. and T. Dietz. 2020. "A Broader Social Science Research Agenda on Sustainability: Nongovernmental Influences on Climate Footprints." *Energy Research and Social Science* 60: 101401. https://doi.org/10.1016/j.erss.2019.101401.

Stern, P. C., T. Dietz, T. Abel, G. A. Guagnano and L. Kalof. 1999. "A Social Psychological Theory of Support for Social Movements: The Case of Environmentalism." *Human Ecology Review* 6(2): 81–97.

Stern, P. C., T. Dietz and J. S. Black. 1986. "Support for Environmental Protection: The Role of Moral Norms." *Population and Environment* 8: 204–22. https://doi.org/10.1007/BF01263074.

Stern, P. C., T. Dietz and L. Kalof. 1993. "Value Orientations, Gender and Environmental Concern." *Environment and Behavior* 25(3): 322–48.

Stern, P. C., T. Dietz, L. Kalof and G. Guagnano. 1995. "Values, Beliefs and Proenvironmental Action: Attitude Formation toward Emergent Attitude Objects." *Journal of Applied Social Psychology* 25(18): 1611–36.

Stern, P. C., T. Dietz and E. Ostrom. 2002. "Research on the Commons: Lessons for Environmental Resource Managers." *Environmental Practice* 4(2): 61–64.

Stern, P. C., T. Dietz and M. Vandenbergh. 2022. "The Science of Mitigation: Closing the Gap between Potential and Actual Reduction of Environmental Threats." *Energy Research and Social Science* 91: 102735. https://doi.org/10.1016/j.erss.2022.102735.

Stern, P. C., G. T. Gardner, M. P. Vandenbergh, T. Dietz and J. M. Gilligan. 2010. "Design Principles for Carbon Emissions Reduction Programs." *Environmental Science and Technology* 44(13): 4847–48.

Stern, P. C., K. B. Janda, M. A. Brown et al. 2016. "Opportunities and Insights for Reducing Fossil Fuel Consumption by Households and Organizations." *Nature Energy* 1: 16043. https://doi.org/10.1038/nenergy.2016.43.

Stern, P. C. and L. E. Kalof. 1996. *Evaluating Social Science Research*. New York: Oxford University Press.

Stern, P. C. and K. S. Wolske. 2017. "Limiting Climate Change: What's Most Worth Doing?" *Environmental Research Letters* 12 (9): 091001. https://doi.org/10.1088/1748-9326/aa8467.

Stern, P. C., K. S. Wolske and T. Dietz. 2021. "Design Principles for Climate Change Decisions." *Current Opinion in Environmental Sustainability* 52: 9–18. https://doi.org/10.1016/j.cosust.2021.05.002.

Stern, P. J. 2015. "The English East India Company and the Modern Corporation: Legacies, Lessons, and Limitations." *Seattle University Law Review* 39: 423–45. https://heinonline.org/HOL/LandingPage?handle=hein.journals/sealr39&div=21&id=&page=.

Stevens, S., ed. 2014. *Indigenous Peoples, National Parks, and Protected Areas: A New Paradigm Linking Conservation, Culture, and Rights*. Tucson: University of Arizona Press.

Stevis, D. 2002. "Agents, Subjects, Objects, or Phantoms? Labor, the Environment, and Liberal Institutionalization." *The Annals of the American Academy of Political and Social Science* 581(1): 91–105.

Stevis, D. 2011. "Unions and the Environment: Pathways to Global Labor Environmentalism." *WorkingUSA* 14(2): 145–59.

Stiglitz, J. 2019. *People, Power, and Profits: Progressive Capitalism for an Age of Discontent*. London: Penguin UK.

Stiglitz, J., A. Sen and J.-P. Fitoussi. 2009. *The Measurement of Economic Performance and*

*Social Progress Revisited*. Paris: Commission on the Measurement of Economic Performance and Social Progress.

Stiglitz, J. E., J.-P. Fitoussi and M. Durand. 2018. *For Good Measure: Advancing Research on Well-Being Metrics Beyond GDP*. Paris: OECD Publishing.

Stillman, S. 2017. "Can Behavioral Science Help in Flint." *The New Yorker*, January 15. www.newyorker.com/magazine/2017/01/23/can-behavioral-science-help-in-flint.

Stirling, A. 2006. "Analysis, Participation and Power: Justification and Closure in Participatory Multi-criteria Analysis." *Land Use Policy* 23(1): 95–107.

Stirling, A. 2008. "'Opening Up' and 'Closing Down' Power, Participation, and Pluralism in the Social Appraisal of Technology." *Science, Technology, and Human Values* 33(2): 262–94.

Stokes, D. E. 1997. *Pasteur's Quadrant: Basic Science and Technological Innovation*. Washington, DC: Brookings Institution.

Stoll, H. 2015. "Presidential Coattails: A Closer Look." *Party Politics* 21(3): 417–27.

Stolper, W. F. and P. A. Samuelson. 1941. "Protection and Real Wages." *Review of Economic Studies* 9(1): 58–73.

Stone, C. D. 1972. "Should Trees Have Standing?: Toward Legal Rights for Natural Objects." *Southern California Law Review*. 45: 450–501.

Stone, C. D. 1985. "Should Trees Have Standing Revisited: How Far Will Law and Morals Reach: A Pluralist Perspective." *Southern California Law Review*. 59: 1–154.

Stork, N. 2010. "Re-assessing Current Extinction Rates." *Biodiversity and Conservation* 19(3570371). https://doi.org/10.1007/s10531-009-9761-9.

Stowman, A. M., L. S. Cacciatore, V. Cortright et al. 2022. "Anatomy of a Cyberattack: Part 3: Coordination in Crisis, Development of an Incident Command Team, and Resident Education During Downtime." *American Journal of Clinical Pathology* 157 (6): 814–22.

Stowman, A. M., N. Frisch, P. C. Gibson et al. 2022. "Anatomy of a Cyberattack: Part 1:

Managing an Anatomic Pathology Laboratory During 25 Days of Downtime." *American Journal of Clinical Pathology* 157 (4): 510–17.

Stradling, D. and R. Stradling. 2008. "Perceptions of the Burning River: Deindustrialization and Cleveland's Cuyahoga River." *Environmental History* 13 (3): 515–35.

Suchyta, M. 2020a. "Sense of Place As a Predictor of Beliefs about Energy Development: A Study in Pennsylvania's Marcellus Shale." *Energy Research and Social Science* 70: 101635. https://doi.org/10.1016/j.erss.2020.101635.

Suchyta, M. 2020b. "Environmental Values and American's Beliefs about Farm Animal Well-Being." *Agriculture and Human Values* 38: 987–1001. https://doi.org/10.1007/s10460-021-10206-0.

Suchyta, M. and T. W. Kelsey. 2018. "Employment and Compensation in the Marcellus Shale Gas Boom: What Stays Local?" *Journal of Rural and Community Development* 13(4): 87–106.

Suitts, S. 2019. "Segregationists, Libertarians, and the Modern "School Choice" Movement." *Southern Spaces*, June 4.https://southernspaces.org/2019/segregationists-libertarians-and-modern-school-choice-movement/.

Sumner, A., C. Hoy and E. Ortiz-Juarez. 2020. *Estimates of the Impact of COVID-19 on Global Poverty*: United Nations University World Institute for Development Economics Research.

Sumner, W. G. 1883a. *What the Social Classes Owe to Each Other*. New York: Harper & Brothers.

Sumner, W. G. 1883b. "The Absurd Effort to Make the World Over." Pp. 193–212 in *War and Other Essays*. New Haven, CT: Yale University Press.

Sun, B. 2018. "Heterogeneous Direct Rebound Effect: Theory and Evidence from the Energy Star Program." *Energy Economics* 69: 335–49. https://doi.org/10.1016/j.eneco.2017.11.025.

Sunstein, C. R. 2014. *Why Nudge? The Politics of Libertarian Paternalism*. New Haven, CT: Yale University Press.

Sunstein, C. R. 2020. "The Siren of Selfishness: Review of Mean Girl: Ayn Rand and the Culture of Greed by Lisa Duggan." *New York Review*, April 9. www.nybooks.com/articles/2020/04/09/ayn-rand-siren-selfishness/.

Sunstein, C. R. 2021. "The Distributional Effects of Nudges." *Nature Human Behaviour* 6: 9–10. https://doi.org/10.1038/s41562-021-01236-z.

Sunstein, C. R. and L. A. Reisch. 2019. *Trusting Nudges: Toward a Bill of Rights for Nudging*. London: Routledge.

Surowiecki, J. 2016. "Courting Business." The New Yorker, March 7.

Svenning, J.-C., P. B. Pedersen, C. J. Donlan et al. 2016. "Science for a Wilder Anthropocene: Synthesis and Future Directions for Trophic Rewilding Research." *Proceedings of the National Academy of Sciences* 113(4): 898–906.

Sweezy, P. M. [1942] 1968. *The Theory of Capitalist Development*. New York: Monthly Review Press.

Sweezy, P. M. and H. Magdoff. 1972. *The Dynamics of U.S. Capitalism: Corporate Structure, Inflation, Credit, Gold and the Dollar*. New York: Monthly Review Press.

Szathmáry, E. and H. P.d. Vladar. 2017. "Beyond Hamilton's Rule." *Science* 356 (6337): 485–86.

Sztompka, P. 1999. *Trust: A Sociological Theory*. Cambridge: Cambridge University Press.

Tabuchi, H. 2018. "How the Koch Brothers Are Killing Public Transit Projects around the Country." *New York Times*, June 19.

Taddeo, M. and L. Floridi. 2018. "How AI Can Be a Force for Good." *Science* 361(6404): 751–52.

Tanner, M. D. 2018. *The Inclusive Economy: How to Bring Wealth to America's Poor*. Washington, DC: Cato Institute.

Taufique, K. M. R., K. S. Nielsen, T. Dietz et al. 2022. "Revisiting the Promise of Carbon Labelling." *Nature Climate Change* 12(2): 132–40. https://doi.org/10.1038/s41558-021-01271-8.

Taylor, D. E. 2000. "The Rise of the Environmental Justice Paradigm Injustice Framing and the Social Construction of Environmental Discourses." *American Behavioral Scientist* 43(4): 508–80.

Taylor, P. J. and F. H. Buttel. 1992. "How Do We Know We Have Global Environmental Problems? Science and the Globalization of Environmental Discourse." *Geoforum* 23(3): 405–16.

Tengö, M., R. Hill, P. Malmer et al. 2017. "Weaving Knowledge Systems in IPBES, CBD and Beyond: Lessons Learned for Sustainability." *Current Opinion in Environmental Sustainability* 26–27: 17–25. https://doi.org/10.1016/j.cosust.2016.12.005.

Thabrew, L., D. Perrone, A. Ewing, M. Abkowitz and G. Hornberger. 2018. "Using Triple Bottom Line Metrics and Multi-criteria Methodology in Corporate Settings." *Journal of Environmental Planning and Management* 61(1): 49–63.

Thaler, R. H. 2018. "Nudge, Not Sludge." *Science* 361(6401): 431.

Thaler, R. H. and C. R. Sunstein. 2009. *Nudge: Improving Decisions about Health, Wealth, and Happiness*. New York: Penguin.

Thomasson, E. D., E. Scharman, E. Fechter-Leggett et al. 2017. "Acute Health Effects after the Elk River Chemical Spill, West Virginia, January 2014." *Public Health Reports* 132(2): 196–202.

Thompson, P. B. 2010. *The Agrarian Vision: Sustainability and Environmental Ethics*. Lexington: University of Kentucky Press.

Thompson, P. B. 2015. *From Field to Fork: Food Ethics for Everyone*. New York: Oxford University Press.

Thompson, P. B. 2017. *The Spirit of the Soil: Agriculture and Environmental Ethics*. New York: Routledge.

Thuan, D. D. and N. Van Ngoc. 2018. "The System of Dykes and Water Resources of North Vietnam under the Impact of the

American Air and Naval Attacks (1965–1972)." Pp. 107–22 in *Armed Conflict and Environment*, edited by D. Briesen. Baden-Baden: Nomos Verlagsgesellschaft.

Thuy, D. T. P. and N. Van Bac. 2018. "Impact of American Large Scale Destruction of Forests on Natural Environment and Ethnic Minorities in South Vietnam during the Vietnam War (1954–1975)." Pp. 91–105 in *Armed Conflict and Environment*, edited by D. Briesen. Baden-Baden: Nomos Verlagsgesellschaft.

Tietenberg, T. 2002. "The Tradable Permits Approach to Protecting the Commons: What Have We Learned?" Pp. 197–232 in *The Drama of the Commons*, edited by E. Ostrom, T. Dietz, N. Dolsak, P. C. Stern, S. Stonich and E. Weber. Washington, DC: National Academy Press.

Tietenberg, T. H. 2013. "Reflections: Carbon Pricing in Practice." *Review of Environmental Economics and Policy* 7(2): 313–29.

Tilly, C. 2017. "From Mobilization to Revolution." Pp. 71–91 in *Collective Violence, Contentious Politics, and Social Change*, edited by E. Castañeda and C. L. Schneider. New York: Routledge.

Tollefson, J. 2022. "Climate Pledges from Top Companies Crumble under Scrutiny." *Nature*, February 7. https://doi.org/10.1038/d41586-022-00366-2.

Trip, G. 2014, "Thousands Without Water after Spill in West Virginia", *New York Times*, February 27. www.nytimes.com/2014/01/11/us/west-virginia-chemical-spill.html?_r=1.

Truelove, H. B., A. R. Carrico, E. U. Weber, K. T. Raimi and M. P. Vandenbergh. 2014. "Positive and Negative Spillover of Pro-environmental Behavior: An Integrative Review and Theoretical Framework." *Global Environmental Change* 29: 127–38. https://doi.org/10.1016/j.gloenvcha.2014.09.004.

Tuanmu, M. N., A. Vina, W. Yang, X. Chen, A. M. Shortridge and J. Liu. 2016. "Effects of Payments for Ecosystem Services on Wildlife Habitat Recovery." *Conservation Biology* 30(4): 827–35.

Tuler, S. and T. Webler. 1995. "Process Evaluation for Discursive Decision Making in Environmental and Risk Policy." *Human Ecology Review* 2(1): 62–71.

Turner, B. L. I., R. E. Kasperson, W. B. Meyer et al. 1991. "Two Types of Global Environmental Change: Definitional and Spatial Scale Issues in Their Human Dimensions." *Global Environmental Change* 1 (1): 14–22.

Turner, F. 2006. *From Counterculture to Cyberculture: Stewart Brand, The Whole Earth Network, and the Rise of Digital Utopianism*. Chicago, IL: University of Chicago Press.

Turner, G. M. 2012. "On the Cusp of Global Collapse? Updated Comparison of The Limits to Growth with Historical Data." *GAIA-Ecological Perspectives for Science and Society* 21(2): 116–24.

Turner, G. M. 2013. "The Limits to Growth Model Is More Than a Mathematical Exercise." *GAIA-Ecological Perspectives for Science and Society* 22(1): 18–19.

Tversky, A. 1972. "Elimination by Aspects: A Theory of Choice." *Psychological Review* 79(4): 281–99.

Twenge, J. M. and A. B. Blake. 2021. "Increased Support for Same-Sex Marriage in the US: Disentangling Age, Period, and Cohort Effects." *Journal of Homosexuality* 68(11): 1774–84.

Tyrrell, M. and J.C. Dernbach. 2010. "The Cash for Clunkers Program: A Sustainability Evaluation." *University of Toledo Law Review* 42: 467–91.

US Commission on Population Growth and the American Future. 1972. *Population and the American Future*. New York: Signet.

US National Academy of Sciences. 1971. *Rapid Population Growth: Consequences and Policy Implications*. Baltimore, MD: Johns Hopkins University Press.

US National Research Council. 1986. *Proceedings of the Conference on Common Property Resource Management*. Washington, DC: National Academy Press.

US National Research Council. 1996. *Understanding Risk: Informing Decisions in a Democratic Society*, edited by P. C. Stern and H. Fineberg. Washington, DC: National Academy Press.

US National Research Council. 1999a. *Perspectives on Biodiversity: Valuing Its Role in an Everchanging World*. Washington, DC: National Academy Press.

US National Research Council. 1999b. *Nature's Numbers: Expanding the National Economic Accounts to Include the Environment*. Washington, D.C.: National Academy Press.

US National Research Council. 2007. *Analysis of Global Change Assessments: Lessons Learned*. Washington, DC: National Academy Press.

US National Research Council. 2008. *Public Participation in Environmental Assessment and Decision Making*, edited by T. Dietz and P. C. Stern. Washington, DC: National Academy Press.

US National Research Council. 2010a. *Advancing the Science of Climate Change*. Washington, DC: National Academies Press.

US National Research Council. 2010b. *Climate Stabilization Targets: Emissions, Concentrations, and Impacts Over Decades to Millennia*. Washington, DC: National Academies Press.

US National Research Council. 2010c. *Limiting the Magnitude of Climate Change*. Washington, DC: National Academy Press.

US National Research Council. 2011. *America's Climate Choices*. Washington, DC: National Academies Press.

US National Research Council. 2012. *Water Reuse: Potential for Expanding the Nation's Water Supply through Reuse of Municipal Wastewater*. Washington, DC: National Academies Press.

US National Research Council. 2013. *Using Science to Improve the BLM Wild Horse and Burro Program: A Way Forward*: Washington, DC: National Academies Press.

Umberger, M. L. 2002. "Casting the Buffalo Commons: A Rhetorical Analysis of Print Media Coverage of the Buffalo Commons Proposal for the Great Plains." *Great Plains Quarterly* 22(2): 99–114.

UN-Energy. 2005. *The Energy Challenge for Meeting the Millennium Development Goals*. New York: United Nations.

Underwood, P. and F. Howell. 1983. *Who Speaks for Wolf*. Bayfield, CO: Tribe of Two Presses Publishing.

United Nations Department of Economic and Social Affairs. 2020. *World Social Report 2020: Inequality in a Rapidly Changing World*. New York: United Nations.

United Nations Development Program. 2019. *Human Development Report 2019. Beyond Income, Beyond Averages, Beyond Today: Inequalities in Human Development in the 21st Century*. New York: United Nations Development Program.

Uppenbrink, J. 1997. "Arrhenius and Global Warming." *Science* 272(5265): 1122.

Uslaner, E., ed. 2018. *The Oxford Handbook of Social and Political Trust*. Oxford: Oxford University Press.

Vaisey, S. 2021. "Welcome to the Real World: Escaping the Sociology of Culture and Cognition." *Sociological Forum* 36(S1): 1297–315.

Van Aaken, A. and C. List. 2017. *Deliberation and Decision: Economics, Constitutional Theory and Deliberative Democracy*. New York: Routledge.

Van Alstyne, A. D. 2015. "The United Auto Workers and the Emergence of Labor Environmentalism." *WorkingUSA* 18(4): 613–27.

van den Belt, M. 2004. *Mediated Modeling: A Systems Dynamics Approach to Environmental Consensus Building*. Washington, DC: Island Press.

Van der Bles, A. M., S. Van Der Linden, A. L. Freeman et al. 2019. "Communicating Uncertainty about Facts, Numbers and Science." *Royal Society Open Science* 6(5): 181870. https://doi.org/10.1098/rsos.181870.

van der Linden, S. 2016. "A Conceptual Critique of the Cultural Cognition Thesis." *Science Communication* 38(1): 128–38.

van der Linden, S., E. Maibach and A. Leiserowitz. 2019. "Exposure to Scientific Consensus Does Not Cause Psychological Reactance." *Environmental Communication*. https://doi.org/10.1080/17524032 .2019.1617763.

Van der Werff, E., L. Steg and K. Keizer. 2013. "It Is a Moral Issue: The Relationship between Environmental Self-Identity, Obligation-Based Intrinsic Motivation and Pro-environmental Behaviour." *Global Environmental Change* 23: 1258–65. https://d oi.org/10.1080/17524032.2019.1617763.

Van der Werff, E., L. Steg and K. Keizer. 2014. "I Am What I Am, By Looking Past the Present: The Influence of Biospheric Values and Past Behavior on Environmental Self-Identity." *Environment and Behavior* 46 (5): 626–57.

Van Jaarsveld, J. 2020. "Nussbaum's Capability Approach and African Environmental Ethics: Is the African Voice Heard?" *Oxford Development Studies* 48(2): 135–47.

Van Leuven, N., L. Highleyman, R. Fujita and A. Kellerman. 2022. *Making Shift Happen: Designing for Successful Environmental Behavior Change*. Gabriola Island, BC: New Society Publishers.

Van Liere, K. D. and R. E. Dunlap. 1978. "Moral Norms and Environmental Behavior: An Application of Schwartz's Norm-Activation Model to Yard Burning." *Journal of Applied Social Psychology* 8(2): 174–88.

van Valkengoed, A. M. and L. Steg. 2019. "Meta-analyses of Factors Motivating Climate Change Adaptation Behaviour." *Nature Climate Change* 9(2): 158–63.

van Valkengoed, A. M., L. Steg, G. Perlaviciute et al. 2021. "Theory Enhances Impact. Reply to: 'The Case for Impact-Focused Environmental Psychology'." *Journal of Environmental Psychology* 75: 101597. https://doi.org/10.1016/j.jenvp.2021.101597.

van Vliet, M. and K. Kok. 2015. "Combining Backcasting and Exploratory Scenarios to Develop Robust Water Strategies in Face of Uncertain Futures." *Mitigation and Adaptation Strategies for Global Change* 20(1): 43–74.

Van Wensveen, L. 2001. "Ecosystem Sustainability As a Criterion for Genuine Virtue." *Environmental Ethics* 23(3): 227–41.

Vandenbergh, M., P., T. Dietz and P. C. Stern. 2011. "Time to Try Carbon Labelling ." *Nature Climate Change* 1(1): 4–6.

Vandenbergh, M. P., and P. Moore. 2022. "Governance by Contract: The Growth of Environmental Supply Chain Contracting. *Michigan Journal of Environmental and Administrative Law*: in press. https://papers.ss rn.com/sol3/papers.cfm?abstract_id=4098237

Vandenbergh, M. P. 2017. "Private Actors: Part of the Problem, Part of the Solution." Vanderbilt Law Research Paper No. 17-14. https://ssrn.com/abstract=2933178.

Vandenbergh, M. P. and J. A. Gilligan. 2015. "Beyond Gridlock." *Columbia Journal of Environmental Law* 40: 217–303.

Vandenbergh, M. P. and J. M. Gilligan. 2017. *Beyond Politics: The Private Governance Response to Climate Change*. Cambridge: Cambridge University Press.

Vandenbergh, M. P. and K. T. Raimi. 2015. "Climate Change: Leveraging Legacy." *Ecology Law Quarterly* 42: 139–79.

Vandenbergh, M. P., P. C. Stern, G. T. Gardner, T. Dietz and J. M. Gilligan. 2010. "Implementing the Behavioral Wedge: Designing and Adopting Effective Carbon Emissions Reduction Programs." *Environmental Law Reporter* 40(6): 10547–54.

Vandenbergh, M. P., P. C. Stern, G. T. Gardner, T. Dietz and J. Gilligan. 2011. "Implementing the Behavioral Wedge." *The Environmental Forum* 28(4): 54–63.

Vargas, A., A. Y. Lo, N. Rohde and M. Howes. 2016. "Background Inequality and Differential Participation in Deliberative Valuation: Lessons from Small-Group Discussions on Forest Conservation in Colombia." *Ecological Economics* 129: 104–11. https://doi.org/10.1016/j .ecolecon.2016.06.009.

Vayda, A. P. 1988. "Actions and Consequences As Objects of Explanation in Human Ecology."

Pp. 9–18 in *Human Ecology: Research and Applications*, edited by R. J. Borden, J. Jacobs and G. L. Young. College Park, MD: Society for Human Ecology.

Vayda, A. P. 2009. *Explaining Human Actions and Environmental Change*. Lanham, MD: Altamira Press.

Vayda, A. P. and R. A. Rappaport. 1968. "Ecology, Cultural and Noncultural." Pp. 477–97 in *Introduction to Cultural Anthropology*, edited by J. A. Cliffton. Boston, MA: Houghton Mifflin.

Veblen, T. [1933] 1954. *The Engineers and the Price System*. New York: Viking Press.

Vecchione, M., S. H. Schwartz, G. V. Caprara et al. 2014. "Personal Values and Political Activism: A Cross-National Study." *British Journal of Psychology* 106(1): 84–106. https://doi.org/10.1111/bjop.12067.

Venhoeven, L., L. Steg and J. W. Bolderdijk. 2017. "Can Engagement in Environmentally-Friendly Behavior Increase Well-Being?" Pp. 229–37 in *Handbook of Environmental Psychology and Quality of Life Research*, edited by G. Fleury-Bahi, E. Pol and O. Navarro. Cham: Springer.

Venhoeven, L. A., J. W. Bolderdijk and L. Steg. 2013. "Explaining the Paradox: How Pro-environmental Behaviour Can Both Thwart and Foster Well-Being." *Sustainability* 5(4): 1372–86.

Venhoeven, L. A., J. W. Bolderdijk and L. Steg. 2016. "Why Acting Environmentally-Friendly Feels Good: Exploring the Role of Self-Image." *Frontiers in Psychology* 7. https://doi.org/10.3389/fpsyg.2016.01846.

Villasenor, J. and V. Foggo. 2020. "Artificial Intelligence, Due Process, and Criminal Sentencing." *Michigan State Law Review* 2020(2): 295–354.

Vine, E. and D. Crawley. 1991. *State of the Art Energy Efficiency: Future Directions*. Washington, DC: American Council for an Energy-Efficient Economy.

Vine, E., D. Crawley and P. Centolella. 1991. *Energy Efficiency and the Environment: Forging the Links*. Washington, DC:

American Council for an Energy-Efficient Economy.

Vine, E. L. 1981. *Solarizing America: The Davis Experience*. Washington, DC: Conference on Alternative State and Local Policies, Energy Project.

Visschers, V. H. 2018. "Public Perception of Uncertainties within Climate Change Science." *Risk Analysis* 38(1): 43–55.

Vohland, K., A. Land-Zandstra, L. Ceccaroni et al., eds. 2021. *The Science of Citizen Science*. Cham: Springer.

Vollan, B. and A. D. Henry. 2019. "Diversity in Decision-Making." *Nature Climate Change* 9 (4): 258.

von Mises, L. [1949] 1998. *Human Action: A Treatise on Economics*. Auburn, AL: Ludwig Von Mises Institute.

von Neumann, J. 1928. "Zur Theorie der Gesellschaftsspiele." *Mathematische Annalen* 100(1): 295–320.

von Neumann, J. 1959. "On the Theory of Games of Strategy." Pp. 13–42 in *Contributions to the Theory of Games*, Vol. 4, edited by A. W. Tucker and R. D. Luce. Princeton, NJ: Princeton University Press.

von Neumann, J. and O. Morgenstern. 1944. *Theory of Games and Economic Behavior*. Princeton, NJ: Princeton University Press.

von Rueden, C. 2020. "Making and Unmaking Egalitarianism in Small-Scale Human Societies." *Current Opinion in Psychology* 33: 167–71. https://doi.org/10.1016/j.copsyc.2019.07.037.

von Spakovsky, H. and J. C. Adams. 2019. *Ranked Choice Voting Is a Bad Choice*. Washington, DC: The Heritage Foundation.

von Winterfeldt, D. 2013. "Bridging the Gap between Science and Decision Making." *Proceedings of the National Academy of Sciences* 110(Suppl. 3): 14055–61.

Voorberg, W. H., V. J. Bekkers and L. G. Tummers. 2015. "A Systematic Review of Co-creation and Co-production: Embarking on the Social Innovation Journey." *Public Management Review* 17(9): 1333–57.

Voosen, P. 2021. "Trump Downplayed the Cost of Carbon. That's About to Change." *Science* 371(6528): 447–48.

Voosen, P. 2022. "Bids for Anthropocene's 'Golden Spike' Emerge." *Science* 376(6593): 562–63.

Vrla, S. 2019. "Who Speaks for Deer? Including Nonhumans in Deliberative Democracy through Multispecies Communicative Democracy and Democratic Education." PhD thesis, Michigan State University.

Wagner, G. 2022. "Climate Risk Is Financial Risk." *Science* 376(6598): 1139.

Walker-Munro, B. 2022. "Drones over Ukraine: Fears of Russian 'Killer Robots' Have Failed to Materialise." *The Conversation*, March 29. https://theconversation.com/drones-over-ukraine-fears-of-russian-killer-robots-have-failed-to-materialise-180244.

Wang, H., L. Tong, R. Takeuchi and G. George. 2016. "Corporate Social Responsibility: An Overview and New Research Directions: Thematic Issue on Corporate Social Responsibility." *Academy of Management Journal* 59(2): 534–44.

Wang, X., E. Van der Werff, T. Bouman, M. K. Harder and L. Steg. 2021. "I Am vs. We Are: How Biospheric Values and Environmental Identity of Individuals and Groups Can Influence Pro-environmental Behaviour." *Frontiers in Psychology* 12. https://doi.org/10.3389/fpsyg.2021.618956.

Ward, L. F. 1884. "Mind As a Social Factor." *Mind* 9(36): 563–73.

Waring, T. M., S. H. Goff and P. E. Smaldino. 2017. "The Coevolution of Economic Institutions and Sustainable Consumption via Cultural Group Selection." *Ecological Economics* 131: 524–32. https://doi.org/10.1016/j.ecolecon.2016.09.022.

Waring, T. M., M. Kline Ann, J. S. Brooks et al. 2015. "A Multilevel Evolutionary Framework for Sustainability Analysis." *Ecology and Society* 20(2). www.jstor.org/stable/26270218/.

Warren, C. 2001. *Brush with Death: A Social History of Lead Poisoning*. Baltimore, MD: Johns Hopkins University Press.

Washington, H. and P. Twomey. 2016. *A Future beyond Growth: Towards a Steady State Economy*. London: Routledge.

Waters, C. N., J. Zalasiewicz, C. Summerhayes et al. 2016. "The Anthropocene Is Functionally and Stratigraphically Distinct from the Holocene." *Science* 351(6269): aad2622.

Watt, K. E. F. 1974. *The Titanic Effect: Planning for the Unthinkable*. New York: Dutton.

Watt, K. E. F. 1977. "Why Won't Anyone Believe Us ?" *Simulation* 28(1): 1–3.

Weart, S. R. 2004. *The Discovery of Global Warming*. Cambridge, MA: Harvard University Press.

Weaver, V. M. and G. Prowse. 2020. "Racial Authoritarianism in US Democracy." *Science* 369(6508): 1176–78.

Webber, D. J. 2008. "Earth Day and Its Precursors: Continuity and Change in the Evolution of Midtwentieth-Century US Environmental Policy." *Review of Policy Research* 25(4): 313–32.

Weber, M. [1919] 2015. "Politics As Vocation." Pp. 129–98 in *Weber's Rationalism and Modern Society: New Translations on Politics, Bureaucracy, and Social Stratification*, edited by T. Waters and D. Waters. New York: Springer.

Weber, M. [1949] 2017. *Methodology of Social Sciences*, translated by E. A. Shils and H. A. Finch. Abingdon: Routledge.

Webler, T. 1993. "Habermas Put into Practice: A Democratic Discourse for Environmental Problem Solving." Pp. 60–72 in *Human Ecology: Crossing Boundaries*, edited by S. D. Wright, T. Dietz, R. Borden, G. Young and G. Guagnano. Ft. Collins, CO: Society for Human Ecology.

Webler, T. 1995. "'Right' Discourse in Citizen Participation: An Evaluative Yardstick." Pp. 33–84 in *Fair and Competent Citizen Participation: Evaluating New Models for Environmental Discourse*, edited by O. Renn, T. Webler and P. Wiedemann. Dordrecht: Kluwer.

Wehn, U., M. Gharesifard, L. Ceccaroni et al. 2021. "Impact Assessment of Citizen Science:

State of the Art and Guiding Principles for a Consolidated Approach." *Sustainability Science* 16(5): 1683–99.

Weible, C. M., K. Ingold, D. Nohrstedt, A. D. Henry and H. C. Jenkins-Smith. 2020. "Sharpening Advocacy Coalitions." *Policy Studies Journal* 48(4): 1054–81.

Weinstein, L. and X. Ren. 2009. "The Changing Right to the City: Urban Renewal and Housing Rights in Globalizing Shanghai and Mumbai." *City and Community* 8(4): 407–32.

Weiss, M. and C. Cattaneo. 2017. "Degrowth: Taking Stock and Reviewing an Emerging Academic Paradigm." *Ecological Economics* 137: 220–30. https://doi.org/10.1016/j.ecolecon.2017.01.014/.

Weissman, S. 1970. "Why the Population Bomb Is a Rockefeller Baby." *Ramparts* (May): 27–41.

Wenzel, J. 2017. "Decolonization." Pp. 449–64 in *A Companion to Critical and Cultural Theory*, edited by I. Szeman, S. Blacker and J. Sully. New York: John Wiley & Sons.

Werfel, S. H. 2017. "Household Behaviour Crowds Out Support for Climate Change Policy When Sufficient Progress Is Perceived." *Nature Climate Change* 7(7): 512–15.

West, C. 1999. *Restoring Hope: Conversations on the Future of Black America*. Boston, MA: Beacon Press.

Weyant, J. P. 2008. "A Critique of the Stern Review's Mitigation Cost Analyses and Integrated Assessment." *Review of Environmental Economics and Policy* 2(1): 77–93.

White, D. and G. VanLandingham. 2015. "Benefit-Cost Analysis in the States: Status, Impact, and Challenges." *Journal of Benefit-Cost Analysis* 6(02): 369–99.

White, D. F., A. P. Rudy and B. J. Gareau. 2016. *Environments, Natures, and Social Theory: Toward a Critical Hybridity*. London: Palgrave.

The White House. 2017. "Executive Order: Using Behavioral Science Insights to Better Serve the American People." Office of the Press Secretary, September 15. https://oba mawhitehouse.archives.gov/the-press-office/2015/09/15/executive-order-using-behavioral-science-insights-better-serve-american.

The White House. 2021. "Fact Sheet: President Biden Sets 2030 Greenhouse Gas Pollution Reduction Target Aimed at Creating Good-Paying Union Jobs and Securing U.S. Leadership on Clean Energy Technologies." April 22. www.whitehouse.gov/briefing-room/statements-releases/2021/04/22/fact-sheet-president-biden-sets-2030-greenhouse-gas-pollution-reduction-target-aimed-at-creating-good-paying-union-jobs-and-securing-u-s-leadership-on-clean-energy-technologies/.

Whitfield, S., E. A. Rosa, T. Dietz and A. Dan. 2009. "The Future of Nuclear Power: Value Orientations and Risk Perceptions." *Risk Analysis* 29(3): 425–37.

Whitley, C. T. 2019. "Exploring the Place of Animals and Human–Animal Relationships in Hydraulic Fracturing Discourse." *Social Sciences* 8(2): 61. https://doi.org/10.3390/socsci8020061.

Whitley, C. T. and M. Bowers. 2020. "Applying Schwartz's Theory of Basic Human Values to Public Opinion of Transgender Rights." Paper presented at the Society for the Study of Social Problems, August 7, Seattle, Washington.

Whitley, C. T., L. Kalof and T. Flach. 2021. "Using Animal Portraiture to Activate Emotional Affect." *Environment and Behavior* 53(8): 837–63.

Whyte, K. P. 2012a. "Indigenous Peoples, Solar Radiation Management, and Consent." Pp. 65–76 in *Engineering the Climate*, edited by C. J. Preston. Lanham, MD: Lexington Books.

Whyte, K. P. 2012b. "Now This! Indigenous Sovereignty, Political Obliviousness and Governance Models for SRM Research." *Ethics, Policy and Environment* 15(2): 172–87. https://doi.org/10.1080/21550085.2012.685570.

Whyte, K. P. 2013. "On the Role of Traditional Ecological Knowledge As a Collaborative Concept: A Philosophical Study." *Ecological Processes* 2(1): 1–12.

Whyte, K. P. 2017a. "Indigenous Climate Change Studies: Indigenizing Futures, Decolonizing the Anthropocene." *English Language Notes* 55(1): 153–62.

Whyte, K. P. 2017b. "The Dakota Access Pipeline, Environmental Injustice, and US Colonialism." *Red Ink: An International Journal of Indigenous Literature, Arts, & Humanities* (19.1).

Whyte, K. P. 2017c. "Our Ancestors' Dystopia Now: Indigenous Conservation and the Anthropocene." Pp. 206–15 in *Routledge Companion to the Environmental Humanities*, edited by U. Heise, J. Christensen and M. Niemann. Abington: Routledge.

Whyte, K. P. 2018. "Indigenous Science (Fiction) for the Anthropocene: Ancestral Dystopias and Fantasies of Climate Change Crises." *Environment and Planning E: Nature and Space* 1(1–2): 224–42.

Whyte, K. P. 2020. "Too Late for Indigenous Climate Justice: Ecological and Relational Tipping Points." *Wiley Interdisciplinary Reviews: Climate Change* 11(1): e603.

Whyte, K. P., J. P. Brewer II and J. T. Johnson. 2015. "Weaving Indigenous Science, Protocols and Sustainability Science." *Sustainability Science* 11(1): 25–32.

Whyte, K. P. and C. J. Cuomo. 2016. "Ethics of Caring in Environmental Ethics." Pp. 234–47 in *The Oxford Handbook of Environmental Ethics*, edited by S. M. Gardiner and A. Thompson. Oxford: Oxford University Press.

Whyte, K. P., N. J. Reo, D. McGregor et al. 2017. "Seven Indigenous Principles for Successful Cooperation in Great Lakes Conservation Initiatives." Pp. 182–94 in *Biodiversity, Conservation and Environmental Management in the Great Lakes Basin*, edited by E. Freedman and M. Neuzil. Abington: Routledge.

Wilkins, E. 2019. "Low Fertility: A Review of the Determinants." United Nations Fund for Population Activities, Working Paper No. 2.

Williams, R. M. J. 1979. "Change and Stability in Values and Value Systems: A Sociological Perspective." Pp. 15–46 in *Understanding Human Values*, edited by M. Rokeach. New York: Free Press.

Wilson, A. E., V. A. Parker and M. Feinberg. 2020. "Polarization in the Contemporary Political and Media Landscape." *Current Opinion in Behavioral Sciences* 34: 223–28. https://doi.org/10.1016/j.cobeha.2020.07.005.

Wilson, D. S. 1983. "The Group Selection Controversy: History and Current Status." *Annual Review of Ecology and Systematics* 14: 159–88.

Wilson, E. O. 1984. *Biophilia*. Cambridge, MA: Harvard University Press.

Wilson, K. A., M. F. McBride, M. Bode and H. P. Possingham. 2006. "Prioritizing Global Conservation Efforts." *Nature* 440(7082): 337.

Wilson, M. A. and R. B. Howarth. 2002. "Discourse-Based Valuation of Ecosystem Services: Establishing Fair Outcomes through Group Deliberation." *Ecological Economics* 21: 431–43. https://doi.org/10.1016/S0921-8009(02)00092-7.

Wimsatt, W. C. and W. K. Wimsatt. 2007. *Re-engineering Philosophy for Limited Beings: Piecewise Approximations to Reality*. Cambridge, MA: Harvard University Press.

Winnie J., Jr. and S. Creel. 2017. "The Many Effects of Carnivores on Their Prey and Their Implications for Trophic Cascades, and Ecosystem Structure and Function." *Food Webs* 12: 88–94. https://doi.org/10.1016/j.fooweb.2016.09.002.

Wischmeyer, T. and T. Rademacher. 2020. *Regulating Artificial Intelligence*. Cham: Springer.

Wish, H. 1939. "The Pullman Strike: A Study in Industrial Warfare." *Journal of the Illinois State Historical Society* 32(3): 288–312.

Witt, B. 2019. "Evaluating the Effects of a Minimalist Deliberative Framework on the Willingness to Participate in a Payment for Ecosystem Services Program." *Resources* 8 (2): 112. https://doi.org/10.3390/resources8020112.

Wolske, K. S. and P. C. Stern. 2018. "Contributions of Psychology to Limiting

Climate Change: Opportunities through Consumer Behavior." Pp. 127–60 in *Psychology and Climate Change: Human Perceptions, Impacts, and Responses*, edited by S. Clayton and C. Manning. San Diego, CA: Elsevier.

Wolske, K. S., P. C. Stern and T. Dietz. 2017. "Explaining Interest in Adopting Residential Solar Photovoltaic Systems in the United States: Toward an Integration of Behavioral Theories." *Energy Research and Social Science* 25: 134–51. https://doi.org/10.1016/j .erss.2016.12.023.

Wolske, K. S., P. C. Stern and T. Dietz. 2020. "Design Principles for Climate Change Decisions." *Current Opinion in Environmental Sustainability* 52: 9–18. http s://doi.org/10.1016/j.cosust.2021.05.002.

Woodcock, G. 2004. *Anarchism: A History of Libertarian Ideas and Movements.* Peterborough, ON: Plainview Press.

Woodward, C. V. 1955. *The Strange Career of Jim Crow.* Oxford: Oxford University Press.

Woodward, C. V. 1988. "Strange Career Critics: Long May They Persevere." *The Journal of American History* 75(3): 857–68.

World Commission on Environment and Development. 1987. *Our Common Future.* Oxford: Oxford University Press.

World Meteorological Organization. 2019. *Scientific Assessment of Ozone Depletion: 2018.* Report No. 58. Geneva: World Meteorological Organization.

Worster, D. 1977. *Nature's Economy.* San Francisco, CA: Sierra Club Books.

Worster, D. 2001. *A River Running West: The Life of John Wesley Powell.* Oxford: Oxford University Press.

Worster, D. 2008. *A Passion for Nature: The Life of John Muir.* New York: Oxford University Press.

Worster, D. 2016. *Shrinking the Earth: The Rise and Decline of American Abundance.* New York: Oxford University Press.

Wright, E. O. 2010. *Envisioning Real Utopias.* London: Verso

Xu, X. and C.-f. Chen. 2019. "Energy Efficiency and Energy Justice for U.S. Low-Income Households: An Analysis of Multifaceted Challenges and Potential." *Energy Policy* 128: 763–74. https://doi.org/10.1016/j .enpol.2019.01.020.

Xu, Z., S. Chau, X. Chen et al. 2020. "Assessing Progress towards Sustainable Development over Space and Time." *Nature* 577(January): 74–78. https://doi.org/10.1038/s41586-019-1 846-3.

Xu, Z., Y. Li, S.N. Chau et al. 2020. "Impacts of International Trade on Global Sustainable Development." *Nature Sustainability* 3(11): 964–71. https://doi.org/10.1038/s41893-020- 0572-z.

Yang, H., T. Dietz, Y. Li et al. 2022. "Unraveling Human Drivers behind Complex Interrelationships among Sustainable Development Goals: A Demonstration in the Wolong Nature Reserve." *Ecology and Society* 27(3): 14. https://doi.org/10.1016/j .cosust.2021.05.002.

Yang, W., T. Dietz, D. B. Kramer, Z. Ouyang and J. Liu. 2015. "An Integrated Approach to Understand the Linkages between Ecosystem Services and Human Well-Being." *Ecosystem Health and Sustainability* 1(5). http://dx.doi.org/10.1890 /EHS15-0001.1.

Yang, W., M. C. McKinnon and W. R. Turner. 2015. "Quantifying Human Well-Being for Sustainability Research and Policy." *Ecosystem Health and Sustainability* 1(4): 1–13.

Yap, M. L.-M. and K. Watene. 2019. "The Sustainable Development Goals (SDGs) and Indigenous Peoples: Another Missed Opportunity?" *Journal of Human Development and Capabilities* 20(4): 451–67.

Yeats, W. B. [1921] 1997. "The Second Coming." Pp. 189 in *The Collected Works of W.B. Yeats, Vol. 1: The Poems*, edited by R. J. Finneran. New York: Scribner

Yoo, D. and E. Azuma, eds. 2016. *The Oxford Handbook of Asian American History.* Oxford: Oxford University Press.

York, R. 2006. "Ecological Paradoxes: William Stanley Jevons and the Paperless Office." *Human Ecology Review* 13(2): 143–47.

York, R. 2012. "Do Alternative Energy Sources Displace Fossil Fuels?" *Nature Climate Change* 2: 441–43. https://doi.org/10.1038/nclimate1451.

York, R. 2013. "Metatheoretical Foundations of Post-Normal Prediction." Pp. 19–29 in *Structural Human Ecology: New Essays in Risk, Energy and Sustainability*, edited by T. Dietz and A. K. Jorgenson. Pullman: Washington State University Press.

York, R. 2017a. "Environmental Consequences of Moral Disinhibition." *Socius* 3: https://doi.org/10.1177/2378023117719612.

York, R. 2017b. "Why Petroleum Did Not Save the Whales." *Socius* 3: https://doi.org/10.1177/2378023117739217.

York, R., L. Adua and B. Clark. 2022. "The Rebound Effect and the Challenge of Moving beyond Fossil Fuels: A Review of Empirical and Theoretical Research." *WIREs Climate Change* 13(4): e782. https://doi.org/10.1002/wcc.782.

York, R. and S. E. Bell. 2019. "Energy Transitions or Additions? Why a Transition from Fossil Fuels Requires More Than the Growth of Renewable Energy." *Energy Research and Social Science* 51: 40–43. https://doi.org/10.1016/j.erss.2019.01.008.

York, R. and B. Clark. 2006. "Marxism, Positivism and Scientific Sociology: Social Gravity and Historicity." *The Sociological Quarterly* 47(3): 425–50.

York, R. and B. Clark. 2011. *The Science and Humanism of Stephen Jay Gould*. New York: Monthly Review Press.

York, R. and P. Mancus. 2009. "Critical Human Ecology: Historical Materialism and Natural Laws." *Sociological Theory* 27(2): 122–49.

York, R. and P. Mancus. 2013. "The Invisible Animal : Anthrozoology and Macrosociology." *Sociological Theory* 31(1): 75–91.

York, R. and J. A. McGee. 2016. "Understanding the Jevons Paradox." *Environmental Sociology* 2(1): 77–87.

York, R. and J. A. McGee. 2017. "Does Renewable Energy Development Decouple Economic Growth from $CO_2$ Emissions?" *Socius* 3: https://doi.org/10.1177/2378023116689098.

York, R. and S. B. Longo. 2017. "Animals in the World: A Materialist Approach to Sociological Animal Studies." *Journal of Sociology* 53(1): 32–46.

York, R., E. A. Rosa and T. Dietz. 2010. "Ecological Modernization Theory: Theoretical and Empirical Challenges." Pp. 77–90 in *The International Handbook of Environmental Sociology, Second Edition*, edited by M. R. Redclift and G. Woodgate. Cheltenham: Edward Elgar.

Young, A., K. A. Khalil and J. Wharton. 2018. "Empathy for Animals: A Review of the Existing Literature." *Curator: The Museum Journal* 61(2): 327–43. https://doi.org/10.1111/cura.12257.

Young, G. L. 1974. "Human Ecology As an Interdisciplinary Concept: A Critical Inquiry." Pp. 1–105 in *Advances in Ecological Research*, Vol. 8, edited by L. Freese. New York: Elsevier.

Young, O. R. 2002. "Institutional Interplay: The Environmental Consequences of Cross-Scale Linkages." Pp. 263–91 in *The Drama of the Commons*, edited by E. Ostrom, T. Dietz, N. Dolśak, P. C. Stern, S. Stonich and E. U. Weber. Washington, DC: National Academy Press.

Załuski, W. 2016. "Rational Choice Theory, Moral Decision-Making, and Folk Psychology." Pp. 171–87 in *The Normative Mind*, edited by J. Stelmach and B. Brożek. Krakow: Copernicus Center Press.

Zarefsky, D. 1986. "The Lincoln–Douglas Debates Revisited: The Evolution of Public Argument." *Quarterly Journal of Speech* 72: 162–84. https://doi.org/10.1080/00335638609383766.

Zarefsky, D. 1993. *Lincoln, Douglas, and Slavery: In the Crucible of Public Debate*. Chicago, IL: University of Chicago Press.

Zhong, R. and N. Popovich. 2022. "How Air Pollution across America Reflects Racist Policy From the 1930s." *New York Times*, March 9.

Zhu, X., L. Li, K. Zhou, X. Zhang and S. Yang. 2018. "A Meta-analysis on the Price Elasticity and Income Elasticity of Residential Electricity Demand." *Journal of Cleaner Production* 201: 169–77. https://doi.org/10.1016/j.jclepro.2018.08.027.

Zimmerman, J. F. 1999. *The New England Town Meeting: Democracy in Action*. Westport, CT: Greenwood Publishing Group.

Zipf, G. K. 1932. *Selected Studies of the Principle of Relative Frequency in Language*. Cambridge, MA: Harvard University Press.

Zipf, G. K. [1949] 2016. *Human Behavior and the Principle of Least Effort: An Introduction to Human Ecology*. Cambridge, MA: Addison-Wesley.

# Index

CPSIA information can be obtained
at www.ICGtesting.com
Printed in the USA
LVHW021231240623
750706LV00004B/206